NETHERLANDS REPORTS TO THE ELEVENTH INTERNATIONAL CONGRESS OF COMPARATIVE LAW

THIS BOOK IS PUBLISHED IN COOPERATION WITH
THE NETHERLANDS COMPARATIVE LAW ASSOCIATION, AMSTERDAM,
AND THE T.M.C. ASSER INSTITUUT, THE HAGUE.

NETHERLANDS REPORTS TO THE XITH INTERNATIONAL CONGRESS OF COMPARATIVE LAW CARACAS 1982

Editor

Hans Ulrich
JESSURUN D'OLIVEIRA

Springer-Science+Business Media, B.V.

Netherlands Comparative Law Association, Oudezijds Achterburgwal 217-219, Amsterdam

The Netherlands Comparative Law Association was founded in 1968 and aims at advancing the study of comparative law and stimulating interest in comparative law, by organising meetings and publishing studies in comparative law.

Interuniversitair Instituut voor Internationaal Recht T.M.C. Asser Instituut
20-22 Alexanderstraat, The Hague.

The T.M.C. Asser Instituut is an interuniversity institute founded in 1965 by the eight Dutch universities offering courses in international law. The Institute is responsible for the promotion of education and research in international law, particularly by carrying out documentation and research programmes, in the fields covered by the three departments. It participates in both the editing and publishing of the Netherlands International Law Review and the Netherlands Yearbook of International Law.

ISBN 978-90-6544-073-0 ISBN 978-94-017-4443-0 (eBook)
DOI 10.1007/978-94-017-4443-0

Preface

Last year I addressed the Netherlands Comparative Law Association with the following question: 'Does Comparative Law Exist At All?' (My intention then was to flog the dead (?) horse of the merger of comparative law and the sociology of law.) In presenting this voluminous collection of Netherlands national reports to the eleventh congress of the International Academy of Comparative Law I feel my misgivings giving way to the suspicion, that comparative law indeed exists.
Of course national reports do not, as such, prove the existence of comparative law. It is the general reports together with the national reports, which embody the comparative effort. That is why the Netherlands Comparative Law Association took the initiative to propose the publishing of the materials on a subject to subject basis instead of publishing collections of national reports. From a comparative legal point of view, it is the topic that should form the basis of the publication, and not the origin of the materials. The general reporter for each topic should be prepared to take up the responsabilities of editing the volume, and would have to be given the right to select those national reports which he considers to be useful both in regard to their quality and the relevance of the material to the basic problems in the questionnaire.
This proposal met with very favourable comments from the national committees and general reporters of some fifteen countries. Although some practical problems remain yet to be solved, the Board of the Netherlands Association is confident that these problems will be overcome, and that the Board of the International Academy of Comparative Law will decide to follow the idea behind the proposal, in the Caracas meeting.

As for the present volume, I am nevertheless very glad to be able to present it to the Comparative Lawyer at large. In these times of recession it proves to be increasingly difficult to produce and finance a book of this size. We were, therefore, forced to decide to be less generous than we had been at the previous congresses, and to provide the participants not with the complete volume of Dutch contributions, but only with separata of each topic in which he or she is interested. Even this less lavish arrangement would have been impossible without the financial support of the Ministry of Justice, to which we are greatly indebted.

A tremendous amount of work was done by the staff of the Centre for Foreign Law and Private International Law of the University of Amsterdam, which took an active part in the production of the volume. Special mention should be made in the first place of Ms. Tineke Kerstens, secretarial staff member of the Centre, who with incredible energy and undiminished patience prepared the texts for the volume and upheld the contacts with writers and editors. The Netherlands Association is very grateful for her dedication. Th.M. Bervoets LL.M., former Secretary of our Association and senior lecturer at the Centre, helped to collect the reports and raise the funds. Both were assisted by the students Nico Zwikker and Petra Cramer.

I should finally like to express the wish this will be the last time that the Dutch reports will be presented in this national collection, and that they will contribute to the success of the eleventh congress in Caracas.

Amsterdam, June 1982

Hans Ulrich Jessurun d'Oliveira

President of the Netherlands
Comparative Law Association

Contents

I.A.2.
FRANZ VON BENDA-BECKMANN
The development of folk property laws in complex societies: an overview of Dutch scholarship, with special references to the property law of the Minangkabau, West Sumatra 1

I.B.3.
H.Ph. VISSER 'T HOOFT
La logique juridique et l'activité judiciaire aux Pays-Bas 19

I.C.1.
JAN M. VAN DUNNÉ
The use of comparative law by the legislator in the Netherlands 37

II.A.2.
M. ROOD-DE BOER
Le placement d'enfants dans des familles de remplacement aux Pays-Bas 69

II.A.3.
FRANS J.A. VAN DER VELDEN
The Dutch law of pretium doloris 99

II.B.1.
D. KOKKINI-IATRIDOU
Le droit applicable à la détermination de la personne physique ou morale qui contrôle une société anonyme dont une filiale a son activité à l'étranger 125

II.B.3.
C.J.J. VAN MAANEN
Le régime juridique applicable aux rapports de travail sur le plan international 149

II.C.1.
TACO STERK
Le défaut et l'opposition 167

II.C.3.
H. WINKEL
La responsabilité des juges 185

II.D.1.
G. HEIDA
Législation agricole des Pays-Bas 207

III.A.1.
A.N. HUIZENGA
Co-operation according to Dutch law 227

III.A.2.
B. WACHTER & JOS NETTEN
Abus d'information préalable en droit néerlandais 241

III.A.3.
CH.P. VERWER
Piped transportation in the Netherlands 257

III.B.1.
D.W.F. VERKADE
Computer programs as subject matter of intellectual property rights 269

III.B.2.
M. VAN EMPEL
Use of industrial property as a clandestine cartel 279

III.D.1.
WYBO P. HEERE
The legal status of hovercraft in the Netherlands 305

IV.B.3.
INGE C. VAN DER VLIES
The role and powers of the council of ministers 311

IV.C.1.
HERMAN COHEN JEHORAM
The unique Dutch broadcasting system on the eve of the revolution in teletechnics and the freedom of information 327

IV.C.2.
E.A. ALKEMA
Conscientious objections in the Netherlands 345

IV.D.2.
WILLEM KONIJNENBELT
La commune néerlandaise 359

IV.E.1.
CHRISTIAN M. STRIK
Tax avoidance in international transactions 383

V.A.2.
NICO KEIJZER
Aut dedere, aut judicare 411

V.B.1.
G. SPONG
The problem of the lawyer and client in criminal cases 421

The development of folk property laws in complex societies: An overview of Dutch scholarship, with special references to the property law of the Minangkabau, West Sumatra

FRANZ VON BENDA-BECKMANN

Professor at the University for Agriculture, Wageningen

I.A.2.

A. THE EVOLUTION OF FOLK PROPERTY LAWS[1] IN RECENT DUTCH LEGAL AND ANTHROPOLOGICAL SCHOLARSHIP

I

The evolution of property law in traditional societies has during the past fifteen years not been a topic of great concern for Dutch lawyers and anthropologists.[2] There is, in fact, only one study which systematically addresses the theme of this section, my own *Property in Social Continuity: The Maintenance of Property Relationships Through Time in Minangkabau, West Sumatra* (1979a). It describes and analyses the present state and historical development of Minangkabau rules, concepts and institutions of property and inheritance as well as the behaviour of managing property and inheritance affairs and the changes which have occurred in this behaviour. The legal development is set into the wider context of legal pluralism and the political, social and economic changes in West Sumatra during the past 150 years.[3] There is, on the other hand, quite a number of publications dealing with selected aspects of property law, types of property objects such as fishing nets (Lette 1981) or cattle (Trouwborst 1956) and the handling of property rights in a situation of legal pluralism (Van Rouveroy van Nieuwaal 1975, 1977). Most of these studies, some of which shall be explicitly mentioned, are concerned with land law and land rights in various geographical areas. Slaats en Portier in their *Grondenrecht en zijn verwerkelijking in de Karo Batakse dorpssamenleving* (Land Law and its Realisation in Karo Batak Village Society) (1981a) present a fine-grained description of the folk (adat) land law of the North Sumatran Karo Batak. Land law is described as an integral part of the overall and political organization of Karo Batak communities, and the realisation of land rights in decision making processes about distribution and

inheritance of land is vividly illustrated with a number of very extensive case-histories. Their descriptive account of Karo Batak land law is, however, rather static; it tells little about the changes which may or may not have occurred in Karo Batak adat law.
Den Ouden's study of changes in land tenure and land use in a Bamiléké chiefdom in Cameroon is less concerned with the conceptual and rule level of the Bamiléké folk system, but with the changing social and economic significance of property rights He traces in detail the processes of land control, use, circulation, distribution and inheritance in two patrilineages through a period of 80 years and analyses these property histories in the context of the changing political and economic conditions (1981). Also more concerned with the economic and social significance of property law rather than with the development of the legal system itself are Sypkens Smit's study on land borrowing in Senegal (1976) and Strijbosch's account of credit operations on Lombok, Indonesia (1981a)[4].
A topic which also has drawn considerable attention is the one of land reform in third world countries. However, only a small number of studies explicitly focus upon the legal dimension of such reforms (Sonius n.d., Van der Klei and Hesseling 1979, Tan 1977, Van Rouveroy van Nieuwaal 1975, Van Rouveroy van Nieuwaal and Amega (eds.) 1979). In most studies dealing with agrarian reform the emphasis is on property as an economic and political resource, and the studies focus upon the overall distribution of productive resources, peasant mobilisation and the development of new inequalities[5] - on poverty rather than on property.

II

This situation is in striking contrast to the pre-war period when property law, in particular of the ethnic groups in the Indonesian archipelago, had received considerable attention in the writings of Dutch scholars of Indonesian adat law. The law relating to all types of property and inheritance was systematically set out in the classical monographs on the law of individual societies, and the comprehensive accounts of the different adat land laws in Indonesia[6].
In the Dutch East Indies land law was a most important and politically most sensitive subject, in particular since the Dutch had issued declarations of state domain for most parts of the colony between 1870 and 1874, assuming state (private) ownership rights not subject to "ownership" by Indonesians. The politically and economically important question then arose of whether the adat rights of Indonesian communities and individuals could or should be recognized as being comparable with ownership and thus be exempted from the state domain or not; a

question heatedly debated by colonial politicians, lawyers and adat law scholars ever since.[7] The great practical importance of this question led the Dutch scholars to an intensified research and analysis of Indonesian land law and of its differences and similarities with western (Dutch) notions of property rights. Neologisms to typify specifically Indonesian land rights were developed, the best known of which are the "communal right of avail" (or disposal, *beschikkingsrecht*) and the "native law of possession" (*inlands bezitrecht*)[8]. The efforts of Dutch adat law scholars to view "eastern law with eastern eyes" (Van Vollenhove) also led them to devote considerable attention to folk conceptual systems and made them aware of the dangers of translating Indonesian folk concepts into the terminology of Dutch law.[9]

III

The comparison of the pre-war colonial with the present situation reveals the importance of the political and cultural context in which Dutch scholars used to operate and operate now. Upon losing its colony, Dutch lawyers and anthropologists shifted their regional interest, mainly to Africa[10].
As far as Indonesian law was concerned, much more attention was given to state law than to folk law[11]. Besides, legal anthropology as an emerging anthropological subdiscipline increasingly focussed upon processes of dispute settlement, and systematic studies of other fields of law became increasingly rare[12].
Only one writer, Sonius, formed a link between the pre- and post war period. Though also primarily concerned with African law, he presented a number of comparative analyses of Indonesian and African systems of property law, land law in particular, using the conceptual and analytical framework developed by the Leiden adat law school (1963, 1965, 1968).

The "evolution of property law" in the sense of evolutionist theory, and the question of whether primitive societies knew of individual ownership or communal ownership - topics of central theoretical and ideological importance in pre-war anthropology - were blown away when the winds of change reached social anthropology. Not the law, but the political economy of property systems in Third World countries constitutes the major topic of interest, theory and action-directed research. The changing political and economic conditions with which traditional local communities are faced all over the world, the processes of incorporation into state structures and the world market economy, also in Holland increasingly provided the context for the study of property systems[13].

IV

Given the present state of Dutch studies on the development of property law in traditional societies, which does not afford the opportunity to describe and analyse the development of the law of several societies on a comparative basis, I shall therefor in this report describe the most important changes in the law of the society most intensively studied, the Minangkabau in West Sumatra, Indonesia. I shall first give an outline of the basic principles and institutions of the Minangkabau folk property and inheritance law as it can be reconstructed for the beginning of the 19th century[14], and then describe the most important developments in that law due to the impact of the Islamic religion, the incorporation of Minangkabau society into the political system of the Dutch East Indies colony and the changing economic conditions[15].

B. CHANGES IN MINANGKABAU PROPERTY LAW.

I

The Minangkabau inhabit the westcoast of Sumatra. Whereas some coastal places had come under Dutch control in the second half of the 17th century, the Padang Highlands, the centre of Minangkabau, only were colonized during the 1820-1840's when the Dutch intervened in a civil war between an orthodox Islamitic movement and the traditional Minangkabau. Minangkabau society consisted of more or less autonomous village republics, *nagari*. According to adat constitutional law each *nagari* had to be constituted by at least four local matriclans, *suku*. The matriclans were constituted by matrilineages under the leadership of a lineage head, the *panghulu*. Lineages could be true matrilineal descent groups, but could also be internally stratified. Lineage internal stratification came into existence when persons of different social and political rank, immigrated strangers or descendants of former slaves, were incorporated. The *nagari* were governed by the adat council consisting of all lineage heads. The *nagari* territory was divided into two basic categories:
1. The land under cultivation and the area used for housesites, divided between the lineages and being part of their heritage, *pusako*.
2. Undivided and not systematically exploited village land, *ulayat*, which was controlled by the lineage heads as representatives of their clan-segment or the whole village.
The *nagari* were strictly endogamous, the matriclans were exogamous. Political residence was matrilocal for both sexes during all stages of the life cycle. Domestic post-marital resi-

dence was uxorilocal for men. The women remained in their lineage longhouse, where each married woman had a room for herself, her husband and children. Married males to a large extent worked on the land of their sisters and often stayed only at night in their wives' house.
Primarily, the villagers were farmers, cultivating rice on dry and wet rice fields. Coffee, pepper, indigo, cloves, nutmeg were grown for cash-crops. The local and interlocal trade was highly developed (Dobbin 1977). Many villages were also specialized in commodity production such as weaving, black-smithing, gold- and silversmithing, woodcarving.
The system of property relations and inheritance was an integral part of the overall political and social organization within the lineage and clan constitution. In the *adat pusako*, the adat of matrilineal heritage, or *adat kamanakan*, the adat of the sisters' children, public and private, political, kinship, economic relations and property and inheritance law were only minimally differentiated. Lineage membership, generally acquired by matrifiliation, was relevant for *nagari* citizenship, socio-political status, residence, access to agrarian resources, dispute settlement, economic cooperation and ceremonial life. In adat, but also from an analytical point of view, the lineages formed the basic socio-political units of village organization. In the adat conceptual system, this unity was quite elaborately expressed and stressed.

In the Minangkabau thinking about valuable goods the concept *pusako*, matrilineal heritage, stood at the apex of the conceptual system. Material and immaterial heritage and the relationships of groups and individual group members to them were dominated by the idea of lineage continuity. *Pusako* could not be definitively alienated: "Its water may be drunk, its fruit may be eaten, but its stem remains and remains", as a Minangkabau saying goes. Property objects were classified by reference to the means by which they originally had been acquired and to the relative distance in time from the moment of their acquisition: *Pusako* property was subdivided into four categories:
1) property originally cultivated by the ancestors, since long lineage property; 2) property originally bought or pawned; 3) property which only in recent time had come under cultivation; and 4) property acquired on the basis of good social relationships, land given to immigrated strangers who had become lineage members, or land acquired by temporary gifts. Besides inherited goods, the category of *harato pancaharian* referred to property objects which the holder had acquired during his/her lifetime by own efforts. *Harato suarang* were the properties acquired by a married couple during their marriage. No basic distinctions were made along the natural or physical characteristics of property objects, such as movable/immovable property. Land could be both heritage or self-acquired, and the rules about

land transfers differed according to the *pancaharian* or *pusako* status of land. The status of self-acquired and marital property were temporary: upon the death of the property holder such property became *pusako* property for his or her heirs, the members of the holder's smallest lineage segment. These temporary property categories were overshadowed by and absorbed in the diachronic notion of *pusako* continuity. All property "was" heritage in the diachronic dimension because it would be heritage in time.

Pusako property by definition was property held by a matrilineal descent group. However, an important distinction must be made between group-external and internal relationships. *Externally*, all inherited property was attributed to a matrilineage or to its *panghulu*(ship), the symbol of group unity and leadership. In external relations e.g. in inter-group transfers, the group as a whole represented by its headman, dealt with "its" *pusako*.
In its internal relations, however, the lineage and its members' property relations could be, and usually were, differentiated. In a true matrilineal descent group, this differentiation was the result of the group internal mechanisms of distribution and allocation of *pusako* property and inheritance. A right to be considered in the distribution of *pusako* only existed for those lineage members for whom the property was really common in the sense that they were direct matrilineal descendants of the person(s) who originally had acquired this particular property. This could, in principle, be the whole lineage. Usually, however, there were within one lineage different complexes of such property held by smaller segments. Such complexes came into existence either by inheritance of self-acquired property by such segments or by a privileged loan/temporary gift of *pusako* property by a father's matrilineage (the *bako*) to the children of a male lineage member (its *anak pisang*). Whereas such property externally was included and represented by the *panghulu*, internally only the heirs of the ex-*pancaharian* property or the recipients of a gift were entitled to economically exploit it.

However, the main portion of the lineage property usually was common heritage property for all lineage members. The relation of the group members to that *pusako* was an unspecified "having" or "holding in common", which was expressed through possessive pronomina or references to the group. This "having in common" was the legal basis to acquire concrete rights to use and exploit *pusako* property; it was not identical with these concrete rights. Concrete rights could only be acquired as a result of a decision making process. This process was (ideally) organized by the group head and should lead to a consensual decision of all adult group members.

FOLK PROPERTY LAWS

The most important concrete rights were the *ganggam bauntuek*, the *pambaoan* and *dapatan*. They all were temporary in character according to adat, for definitive division of *pusako* property within the lineage was not allowed. When it occurred, it also meant a cleavage of the lineage into two lineages, each of which then was holding "one pusako in common".
The *ganggam bauntuek* was distributed to segments of ideally equal genealogical depth. It remained in the segments unless a redistribution occurred. It gave its recipients, in principle both men and women, the exclusive right to use the property. The actual use was determined by the segment's members. The exploitation of *ganggam bauntuek* property was generally left to the women. The actual distribution of *ganggam bauntuek* depended upon the concrete needs of the women/their segment - e.g. number of children, of female children in particular, their and their husbands' economic situation. The distribution in principle was subject to redistribution, if changes in the circumstances should make it desirable.
The allocation of *pambaoan* and *dapatan* had a more temporary character. *Pambaoan* could be given to a married man for exclusive use in his nuclear family. After his death, it in principle reverted to the group which had given it (*pambaoan kumbali*). If the relations between the man's lineage and his children were good, the lineage could decide to leave the property with the children for a longer time, or one could formalize this by a privileged loan or temporary gift. Decisions about *pambaoan* had to be taken by the whole group. Whether or not *pambaoan* should be given, how much, for how long, depended upon the circumstances of the concrete situation - the economic situation of the man's wife, the relation between her and her husband's groups, eventual further marriages to strengthen the inter-group relationship, etc. *Dapatan* was *pusako* property usually given to women at/after marriage. Until their marriage, women had no separate household but lived and worked with their mothers. After divorce or the woman's death, the *dapatan* remained with the group which had allocated it.

In a stratified lineage, there was an additional differentiation, for lower ranking lineage members were not entitled to share in the processes of distribution (*pambahagian*) but only to a gift (*pambarian*). The group's core members (the blood relatives) would decide how much of the lineage's property was to be given to the lower ranking lineage members. This property remained subject to the ultimate control of the core members and the *panghulu*. If the blood relatives of the lineage were extinct, their *pusako* property could be transmitted to the lower ranking lineage members. The lower ranking lineage members were in principle excluded from succeeding to the lineage's *panghulu* title. Within their group, however, the property they had been given was treated as "their" *pusako* and this property complex was subject to the same rules about distribution, allocation and inheritance as *pusako* in general.

Alienations of *pusako* property were severely restricted. In principle, only temporary alienations were allowed and these had to be based upon, or had to newly create, social relationships. There were two main types of such transfers: 1) Transfers to the group's *anak pisang*, the children of male group members, which had the character of a privileged loan or temporary gift. The property reverted to the *bako* after the death of the children or when the children's segment became extinct. 2) The other important category of temporary alienations were *pagang gadai* transactions, best translated as pawning or pledging. The pawner transferred the right to use the land in exchange of a sum of money/gold to the pawnee. Pawnings were allowed only when a lineage required money for the marriage feast of a female group member, the installation of a *panghulu*, for the costs of a burial and for the reparation of the lineage house. Pawning required the consent of all members of the group who held the *pusako* as common heritage. The pawned property kept its status of *pusako* of the pawner lineage. For the pawnee, the status of the right to use the land was determined by the status of the money he had given. If the money/gold was *pusako* or derived from *pusako*, the use right for the pawnee also had the character of *pusako*; if it was self-acquired property, it had *pancaharian* character as well. The *pagang gadai* relationship could be ended by the "transfer of the pawning" (*mangisah gadai*) to a new pawnee. Redemption terminated the pawning relationship. The right to redeem could not be abrogated and was not subject to limitation.

In economic exchange transactions Minangkabau individuals could dispose freely of their *pancaharian* property. Disposition in the form of gifts, in practice gifts from a father to his children which threatened to withdraw future *pusako* from his lineage segment, were subject to restrictions. Such gifts, generally termed *hibah*, were allowed and valid only *satahu saizin ahli warih* with the "acknowledgement" ("knowledge and consent") of the lineage members who were the future heirs to this property and with the "cooperation" of the *panghulu*.

II

The Minangkabau law briefly sketched in the preceding paragraph by no means was a "pure autochtonous" law. Since the 16th century, when the Islamic religion penetrated the Padang Highlands, the adat Minangkabau co-existed with a competing legal system, Islamic law, which in its basic tenets relating to property and inheritance was radically at variance with the matrilineal sys-

tem of the *adat pusako*. The relationship between adat and Islamic law has always been of a dual nature.
1. Some elements of Islamic law and legal terminology have been incorporated into adat or accepted besides adat on the village level. Once Islam had been established as the dominant religion, religious offices were created but became clan or lineage offices to be inherited matrilineally. Large parts of Islamic marriage law and burial customs were accepted into the village law, not replacing but being added to adat law and customs. Many legal concepts of Islamic law, such as *hak* ("right"), *milik* ("property, ownership"), *hibah* (gift) or *warith* (heir) were used in adat. A comparison of the adat institutions expressed in Islamic terms and the meaning these terms have in Islamic law reveals, however, that the original adat rules were not suppressed by Islamic legal institutions.
2. No matter to which extent Islamic legal elements were translated into or accepted beside adat, Islamic law as a separate system was also known and reproduced through time in Minangkabau.

The relationship and conflicts between adat and Islamic law has varied considerably in Minangkabau, mainly with the relative power of the proponents of the systems (cf. Taufik Abdullah 1966, 1972). But there is no evidence from which it could be inferred that Islamic law as a whole ever succeeded in superseding adat as a system of property and inheritance law[16]. This does not preclude, however, Islamic legal precepts to have considerable influence upon the legally relevant behaviour in property and inheritance affairs, e.g. by urging men to make a gift or testament - actions considered to be advisable (*mandub*) in Islamic law - even if the form and consequences of such actions remained subject to adat norms.

III

A situation of legal pluralism thus already existed before Minangkabau was incorporated into the colonial state. However, it assumed a new dimension and had a much greater practical significance after this incorporation had taken place.
The Dutch promises to recognize village autonomy were quickly broken. Already in the 1820's, market and opium taxes were introduced, and gradually a colonial administration of indirect-rule type was built up: On *nagari* level, the Dutch created the office of a head *panghulu*, and they also established on supra-*nagari*-level a district (*laras*), administered by a Minangkabau district head. When in 1847 the system of forced cultivation and delivery of coffee was introduced, the Dutch appointed in each *nagari* some *panghulu* as functionaries responsible for the execution of the new economic policy in their clan segments.

Whereas these measures had but little effect upon the property law, the new constitutional pluralism slowly brought about new differentiations in adat law. A new frame was set for the differentiation of public and private law - the public level being newly constituted by Dutch government law. As the degree of Dutch encroachment upon village law and constitution was still limited, this did not, yet, obliterate the politico-public aspect of adat law and of adat leaders' functions. A radical change then occurred during the 1870's. Within five years' time three important measures were taken:
1) A new judicial system was established by the colonial administration. The judicial autonomy of the villages' adat councils, until then recognized by the Dutch, was declared "unofficial". A set of "native" courts was established with as courts of first instance the district head-courts and as main court the *Landraad* constituted by a Dutch colonial administrator as chairman and Minangkabau adat heads as assessors. These courts had to apply adat law in civil matters; their procedures, however, were modelled upon Dutch procedural law.
2) A penal code was introduced, declaring invalid the adat "criminal law".
3) The West Sumatran Domain Declaration declared "all waste land" to the state's domain, "unless members of the indigenous population exercise rights over it deriving from the right of reclamation". In the government's interpretation, the new state domain embraced the *ulayat* land of the *nagari*.

The direct impact of these measures on Minangkabau behaviour in property and judicial affairs seems to have been small. The adat councils continued to exercise adat judicial function, also in most "criminal affairs", often under the benevolent eyes of the Dutch *Landraad* judges. The domain declaration was not really carried out but largely existed on paper only. Yet these measures had another important consequence: On the level of legal ideology, the differentiations of western law imposed upon adat law absorbed nearly all important public aspects of adat law and of adat leaders' functions: the control over *ulayat* land, the judicial function and the criminal aspects of adat law. Thus a "private" adat law was created, private adat property law in particular, divested of its public aspects and thereby more amenable to interpretation in terms of Dutch legal logic. The basis was laid for a new type of legal pluralism in Minangkabau, the co-existence of different forms of adat law: adat law as perceived and operated on the village level, and adat law as perceived and operated by colonial judges and writers on Minangkabau adat law (cf. K. von Benda-Beckmann 1981b).

In the latter sphere, the property relationships to *ulayat* land were thought to fall into the public domain. All other property rights were considered to fall into the private domain and were transformed along Dutch notions about ownership: The *pusako* holding group which in its external property relations appeared as a unit - but which in adat functioned as such in external, largely political matters only - was conceived as a property holding unit in terms of private law. Thus the notion of the "family" (*familie*, lineage) as a legal person holding property in common ownership was created. The right of ownership (but also the neologism *inlands bezitrecht*[17]) implied that use and exploitation rights must be derived from it. The concrete adat rights of lineage members were therefore translated into such rights, and the important and legally relevant adat distinctions within the *pusako* property complex (*ganggam bauntuek, dapatan, pambaoan*) were pushed into the background. Besides, this construction presupposed the existence of a legal person different from the sum of its members. Within the unit of common ownership of *pusako*, there could not be a smaller unit having equal rights to a part of these common *pusako* goods. Consequently, only the "family" (lineage) was considered to be a legal community and not its segments. This led to the notion, that self-acquired property was not, as in adat, inherited by a lineage segment - as these could not hold the right to *pusako* - but by the whole lineage.

This transformation of the relations to *pusako* also became manifest in the changing conceptualization of property categories The manner of categorization was adapted to Dutch legal thinking, in which property is distinguished in the synchronic dimension by reference to individual property holders. Thus the distinction between inherited and self-acquired property became to be the basic one. The elaborate distinctions of *pusako* property in the diachronic dimension were trivialized as the legally relevant distinctions they indicated in adat were not reproduced in the western conceptualization of relations of *pusako*.

Another distortive element was introduced with respect to the size of the groups holding *pusako* in common. In the 1880's the colonial government had "frozen in" the number of *panghulu*-ships in the *nagari*. As the installation of a new *panghulu* in adat meant the formation of a new lineage and an official division of one into two complexes of *pusako* held in common, this Dutch measure in fact amounted to putting an end to the customary processes of lineage- and property splitting. In practice it led to irregular cleavages of lineages and to the dissociation of the functions of common leadership by *panghulu* and common property holding. This situation worsened when in 1908 the Dutch introduced the *kaum* as term for the standard-lineage holding *pusako* in common to become reponsible for the newly introduced tax, as *kaum* referred to groups of different size (lineage, sublineage) in different *nagari*.

The practical importance of these interpretations remained limited to group external matters during the 19th century, as the colonial courts only in the beginning of the 20th century began to accept lineage-internal disputes about *pusako* property.

IV

During the 20th century, some important changes occurred in the rules about disposition and inheritance as a result of, and at the same time reinforcing, changes in social and economic life. The most obvious change is the change in the rules relating to the disposition and inheritance of self-acquired property. In the 1930's it was accepted - in local level adat as well in the courts' interpretation - that men could dispose freely of all their *pancaharian* properties during their lifetime by way of gift or testament. This was the recognition of much closer social bonds within the conjugal family. With losing much of their former political and economic functions, the lineages slowly desintegrated. Adat long houses became less used, and increasingly married couples lived together in one-family houses - although until today these houses are built on the wife's *pusako* land, thus not changing the uxorilocal residence for married men.

In the domestic sphere, men took, and were given, more responsibility for the upbringing of their children and shifted their educational and economic activities from their own matrilineage to their conjugal family and their wife's matrilineage. It became a customary way of behaviour that men donated most of all of their self-acquired property to their children. The new *pancaharian*-disposition rules recognized that this could be done also without or against the consent of a man's matrilineage. In the 1960's it was accepted - again both on village level and in the state courts - that a man's *pancaharian* property was inherited by his children also if he had not disposed of it during his lifetime. This new rule, however, only operates for inheritances within the conjugal family. If a man leaves no children, his self-acquired properties are still inherited by his matrilineal relatives. Besides, the property becomes *pusako* for the children, and in the future follows the rule about *pusako* property in their lineage.

The law concerning alienations and inheritance of *pusako* property has not principally changed. Only the restrictions on pawning have become less severe: In contemporary Minangkabau, the *pusako* holding group can pawn its *pusako* in all cases where the group is in need of money for common purposes.

V

Besides these changes of norms, important changes occurred in the social and economic significance of property categories and the norms about distribution and inheritance - "changes of function" in the sense of Renner (1929) - as consequence of the increasing monetarization and the incorporation of the Minangkabau economy into the world market economy (cf. Schrieke 1955, Kahn 1980b). In 1908 the system of forced cultivation was abandoned and a tax system introduced; simultaneously Minangkabau was openend to the influx of foreign commodities and capital. As a consequence, there was a growing need for money; through the growth of the colonial administration and of cash cropping activities the opportunities to earn money also increased. Through this development, the significance self-acquired property played in social and economic relationships of Minangkabau individuals became much greater than it had been before. As self-acquired property became *pusako* after its holder's death, this development did not affect the *pusako* system as such. However, there was, and still is, a countervailing tendency of "*pancaharian*ization" of *pusako* relationships due to an increase in land pledges. Land pledges offered the pledger the opportunity to get money - for the pledgee the land could be used to cultivate cash-crops and thus also earn money. Once pledged, the right to exploit the *pusako* land could rather easily be transferred to third parties, also to individual members of the pledger-lineage. Proper redemption only occurred when the lineage as a whole redeemed its *pusako*. As the right to exploit the *pusako* property - of one's own lineage or of a different lineage - based upon the investment of self-acquired property into the transfer of the pledge had *pancaharian* status, the Minangkabau could dispose of it freely according to the new rules of *pancaharian*-disposition; in particular, they could also freely donate these rights to their children. Since the 1960's such rights are also inherited (intestately) by a person's children.

Thus a large part of *pusako* property, or better: rights to economically exploit *pusako* property, could on this basis be used, disposed of and be inherited according to the rules about self-acquired property. The traditional mechanisms of distribution and allocation of *pusako* property became supplemented by a new mechanism: the investment of money. Although temporary in nature - the *pancaharian*ized exploitation rights also become *pusako* and all pledges and transfers of pledges remain subject to redemption by the original pledger-lineage - the monetarization of *pusako*-relationships and the developing land-right market have considerably changed the social and economic life of the Minangkabau[18].

VI

Concludingly, a brief comment upon the contemporary and future development. The increasing *pancaharian*ization of rights to exploit *pusako* has effaced the sharp distinction between *pancaharian* and *pusako* property. Disputes about *pancaharian* to an increasing extent become disputes about rights to *pusako*. Therefore new interpretations and redefinitions of *pancaharian* as consequence of the new rules about the disposition, and later inheritance, also affect the rights to *pusako*. It seems premature to speak of a new development which would have led to a new system of adat law. We rather have to do with new tendencies, which coexist with older adat interpretations and practices. The most important tendency is the redefinition of *harato pancaharian* in terms of *hak milik* (ownership) and the often implicit weakening or abolition of the rule that *pancaharian* property becomes *pusako* after its holder's death. This *pusako*ization of *pancaharian* is of basic importance for the maintenance of the *pusako* system, for it guarantees that, through time and inheritance, all property will be *pusako* property. As has been noted, this rule has not been changed by the new rules of *pancaharian* inheritance within the nuclear family, as *pancaharian* is held to become *pusako* in the childrens' segment. There is, however, the tendency to cut off this rule from the legal status of *pancaharian* property. This shows itself in the attempt to reduce the adat property distinctions to one basic distinction between *pancaharian* and *pusako* and in the redefinition of the legal status of *pancaharian*. Once the equation *harta pancaharian* = ownership (*hak milik*) has been made, it is easy to stick to the ownership characteristics also when inheritance is concerned. In western legal thinking, ownership keeps its status after inheritance; it would not become *pusako* property any more. As rights to use *pusako* often have *pancaharian* character, these transformations tend to affect and change the rights to *pusako* themselves and give rise to categories of *pusako* property, such as "private *pusako* property" or "properties which originate from *pancaharian* and which have according to their development become *hak milik*" (see F. von Benda-Beckmann 1979a: 348 ff.). These notions cannot be accommodated by the legal logic of the *adat pusako* any more.

If these new legal notions should become predominant in the future, the basis would be provided for a real breakdown of the adat law system which substantively is still informed by the adat principles of the *adat pusako*. These tendencies are further strengthened by the fact, that the Indonesian government in 1960 has issued an agrarian law prociding for categories of rights in land along western notions of property law and for the conversion of adat rights into these new rights. Although until the present day the direct effect of this new law in Minangkabau is minimal, it may eventually contribute to the further weakening of the Minangkabau law of property and inheritance.

NOTES

1. I am using the term "folk law" in the way it has been characterized in the terms of reference of the Commission on Folk Law and Legal Pluralism of the International Union of Anthropological and Ethnological Sciences, see Newsletter I of the Commission.
2. A rather comprehensive survey of Dutch anthropological publications during the past 30 years is given by Kloos and Claessen (eds.) 1981.
3. And even here it may be questioned whether the book is a *Dutch* work, as the research was carried out by a German national working at a Swiss university. It is included here, as the author held a permanent position at a Dutch university when the book was published and as his later publications were written in a Dutch university context.
4. In 1971-'73 a combined research project on property law on Bali and Lombok has been carried out by the Universities of Nijmegen and Surabaya. Koesnoe (1975, 1977) has published a report on this research. Strijbosch's publication is the first of a series dealing with selected aspects of the research on Lombok.
5. See the studies of Breman (1974) on India, Buve (1977) on Mexico, Van Binsbergen and Geschiere (eds.) (1981) on Africa, Doornbos (1975) on Uganda, Geschiere (1978) on Cameroon, Van der Klei (1978) and Venema (1978) on Senegal, Hekken and Thoden van Velzen (1972) and Konter (1978) on Tanzania, Huizer (1974, 1979) on Indonesia and Latin America.
6. See e.g. Willinck (1909) on Minangkabau, Korn (1932) on Bali, Vergouwen (1933) on the Toba Batak. See also the systematic studies of Van Vollenhoven (1918) and Ter Haar (1939). In the bibliography on adat law published in 1927 by the Adat Law Foundation, 70 titles are given alone for adat land law in Indonesia in general.
7. See a.o. Van Vollenhoven 1919, Logemann and Ter Haar 1927, Korn and Van Dijk 1946, Nolst Trenité 1912, 1920, 's Jacob 1945. For a recent overview of Dutch agrarian policy in Indonesia see Sonius 1980.
8. See Logemann and Ter Haar 1927, Van Vollenhoven1919. For a discussion of these terms from a later legal anthropological perspective see Gluckman 1972: 89.
9. Classical is Van Vollenhoven's *Miskenningen van het Adatrecht* (1909).
10. In 1958, the African Studies Centre was established. J.F. Holleman, a legal anthropologist with an Africanist background, was director of the centre during most of the 1960's and later professor in legal anthropology. The Institute for Folk Law of the University of Nijmegen devoted most of its attention to Indonesia during the 60's and 70's (see Van den Steenhoven 1970, 1973). Van den Steenhoven, the Institute's director until 1981, did his main field research on the Eskimo (see Van den Steenhoven 1962).
11. An outward manifestation of this development was the rapid decline of the Adat Law Foundation, and the establishment of the Documentation Bureau for Law Overseas in the early 1950's, which focussed upon the development of state law in Indonesia. The situation changed when the Institute for Folk Law was established in 1973 at the University of Nijmegen and when in 1978 the Documentation Bureau for Law Overseas and the heritage of the Adat Law Foundation were united to form the Dutch Research Centre for the Law in South East Asia and the Caribbean in Leiden.
12. Special attention upon the law as manifest in decision making processes in Holland antedated the reign of the trouble-case method in Anglo-American legal anthropology, based upon the theoretical framework of Ter Haar's *Beslissingenleer* (1937), cf. Strijbosch 1980. For dispute process oriented studies in Holland see Van den Steenhoven 1970, 1973, Holleman 1974, Van Rouveroy van Nieuwaal 1976, Van Rouveroy van Nieuwaal and Van Rouveroy van Nieuwaal-Baerends 1981, K. von Benda-Beckmann 1981a, 1981b, Strijbosch 1981b, Slaats and Portier 1981b. For a systematic treatment of marriage law in Surinam, see Zevenbergen 1980.
13. See note 5.
14. Such reconstructions inevitably involve a considerable amount of speculation. About the dangers involved see Kahn 1976, 1980a, F. and K. von Benda-Beckmann 1981a, 1981b.
15. The account presented here is based on F. von Benda-Beckmann 1979a and F. and K. von Benda-Beckmann 1981. No detailed references will be made to these publications. For further accounts see Dobbin 1977, Guyt 1936, De Josselin de Jong 1951, Joustra 1923, Kato 1977, Schrieke 1955, Tanner 1971, Taufik Abdullah 1966, 1972, Thomas 1977, Westenenk 1918, Willinck 1909, Kahn 1980.
16. For more detailed accounts of the relationship between adat and Islam in Minangkabau see Prins 1953, 1954, Hamka 1968, Taufik Abdullah 1966, 1972.

17. The introduction of the neologism *"inlands bezitrecht"* did not change this impression. It was a well-meant effort to conceive of "eastern" property relations in non-ethnocentric terms. But this "easternization" of ownership was mainly concerned with the external relations and rights of the property holding units, the rights to dispose of property by means of sale, gift, etc., and did not change the idea that the group was holding one property in common on the basis of a communal *right*.
18. I have analyzed this development in more detail in F. von Benda-Beckmann 1979a, 1979b. It should be noted that several factors in this development also reinforce the *pusako* system, cf. 1979a: 373 ff.

BIBLIOGRAPHY

Anas, "Masalah Hukum Waris menurut Hukum Adat Minangkabau", in: Naim (ed.), *Menggali Hukum Tanah dan Hukum Waris Minangkabau*, Padang: Center for Minangkabau Studies (1968).

Benda-Beckmann, F. von, *Property in Social Continuity: Continuity and Change in the Maintenance of Property Relationships Through Time in Minangkabau, West Sumatra*, Den Haag: M. Nijhoff (1979a).

Benda-Beckmann, F. von, Modernes Recht und Traditionelle Gesellschaften, *Verfassung und Recht in Ubersee* 12: 337-351 (1979b).

Benda-Beckmann, F. von (ed.), *Rechtsanthropologie in Nederland*, Sociologische Gids no. 4 (1981).

Benda-Beckmann, K. von, Forum Shopping and Shopping Forums, *Journal of Legal Pluralism* 19: 117-159 (1981a).

Benda-Beckmann, K. von, *Folk Law and State Courts in West Sumatra, Indonesia*, paper presented to the IUAES-symposium on Folk Law in State Institutions, Bellagio (1981b).

Benda-Beckmann, F. and K. von, *Transformation and Change in Minangkabau Adat*, paper presented at the IUAES-Intercongress, Amsterdam (1981a).

Benda-Beckmann, F. and K. von, Rechtsveranderingen in Minangkabau, in: F. von Benda-Beckmann (ed.) 1981 (1981b).

Binsbergen, W.M.J. van and P. Geschiere (eds.), *Oude produktiewijzen en binnendringend kapitalisme*, Masbree: Corrie Zelen (1981).

Breman, J., *Patronage and Exploitation. Changing Agrarian Relations in South Gujarat, India*, Berkeley: University of California Press (1974).

Buijtenhuis, R. and P. Geschiere (eds.), Social Stratification and Class Formation, *African Perspectives* 2, Leiden (1978).

Buve, R.T.J., *Boeren, mobilisatie en landhervorming tijdens en na de Mexicaanse revolutie: de vallei van Nativitas, Tlaxcala, tussen 1910 en 1940*, Amsterdam: CEDLA Incidentele publicaties no. 9 (1977).

Dobbin, "Economic Change in Minangkabau as a Factor in the Rise of the Padri Movement , 1784-1830", *Indonesia* 23: 1-38 (1977).

Doornbos, M.R., Land Tenure and Political Conflict in Ankole, Uganda, *Journal of Development Studies* 12: 54-74 (1975).

Gluckman, M., *The Ideas in Barotse Jurisprudence*, reprinted, with minor amendments and a new preface considering later work, Manchester: Manchester University Press (1972).

Geschiere, P., The Articulation of Different Modes of Production: Old and New Inequalities in Maka Villages (Southeast Cameroon), in: Buijtenhuis and Geschiere (eds.) (1978).

Guyt, H., *Grondverpanding in Minangkabau*, Leiden (1936).

Haar, B. ter, *Het adatrecht van Nederlandsch-Indië in wetenschap, practijk en onderwijs*, Rede, Batavia (1937).

Haar, B. ter, *Beginselen en Stelsel van het Adatrecht*, Groningen-Batavia: Wolters (1939).

HAMKA (Haji Abdul Malik Karim Amrullah), "Adat Minangkabau dan Harta Pusakanja", in: Naim (ed.), *Menggali Hukum Tanah dan Hukum Waris Minangkabau*, Padang: Center for Minangkabau Studies (1968).

Hekken, P.M. & H.U.E. Thoden van Velzen, *Land Scarcity and Rural Inequality in Tanzania*, The Hague: Mouton (1972).

Holleman, J.F., *Shona Customary Law*, London: Oxford University Press (1952).

Holleman, J.F., *Issues in African Law*, The Hague: Mouton (1974).

Huizer, G., Peasant Mobilization and Land Reform in Indonesia, *Review of Indonesian and Malayan Affairs* 8: 27-56 (1974).

Huizer, Peasant Participation in Agrarian Reform: Mexico, Bolivia, and Venezuela, in: B. Berdichewski (ed.), *Anthropology and Social Change in Rural Areas*, The Hague: Mouton (1979).

Jacob, E.H. 's, *Landsdomein en Adatrecht*, Utrecht: Kemink en Zn. (1945).

Josselin de Jong, P.E. de, *Minangkabau and Negri Sembilan; Socio-Political Structure in Indonesia*, Leiden: IJdo (1951).
Joustra, M., *Minangkabau*, tweede uitgave, Leiden: M. Nijhoff (1923).
Kahn, J.S., 'Tradition', Matriliny and Change among the Minangkabau in Indonesia, *BKI* 132: 64-95 (1976).
Kahn, J.S., Review of F. von Benda-Beckmann, Property in Social Continuity (1979), *Indonesia Circle* 22: 81-88 (1980a).
Kahn, J.S., *Minangkabau Social Formations; Indonesian Peasants and the World Economy*, Cambridge University Press, Cambridge (1980b).
Kato, T., *Social Change in a Centrifugal Society: The Minangkabau of West Sumatra*, Ph.D.Thesis, Cornell University (1977).
Klei, J. van der, Customary Land Tenure and Land Reform: The Rise of New Inequalities among the Diola of Senegal, in: Buijtenhuis and Geschiere (eds.) (1978).
Klei, J. van der and G. Hesseling, Anciens et Nouveaux Droits Fonciers chez les Diola au Sénégal et leurs Conséquences pour la Répartition des Terres, in: Van Rouveroy van Nieuwaal et Améga 1979 (1979).
Kloos, P. and H. Claessen, *Current Issues in Anthropology: the Netherlands*, Rotterdam (1981).
Koesnoe, M., *Penelitian Hukum Adat di Bali dan Lombok 1971-1973*, Laporan Pokok, Surabaya (1975).
Koesnoe, M., *Report Concerning a Research of Adat Law on the Islands of Bali and Lombok 1971-1973*, Nijmegen: Publikaties over Volksrecht IV (1977).
Konter, J.H., *Ujamaa: De ontwikkeling van een Afrikaans socialisme*, Assen: Van Gorcum (1978).
Korn, V.E., *Het Adatrecht van Bali*, The Hague: Naeff (1932).
Korn, V.E. and R. van Dijk, *Adatgrondenrecht en domeinfictie. Twee critieken*, Gorinchem (1946).
Lette, J., *Incorporation and Ownership: A Case of a Bajau Village in Sabah, Malaysia*, paper presented to the Symposium on Law and Development, Leiden (1981).
Logemann, J.H.A. and B. ter Haar, Het beschikkingsrecht der Indonesische rechtsgemeenschappen, *T* 125: 347-464 (1927).
Moore, S.F., "Law and Anthropology", in: B. Siegel (ed.), *Biennial Review of Anthropology*, 1969, Stanford: Stanford University Press (1970).
Nader, L., "The Anthropological Study of Law", *AA* 67, no. 6, part 2: 3-32 (1965).
Nolst Trenité, G.J., *Domeinnota*, Batavia (1912).
Nolst Trenité, G.J., *Inleiding tot de Agrarische Wetgeving* (1920).
Ouden, J.H.B. den, *The Process of Incorporation With Regard to the Relations Between Local Population and Outside World. The case of two Bamiléké chiefdoms, Cameroon, in the period 1900-1970*, Agricultural University Wageningen: Department of Rural Sociology of the Tropics and Subtropics (1979).
Ouden, J.H.B. den, *Changes in Land Tenure and Land Use in a Bamiléké Chiefdom, Cameroon 1900-1980: An Historical Analysis of Changes in Control over People, Land and Production*, paper presented to the 41st Annual Meeting of the Society of Applied Anthropology, April 1981, Edinburg (1981).
Prins, J., Rondom de oude strijdvraag van Minangkabau , *Indonesië* 7: 320-329 (1953).
Prins, J., *Adat en Islamietische Plichtenleer in Indonesië*, 3e druk, 's-Gravenhage: W. van Hoeve (1954).
Renner, K., *Die Rechtsinstitute des Privatrechts und ihre soziale Funktion*, Tübingen (1929).
Rouveroy van Nieuwaal, E.A.B. van, The Plot of the Sophisticated Son-in-Law: Disparity Between Old and New Ways of Establishing Rights Over Land in N'zara (Sansanné Mango), North Togo, *Kroniek van Afrika* 1: 47-58 (1975).
Rouveroy van Nieuwaal, E.A.B. van, *A la recherche de la justice: quelques aspects du droit matrimonial et de la justice de juge de paix et du chef supérieur des Anufòm de Mango dans le Nord du Togo*, Leiden: Afrika Studiecentrum (1976).
Rouveroy van Nieuwaal, E.A.B. van, Qui Terre A Guerre A: Disparité entre le Droit Foncier Moderne et le Droit Foncier Coutumier au Nord-Togo, *Receuil Penant* 756: 150-169 (1977).
Rouveroy van Nieuwaal, E.A.B. van and E. van Rouveroy van Nieuwaal-Baerends, Het mogelijke en onmogelijke in verzoening bij de Anufòm in Noord-Togo (West-Afrika), in: F. von Benda-Beckmann (ed.) 1981.
Rouveroy van Nieuwaal, E.A.B. van and A.K. Améga (eds.), La Réforme Agro-Foncière dans les Pays du Conseil de l'Entente en Afrique de l'Ouest, *African Perspectives*, Leiden (1979).
Schrieke, B., "The Causes and Effects of Communism on the West Coast of Sumatra", in: *Indonesian Sociological Studies; Selected Writings of B. Schrieke*, part 1, The Hague: W. van Hoeve (1955).

Slaats H.M.C. and K. Portier, *Grondenrecht en zijn verwerkelijking in de Karo Batakse Dorpssamenleving*, Nijmegen: Publikaties over Volksrecht IX (1981a).

Slaats, H.M.C. and K. Portier, Verwerkelijking van adatrecht in de Karo Batakse samenleving, in: F. von Benda-Beckmann (ed.) 1981 (1981b).

Sonius, H.W.J., *Introduction to Aspects of Customary Land Law in Africa as Compared with Some Indonesian Aspects*, Leiden: University Press (1963).

Sonius, H.W.J., Grondbezitsverhoudingen in ontwikkelingslanden, *Internationale Spectator* XIX no. 10: 811-836 (1965).

Sonius, H.W.J., *Rhodesia - een dilemma van ras en grond*, Leiden: University Press (1966).

Sonius, H.W.J., Introduction comparative à quelques aspects des droits coutumiers africain et indonésien en matière foncière, *Tropical Man* 1: 1-58 (1968).

Sonius, H.W.J., *Binnenlands Bestuur en Agrarisch Recht in Nederlands-Indië*, Nijmegen: Publikaties over Volksrecht VIII (1980).

Sonius, H.W.J., *Het recht op de grond in Kenya*, MS, Leiden: Afrika-Studiecentrum (n.d.).

Steenhoven, G. van den, *Leadership and Law among the Eskimos of the Keewatin District*, Den Haag: Excelsior (1962).

Steenhoven, G. van den, *The Land of Karenda*, Nijmegen: Instituut voor Volksrecht (1970).

Steenhoven, G. van den, Musyawarah in Karo-Land, *Law and Society Review* 7: 693-718 (1973).

Strijbosch, A.K.J.M., *Methods and theories of Dutch juridical-ethnological research in the period 1900 to 1977*. Netherlands Reports to the Tenth International Congress of Comparative Law, Deventer: Kluwer (1978).

Strijbosch, A.K.J.M., *Juristen en de studie van volksrecht in Nederlands-Indië en Anglofoon Afrika*, Nijmegen: Publikaties over Volksrecht 7 (1980).

Strijbosch, A.K.J.M., Krediethandelingen op het eiland Lombok, in: F. von Benda-Beckmann (ed.) 1981: 327-346 (1981a).

Strijbosch, A.K.J.M., *Recognition of Folk Institutions For Dispute Settlement in Lombok - Indonesia*, paper presented at the IUAES-Symposium on Folk Law in State Institutions, Bellagio (1981b).

Sypkens Smit, M., *Landbouwrelaties in de Basse Casamance (Senegal)*, Leiden: Afrika-Studiecentrum (1976).

Tan, K.L., *De Agrarische Basis Wet 1960; Enige Principes*, Leiden: Documentatiebureau voor Overzees Recht (1977).

Tanner, N., *Minangkabau Disputes*, unpublished PhD thesis, University of California, Berkeley (1971).

Taufik Abdullah, "Adat and Islam; An Examination of Conflict in Minangkabau", *Indonesia* 2: 1-24 (1966).

Taufik Abdullah, "Modernization in the Minangkabau World", in: C. Holt (ed.), *Culture and Politics in Indonesia*, Ithaca, N.Y.: Cornell University Press (1972).

Thomas , L.L., *Kinship Categories in a Minangkabau Village*, unpublished PhD thesis, University of California, Riverside (1977).

Trouwborst, A.A., *Vee als voorwerp van rijkdom in Oost-Afrika*, doctoral thesis, University of Leiden, (1956).

Venema, L.B., *The Wolof of Saloum: Social Structure and Rural Development in Senegal*, Wageningen (1978).

Vergouwen, *Het rechtsleven der Toba Bataks*, Den Haag (1933).

Vollenhoven, C. van, *Miskenningen van het Adatrecht*, Leiden: E.J. Brill (1909).

Vollenhoven, C. van, *Het Adatrecht van Nederlandsch-Indië*, vol. 1, Leiden: E.J. Brill (1918).

Vollenhoven, C. van, *De Indonesiër en zijn Grond*, Leiden: E.J. Brill (1919).

Westenenk,L.G., *De Minangkabausche Nagari*, Mededelingen van het Bureau voor de Bestuurszaken der Buitenbezittingen, bewerkt door het Encyclopaedisch Bureau, afl. 17, 3e uitgave (1918).

Willinck, G.D., *Het Rechtsleven bij de Minangkabausche Maleiërs*, Leiden: E.J. Brill (1909).

Zevenbergen, J.A., *De Surinaamse huwelijkswetgeving in historisch en maatschappelijk perspectief*, Deventer: Kluwer (1980).

ABBREVIATIONS:

AA American Anthropologists
BKI Bijdragen tot de Taal-, Land- en Volkenkunde
T Indisch Tijdschrift voor het Recht

La logique juridique et l'activité judiciaire aux Pays-Bas

H. Ph. VISSER 't HOOFT
Professeur à l'Université d'Utrecht I.B.3.

1. La "logique juridique" consiste en l'ensemble des procédés argumentatifs propres au juriste: son étude peut donc être conçue comme étant celle de l'argumentation juridique dans ce qu'elle a de particulier. L'expression "argumentation juridique" est peut-être plus sûre, car le terme de "logique" pourrait suggérer qu'il s'agit principalement de logique au sens strict, c.à.d. de logique formelle (étude des structures de la déduction); or, si la logique formelle fait certainement partie d'une théorie de l'argumentation juridique, elle n'en constitue pas l'aspect le plus intéressant. Le raisonnement juridique doit pouvoir être contrôlé, quant à la validité du rapport entre prémisses et conclusion, par sa "traduction" en un schéma logique permettant d'opérer ce contrôle sans équivoque (pensons au syllogisme), mais l'enjeu véritable de l'argumentation ne se situe pas, en général, sur le plan de ce rapport de validité formelle. Il concerne bien plutôt l'élaboration des prémisses elles-mêmes. La logique formelle ne concourt pas à cette élaboration; ce à quoi elle peut contribuer, par la contrainte qu'exercent ses schémas déductifs précis, c'est à une prise de conscience plus nette des prémisses établies, elles-mêmes, par d'autres moyens. La clarté terminologique exige donc une distinction nette entre deux niveaux d'examen du discours juridique: argumentation productrice d'une part, validité formelle d'autre part. L'originalité de la "logique juridique" se situe à ce premier niveau; les règles de la logique formelle, par contre, sont les mêmes pour tout le monde. Il est donc erroné de parler d'une application *sui generis* de la logique formelle par le juriste. Concluons de ce qui précède que les termes d' "argumentation juridique" ou "raisonnement juridique" doivent être préférés à celui de "logique juridique", qui peut causer des confusions.

2. L'argumentation juridique jouit actuellement d'un intérêt fort soutenu aux Pays-Bas. Nous n'essayerons pas d'expliquer ici cet état de choses, dont les causes sont assez complexes et d'ailleurs non particulières à notre pays (mentionnons seulement l'importance accrue de l'activité judiciaire dans l'évolution du droit, accompagnée d'une insatisfaction assez répandue à l'égard du degré de transparence de la motivation judiciaire; mentionnons également, sur un plan plus théorique, le défi que constitue, pour le juriste, l'esprit scientifique de notre époque: comment définir, en somme, la "rationalité" particulière dont il s'estime être le défenseur? Deux facteurs spécifiques favorisent cependant, aux Pays-Bas, l'intérêt porté au raisonnement juridique. Le premier est que la doctrine néerlandaise est traditionnellement très ouverte à ce qui se passe à l'étranger; ainsi, les travaux de *Esser*, *Perelman* ou *Dworkin* (pour ne mentionner que quelques noms) ont rapidement influencé ses discussions. Le second facteur est que cette doctrine dispose d'un ouvrage capital sur le raisonnement judiciaire, publié en 1931 (mais très en avance à cette époque sur beaucoup d'analyses étrangères): la "Partie générale" du Traité de droit civil néerlandais de *M. Asser*, rédigée par *P. Scholten*, dont le rôle de cadre de référence pour la doctrine n'a guère diminué depuis sa parution[1]. Néanmoins (et ceci peut être attribué en partie à la pénétration rapide, qu'on vient de signaler, de perspectives théoriques élaborées à l'étranger), les études consacrées aux Pays-Bas au raisonnement juridique se caractérisent par une grande variété.

3. Comment définir, et analyser, notre objet d'étude? Le présent rapport implique à cet égard les options suivantes.
Le raisonnement juridique: nous précisons d'abord le sens de cette expression comme étant synonyme des opérations discursives qui justifient la détermination du droit applicable au cas d'espèce. En néerlandais, on utilise volontiers, pour parler de ces opérations, le terme de *rechtsvinding*, soit activité tendant à "trouver" le droit.
Or, ces opérations sont extrêmement complexes, et il est difficile, par conséquent, d'en proposer un "modèle" satisfaisant. Cette complexité s'accompagne d'un fréquent manque de transparence: la doctrine dresse, à cet égard, un acte d'accusation permanent contre le juge. Enfin, l'analyse du raisonnement juridique exige qu'on soit muni de moyens théoriques sûrs; or ces moyens, la doctrine en offre de très divers et même de très divergents, ce qui oblige l'analyste de procéder à un arbitrage risquant d'outrepasser ses compétences. Il résulte, de tout ceci, une littérature fort riche mais également fort confuse.
Le présent rapport, obligé de trancher dans le vif, propose le schéma d'étude suivant. Il oppose d'abord une analyse de style descriptif (§ 4-7) à une analyse d'allure philosophique

(§ 8). A l'intérieur de l'analyse descriptive, il distingue les trois étapes suivantes: typologie des arguments (§ 4), justification concrète de la décision (§ 5-6), recherche de cohérence avec le droit positif (§ 7). Ces trois étapes ne reflètent pas une séquence temporelle; nous pensons qu'elles correspondent à trois niveaux du raisonnement, que ce dernier actualise en même temps.

4. L'étude du raisonnement juridique, cela suggère en premier lieu une analyse des divers types d'arguments (*argumentatiepatronen*) qui caractérisent le discours juridique et partant, la motivation du prononcé judiciaire. Il s'agit de figures du raisonnement bien connues de la tradition, et qu'on peut considérer globalement comme reflétant les diverses stratégies selon lesquelles le juriste accède au sens du droit positif ("interprétation", au sens large du mot). Pour la doctrine néerlandaise, le *locus classicus* d'une telle analyse est certainement fourni par l'ouvrage précité de *Scholten*. En décrivant les opérations de *rechtsvinding*, *Scholten* procède comme suit. Il explique, d'abord, pourquoi le juge n'est pas l'automate envisagé par *Montesquieu*. Les raisons qu'il avance à cet égard dérivent, selon lui, d'une tension irréductible entre ce qu'il nomme la "règle" (la norme de droit positif) et le "cas" tel qu'il doit être résolu de manière conforme à la justice (*Scholten* parle également de la "décision"). Comment est recherchée, dans ce contexte, la règle de droit positif? Le juge la trouve par l'intermédiaire d'un ou plusieurs des types d'arguments précités, dont les stratégies respectives doivent leur statut aux "facteurs ayant autorité" (*gezaghebbende factoren*) qui s'imposent à l'attention du juge (facteurs que nous retrouverons plus loin). *Scholten* établit, pour l'essentiel, la typologie suivante: les divers modes d'interprétation de la loi (interprétation grammaticale, volonté du législateur, interprétation systématique, sociologique, téléologique), le recours à l'histoire des institutions, et l'autorité du précédent et de la doctrine. L'interprétation systématique sert de cadre à l'étude de la conceptualisation ("construction") juridique, du raisonnement par analogie, des principes généraux du droit, etc.
Tenons nous pour un instant à ce niveau d'un inventaire et d'une description séparée des divers types d'arguments, tels que nous les offre - en premier lieu - l'ouvrage de *Scholten*. La typologie de *Scholten* fait encore largement autorité aux Pays-Bas, bien que certains accents se soient certainement déplacés depuis lors.

Ainsi, les raisonnements fondés sur l'histoire du droit (*rechtshistorische argumentatie*) ne jouent plus guère de rôle dans la jurisprudence[2]. D'autre part, la typologie de S. peut être complétée par un mode de raisonnement décrit pour la première fois par *Wiarda*[3], celui de la "comparaison des cas" (*gevalsvergelijking*). Ce type d'argumentation, utile surtout pour l'application de critères d'ordre très général (*vage normen*, *"unbestimmte Rechtsbegriffe"* en allemand), consiste à créer, pour le cas d'espèce, un cadre de comparaison défini par deux cas-type aux caractéristiques opposées, et dont la solution ne fait pas de doute. Il s'agit alors de déterminer duquel de ces deux extrêmes se rapproche la plus le cas d'espèce[4]. Signalons enfin, dans un ordre d'idées plus général, l'évolution vers une réalité encore plus "prétorienne" que celle que décrit *Scholten*, évolution reflétée par le fait que la Cour de Cassation néerlandaise (*Hoge Raad*) peut casser depuis 1963 pour cause de violation du "droit" (et non plus seulement de la "loi"), ce qui facilite le contrôle de la Cour à l'égard de modes d'argumentation tels que le recours aux principes généraux du droit.

La typologie de *Scholten* doit être contrastée, selon nous, avec une étude des "topiques juridiques"[5] qui risque de mêler les *types* d'arguments avec des principes, maximes, ou adages tenant à la procédure ou aux contenus du droit. *Scholten* suit une voie plus claire, et conforme à la nature des choses: il accorde un statut particulier aux types d'arguments parce que ceux-ci dérivent d' "autorités" (*Scholten* parle de "facteurs ayant autorité") inscrites dans la nature propre du droit, dans son contexte historique, dans ses finalités: autorité du texte, de la volonté du législateur, d'un principe de justice consistant à traiter également des situations égales, d'une adéquation nécessaire aux besoins actuels de la société, etc. La typologie de *Scholten* renvoie donc directement à une théotie du droit: les stratégies d'accès au droit positif doivent être comprises en fonction des structures, des valeurs constitutives de ce dernier, telles que la positivité, la systématicité ou la justice; le juriste argumente comme il le fait parce qu'il est juriste, et c'est donc par ces traits fondamentaux de l'institution "droit" qu'il faut, d'abord, expliquer son argumentation. On ne voit pas quel pourrait être, ici, un meilleur instrument de travail[6].

5. L'inventaire et l'étude séparée des divers types d'arguments qui caractérisent le discours juridique: cette approche, aussi importante qu'elle soit, n'épuise nullement la problématique dont nous traitons dans le présent rapport. *Scholten* lui-même va beaucoup plus loin lorsqu'il décrit la tension entre la "règle" et le "cas": le juge cherche la règle propre au cas d'espèce, son intuition doit donc ratifier l'opération intellectuelle qui consiste à dégager, à travers les "facteurs ayant autorité", la règle de droit positif applicable[7]. Mais

cela revient, semble-t-il, à introduire dans le raisonnement une instance aussi mystérieuse que décisive, qui échappe à toute raison (*Scholten* attribue en effet un aspect "irrationel" à la décision[8]). On peut, si l'on veut, interpréter la doctrine néerlandaise plus récente comme un commentaire prolongé de cette dialectique entre la "règle" et le "cas".

(a) Que le "cas" impose, en un sens, sa propre loi (nous verrons que cette expression ne peut être prise à la lettre!), cela paraît rendre incertain le poids des "facteur ayant autorité": ceux-ci déterminent ensemble des stratégies d'accès au droit positif dont le juge ne peut (ni ne doit) se passer, mais l'usage concret de ces moyens reste soumis au contrôle d'un jugement portant sur la justice de la décision. Or, le statut incertain de la typologie des arguments, il faut peut-être admettre qu'il lui est inhérent dès l'abord: *Scholten* nous expose les divers "facteurs" dont doit tenir compte le juge, il ne dit nulle part au juge comment *choisir* entre les stratégies concurrentes qui en forment le reflet. Sans doute le juge n'est-il-pas, en général, confronté à toutes ces stratégies à la fois; de plus, il arrive que plusieurs stratégies suggèrent une conclusion identique; mais la nécessité d'effectuer un choix véritable paraît néanmoins fréquente. Cette marge de liberté, *Scholten* ne tente pas de la combler, et pour cause: parlant des "facteurs ayant autorité", il déclare que la valeur de ceux-ci pour des cas concrets ne peut être ni précisée ni classée dans un ordre bien déterminé. "Il en est ainsi déjà pour la seule raison que toute détermination du droit tend à la recherche de la justice"[9]. La doctrine ultérieure le suit sur ce point. On s'accorde en effet pour admettre qu'il n'existe pas de hiérarchie évidente entre les diverses "autorités" identifiées par *Scholten*, et il est clair que seule une telle hiérarchie pourrait fonder de réelles directives en matière de *rechtsvinding*[10]. La jurisprudence confirme cette absence de méthode (au sens précis du mot): le *Hoge Raad* n'élabore aucune règle générale en ce qui concerne le choix entre types d'arguments[11]. La seule chose qu'on peut affirmer, peut-être, c'est que le juge argumente, à chaque époque, dans le cadre d'une certaine conception plus ou moins implicite du droit, et de sa fonction à lui, qui influe sur le poids respectif des "patterns of argument"[12], mais sans que cela puisse être exprimé par des priorités quelque peu tangibles. Que le juge n'est pas l'automate conçu par *Montesquieu*, cela dérive - en partie - de ce que le droit positif ne dicte pas, lui-même, de quelle manière il doit être "approché" aux fins de son application: ce qui veut dire en somme que cette application révèle, dans le droit, une structure potentiellement antinomique; les autorités de *Scholten* se font mutuellement concurrence (ce qui n'exclut pas la *possibilité* d'une convergence); les valeurs qu'elles représentent ne se laissent pas soumettre à une hiérarchie même imprécise. On

peut conclure que même avant toute insistance sur le rôle du "cas" dans le raisonnement juridique, l'analyse de ce mode de discours pose un problème de justification dont la solution échappe à la typologie des arguments.
Mais ce "flou", cette indétermination que démontre la nécessité d'un *choix* entre types d'arguments, même s'il était supprimé, on le retrouverait dans l'usage précis du type d'argument utilisé. Le juge doit très souvent se décider "à l'intérieur" d'un seul type d'argument: que faut-il conclure, exactement, des travaux parlementaires, comme évaluer, entre thèses opposées, la consistance de la *ratio legis*, etc.? Et que dire de la qualification des faits à l'aide de notions aussi protéiformes que la "faute" ou la "bonne foi"? Inhérente d'un côté à l'absence de hiérarchie entre les types d'arguments, l'indétermination propre à la typologie renvoie directement, de l'autre, à l'appréciation du cas d'espèce, et confirme ce que dit *Scholten* de la dialectique entre "règle" et "cas"[13].

(b) Est-ce à dire que le raisonnement juridique ne peut en réalité livrer qu'une justification fort approximative de la décision, l' "intuition" du juge en formant, en quelque sorte, le centre invisible? Le recours à une statégie reconnue pour dégager la règle de droit applicable justifie la décision, puisque celle-ci est ainsi rattachée au droit positif (par l' intermédiaire de l'un des "facteurs ayant autorité"); mais cette justification reste très partielle du moment que le choix et l'usage précis de l'approche stratégique dépend d' une appréciation (relative au résultat à atteindre par la décision) qui semble refuser tout motif. En fait, la doctrine ne s'est pas limitée à un tel constat, elle s'est efforcée de réduire la portée de l' "intuition" judiciaire en postulant, plus près du "cas" que de la "règle", un ordre de *raisons* sous-jacent à la typologie des arguments. La décision (synthèse de ce qu'exige la "règle" et de ce qu'exige le "cas"), *Scholten* la fait reposer en dernière analyse sur la conscience du juge.
On a pu voir, dans cette "conscience", un principe de certitude métaphysique, dont le juge n'a pas à rendre compte envers le justiciable. Il nous paraît plus vraisemblable que *Scholten* met seulement l'accent sur le sérieux de la décision judiciaire: le juge doit avoir pleinement conscience de ses responsabilités. La question de savoir ce qui détermine, au juste, la décision, reste donc posée. *Scholten* lui-même y répond à certains endroits, lorsqu'il fait voir le rôle de jugements de valeur précis dans la prise de position judiciaire[14]. Qu'un style de motivation plus transparent soit possible, *Polak* le sous-entend lorsqu'il conclut dans une étude datant de 1953 que le *Hoge Raad* n'explique pas suffisamment pourquoi il choisit tantôt tel type d'argument, tantôt tel autre[15]. (La situation ne s'est guère améliorée depuis.) Pour la doctrine d' après-guerre, influencé par des auteurs tels que *Esser*, le

rôle déterminant de considérations de justice ou d'utilité contemporaines constitue une sorte de postulat: le juge fait en réalité de la "politique"[16], et il vaudrait mieux qu'il le fasse en plein jour. Les motifs véritables, dit-on, restent trop souvent cachés; et il arrive fréquemment que le juge s'appuie sur des "motifs" sans valeur argumentative réelle (citons par exemple le recours sommaire à la notion de *redelijkheid* (conformité au standard du "raisonnable"), qui ne livre en fait qu'une justification de pure forme)[17].

6. Revenons un instant sur ce qui précède. Le juge n'est pas l'automate qu'y a vu *Montesquieu*: il doit interpréter, au sens large du mot. La typologie des arguments met en lumière une pluralité de stratégies qu'il peut suivre à cet effet (stratégies découlant, elles-mêmes, de traits ou d'exigences propres au droit). Or, cette typologie ne permet pas de retrouver, que ce soit sous une forme atténuée, l'automatisme initialement refusé à la recherche du droit applicable. (La recherche d'une "méthode", ne tente-t-elle pas de réintroduire par un détour l'idée, dès longtemps dépassée, que la décision relève d'un mécanisme cognitif?) La pluralité des stratégies n'est pas réglée: au lieu d'une hiérarchie, on découvre plutôt une rivalité. Par ailleurs, l'usage autant que le choix de ces stratégies connaît une forte marge d'indétermination. La typologie confirme elle-même le statut propre du "cas" (au sens de *Scholten*). Sans doute ce dernier est-il toujours plus ou moins préformé par la "règle" (il n'y a pas de faits bruts, les "faits" sont toujours vus dans la perspective de ce qui est, juridiquement, intéressant et possible), mais étant donné le "flou" inhérent à cette préformation (c.à.d. la marge qu'elle ouvre à ces choix véritables) il est clair qu'elle ne peut mener qu'à une justification très partielle de la décision. La doctrine postule par conséquent un ordre de raisons sous-jacent, relatif à la "plausibilité contemporaine" de la solution retenue. Quels sont les thèmes principaux auxquels elle s'attache dans ce contexte? Nous en voyons deux: la structure du raisonnement et les conditions formelles de transparence de celui-ci; et les problèmes d'une "politique" au niveau judiciaire.

(a) Le raisonnement juridique est d'autant plus intéressant à suivre que le cas d'espèce est plus difficile à trancher: l'analyste présuppose (il l'oublie quelquefois) ce qu'on appelle, en anglais, un *hard case*. Mais cette présupposition étant admise, suivons-en les implications. Le juge est appellé à décider entre prétentions contraires, le cas "fait problème", il consiste en somme en un problème. Il a surgi, comme problème, par la rencontre de plusieurs argumentations possibles. Les raisonnements qui feront pencher la balance dans l'un ou l'autre sens seront par conséquent des raisonnements préférés. La doctrine insiste volontiers sur cet aspect "concurrentiel" du champ de

la décision, en précisant que c'est seule la particularité du cas d'espèce qui permet, en un sens, de trancher: la préférence ne se dessine jamais globalement, l'estimation du sens et du poids des raisons en conflit a un aspect irrémédiablement casuïstique. C'est là, sans doute, ce que veulent dire les expressions fréquemment employées de *probleemdenken* ou de *topisch denken*[18]; comme le dit *Scholten*, le "cas" introduit une dimension spécifique. Mais on en déduit - plus clairement que chez *Scholten* - une sorte de modestie congénitale de la décision: qu'il y ait préférence, cela veut dire qu'il n'est jamais totalement impensable qu'on ait pu décider autrement, les raisons qui s'opposent ont toutes un certain pouvoir convaincant, elles ne s'entre-détruisent pas à 100%[19]. Signalons que la nature "problématique" ou "topique" du champ de la décision, déjà manifeste au niveau d'une typologie des arguments par la rivalité entre "facteurs ayant autorité", y est trouvée aussi par la doctrine dans la structure-même d'un type d'argument très important: le recours aux principes généraux du droit. *Scholten* observe déjà que ces principes ont tendance à s'entreheurter lors de la formation des règles du droit dont ils constituent le substrat[20], et un auteur récent décrit les principes généraux non pas comme formant ensemble un système cohérent, mais comme constituant un appareil de poids et contrepoids (*checks and balances*) dont l'équilibre doit être réalisé chaque fois dans le concret[21].
Que la décision ait un aspect irrémédiablement casuîstique, cela a pu suggérer la formule selon laquelle le cas impose "sa" justice propre (aux Pays-Bas, on utilise volontiers à ce propos l'expression allemande de *Einzelfallgerechtigkeit*). Mais on risque, ici, de commettre une erreur de pensée. La "cas" n'est jamais, et ne peut être, un cas strictement individuel, c.à.d. non susceptible de répétition[22]. On pourrait l'établir par la voie philosophique: il n'y a de saisie que générique, "typique" de la réalité. Qu'il suffise de dire que la décision judiciaire implique, par nature, la volonté de trancher pareillement des cas pareils (comment expliquer autrement la valeur de précédent qu'a en principe toute décision?). Le fait que la motivation judiciaire se borne fréquemment à renvoyer aux circonstances de l'espèce[23] n'y change rien: cela peut rendre difficile de préciser *a posteriori* ce qui a été décidé au juste, mais si l'on admettait que le juge s'est laissé guider par une intuition ineffable et strictement particulière, on porterait un coup mortel à son autorité.
Les remarques qui précèdent suggèrent que la motivation judiciaire est soumise - idéalement - à ceux critères formels de transparence: faire état du raisonnement écarté, pour mieux faire ressortir les motifs de la préférence exercée, et dégager dans la mesure du possible les aspects généraux du cas d'espèce, tels qu'ils conditionnent la portée du problème résolu. Sous le premier rapport, les auteurs sont d'accord pour

déplorer le silence du juge néerlandais, qui contraste fortement avec la pratique anglo-saxonne[24]. Sous le second, on peut saluer les récents efforts du *Hoge Raad* tendant à situer les règles qu'il établit dans le silence de la loi à un niveau de généralité relativement élevé[25]. Il faut mentionner, dans le même ordre d'idées, la technique consistant à fournir au juge du fait une liste des points de vue (*oriëntatiepunten*) selon lesquels il peut organiser son appréciation du cas d'espèce[26] ainsi que le procédé déjà cité de la "comparaison des cas" (*gevalsvergelijking*), utile surtout pour l'application de ce qu'on nomme, en Allemagne, les *unbestimmte Rechtsbegriffe*.

(b) Si le juge fait de la "politique" (juridique), quelles sont à cet ègard ses sources, et ses limites? Ce thème de discussion fort important, nous n'en dessinons que les traits principaux. Il est lourd d'implications théoriques, car qu'est-ce en somme que le droit vivant, dans quelle mesure est-il inscrit dans nos pratiques et nos convictions, dans quelle mesure est-il au contraire fonction de choix conscients et toujours plus ou moins risqués? *Ter Heide*[27] défend un point de vue très proche de ce que l'on pourrait appeller un sociologisme du droit vivant: la réalité du droit, c'est un réseau de "confiances légitimes" que nous plaçons réciproquement dans le comportement d'autrui, et la mission du juge est d'en préciser le sens en "écoutant" ce que nous dit, ici et maintenant, la norme inscrite dans nos pratiques effectives. Les textes n'ont qu'une valeur de directive: ce qui prime, c'est l'état présent de notre sentiment du juste. Ces vues ont eu une influence notable; elles ont été comprises comme un appel au dynamisme judiciaire (le juge doit fidélité aux orientations actuelles de la société, plutôt qu'aux jugements de valeur "historiques" du législateur)[28]; mais elles tendent curieusement, en même temps qu' elles le libèrent de la loi, à interdire au juge une "politique" autonome: le juge est là pour dire un droit qui a son assise hors de lui, dans l'opinion. *Ter Heide* demande-t-il peut-être trop à notre *Rechtsgefühl*? *Scholten* remarque déjà que le sentiment de justice a une portée surtout négative: toute collectivité sait à peu près ce qu'elle n'acceptera jamais, elle sait beaucoup moins ce qu'elle veut positivement, à l'intérieur de la marge définie par ses refus[29]. Or c'est à l'intérieur d'une telle marge que doit trancher le juge (sinon, l' autait-on saisi?)[30]. On a pu insister, exemples à l'appui, sur la fréquente absence de convictions précises chez le public (et même, les milieux intéressés) en ce qui concerne les questions soumises aux tribunaux[31]. C'est pour autant le for juridique, plutôt que la collectivité tout entière, qui sert de "caisse de résonance", le juge cherchant par ailleurs un appui maximum dans le "système" (voir par. suivant). Mais s'il s'agit moins d'une incertitude ou d'une inconsistance de l' opinion que d'un conflit ouvert entre convictions ou intérêts de groupes, le juge, évidemment, risque de perdre pied en l'absence d'une intervention du législateur (questions d'ordre "politique"). Reste le problème suivant: s'il existe quand-même, sur quelque questions posée aux tribunaux, une opinion nettement majoritaire, est-il conforme à sa mission que le juge puisse s'en distantier? Les vues de *Ter Heide* lui rendent difficile de l'affirmer, ceux qui ne partagent pas ses opinions reconnaîtrons, au juge, la mission de défendre certains intérêts permanents de la société que l'opinion aura pu perdre de vue[32]. Le problème se situe près de celui des rapports entre le juge et le législateur: les intérêts permanents dont la défense incombe à l'institution judiciaire, il est attrayant de les chercher surtout du côté des libertés fondamentales, ce qui met à l'ordre du jour la question du contrôle de constitutionnalité des lois[33].

7. Mettre l'accent sur la substance "politique" de la décision, cela risque cependant de nous faire oublier que *Scholten* décrit les opérations de *rechtsvinding* comme une dialectique entre *la règle* et le "cas". Sans doute: la typologie des arguments ne livre pas de méthode, elle ne dit pas elle-même comment il faut exercer une préférence tantôt pour tel mode d'argumentation, tantôt pour tel autre, et la vérité du raisonnement paraît donc refluer vers un ordre de raisons sous-jacent, celui des considérations fort diverses qui déterminent la justice, l'utilité, la "plausibilité" contemporaine de la solution du cas d'espèce. Mais la réalité est, évidemment, plus complexe. En effet, que reste-t-il dans l'optique précité du raisonnement juridique? On lui refuse d'une part toute méthode; et on suggère implicitement, d'autre part, que sa juridicité est factice, puisqu'en accusant la typologie de ne pas refléter la vérité du raisonnement, on expulse en fait les textes, la *ratio legis*, le système, et même la recherche d'une interprétation *de la loi* en fonction des réalités contemporaines, soit virtuellement le droit positif, le *donné* normatif tout entier, tel que la typologie des arguments en définit les diverses approches. (Dira-t-on que le *hard case* surgit précisément dans le silence des textes, des précédents etc., et que le juge doit alors se faire législateur à 100%? Ce serait privilégier un cas extrême, point caractéristique du tout de l'activité judiciaire en matière de *rechtsvinding*.) Il nous faut, manifestement, un modèle plus subtil. Les observatuers de la jurisprudence s'accordent pour constater que le juge cherche à trouver une solution dans le cadre de la loi, équilibrée par un jugement portant sur le caractère "socialement acceptable" de la décision. Et cette constatation, il est clair qu'elle n'attribue pas au "cadre de la loi" un statut purement artificiel: d'une façon ou d'une autre, le raisonnement des juges trouve, dans ce cadre, en élément capital de sa substance[34]. La doctrine suit le pas, car elle corrige

partout l'accent mis sur la "politique" judiciaire par un accent complémentaire sur la fonction régulatrice du "système" (expression employée de manière si large qu'elle dénote quasiment l'ensemble du droit positif, du "donné" juridique). Ce qui veut dire, en somme, qu'il faut penser ensemble, d'une manière ou d'une autre, *et* l'absence de méthode au niveau d'une typologie des arguments (c.à.d. le rôle crucial du jugement relatif au cas d'espèce) *et* le réalité des valeurs qui fondent cette typologie (c.à.d. le poids réel du droit positif, du donné, tel qu'il se livre au juge *à travers* les divers "facteurs ayant autorité"). Par son affirmation qu'il existe une dialectique permanente entre la "règle" et le "cas", *Scholten* va déjà dans ce sens (l'absence de méthode ne signifie pas qu'il n'y a rien de donné); il fournit de plus les éléments d'une réponse plus précise lorsqu'il conclut sa description du mode d'interprétation "systématique" en dégageant la notion d'un "système ouvert" (*open systeem*)[35]: ce qu'il faut arriver à comprendre, c'est que la décision judiciaire cherche à réfléter en même temps un travail intellectuel qui a pour matière le donné (la loi positive) et un jugement de valeur de nature créatrice orienté sur la juste solution du cas d'espèce. En d'autres termes: une liberté de jugement disciplinée par le droit positif, et un droit positif dépendant, pour sa vie, de cette liberté de jugement. Mais essayons d'être plus exacts. La synthèse qu'évoque *Scholten*, et que la doctrine commente après lui[36], on peut dire qu'elle tend à fusionner le jugement de valeur contemporain et l'interprétation du "système" (au sens large du mot): le juge cherche un appui, pour le jugement de valeur qu'il opère, dans le droit positif, tandis qu'il attend en même temps, de ce droit positif, certaines indications de politique juridique (recherche et attente qui n'excluent certainement pas l'insuccès: pensons au cas d'un conflit manifeste entre les besoins actuels et l'évaluation opérée en son temps par le législateur). Si elle peut diriger, sans doute, l'usage de tout mode d'argumentation (pensons par exemple à la *ratio legis* ou à l'analogie), cette fusion trouve sa forme la plus claire dans le recours aux principes généraux du droit: la formulation et l'application de ces principes tend à établir un lien cohérent entre le jugement de valeur contemporain et le "donné", en ce qu'elle fournit la "raison" (la "politique") de tel ou tel ensemble de règles positives, tout en dépendant à cet égard d'un choix *hic et nunc*[37]. Le raisonnement juridique ne connaît pas de méthode au sens propre du mot: mais il connaît bel et bien une recherche de cohérence, et donc une discipline (il ne peut aller dans tous les sens, il lui faut des points d'appui).

Ces remarques, on peut estimer qu'elles valent pour tout raisonnement juridique, et même qu'elles en caractérisent la nature profonde; elles dépassent pour autant le cadre du mode d'interprétation "systématique" au sens strict du mot (le donné, cela peut être par exemple, et cela est effectivement dans nombre de cas, une jurisprudence constante, une "ligne" dans la série des précédents).

Dans son arrêt du 30.1.1959 (*NJ* 1959, 548), le *Hoge Raad* précise comme suit le contrôle auquel doit se soumettre toute prétention fondée sur le "droit non écrit" (il s'agissait en l'occurrence d'une prétention fondée sur l'enrichissement sans cause): ayant à interpréter l'art. 1269 du CC néerlandais, qui prévoit que toute obligation naît soit d'un engagement conventionnel soit "de la loi" (*uit de wet*), la Cour décide que ces derniers mots ne signifient pas que toute obligation doit être fondée directement sur une disposition légale, mais seulement que dans les cas non expressément réglés par la loi, il faut accepter la solution "qui se laisse intégrer au système de la loi" (*in het stelsel van de wet past*) et qui se laisse harmoniser avec les solutions faisant l'objet de dispositions expresses (*aansluit bij de wel in de wet geregelde gevallen*). On peut estimer que ces formules expriment, en fait, l'esprit caractéristique du raisonnement juridique en général.

8. Ces dernières années, l'étude de l'argumentation juridique s'est également développée aux Pays-Bas dans un sens plus philosophique, qu'on pourrait dire intéressé par la rationalité de ce mode de raisonnement. De quoi s'agit-il au juste? Constatons, pour commencer, que la description du raisonnement juridique soulève, elle-même, une foule de problèmes théoriques: décrire n'est pas enregistrer, c'est chercher une modèle, c'est organiser l'objet d'étude autour de certaines notions. Or il est clair que ces notions, on doit pouvoir les fonder en dernier ressort sur une conception de ce qu'*est* le raisonnement juridique, défini en fonction d'un cadre plus étendu. Ce cadre plus étendu, c'est d'une part une théorie du droit: on a vu que celle-ci est à l'arrière-plan de toute typologie des arguments (§ 4). Mais c'est aussi une théorie de la "Raison": qu'est-ce en somme que justifier une décision? Les deux lignes convergent, en ce que toute théorie de la "Raison" doit pouvoir, ici, situer, assigner sa place à, la juridicité du raisonnement.
Nous ne pouvons faire mieux, pour illustrer l'état présent des discussions aux Pays-Bas dans l'espace très restreint qui nous est alloué, que de résumer les thèses principales de deux ouvrages récents aux conclusions diamétralement opposées, et dont la divergence prouve que l'étude philosophique du raisonnement juridique est fonction de certaines options fondamentales.
De Wild[38] se pose le problème de savoir sous quelles conditions

une décision judiciaire - ou mieux encore, une série de décisions judiciaires - peut être considerée comme étant le résultat d'un *decision-making* rationnel. Il établit à cette fin une distinction entre le point de vue "interne" des participants au système juridique, qui gouverne le processus de justification de la décision (cette justification s'adresse au for juridique) et le point de vue "externe" de l'observateur en quête d'un critère de rationalité. Selon lui, la "justification" de la décision, telle qu'elle est comprise depuis *Scholten*, concerne en fait la composante heuristique du travail judiciaire, c.à.d. la question de savoir comment le juge *cherche* le droit applicable; or (*Scholten* le dit lui-même) cette recherche n'est pas réductible à une méthodologie précise, elle comporte une part d' "irrationnel" (l'intuition du juge); *De Wild* estime par conséquent qu'elle doit être soumise à une critique fondée sur un concept de "rationalité" qui ne peut que lui être extérieur: ce concept détermine dès lors ce qui est, ou n'est pas, "rationnel" dans la justification établie par les participants au système. Mais comment définir ce concept? *De Wild* écarte à cet effet l'idée fort répandue d' une cohérence de la décision avec le droit positif (le "système" au sens large du mot); cette idée, selon lui, est trop diffuse, la question de savoir si une telle cohérence existe, ou non, faisant précisément l'objet de la décision elle-même. Il lui préfère la notion (analogue à celle que propose *I. Lakatos* pour les théories scientifiques) d'une cohérence propre à la jurisprudence comme telle: la décision serait "rationnelle" dans la mesure où le juge cherche à contribuer de la manière la plus adéquate à une "programme de développement du droit" (*rechtsontwikkelingsprogramma*), cette adéquation maximale étant déterminée chaque fois par comparaison avec d'autres décisions possibles. Mais *De Wild* semble penser que ce n'est que rétrospectivement, et à l'aide de données empiriques relatives à la société (croyances, comportements) qu'on pourra définitivement évaluer si la jurisprudence s'est effectivement développée d'une telle façon "progressive".
Nous ne pouvons entrer, ici, dans le détail de l'analyse proposée par *De Wild* (qui soulève d'ailleurs des difficultés notables: ainsi, sa thèse ne l'oblige-t-elle pas à accuser d' "irrationalité" tout retournement de jurisprudence?). Qu'il suffise de constater son orientation de base, qui consiste en la recherche d'un critère de rationalité "extérieur" au raisonnement juridique lui-même, emprunté à la philosophie des sciences. Un cadre de référence tout à fait différent est adopté par *Vranken*[39]: la recherche du droit applicable est située par lui dans l'orbite d'une théorie de la compréhension des textes (l'hermeneutique de *G. Gadamer*) dont il découle que l'application du droit est tributaire d'une pré-compréhension (*Vorverständnis*) du cas d'espèce orientée sur le contenu idéel du droit (*die Sache Recht* dans la terminologie de

Vranken); le raisonnement juridique ne peut être compris, par conséquent, si l'on néglige sa composante "volitive", c.à.d. si l'on ne voit pas que c'est un discours intégrant des jugements de valeur. On pourrait dire - en risquant une simplification abusive - que *Vranken* propose, au lecteur de *Scholten*, le complément philosophique de sa lecture. Il n'est donc pas question, chez lui, d'un critère de rationalité extérieur au raisonnement juridique, ni d'un rejet (concomitant) de ce dernier vers la seule "heuristique": l'argumentation juridique fait en principe ce qu'elle se propose de faire, c.à.d. *justifier* la décision, mais il lui faut, à cet égard, plus de transparence qu'elle n'en a d'habitude, elle doit être plus explicite quant aux conceptions en matière de justice qui en forment la substance véritable.
Le présent rapport, avouons-le, est écrit dans une optique beaucoup plus favorable à *Vranken* qu'à *De Wild*[40]: nous croyons en effet que la "rationalité" du discours juridique ne peut être mesurée par des concepts applicables au discours scientifique (sinon au sens tout à fait général, mais d'autant plus vide, que tout discours digne de ce nom doit obéir à certaines conditions de cohérence). Le discours juridique doit d'abord être compris pour ce qu'il est en lui-même: comme une variante - très formalisée et très institutionalisée évidemment - du discours moral, ou, si l'on veut, de la Raison pratique, telle que la définit une longue tradition commençant avec *Aristote*. Un courant important se dessine en ce sens dans la théorie plus récente[41]: définir les conditions de rationalité du discours juridique, c'est en dernière analyse définir les conditions de rationalité de tout choix dans le domaine de l'action. Et c'est alors que la juridicité de ce discours, qui entraîne une recherche de cohérence plus explicite et mieux encadrée qu'elle ne l'est dans nos pratiques quotidiennes, peut être étudiée avec le plus de fruit.

NOTES

1. *Traité de droit civil néerlandais. Partie générale*, par P. Scholten, Traduction B.E. Wielenga, préface G. Ripert, Tjeenk Willink/Pichon & Durand-Auzias, 1954. Il semble que cette traduction n'ait pas eu, hors des Pays-Bas, l'audience qu' elle mérite.
2. Snijders, *Rechtsvinding door de burgerlijke rechter*, Deventer 1978, p. 36-37. L'étude de Snijders consiste en une recherche d'ordre statistique portant sur la fréquence relative des divers types d'arguments utilisés par la chambre civile du *Hoge Raad* et par les chambres civiles des Cours d'Appel de 1970 à 1974. V.ég. *HR* 7.3.1980, *RvdW* 1980/42 (réinterprétation de l'art. 1404 du CC néerlandais concernant la responsabilité pour les dommages causés par les animaux): le *HR* dit qu'on ne peut attribuer une importance décisive aux arguments tirés de l'histoire de la loi et du droit; plus important est le développement des opinions sur la question.
3. Wiarda, *Drie typen van rechtsvinding*. Zwolle 1972 (herz.uitg.), p. 62-65. L'auteur se réfère à un arrêt du *HR* du 26.6.1953, *NJ* 1954, 90.
4. Un bon exemple se trouve dans l'arrêt du *HR* du 7.5.1976, *NJ* 1977, 55, relatif au droit au salaire d'ouvriers qui ne participent pas à une grève obligeant l'entreprise à fermer son usine. Le *HR* donne une réponse pour le cas d'une grève organisée, d'une part, et pour celui d'une grève sauvage (ou "action individuelle de protestation") d'autre part: le cas précis doit alors être situé entre ces deux pôles, comme étant plus près de l'un ou plus près de l'autre. V.ég. sur la technique en question: Schoordijk, Typologiseren en moduleren in de rechtsvinding, dans: *Bundel rechtsvinding, opstellen aangeboden aan Prof.dr. J.M. Pieters*, Deventer 1970, et Snijders, op.cit. p. 87 et s.
5. Perelman, *Logique juridique (Nouvelle rhétorique)*, Paris 1976, p. 54 et s.(Tarello), 87 et s. (Struck).
6. Perelman, op.cit., suit une approche quelque peu analogue, l'argumentation juridique étant étudiée chez lui en fonction d'une évolution de nos conceptions du droit (v.ég. note 12 ci-dessous). Observons ici que l'étude des figures du raisonnement juridique peut également suivre une voie purement analytique, pour se consacrer par exemple à la différence exacte entre arguments par analogie, *a contrario*, *a fortiori*, etc.; mais cela relève plutôt d'une théorie de l'argumentation en général, qui ne livre pas de typologie du raisonnement juridique en particulier. On peut également ranger, dans cette rubrique, toutes les informations utiles pour le juriste qui ont trait à l'analyse du langage.
7. Scholten, op.cit. p. 168-169.
8. Ibid., p. 182.
9. Scholten, op.cit. p. 51.
10. Sur l'absence de tout arbitrage "préalable" entre modes d'interprétation: voir également: Vranken, De betrekkelijke waarde van een juridische methodenleer voor de rechtspraktijk, *Ars Aequi* 1979, jg. 28-11 (déc.) p. 189. Le poids respectif d'exigences telles que la sécurité juridique, la systématicité, etc., fait tout au plus l'objet de certaines contraintes assez lâches, d'ordre sectoriel: ainsi, on s'accorde traditionnellement pour attribuer une valeur relativement importante à l'interprétation "stricte" dans le droit pénal.
11. Snijders, op.cit. p. 115 et s. L'auteur remarque aussi que l'établissement de tout "ordre" entre types d'arguments se heurte au fait que le poids de chaque type d'argument en particulier est largement fonction des circonstances: par exemple, l'importance des travaux parlementaires faiblit nettement à mesure que la loi provient d'une époque plus reculée.
12. Voir Perelman, op.cit., pour une telle vision évolutive du raisonnement des juge, sur la base de la jurisprudence belge et française (qui suggère un dynamisme judiciaire plus tardif, dans ces pays, qu'aux Pays-Bas); voir également, pour les Pays-Bas, Pitlo, *Evolutie in het privaatrecht*, Haarlem 1969, qui accentue plutôt l'évolution de certaines "manières de penser" propres à chaque époque en général.
13. Mentionnons également, dans ce cadre, un genre d'indétermination que prouve déjà une analyse purement formelle: il est clair que rien ne vient dicter au préalable s'il faut préférer, dans le cas précis, un raisonnement par analogie à une interprétation restrictive, ou vice-versa.
14. Scholten, op.cit. p. 103-104 (par exemple). On pourrait dire aussi qu'en recherchant les raisons déterminantes "sous" la typologie des arguments, la doctrine regarde en fait vers l'*une* des "autorités" sur lesquelles Scholten fonde cette typologie elle-même: soit, l'adéquation du droit aux réalités contemporaines.

15. J.M. Polak, *Theorie en praktijk der rechtsvinding*, Zwolle 1953.
16. W. van Gerven, *Het beleid van de rechter*, Antwerpen-Zwolle 1973. La terminologie de la doctrine est ici fort confuse: politique (juridique), motifs-extra-systématiques, considération des intérêts en présence, jugements de valeur en matière de justice, etc. Une analyse distinguant "intérêts" et "valeurs" est tentée par Van Gerven, p. 133 et s. Il est clair que la confusion terminologique reflète la très grande variété des motifs en cause, dont il n'existe pas de principe de classification évident; l'analyse relève, à notre sens (en partie du moins) d'une réflexion sur les "valeurs juridiques" (*legal values*) qui dirigent l'évolution des différents secteurs du droit. Nous retenons nous-mêmes les termes de "politique" (juridique) et de "plausibilité contemporaine de la décision".
17. Mais toute règle connaît ses exceptions: ainsi, Snijders, op.cit. p. 80 et s., signale quand-même un certain nombre de décisions du *HR* (2,4 %) et des Cours d'Appel (6,7 %) qui procèdent à une évaluation explicite des "intérêts en cause". D'autre part, on s'accorde pour saluer la motivation très *rechtspolitisch* d'un arrêt tel que celui du 7.5.1976 (voir note 4 ci-dessus).
18. J.C.M. Leyten, dans: W.v. Gerven/J.C.M. Leyten, *Theorie en praktijk van de rechtsvinding*, Zwolle 1977, p. 40, 48. Comp. ég. pour l'arrière-plan philosophique: Th.Viehweg, *Topik und Jurisprudenz*, 1954. L'expression de *topisch denken* ou de *topische controle* est cependant employée également pour dénoter une politique judiciaire soumettant l'application de la loi aux impératifs d'un "consensus social" actuel (voir § 6(b)).
19. Leyten, op.cit. p. 51; v.ég. Viehweg, op.cit. p. 106. Mais il est clair, inversement, que c'est la fonction du débat judiciaire que de dégager dans la mesure du possible une inégalité dans la vraisemblance respective des thèses en présence. L'horizon des arguments ne se clarifie qu'à travers le débat lui-même; celui-ci peut donc mettre à jour des préférences déjà latentes dans nos évaluations communes.
20. Scholten, op.cit. p. 88.
21. J.H. Nieuwenhuis, *Drie beginselen van contractenrecht*, Deventer 1979, p. 4-5. Comp. Viehweg, op.cit. p. 107, pour la mention d'une analyse du droit de la responsabilité civile en termes de principes de responsabilité concurrents, entre lesquels s'imposent de constants arbitrages. On peut opposer au principe général qui vit en régime de concurrence, la "règle" qui elle, cherche à obtenir un monopole: Nieuwenhuis, op.cit. p. 5, Dworkin, The Model of Rules, dans: *Taking rights seriously*, Londres 1977. Cette opposition a soulevé certaines critiques que nous n'examinerons pas ici.
22. Scholten, op.cit. p. 172.
23. Snijders, op.cit. p. 177 et s., 225: les décisions des Cours d'Appel (*Gerechtshoven*) relatives à l'application de "normes vagues" (*vage normen*) telles que le standard du "raisonnable", la "bonne foi", etc., se bornent dans leur très grande majorité à l'énumération des circonstances auxquelles est attribuée ou refusée la qualification en cause, sans que les Cours formulent une règle à ce propos. Mais voir Scholten, op.cit. p. 173: il se peut que le juge ne soit pas en mesure de formuler une règle, c.à.d. "d'indiquer séparément les éléments généraux et spéciaux de sa sentence". A ceux qui jugent après lui que de déterminer alors la portée de sa décision.
24. Snijders, op.cit. p. 108; Wiarda-symposium, *Nederlands Juristenblad* 1977, p. 504 et s. (voir: *stellingen van Prof.mr. J.P. Verburgh*). Signalons qu'en 1973, l'Association des juristes néerlandais (*Nederlandse Juristenvereniging*) s'est prononcée dans sa majorité pour l'introduction des *dissenting opinions* dans la pratique judiciaire.
25. Wiarda-symposium, loc.cit.: Verburgh parle d'une *groepscasuïstiek*; les exemples qu'il tire de la jurisprudence ont trait au droit au salaire en cas de grève, à l'invocation des clauses limitatives de responsabilité, à la responsabilité du transporteur de personnes, à la responsabilité pour le matériel utilisé lors de l'exécution d'une obligations contractuelle, etc.
26. Ibid.
27. J. ter Heide, Iudex Viator, *Ars Aequi* 1967, p. 3 et s.; id. Rechtsvinding, *Inleiding voor de Nederlandse Vereniging voor de Wijsbegeerte des Rechts*, Zwolle 1965; id., *De onafhankelijkheid van de rechterlijke macht*, Amsterdam-Brussel 1970; etc. V.ég. Van Gerven, op.cit.
28. Van Gerven, op.cit. p. 147 et s.
29. Scholten, op.cit. p. 178: le sentiment de la justice est surtout un sentiment de l'injustice; v.ég. p. 177. Les vues de Ter Heide ont été critiquées par *Langemeijer* avec des arguments très analogues: le public réagit de façon frag-

mentaire et inconsistante aux grands problèmes du jour; le juge doit donc lui-même aller de l'avant, en cherchant à raisonner (par exemple, par la voie de l'analogie) la compatibilitédes solutions qu'il retient avec les orientations fondamentales de l'opinion. Voir Van Gerven, op.cit. p. 108 et s.

30. Remarquons cependant que certains grands arrêts du *HR* sont clairement soutenus par une évolution globale de l'opinion dans le sens "négatif" précité: la décision consiste pour autant à mettre au pas la jurisprudence avec une telle évolution des esprits.

31. Sur l'impossibilité fréquente de dégager des vues précises dans les milieux intéressés, lorsqu'il s'agit de questions quelque peu complexes, v. *Ars Aequi* 1969, jg. 18-10 (déc.), *HR* 5.1.1968 et 13.12.1968, note Köster, p.439. Mais v. *HR* 14.2.1969, *NJ* 1969, 189, pour un raisonnement fondé sur une absence de consensus positif chez le public (devoir général des parents de conclure une assurance-responsabilité pour leurs enfants).

32. Comp. Van Gerven, op.cit. p. 106 et s.

33. Les Pays-Bas ne connaissent pas le contrôle de constitutionnalité des *lois*: le juge n'exerce un tel contrôle qu'à l'égard de "produits réglementaires" d'ordre inférieur.

34. Wiarda-symposium, loc.cit. (Verburgh). Il faut ici commencer par reconnaître que les juges argumentent, en effet, comme le décrit la typologie de Scholten, soit, en se référant au donné, à la loi. Snijders, op.cit. p. 223-224: la loi occupe encore toujours une position éminente dans l'argumentation du *HR* (et des Cours d'Appel), et les thèses de Ter Heide, selon lesquelles la volonté du législateur doit toujours capituler devant un jugement de valeur contemporain, ne reflètent donc pas la réalité; comp. Snijders, p. 40 et s. pour l'importance du recours aux travaux parlementaires (*wetshistorie*), et p. 75 pour le recours, également très fréquent, à la *ratio legis* (déterminée, souvent, par référence aux travaux parlementaires). Ibid. p. 171: le *HR* n'aurait décidé *contra legem* que dan 2,6 % des cas étudiés (c.à.d. contrairement à ce que *permet* de conclure le "sens normal" du texte applicable). V.ég. Leyten, loc.cit. p. 58 et s.: s'il est vrai que le juge cherche une décision "raisonnable", conforme aux exigences d'une plausibilité contemporaine, la loi (c.à.d. la volonté clairement exprimée du législateur) constitue néanmoins, à l'intérieur de cette recherche, un *topos* indépendant, ayant un poids certain (Leyten lui-même veut lui accorder un poids décisif), et ceci, quelle que soit la *policy* exprimée dans le texte législatif. Et s'il faut choisir entre plusieurs solutions également "raisonnables", l'appui de la loi fait alors certainement pencher la balance.

35. Scholten, op.cit. p. 107.

36. V. par exemple Van Gerven, Over recht en systeem, *Rechtsfilosofie en Rechtstheorie* 1973, jg. 2 (déc.).

37. En ce sens, à notre avis: Scholten, op.cit. p. 88 et s., et J. Eggens, *Iets over de verhouding van wet en recht*, Afscheidscollege 16.12.1961. Ceci ne veut pas dire qu'un recours explicite aux principes généraux du droit -dans le sens indiqué- soit très fréquent chez le *HR*, au contraire: Snijders, op.cit. p. 71 et s. La doctrine est moins réticente.

38. A.H. de Wild, *De rationaliteit van het rechterlijk oordeel*, Deventer 1979.

39. J.B.M. Vranken, *Kritiek en methode in de rechtsvinding*, Deventer 1978.

40. Ce qui ne veut pas dire que les conclusions de De Wild ne pourraient pas trouver place, selon nous, dans un cadre théorique différent.

41. Perelman, *Logique juridique*, Paris 1976; R. Alexy, *Theorie der juristischen Argumentation*, Frankfurt 1978; Neil MacCormick, *Legal reasoning and legal theory*, Oxford 1978.

The use of comparative law by the legislator in the Netherlands

JAN M. van DUNNÉ *

Professor of Law, Erasmus University, Rotterdam

I.C.1.

'Schlechte Rechtsvergleichung ist schlimmer als keine' — Paul Koschaker

A topic like the one taken for this report is very suitable to leave an author crossed-armed, staring at the empty space beneath the title. Even when restricted to private law, the field is so broad, that a fair amount of hesitation where to start seems justified. On the other hand, this gives an author a *freies Ermessen* in his treatment of the subject, as the odds of incurring a *culpa in eligendo* will not be very high. The words of *Kahn-Freund* come to mind: 'On the professor of comparative law the gods bestowed the most dangerous of all their gifts, the gift of freedom'. However, law still has something to do with order, and some structure in this essay might be helpful. This also gives the opportunity to deal with the intriguing questions posed by the general-reporter.

I intend to start with a general part, offering a frame-work for the treatment of the subject. Attention is given to the international discussion on the use of comparative law in law reform, which leads to the formulation of some starting points for our inquiry into law making in The Netherlands. At the same time an effort is made to obtain clarity on the different uses of comparative law, or should I say, the different forms of comparison of law, by the legislature.

The categories developed in the first chapter are being used in the second chapter, where illustrative examples of the use of comparative law in legislation are brought together. In the last chapter, finally, one finds an analysis of the subject, or rather an attempt in this direction, and further some critical remarks and conclusions.

* The author wishes to express his gratitude to Mr. J.van der Meer, research-assistant, for his energy, and several staff members of the ministry of Justice and colleagues for their information and helpful suggestions. The standard-clause on faults being my own is applicable.

I. THE FRAMEWORK

1. *Comparative law and law reform*

The use of comparative law as tool of law reform is treated by *Kahn-Freund* in his Chorley lecture, published in 1974 under the title 'On uses and misuses of comparative law'[1]. His bold description of the purposes pursued by those who use foreign law in law making, a process characterised as 'legal transplantations', was the start of an animated debate. *Kahn-Freund* distinguishes three purposes: first, the object of preparing the international unification of law; secondly the object of giving adequate legal effect to a social change shared by the foreign country with one's own country, and thirdly, the object of promoting at home a social change which the foreign law is designed either to express or to produce. The debate which followed was concentrated on the second and third categories, the first being of less interest and non-controversial. In the wording of *Marsh*, these categories can be phrased as reforms based on foreign law, which are intended to *reflect* a social change, respectively, *to effect* a social change[2].

Kahn-Freund is using the metaphore of 'transplantation' to stress the effects of this operation: like in the case of a surgical operation there is the risk of rejection by the home environment, which phenomenon is the main point of interest for the author. Through an analysis of some recent transplantations by the legislator in England and abroad (concerning divorce law and family law in general, law of procedure, and the law of labour relations), he comes to the formulation of preconditions for a successful transplantation. These have to do with the socio-political power structure in the recipient country. *Montesquieu* could in his days only think of factors like the climate, and more generally geographical, social, economic and cultural elements, which could be prohibitive for the acceptation of foreign law, or in his own words, which would lead to 'un grand hazard'. *Kahn-Freund*, however, is pointing out the greatly diminishing importance of these factors, not fitting into the western world of today, and discerns on the other hand three important factors unknown to *Montesquieu*: the system of government, democratic or non-democratic, in other words the East-West split; the presidential type of government (USA) or the parliamentary type (Western-Europe); and finally, most important, the role of pressure-groups, 'organised interests in the making and maintenance of legal institutions'. These interests may be in the economic sense, like big business, trade unions, consumer organisations, etcetera, but also in the cultural sense, religious groups, and the like.

This last factor, the organisation of power, is often overlooked in the process of legal transplanting, but the obstacles to transplanting may be formidable. The illustration given by *Kahn-Freund* is the English Industrial Relations Act of 1971, where, as he suggests, the American solution in structuring labour relations was not suited at all to be transplanted into the English situation.

This model presented by *Kahn-Freund* is, to my judgment, very useful, not for the sake of discussion only. It shows some similarity with *Hellner*'s model for the purposes of the legislative process in general: first, the codification of existing law, customary or case-law; secondly, a juridical-technical reform; thirdly, a reform of policy[3]. Reference can also be made to the model for law reform used by *Merryman*, consisting of three kinds of law reform: 'tinkering', 'following', and 'leading'[4].
Returning to *Kahn-Freund*'s model, in the debate which followed the model has been criticised, on the one hand, and has been elaborated on the other hand. The contribution of *Marsh* in this respect is very substantial. He indicates some factors derived from the praxis of law reform, which are missing in the model, that is, in the description of the socio-political power structure: the pressure of time as a practical limit to the use of comparative law, the particular needs of the reform project which do not always correspond with the legal situation elsewhere, the time limit for discussion in parliament. His only criticism of the model is, that it is hard to draw a line in practice between reforms merely reflecting social change and those which are trying to effect social change. The example *Marsh* is giving in this respect is the introduction of the *Ombudsman* in England in an Act of 1967.
A strong opposition to *Kahn-Freund*'s model is coming from the side of *Watson*[5]. His main argument is, that in 'legal borrowing' usually what is borrowed is not the legal rule, but the idea. Legal rules also operate on the level of ideas; the way a rule works in practice is often unknown to the transplantors anyway. More important is his objection against the influence of socio-political factors. The knowledge of the power structure in the donor country in his opinion is quite irrelevant, the home situation prevails[6]. Presumably this has to do with *Watson*'s point of view that there is no natural, close relationship between law, institutions and rules on the one hand and the needs and desires and political economy of the ruling élite or of the members of the particular society on the other hand[7]. It seems that we have to do with a clash of ideas of the historian *Watson* and the lawyer-sociologist *Kahn-Freund*.
This last observation is taken from *Stein*, in his American contribution to the debate; his criticism of *Watson*'s challenge to the *Kahn-Freund* model seems justified[8].

The interesting part of *Stein*'s essay is his stressing of the importance of environmental factors besides the political factors, the latter ones which *Watson* was losing out of sight. Thus *Montesquieu* is put in the spotlights again. The author uses some convincing examples to illustrate the influence of psychological, cultural, and traditional elements in law reform based on comparative law, taken from the development of company law in Western Europe. Here too, it is hard to draw a line between environmental and political or power factors, as *Stein* concedes. Good examples given of the last factor are the 1966 French Law on Commercial Companies, borrowing German law, and, more recently, the 'European' Company Statute, where dissimilarities between donor and recipient countries in the attitudes of the business communities and in the status, ideology and power of the national labour unions have stalled the transplanting process[9]. The home environment in France, but in England as well, considered as *Fremdkörper* the German concept of the two-tier company-board system, consisting of a supervisory board and a management board, and the related concept of worker codetermination. The strong opposition here was clearly of a political nature; decisive factors were in *Stein*'s observation:"the relative power and institutional arrangements of business and labour, of the management and the shareholders, of the bar, of the banks, and of the national and transnational bureaucracy"[10]. Nonetheless, 'environmental factors' also play a role, sometimes even a more decisive role, as *Stein* suggests: the opposition of lawyers (usually of the bar) is sometimes based "on their passionate attachment to national legal doctrine and traditions rather than on vested professional interests"[11].

I would propose to leave the discussion on the use of comparative law in law reform at this stage, and postpone my own observations until we have looked into the Dutch legislative process. So much is clear, that there is a crucial borderline between the transplantation of foreign legal institutions or rules as a consolidation of a social change realised in the home country on the one side, and as an instrument of social change desired for the home country on the other side. In both cases, however, there may be opposition against the proposed operation, though this will be sooner the case in the latter situation. The problem with the phenomenon of social change seems to be, that at first it is being proclamed by a (strong) minority in society, and when it gradually has been realised, it is being resisted by, again, a (strong) minority. There also is the problem of how to establish the existence of a minority or majority in relation to a certain issue; usually it is not only a matter of numbers, but essentially of the power structure and of social and administrative stratification.

At this moment the presentation of the issue will suffice, with the remark that the reason for refusing the transplantation of a foreign institution or rule is of equal interest as the reasons for acceptation of the transplant. We will return to this subject later. Another issue which came out of the debate, also deserving our attention, is the relation between the 'environmental factors' and the 'socio-political factors'. Again, some remarks on my part in advance.
One should take into consideration, to my judgment, that the process of law making, here and elsewhere - in the courts and in the 'streets' - is not strictly a rational process, where pro and contra are being weighed on the scales of reason and logic. Drafts are prepared, made, discussed in legal periodicals, defended and accepted or rejected in parliament, by lawyers and other human beings. Therefore, not only human shortcomings should be reckoned with but also, which is more important, psychological factors such as prejudices in favor or against certain foreign legal systems or institutions - the 'transplant bias' *Watson* is speaking of.
Besides these psychological factors, we may also think of extremely prosaic factors which come close to coincidence, like the command of a certain language, the acquaintance with a particular influential foreign lawyer, the attendence of a particular international conference, etcetera.[12]
A closer look at the socio-political factors also reveals some lacunae which I would like to indicate aforehand.
One can think of this category in the sense of policy-oriented strategies - labour relations offer an excellent illustration. But here we find also the personal element: the party affiliation or involvement with particular political issues of a certain minister of justice or of the civil servants engaged in the drafting process, members of law commissions. Every jurisdiction will have its own illuminating examples. Sometimes a legal idea is ripe for codification, but just waiting for the right person pushing it through treadmills of legislation, using his personal prestige and influence[13]. This is of course becoming more and more exceptional in modern times, the causes of which I leave to the reader's imagination.

The point I wanted to make though, is that one should not lose out of sight the 'bread and butter' politics, which also greatly influence the law making process on a comparative basis. It is not just the time factor playing a role in the game, as a neutral entity. There may be a hurry on the side of a minister in the view of the oncoming general elections, after which his position will be at stake. He may even try to 'buy votes' with the proposal of a specific draft, and the opposition may have the same objective. The enactment of the German *Allgemeine Geschäftsbedingungen Gesetz* (Standard Terms Act) of 1976 is an amazing story of fighting for consumer-

votes by all parties in the legislative process[14]. Finally there is the situation that in regard of the political division of powers, a certain minister is not willing to stick his neck out with the proposed draft concerning a politically touchy issue. The personality of the minister may be as important in this respect as is the soundness of his evaluation of the political situation.
In short, policies which we are dealing with are not necessarily of the star-reaching type but, more often as it seems, down-to-earth policies of political survival or personal interest. Whether this is a general aspect of politics I am not qualified to consider.
A factor not yet mentioned in the debate over the last years is the economic factor which proves to be very influential at times. The field of risk-allocation in specific torts gives a variety of illustrations. The struggle most legal systems are going through, moving from fault-liability to no-fault-liability, with bottlenecks as the aspects of costs, insurance, and the allocation of liability to a group in society, is to a large extent similar to the situation on the socio-political battle-grounds. It deserves special attention though, even when disregarding the recession we are going through recently and its influence on legal solutions for liability questions. In this field the power-structure in society is of crucial importance, and with it the functioning of 'organised interests', insurance companies standing in the first ranks.
So far for the framework on the use of comparative law in legal reform. However, before getting into the field-work, some other uses of comparative law in the legislative process have to be mentioned and furthermore, we have to go into the method of comparative law.

2. *Other uses of comparative law by the legislator*

In the last paragraph we investigated the more spectacular use of comparative law in the legislative process: as a tool for law reform. This, however, is by far not the only use or the most frequent use made of comparative law at legal departments. As indicated by several sources, we have in the first place a common use of comparative law at the pre-drafting stage [15]. The function of comparative law is here,with its '*Vorrat an Lösungen*',('stock of solutions', *Zittelman*), is to clear the ground, to find inspiration or stimulus to realize certain aims. The newer the legal institution or concept which asks for legislation and the less experience with its practice, the greater need for a comparative investigation: compare the introduction of the *Ombudsman*, or of products liability, or security transactions.

This stage may be described as the looking for ideas, and the taking-over of ideas of foreign legal systems. Some authors speak of 'happy plagiarism'; perhaps *Watson* had this in mind when proposing his thesis that no legal rules are being borrowed, but legal ideas. Another use that can be distinguished is the use of foreign law as illustration for the proposed new domestic rule, to reach a greater clarity as far as the future application of the rule or institution is concerned, given the lack of imaginative examples in the own case law or practice. We may think for instance of the introduction, in cases of unjust enrichment, of an action of restitution (*ungerechtfertigte Bereichung*) or of the modification of contract based on changed circumstances (*imprévision*).
A variation on this theme is the use of foreign law as window dressing, just to impress the reader ('Compare Hungary, § 313; Egypt, § 212; Ethiopia, § 164), or more specifically, to sell a controversial rule. Especially in the last case these citations are not always free of an element of fashion or trend, and one wonders whether there is a symbolic function as well. Consumer law cannot go without Swedish law, for instance. A complicating factor here, is the iceberg-aspect of the drafting process. To a great extent the preparatory work, including comparative studies, is staying below the surface of the official documents forming a bill presented to parliament and the legal world at large. As will become clear from the following, this circumstance, a source for frustration for the civil servant and the legal scientist alike, is typical for our subject and contains the danger of making scholarly observations even more academic than they already are by nature. We will return to this aspect later.

Little has been said thusfar about the nonuse of comparative law by the legislator. Leaving aside factors as sheer ignorance, tradition [16], habit, incompetence, shortage of assistance and the like, it may be the case that the domestic situation calling for legislation is unique in its social or political setting, which makes comparison of law rather senseless. The problem of squatting for instance, cannot be detached from the local, Dutch socio-economic context - in a neighbouring country like Belgium the phenomenon even is unknown, due to the nonexistence of a housing-shortage in that country. Then it may be the case that the home-made solution is the fruit of long debates and negotiations with specialists and interest-groups, which makes a comparative excursion also superfluous. Another reason for disinterest in foreign law may be that the solution sought for has to fit into a domestic legal system which is essentially different from the systems abroad in general, or from that of a specific country with a high-standing legal reputation in the field in question. Examples may be found in the Law of Property, of Civil Procedure, Family Law

and in the borderline territory with Administrative Law. The specific solution reached under foreign Law, attractive as it may be in itself, defies transplantation due to excessive costs of altering the surrounding system which is supporting it. Sometimes even a landslide will be caused in the sphere of the legal profession concerning work load and income, when a radical change would be effected by new legislation. This not always needs to be prohibitive, compare the new divorce procedure in England, enacted in 1977, cutting compulsory legal assistance in court - a topic under recent discussion in The Netherlands[17]. The fear to tread, and the inclination to rush will be competing drives in a legislator's mind. Again, we encountered the economic aspects of law reform.
Finally we have the case that the own solution might be considered of exceptional value, which does not invite for code-shopping. It will be increasingly clear that we have entered the soft-ware department now, as one can only go by his own guess, which has little normative value as will be known. For understandable reasons it will not be very likely that the legislator will be very explicit on this point.

3. *The method of comparative law*

An essential part of the framework set up for the treatment of our subject is the method of comparative law. Again, my remarks on the state of the methodology in this field must be seen as an effort to supply rough standards for the evaluation of the activities of the legislator, nothing more.
The abundant literature on this topic offers the obstinate reader a definite structure which, to my surprise, has not seen a fundamental change since the beginning of the century. If one compares the leading textbooks on comparative law, by *Zweigert* and *Kötz*, and by *Constantinesco* on the one hand, and the literature of the first decades of this century on the other hand there is a striking resemblance between the standpoints concerning the character of comparative law and its methodology. Let us take the famous Paris conference of 1900, seen by many authors as the cradle of the science of comparative law. The views expressed by the great French *Saleilles* in his report for the conference, elaborated in later publications, still form the essence of comparative law[18]. The central issues are: the method of the comparative process, the role of sociology of law, and the need for a supra-national system of law. The view of *Saleilles* on these issues is basically the *communis opinio doctorum* of our era: comparative law should be based on a functional approach, directed at law in action and not at black-letter rules; this approach should make use of sociology to get an insight of the functioning of legal rules and institutions; and finally, the comparatist

needs a supra-national system to get some structure in his observations. The functional method to begin with, was defended by *Saleilles* with statements like the following:

> *On croit en effet avoir suffisamment constaté le droit étranger lorsqu'on connaît les textes qui résument. Or, d'abord le tout, les textes ne sont rien sans l'interprétation; et, au point de vue de la critique législative, l'interprétation elle-même n'est rien sans les résultats. Ce sont ces derniers, en définitive, qu'il importe de connaître.*[19]

Function is the paradigm of contemporary comparative law. In the words of *Zweigert* and *Kötz*: 'Function is the start-point and basis of all comparative law'[20].
In the German literature the acceptance of the principle of functionality is attached to the names of *Kohler*, *Rabel* and *Radbruch*[21], in the American sphere the pioneers were *Pound*, *Rheinstein* and *Yntema*[22]. As to the role of sociology of law in comparison of law the state of discussion is characterised by the argument of some authors that comparative law is not just a sub-section of sociology of law[23]. For several reasons the weight given to sociology of law nowadays seems largely overdone. First there is the circumstance that this science, after almost a century, still is a young, promising science. The great expectations, also of comparatists, have not been fulfilled; according to *Constantinesco*[24] no considerable influence by sociology of law can be found in the legal science of France and Germany, and one may add The Netherlands. In the last mentioned country it is still not possible to find enough Dutch candidates for the chairs of sociology of law at the faculties of law; in West-Germany they are starting to abolish the chairs recently. Secondly, it should be possible to distinguish questions in comparative law where sociology of law could be very helpful, and questions where the assistance is of little use. An interesting proposal is made by *Gessner*[25]; in his view a scale can be drawn with on the extreme one end dogmatic legal problems, only to be formulated with the use of legal concepts. On the extreme other side one finds problems which can only be object of a social description as a legal setting fails. In between there are the social problems put into legal categories, usually the traditional categories; then we have also problems where the legal construction is only partially covering the problem in its social context, due to shortcomings of the legal model being out of tune with society, or to the novelty of the problem itself. This scale is in the form of a continuum; *Gessner*'s argument is that only for problems on the half of the scale opposite to the dogmatic problems, that is, the more socially defined problems, the application of sociology

of law makes sense. In the sphere of the other, more dogmatically defined half, the comparatist may with a clear conscience use the traditional legal tools[26]. The proposal makes the impression of a wise self-constraint; furthermore one may call it a functional use of sociology of law.
The general acceptance of the functional method in comparative law, with the aid of sociology of law in certain fields, leads to the conclusion that the process of merely comparing legislative rules of different countries, or I may add, the comparison of cases, institutions and the like, taken by themselves, has little to do with the science of comparative law. In the image of *Saleilles*, statute law is only the skeletton of the law of a country, with flesh, blood and muscles of the living law lacking. For this reason some authors make a distinction between *Rechtsvergleichung* and *Auslandsrechtkunde*, comparative law and on the other hand the study of foreign law. This observation will gain importance when we will come to the investigation of the use of comparative law by the legislature: seeing the custom of only comparing statute texts one wonders whether there is any comparative law in the strict sense involved at all. But let us not run ahead.
What has been said thusfar will obtain some more depth when we give some attention to the models developed for the process of comparison. We will also be able then to comment on the third issue mentioned, the proposal of a supra-national system of rules and concepts. Here again, we find a remarkable similarity in the structure of ideas in this century. As will be known, all good things come in three. Therefore, all models of some importance consist of three stages or categories or phases. Even more strikingly, there is a consistance in the content of every separate stage. In the following survey the model of *Saleilles*, developed in 1900, is compared with the recent models of *Zweigert/Kötz* and of *Constantinesco*.
The three stages are, in the terminology of *Saleilles*,
1. *'constatation'*, 2. *'comparaison'* and 3. *'adaptation'*.
In the first stage the materials are being collected concerning the law of the countries under investigation. This is seen as an objective, descriptive process aimed at the gathering of basic material to give the comparatist access to foreign legal systems. *Zweigert* and *Kötz* and *Constantinesco* are on the same line. After this preliminary step the comparison proper takes place: the second stage. In this stage the differences and similarities of comparable legal figures are being studied, not by way of a simple juxtaposition. In the formulation of *Zweigert* and *Kötz*:...' the solutions we find in the different jurisdictions must be cut loose from their conceptual context and stripped of their national doctrinal overtones so that they may be seen purely in the light of their function, as an attempt to satisfy a particular legal need. It means also that we must look to function in order

to determine the proper ambit of the solution under comparison...'[27]. In the vision of *Constantinesco* in this analytical stage there is the need for a common comparative scheme to investigate a legal figure stripped to its elements, and rearrange common elements according to specific characteristics. Consideration is also given to the relations with the legal system in question and to the meta-legal '*Umwelt*'[28].
This all serves a preparation for the third and final stage: the critical evaluation and possible 'adaptation' in the domestic legal system, the legal transplantation we discussed earlier. As we have seen *Saleilles* stresses the focus on the real results in the practice of legal rules. His approach is also policy-oriented: comparative law serves as an instrument for the development of the law and even law reform. In his view this is the task of the legislator and the judiciary as well[29]. For this purpose the comparatist should develop types of legal institutions, extracted from the different legal systems as the legislator's ideal form: '*le type idéal tout relatif*'. This 'droit commun international' however, is in his view based on the functioning of legal rules, on the results in the solving of social problems. In later publications *Saleilles* also speaks of '*droit commun de l'humanité civilisée*' and shows some natural law influences in his thinking[30].
Compared to the modern view there is much in common. According to *Zweigert* and *Kötz* in the third stage one needs the building of a system of structural concepts which should be achieved inductively during the comparison of different legal systems. 'A system of comparative law will thus seem to be rather of a loose structure. The component concepts cast a wider net than those of national systems: this is because the functional approach of comparative law concentrates on the real live problem which often lurks unseen behind the concepts of the national systems'[31]. Only thus comparative studies can rise above the level of 'national comparative law' and reach the level of truly 'international comparative law' which could form the basis for a universal legal science. The authors also stress the need for critical evaluation.
This last aspect is also an important element in *Constantinesco*'s vision of the third stage, which he calls the synthetic stage. On basis of the analytic scheme used in the second stage the aim of investigation now is by comparing elements in the social functioning to find the basic causes for difference and similarity. This calls for an universalistic approach[32]. In contrast with *Zweigert* and *Kötz* however, he sees no use in the development of universal concepts or types, not even in the restricted sense in *Sandrock*'s approach[33]. In this context *Constantinesco* nor *Zweigert* and *Kötz* are giving much attention to the subject of comparative law as an instrument of law reform. Only the first author has some remarks on *Rechtspolitik* and what he calls the

orientation and control function of comparative law. He observes that in the case of legal-technical reforms a broad comparison of foreign legal systems is useful, which is not the case when the legal institution at stake has ideological, political, national or social characteristics. The foreign solution in the last field may be superior but will as a rule not be suited to fit into the domestic legal order. Political motives outweigh legal motives in this field anyway[34].

II. COMPARATIVE LAW AND THE LEGISLATIVE PROCESS

Before starting our survey of the use of comparative law in the practice of statute drafting I would like to make some preliminary remarks. Like there is a theoretical framework for our topic, there is a practical framework as well. Reference to this framework was made earlier, when we discussed the influence of political and personal factors, the time-factor, and the like. We have to return to this matter first, in order to see the role of comparative law in its proper perspective. What came out of the interviews I held with staff members of the legislation department of the Ministry of Justice is that, seen in whole context of the legislative process, the legal construction plays a very modest role, and so does the aid of comparison of law. As a rule the preparation of a draft is policy-oriented: what kind of a regulation do people want? Then comes the consulting stage on a national and international basis; all kinds of organizations and pressure groups have their say and after an exchange of several drafts a compromise is reached. The results of this stage are binding for the next stage, that of the legal construction. Then there is little room left for experiments, alternatives, and the niceties of comparative law in general.
This model will often hold true: on the other hand, a common model can be construed also with a use of comparative law at the second, consulting stage. A pressure group or interest group is usually looking for examples to back up her position which one often can find in other countries. I will give some illustrations shortly. An other aspect I want to mention which is distorting the comparative scene, is the abundance of international treaties, conventions and the like, which usually are based on a comparative study and which only ask for implantation of certain rules by the national legislator. The pre-fab character of this all sounds attractive, at the presumption that the preparatory work done is of high quality, but a great disadvantage is the time-claim which is laid on the domestic legislation department. Little time thus is left for comparative research in preparing other, self-initiated drafts[35].
The influence of harmonization of the law being a typical aspect of the legislative process of the Western world, less

typical is the codification-project taking place in The Netherlands in the last decades. The New Civil Code is on its way; started in 1947, partially in force since 1970, the complete enactment is planned for 1984. The work on the new code definitely gave an impulse to comparative law. One may doubt however, whether the enormous energy needed for this gigantic project has not been spent at the cost of the quality of the substantive law in its revised form, the form and content of the new legal rules. The speeding up of the procedure in recent years in a 'point of no return'-mood, does not seem to be a guarantee for quality either. In the following I will only incidentally refer to the New Civil Code, as this is the topic of an other reporter. The point I wanted to make in this context, is the time-consuming aspect of the re-codification procedure comparable with the harmonization movement. To my judgment this is not in the interest of law reform based on fundamental comparative research.
As observed above, the evaluation of the use of comparative law in the practice of legislation is being hampered by the iceberg-aspect. As I was told it is almost a standard procedure that in preparing a draft the first step taken is a comparative survey in regard of the subject by way of orientation. It depends on the subject and on circumstantial factors whether a more substantial use of comparative law will follow. This part of the process and the motivation for the decision making stays below surface.

We now come to the survey of the legislation in private law of the last years. It will be by no means an exhaustive treatment, I tried to select illuminating examples of pieces of legislation to support the discussion in the preceding chapter. The arrangement of the materials, reports, drafts, bills and laws, created a problem. I decided to take one category apart, namely drafts influenced by economic factors, and treat the rest on the basis of the intensity of the use of comparative law. I hope that the outlines of the field will become clear and an overall picture can be obtained, revealing tendencies and the legal climate in general.

1. *Economic factors*

It is not uncommon that a change in the national private law will have repercussions in the field of international trade. Thus the market position can be at stake, due to a change in the legal situation. Much of the harmonization endeavour in Europe and elsewhere is based on this very thought and is therefore directed at ironing out legal differences between states. On a smaller, national basis one sometimes sees the same phenomenon and here too, comparative law is used as an instrument.

A first example is the reform of the Pilotage Act 1957. The report of the commission preparing the reform was published in 1981 and contains a considerable amount of comparative work[36]. One of the issues was the liability of the pilot and as consequence of his status as civil servant, the state liability. The commission is stressing the need for a regulation which is in accordance with the situation in neighbouring countries and which takes the insurance aspects into account[37]. An interesting remark was made by the municipality of Rotterdam, pleading for the acceptance of the legal solution found in surrounding countries in view of competitive position of the port of Rotterdam. Laying a greater liability on the pilot or the state could lead to a raise of pilotage fees, and thus make a stay in Rotterdam less attractive.
Another example of the need of keeping up with international developments, be it for less specific reasons, is the Securities Transactions Act 1977 (*Wet Giraal Effectenverkeer*). The international trade in securities in The Netherlands is an estimated 9% of the total trade in this sector. Many Western countries already had introduced a securities transactions system; for several reasons there was a feeling that the Dutch law could not stay behind, among aothers the need for connecting with foreign transactions systems in the international trade. In the report of the drafting commission attention is given to these systems in the countries of Western-Europe, and incidentally, the United States, Japan and Canada. There is a preference for French, Belgian and German law[38]. Only in exceptional cases reference is made to the experience in other countries with the new system, in a casual manner. The most radical change made in Dutch law through this reform is the acceptance of the institution of joint-ownership for this purpose, defended in the past by several authors, but thusfar rejected by the *Hoge Raad* (Supreme Court). The comparative basis given in the report for the introduction of this legal construction is not very impressive[39]. In the 'evaluation' of the commission, qualified as a legal evaluation, it is pointed out that the central theme is the creation of a strong position of the security-owner. At the same time, a stronger argument seems to be of economic nature: the acceptance of the system applied by neighbouring countries which takes out thresholds in the international trade (p. 18). Section 6 of the German *Depotgesetz* stood model for the joint-ownership construction (also followed by legislation in Austria and Switzerland), which is also generally accepted by French and Belgian authors.
In the following the material is put into categories on the basis of the amount of comparative law used in the legislative process, varying from zero to a substantial part.

2. *No or little comparative law used in drafting*

An example of drafting without the use of comparative law is the new Land Registry Act *(Kadasterwet)* which will be presented to the parliament very soon. The motives for this restriction are apparently the unique character of the Dutch system for the transfer of immovables. Like the German system it operates with a land register, opposed to the conveyancing system in Anglo-American law, but the reliance on the register according to Dutch law is relative: it is a so-called 'negative system', whereas German law has a 'positive system'[40].
Another field where almost no comparative law can be found is the legislation concerning leases. This is probably due to the political issues involved, and the typical Dutch setting, with its great housing shortage. This observation also holds true for the solutions sought by the legislator for the squatting phenomenon[41].
In the Door-to-door Sales Act 1973 (*Colportagewet*) the role of comparative law has been very restricted. In the presentation of the draft and in the report on which it was based almost no reference to foreign law was made, let alone a comparison of law. The parliamentory Standing Committee on Justice brought in the comparative aspects: especially in regard of the introduced 'cooling off period' questions were asked about the regulations in other countries and the experience had with the new construction[42]. In response brief information is given by the ministers responsible for the draft, mainly in an illustrative manner: some remarks on the Belgian and Austrian system, and simply a mentioning of countries with a cooling off period accepted in the legislation for this type of sales (Canada, England, Sweden, Luxemburg, USA, Switzerland, and in preparation, Germany and France), with an indication of the length of the period. The answer to the more important question regarding the effects of foreign regulations using the cooling off period, the reply is evasive. An efficient comparison of the draft with foreign regulations is impossible, it is said; the difference in legal systems and commercial customs prevents the drawing of conclusions of value for the legislation in the Dutch situation[43]. A further argument is the lacking of a registration of cases where the contract was repudiated during the cooling off period, in the countries mentioned. No literature has been cited, nor any effort made to put any flesh to the bones of the black-letter rules. It appears highly improbable that no information whatsoever concerning the functioning of all these regulations could be obtained from consumer organisations, institutes, experts, and the like.
It is not clear whether the parliament was convinced by this information; the period was extended from 6 to 8 days, and leaving aside many other objections the policy followed was that some legislation seemed to be better than none.

Another act drafted with little or no use made of comparative law is the Protective Trust for Older Adults Act 1981 (*Wet Onderbewindstelling ter bescherming van meerderjarigen*). The basis for this act were reports brought out for the Netherlands Jurists Association in 1974, by *C.J. van Zeben* (professor of law) and *W. Heuff* (notary-public). In the annual meetings of this *Nederlandse Juristen Vereniging* a standing issue is the need for legislation concerning subjects discussed. The positive reaction of the assembly resulted in the present act. In the draft presented and the comments from the minister almost no signs of comparative law can be found. This was also the case with the *NJV*-reports mentioned: apart from some cursory remarks, *Van Zeben* only briefly refers to the French 1968 act '*portant la réforme du droit des incapables majeurs*', adapting the Code Civil, and to an American 'Report of the national protective services project for older adults'[44]. This time the Committee on Justice of the House of Commons proves less inquisitive: only one suggestion in this respect is made, by the socialist delegation (*PvdA*), to change section 953 *BW* along the line of section 1125-1 of the French *CC*, concerning gifts by deed or will. This suggestion, also made in 1974, was taken over by the minister, as a bye-product of the present act. It is puzzling why with the passing this piece of legislation no need was felt for an extensive comparison with solutions found in other legal systems and, more important, for a survey of the experience with the new institution which is by no means without hazards.

The draft for a Postbank Act (1977) seems to be an example of a legislative effort where the political aspects are a hindrance for an efficient use of comparative law. The motives for activity by the legislator are reasons of efficiency on the one hand, and reasons of policy on the other hand. At stake is the fusion of the *Rijkspostspaarbank* and the *Postcheque- en Girodienst* as a reaction to increasing competition from the side of the banks. Then we also have the consumer interests and anti-trust aspects. Due to concentration in the banking world of the 114 banks of 1963, 18 remained in 1975, of which only 6 are of importance, of which the 2 biggest take 65% of the balance total of the general banks. Thus the creation of a 'Postbank' could promote a healthy competition in banking affairs. Although the development described and endeavours to cope with it by the legislature are a common feature in the Western world, little use of comparative law is made by the draftors. In the comments a remark is made that the solutions found in neighbouring countries are in the same direction the present draft is following, and in an appendix a brief survey is given of the banking situation in the European Common Market - countries, Sweden and Finland[45]. No citations though, and no information about the legal constructions and their functioning. At the moment the future

of the draft is uncertain.
The law of civil procedure is another arid territory for comparative law. In the course of the introduction of the New Civil Code changes had to be made in the Code of Civil Procedure. A special topic was the role of the bailiff and the law of seizures. In the 1981 draft references to foreign legal systems are rare, and usually by way of illustration[46]. The influence of the consultations with professional groups, like the Association of Bailiffs, seems to have been stronger than that of comparison of law[47]. The position of the bailiff in the civil procedure according to the draft has gained considerable importance. One novelty is the introduction of the *deurwaarders-kort geding* (bailiff-injunction procedure) in the field of execution.
Started as an adaptation of the Code of Civil Procedure, what remained in the end was a complete reform of the law of seizures. The minor role of comparison of law is a striking feature.

3. *A substantial use of comparative law in drafting*

It is hard to draw a line between the last category and the present one, some of the legislative products discussed below would also fit into the foregoing category. The Misleading Advertising Act 1980 (*Wet Misleidende Reclame*) is based on a 1975 draft which contained hardly any references to foreign law. A broad statement mentioning the law in Belgium, Western-Germany, England, France and Sweden, and a reference to the resolution of the Council of Europe and the International Code of Advertising Practice is all that can be found[48]. The committee on Justice of the House of Commons was highly disappointed by the draft, and pointed out that the legislation in other countries is of superior quality. The Committee asked for information concerning these regulations in the countries of Western-Europe, and especially about the experience with the Belgian solution to misleading advertising by the introduction of a group action.
In the answer of the ministers a survey is given of the legislation in this field in Western-Germany, England, France, Austria, Sweden and Switzerland. No information is given on the practice in Belgium of collective action, with the motivation that the activities of consumer organisations of different countries are not comparable. Moreover, it is deemed of more importance to wait for experience with the present act[49]. One of the important changes made in the draft is the reversal of the burden of proof in the advantage of the consumer. Without further objections the bill was passed. Here we have another example the initiative for comparison of law coming from the parliament as support for law reform. The level of comparative law presented by the draftors however,

is not impressive at all, but proved nonetheless acceptable to the Commission of Justice in the end.
The 1981 Draft Data Protection Act is based on work done by a state-commission (1976) and resolutions of the Council of Europe OESO, (*OECD*) and EC. In the draft itself reference to foreign law is scarce, recent data acts in Western-Germany, France and Sweden are mentioned, the last one being cited several times[50]. Finally there is the 1981 Treaty of the Council of Europe which has been incorporated in the draft. This setting makes the draft a typical product of the harmonization movement. An interesting aspect though, is that the draftors have joined the general criticism against the report of the state-commission, namely the lack of information about the functioning of data registration systems in other countries (p.3) In regard of the institution of a registration office it is said that research will be undertaken about the practice in Sweden, Western-Germany and France, to get an insight in the personal and material consequences of such an institution. Thus also a basis can be found for the financial aspects (p.24) In the drafting tradition, this is a completely new sound. Is this the influence of the new, progressive minister of Home Affairs and secretary of state of Justice?, one wonders.
In 1979 a report was presented to the House of Commons containing a study of the need for a section in the constitution dealing with the protection of the human body. This study was undertaken at the request of the House several years before. The comparison of law involved is of a general character; most attention is given to German literature and case-law concerning the comparable section 2 of the constitution in a short exposé. In an appendix one finds a brief survey of the regulations in European constitutions and in international documents[51]. The government is opposing the introduction of a specific basic right of protection of the human body in the constitution, with arguments found in the system of the constitution and the suffiency of the section on the protection of the personal way of life, which would include that of the human body. The ministers could not convince the House and an amendment to insert a section on the protection of the human body was accepted unanimously[52]. A remarkable procedure, as the same amendment was defeated years before, in a session leading to the promised study by the government. It seems that this study, shaky as it is, only worked in favor of the emendment. The many examples of foreign legislation apparently spoke a clear language.
Traffic accident liability is the subject of a studygroup formed by the minister of Justice in 1973. The reports came out in 1978 (personal injury) and 1980 (damages) and are based on an intensive use of comparative law. Attached to the reports are preliminary drafts: for personal injury one based on no-fault liability and an alternative one based on a traffic

compensation system; for material damages the draft is based on the so-called barema-system, known in Belgium and France, which is essentially a fault-system[53]. A sharp criticism is formulated by an expert in this field, *Bloembergen*, who may be considered the Dutch *Tunc*. Besides objections against the content of the reports and the drafts, he also criticizes the quality of the comparison of law involved. As he points out, the study-group has insufficiently studied the abundant literature, legislation and case-law on this subject. The description of the no-fault systems in the USA are partially out of date and no endeavour has been made to obtain information on the functioning of these systems.[54] *Bloembergen*'s general complaints about the functioning of the commission have to do with its composition, as being one-sided (civil servants and representatives of the insurance world), and with the poor staff assistance provided. Representatives of other interest groups are missing and so is the know-how of economists, social scientists, social security lawyers. Looking at the legislative activities at large, his criticism seems to be of general importance.

Of the last group of drafts I would like to discuss all drafts have to do with the New Civil Code. Usually they form an integrated part of the code in preparation, but are sent to parliament as a separate bill, to be enacted aforehand for reasons of policy, as a so-called 'front-train'. This policy is based on different motives. Sometimes international treaties or conventions ask for national legislation in a short term, but as a rule there is an urgent need felt for legislation in a specific area of the law, which cannot wait for the completion of the code, planned for the mid-eighties. There is also the motive of promoting the New Civil Code idea, a project which proved more time and energy consuming than ever expected, by presenting some tangible results of all labour. The way it turned out in practice, most subjects taken for a front-train bill were found to be more complicated than initially expected, others were highly controversial. Illustrations of this development will be given below.

The Draft Contract of Road Transportation Act (*Wet Overeenkomst Wegvervoer*) was presented to parliament in 1979 simultaneously with the identical Draft Book 8 New Civil Code, 2nd Part[55]. An increasing need for modernizing the 1950 General Transportation Conditions (modified in 1972) was felt among consumers and transportation companies alike, which explains the introduction of this front train[56]. Domestic law is brought closer to the regulations of the CMR Convention, ratified by The Netherlands in 1960. Comparison of law therefore, is scarce in the draft. Reference is made, and no more, of the Swedish Domestic Road Transportation Act of 1975[57]. This act was not mentioned in the 1976 draft of Book 8, which leaves the impression that no comparison with the recent

Swedish law has been made, at least not overtly. There seems to be no reason, however, to refrain from such a comparative study in 1979, although it may jeopardize the identical status of both 1979 drafts.
The reform of the law of succession is characterized by emotional and political issues and the need for information by comparison of law is amazingly small. In 1969 Book 4 of the New Civil Code was accepted by parliament; the draft dating from 1954 received a substantial opposition from the side of the notaries public. In 1969 the minister promised the introduction of a front train draft covering the issues which were of the greatest political and social interest: the position of illigitimate children and that of the remaining spouse. Reconsideration of the regulation in question and intensive consultation with representatives of the association of notaries public also intended, partially to satisfy the opposition to the law reform. Especially the last subject proved very controversial: the 1974 draft was rejected by the Committee on Justice of the House. This draft was not based on comparative research, the proposed construction, known as 'the longest-living-all' seemed unique in the legal world. As some members of the Committee stated, the deprivation of the children of their position as heir-at-law is a legal novelty. Citing the President of the *Hoge Raad* (Supreme Court) they remark that most European, American and Asean countries place children first in the parential inheritance[58]. Other members question the consequences in relation to the legal systems in surrounding countries (p.12). General remarks made are, the draft being too theoretical in approach and too little focussed on societal developments and on the legal practice (p.7,11). The Committee also asked for the legal-philosophical and sociological foundation of the new construction. In response to the last request the minister conducted an inquiry under the population regarding this question, the results of which were published in a letter presenting the main lines of a modified draft to the Committee[59]. The foreign law referred to in this document consists of two sentences and one footnote, describing the general international development and mentioning a Belgian draft[60].
In 1981 the minister gave up the idea of a front train and reincorporated the subject in the Draft Introductory Act Book 4 NCC[61], presented to parliament October 1981. As a result of the consultations with practicioners and the House of Commons the construction concerning the remaining spouse had been modified into a special usufruct. Judging from the comments that appeared thusfar, like the one by *Van Mourik*, the draftors are still kicking up a lot of dust. Considering all technical questions raised by the draft the acceptance of the bill probably will take some time.

Standard form contracts have been a field of interest of the legislator for a considerable time. In the 1961 preliminary draft Book 6 NCC two sections dealt with unfair contract terms. In 1975 the government announced a front-train draft for this subject and asked advice from the SER, the Social Economic Council, which Commission for Consumer Matters (CCA) presented a report in 1978. In the meantime a combination was sought with the preliminary draft on consumer sales, which appeared in 1978. Here again the idea of putting up a front train vanished after confrontation with the reality of the drafting process. The final draft on the present subject was presented to parliament in 1981 as a part of Book 6 NCC[62]. The consultations of interest groups took place through the work of this CCA-commission where consumer organisations and the business world were represented. Due to the conflicting interests a description the work of the commission as 'a battle of forms' is not unrealistic. The final report, after half a dozen drafts, was clearly a compromise. Very influential were the Swedish consumer acts and the German *AGB-Gesetz*, from which ideas about a 'black list' and a 'grey list' were borrowed. It took three years before the legal department of the ministry of Justice completed a draft, which is an indication of the political implications of the draft.
In the draft the use of comparative law is very moderate indeed. A brief survey of less than half a page is given where consumer legislation from Western-Germany, Austria, France, England, and the Council of Europe is only mentioned, with reference for the contents to the literature[63]. With it goes a general remark that the present draft has been influenced by these acts in many respects, but that, as a rule, they are a valuable source of inspiration but seldom offer ready-made solutions. Very few citations of foreign regulations are given, in a cursory manner, and furthermore some general observations.[64] The reason for this unimpressive use of comparative law could be, in my opinion, that the political choices made outweigh the importance of comparative study. Nonetheless, for a proper evaluation of the proposed legislation and an insight in its functioning the instrument of comparative law is indispensable.
In 1981 another front-train draft was brought on a regular schedule, the Consumer Sales Act already mentioned. The preliminary draft of 1978 was incorporated in Book 7 NCC on Sales[65], which was published in 1972 as a preliminary draft. This book is to a great extent based on a 1970 Benelux Convention on Sale and Exchange and the ULIS (*LUVI*) regulations. The legislative developments concerning consumer sales have much in common with those in the field of standard forms, which just have been described. Here the conflict of interests was even stronger though, and no compromise between representatives of consumer organisations and of business organisations could be reached in the CCA-commission of the SER. The last

group opposed the legislation of consumer sales; the advise came out in 1980.
In the 1981 draft of Book 7, containing the regulation of consumer sales, the use of comparative law, again, is very restricted[66]. At several places references are made to the CCA-advise, e.g. in defending the compulsory character of some crucial sections, a central issue in the opposition from the representatives of business organisations, being the minority in the CCA-commission[67]. In the report of this commission support for a compulsory regulation is found in consumer acts from England, Sweden, USA and Denmark.

III. CONTOURS OF THE USE OF COMPARATIVE LAW BY THE DUTCH LEGISLATOR. CONCLUSIONS.

For an insight in the use of comparative law in the legislative process the materials of the previous chapter are very instructive, at least for the present author. Although a profound analysis would be justified, at this stage of the report I can only give some brief observations, as an aid for the interested reader to draw his own conclusions.
A general impression is that the discussion in Chapter I on uses, nouses and misuses of comparative law finds ample illustration in the materials gathered. The way economic factors are of influence (e.g. Pilotage Act), the influence of political factors (e.g. Postbank Act) or of the uniqueness of the domestic solution for the legal need (e.g. the bill on the law of succession) and its consequences for the use of comparison of law, came out clearly. The role of interest or pressure groups varying from consumers to bailiffs, also came to the fore. The influence of treaties and conventions was considerable too, and with it the negative aspects of the international harmonization circuit: parliament is left out, they concur often with national legislation, they come in high sequence, their text is frequently complicated, their basis usually compromises, which are leading to rigidity. In this sense recently, *Neuhaus* and *Kropholler*[68]. In practice it gives the ministry responsible for a bill on a subject dealt with in a treaty or convention an excuse for refraining from a motivation for legislation and from comparative research.
One of the outcomes of the present study and a surprise to this author, is the active role of the House of Commons, especially the Standing Committee on Justice, in the use of comparative law. As we have seen, in many cases the Committee took the initiative for (additional) comparative research, which the ministry carried out consequently (compare e.g. the bills on Misleading Advertising, Door-to-door Sales, Law of Succession).
As to the quantity of comparative law research used in the legislative process in civil law, the conclusion must be that

it is disappointingly small. But the more important question, in scientific work too, is the one concerning quality. We now come to an evaluation of the method of comparative law applied by the legislator and his purposes for using this instrument, the subject of Chapter I. It seems appropriate at this place to cite a thought-provoking statement of *Kahn-Freund*. At the end of his 1974 article we met earlier in this report, he gives a summing up of his treatise of the comparative method:

> *"All I have wanted to suggest is that its use requires a knowledge not only of the foreign law, but also of its social, and above all its political, context. The use of comparative law for practical purposes becomes an abuse only if it is informed by a legalistic spirit which ignores this context of the law"*[69].

To my judgment, most civil law legislation passed in The Netherlands would fit into this last category of *Kahn-Freund*. The foreign law taken in comparison in ministerial drafts is almost without exception 'black-letter law', the comparison is one of code-texts. A happy exception is the bill on Data Protection and also the initiative of the House in the case of the bill on Law of Succession should be mentioned. In general the functioning of rules of foreign law and legal institutions seems to be of no interest to the draftsmen. Thus, the functional method of comparative law which finds its starting-point at the Paris conference in 1900 and became the leading doctrine after some decennia and is firmly rooted now, in the practice of legislative drafting seems to be of academic value only. The comparative law study in the preparation of drafts, in this observer's impression, as a rule is not going beyond the first of the three stages discussed above, the stage of 'constatation' (*Saleilles)*. An indication for this is the statement made by several draftsmen about the function of foreign law at the start, the period of orientation, as a source of inspiration. The conclusion may be that according to the international scientific standards we have to do with '*Auslandsrechtkunde*' and not with 'Comparative Law'.
In this context the influence of international legal harmonization on national legislation is also of importance. As *Lando* states, uniform laws are often drafted at conferences were academics predominate, who seem to have a professional preference for codified law[70]. His observations regarding the 1964 ULIS (*LUVI*) law is, in my opinion, of general importance.

> *"The basis was a careful analysis of how the sales laws of the world's leading commercial countries were framed. The influence of the existing sales statutes, many of which were of venerable age, was considerable.*

No systematic effort was made to base the draft laws on the experiences of the business communities. We have now, since 1972, seen how numerous enterprises in the countries which have adopted the Uniform Laws have taken advantage of their option to contract out of the Uniform Laws".

Of course there is much which can be said in defense of the hard-working drafting departments at the ministries, as a matter of fact many arguments for the actual process in drafting have been discussed yet, like the time-pressure, understaffing, political aims, et cetera. An argument not yet brought forward which also can be heard at the ministry of Justice, is that the draftors find little support for comparative study in Dutch literature. This observation seems correct, comparative law as a branch of legal science is still in its infancy in The Netherlands [71]. But it was by no means my intention to be an inquisitor, this report must be seen as an investigation by an interested consumer of legislation.
However, legislation is a matter to be taken seriously. It effects by its nature many people and in practice it proves hard to change and therefore it may effect generations to come. Consequently, demands relating to the quality of legislative products are justified, and excuses should be dealt with healthy suspicion if the products are of poor quality or if the treatment in parliament is ill-prepared. Bad laws make hard cases, one case being the effects of dead-letter rules, or the loss of confidence in the abilities of the legislator.
Parliament should get real information about the expected functioning of proposed regulations and not just a survey of countries where the same rules were sent through the House. Only thus the members of parliament are in the opportunity to weigh pro and contra of the law presented on a more realistic basis, namely in its effects in society. Their role should not be restricted to the scrutiny of texts which have been gone already through many hands (even foreign hands) before. For matters of a more dogmatic nature the scale developed by *Gessner*[72] indicates a traditional use of foreign law which is an attractive suggestion.
Of course, the field of study in a functional approach is not without difficulty, and one should also be realistic in the demands formulated[73]. But the current level of study is clearly insufficient in this respect. There is no reason for leaving foreign comparative studies unnoticed (compare e.g. the Traffic Accident Liability Reports). It also seems a too readily made excuse for the omission of comparison of law to point at the 'environmental differences' of countries (compare e.g. the Door-to-Door Sales Bill and the

Misleading Advertising Bill). If one is to characterize the 'style' of civil law drafting in the Netherlands the description would be traditional and rather conservative. The cause is basically the composition of commissions, study-groups et cetera preparing drafts, in which no economists, statisticians, sociologists and others take part. We met the criticism of *Bloembergen* in regard of the law of traffic accident liability, in the same direction is a general observation by *Lando*[74]. In the words of *Lord Wilberforce*, law reform is a too serious matter to be entrusted to the lawyers. Or, as put by *Farrar*: 'For too long law reform has been carried out on the basis of *a priori* assertions or intuitive assessments of social facts and social consequences by lawyers'[75]. The point I want to stress is that the draftors cannot refrain from motivating their proposal for law reform (or any regulation) in the light of its prospective functioning. Comparative law, the '*Kritikweckend*' science in the word of *Zittelman*, is an indispensable instrument here.

Finally a few words on the much debated question on the use of comparative law as 'tinkering', 'following' or 'leading', which we came across in Chapter I. The remark by *Marsh* about the difficulty in practice to draw a line between reflecting and effecting social change by law reform with the aid of comparative law is, looking at the results of our study, justified. Especially where the reform proposed is controversial it is hard to say whether the legislator is following a social change or leading. Compare the introduction of the black list in consumer law, import from Germany and Sweden. The qualification of the role of the legislator is also hindered by the lack of information and motivation in the drafts. An improvement would unquestionably be the accessibility of all *travaux préparatoires*, as is the case in Sweden[76]. In the Netherlands too, we have a '*Gesetzgebung durch Vorarbeiten*[77]. If for instance social research is used the results should also be open to scientific evaluation.

Coming to a conclusion, I would suggest that reform of the legislative process as far as the use of comparative law is concerned, is even more important than law reform in itself. It is only realistic not to increase the workload of the hard-pressed civil servants at the drafting departments of the ministries. Realization of the proposed reform can only be obtained with the use of other means. I would like to make a few suggestions.

A most obvious solution would be the extension of the staff of these drafting departments. At the Ministry of Justice this section consists of some 30 lawyers, of which 7 are occupied with the New Civil Code and 16 with the other civil legislation[78].

This is not a popular thought though, in a time of economy, and moreover this is a political issue. A cheaper solution and perhaps easier to realize, is the search for cooperation in comparative research at the universities. The basis could be contract-research, whether or not on a commercial basis, or the hiring or borrowing of assistants, accepting students [79] as research assistants, and the like. There are no Max Planck-Institutes in The Netherlands, so no ready-made structures are available [80]. It should be worth while the effort. In Sweden judges are working during some time in their career at the Ministry of Justice to assist in drafting.
Another solution, perhaps besides the previous one, would be the staffing of the Standing Committee on Justice of the House of Commons (and of the Senate too, perhaps), along the same lines drawn above. The Committee deserves it, considering her role in the process and moreover some independance in relation to the ministry in question seems to be of importance. The practice in regard of the New Civil Code where the Committee obtained a special secretary for assistance is not a happy example. This secretary is furnished by the department to further a smooth procedure, which in practice means that he functions as '*bouche de la loi*', a loi *in statu nascendi*. Here too, clear structures are not yet available but there is room for inventive action. What could be a more striking thought when dealing with comparative law?

NOTES

1. O.Kahn-Freund, 37 *M.L.R.* 1 (1974).
2. Norman S. Marsh, Comparative law and law reform, 41 *RabelsZ.*, 649 (1977),at p. 661 et seq., originally a paper for the Fourth European Conference of Law Faculties, *Council of Europe*, Strassbourg 1976.
3. Jan Hellner, Rechtsreform durch Gesetzgebung im Bereich des Verbraucherschutzes, in: *Festschrift Zweigert*, 1981, 827, at 833. The first type he distinguishes, is the traditional type, the 'Ubersetzung' of the 'herrschende Lehre' by codification. The second type 'rechtstechnisch reformierende Gesetzgebung', deals with adaptation or extension of existing statutes, without the pursuit of new goals. In the last type however, the 'rechtspolitisch reformierende Gesetzgebung', new (political) goals are set, to change an unsatisfactory legal situation.
4. John Henry Merryman, *Comparative Law and Social Change*: On the Origins, Style, Decline & Revival of the Law and Development Movement, 25 *Am.J. of Comp.L.* 457, at 462 (1977). 'Tinkering' stands for accepting the existing system, keeping it operating, 'following' for adjusting the legal system to social change, 'leading' for the use of law to change society. Compare also J.H. Merryman, D.S.Clark and L.M.Friedman, Law and Social Change in Mediterranean Europe and Latin America, 1979, 2; Merryman, 17 *Stanford J. of Int.L.*357, at 367 (1981). The topic of legislation and law reform is by no means a recent feature. Merryman, 1977, 462, refers to the Thibaut - Von Savigny debate about German codification in the early 19th century: codification seen as a way of achieving a number of important social objectives (Thibaut), contra codification as the finding and crystallizing of German law into statutory form (Savigny).
5. Alan Watson, legal transplants and law reform, 92 *L.Q.R.*, 79 (1976); Comparative law and legal change, 37 *Cam.L.J.*313 (1978). Compare also his Legal transplants, Edinbourgh 1974, 17; Society and legal change, Edinbourgh 1977. In his first mentioned article Watson points out that Montesquieu is closer to Kahn-Freund than the latter realizes: Montesquieu also stresses the importance of political factors and the knowledge of the foreign political context.
6. 1976, 82.
7. 1978, 315. Watson observes 'that private law in most countries of the Western world is in large measure out of step with the needs and desires of all classes of society and yet can continue unchanged for centuries'. His views on 'the transmission and longevity of rules' are based on a study of the reception of Roman law in the Western world and of the French, German and Swiss Codes in other parts of the world. For a criticism on the last part, see Stein, infra.
8. Eric Stein, Uses, Misuses and Nouses of Comparative Law, 72 *Northw. U.L.R.*, 198 (1977).
9. The French act took a preparation of 25 years, and despite the immense amount of preparatory work, indicated with impressive figures by the author, the resulting text of 1966 was a bleak version of the original draft. This draft met more than 400 amendments in the National Assembley and 548 in the Senate.
10. p. 208. See for this subject also: Eric Stein, *Harmonization of European Company Law - National Reform and Transnational Coordination*, 1971.
11. A striking - and well-known - example the author gives, is 'the lingering devotion on the part of some Italian and French lawyers to the theoretical concept of a company as a contract as distinguished from the modern concept of a company as a legal person' which seemed to have played a greater role than any policy differences in determining the parameters for the 'one-man' company or the circumstances under which a company may be declared null and void', at p. 208.
12. An example: in the Preliminary Draft Book 6 New Civil Code (Obligations) references to Italian law are made frequently, contrary to later drafts. This was a result of the special interest of F.J. de Jong, one of the draftsmen, who had a command of Italian.
13. An illuminating example is J.C. van Oven, who as a retired professor of law at the age of 74 was called upon as minister of justice, and through his personal efforts lead the 1957 act through parliament, granting women legal capacity, a reform which Van Oven had defended vigorously in the twenties. Due to a cabinet crisis he stayed longer than foreseen and took the opportunity to get also other pieces of important legislation through.

A recent example of a draftsman whose skill and prestige make the legislative process run smoothly, is H. Schadee, who drafted Book 8 New Civil Code, on Transport.

14. Information obtained from E.H.Hondius. On the relation between special acts and the legal (code) system, compare Reinhard Damm, Verbraucherrechtliche Sondergesetzgebung und Privatrechtssystem, *JZ* (1978), 173.
15. Compare for instance, Ole Lando, The Contribution of Comparative Law to Law Reform by International Organizations, 25 *Am.J.Comp.L.*641, at 647 (1977) ('investigation stage'); Klaus A. Ziegert, Juristische und soziologische Empirie des Rechts, 45 *RabelsZ.* 51, at 70 (1981).
16. Compare for the American situation where law reform is seldom preceded by systematic, conscious comparative study: Stein o.c. 210; Edward M. Wise, Legal Tradition as a Limitation on Law Reform, 26 *Am.J.Comp.L.*, 1 (1978), at 14.
17. Compare H.U. Jessurun d'Oliveira's lecture at the meeting of the Netherlands Comparative Law Association, January 1982, published in 57 *NJB* 309 (1982). The subject was also treated by Zander in his lecture at the 1981 conference of the Deutsche Gesellschaft für Rechtsvergleichung in Frankfurt.
18. For Saleilles, his work and ideas, compare Léontin-Jean Constantinesco Rechtsvergleichung I, *Einführung in die Rechtsvergleichung*, 1971, 161, 234, (French translation 1972) and recently Klaus A. Ziegert, O.C., at 61. The views of Saleilles were shared by several other French authors of that period, like Lambert, Tarde, Deslandres.
19. Citation by Ziegert, 61.
20. Konrad Zweigert and Hein Kötz, *An Introduction to Comparative Law, I The Framework*, Amsterdam 1977, translated from the German by Tony Weir, 36.
21. Ibid.,23; Constantinesco I, 143, 178. Compare also the essays collected in *Rechtsvergleichung*, K. Zweigert and H.J.Puttfarken, Eds., Darmstadt 1978.
22. Compare Constantinesco II, *Die Rechtsvergleichende Methode*, 1972, 189, 263 (also in French translation, 1974); Jerome Hall, Comparative Law as Basic Research, 4 *Hastings Int. Comp., L.R.*, 189 (1980). Rheinstein's collection of essays appeared also in a German translation, Einführung in die Rechtsvergleichung, 1974. For the functional method, compare further Michael Bogdan, Different Economic Systems and Comparative Law, *Comp. L. Yearbook* 1978, 89, at 93, and recently Efstathios K. Banakas, Some Thoughts on the Method of Comparative Law: The Concept of Law Revisited, 67 *Archiv f.R.u.Soz.phil.* 289 (1981).
23. Constantinesco II, 265. For the role of sociology of law compare also Bogdan, o.c., 94; J. Carbonnier, l'Apport du droit comparé à la sociologie juridique, in: *Livre du centenaire de la Société de Législation Comparée*, Paris 1969, 75; H.A. Schwarz-Liebermann von Wahlendorf, *Droit Comparé, Théorie générale et Principes*, Paris 1978, 44, and for an impressive survey, Keebet von Benda-Beckmann, Einige Bemerkungen über die Beziehung zwischen Rechtssoziologie und Rechtsvergleichung, 78 *Zeitschr.f.Vergl.Rw.* 51 (1979).
24. o.c. 263
25. Volkmar Gessner, Soziologische Überlegungen zu einer Theorie der angewandten Rechtsvergleichung, 36 *RabelsZ.* 229 (1972).
26. o.c. 240. Support for this point of view is given by Zweigert, Die Soziologische Dimension der Rechtsvergleichung, 38 *RabelsZ.* 299, at 312 (1974). In the same sense also Drobnig, compare Von Benda-Beckmann, o.c. 52.
27. o.c., 37.
28. o.c. II, 147, 280.
29. o.c. I, 168.
30. o.c.II, 357, where besides Saleilles also Lambert and other authors accepting 'La structure conceptuelle de la science de droit comparé' are being treated by Constantinesco.
31. o.c., 38. Reference is made in this context to the work of Drobnig, and the approach of Sandrock is rejected, at p. 40.
32. o.c. II, 280, 294, 323, compare also 371.
33. o.c. II, 361.
34. o.c. II, 371.
35. Compare the complaint in the Comment on the Draft Data Protection Act, 1981, Memorie van Toelichting p. 4, stating that the time-consuming international consulting went at the cost of the preparation of the Act. Compare in general on the overburdening of the national legislature: Jan Kropholler, *Internationales Einheitsrecht. Allgemeine Lehren*, 1975, 23; Hein Kötz, Gemeineuropäisches Zivilrecht, in: *Festschrift Zweigert*, 1981, 481, at 483. See for a critical review of harmonization also Paul Heinrich Neuhaus and Jan Kropholler, Rechtsvereinheitlichung - Rechtsverbesserung? 45. *RabelsZ.* 1981, 73 at 78.

36. Final Report of the Commission for the reform of the Pilotage Act 1957 (Loodswet), Ministry for the Maintenance of Ways and Waterways, sept. 1981. Reference is made to the law in Belgium, W.-Germany, France, England, Canada, USA, Japan, including the work of Law Commissions in this field. No citations are given in the report, however.
37. p. 76, 88. The commission is advising further study by qualified experts as preparation for a draft. The 1957 Act contains exemptions clauses for civil liability of the pilot (with cases of gross or international negligence excepted) and for state liability, the last being severely criticised by the group of 'users', p. 74.
38. Rapport van de commissie giraal effectenverkeer, 1974. The commission started the work in 1970, the draft appeared in 1976 and passed parliament in 1977.
39. p. 16 et seq. Compare for this subject F.H.J. Mijnssen, 53 *De NV* 1975, 199, at 200, where also Dutch law is discussed as it was before the proposed Draft, a matter one is missing in the report.
40. Compare for the choice made in the New Civil Code the discussion in the House of Commons, *Parlementaire Geschiedenis NBW, Boek 3*, 107.
41. Unoccupation Act 1981 (Leegstandswet).
42. Voorlopig Verslag, *Tweede Kamer* 1971, 11106 nr. 6, p. 7. The cooling off period proposed was one of 6 days. General information was asked about periods in other countries and specific information on the experience in Belgium and Austria. The advisory commission preparing the draft, a SER-commission (Social-Economic Council) had taken a position against the cooling off period.
43. Memorie van Antwoord, 1972, 11106 nr. 7, p.11.
44. *Handelingen NJV* 1974, I p. 61 note 2; passim, e.g. 52, 63. In Van Zeben's proposal for legislation connection is sought with the New Civil Code, especially the regulation of 'bewind' (trust) in general. This became also the approach of the draft.
45. *Tweede Kamer*, 1977, 14632 nr. 3, 14; 50, 51; Compare also nr. 7 (1981). The draft was issued by the minister of Finance and the secretary of state for the Maintenance of Ways and Waterways.
46. Introductory Act Books 3-6 New Civil Code, first part, containing the change of the Code of Civil Procedure, the Code of Judicial Organisation and the Bankruptcy Act, *Tweede Kamer* 1981, 16593, nr. 3. Compare p. 10, costs of litigation, Belgian and German law; p. 6, execution, Belgian and French law, p. 111, seizure, French, Belgian and German law; p. 142, bankruptcy, German law. Only sections of codes are referred to.
47. Compare M. Teekens, 91, *De Gerechtsdeurwaarder*, 53. (1981). For a survey of the reform of the law of seizures, H. Stein, 61 *Advocatenblad* 1981, 85; 106.
48. *Tweede Kamer* 1975, 13611, nr. 3, 4, 9; nr. 4, 17.
49. nr. 6, 16; nr. 8, 2. The point of interest to the Commission was the role of the Government in the Belgian legislation. Compare also nr. 9, 3, where the ministers are requested to reconsider this issue.
50. Regels ter bescherming van de persoonlijke levenssfeer in verband met persoonsregistraties (Wet op de persoonsregistraties), *Tweede Kamer* 1981, 17207 nr. 3, 4; 6; 27; 48.
51. *Tweede Kamer* 1979, 15463 Nota over de vraag of een bepaling over het recht op onaantastbaarheid van het menselijk lichaam in de Grondwet zou moeten worden opgenomen, nr. 2, 4; 21.
52. *Handelingen Tweede Kamer* 1979, 5678. The amendment was from Kappeyne van de Copello c.s.
53. Studiegroep Verkeersaansprakelijkheid over de Vergoeding van schade door dood en letsel; the reports are discussed at length by A.R. Bloembergen, 53. *NJB*, 693; (1978) 1980, 925.
54. *NJB* 1980, 928. Bloembergen is supporting his standpoint and his criticism of the reports with an impressive use of comparative law. He also cites studies on the functioning of no-fault systems in several jurisdictions.
Compare also his remarks in 56 *NJB* 1981, 910, on the legislative procedure.
55. *Tweede Kamer* 1979, 15963 and 15966.
56. Compare 15963 nr. 3, 1 and also R. Cleton, 30 *Ars Aequi* 1981, 247. The proposed act corresponds with titel 13 of Book 8 CC.
57. 15963, nr. 3, 5, in the sense that the Swedish act is not identical to the CMR Convention, as is the Dutch draft. Reference is made only to the article by Petersson and Wetter in *Lloyd's MCLQ* 1978, 567.
For a discussion of the draft Book 8, see K.F.Haak, 108 *WPNR* 513, 529 (1977).

58. *Tweede Kamer* 1974, 12863 nr. 4, 6. Compare for the history of the draft also M.J.A. Van Mourik, 57 *NJB* 1 (1982).
59. 12 863, nr. 5 (1978). Statistical information is given also. In the new proposal the position of the remaining spouse is in the form of a special usufruct, also known in a Belgian draft. The Association of Notaries Public also held an inquiry under their members in 1974.
60. at p. 9. In the Belgian draft the usufructuary's authority to act is depending on permission of the judge, contrary to the Dutch draft.
61. 17141, appearing as part 3 of the Introductory Acts Books 3-6 NCC. Compare for a survey of the reform in inheritance law according to Book 4: Commissie Erfrecht, 112 *WPNR* 5590-93, (1981); Van Mourik, o.c. The regulation of the position of illegitimate children has been presented earlier, under nr. 16585, as a consequence of the Marckx-case of the European Court (1979).
62. *Tweede Kamer* 1981, 16983, Introductory Act Books 3-6 New Civil Code, 2nd Part, Standard Forms (Algemene Voorwaarden).
63. nr. 3, 13; general reference is made to the Israelean, and Swedish acts, a Luxembourg and a Belgian draft and the Italian CC.
64. Compare p. 12, 28, 30, 66. A preliminary draft on this subject remained unpublished but has been discussed with interest-groups and experts. This predraft contains more references to foreign law than the final draft. The AGB-Gesetz is cited most and further one finds European legislation mentioned cursorily. No reference is made to Swedish law; a staff member of the department however, spent some time in Sweden to study consumer law there, as I was informed.
65. Draft of an Act Establishing and Introducing Title 7.1 (Sale and Exchange) of the New Civil Code, *Tweede Kamer* 1981, 16979.
66. nr. 3, e.g. 12, 16.
67. 14, 16.
68. o.c., 78. Compare also Kötz, o.c. 483: Lando, o.c. 651. Compare also, on the compromise character of the ULIS (LUVI) convention, the draft Consumer Sales Act, o.c.3.
69. o.c., 27.
70. o.c. 651. In contrast to the 'professorial' way the Hague Uniform Laws were drafted Lando points at the empirical way of drafting in the case of the American Uniform Commercial Code, using extensive studies in the field of business life in the various commercial centers of the US.
71. For a survey, compare E.H.Hondius, Teaching and research in comparative law in the Netherlands, 24 *Neth. Int.L.Rev.* 560 (1977) At the moment not every faculty of law has a full chair in (civil) Comparative Law; two chairs are presently occupied by foreign scholars.
72. Supra, p.
73. For a sympathetic but rather utopian proposal for multi-disciplinary methodology and research, compare A. Esin Orücü, Symbiosis between Comparative Law and Theory of Law - Limitations of legal Methodology, Inaugural lecture Erasmus University Rotterdam 1982, *Meded. Juridisch Instituut nr. 16*, 1982.
74. o.c., 651.
75. J.H. Farrar, *Law Reform and the Law Commission*, London 1974, 78. For a general criticism in this sense in regard of the New Civil Code, see my article in 52 *NJB* 342, at 345 (1977).
For a stimulating example of broadening the process of consultation, compare the practice of the Australian Law Reform Commission which goes much further than the publication of working Papers like the English Law Commission does. Compare Michael Zander, *The Law-Making Process*, London 1980, 301.
76. Compare Hellner, o.c. 647; William Dale, *Legislative Drafting: A New Approach*, London 1977, 101. This is based on the Swedish Administrative Publicity Act. Under the Dutch Act (Wet Openbaarheid Bestuur) the publicity of these materials in principle is excluded, in view of policy questions.
77. An example of the publishing of preparatory work is the report by J.R.A. Verwoerd, *on the Reform of the Judicial Organization in Belgium*, 1978, a literature study done at the request of the State Commission for Reform of the Judicial Organization.
78. In the Dutch system most ministries have their own drafting department; for a survey compare J.M. Polak, Preadvies NJV 1979, Hand. *NJV* 1, 1979, 20. For the English system, using one central department, the Office of Parliamentary Counsel, serving all ministries, compare Zander, o.c. 1; Dale o.c. 331 (with also a description of the French, German and Swedish systems).

79. In the consumer legislation a draft on consumer sales was prepared by Tilburg students which was discussed in the bill.
80. The Inter-Universitary Asser Institute is dealing with international law, private international law and European law. Compare also Hondius' survey, o.c., 568.

Le placement d'enfants dans les familles de remplacement aux Pays-Bas

M. ROOD-DE BOER
Professeur à l'Université d'Utrecht II.A.2.

INTRODUCTION.

1. Dans l'article qui suit, il est répondu à quatorze questions formulées par Monsieur le Professeur W. Czachorski (Varsovie), qui a été désigné comme rapporteur général pour le thème "Famille de remplacement", dont il sera question lors de la Conférance de l'Académie Internationale de Droit Comparé devant avoir lieu au cours de l'été 1982 à Caracas. La questionnaire établi par Monsieur le Professeur Czachorski a surtout trait aux aspects formels du cadre juridique des placements en famille de remplacement, a l'ensemble des problèmes de financement et aux questions de gestion. Il va donc de soi que dans les réponses à ce questionnaire ce sont des points juridiquesformels, des points financiers et des points de gestion qui ont été traités.
Il s'agit point par point de questions importantes, mais cela ne signifie pas pour autant que, sur les placements en famille de remplacement aux Pays-Bas, il n'existe pas de littérature ni plus abondante ni différante de celle ayant été mentionnée dans les réponses aux questions officielles. L'exposé du cadre juridique, avec les réglementations de subvention qu'il comporte, est en effet une chose, la pratique vécue de placements dans des familles de remplacement en est un autre, bien spécifique.
Quelques-uns de ces points d'application seront signalés ci-dessous.

2. Les *objectifs* factuels des placements en famille de remplacement n'ont pas été traités de façon substantielle dans les réponses au questionnaire. Les études effectuées aux Pays-Bas mettent souvent en évidence une attitude ambivalente de la part des organismes de placement. Il semble qu'il y ait "une tendence à maintenir toutes les options ouvertes" (Junger-Tas), et qu l'on puisse même parler d'une

certaine préférance à replacer l'enfant dans son milieu d'origine au moment opportun. Il va de soi qu'une telle ambivalence constitue une source d'incertitude permanente, tant pour les parents de remplacement que pour l'enfant confié à leur garde (Weterings). Des recherches ont été effectuées concernant la *selection* des parents de remplacement ainsi que leur *motivation* (Wit, Weterings). Mais on ne sait pas avec certitude quelles motivations sont liées au succès ou à l'insuccès des placements en famille de remplacement. On n'est pas non plus renseigné sur la présence d'un rapport manifeste entre la sélection des parents de remplacement et l'insuccès éventuel du placement.
Selon toute probabilité *l'attitude pédagogique* des parents de remplacement à légard de l'enfant adoptif constitue un facteur de réussite d'un placement dans une famille de remplacement tout aussi important que la sélection et la motivation précédemment mentionnées. Il est évident qu'il ne peut être fait ici abstraction de la *personnalité* même de l'enfant. Un placement en famille de remplacement est à ce point le résultat d'un processus d'interaction qui ne peut être fait à l'avance de pronostic réel sur le succès du placement. Il est impossible dans le cadre qui nous est imparti de traiter en détail toutes les recherches ayant été effectuées aux Pays-Bas dans le domaine des placements en famille de remplacement.
Il faut toutefois mentionner que la réponse aux questions officielles n'est guère plus que l'esquisse d'un cadre formel. La matérialisation de ce cadre présente un aspect très varié et trop nuancé pour qu'il puisse en être rendu compte ici.

Bibligraphie:

O.C. Wit, *"Recht en billijkheid"* 1972
A.M. Weterings, *"Het opvoedingsproces in een pleeggezin"* 1977
J. Junger-Tas, *"Pleeggezinplaatsingen: een overzicht"* 1981.

FAMILLES DE REMPLACEMENT

QUESTION I:

La famille de remplacement est-elle reconnue comme institution légale dans votre système?
Si tel est le cas, quelles sont les sources formelles à citer dans ce domaine?

RÉPONSE:

La famille de remplacement est reconnue comme institution légale dans le système juridique néerlandais.
Les sources formelles à cet égard sont les suivantes:
- Le Code civil
- Le Code de procédure civile
- La Loi de principes pour la protection de l'enfance et la Décision exécutoire
- La Loi sur les enfants confiés à la garde de familles de remplacement et la Décision exécutoire.

Ainsi que:

- Lois fiscales
  - Loi sur les successions
  - Loi sur l'impôt sur le capital
  - Loi sur l'impôt sur le revenu

- Lois sociales
  - Loi sur les allocations familiales
  - Loi sur l'aide sociale générale
  - Loi sur l'assurance-maladie
  - Loi sur les indemnités de maladie
  - Loi générale sur les frais de maladie particuliers.

Le Code civil adopte comme point de départ la situation normale, dans laquelle les enfants grandissent entre leurs parents d'origine. La loi tient néanmoins compte du fait que, dans certains cas, la situation est différente, soit parce que les parents sont décédés, soit parce qu'ils ne jouissent plus de l'autorité parentale, soit encore parcequ'il est préférable pour l'enfant qu'il grandisse ailleurs, dans une famille de remplacement par exemple. Notre Code civil ne connaît qu'une clause spécifique, à l'égard de la famille de remplacement: il s'agit du droit d'obstruction dont jouissent les parents de remplacement et qui prévoit que, si l'enfant a été pris en charge et élevé, avec l'accord des parents d'origine, pendant au moins un an dans la famille de remplacement, les parents d'origine ne peuvent reprendre l'enfant dans leur propre famille que moyennant l'accord des parents de remplacement. Les parents de remplacement peuvent donc en quelque sorte faire obstacle au retour de l'enfant dont ils ont la garde dans la famille des parents d'origine.

Si les parents de remplacement font ainsi obstacle au retour de l'enfant, souhaité par les parents d'origine, ceux-ci peuvent demander au juge des enfants une autorisation suppléante, ce qui veut dire que l'autorisation du juge se substituera au refus des parents de remplacement.
Le juge des enfants ne rejettera cette demande des parents de remplacement qu'en cas de crainte fondée que, s'il donnait son assentiment, les intérêts de l'enfant ne soient négligés (Code civil, article 246a).

Le *Code de procédure civile* décrit la procédure à suivre lorsque les parents de remplacement ne donnent pas au parents d'origine de l'enfant l'autorisation de modifier le lieu de séjour de celui-ci (Code de procedure civile, article 955 a-c).

La *Loi de principes pour la protection de l'enfance* (1961) a pour but de fixer des règles concernant la mise à exécution des mésures et des sanctions pénales pouvant être prononcées à l'égard de mineurs en vertu des stipulations du Code civil et du Code pénal. Il y est indiqué les oeuvres privées, les établissements, les foyers et les familles de remplacement auxquels peuvent être confiés les enfants placés sous la tutelle d'une personne civile ou provisoirement confiés au Conseil pour la protection de l'enfance ou mis (provisoirement) sous la surveillance ou à la disposition du gouvernement.

La *Décision exécutoire de la Loi de principes pour la protection de l'enfance* pose des conditions concernant le personnel attaché à l'organisme, à l'organisation de l'administration, à la surveillance des mineurs, à leur santé physique et psychique, à leur éducation et à leur placement dans des familles de remplacement, dans des institutions et des foyers. Il ressort de la Loi de principes et de la Décision exécutoire que la prise en charge des enfants confiés à la protection de l'enfance relève en premier lieu dans notre système de l'initiative privée (des oeuvres privées).

La *Loi sur les enfants confiés à la garde de familles de remplacement* a été élaborée en 1951 parce que le législateur a considéré comme d'interêt public que le soin et l'éducation des mineurs dans les institutions et les familles de remplacement remplissent des conditions raisonnables. La loi résulte principalement de la nécessité de mettre fin au prises en charge incontrôlées où des enfants étaient placés par leurs propres parents ou par les personnes en ayant la garde dans des familles de remplacement, sans que cela ne soit signalé aux organes publics concernés, de telle sorte qu'il n'existait aucun contrôle. Toutes sortes d'abus en étaient la conséquence. Il a en premier lieu été recherché une solution sous la forme d'ordonnances locales, mais celles-ci présentaient souvent tant de divergences qu'il n'y avait plus trace ni d'aucune unité, ni de contrôle réel. La Loi sur les enfants confiés à la garde de familles de remplacement confie au Conseil pour la protection de l'enfance le contrôle des familles de remplacement et de l'observation des conditions en matière d'habillement, d'alimentation, de logement, d'enseignement, de soins physiques et psychiques et de traitements médicaux, telles qu'elles sont énumérées dans la Décision exécutoire.

QUESTION 2 A):

Comment peut-on préciser la fonction fondamentale de la famille de remplacement, dans le cas où celle-ci existe?

RÉPONSE:

La tâche fondamentale d'une famille de remplacement consiste à offrir à l'enfant lui étant confié la sécurité et la chaleur d'un foyer. Dans une bonne famille, l'apport d'une sécurité fondamentale et d'une éducation entourée d'amour et de chaleur constitue pour les enfants qui grandissent dans cette famille des fonctions allant de soi.
Pour les enfants à qui cet apport a fait défaut dans leur famille biologique d'origine, un placement dans des familles de remplacement peut être préparé. Le choix de la famille de remplacement recherché depend néanmoins du cas spécial de l'enfant et du degré selon lequel celui-ci a été défavorisé.

QUESTION 2 B):

En cas de placement dans une famille de remplacement, s'agit-il de l'éducation et des soins de l'enfant ou, en plus, de sa représentation sur le plan juridique ou de la défense de ses intérêts?

RÉPONSE:

Dans la plupart des cas de placement dans des familles de remplacement, il s'agit de l'éducation et des soins de l'enfant par les parents de remplacement. Lorsque le juge confie aux parents de remplacement l'autorité (tutelle), la représentation légale de l'enfant et la défence de ses intérêts leurs incombent alors aussi.

La littérature publié sur ce sujet fournit diverses descriptions des differentes sortes de familles de remplacement.

1. *Familles de remplacement adoptives*
Les parents adoptifs présentent aussi vite que le délai légal le leur permet une demande d'adoption de l'enfant se trouvant déjà dans leur famille au juge compétent.

2. *Famille de remplacement permanente*
Si l'enfant n'a pas ou peu de contact avec ses parents d'origine, il peut se constituer dans la famille de remplacement une situation ressemblant à un haut degré à la situation usuelle d'une famille courante. Il peut y avoir des raisons pour lesquelles il ne peut être procédé à une demande d'adoption. La différence d'âge entre les parents de remplacement et l'enfant peut par example être si grande que les conditions posées par la loi sur l'adoption ne sont pas remplies.

3. *Famille de remplacement provisoire*
Certains placements dans des familles de remplacement sont de très courte durée et ont un objectif provisoire. Examples:
- *Familles de vacances*: l'enfant élevé dans un pensionnat passe ses vacances dans une famille. Le point de départ adopté est de vouloir donner à des enfants vivant généralement dans un foyer d'enfants de véritables vacances, afin de rompre la monotonie de la routine journalière. Une famille de vacances peut favoriser l'implantation dans une autre famille. Il arrive aussi qu'une famille de vacances se transforme au bout d'un certain temps en famille de remplacement.
- *Placement en "terrain neutre"*: dans le cadre de l'aide aux mères célibataires - il s'agit généralement de bébés dont la mère hésite à l'abandonnement — des nouveaux-nés sont placés dans une famille de remplacement provisoire jusqu'à ce que l'on ait obtenu davantage de certitude sur leur avenir.
- *Familles d'accueil*: Les placements dans ces familles sont utilisés pour l'acceuil provisoire, éventuellement comme adresse d'hébergement en cas de fuges ou de crises. Les enfants placés dans des familles de remplacement provisoires sont généralement plus âgés (à partir de 14, 15 ans).

4. *Famille-pension*
Lorsqu'il s'agit d'un placement provisoire où l'accent est mis sur la prise an charge matérielle, c'est une famille-pension qui est recherchée. Les rapports sont plus extérieurs que dans le cas d'une famille de remplacement ordinaire. Il s'agit en générale de jeunes de 17 à 19 ans ayant déjà

été confiés à la protection de l'enfance à un stade antérieur. Ces jeunes cherchent à se faire une place dans la société mais ne sont pas encore en mesure d'assumer totalement leur indépendance. Une famille-pension peut constituer une solution dans de tels cas. D'autre part on parle de *famille de remplacement-pension* lorsque indépendance et liberté sont combinées à un certain degré d'encadrement de supervision et de vie de famille.

5. *Famille de remplacement professionnelle*

La famille de remplacement professionnelle est caractérisée par quelques aspects marquants:

1. Les parents de remplacement possèdent le plus possible d' aptitudes sur le plan des rélations et de la collaboration avec un groupe de consultation et d'encadrement/ de supervision.
2. La famille doit être spécialement organisée en fonction du travail avec les enfants leur étant confiés. La maison doit être adéquate ou rendue adéquate. Une aide suffisante doit être disponible.
3. Le nombre d'enfants confiés à une telle famille est de 4 ou 5. Ce nombre n'a pas tellement de signification économique; il est plutôt destiné à créer un climat psychologique approprié dont les enfants pour lesquels cette forme d'aide familiale a été préconisée ont besoin pour s'épanouir (dans une certaine mesure).
4. Il est pris des mesures financières telles que le travail de la femme y est pris en considération. On part du principe que l'homme possède son propre emploi.

Malgré cette attitude objective et malgré une tendance au professionnalisme il existe des rapports assez marqués avec une vie familiale ordinaire: la présence continue d'éducateurs, le fait d'habiter ensemble dans une même maison, la vie dans un quartier ordinaire

6. *Famille de remplacement thérapeutique*

Le but du placement dans une tele famille est de permettre un traitement thérapeutique, en règle générale dans une clinique psychiatrique pour enfants. Les parents de remplacement collaborent avec une équipe de spécialistes auxquels incombe la responsabilité du traitement. Il s'agit d'enfants devant faire l'objet de beaucoup d'attention et de soins et ayant besoin pour leurs conflits intérieurs d'une aide psychothérapeutique quotidienne ou au moins régulière. Il est recherché pour ces enfants des familles de remplacement possédant aussi des qualités thérapeutique, pour les périodes pendant lesquelles les enfants ne sont pas en traitement. Les familles ont été la plupart du temps recherchées et sélectionnées par une clinique (psychiatrique) pour enfants.

Des fondations spéciales sont actuellement chargées du recrutement et de la sélection.

7. *Maisons familiales*

Dans le cadre de leur programme de services les institutions privées de protection de la jeunesse exploient parfois des maisons familiales. Les parents de remplacement demeurant dans la maison familiale sont en quelque sorte employés par l'institution. Ce sont en même temps les éducateurs de l'enfant.
Ils remplissent les fonctions habituellement remplies par les parents à l'égard de leurs enfants dans une famille normale.
L'une des principales considérations (par exemple à l'intérieur du Centre Socio-Agogique d'Amsterdam) ayant conduit à la mise en place de maisons familiales est la demande d'une 'suite' pour les enfants dans les cas desquels le but du traitement en foyer de la protection de l'enfance a été atteint.
Après le traitement en foyer, il serait souhaitable que ces enfants vivent de nouveau en milieu familial. Pour diverses raisons ces enfants ne peuvent toutefois ni retourner dans leur famille d'origine ni aller dans une famille de remplacement. Il s'agit surtout d'enfants ayant entre 10 et 16 ans et dont les parents d'origine ne peuvent plus, pas ou pas encore reprendre l'éducation. Il s'agit souvent aussi d'enfants qui entretiennent des contacts intensifs avec leurs parents d'origine et ne peuvent supporter des liens trop émotionnels avec d'autres adultes. Pour eux les parents sont vraiment des parents mais non des éducateurs.
La forme de famille en maison familiale a été choisie pour deux raisons:

- la famille est actuellement la forme la plus courante de vie communautaire:
- ces enfants viennent en outre la plupart du temps de familles brisées ou fonctionnant mal, ce qui explique que la demande d'aide ait précisément une orientation familiale.

Le modèle de maison familiale recherché est le suivant:
un ménage ayant un ou deux enfants, de préférence petits, demeure dans une maison appartenant à l'institution de protection de l'enfants (SAC par exemple). Cette famille prend en charge quatre enfants ayant la plupart du temps déjà séjourné en foyer. Il s'agit parfois d'enfants ne pouvant être normalement placés dans des familles de remplacement parce qu'ils s'y opposent en raison de leur relation avec leurs parents d'origine ou parce qu'ils ont déjà fait une ou plusieurs expériences malheureuses dans des familles de remplacement. Il peut aussi s'agir d'adolescents et d'enfants assez difficiles qui de temps en temps commettent des vols, sont agressifs ou font des fugues.
Dans le ménage en question l'homme possède un emploi à l'extérieur et la femme reçoit un salaire, partiellement sous forme de logement gratuit etc. Toutes les dépenses faites pour les

enfants sont remboursées, à condition qu'elles restent dans les limites raisonnables. La famille bénéficie d'un encadrement/supervision intensif de la part d'un assistant social qui peut à son tour bénéficier du soutien de l'équipe de l'organisation, composée d'orthopédagogues, de psychologues et de psychiatres.
Dans la plupart des organisations, il est conclu avec les 'parents' des maisons familiales un contrat prévoyant les frais respectivement à la charge des deux parties, la durée pour laquelle les deux parties se lient et la procédure à suivre en cas de fermeture de la maison familiale. Les parents reçoivent un dédommagement qui était de 15,60 Florins par jour au milieu de l'année 1981 et, bien que cela soit supérieur au prix que reçoivent pour les soins donnés les familles de remplacement ordinaires par enfant et par jour, cela est absolument insuffisant pour qu'il soit possible d'en vivre. Le revenu principal est donc généralement assuré par le salaire d'un des deux époux.
La maison est et demeure la propriété de l'institution de protection de la jeunesse (SAC, par exemple), car le point de départ adopté est que la maison doit en premier lieu fonctionner pour les enfants. Si quelque chose va mal dans les rapports de travail entre l'institution et le ménage faisant fonction de parents, les enfants continuent d'habiter dans la maison et un nouveau ménage est recherché pour tenir lieu de nouveaux parents de remplacement. Les objectifs du séjour dans une maison familiale sont que :

- L'enfant pourra faire l'expérience de liens positifs et constants avec des adultes;
- L'aptitude sociale et l'indépendance de l'enfant seront accrues;
- L'enfant fera partie d'un petit groupe solide; l'approche y sera très personnelle;
- Les contacts avec les parents d'origine de l'enfant resteront le plus possible intacts;
- L'enfant ne devra plus nécessairement se trouver dans la situation d'exception et dans l'isolement d'un foyer pour enfants plus longtemps que cela n'est strictement nécessaire.

QUESTION 3 :

Utilise-t-on la garde d'enfants au sein de familles de remplacement :

- *dans les cas où les liens avec la famille d'origine sont ou doivent être complètement rompus,*
- *ou bien aussi dans les cas où les liens en cause sont considérés comme passagèrement nuisibles ou affaiblis, sans éliminer toutefois la possibilité d'un changement ultérieur ?*

RÉPONSE :

Comme on a pu le constater dans la réponse à la question 2, il est possible de recourir à la garde de l'enfant dans ces deux cas. Il est possible que les parents d'origine confient de leur plein gré l'enfant à la garde d'une famille de remplacement. Le placement peut néanmoins aussi être la conséquence d'une mesure émanant de la protection de l'enfance, telle que la mise sous tutelle de l'enfant ou bien le relèvement la décharge ou la déchéance des parents de l'autorité parentale.

Commentaire :

- Placement de plein gré
Les liens avec les parents d'origine sont conservés. Les parents ont eux-mêmes confié leur enfant à la garde d'une famille de remplacement pour qu'il y soit pris en charge et éduqué; ou bien ils ont accepté que l'enfant soit placé ailleurs, après que l'enfant a quitté le domicile parental. Les parents conservent l'autorité juridique.

- Mise sous tutelle de l'enfant
En général un enfant sous tutelle reste dans sa famille d'origine. Les parents doivent alors se conformer aux indications du tuteur familial.
Le placement de l'enfant à l'extérieur de la famille s'effectue seulement dans les cas cités aux articles 262 et 269 I du Code civil, c'est-à-dire dans les cas où l'intérêt des soins et de l'éducation de l'enfant le rendent nécessaire. Les parents peuvent rendre régulièrement visite à l'enfant et celui-ci peut passer ses vacances chez lui. Un tel placement est prononcé par le juge des enfants.
En vertu du paragraphe 3 de l'article 263, le juge fixe la durée du séjour de l'enfant hors de son foyer d'origine à un an maximum. Il peut prolonger ce délai jusqu'à deux ans maximum et le réduire à n'importe quel moment. Ce déplacement de l'enfant peut prendre la forme d'un séjour dans un internat ou bien d'un placement dans une famille de remplacement.

- Décharge, et déchéance des parents de leur autorité parentale
Lorsqu'une telle mesure émanant de la protection de l'enfance a été prise, les enfants sont pour la plupart confiés à des associations de tutelle. Ceux-ci placent les enfants dans un établissement ou dans une famille de remplacement.
Les parents n'ont plus aucune autorité juridique. Le rétablissement de l'autorité qui est possible demeure cependant rare (article 278 du Code civil).

QUESTION 4 :

Le but de resocialisation de l'enfant délinquant ou en danger de délinquance est-il réalisé par ce moyen ?
Si tel est le cas, les règles juridiques sont-elles les mêmes?

RÉPONSE :

Le placement de jeunes délinquants dans des familles de remplacement dans le but de resocialisation est très peu en usage. Au cas où le placement dans une famille de remplacement serait jugé utile pour un enfant s'étant rendu coupable d'un délit répressible, les règles généralement appliquées aux placements dans des familles de remplacement valent aussi dans ce cas particulier.

QUESTION 5 :

Utilise-t-on l'institut en question (famille de remplacement) comme étape préparatoire à l'adoption de l'enfant = familles de remplacement pré-adoptives ? Si tel est le cas, quelles sont les règles juridiques en vigueur ?

RÉPONSE :

Le placement dans des familles de remplacement peut parfois, mais parfois seulement, être utilisé comme étape préparatoire à l'adoption de l'enfant. La loi pose des conditions plus sévères aux parents susceptibles d'adopter un enfant qu'aux parents de remplacement. Ces conditions concernent principalement les limites d'âge, la durée de mariage des parents pré-adoptifs ainsi que la durée de prise en charge (articles 227 et 228 du Code civil).
Quelques autres règles sont en outre en préparation :
Le 5 mai 1980 a été publiée la Note "Marche pratique à suivre en matière d'adoption et de préparation à l'adoption", appelée encore "Note sur l'Adoption" du Secrétaire d'Etat à la Justice. Les règles élaborées concernent spécialement les enfants étrangers devant être adoptés par des parents adoptifs néerlandais. Les règles en question seront incluses dans la Loi sur les enfants confiés à la garde de famille de remplacement.

QUESTION 6 :

1. *La garde de l'enfant au sein de la famille de remplacement a-t-elle une base contractuelle? Si tel est le cas, quelles sont les parties contractantes? Quel est l'objet du contract? A quelles exigences de forme est-il soumis?*

2. *Lorsque la base contractuelle n'est pas admise ou utilisée, s'agit-il d'une décision du tribunal ou d'un organe de l'administration publique ou d'un autre organe? Quelles règles détaillées existe-t-il dans ce domaine?*

RÉPONSE 1. ET 2. :

Le placement dans une famille de remplacement a toujours une base contractuelle (voir en annexe un exemple de contrat-modèle de garde).
Les parties contractantes sont :
- les parents d'origine et les parents de remplacement ou
- l'autorité procédant au placement et les parents de remplacement.

L'autorité procédant au placement est parfois le juge des enfants, parfois une association de tutelle.
Le contenu du contrat porte en règle générale sur la prise en charge et sur l'éducation de l'enfant dans la famille de remplacement. Il n'existe aucune exigence de forme.

QUESTION 6 - ANNEXE

MODÈLE DE CONTRAT ENTRE PARENTS D'ORIGINE ET PARENTS ADOPTIFS, CONCERNANT LE PLACEMENT D'UN ENFANT DANS UNE FAMILLE DE REMPLACEMENT

Parents (d'origine)
nom et prénoms du père :
adresse du père :
nom et prénoms de la mère :
adresse de la mère :

Parents de remplacement
nom et prénoms du mari :
nom et prénoms de la femme :
adresse :

Enfant
nom et prénoms :
date et lieu de naissance :

Parents (d'origine) et parents de remplacement *conviennent* que l'enfant susmentionné, sur qui les parents d'origine ont autorité, entre dans la famille de remplacement comme enfant confié à la garde des parents de remplacement à dater du..........
Les soins et l'éducation journaliers - parmi lesquels figurent l'éducation religieuse et/ou morale sont confiés aux parents de remplacement, le tout en accord avec les parents d'origine et sous leur responsabilité.

Les parents d'origine contribuent à ce que les parents de remplacement puissent s'acquitter au mieux de leur tâche.

Durée du contrat

Le contrat est conclu pour une durée indéterminée/ pour .... ans/ pour .... mois.
Lorsque le contrat n'est pas conclu pour une durée indéterminée, si les parents ne reprennent pas l'enfant confié à la famille de remplacement une fois le délai écoulé, celui-ci est de plein droit prolongé pour la durée conclue.*
Le contrat peut prendre fin à tout moment avec l'approbation des deux parties.
Le contrat peut en outre être résilié par chacune des deux parties. Dans ce cas, avec l'accord mutuel des deux parties, le moment d'expiration sera fixé mais ne sera pas en principe situé en deçа de deux mois.
Cependant, si la prise en charge et l'éducation ont duré un an ou plus, avec l'accord des parents d'origine, ceux-ci ne pourront apporter de modification au séjour de l'enfant, qu' avec l'autorisation des parents de remplacement, ou - si celle-ci n'est pas obtenue - qu'avec l'autorisation du juge pour enfants.

Clauses supplémentaires

(Pouvant inclure ce que parents d'origine et parents de remplacement jugent nécessaire ou souhaitable en vue de la prise en charge et de l'éducation de l'enfant. La rémunération à verser par les parents d'origine peut, par exemple, y être fixée.)

Ainsi rédigé en deux exemplaires à ....
le

Les parents (d'origine), Les parents de remplacement,

* Cet alinéa n'est pas valable si le contrat a été conclu pour une durée indéterminée

QUESTION 7 :

Dans votre pays (système national), l'organe de contrôle prenant soin des intérêts de l'enfant de la part de l'Etat est-il un tribunal (éventuellement un tribunal dit de famille), un organe de l'administration publique ou une autre organisation à caractère social?
La coopération simultanée des différents organes en cause est-elle admise? Si tel est le cas quelles sont les formes que prend cette collaboration? Celle-ci est-elle efficace?

RÉPONSE :

Dans notre pays, l'organe administratif public prenant soin des intérêts de l'enfant et y veillant est le Conseil de la protection de l'enfance (voir Code civil, articles 238-242 et Décision exécutoire des comités de protection de l'enfance).

La *Loi sur les enfants confiés à la garde de familles de remplacement* comporte également plusieurs articles concernant les Conseils de la protection de l'enfance. Globalement, leur contenu est le suivant : Le chef d'une famille ou d'un établissement dans lequel un enfant est pris en charge et éduqué doit obligatoirement, dans un délai d'une semaine, aviser le maire et les conseillers de la municipalité en question de la prise en charge de l'enfant. Un tel avis est immédiatement transmis au Conseil de la protection de l'enfance dans le ressort duquel la municipalité en question est située. Après réception de cet avis, le Conseil ouvre une enquête sur l'enfant et sur la famille ou l'établissement auquel il a été confié. Une telle enquête n'a lieu qu'en cas de présomptions raisonnablement fondées de l'existence ou de l'imminence d'anomalies dans la famille ou dans l'établissement. Le chef de la famille ou de l'établissement où l'enfant est pris en charge et éduqué doit obligatoirement fournir au Conseil tous les renseignements désirés et il doit également présenter l'enfant.

Au cas où il s'avérerait que l'intérêt de l'enfant confié à la garde d'une famille le requiert expressément, le Conseil de la protection peut décider que l'enfant ne pourra rester plus longtemps dans la famille ou dans l'établissement où il est pris en charge et éduqué.
D'autre part, en cas de présomptions fondées de negligence des intérêts d'un ou de plusieurs enfants, le Conseil de la protection de l'enfance peut décider qu'il ne peut plus être pris en charge et élever d'enfants dans la famille ou l'établissement.
Le contrôle des placements dans des familles de remplacement incombe donc en général au Conseil de la protection de l'en-

fance. Cependant, le Ministère de la Justice a également une fonction de surveillance car le Ministère de la Justice est précisément l'organe exerçant une surveillance sur les Conseils.

Il faut distinguer trois sortes de placements dans des familles de remplacement :
- le placement par des associations de tutelle: c'est l'organisme qui assure lui-même le contrôle
- le placement par des associations de tutelle familiale (dans le cadre de mises sous tutelle); dans ce cas, c'est le Juge des enfants et l'Association de tutelle familiale qui constituent les organes de contrôle,
- les placements dits 'libres' par les parents eux-mêmes ou par les services sociaux municipaux et par les autorités de la santé publique : le contrôle est exercé par les parents, par l'organisme ayant procédé au placement et par le Conseil de la protection de l'enfance.

Dans la plupart des cas, à l'origine d'un placement dans une famille de remplacement, il existe une collaboration entre plusieurs organes. Les oeuvres privées prennent en règle générale soin du recrutement et de la sélection des familles de remplacement. C'est parfois par des organisations privées (associations de tutelle) que les enfants sont placés dans des familles de remplacement. Parfois aussi, c'est le Juge des enfants (cas de tutelle familiale) qui s'en charge. D'autres formes de collaboration sont également concevables. Cette collaboration est en général efficace.

QUESTION 8 :

Qui prend l'initiative de l'instauration de la garde de l'enfant au sein de la famille de remplacement?
1. *Cette initiative est-elle liée au contrôle concernant l'exécution de l'autorité parentale par les père et mère d'origine de l'enfant ou par son tuteur?*
2. *Cette initiative est-elle liée dans certains cas à l'activité judiciaire pénale concernant les père et mère d'origine ou l'enfant lui-même? Est-ce que c'est toujours un seul et même organe qui en décide?*

RÉPONSE :

L'initiative de confier la tutelle aux parents de remplacement peut parfois venir: des/du parent(s) d'origine, de l'organisme de tutelle, du Conseil de la protection de l'enfance ou des parents de remplacement eux-mêmes.
1. Il existe effectivement un lien entre la façon dont les

parents exercent leur puissance parentale et l'initiative de confier la tutelle aux parents de remplacement. Dans tous ces cas la tutelle n'est d'ailleurs confiée que par l'entremise du juge.

2. Il y a rarement de lien entre des poursuites pénales contre le mineur lui-même et le placement dans une famille de remplacement et la remise de la tutelle aux parents de remplacement y faisant suite.
   Le placement dans une famille de remplacement et la remise de tutelle aux parents de remplacement peuvent en revanche être liés à des poursuites pénales contre le/les parent(s) d'origine. Il s'agit dans presque tous les cas de poursuites en vertu d'un délit commis envers le mineur en questions (il peut s'agir de sévices abus ou d'atteintes aux moeurs commis par le/les parent(s) d'origine envers leur enfant).

QUESTION 9 :

1. *Quels sont les droits et les devoirs des parents de remplacement envers l'enfant placé sous leur garde? Ces droits et devoirs sont-ils énoncés en détail?*
2. *Traite-t-on en particulier les cas où les parents d'origine ont conservé* de jure *leur puissance parentale totalement ou partiellement?*
3. *Comment le même problème se pose-t-il en cas de coïncidence de la garde par la famille de remplacement et de l'existence d'un tuteur ou curateur formel de l'enfant?*
   Est-il possible que celui qui exerce la garde de la part de la famille de remplacement reçoive en même temps une position juridique de tuteur? de curateur?

RÉPONSE :

1. Tout comme les parents d'origine, les parents de remplacement ont l'obligation de prendre soin de l'enfant dont ils ont la garde et de l'éduquer. L'obligation des parents de remplacement résulte en premier lieu, bien qu'indirectement, de la *loi*. Seule la Décision exécutoire de la Loi sur les enfants confiés à la garde de familles de remplacement fournit des clauses plus précises à ce sujet (et fixe des conditions concernant la situation et l'aménagement de l'habitation, l'alimentation et les vêtements, les traitements médicaux et dentaires, le développement physique et psychique de l'enfant ainsi que l'enseignement et la formation qu'il reçoit). Dans l'éducation de l'enfant, il doit le plus possible être tenu compte des conceptions religieuses et morales dans lesquelles ceux qui détiennent

la puissance parentale ou la tutelle désirent que l'enfant soit élevé.
Le *contrat de garde* prévoit que :
'Les soins et l'éducation journaliers - ce qui englobe également l'éducation religieuse et/ou morale - sont confiés aux parents de remplacement, le tout en accord avec les parents d'origine et sous la responsabilité de ceux-ci'.

2. Non, les contrats sont les mêmes.
Cependant la clause suivante figure dans le contrat:
'Si toutefois les soins donnés aux enfants et leur éducation ont duré une année, avec l'accord des parents d'origine, ceux-ci ne pourront apporter de modification au séjour de l'enfant qu'avec l'autorisation des parents de remplacement, ou - si celle-ci n'est pas obtenue - qu'avec l'autorisation du Juge des enfants'. Cette clause découle à son tour de la loi et plus précisément de l'article 246a du Code civil (droit d'obstruction).

3. Dans ce cas, c'est l'article 336a du Code civil qui sera appliqué.
Si le mineur a été pris en charge et éduqué comme appartenant à la famille pendant au moins un an par une ou plusieurs personnes autres que son tuteur, avec l'accord de celui-ci, le tuteur en question ne peut apporter de modification dans le séjour de l'enfant mineur qu'avec l'autorisation de ceux ayant pris en charge les soins et l'éducation de l'enfant.
En effet, la personne qui, avec l'accord du tuteur, a pris en charge et éduqué pendant au moins un an un enfant mineur au sein de sa famille, peut demander au Juge des enfants de le nommer tuteur. Si le mineur est pris en charge et éduqué par plus d'une personne comme faisant partie de la famille, cette demande ne peut être faite que par ces personnes collectivement.
Le juge des enfants ne donne suite à cette demande que s'il juge que cela est dans l'intérêt de l'enfant et qu'il a suffisamment constaté que le tuteur n'était pas disposé à se laisser démettre de sa fonction. Il nomme de préférence tuteur la personne dont la nomination est demandée (article 299 a, Code Civil).

QUESTION 10 :

1. *Le financement des besoins vitaux de l'enfant, lorsque celui-ci se trouve au sein d'une famille de remplacement, est-il effectué aux parents de remplacement par :*
- le père et la mère d'origine;
- d'autres personnes obligées de se charger de l'entretien

de l'enfant en vertu des règles du droit de la famille;
- *des fonds publics (sur une base contractuelle ou sur celle de la sécurité sociale, etc.);*
- *d'autres fonds sociaux?*

Quelles sont de façon plus précise les règles en question?

2. *Les parents de remplacement reçoivent-ils une rémunération pour les soins dont ils entourent l'enfant? Si tel est le cas, de la part de qui? Et quel en est le montant approximatif?*

RÉPONSE :

- En cas de placement de plein gré, le financement compte en principe parmi les obligations des parents d'origine.
- Le placement dans une famille de remplacement par une association de tutelle ou de tutelle familiales est financé par l'organisation effectuant le placement et en ayant reçu le pouvoir du Ministère de la Justice.
  Les associations de tutelle et de tutelle familiale paient les parents sur une base contractuelle.
- En ce qui concerne les autres personnes qui, en raison des règles du droit de la famille, ont l'obligation de subvenir à l'entretien de l'enfant, on peut songer par exemple :
- Au père qui n'a pas juridiquement de liens familiaux avec l'enfant après qu'une demande d'entretien à cause de paternité aura été accordée par le juge.
- Fonds publics.
  Il n'existe pas de financement public direct des placements dans des familles de remplacement. C'est l'organisme de placement qui paie et, aux Pays-Bas, cet organisme de placement est rarement un organisme public.
- Il existe un certain nombre de fonds privés tels que le Fonds Reine Juliana, le Fonds du comité néerlandais des timbres pour l'enfance, le Fonds 'Jantje Beton', qui fournissent des fonds au profit de recherches et d'expériences scientifiques ayant également trait aux placements dans des familles de remplacement.
  Les placements proprement dits ne sont cependant pas financés par ces fonds particuliers.
  Les parents de remplacement ne sont en général pas rémunérés pour leur travail. Les parents de remplacement collaborant dans le cadre des soins familiaux thérapeutiques constituent cependant une exception. Ils reçoivent, selon l'âge de l'enfant, de 13,90 Fl. à 25,20 Fl. par jour pour les soins donnés à l'enfant leur étant confié. Les parents des maisons familiales reçoivent également une rémunération : celle-ci est de 15,60 Fl. par jour (circulaire du Sécrétariat d'Etat à la Justice du 14 juillet 1980, no. 430/780). Dans tous les cas c'est l'organisme ayant procédé au placement qui veille au paiement des parents de remplacement (Voir Annexe).

QUESTION 10 - ANNEXE

GUIDE FINANCIER

A L'USAGE DES PARENTS DE REMPLACEMENT

allocations de soins
cours
frais médicaux
enseignement
frais de déplacement
frais de scolarité
(formulaires de déclaration)
responsabilité civile
argent de poche
sécurité sociale

Important

Parents de remplacement, vous êtes pour notre organisation des auxiliaires précieux. S'il nous est guère possible de rémunérer votre sollicitude et vos efforts, nous essayons en revanche de vous dédommager le plus possible de vos frais. Nous ne pouvons vous payer que ce qui nous est remboursé par l'Etat. Cela est régi par des règles strictes (comportant notamment un contrat écrit avec vous).
Il est important que vous connaissiez ces règles; sinon vous attendrez de nous plus que nous ne pouvons faire, ou bien vous vous inquiéterez inutilement à propos de dépenses qu'il nous est au contraire possible de vous rembourser.
Il y a des dépenses que nous pouvons automatiquement vous restituer, en plus de l'allocation mensuelle de soins usuelle, du fait qu'elles nous sont à notre tour restituées par l'Etat.
En revanche, certaines autres dépenses ne nous sont restituées que lorsque nous en avons préalablement demandé l'autorisation à l'Etat et qu'une telle autorisation nous a ensuite effectivement été accordée.
Il vous faut savoir quelles sont ces dépenses, car elles ne peuvent vous être remboursées que si vous nous en avez préalablement demandé l'autorisation et que nous vous avons donné cette autorisation.
Pour tous les frais que nous vous restituons en plus de l'allocation de soins, nous devons - même lorsque nous n'avons pas besoin d'autorisation spéciale - remettre les factures que vous avez payées. Veuillez donc toujours demander et garder factures et quittances afin de nous les remettre.
Nous faisons tout notre possible pour que les règlements financiers s'effectuent le plus rapidement possible. Dans

votre intérêt et dans le nôtre, vos demandes de remboursement de frais spéciaux devront donc être remises à temps. Pour savoir comment procéder dans les cas douteux, vous pouvez consulter l'assitant(e) social(e) ou demander des renseignements par téléphone.
Enfin, une dernière remarque générale : les parents de remplacement n'ont généralement pas droit aux allocations familiales concernant les enfants dont ils ont la garde.

1. *Allocations de soins*

Les allocations de soins vous sont versées régulièrement, tous les mois ou tous les trimestres, par exemple.
Le montant en est calculé d'après les prix journaliers de soins fixés par l'Etat. Les sommes augmentent avec l'âge de l'enfant. Elles sont ajustées chaque année au coût de la vie.
A dater du 1er janvier 1981 les sommes journalières maximales pouvant être versées sont les suivantes :

pour les enfants de 0 à 8 ans	Hfl.	13,90
pour les enfants de 9 à 11 ans	Hfl.	15,50
pour les enfants de 12 à 15 ans	Hfl.	18,60
pour les enfants de 16 à 17 ans	Hfl.	22,05
pour les enfants de 18 à 20 ans	Hfl.	25,30
En cas de logement indépendant		
pour les enfants de moins de 18 ans	Hfl.	23,95
pour les enfants de 18 ans et plus	Hfl.	25,20

Outre les frais évidents tels que frais de logement et d'alimentation, ces allocations mensuelles de soins devront couvrir les dépenses suivantes :
- vêtements et chaussures
- coiffeur et articles de toilette
- réparations de byciclette et de vélomoteur (pour les non-salariés)
- sports et loisirs
- argent de poche (pour les non-salariés)
- frais normaux pour l'école primaire et l'enseignement spécial (type LOM, par exemple), tels que crayons, cahiers, menus frais, etc.
- frais de déplacement scolaire jusqu'à concurrence de Hfl. 22,25 par mois
- frais de voyage pour les visites de fin de semaine.

Pour les enfants salariés, vois sous 4.

N.B. L'allocation de soins est un dédommagement pour les frais devant être faits pour les soins et l'éducation de l'enfant. Il ne s'agit donc pas d'une rémunération (c'est-à-dire d'un salaire).

2. *Frais que nous remboursons sans autorisation préable*

En plus de l'allocation de soins, nous pouvons vous rembourser les frais suivants, sans que vous ayez à en demander préalablement l'autorisation.

Frais médicaux
Remarque préliminaire générale : les enfants confiés à la garde de familles ne doivent pas être inscrits séparément ou avec les parents de remplacement à une caisse de sécurité sociale ou d'assurance-maladie. Les primes versées ne sont pas remboursées, sauf dans des cas exceptionnels.
La situation est évidemment différente lorsqu'un enfant travaille et qu'il est inscrit individuellement, en tant que salarié, à une caisse générale de sécurité sociale.
Les frais médicaux suivants sont remboursés sans autorisation:
- médecin et pharmacie
- traitement de spécialiste ne nécessitant pas d'hospitalisation, mais toutefois uniquement sur indication du médecin traitant. La lettre du médecin traitant devra donc nous être envoyée avec les notes et les quittances.
- hôpital et sanatorium (sur indication du médecin traitant)
- soins dentaires normaux (consultations, arrachages, obturations, etc.)
- montures de lunettes jusqu'à concurrence de Hfl. 97,-*
- verres de lunettes
- semelles orthopédiques

Enseignement
- Enseignement secondaire général élémentaire, moyen et supérieur; enseignement donné dans les lycées (Atheneum et Gymnasium),
  Enseignement technique élémentaire et moyen, écoles de commerce de détail,
  Enseignement économique et administratif élémentaire et moyen, enseignement ménager, etc.
  (voir aussi sous 3 et 4)

N.B. Ne pas remplir les formulaires de déclaration pour le montant des rétributions scolaires, mais nous les envoyer.

Les factures peuvent si nécessaire - par exemple lorsqu'il s'agit de sommes assez élevées - nous être envoyées, de sorte que nous nous chargeons alors directement du paiement à la personne en question.

---

* Sous réserve, cette somme peut également être portée à Hfl. 125,-.

3. *Frais que nous remboursons seulement après autorisation*
Nous ne pouvons rembourser les frais suivants que lorsque vous nous en avez préalablement demandé l'autorisation et que nous vous avons accordé cette autorisation.

Frais médicaux
- traitements dentaires spéciaux (correction, dents-pivots, couronnes, etc.)
- traitements paramédicaux (orthophonie, gymnastique corrective, massage)
- traitement psychologique et psychiatrique
- prothèses (prothèses dentaires incluses)

Prière de joindre aux demandes une spécification de frais.

Enseignement
- cours, par exemple de sténographie, dactylographie, esthéticienne
- cours par correspondance
- enseignement professionnel supérieur (par exemple : école technique supérieure, école économique et administrative supérieure, académie d'études sociales)
- enseignement supérieur (université ou école de hautes études)
- frais de déplacement supérieurs à Hfl. 22,25 par mois.

N.B. Veillez à vous renseigner sur les abonnements les plus avantageux (abonnements scolaires ou pour jeunes, par exemple) et à nous envoyer les cartes d'abonnement périmées.

Bicyclettes, vélomoteurs, casques
Nous remboursons au maximum Hfl. 275,- pour l'achat d'une bicyclette, Hfl. 365,- pour celui d'un vélomoteur et Hfl. 67,- pour l'achat d'un casque de sécurité (pour enfants non salariés).
Pour les enfants transportés comme passagers par les parents de remplacement, l'achat d'un casque de sécurité peut également être remboursé, à raison de Hfl. 67,- maximum.

Responsabilité civile
Dans la plupart des cas les enfants pris en charge sont assurés civilement par l'association.
Renseignez-vous à temps pour savoir si tel est aussi votre cas. L'assurance de responsabilité civile de l'association n'est pas responsable lorsque les dommages sont recouvrables en vertu d'une autre police d'assurance. Nous insistons sur le fait que pour toutes les dépenses supplémentaires, quittances et factures doivent être conservées et envoyées, et que les autorisations doivent être demandées à temps.

4. *Enfant salariés*
Des règles particulières s'appliquent aux enfants, garçons ou filles, subvenant à leur entretien, mais dont le salaire n'y suffit pas encore entièrement. Vous devez donc savoir quand un jeune est censé pouvoir subvenir à son entretien personnel.
Pour pouvoir établir cela, il faut soustraire du salaire net ayant été versé au jeune les sommes nettes correspondant aux heures supplémentaires, aux primes de rendement et de vacances. Il est soustrait comme argent de poche/économies un tiers de la somme restante. Il est encore soustrait des deux tiers restants les frais éventuels liés à l'exercice de la profession et non remboursés par l'employeur. Ces frais comprennent notamment : vêtements de travail, outils, cotisation syndicale, littérature spécialisée, casque de sécurité (Hfl. 67,- maximum), frais de bicyclette et de vélomoteur, et autres frais de transport pouvant s'avérer nécessaires.
Lorsque la somme obtenue est supérieure à l'allocation de soins applicable, le jeune est considéré comme pouvant subvenir à son entretien. Pour ces jeunes, il n'est pas versé d'allocation de soins et il n'est pas remboursé de frais spéciaux.
Lorsqu'un jeune ne gagne pas assez pour pouvoir subvenir à son entretien, les règles suivantes sont appliquées :
- tout salaire doit nous être communiqué, par conséquent également heures supplémentaires, primes de rendement et de vacances, ainsi que tous dédommagements pour vêtements de travail et frais de déplacement.

Conserver et envoyer les bulletins de paye.
- Les montants nets de primes de vacances, de primes de rendement (à condition qu'elles ne soient pas supérieures à 10% du salaire brut) et les heures supplémentaires reviennent au jeune comme argent de poche/économies.
- un tiers du montant restant du salaire net versé est également considéré comme argent de poche/économies
- les deux tiers restants servent à couvrir partiellement les frais de soins et ils sont complétés par l'allocation de soins, après toutefois que les frais suivants auront été déduits :

  frais liés à l'exercice de la profession, non remboursés par l'employeur (par exemple pour outils, vêtements de travail, voir ci-dessus)

  frais de cours et d'auto-école faits à la demande de l'employeur et moyennant une demande écrite de celui-ci; l'autorisation de l'organe de subvention est requise.

En cas de licenciement, les mêmes règles s'appliquent aux allocations d'attente et de chômage qu'au salaire.

N.B. Pour les enfants pupilles de la protection de l'enfance il n'y a pas d'allocations R.W.W.

5. *Prolongation du paiement de l'allocation de soins lorsque l'enfant n'est pas chez vous*

Le paiement de l'allocation de soins est prolongé pendant 14 jours lorsque :
- l'enfant est entré dans un hôpital ou un sanatorium
- l'enfant a fait une fugue
- l'enfant doit subir une détention

et qu'il est sûr que l'enfant sera replacé chez vous après son séjour ailleurs.

Si le séjour à l'hôpital ou en sanatorium dure plus de 14 jours, il peut être versé Hfl. 3,25 maximum par jour, à partir du quinzième jour, pour les éventuels frais de visite, etc.
Lorsqu'un enfant faisant un séjour prolongé dans un hôpital ou une clinique passe régulièrement les fins de semaines chez vous, il vous est possible de nous demander le paiement intégral de l'allocation de soins pour les jours que l'enfant passe chez vous.

mai 1981 8e édition sous réserve de modifications

Ed.: Werkverband Integratie Jeugdwelzijnswerk Nederland (WIJN) Utrecht (Département de Documentation et de Publicité).

FAMILLES DE REMPLACEMENT

QUESTION 11 :

La garde de l'enfant accomplie dans le cadre d'une famille de remplacement peut-elle prendre fin avant l'écoulement du terme établi? Pour quelles raisons?
Y a-t-il des règles plus détaillées pour une telle éventualité?

RÉPONSE :

La garde de l'enfant par la famille de remplacement peut effectivement prendre fin avant l'expiration du terme convenu. Les raisons à cela peuvent être :

Situations problématiques	- Difficultés survenant dans les rapports entre enfant et famille de remplacement, entraînant le transfert dans une autre famille ou le retour dans la maison d'enfants initiale. L'échec du placement peut être lié à une fugue ou au comportement inapproprié du mineur ou des parents de remplacement, au divorce des parents.
Raisons formels	- Si l'enfant se marie; s'il atteint sa majorité; s'il effectue son service militaire ou s'il a un emploi ailleurs dans ces cas la fonction de famille de remplacement changera.

Il n'existe pas de règles détaillées concernant cette situation. Le contrat de garde comporte cependant la clause suivante : ' Le contrat peut prendre fin à tout moment avec l'approbation mutuelle des parties. Le contrat peut en outre être résilié par chacune des parties. Dans ce cas la date d'expiration sera fixée d'un commun accord par les parties. Cette date ne sera en général pas située en deça de deux mois.'

QUESTION 12 :

Quelles sont selon la doctrine les modifications législatives nécessaires à l'amélioration de l'institution de la famille de remplacement et de son fonctionnement?
Dans votre pays, des travaux préparatoires ont-ils déjà été entrepris dans ce domaine?

RÉPONSE :

Il faut préciser en préambule que la doctrine juridique ne s'occupe quère des familles de remplacement et des placements dans ces familles. Depuis l'introduction du droit d'obstruction (voir la réponse à la question 1) les auteurs de textes juridiques ne se sont pratiquement pas exprimés à ce sujet. En revanche, dans des considérations pratiques, il a été formulé des souhaits relativement à l'assistance sociale.

Le rôle des parents de remplacement
Les parents de remplacement devraient avoir un rôle plus indépendants; ils sont encore actuellement trop souvent considérés comme des clients au lieu de véritables collaborateurs de l'organisme de placement. Cela se manifeste par exemple dans le fait que si des difficultés surgissent dans la famille de remplacement, les parents doivent en premier lieu s'adresser à l'organisme qui cherche alors une forme d'assistance adaptée. Pourquoi les parents de remplacement ne pourraient-ils pas s'adresser eux-mêmes, de façon autonome, à la forme d'assistance (par exemple à un bureau MOB = Bureau médico-pédagogique) qu'ils considèrent adéquate et souhaitable, tout comme une famille ordinaire peut le faire?

Conditions devant être posées aux parents de remplacement
Des conditions plus nombreuses devraient en outre être posées aux parents de remplacement :
Les rapports devraient avoir un caractère moins facultatif, en ce sens que les parents ne doivent pas pouvoir mettre fin à leur tâche de parents de remplacement lorsqu'ils n'en ont plus envie. Actuellement la situation est telle qu'avec l'approbation réciproque il peut à tout moment être mis fin au contrat de garde. L'expérience a montré que cette situation était trop libre/gratuite. Il devrait pouvoir être exigé des parents qu'ils remplissent un terme donné. Il ne devrait pas pouvoir être mis fin à un placement dans une famille de remplacement avant l'expiration du délai prévu sans raisons urgentes telles que l'échec total du placement, des problèmes conjugaux survenant entre les parents de remplacement ou bien l'inconduite grave de l'enfant ou des parents de remplacement
La qualité de parents de remplacement pourrait peut-être être spécifiée dans un contrat de travail spécial.

Système de rénumération
Un système de rémunération peut constituer un facteur permettant de spécifier le contrat de travail et d'en faire disparaître le caractère facultatif. Le paiement aboutira à ce que les parents de remplacement soient considérés plus que cela n'est actuellement le cas comme des collaborateurs de l'organisme chargé du placement. Le travail accompli par les

familles de remplacement pourrait être ainsi mieux valorisé. Cela peut exercer une influence positive à l'égard de la femme en particulier.
La rémunération des parents de remplacement comporte un risque : l'accent pourrait ainsi être mis davantage sur l'aspect financier et moins sur la motivation d'assistance.

Parents de remplacement originaires de toutes les couches de la société
Il y a actuellement une offre en nombre suffisant de familles de remplacement, mais la différence entre les familles-candidates et les enfants devant leur être confiés est trop grande. Les parents-candidats ont souvent une origine différente, une formation trop poussée, un autre mode de vie, etc. que les enfants à placer. Pour ces derniers la transition est trop grande.

Indépendamment de tout ceci, un projet de loi est actuellement en préparation concernant les placements en famille de remplacement envisagés comme préparation à l'adoption. Des règles plus précises seront prévues concernant les préparatifs en vue d'adoptions entre pays. Il sera par exemple introduit un système d'autorisation pour les organisations ou les personnes faisant office d'intermédiaires lors du placement d'enfants étrangers. En même temps il sera publié de nouvelles règles concernant l'autorisation de principe en possession de laquelle une famille de remplacement candidate devra se trouver avant qu'un enfant étranger puisse être placé dans cette famille.
Cependant, la date à laquelle un tel projet de loi sera présenté est encore incertaine. Le continu du projet de loi à paraître demeure également incertain.

QUESTION 13 :

Votre système national connaît-il l'institution des maisons d'enfants :
- de type familial, hébergeant un nombre d'enfants plus élevé et provenant de différentes familles d'origine?
- de type plus collectif (home familial) ?
Si tel est le cas, quelles sont les sources formelles de ces institutions et quelle est la position des institutions en question par rapport à celle des familles de remplacement? Quelle est aussi leur importance dans la pratique?

RÉPONSE :

Notre système connaît différentes espèces de homes d'enfants soit privés soit publics :

- Etablissements privés (Loi de principes article 5)
  - foyers d'observation
  - foyers d'accueil
  - établissements pédagogiques comprenant des établissements pour :
    a. mineurs normaux;
    b. mineurs normaux ayant un emploi; établissements destinés à l'éducation de mineurs n'étant plus soumis à la scolarité obligatoire et dont la tâche journalière consiste principalement en travail rémunéré ou en études;
    c. passage précédant le traitement familial; établissements destinés à l'éducation temporaire de mineurs pour qui le traitement familial a été prescrit mais pour qui aucune famille de remplacement n'est encore disponible;
    d. mineurs déficients mentaux; établissements destinés à l'éducation de mineurs dont l'intelligence présente un développement défectueux;
    e. mineurs déficients mentaux ayant un emploi; établissements destinés à l'éducation de mineurs n'étant plus soumis à la scolarité obligatoire, dont l'intelligence présente un développement défectueux et dont l'emploi du temps consiste principalement en travail rémunéré ou en études;
    f. mères célibataires et leurs enfants: établissements destinés à l'éducation de jeunes filles mineures avant et après leur accouchement ainsi qu'à l'éducation des enfants de ces mineures;
    g. traitement; établissements destinés à l'éducation de mineurs ayant besoin de traitement psycho-thérapeutique;
    h. formation professionnelle; destinée à l'éducation de mineurs qui, pendant leur séjour, sont formés en vue de l'exercice d'une profession.
    (Décision exécutoire article 96)
  - Etablissements publics (9 à affectation multiple).

Les homes d'enfants hébergeant un grand nombre de pupilles ne jouent plus un rôle aussi important que par le passé à l'intérieur de la protection de l'enfance; il a été pris conscience du fait qu'il était préférable pour un enfant de grandir dans une petite groupe, à caractère familial ou non. On note une tendance à la réduction et l'on peut citer à titre d'illustration les maisons familiales où un ménage accueille et prend soin de 3 ou 4 mineurs (voir question 2).

FAMILLES DE REMPLACEMENT

QUESTION 14 :

Quel est votre avis sur la valeur pratique et sur l'avenir des familles de remplacement ?

REPONSE :

La famille continue d'être à un haut degré le pivot de notre société. Il apparaît sans cesse que des liens familiaux solides sont bénéfiques à un enfant. Dans une famille attention et approche individuelles sont au premier plan, contrairement à l'éducation et à la prise en charge en établissement.
Dans un établissement la plupart des enfants ne parviennent pas à un développement optimal, malgré les bonnes intentions et les gros efforts des responsables.
La valeur pratique des placements en familles de remplacement est donc élevée et elle continuera d'augmenter. Bien sûr, il y aura toujours des mineurs pour qui une famille de remplacement ne constituera pas un environnement adéquat en vue de leur développement, soit parce qu'ils ont déjà eu trop de difficultés, soit peut-être parce-qu'ils mènent une vie trop personnelle pour pouvoir encore s'implanter dans une famille étrangère.
Néanmoins les enfants difficiles peuvent être pris en considération pour être placés dans des familles de remplacement, à condition que ces enfants et que les parents de remplacement soient bien accompagné par l'organisme de placement et à condition que les parents de remplacement soient accessibles aux problèmes de l'enfant qui leur est confié et de ses parents d'origine. Un trait d'évolution favorable réside actuellement dans le fait que le nombre de familles disposées à accueillir des enfants moins favorisées est en hausse.
Les gens décident en outre de plus en plus souvent de ne pas avoir eux-mêmes d'enfants mais sont prêts à accueillir en tant que parents de remplacement des enfants d'autres parents.
Cela ne peut qu'être favorable au développement de la famille de remplacement.
Un autre tendance actuelle est l'intérêt croissant manifesté par le gouvernement pour la stimulation des placements en familles de remplacement. Il y a tout lieu de considérer ces efforts avec quelque réserve. Il ne s'agit en effet ici pas tant de l'intérêt de l'enfant à qui un placement en famille de remplacement serait plus profitable que du fait qu'un placement en famille de remplacement revient moins cher que la prise en charge dans un foyer de la protection de l'enfance.

FAMILLES DE REMPLACEMENT

LITTÉRATURE

'Het Personen- en Familierecht', titels 12, 13, 14, 15, 17
A. Pitlo, 6e druk, 1979; bewerkt door J.E. Kasdorp en M. Rood-de Boer
Gouda Quint B.V. - Arnhem
'Kinderrecht', civielrechtelijk deel, met name hfdst. XII
G. Delfos, J.E. Doek, 5e druk 1974
Tjeenk Willink - Zwolle
'Kinderrecht' I en II, losbladige uitgave
J.W. Knottenbelt en G. Delfos
VUGA - boekerij - 's-Gravenhage
'Nieuw Jeugdrecht', losbladige uitgave
G. Delfos, J.E. Doek en J. Jansen
VUGA - boekerij - 's-Gravenhage
'Het Personen- en Familierecht in het Nieuwe Burgelijk Wetboek'
onder redaktie van E.A.A. Luyten, tweede druk 1977
Tjeenk Willink - Zwolle
'Hoofdtrekken van het Nederlands familierecht'
Ch. Petit, 1970
De Erven F. Bohn N.V. - Haarlem
'Personen- en Familierecht',
losbladige uitgave,
Kluwer - Deventer.
'Kind en Pleeggezin' hoofdstukken II, III, VIII, IX
M.J. van Spanje, 2e gewijzigde druk 1976
Van Loghum Slaterus - Deventer
'Kinderbescherming in de maatschappij 1905 - 1980' , hoofdstuk 15
Dik Roeland, 1980
Basisboeken AMBO - Baarn
'Recht en billijkheid'
O.C. Wit, proefschrift R.U.Utrecht, 1972
Stichting Paedagogisch Onderzoek, Utrecht
'Facetten van jeugdbescherming 4/5'
Nieuwe vormen van inrichtingswerk als hulpverlening, 2e druk 1976
Gezamenlijke uitgave van het W.I.J.N. en de Stichting v.h. Kind, Amsterdam
'Internaat of pleeggezin' 1980
Gezamenlijke uitgave van het W.I.J.N. en de Stichting v.h. Kind, Amsterdam

The Dutch law of pretium doloris

FRANS J.A. VAN DER VELDEN
Assistant Professor at the University of Utrecht II.A.3.

1. A CAR ACCIDENT - DECISION IN 1943

In The Hague on the 21th of October 1933 a car accident occurred; a van driver, named Bessem, knocked down a young man, Van Kreuningen. Van Kreuningen, a motor mechanic at his father's garage at the time of the accident, was seriously injured and had to undergo medical treatment and physical rehabilitation for a long period.
After a year Van Kreuningen's disability stabilized at 50%. Meanwhile Van Kreuningen had acquired a job at his brother's shoeshop.
In addition to material damages for recovery cost and loss of earnings, and for loss of earning capacity, Van Kreuningen claimed non-material damages for pain and suffering and loss of enjoyment of life. The Hague District Court and the Court of Appeal both rejected the claim for non-material damages, stating that the Dutch Civil Code (*Burgerlijk Wetboek*, abbr: *B.W.*) does not either in general or specifically in art. 1407 *B.W.* award plaintiff the right to claim pecuniary compensation for pain and suffering or for loss of enjoyment of life. Van Kreuningen appealed to the *Hoge Raad*, the Dutch Supreme Court, asking for *cassatie* of the judgment of the Court of Appeal.
In accordance with a very learned advisory opinion of the *Procureur-Generaal*[1] the *Hoge Raad*[2] annulled the decision of the Court of Appeal and accepted non-material damages as part of Dutch law in cases of personal injury to the claimant.

> *"Art. 1407 BW comprises in its subsection 2 a* lex specialis *for the assessment of the damage in cases of injury or mutilation, be it intentional or by negligence to any part of the body."*
> *"Subsection 3 of the said article declares this* lex specialis *to apply as well to crimes against a person as in case of rape, abduction or false arrest, examples given when this Code was enacted."*

"Under the consequences of these actions described in the subsections 2 and 3 of art. 1407 BW against the body and the personality of somebody, the so-called non-material damage takes an important place next to loss which affects property."
"In conformity with rules which had been in force in our country for a long time and with rules at present in force in neighbouring countries, the adjudgment of compensation for non-material damage, arising in consequence of the above-mentioned actions should be considered reasonable and fair."
"For that reason the Hoge Raad prefers, now that there is some doubt as to what the legislator in 1838 meant by art. 1407 subsection 2, to interpret this article in such a way that non-material damage is taken into account when estimating the damage."

2. HISTORICAL BACKGROUND OF THE DUTCH LAW OF PRETIUM DOLORIS

2.1. *Roman Dutch Law*

Until the 17th century non-material damage could be claimed by means of "*weregild*" (*zoengeld*), composition in Dutch customary law. *Weregild* was the pecuniary punishment of homicide or other atrocious personal offences. Generally these offences were prosecuted by the Government, but they could also be charged by the victim or by his widow or her widower, children and other close relatives. If the government did not insist upon *weregild*, the victim or his family could do so for their own benefit or for distribution among the poor as the price of the composition.
In the 17th century the *weregild* of the widow or widower and of the children and close relatives of the killed victim still existed and could be claimed under the condition mentioned above in addition to compensation for pecuniary damage[4]. *Weregild* for the victim had evolved into the right to claim non-material damage in case of wrongs against the victim's body. In his "Inleidinge" *Grotius* (1583-1645) states that these wrongs, "acts whereby a man loses a limb, is maimed, wounded or otherwise hurt", give a right to compensation not only for pecuniary damage as, e.g., the surgeon's fee and present and future losses, including loss of profit, but also for non-material losses. "Pain and bodily disfigurement, though properly speaking incapable of compensation, are assessed in a sum of money, if such is demanded."[5]
About a century later the *weregild* seems to have fallen in abeyance. In his "Commentarius ad Pandectas" [6] *Johannes Voet* (1647-1713) does not mention it any more. He notes that the action for wounding a man is not only directed at compensation

of pecuniar damage, "but also by custom an assessment for scarring and pain and disfigurement falls to be made good, if it has been claimed by the man or woman hurt; although no account was taken in Roman law of such things, since the body of a free person admits properly of no assessment"[7]. On the other hand the claim for *weregild* of the widow(er), children and other relatives was not transformed into a right of compensation for non-material damage. In the discussion of the contemporary (= 17th century) custom to extend an action in tort to the wife and children of a killed free man, *Voet* said:

> *"There is no doubt that in modern practice this power of suing has been womewhat widely extended in so much that an action is granted to wife and children on account of the killing of a free man by negligence for whatever shall seem fair to the conscientious mind of the person judging, after taking account of the sustenance which the person killed had been able and wont to furnish by his service to wife, children and other relatives."*

This action was granted to wife and children not as payment of a penalty, but as compensation for damage caused to them; nor was it granted to them as heirs of the killed person, but as claimants who have been injured by the act of the killer.[8]

2.2. *Nineteenth century's Dutch law*

The French invasion in the Netherlands in 1795 not only transformed the Union-of-Utrecht-federation into a unitary state, as it is still now, but also led to the unification of the law of the Netherlands. The first uniform civil law codification, the "*Code Napoléon* adapted for the Kingdom of Holland" (1809), although in a larger part a copy of the French *Code civil*, contained quite a number of Roman-Dutch law rules.
With regard to the subject to be studied here, the 1809 code comprised in its article 1313 the general rule concerning compensation in tort, but added two provisions not figuring in the *Code civil*, the first one a provision on the right of the widow(er) and the children to claim compensation for loss of sustenance given by the killed person, and secondly a provision on the right of the injured claimant to be compensated not only for pecuniar damage but also for pain and sorrow and disfigurement of the body (arts. 1318, 1319). This interesting 1809 code survived only one year. It was abolished and substituted by the French *Code civil* when Napoleon openly annexed the Kingdom of Holland in 1810. The actual Dutch civil code which replaced the French *Code civil* in 1838 is in many a part a replica of this French code, but contains in contrast with the French code the two provisions on compensation in case of injury to and death of a human being, as indeed did the 1809 code, though with a

major difference compared to the customary rule of the XVIII century Roman-Dutch law as described by *Voet* and set down in the 1809 code. No explicit reference was made to the right of an injured person to claim compensation for pain and suffering and for disfigurement. Exactly on that point of law the *Hoge Raad* in 1942 had to decide in order to end the discussions in courts and among the legal writers focusing on the question: "Did the 1838 legislator take it for granted that compensation for non-material damage was part of Dutch private law, or did he, on the contrary, express by not mentioning it, a denial of that kind of compensation?"[9] As we have seen the *Hoge Raad*, without answering this historical question, reintroduced *pre-rium doloris* as an item reparable under article 1407 *B.W.*

2.3. *Modern times*

By quoting the 1943 decision of the *Hoge Raad* on the compensation for non-material damage and by delineating the historical data leading to this decision, we have at our disposal the rough but clear elements of the Dutch law on compensation for non-material damage:

a. in case of an injury to the body or personality of the claimant compensation for non-material damage can be adjudged;
b. relatives and the surviving spouse have a right to be compensated for the maintenance lost by the death of the victim, but have no right to a *pretium doloris*.

In order to obtain a more detailed view of this part of Dutch law we will first specify the legal sources on which the compensation for non-material damage is based.

3. PRETIUM DOLORIS: LEGAL SOURCES

3.1. *Legislation*

In modern Dutch law compensation for non-material damage is explicitly mentioned in several legal provisions. These provisions are:

(1) Articles 1408-1416 *B.W.* (defamation):
In case of defamation the victim can claim compensation for present and future loss, and for non-material detriment to his honour and good name.[9a]

(2) Article 1637w *B.W.* (labour contract):
A party to a labour contract who willingly or by negligence acts in violation of his obligations, must provide compensation not only for material damage, but also for non-material damage done to his co-contractor.[10]

(3) Article 89 Code of Criminal Procedure:
If a person without good cause has been taken into custody or into detention awaiting trial, he or she can ask the

judge to award compensation for the damage sustained, to be paid by the Crown. Non-material damage is included in explicit terms.

(4) Article 4 Act on the indemnification of crime victims 1975[11]:
Victims of violent crimes who cannot be compensated because of the insolvency of the assailant, may ask the government for an indemnification to be paid out of a special fund. A regulation sets the maximum amount of indemnification per incident at Hfl. 25.000 for material damage and at Hfl. 10.000 for non-material damage.

No other legal provisions refer to non-material damage as such; all other articles on liability use the word 'damage' without further specification in the sense in which we are interested here.

The two main code provisions on liability are article 1282 *B.W.* on contractual, and article 1401 *B.W.* on tortious liability:

(5) Article 1282 *B.W.*[12]:
"Damages due to a creditor are, in general, the loss which he incurred and the gain of which he was deprived, apart from the exceptions and modifications, mentioned hereafter."

(6) Article 1401 *B.W.*[13]:
"Any illegal act which causes damage to another obliges him by whose fault it occurred to make reparation."

The general provision on tort liability given in art. 1401 *B.W.* is specified in subsequent articles. These are art. 1403, on vicarious (strict) liability and on parent's (fault) liability, art. 1404 on (strict) liability for animals and art. 1405 on (strict) liability for collapsed buildings; art. 1406 on liability in case of a dead victim - an article we will discuss hereafter -, art. 1407 on liability for injuries done to the victim's body or mind or to his personality - the *de facto* main provision on non-material damage -, artt. 1408-1416 on defamation and artt. 1416 a-c on misleading advertising. As we have mentioned, art. 1408 is the only article within the *B.W.* in which non-material damage is explicitly referred to. Although the legislature rarely and rather without system mentions in explicit words non-material damage as an item fit for compensation, we can, as a consequence of the recodification of the Dutch civil code acquaint ourselves with the actual view of government and parliament on this particular subject. While postponing the discussion of the *ius constituendum* to a further chapter, we can reveal at this point that their view is rather a restricted one.

3.2. *Judicial decisions*

In Dutch legal theory the decisions of the courts have no binding authority. They do not establish a precedent as judicial decisions in Anglo-American law do, not do they become customary law as *ständige Rechtsprechung* is in Austria, Switzerland and Germany.
In practice, however, decisions of (higher) courts have persuasive authority and are - at least as far as the *Hoge Raad* decisions are concerned - usually followed. As a result of the very restricted explicit legislation on non-material damage - very few legal provisions, and only pertaining to particular items, could be quoted - judicial decisions are in fact the most important source in this part of the law.

3.2.1. *The Hoge Raad*

As we have seen above, the *Hoge Raad* - the Dutch Supreme Court which decides by way of *cassatie*[14] - expressed the opinion in 1943 that in article 1407 *B.W.* - a provision focusing on the compensation for damage caused by a wanton or negligent act against the body or the personality of the victim - the word 'damage' has to be interpreted as including non-material damage. One might question whether this interpretation of the word 'damage' has to be restricted only to article 1407 *B.W.*, or whether the term may be applied to all provisions on the compensation of damage based on tort-liability, perhaps even to contractual liability as well.
In the 1943 decision, discussed above, uncertainty is created by the *Hoge Raad*'s reference both to Dutch legal history - while in seventeenth century Dutch law, as we have seen, compensation of non-material damage was restricted to torts causing bodily harm and the like - and to the legal rules in neighbouring countries - while German, French and Belgian law apply non-material damage on a more extensive basis.
In three other cases the *Hoge Raad* was asked to decide whether the word 'damage' as used in the Dutch civil code includes non-material damage or not. In 1937 in two nuisance cases[15] (by lack of special provisions nuisance has to be decided according to the general tort-rule of article 1401 *B.W.*) the *Hoge Raad* ruled that elimination or diminution of the enjoyment a person is entitled to under his property right, be it by stench or noise or other interferences, is damage reparable under article 1401 *B.W.* Since in both cases the *Hoge Raad* referred[16] the final decision to a lower court without indicating whether the different items of actual damage claimed - leading to material damage (as does unusual and frequent disturbance of the night's rest) as well as to non-material damage (as is the nervousness caused to the claimant's pregnant wife) - are included in the rule it had formulated, no positive conclusion

as to non-material damage can be drawn from this decision.[17] A second opportunity arose in 1959[18], when an action was brought for interference with the plaintiff's good name. The *Hoge Raad* decided that, since the kind of interference sued for did not satisfy the essentials of the tort of defamation, which are required by art. 1408 *B.W.* (the *lex specialis* on defamation explicitly awarding compensation for non-material damage[19]), the plaintiff was not entitled to claim non-material damage under the *lex generalis* of art. 1401 *B.W.*

In short, we may conclude that the *Hoge Raad*, apart from its judgment on article 1407 *B.W.* (injury to a man's body or personality), never explicitly decided on the item of non-material damage; implicitly it evaded the question by using, on several occasions[20], an *obiter dictum* formula: "..., leaving aside what purport may be given to the concept of damage in the articles 1401 to 1403 B.W., ...".

3.2.2. *Lower courts*

As a consequence of the few opportunities given to and accepted by the *Hoge Raad* to decide whether or not the word 'damage' as used in the different legal provisions on compensation includes non-material damage, lower courts have been given ample scope for their own elucidation of this point of law.
If we review the different judgments on non-material damage rendered by the lower courts, the following facts and tendencies emerge.
Lower courts unanimously observe the interpretation of damage given by the *Hoge Raad* in its 1943-decision on art. 1407 *B.W.*, and award compensation for non-material damage caused by injuring the victim's body or personality. They seem to be unanimous too in their decision, that art. 1406 *B.W.* entitles the relatives of a killed person only to a fair compensation for the loss of maintenance they used to receive from the victim, but not to a compensation for other damage or for expenses caused by his death.[21] There, unanimity in the lower court decisions on non-material damage ends. Nevertheless, without quantifying their acceptance, we will point out a few very interesting developments in this field.
There is e.g. a tendency in lower courts to apply the extensive interpretation of the word damage - that is to say as including non-material damage - not only to cases based on art. 1407 *B.W.*, but also to cases based on the general provisions of tort liability as laid down in art. 1401 *B.W.*[22], especially if part of the tortious act consists of an injury to the victim's body or personality.[23] In a recent case, for example, the President of the *Arrondissementsrechtbank* Haarlem decided that the defendants, by disclosing medical documents about the plaintiff as evidence in their defence, had acted illegally

even in this trial *in camera* where only the judge and the lawyers of both parties were present. By doing so they had caused non-material damage to the plaintiff.[24]
In a restricted number of cases lower courts have awarded compensation for non-material damage in case of liability *ex contractu*.[25] Some of these decisions hold that the restricted application of non-material damage in case of tortious liability can be applied analogously to contract law. Compensation was therefor awarded for non-material damage if the breach of contract included injury to the body or personality of the claimant.[26] Here, especially in cases of unskillful medical treatment, non-material damage was given for unnecessary pain, disfigurement and the like.[27]
Other judgments have extended the right to compensation for non-material damage in case of breach of a labour contract, legally recognized by art. 1637w *B.W.* - quoted above -, to all cases of breach of contract. Using this argument the *Kantongerecht* Rotterdam awarded compensation for non-material damage to a newly married couple to be paid by the professional photographer who had lost the films made on the wedding day.[28]
Among the few judgments on non-material damage in contractual liability some cases in particular attract attention: the travel- and hotel contracts. Several courts hold the opinion that notably misrepresentations in travel- and holidays prospectusses not only give right to compensation for material damage, but also to compensation for non-material damage suffered as a consequence of the caused inconvenience and annoyance.[29]

3.3. *Legal doctrine*

In Dutch law legal writings are only a minor source of law. Therefore, one remark must suffice here, while doctrine will be discussed in more detail in the chapters below.
It will not be a surprise that authority can be found for almost every possible opinion; but in recent years the majority of the legal writers seems to favour compensation for non-material damage on a larger scale than is usual in court practice at this moment.[30]

Although this cursory panorama of the legal sources of compensation for non-material damage in Dutch law has shown that in quite a number of situations compensation of this kind has been recognized by law and by the courts as a matter of fact, compensation for non-material damage is in practice only claimed if the plaintiff has been wounded by the tortious act and is therefore able to base his claim on article 1407 *B.W.*, unless a special provision applies.
Now that we have uncovered the legal sources of compensation

of non-material damage, we will research its substance by the following questions:

- What damage is material and therefore ruled by the general regime of compensation, what damage is non-material and ruled by a restricted regime?
- In what way will the compensation for non-material damage be measured now that non-material damage seems to have no direct economic value?
- To what extent will the right of compensation for non-material damage be recognized in the recodified Dutch civil code?

4. DAMAGE; MATERIAL AND NON-MATERIAL DISTINGUISHED

Non-material damage is that kind of damage which is not material. Using this definition necessitates describing the meaning of 'material damage' in Dutch law.

Material damage[31] is that part of the prejudice created by the tortious act, which can be repaired, neutralized or mitigated by paying a sum of money. If, for example, the factual damage caused by an accident consists of a wrecked car and a shattered foot, the material damage amounts not only to the devaluation of the car, the costs for medical treatment and hospitalization, and the loss of income until the end of revalidation, but also to the diminution of the victim's future income and to the expenses of a car adapted to the victim's needs and an artificial foot if the victim wants one, even if these expedients are only needed for social and recreative purposes.[32]

When material damage is that kind of damage that directly or indirectly creates a loss of property, then the character of non-material damage[33] consists in the fact that economic loss or diminution of the victim's present or future property neither has taken place nor will ever take place. Compensation of this kind of damage does not repair the shrinkage of the victim's fortune, but, on the contrary, adds a sum of money to the victim's means.[34]

The distinction between material and non-material damage is not a phenomenological but a legal one. The actual damage of e.g. battery can be material - broken glasses, a wounded face - or immaterial - a mental shock, pain and sorrow -, but it does not in the least determine the legal distinction of material and non-material damage. A wounded face needs medical treatment and will create grief if permanently disfigured, a nervous shock can often be healed by a trip abroad and diminishes the enjoyment of life temporarily. Even the actual damage in case of the destruction of the merest trifle which is of great emotional value to its owner can be repaired or at least mitigated by buying - if claimed by the owner - a replica of the lost object, and that compensation too constitutes compensation for material damage by its very nature.

The legal distinction of material and non-material damage is not linked with the kind of remedy claimable either. Compensation in kind or by way of money, restoration of the original kind, rectification and an injunction to restrain interference can be claimed regardless of the kind of damage ahead. In recent years some Dutch writers[35] have suggested replacing the negative definition of non-material damage, that is to say damage that is not material, not reparable in an economic way, by a definition that concentrates on the loss of enjoyment of life, on the bodily disfigurement, pain and defamation. Although such a definition is better suited to the literal meaning of *pretium doloris*, it is not a precise one. For if the pain can be assuaged by an anodyne, if the disfigurement can be lessened by plastic surgery, the expenses constitute material damage, as does the letter a defamed merchant has to send to his business relations to deny the alleged facts. The inconsistency of this positive definition lies in the fact that it concentrates on the phenomenological damage itself, while private law, *in casu* tort law, is only interested in the question whether and in what way actual damage has to be remedied, has to be compensated. For simplicity's sake non-material damage is said to be mainly connected with the following phenomena: pain, suffering, disfigurement, defamation, sorrow and the like. However, the loss of enjoyment which these injuries have in common, is not characteristic; the value of a Rembrandt is for almost a hundred percent indicated by the - objectivized - enjoyment the painting gives, its destruction is nevertheless very material damage. Although there is no reason to expect the given and in Dutch law generally accepted definition of non-material damage depending on the character of its compensation to be changed into a definition that focusses on the actual damage caused, this actual damage plays its role in awarding compensation for non-material damage, as can be seen in the reference in article 1407 *B.W.* to "damage to the body or personality of the victim".

Summarizing in short our definition of non-material damage: non-material damage is that damage that does not create a decrease of the victim's economic assets, neither in a direct way, because the detriment has no objective pecuniary value, nor in an indirect way, as the detriment cannot be repaired or diminished by paying a sum of money.
Regarding the distinction between material and non-material damage as made in Dutch law, a few remarks are necessary.
(a) Courts and writers do agree that material damage not necessarily means that the damage is calculable in a direct, concrete way, or that it can be expressed in an exact sum of money. Compensation not only for future losses, but also for loss already suffered, can often only be assessed *ex aequo et bono*[36] as is compensation for non-material damage.

(b) On the other hand, the denomination of non-material damage is often used by the courts, and by adjusters as well, to assess in one comprehensive sum of money all kinds of damage that are material in fact but difficult to calculate, or are very credible but not possible to prove in the right way. In adjusters' practice the denomination 'non-material damage by loss of future earning capacity' seems to be preferred above '(material) loss of future income', now that the first denomination has a greater chance not to be charged with income tax than the second one has.[37]
(c) While the enjoyment of property, especially of immovables, or of some right to property, is surely not material in the sense of having a separate commerciable value, its unlawful interference is nevertheless a material damage as described above, being the difference in the objective value of the property with and without this interference.[38]
(d) Expenses made for the victim's physical or mental recovery are considered material damage. The victim has a right to seek, in a reasonable way, reparation (even if only partially possible) of the damage caused, and to ask for compensation of the cost involved. We already mentioned that the claim, if reasonable, for an artificial leg makes that part of the damage resulting from an amputation, material damage. The journey prescribed by a doctor as a medicine for the recovery of the illness caused by the wrongful act is material damage too.[39] One could even ask whether the payment of a *pretium doloris* is compensation of material damage if a doctor holds the view that its payment is propitious to the recovery of the victim.

BUT: Although in theory we are able to distinguish sharply between material and non-material damage, in practice the distinction is less easy.
An employee whose career as planned in his labour contract is ended by the damaging accident, can claim compensation for material damage, being the loss of future salary increases (as far as reasonable). But a schoolboy's claim for compensation of the same damage is held to be a claim for compensation of non-material damage[40], though it is quite reasonable to assume that he will not reach as high a social and economic status as he would have done without the handicap caused by the accident. Other examples of the overlapping areas of material and non-material damage, where both kinds of damage merge with one another, have been given above.
A second restriction has to be made. In this chapter non-material damage is described in relation to its compensation: non-material is that part of the damage that cannot be balanced in an economic way. Although this description complies perfectly with its legal context, it is philosophically unsatisfactory in that no intrinsic definition can be given which links the concept of non-material damage to a phenomenological damage.[40a]

Most courts seem to feel embarrassed by the lack of a concept of this kind; they only award compensation if the non-material damage is linked to a damage which can be established objectively, like a crashed object, an injured part of the body or a face visibly ridden with pain. And, with the exception of the few cases based on contractual liability cited above, they award no compensation, at least in the cases published, if the non-material damage is only linked to strictly subjective feelings of damage as sorrow and lost affection; a genuine application of Salmond's maxim: "tears do not permit calculation in money"[41].

5. ELEMENTS OF LIABILITY

Iniuria, causa, culpa: elements that determine the right of compensation of the damage.[42] A description of these elements, even an elementary one, is outside the scope of this article. But, indispensable as these elements are to an explanation of the full context of the compensation for non-material damage, we will give here a few glimpses of Dutch tort law, by providing rather personal[43] definitions of its elements: causation, fault and illegality.

Causation: the (illegal) act is the cause of the damage if it is a condition *sine qua non*, unless the damage is, in reason, unimputable to its author for being too exceptional or too uncharacteristic a consequence of the damaging act. Therefore, a truck driver who had lost barrels containing toxic liquids has been obliged to compensate the water supply company for the expenses necessary to prevent the liquids to penetrate the soil as deep as the level of the subsoil water, used for water supply. The *Hoge Raad*[44] held, that "damage to subsoil water basins by flowing toxics is, in our country, not that exceptional a damage nor that remote to the accident that this damage caused by the accident, could reasonably not be imposed on the person liable in law".
Fault: fault can be defined as the duty to foresee and prevent the injustice (not the damage) as a reasonable person in the same position as the author should have done. Fault is not an element of liability in all tortious acts. Dutch law recognizes non-fault (or: strict) liability in case of vicarious liability and liability for animals, as well as in case of liability for defective structures, nuclear energy and, in a restricted way, for car accidents.[45]
As far as causation and fault are concerned, neither the law nor the courts seem to hold different views on material and non-material damage.

Illegality: the main element of tort liability is *iniuria*, illegality. Damage, including non-material damage, will only be legally remedied if the damage has been created by an infringement of a legally protected interest. Although an all-embracing definition of this kind of interest has not yet been developed in Dutch law - if possible at all -, interest includes not only property right but also, as we have seen, interests like the enjoyment of life, the right of personality and of good name. Non-material damage seems to arise only in interferences with this second kind of interests, which comprises all that is said to be inherent to man: his right to have a future and his hopes for that future, his free will and his faculty to control his own destiny. But, as we have seen, damage to these interests can be material as well as non-material.

6. ENFORCEMENT OF PRETIUM DOLORIS

Although under the above mentioned restrictions, liability in tort (and in contract[46]) creates a duty to compensate non-material damage, the claim is, according to Dutch law, strictly personal at the outset. Only by some kind of 'crystallization' this claim loses its personal character and can be enforced not only by the victim himself but also by his legal representatives and his heirs (under universal title).[47] This 'crystallization' occurs when the victim himself openly expresses his wish to make a demand for compensation, either by concluding or trying to conclude an agreement assessing this compensation, or by summoning the *laedens* or by preparing legal proceedings against him.[48]

This strictly personal character of the claim for compensation of non-material damage has its consequences. Compensation can not be recovered so long as the victim is unable to express a wish to that effect; the claim does not constitute part of the victim's property if that is subjected to attachment or bankruptcy, unless crystallization took place. And at the victim's death only a crystallized claim for compensation of non-material damage is considered to be part of the inheritance.

On the other hand a claim for compensation of non-material damage, even if not yet crystallized, qualifies for assignment by the victim, because the assignment itself expresses the victim's wish to crystallize the claim.[49]

7. MEASURE OF DAMAGE

7.1. *Purpose of compensation*

Compensation for non-material damage seems to serve a two-fold purpose at least.
It is not disputed that this kind of compensation is first and foremost aimed at the victim's indemnification. Indemnificatio of non-material damage in an economic way, monetary way is nc self-evident, but contradictory, for the very character of non-material damage is the impossibility of a pecuniary reparation. But private law, at least Dutch private law, has *in ultimo* no instruments to repair the damage, other than economically. Judges have no legal instruments to impose on the author of the damage a duty to reduce sorrow by regularly taking the crippled victim out for a walk, by visiting him when he is in hospital, by offering excuses to the defamed, or by sending flowers to a victim suffering from stench.
The only reason to indemnify non-material damage in a pecuniar way is the lack of a more appropriate means of compensation; or, as a French writer states: "*Si l'argent ne remplace pas le bonheur perdu, il est quand même une bonne chose*"[50].

Next to the above described aim compensation serves a second and additional purpose , for indivisible parts of this compensation are considered to be punitive damage, atonement or solace. Some writers[51] underline the punitive character: the victim's sense of injustice will be alleviated because a sacrific is demanded from the other party. Others[52] point out the solac character: this compensation helps the victim to reconcile himself with the sustained injustice, to acquiesce in his fate.

7.2. *Determinants of compensation*

Article 1407 *B.W.*, which provides, as we have seen above, compensation for material and non-material damage in case of an injury to the body or mind and is considered, by some courts and writers, to be the general rule on this subject, gives, in rather vague terms, a concrete instruction for the measurement of compensation for non-material damage. Section 2 of this article rules that the compensation has to be assessed "according to each party's status and fortune". As this is a rule not for the calculation but for the mitigation of the compensation of damage, it will be discussed below.
In measuring the compensation for non-material damage the judges have no other legal calculating rules to go by. Nevertheless, if we take stock of the published cases, several recurrent elements can be observed. Determinants seem to be at least the seriousness of the injury - a broken finger is less serious than a broken leg -, the amount of pain sustained -

was the operation a minor or a major one, were more operations necessary or just the one -, the extent of the permanent consequences for body and mind - what is left of her pretty face, has his character changed for the worse -, and the duration of the recuperation. The seriousness of the injury plays another part, at least in the decisions of many Dutch courts , for if in the opinion of the court the injury is not serious enough, the plaintiff will only get compensation for his material damage, but is refused compensation for his non-material damage.[53]
The age of the victim - the number of the years ahead to live with the handicap of caused sorrow - is determinent too. This element was used in a case in which the 43-old victim died twelve years after the accident, while his case was still in trial. The court held that the victim, were he still alive, would have been entitled to Hfl. 25.000 as compensation of non-material damage based on a life expectancy of 69 years. But since he had died at 43 years, the compensation would be set at Hfl 15.000.[54]
Remarkable too are the case where the courts took account, especially if young people were involved, of the reduced chance of getting married, and where they awarded compensation when the inflicted bodily or mental injury had occasioned a divorce.[55]
In some cases the lost chance of promotion at school or at work and the lost enjoyment of hobbies or of holidays are considered to be determinants of compensation for non-material damage.[56]

7.3. *Reduction*

In general the amount of compensation is directly influenced by contributory negligence on the part of the victim and by collateral benefits.
If the suffered damage results partly from the claimant's fault, the recoverable compensation thereof will be reduced. The reduction will be measured in a certain percentage and the total amount of damage will be apportioned accordingly. No special rule for non-material damage seems to exist in case of reduction for contributory negligence.[56a]
Collateral benefits realised as a result of the accident are generally calculated in the total amount of compensation for material damage (albeit with some complications in cases of payments by insurance companies; here at least the recoverable amount under an insurance-contract that is not for indemnity - like a life-insurance - may not be set against the damages[57]). But does the compensation for non-material damage have to be counterbalanced by the caused immaterial or material gain? What is the influence of, e.g., the timely discovery of a malignant cancer during the victim's hospitalization after a car accident; what of the escape from a fatal aircrash when

as a result of the car accident the death-carrying airplane was missed? May the defendant object that the now-crippled claimant at least saves the price of an annual pair of shoes? No positive or negative answer can be distilled from the reports, while in adjusters' practice gains do not appear, at least not explicitly, to be neutralized; yet with exception. When income tax is levied on compensation for non-material damage - as is the case when the right of compensation is directly linked with a source of income (e.g. in the case of the compensation for non-material damage ex art. 1637w *B.W.*, cited above, a compensation based on a breach of the labour contract) - then the amount of compensation differs in order to neutralize this taxation.

7.4. *Mitigation*

Now that we have reached the point where, whether or not by comparison to other cases, and after reduction of deductible profits, the amount of compensation is determined in an objective way, we must recall section 2 of art. 1407 *B.W.*, imposing a duty to set the amount of compensation in a subjective way: "according to status and fortune of the parties, and to the circumstances".
This mitigation rule is often used in cases in which the *laedens* is not insured for his liability and unable to bear the obligation of full compensation. The well-to-do victim, on the other hand, sometimes receives a lower compensation; his need for money is judged to be lower than average.
As fortune has its mitigating influence, status on the other hand does not, at least no positive or negative decision can be cited here. In only a few cases the courts have mitigated compensation using other circumstances for reduction as in case of family relationship between author and victim, or of a non-paying passenger injured by a tortious act of the car driver.[58]

7.5. *Systematization*

As we have seen the very character of non-material damage is that there is no economic measure to calculate the caused damage. Therefore it has to be achieved by using moral standards. In Dutch law a certain kind of uniformity regarding these standards is reached by an index of court decisions on compensation for non-material damage. This index, started in 1964 by a barrister *Van der Veen* and republished at regular intervals, is generally accepted by the courts and the adjusters as their guideline for assessment.[59] Judges seem to abide by this index, adjusters use it too, but they try - increasing the indexed sum by an extra amount - to settle the compensation by agreement in order to prevent litigation, which, so they

fear, will be more expensive. *Van der Veen*'s index on compensation systematizes the various judgments on non-material damage according to the sustained bodily harm. By consulting the index one can find examples of a casualty and the amount of compensation awarded.
The rather rough method of calculating compensation by comparison with decided cases has been criticized on several occasions. Suggestions have been made to replace this index by a point system where every injury causing non-material damage receives its fixed number of points and every point in its turn a fixed sum of money, so that by adding the points resulting from the various injuries sustained in e.g. an accident, the total amount of compensation for the non-material damage should be indisputable. Mainly because of their inflexibility these proposals did not receive general acclaim; they have only a very limited chance to be introduced in the near future.[60]

7.6. *Nominal value of the compensation*

The act of measuring the compensation of non-material damage results in determining a nominal amount of money. In several examples given above the awarded sum of money has been added as a specimen of the judge's calculation of the particular non-material damage. It is impossible to give a detailed exposition of the specific amounts usually awarded by Dutch courts, only a few major points can be mentioned.
- Victims usually claim as compensation for non-material damage a sum of money more or less in accordance with the amount specified in *Van der Veen*'s index. The judge is bound by this sum as a maximum.
- In cases where the victim is not bodily or mentally injured judges award a rather low sum as compensation for non-material damage; up to the present the maximum is about Hfl. 2.500. In cases of a bodily or mentally injured claimant Dutch courts award - in comparison with e.g. American or French courts - a rather limited sum; the absolute maximum until now is Hfl. 80.000.[61]

When studying these figures we must keep in mind that the amount of compensation awarded for non-material damage is directly influenced by the Dutch social economic system. For that very reason perhaps, a comparison of the Dutch compensation-index of *Van der Veen* to the German index yield - be it with the exception of the maximum amount - strikingly similar amounts of money awarded in comparable cases, now that these countries are comparably high in the scale of Welfare States.

8. PERSONS ENTITLED TO NON-MATERIAL DAMAGE

In the previous chapters we used the terms 'victim', 'plaintiff' and 'claimant' to denote the natural person who was directly damaged by the tortious act and had sustained the created actual damage. Still to be reviewed is the position of legal entities claiming non-material damage and that of relatives who were hurt in their emotional feelings for the victim without being actually damaged.

8.1. *Legal entities*

Legal entities, like companies and associations, are not explicitly excluded by the law from compensation for non-material damage.
In defamation cases, based on art. 1408 ff. *B.W.*, their right to claim compensation for such damage is only accepted by part of the legal writers, while the courts too hold a reticent view[61a].
No decisions can be cited of tort liability cases other than for defamation, where compensation for non-material damage was claimed by legal entities, and was awarded. But for one exception, where damage was done to a trade union's reputation for reliability. Here the *Hoge Raad* decided that the damage the union claimed compensation for was not non-material damage, since it was directly related to a loss of its members[61b].

8.2. *Relatives and pretium doloris*[62]

The damage a relative (or spouse) can claim in case of the death of a victim caused by a tortious act, can be claimed *pro herede*, as being the heir of the victim's inheritance, or *pro se*, as being directly injured by the act. As we have seen before, compensation of non-material damage will become part of the victim's inheritance only if the victim himself has 'crystallized' the claim.
The relative's right to claim *pro se* in case of death is codified in article 1406 *B.W.* This article - at the time of its introduction a very social maintenance rule - reads as follows:

> *"In case of a willingly or negligently caused homicide the spouse, the children and the parents of the killed person, who used to be maintained by his labour, are entitled to claim damages to be estimated according to the parties' status and fortune and to the circumstances."*

The restriction in this provision "who used to be maintained by his labour" is extensively interpreted by the courts and legal writers; therefore it has to be read as "who used to be maintained *and* in so far they are maintained by his labour"[63]. There is no doubt that under this interpretation, that is generally used in the courts, relatives have a right of maintenance only, not of compensation for other material damage, not even for the material damage like the funeral costs and certainly not of compensation for non-material damage.

If the victim has not been fatally wounded, the position of his or her spouse and relatives is in principle the same.[64] Nevertheless, some courts as well as adjusters award a higher amount of compensation for non-material damage to the child when, e.g., the mother had to nurse her injured child, or when by the accident the child turned into an *enfant terrible*[65]. Although many legal writers[66] do not agree with this negation of an *ipso iure* right of compensation for non-material damage of the spouse and relatives, this right has been firmly rejected by the legislature, as we will see in the next chapter.

9. NON-MATERIAL DAMAGE IN THE NEW DUTCH CIVIL CODE

At this moment the Dutch codes of private law are subjected to a thorough recodification. Parts of the 1838-civil and commercial codes are still in force, while the other parts of both codes have been rewritten and transferred to the new civil code.
The Dutch new civil code will be divided into eight books, containing civil and commercial law. Two of these books have already entered into force, the others will be introduced - if possible - in 1984. In this New Civil Code the law of damages is incorporated in Book 6, The Law of Obligations.
The new law of damages only recognizes non-material damage as a cause for compensation in a very limited way. In Book 6 - article 6.1.9.1 *N.B.W.* - the general rule for compensation reads as follows[67]:

> *"Damage to be indemnified under a legal duty of compensation consists in material damage and in other loss; this other loss shall be compensated only in so far as statute does provide."*

It is clear that the new civil code in this article uses the term 'other loss' as synonymous with non-material damage. The question now is: which statutory provisions provide compensation for these losses? We did mention already the specific acts containing provisions for non-material damage. To these one special provision in the new civil code on material damage can be added, article 6.1.9.11 *N.B.W.*[68]:

"1. *For loss other than material damage the injured party may claim damages to be estimated* ex aequo et bono*:*

a. if the person liable deliberately inflicted such loss;

b. if the injured party has sustained bodily harm, has been injured in his honour or good name, or if in any other manner an attack has been made on his personality;

c. if by discrediting a deceased person's character loss is inflicted upon the surviving spouse (whose marriage was not partly dissolved by judicial separation), or to consanguinei *of the first or second degree, in case the discredition should have been actionable as defamation if the deceased were still alive.*

2. The claim for compensation referred to in the preceding paragraph is not susceptible for transfer or attachment, unless there is a contractual provision to that effect or judicial proceedings have been instituted. In case of transfer by universal title the claim for compensation passes to the transferee once the injured person has communicated to the laedens *to submit such a claim."*

Comparing this new non-material damage provision, which will be introduced as it is in 1984, with the actual state of the law as developed by the courts, its restraining effect is unmistakable.

In the thirty years during which the new civil code was drafted government and parliament - represented by its standing committee on legal affairs - were more or less unanimous on a restricted recognition of right of compensation for non-material damage. The compromisory nature of this unanimous recognition is deductible from the arguments used by the government in its explanatory report.

- To those political parties in parliament that had declared themselves to be opposed to a *pretium doloris* for motives of principle (a respectable minority in parliament, including the (former) protestant parties) the government pointed out that compensation for non-material damage serves a useful purpose because it covers all damage that is material in kind but impossible to prove in a legally sufficient way.

- To those parties (socialist and liberal) that had asked for a broader acceptance in the new code of the right of compensation for non-material damage than was given by the *Hoge Raad* in its 1943-decision and to give at least to the parents of a wounded or killed child a compensation for fear, anxiety and sorrow, the government pointed out that what it called the the general sense of justice in Dutch society would only ac-

cept a very resticted application of the non-material damage compensation.
In the explanatory report at the last version of this part of the new civil code the government (i.e. its drafter *Snijders*) - in contrast to earlier reports (drafted by *E.M. Meijers*) - has made some more interesting remarks on our subject. The report starts by saying that material and non-material damage are not of the same kind and that an excessive development of *pretium doloris* should therefore be prevented; its application must be restricted to cases in which it is indispensable. The report openly refuses to accept emotional damage (*pretium affectionis*) as a kind of injury to person, entitling the victim to compensation, unless the emotional damage has been caused intentionally.[69]

CONCLUSION

When in 1984 Book 6 of the New Dutch Civil Code comes into force, the formulative era of the law of non-material damage, that started some forty years before at the moment the *Hoge Raad* decided in the *Van Kreuningen/Bessem* case, will have an end. In article 6.1.9.11 the New Civil Code then resettles Dutch law of non-material damage in its general outline on its Roman - Dutch law basis. Neither the negation of non-material damage, which existed since the nineteenth century and, even after the *Hoge Raad*'s decision of 1943, still has its supporters, nor the attempts made by judges and writers to enlarge the scope of non-material damage by its integration into the general rules of damage, were honoured in the new code.
In future, as it was in the seventeenth and eighteenth centuries and is practised nowadays by the majority of the courts the right of compensation for non-material damage will be mainly reserved to a victim who has sustained harm to his body or personality; only in rare occasions - in case of deliberately inflicted losses and defamation of a dead person's memory - it will have a more extensive application. The New Civil Code contains no provision on the measure of compensation; the rather restricted practice of the courts will therefore continue.
One may ask why the right of compensation of non-material damage is so reticently accepted by Dutch law and practice, and why only rather reduced amounts of compensation are awarded. The answer is hard to give. But, as some writers have suggested[70], the law is if not in general, particularly on this point greatly influenced by broadly accepted ethical standards in Dutch society and by the highly developed socio-economic security of the Dutch welfare state. Especially the comparison of rules of *pretium doloris* in the Dutch legal system to those of other legal systems is highly conditioned by these influences of a cultural, religious and socio-economic kind.

REFERENCES AND ABBREVIATIONS

Asser 4, I	Asser-Rutten, *Verbintenissenrecht, I: De Verbintenis in het algemeen*, 6th ed., 1981 (manual on the Law of obligations in general).
Asser 4, III	Asser-Rutten, *Verbintenissenrecht, III: De Verbintenis uit de wet*, 5th ed., 1979 (manual on the Law of tort obligations).
Eykman	L.G. Eykman, Smart en Geld, in: *WPNR* 5572 (1981), p. 461 (review of Overeem's book).
Greebe	J.J.A. Greebe, *Eenige rechtsvergelijkende beschouwingen over de vergoeding van onstoffelijke schade bij niet-nakoming van overeenkomsten en bij onrechtmatige daad*, Amsterdam 1935 (comparative study of pretium doloris).
De Groot	G.R.J. de Groot, *Schaderegeling bij verkeersongevallen*, 1979 (sociological study of adjuster's practices in case of road-accidents).
Mok	L. Mok, Recensie R. Overeem's Smartegeld, in: *Verzekeringsarchief* 56 (1979), p. 230 (review of Overeem's book).
Mout	P. Mout, Bescherming van het individu tegen ongefundeerde aantijgingen in massamedia, *Handelingen NJV* 1979, p. 81 (report on the protection against defamation uttered in mass-media).
OD II	*Onrechtmatige daad, II: Schadevergoeding en andere rechtsgevolgen*, A. Bloembergen (looseleaf on torts, part II: Compensation).
OD IX	*Onrechtmatige daad, IX: Artikelen 1408-1416 BW*, I. Michiels van Kessenich-Hoogendam (looseleaf on torts, part IX: Defamation).
Overeem	R. Overeem, *Smartegeld*, 1979 (comparative study on pretium doloris).
Parl.Gesch.	C.J. van Zeben & J. du Pon, *Parlementaire Geschiedenis van het N.B.W., Boek 6: Algemeen gedeelte van het verbintenissenrecht*, 1981 (parliamentary history of the codification of Book 6: Obligations, of the New Civil Code).
VdV	Van der Veen, Overzicht van Smartegeld uitspraken, 7th ed., with Preface, in: *Verkeersrecht* 1979, p. 121 (index of amounts of compensation awarded for non-material damage).

BNB	Beslissingen in Belastingzaken - Nederlandse Belastingrechtspraak (Dutch Tax Law Reports)
BW	Burgerlijk Wetboek (Dutch civil code)
Hof	Gerechtshof (Court of Appeal)
HR	Hoge Raad (Dutch Supreme Court)
NBW	Nieuw Burgerlijk Wetboek (Dutch new civil code)
NJ	Nederlandse Jurisprudentie (Dutch Law Reports)
Pres.	President van de Rechtbank (esp. when deciding in summary proceedings)
Rb.	Rechtbank (District Court)
RvdW	Rechtspraak van de Week (Dutch Weekly Law Reports)
VR	Verkeersrecht (Review of Road Traffic Law)

NOTES

1. This advisory opinion of Procureur-Generaal Berger is published as an annex to the decision mentioned in note 2.
2. HR, *RvdW* 1943-15; *NJ* 1943-455. See note 16.
3. From 1579 till 1795 the Netherlands were a union of seven independent provinces. Each province had its own legal system, although the differences between these systems were of minor importance. In 1795 the Netherlands were occupied by the French.
4. The history of the *were* is described by Grotius in his *Inleidinge tot de Hollandsche Rechtsgeleerdheid*, Book III, Ch. 32 no. 7. *Inleidinge*'s English translation is: Hugo Grotius, *Jurisprudence of Holland*, translated with brief notes and a commentary by R.W. Lee, Oxford 1926.
5. Grotius, *Inleidinge*, Book III, Ch. 33 s. 1 and 3, see note 4.
6. Johannes Voet, *Commentarius ad Pandectas*, IX, 2, 11. Translation used: *The selective Voet, being the Commentary on the pandects by Johannes Voet*, translated by P. Gane, Durban 1955.
7. Only Frisian law did not give a right to compensation for non-material damage, as is noted by P-G Berger in his opinion mentioned in note 1.

8. Voet, *Commentarius*, IX, 2, 11; see note 6.
9. Greebe p. 19.
9a. See Mout p. 141 ff.
10. An incidental provision is given in art. 16 of the Collective Labour Contracts Act 1927 (*Wet C.A.O.*), and in art. 3 of the Act on the General Binding Effect of Collective Labour Contracts (*Wet Algemene Verbindend en Onverbindend Verklaring van CAO's*).
11. *Wet Voorlopige Regeling Schadefonds Geweldmisdrijven.*
12. Cf. art. 1149 French civil code.
13. Cf. art. 1382 French civil code.
14. See note 16.
15. HR, *NJ* 1937-570 (*Voorste Stroom III*); HR, *NJ* 1938-517 (*Unitas*).
16. In Dutch law of procedure the Supreme Court (*Hoge Raad*) appeal is decided by way of *cassatie*. Having decided the legal question the claim is based on, the *Hoge Raad* refers the case to an appeal court (*Gerechtshof*) to give a final judgment in accordance with the *Hoge Raad*'s decision.
17. So Asser 4, III p. 85. Meijers (annotations *NJ* 1937-570 and *NJ* 1938-517) holds that the *Hoge Raad* in these decisions maintained a positive acceptance of compensation of non-material damage.
18. HR, *NJ* 1959-15 (*Van Herwaardens Kalkzandsteenfabrieken*).
19. See nr. 3.1.1.
20. Cases cited in notes 15 and 18.
21. See nr. 3.1.6. Concerning this refusal of compensation for non-material damage: Rb. 's Hertogenbosch, *NJ* 1953-168; idem *NJ* 1952-132; Rb. Assen, *NJ* 1953-99; Rb. 's Gravenhage, *NJ* 1953-496.
22. See nr. 3.1.6.
23. So e.g. Rb. Groningen, *NJ* 1950-433; Rb. Alkmaar, *NJ* 1968-335; Pres. Groningen, *NJ* 1971-403.
24. Pres. Haarlem, *RvdW* KG 1981-108.
25. For compensation of non-material damage in case of a labour contract, see nr. 3.1.2.
26. So e.g. Kantongerecht Terborg 11.8.1977, *VdV* 578. The *Kantongerecht* (see note 28) gave judgment for the tenant who had to move after the landlord's announcement that he needed the house himself. Immediately after the removal the landlord sold the house. The former tenant was granted compensation ex art. 1623e BW not only for material damage but also for non-material damage caused by the substantial inconvenience and annoyance sustained (Hfl. 2.500).
27. Hof 's Hertogenbosch, *VdV* 268: a dentist drops an extirpation-needle which is swallowed by the patient, who needs to be operated afterwards; compensation Hfl. 2.000. Hof 's Hertogenbosch, *VdV* 322: X-ray treatment of face results in disfigurement ; compensation Hfl. 15.000.
28. Kantongerecht Rotterdam, *Praktijkgids* 1978-1307, compensation Hfl. 1.000. The *Kantongerecht* is a court of first instance competent for small claims and for *all* rent and labour disputes.
29. So Kantongerecht Utrecht, *VdV* 569 (Hfl. 100). Most disputes of this kind have, by the standard clauses used, to be decided by special arbitration. The Arbitration Commission often awards compensation for non-material damage in its decisions: see *NJ* 1974-384. In its uniform Standard Form Contracts Regulation the ANVR, the most important Dutch association for tour-operators, obliges clients to accept arbitration. In its regulation of this arbitration the ANVR allows the Arbitration Committee to give compensation not only for material but also for non-material damage (art. 4.3).
30. See *OD* II, 16.
31. Material damage is also called pecuniary, monetary or economic damage.
32. So Eykman p. 463.
33. Non-material damage is used here as synonymous with non-pecuniary damage, moral damage, *solatium* or *pretium doloris*. The term *pretium doloris* (the Dutch word *smartegeld* is a literal translation) is used here as a term of art, not in its literal meaning of smart-money.
34. So Meyers in his annotation to HR, *NJ* 1937-570.
34a. See note 45a.
35. Stein in annotation HR, *NJ* 1980-227. Wachter in annotation HR, *NJ* 1980-482.
36. HR, *NJ* 1933-88, *NBW* art. 6.1.9.3. Asser I, p. 192.
37. Hof Amsterdam, *VdV* 60. Mok p. 231, De Groot p. 20, 106. On income tax: Hof Leeuwarden, *BNB* 1978-200.
    It is remarkable to see that the burden of proof of material damage seems to be heavier then of non-material damage, De Groot p. 37.

38. *OD* II, 16, 3. For the opinion of the *Hoge Raad*: see note 15.
39. *OD* II, 14; *Parl.Gesch.* p. 368.
40. Mok p. 231.
40a. As we have seen, concepts focusing on the enjoyment, pain, sorrow and affection are not appropriate. On the other hand, non-material damage seems to be linked with interferences of interests of a special kind, see below note 45a.
41. Salmond, *On Torts*, 12th ed., 1957, p. 629.
42. Although the following description is partly applicable to contractual liability we limit ourselves here to delictual liability.
43. Recent developments make it difficult to cite generally accepted definitions.
44. HR, *NJ* 1970-251 (*Waterwingebied*).
45. In awarding non-material damage courts do not, until now, differ between fault and strict liability.
45a. If we try to schematize the links between the injured interest, the actual damage sustained, and the legal damage to be compensated, we find the following diagram:

injured interest →	*actual damage* →	*compensation*
1. proprietary interests to (in)corporals (e.g. in case of damage to an - owned or hired - car; interference with a contractual relationship)	reparable	material damage
2. proprietary interests (e.g. in case of a burned painting)	irreparable	material damage
3. non-proprietary interests (e.g. in case of wounds, necessitating hospitalization)	reparable	material damage
4. non-proprietary interests (e.g. in case of sorrow for lost affection)	irreparable	non-material damage

Time is lacking to discuss the interdependances of the four categories of legal damages - especially questionable is here the right of the plaintiff to insist on compensation aimed at reparation (nrs. 1 and 3), if compensation of the other kind (nrs. 2 and 4) would be less expensive to the defendant.
46. See 3.2.2.
47. So the majority of court decisions, see *OD* II, 19.
48. Courts differ in their appreciation. Some courts demand full consciousness of the victim while others accept the faintest expression of will as sufficient for crystallization.
49. Rb. Groningen, *VR* 1960-27; Rb. 's Hertogenbosch, *VR* 1964-27.
50. This effect is recognized by De Groot, p. 106, and by the Special Committee on Traffic Accidents, see note 60.
51. *Toelichting Boek 6* (6.1.9.11), *Parl.Gesch.* p. 369, Eykman p. 463.
52. Mok p. 24; Mout p. 144.
53. Rb. 's Gravenhage, *NJ* 1969-313; plaintiff A, damaged biceps, plaintiff B, head injury. Both unfit for work during one week, no *pretium doloris*. Kantongerecht Groningen, *VdV* 367: 11 years old child, hit by snowball, front teeth broken, to be replaced by crowns, no *pretium doloris*. De Groot p. 104.
54. Rb. Groningen, *NJ* 1973-88. Rb. Haarlem, *VdV* 207.
55. Rb. Amsterdam, *NJ* 1965-42 (marriage chances). Rb. Leeuwarden, *VdV* 442 (divorce).
56. Overeem p. 34.
56a. De Groot, p. 637, discovered that in adjuster's practice contributory negligence is seldom taken into consideration. It usually causes a complete denial or a complete acceptance of the victim's right of compensation of non-material damage.
57. HR, *NJ* 1970-172. On the other hand, life-insurance is a 'circumstance' that - according to the arts. 1406 and 1407 - can be taken into account when mitigating the damage; see below.
58. Overeem p. 29.
59. Van der Veen, *VR* 1979, p. 121.
60. So: Report (Special Committee on Traffic Accidents), Part I, p. 41. Pro a point system: Van der Veen, *VR* 1979, p. 122; Eykman p. 464.
61. *VdV* 373, 510, 553.
61a. *OD* II, 15; *OD* IX, 21.

61b. HR, *NJ* 1980-227.
62. Overeem p. 22.
63. Rb. Assen, *VdV* 74; Hof Leeuwarden, *NJ* 1980-128.
64. E.g. Hof Leeuwarden, *NJ* 1981-128.
65. Rb. Amsterdam, *VdV* 176; De Groot p. 21.
66. See Overeem p. 23. Mok p. 232.
67. At its introduction in 1984 the provisions of the new civil code will be numbered in a different way than is done in the enactment. Each provision will be indicated by the number of the book and a consecutive figure.
68. In comparison to earlier drafts this article was in its last draft amplified in subsection 1c.
69. *Parl.Gesch.* p. 384.
70. Eykman p. 461; Mok p. 232. In their juridico-sociological research of 1967-1968 Bloembergen and Van Wersch found that almost one-third of the victims entitled to compensation of non-material damage abstained from claiming this damage.

Le droit applicable à la détermination de la personne physique ou morale qui contrôle une société anonyme dont une filiale a son activité à l'étranger

D. KOKKINI-IATRIDOU

Professeur à l'Université Libre à Amsterdam

II.B.1.

Sous ce titre ésotérique, nous allons rapporter quelques cas où l'actionnaire (personne physique ou société-mère) entre en ligne de compte, tout en gardant nos doutes sur la signification véritable du sujet et par conséquent sur ce qu'il fallait ou ne fallait pas y inclure. Quelques remarques, fragmentaires et elliptiques, les précéderont.

I. REMARQUES INTRODUCTIVES

A. *Conflits de lois*

Hors du droit conventionnel il n'y a dans le domaine des conflits de lois qu'une seule règle écrite concernant les personnes morales. Celle-ci est formulée de manière négative dans la loi du 25 juillet 1959[1]: "Les Pays-Bas ne sont pas un pays où le siège réel est pris en considération". Le système de l'incorporation n'est cependant pas toujours suivi par le juge néerlandais, les 'yeux fermés'. L'objet du différend, le but de la loi à appliquer, les circonstances de fait qui entourent le cas concret, sont des éléments qui peuvent faire pencher la balance vers le système du siège réel. C'est ainsi que le Président du tribunal de Rotterdam (décision du 21 décembre 1979[2]) jugea "qu'il ne peut pas être exclu pour le moment" que le droit hellénique trouve application à la question de savoir si une société constituée au Libéria est tenue responsable pour les dettes d'une autre société également constituée au Libéria. Comme motif fut avancée la circonstance que les deux sociétés bien qu'étant des personnes morales selon le droit libérien et établies à Monrovia, exerçaient en réalité leur entreprise dans la sphère juridique hellénique, vu qu'elles avaient le même *managing director*, une S.à.R.L. établie au Pirée (Grèce).
Le système de l'incorporation figure en outre dans de nombreuses conventions bilatérales conclues par les Pays-Bas, notamment en matière de coopération économique et de protection des investissements. Mais ici encore, il ne jouit pas d'une appli-

cation exclusive et absolue. A titre d'exemple on peut citer l'article XIV de la Convention avec le Kenya, du 11 septembre 1970[3], en matière de coopération economique:

> *une société peut convenir avec l'Etat d'accueil, selon le droit duquel elle a été constituée et dont elle possède la personnalité juridique, qu'elle sera considerée pour l'application de cette Convention, comme un 'ressortissant' de l'autre Pays contractant lorsqu'un ressortissant ou des ressortissants (personnes physiques ou morales) de ce dernier ont un 'intérêt prépondérant' dans cette société.*

B. *Droit matériel*

La réglementation de la S.A. et de la S.à.R.L. est donnée par le législateur néerlandais dans le Second Livre du Code Civil. Un capital minimum est requis pour les deux types de société depuis le 1er juin 1978. La société dite 'grande' fait l'objet de règles spéciales; est qualifiée comme telle la société, S.A. ou S.à.R.L., qui répond à certains critères énoncés dans le C.C. même. L'appartenance d'une société à un groupe est prise en considération - sous certaines conditions - dans certains domaines, par exemple par rapport à l'enquête judiciaire, aux comptes annuels.
Le privilège de responsabilité limitée des actionnaires de la S.A. ou de la S.à.R.L. vaut aussi pour le cas où toutes les actions de la société sont en fait réunies entre les mains d'une seule personne[4]. Il n'existe pas de principe de responsabilité automatique de l'actionnaire pour les dettes de la filiale, pas plus qu'il n'existe un pouvoir d'injonction formel de celui-ci[5]. C'est à l'arsenal du droit civil qu'on a recours pour juger de la responsabilité de l'actionnaire[6].

II. LE 'LEVER DU VOILE' PAR LE LÉGISLATEUR

1.
Nombreux sont les cas où le législateur néerlandais perce la façade juridique de la personne morale pour tenir compte d'une 'autre réalité'. Ces manifestations de la transparence de la personne morale - on pourrait parler d'un lever de voile au sens large - sont conçues de différentes manières, visent des buts divers et ont lieu dans des domaines si hétérogènes que leur classification systématique s'avère problématique sinon impossible. Nous nous bornerons donc ici à citer quelques dispositions législatives pour ne traiter par la suite que de l'enquête judiciaire et des comptes annuels (v. aussi sous V. Fusions et absorptions)[7].

2. Exemples:

a. Selon la loi du 23 avril 1969[8] concernant la réassurance des investissements accomplis dans les pays en voie de développement, le Ministre des Finances peut refuser le réassurance à une personne morale, constituée selon le droit néerlandais, lorsque, d'après son opinion, elle "n'a aucun caractère néerlandais" (art. 5). Cette compétence lui a été accordée pour pouvoir exclure du système de réassurance la filiale d'une entreprise-mère étrangère qui aurait été constituée aux Pays-Bas uniquement dans le but de profiter des garanties offertes par l'Etat néerlandais[9].

b. Selon l'art. 51 du Code pénal, au cas où la personne morale a commis un acte punissable peuvent être poursuivis pénalement: la personne morale, ceux qui ont donné l'ordre d'accomplir l'acte ou ceux qui ont commandé en fait, ou bien la personne morale et les personnes susmentionnées conjointement[10].

c. L'art. 31 (2,d) de la loi sur les comités d'entreprise du 26 janvier 1971 (telle qu'elle a été modifiée le 5 juillet 1979) prescrit que l'entrepreneur faisant partie d'un groupe d'entrepreneurs, est tenu de donner au comité - au début de chaque période de session - des informations par écrit au sujet des rapports de contrôle par lesquels les entrepreneurs sont liés entre eux ainsi que le nom et le domicile de ceux qui par suite de ces rapports peuvent exercer un contrôle de fait sur l'entrepreneur.

d. L'art. 69 al. 2 du Second Livre du CC prévoit que tout dirigeant est solidairement responsable avec la S.A. pour les actes juridiques liant la société, aussi longtemps que le dépôt d'une copie authentique de l'acte de constitution et l'immatriculation de la société au registre du commerce n'ont pas eu lieu et qu'un certain pourcentage (le minimum est fixé par la loi) pour chaque action souscrite lors de la constitution, n'a pas été libéré. Une disposition analogue, celle de l'art. 180 al. 2, est prévue pour la S.à.R.L.

3.

Dans ce contexte il faut mentionner le projet de loi[11] portant modifications de certaines dispositions du Second Livre du CC et de la loi sur la faillite, dans le but de combattre l'utilisation abusive du concept de personnalité morale[12]. Intéressantes sont les modifications apportées aux articles 138 et 248 du Second Livre du CC ayant trait à la faillite, respectivement de la S.A. et de la S.à.R.L. D'après le projet, chaque dirigeant est responsable pour la somme des dettes (différence entre l'actif et le passif de la société faillie) "si la direction n'a pas accompli sa tâche convenablement et s'il est plausible que ceci est une cause importante de la faillite". Le dirigeant peut cependant dégager sa responsabilité lorqu'il peut prouver que "l'accomplissement incorrect de ses tâches par la direction ne lui est pas imputable et qu'il n'avait pas négligé de prendre des mesures pour en modifier les conséquences". Pour l'application des articles susmentionnés, est assimilé au dirigeant celui qui a défini - seul ou ensemble avec le dirigeant - la gestion de la société "comme s'il avait été un dirigeant". Le projet de loi susmentionné ajoute un article au Second Livre du CC (art. 4a) lequel constitue pour ainsi dire une manifestation de transparence[13]. Selon la nouvelle disposition la responsabilité d'une personne morale comme dirigeant ou commissaire d'une autre personne morale repose en même temps sur toute personne qui au moment où surgit la responsabilité de la première personne morale, est dirigeant de celle-ci. Ce qui signifie qu'à côté de la personne morale-dirigeant sont aussi solidairement responsables ses dirigeants (personnes physiques) dans les cas où la loi prévoit la responsabilité des dirigeants[14].

4.
Comme il a été déjà dit la réglementation de l'enquête judiciaire et celle des comptes annuels, tient compte de l'existence de liens étroits entre personnes morales.

A. *Enquête judiciaire*

1.
La Chambre des entreprises de la Cour d'appel d'Amsterdam - l'instance compétente pour connaître des demandes en enquête - peut autoriser l'enquêteur à examiner les livres, les pièces et à se faire montrer les effets d'une société qui est étroitement liée avec la société au sujet de laquelle a lieu l'investigation. Objet de celle-ci sont "la gestion et la marche des affaires" de la société, S.A. ou S.à.R.L. (art. 345). Il appartient à la Chambre de déterminer ce que constitue dans le cas concret une mauvaise gestion. D'après la jurisprudence il peut en être question tant dans le domaine économique que social[15].

2.
Une décision récente (du 21 juin 1979[16]) trace nettement les limites de la détermination exclusivement nationale du champ d'application des mesures à prononcer. En revanche, l'étendue de l'investigation à exécuter par l'enquêteur, peut déborder les frontières néerlandaises. En l'espèce les organisations syndicales intéressées[17] avaient demandé une enquête au sujet de Batco-Nederland BV, laquelle, bien qu'étant une entreprise lucrative, avait décidé de fermer son usine à Amsterdam et de transférer sa production à Bruxelles. En recevant la requête la Chambre a dit expressément (ordonnance du 5 octobre 1978) qu'on ne saurait négliger lors de l'investigation[18] le fait que Batco-Nederland est une société filiale à 100% de l'entreprise

multinationale BAT-Industries (siège à Londres) et que Batco-Nederland et BAT-Industries détiennent respectivement 71,6% et 28,4% des actions de Batco-Benelux S.A. La Chambre considéra Batco-Nederland et Batco-Benelux comme constituant une "unité" du point de vue de l'organisation au sein de BAT-Industries (pour ce qui concerne la production et la vente des cigarettes) parce qu'elles sont placées toutes les deux sous la direction du Benelux Management Board[19]. Elle statua en ces termes:

> *"Les décisions de cet organe ont eu directement des suites concrètes pour Batco-Nederland et par conséquent elles ne peuvent pas rester hors de cause. À cela ne change rien le fait que les mesures à prendre par la Chambre peuvent porter seulement sur Batco-Nederland et peuvent être prises seulement si d'après l'opinion de la Chambre, il apparaît du compte rendu du rapporteur qu'il y avait eu mauvaise gestion de la part de Batco-Nederland."*

Sur demande des organisations syndicales la décision de Batco-Nederland de fermer son usine à Amsterdam fut annulée. D'après la Chambre il n'y avait eu mauvaise gestion que dans le domaine social[20]. Batco-Nederland s'était acquittée insuffisamment de son obligation de s'entretenir avec le comité d'entreprise conformément à la loi relative aux comités d'entreprise et avec les syndicats conformément au contrat collectif de travail (Batco avait interrompu très tôt les entretiens avec eux) Encore est-il intéressant de noter que la Chambre pour arriver à sa conclusion se référa aussi à la circonstance ("non sans importance") que BAT-Industries avait accepté les directives formulées par l'*OECD*. Comme l'on sait, ces directives obligent dans un cas pareil à la discussion avec les représentants du personnel.

B. *Comptes annuels*

1.
La société-mère est tenue de donner dans son rapport annuel[21] "le plus fidèlement possible toutes les informations" concernant ses sociétés filiales. Cela peut avoir lieu de l'une de trois manières suivantes: reprendre dans le commentaire les comptes annuels complets des sociétés filiales; présenter des comptes annuels consolidés du groupe entier; présenter des comptes annuels combinés des sociétés filiales. De cette obligation est exemptée la société-mère qui à son tour est une société-filiale à 100% d'une autre société (art. 319). Au cas où il s'agirait de consolider ou de combiner les comptes annuels d'une société filiale à responsabilité limitée laquelle est obligée par la loi (art. 214) à publier son bilan, il y a exem tion de cette obligation à condition que la société-mère se

déclare[22] solidairement responsable des dettes de cette société filiale ou bien si le domaine des activités de cette société filiale se trouve "exclusivement ou presque exclusivement hors du territoire de la Communauté Européenne" (ex art. 215 et 343 al. 4 et 5). Au cas où il s'agirait de consolider ou de combiner les comptes annuels d'une société filiale constituée comme société anonyme, l'obligation de cette dernière de publier ses comptes annuels se réduit à une obligation de déposer ses comptes annuels lesquels n'ont pas besoin d'être établis conformément aux conditions requises par la loi; ces comptes annuels peuvent donc être très succincts. Cela est permis à condition que la société-mère se déclare[23] solidairement responsable des dettes de cette société filiale (art. 343 al. 1 et 3). Tant dans le premier cas (S.à.R.L.) que dans le second cas (S.A.) la responsabilité de la société-mère se limite aux dettes dérivant des "actes juridiques" accomplis par la société-filiale (art. 343). La responsabilité de la société-mère ne s'étend pas aux obligations découlant d'un acte illicite commis par la société filiale.

2.
S'agissant des sociétés filiales établies hors des Pays-Bas, la société-mère peut reprendre dans le commentaire les comptes annuels de celle-ci chronologiquement les derniers - combinés ou pas - établis delon les prescriptions du droit étranger applicable, ou bien déposer ces comptes annels auprès du bureau du registre du commerce et renvoyer dans le commentaire à ce dépôt (art. 321). On remarque que le législateur néerlandais reconnaît indirectement la territorialité des lois relatives à l'établissement des comptes annuels mais qu'en même temps cette territorialité ne fait pas obstacle à admettre aux Pays-Bas des comptes annuels établis selon le droit étranger compétent.

3.
La jurisprudence relative de la Chambre des entreprises de la Cour d'appel d'Amsterdam (elle est l'instance compétente pour connaître des demandes en rectification) est peu abondante. Il ressort toutefois de celle-ci le refus de la Chambre de se prononcer sur les objections concernant le fond des opérations effectuées par la société. La Chambre vérifie seulement si la gestion a été correctement présentée dans les comptes annuels.[24]

4.
Un cas récent servira d'exemple[25]: les comptes annuels de Michel Dufour (Holland) BV - une S.à.R.L. filiale à 100% de Michel Dufour S.A. établie à La Rochelle (en France) - furent mis en cause par *Van W.* La société néerlandaise fait fonction de bureau de vente pour les bateaux fabriqués par la société française. *Van W.* avait droit à une provision dont le montant dépendait également des bénéfices réalisés au cours de l'exercice

comptable écoulé. Van W. se plaignit de ce que la société-mère avait chargé des prix plus élévés que ceux qui étaient convenus et qu'ainsi a eu lieu à tort un transfert des bénéfices de la part de la société filiale à la société-mère. La Chambre jugea (décision du 27 mars 1980, no. du rôle 525/78[26]) que dans une procédure relative aux comptes annuels il ne s'agissait pas "de la justification d'une gestion telle que suivant l'opinion d'une partie intéressée, elle devrait être menée par la personne morale, mais de la gestion telle qu'elle a été en fait menée". Par l'acceptation des prix élévés, a dit la Chambre ensuite, la défenderesse avait mené une gestion qui avait trouvé son contrecoup dans ses comptes annuels notamment dans le résultat obtenu. Et d'y ajouter cette condition nouvelle, laquelle toutefois n'avait pas eu des conséquences en l'espèce[27]:

> *"Si, et dans l'affirmative jusqu'à quel point, ce résultat est influencé par la relation entre la société-mère et la société filiale, doit ressortir de l'exposé qui est donné dans le commentaire concernant les comptes annuels au sujet de la détermination des prix pour les bateaux livrés. La même chose vaut pour les frais de financement qui y seront mentionnés."*[28]

III. LE 'LEVER DU VOILE' PAR LE JUGE

D'eux-mêmes les juges néerlandais ont levé le voile dans nombre de cas pour tenir compte, eux aussi, d'une 'autre réalité'. Il y a eu des cas où le voile fut seulement soulevé sans que la personnalité morale eût été mise de côté et des cas de transparence totale où la personne morale fut laissée de côté et où seuls les actionnaires furent pris en considération[29].

A. *Identification*

1.
Les affaires purement internes où le voile fut soulevé pour identifier la personne morale[30] soit avec des personnes physiques soit avec une autre personne morale[31], concernaient entre autres[32] des relations de travail, la protection des locataires, l'assistance judiciaire[33]. Mentionnons ici deux points: une décision[34] - au moins - s'est réferée au lien étroit existant entre les deux sociétés, lien qui d'après elle découlait de la seule circonstance que l'une des sociétés était la filiale à 100% de l'autre; l'utilisation abusive de la forme sociale ne fut pas souvent le motif pour procéder à l'identification.

2.
Les quelques cas qui suivent comportent des éléments d'extraneïté; ils sont les seuls que nous ayons pu trouver. L'identification a eu lieu (ou été refusée) sur base d'une série de faits; aucune référence à un droit quelconque ne fut faite.

a. LPG-Containers Leasing and Trading Establishment, société constituée au Liechtenstein, avait transféré la propriété des bouteilles à gaz, qui étaient louées par la société néerlandaise Eemgaz, à une autre société néerlandaise. Eemgas allégua - en invoquant certains faits - que LPG avait agi contrairement à la bonne foi. La Cour d'appel d'Amsterdam (décision du 10 janvier 1974) rejeta cette allégation: à la situation de fait invoquée par Eemgas avait aussi contribué l'Intercontinental Trading Establishment (ICT), laquelle société, constituée au Liechtenstein, était l'actionnaire principal de Eemgas. La Cour se référa entre autres à la circonstance que Eemgas était "dominée par ICT et dirigée par deux de ses responsables". La Haute Cour - arrêt du 28 juin 1974[35] - estima que "ce jugement de la Cour d'appel n'était ni incompréhensible ni incompatible avec les faits établis par la Cour".

b. Dans l'affaire portée devant le juge d'instance d'Apeldoorn (jugement non publié du 21 juillet 1976[36]), il s'agissait d'une relation de travail entre un Néerlandais et une société en commandite allemande. Le contrat de travail existant, avait été converti en un contrat de travail entre l'employé et une filiale constituée par la société allemande aux Pays-Bas sous la forme d'une S.à.R.L. Le demandeur allégua qu'il n'y avait pas en réalité de changement dans la relation de subordination entre lui et la société allemande. Le juge lui donna raison en décidant que de la correspondance produite au procès, il ressort que c'était la société allemande qui dictait "au demandeur ce qu'il fallait faire ou ne pas faire".

c. La décision de la Cour d'appel d'Amsterdam du 20 juin 1979 (non publiée[37]) concerna un différend dérivant d'un contrat d'agence. Kenitex Chemicals Inc., société constituée en Californie, avait conclu avec un Néerlandais (NTI), domicilié aux Pays-Bas, un contrat d'agence. Ce dernier acquiert les droits de conclure les contrats de licence entre Kenitex et des entreprises établies en Europe. NTI demanda à Kenitex Chemicals Inc. de lui verser une commission sur les royalties reçus de la part de la société Y. Kenitex Chemicals allégua (pour la première fois en appel) qu'elle avait vendu tous ses droits concernant le produit - objet de licence - à Kenitex Liechtenstein et qu'elle-même ne participait sous aucune forme que ce soit à cette société. La Cour jugea "que Kenitex Chemicals Inc. s'identifie tellement dans le domaine des affaires avec Kenitex Liechtenstein, qu'on peut assumer en droit que Kenitex Chemicals Inc. considère les actes accomplis par Kenitex

Chemicals International comme des actes à elle et par conséquent ces actes peuvent être considérés comme les siens." D'après la Cour le rapport contractuel entre Kenitex Chemicals et NTI était régi par le droit néerlandais (les parties n'avaient pas choisi de loi applicable) au motif que NTI lequel devait effectuer la prestation caractéristique, était établi aux Pays-Bas et y avait le centre de ses activités.

d. Dans la même affaire le tribunal d'Utrecht (jugement non publié du 19 décembre 1979[38]), considérant que Kenitex Chemicals Inc. et Kenitex Chemicals International (Liechtenstein) ne s'identifiaient pas envers la société Y (le tiers-saisi), décida que la saisie-arrêt conservatoire à la charge de Kenitex Chemicals Inc. "n'a pas de but".

e. Par contre, le Tribunal d'Amsterdam, devant lequel furent assignées toutes les deux sociétés, valida la saisie-arrêt en décidant laconiquement que NTI avait une prétention contre Kenitex Chemicals International (jugement non publié du 3 décembre 1980[39]).

f. Le tribunal d'Amsterdam (jugement du 30 juin 1939[40]) fut saisi d'une action en nullité d'un contrat, intentée par un cessionnaire. Celui-ci invoquait en outre comme fondement de sa demande, un droit propre au motif qu'il était le seul à avoir un intérêt dans la personne morale (allemande) créancière du débiteur cédé, et que par là il formait avec elle du point de vue économique un tout. Le tribunal, après s'être référé au contenu (non contesté par le demandeur) d'une lettre d'où il ressortait que toutes les actions de la personne morale étaient à partir d'une certaine date entre les mains d'une autre personne, jugea: "en tout cas Freie Deutsche Bühne était du point de vue juridique une personne autonome qui concluait des contrats ... qu'un intérêt, grand ou moindre, dans pareille personne morale ne donne pas à l'intéressé un droit propre à demander l'exécution ou la résiliation des contrats conclus par cette personne morale"[41].

B. *Questions de responsabilité*

1.

Dans les affaires purement internes la responsabilité de l'actionnaire fut le plus souvent retenue grâce au recours à l'art. 1401 CC (concernant l'acte illicite)[42]. Exemples des cas où l'actionnaire pourra engager sa responsabilité: s'il s'est servi de la filiale pour éluder ses obligations contractuelles envers des tiers; s'il a incité la filiale à l'inexécution de ses obligations ou à un acte illicite ou bien s'il a profité de l'inexécution ou de l'acte illicite. Notons que les créanciers de la filiale peuvent à côté de l'action fondée sur l'art. 1401, intenter aussi l'action paulienne (1377 CC) pour les transactions entre l'actionnaire et la filiale, transactions que la filiale n'était pas tenue d'accomplir. Beaucoup plus importante est toutefois une décision récente de la Cour d'appel de La Haye (du 11 avril 1980[43]). Celle-ci statua qu'il n'y a pas de responsabilité d'une société membre d'un groupe pour les dettes d'une autre société du même groupe; l'admission d'une telle responsabilité, dit-elle, constituerait une "dérogation sérieuse au droit des personnes morales actuel".

2.
Les décisions ayant trait à des affaires comportant des éléments d'extranéïté sont, ici encore, très peu nombreuses. Ci-dessous sont citées celles que nous avons pu trouver; en aucune d'elles il n'est question de S.A. (pour les relations de travail v. sous IV).

a. Deux décisions concernent la responsabilité des associés commandités envers des tiers. Les juges ont fait régir la question de leur responsabilité par la loi du pays où la société en commandite avait son siège social. Il s'agit d'une décision du Tribunal de La Haye du 31 janvier 1900 (le droit sud-africain fut appliqué[44]) et de la Cour d'appel de Leeuwarden du 3 décembre 1941 (le droit néerlandais fut appliqué[45]). Il est intéressant de noter que dans le premier cas le droit étranger ne connaissait pas une disposition analogue à celle de l'art. 21 du Code de Commerce néerlandais qui déclare l'associé commandité solidairement responsable pour toutes les dettes et les obligations de la sosiété au cas où celui-ci accomplit un acte de gestion ou exerce des activités dans la société. Cette disposition ne constitua cependant pas un obstacle à l'application du droit étranger. Le tribunal statua que la question de la responsabilité devait être jugée "exclusivement" en vertu de la loi du siège social.
b. Deux décisions concernent la responsabilité des associés de *partnerships* envers des tiers. Il s'agit d'une décision du Tribunal de Rotterdam du 16 février 1916[46] et de la Cour d'appel d'Amsterdam du 24 octobre 1946[47]. Toutes les deux appliquèrent le droit anglais en tant que loi du pays où la *partnership* était établie.
c. Deux décisions concernent des sociétés commerciales en nom collectif. Le Tribunal d'Almelo (jugement du 30 octobre 1901[48]) appliqua à la question de savoir si l'associé était solidairement responsable, le droit romano-hollandais en vigueur au Natal, au motif que le siège social de la société était à Durban. Le Tribunal de Rotterdam (jugement du 19 mai 1909[49]) décida que la question de la responsabilité de deux associés qui au moment de la conclusion du contrat étaient les dirigeants d'une société établie en Italie, était régie par le droit néerlandais; en l'espèce la société était en état de liquidation et selon le droit italien les actions ne pouvaient être intentées que contre le liquidateur.

d. Deux décisions concernent des S.à.R.L. allemandes. Le Tribunal d'Amsterdam (jugement non publié du 17 juin 1969[50]) déclara que la responsabilité de l'actionnaire d'une S.à.R.L. non-immatriculée était régie par le droit allemand. Il ne ressort cependant pas clairement du jugement laquelle de deux circonstances (le tribunal s'était référé à toutes les deux) fut décisive: le fait que la société avait son siège social en Allemagne Fédérale ou bien le fait que les parties avaient inséré dans la lettre contenant les conditions du prêt, une clause renvoyant à l'art. 11 de la loi allemande sur les S.à.R.L. Ledit article dispose que la personne agissant au nom d'une S.à.R.L. non-immatriculée est solidairement responsable pour les dettes de celle-ci. Devant la Cour d'appel d'Arnhem (décision non publiée du 3 février 1970[51]) l'intimé allégua qu'il n'avait pas acheté les biens (qu'il avait reçus mais non payés) en tant que particulier mais "en sa qualité d'actionnaire ou du moins de représentant" d'une S.à.R.L. La Cour jugea que pour cela "était décisive la manière dont celui-ci s'était présenté à l'appelant". D'après la Cour l'intimé avait agi en tant que particulier puisque dans la confirmation de l'ordre il n'avait écrit que son propre nom et son adresse aux Pays-Bas; la loi allemande sur les S.à.R.L. en disposait autrement.
e. D'après le Tribunal de Rotterdam (décision du 26 mars 1974[52]) la question de la responsabilité personelle des 'souscripteurs et dirigeants' d'une société anglaise (Ltd) non consituée au moment de la conclusion du contrat, doit être jugée selon le droit anglais.

IV. RELATIONS DE TRAVAIL

Les relations de travail faisant l'objet d'un autre rapport néerlandais, nous nous bornerons en ce lieu à citer quatre décisions où il était question de la société-mère. Elles concernent des contrats individuels.

1.
La Haute Cour a énoncé dans son arrêt du 6 juin 1973 (connu sous le nom d'arrêt *Mackay II*[53]) des règles de conflit subsidiaires pour le cas où les parties n'ont pas choisi le droit applicable à la relation de travail. Ces règles sont formulées comme *open-ended rules*: le juge peut s'en écarter si les circonstances spéciales du cas concret l'exigent. La première règle subsidiaire est la *lex loci laboris*; elle est applicable au cas où le travail est effectué dans un seul pays. Si le domaine des activités de l'employé s'étend à plus d'un pays, est applicable la loi du pays où se situe, d'après le contrat de travail, le centre principal des activités de l'employé. Si aucun pays ne peut être désigné, est applicable la loi du pays

où l'employeur est établi. La *lex loci laboris* - avec la réserve précitée - est également applicable aux personnes employées par une entreprise multinationale, sauf dans le cas où l'employé est envoyé à l'étranger à partir du pays où la direction centrale de l'entreprise est établie (la Cour emploie les termes: "une entreprise considérable internationalement ramifiée"). On lit dans l'arrêt:

> "... *la circonstance que certains employés travaillant auprès des établissements étrangers d'une telle entreprise 'soient immédiatement en relation avec la direction centrale de l'entreprise comme receveurs d'instructions et rapporteurs', n'offre pas à elle seule un point de rattachement suffisant avec le droit du pays où la direction centrale est établie, pour qu'on admette à l'égard de tels employés comme règle générale que le contrat de travail est régi par le droit de ce pays, même si leur domaine d'activité ne se limite pas au pays où ils ont le centre principal de leurs activités ..., mais que tel serait bien le cas si les employés étaient envoyés par l'employeur dans un établissement étranger à partir du pays où la direction centrale de l'entreprise est établie* ..."

D'autre part la Haute Cour estima que la question de savoir si un déplacement 'international' entraîne un changement de droit applicable à la relation de travail, "n'est pas susceptible d'une réponse générale et dépend des circonstances du cas donné". On constate facilement que sur base de cet arrêt la loi du siège de la société-mère ne trouvera application que dans un nombre de situations très limité.

2.
Les trois jugements qui suivent ont été rendus après l'arrêt *Mackay-II*.

a. La Cour d'appel de La Haye a eu à connaître (décision du 2 mai 1975[54]) du cas suivant: K., de nationalité américaine, fut engagé par Cyanamid International Development Corporation (CIDC), société filiale de American Cyanamid Company (ACC), constituée à Wayne, New Jersey. CIDC est l'actionnaire unique de Cyanamid BV, société constituée aux Pays-Bas. Par décision de CIDC, K. fut nommé membre du conseil de direction et en même temps *managing director* de Cyanamid BV. K. recevait des instructions et rendait compte au titre de *managing director* à Cyanamid International Division (à Wayne), une section de la société-mère (ACC). K., licencié, assigna Cyanamid BV en paiement de certaines sommes, y inclus des dommages-intérêts pour atteinte à sa réputation. Cyanamid BV soutient en appel que le Tribunal de Rotterdam avait eu tort de passer sous silence ses allégations selon lesquelles un contrat de travail n'a jamais existé entre elle et l'intimé et que ce dernier a été détaché auprès d'elle seulement en vertu de son contrat de travail avec CIDC. La Cour rejeta les prétentions de K. comme étant basées sur un contrat de travail qui n'existait pas. Elle a abouti à cette conclusion sans mentionner un droit quelconque mais uniquement une série de circonstances de fait, entre autres que K. n'avait jamais signé un contrat de travail avec Cyanamid BV "comme c'est le cas avec les employés locaux" de celle-ci que K. pendant la période de son détachement aux Pays-Bas restait inscrit à la caisse des retraites de la société-mère à New Jersey. Il ne ressort cependant pas de la décision de la Cour laquelle parmi des sociétés du groupe elle considéra comme étant le véritable employeur de K. On y lit seulement cette phrase vague: "Il ne fait pas de doute que l'intimé ... était employé dans le cadre du groupe Cyanamid selon un contrat de travail, auquel le droit de New Jersey était applicable."

b. C'est une autre sorte de raisonnement qu'on trouve dans le jugement prononcé par le Tribunal d'Amsterdam le 14 décembre 1977[55], lequel considéra l'employé comme étant au service tant de la société-mère que de la société filiale. Ici encore aucun contrat de travail n'avait été conclu entre l'employé et la société filiale. Kr., de nationalité américaine, fut engagé en 1961 par Calcomp Inc. , une société constituée en Californie. De 1963 à 1967, Kr. assuma des fonctions auprès de Calcomp BV, une société constituée aux Pays-Bas, d'abord comme *european salesmanager*, ensuite comme directeur. Calcomp Inc., qui est l'actionnaire unique de Calcomp BV, conclut le 1er avril 1967 un second contrat de travail avec Kr. En vertu de ce contrat il fut 'stationné' aux Pays-Bas, chargé de la direction et de l'organisation de Calcomp BV (sans avoir toutefois exercé les fonctions de directeur jusqu'au 1er septembre 1970), de même que de l'organisation des ventes pour Calcomp Inc. dans certains pays européens. Kr. recevait des instructions et rendait compte à Calcomp Inc. Licencié en 1971, il assigna les deux sociétés en versement d'une partie de ses salaires qui n'était pas payée et des indemnités en vertu du droit néerlandais. Le Tribunal estima qu'il fallait en premier lieu savoir quels étaient les rapports de droit existant entre le demandeur et Calcomp Inc. d'une part et le demandeur et Calcomp BV d'autre part, au moment du licenciement de celui-ci et par quel droit ces rapports étaient régis. Pour ce qui concerne le premier contrat de travail avec Calcomp Inc., le tribunal jugea que ce contrat conclu entre une entreprise établie en Californie et un Américain domicilié dans cet Etat, "est naturellement régi par le droit de cet Etat". Pour ce qui concerne le second contrat de travail avec Calcomp. Inc., le tribunal jugea que c'était également le droit de Californie qui était applicable au motif "qu'il n'est pas apparu que le contrat avait des points de rattachement importants avec un autre pays". Le tribunal estima en outre que la relation d'emploi entre Kr. et Calcomp Inc. ne fut pas terminée le 1er septembre 1970. Par la suite, le tribunal considéra que la relation existant à partir de cette date entre Kr. et Calcomp BV, devait être qualifiée "selon le droit néerlandais" de contrat de travail. Le tribunal fut d'avis qu'il n'y avait pas de raison fondée pour que cette relation fût régie par un droit autre que celui de l'Etat de Californie. On lit dans le jugement:

> *"Cette connexion étroite existant entre la relation d'emploi avec Calcomp Inc. et celle avec Calcomp BV et avec cela portée prédominante des rapports avec la société-mère, Calcomp Inc., entraînent en principe que le droit qui régit la relation d'emploi du demandeur avec Calcomp Inc., régit en même temps la relation avec Calcomp BV dans la mesure où cette relation comprend une relation d'emploi."*

Le tribunal disposa que Calcomp BV "est solidairement tenue avec Calcomp Inc. pour cette partie des salaires qui devait être versée en dollars par Calcomp Inc.". La réclamation des indemnités - basée exclusivement sur le droit néerlandais - fut considérée comme non fondée au motif que le demandeur n'avait pas allégué qu'une action en indemnités "aurait été aussi possible en application du droit de l'Etat de Californie".

c. Un jugement rendu le 19 avril 1977 (non publié[56]) par le même Tribunal, concernait une affaire moins compliquée. Sch. fut engagé par la Compagnie Commerciale Hollando-Africaine (CCHA), société constituée aux Pays-Bas. Il fut par la suite envoyé auprès de Maryland Logging Corporation (MLC), société constituée au Liberia, pour travailler dans l'exploitation forestière. CCHA est l'actionnaire majoritaire de MLC. Sch., licencié, assigna les deux sociétés devant le juge d' instance d'Amsterdam en réclamant, en vertu du droit néerlandais, le paiement de certaines sommes. CCHA et MLC alléguèrent en appel devant le Tribunal d'Amsterdam, que le cocontractant de Sch. était MLC et non CCHA comme le prétendait Sch. et que CCHA avait agi en tant que représentant de MLC. Le tribunal considéra que la question de savoir si CCHA représentait MLC, devait être jugée d'après le droit néerlandais en vertu de la règle de conflit non-écrite néerlandaise qui désigne comme applicable la loi du lieu où le représentant a agi. Le tribunal se basant sur divers éléments de fait jugea qu'il ne s'agissait pas d'un cas de représentation et que CCHA avait été le cocontractant de Sch. Ensuite ce fut la question du droit applicable au contrat de travail qui fut examinée. Après avoir dit que les parties n'avaient pas fait un choix et que le travail avait été effectué au Liberia, le tribunal estima que "des circonstances spéciales existent qui entraînent dans ce cas l'application du droit néerlandais". Ce droit ne trouva toutefois pas application à titre de loi du siège de la société-mère. La nationalité néerlandaise de l'employeur ne fut considérée que comme une 'circonstance' parmi les autres; on note aussi qu'un des éléments de fait qui avait servi à déterminer le cocontractant de Sch. - instructions et rapports - fut nommé à part comme constituant lui aussi une 'circonstance'. C'est de cette manière que le tribunal justifia l'application du droit néerlandais:

"... le contrat a été conclu entre Sch., un Néerlandais, qui a vécu pendant toute sa vie aux Pays-Bas et qui y reste encore domicilié, et CCHA, société établie aux Pays-Bas et ayant la personnalité juridique selon le droit néerlandais, laquelle société a envoyé Sch. travailler au Libéria au profit de l'une de ses sociétés filiales, pendant que Sch. recevait des instructions et rendait compte à CCHA."

V. FUSIONS ET ABSORPTIONS

1.
Le Code de fusion néerlandais peut sous certaines conditions s'étendre à des sociétés étrangères. Par Code de fusion on entend un ensemble de "règles de conduite" émises par le Conseil Economique et Social. Ces règles n'on pas force de loi et leur observation ne peut pas être imposée par le juge[57]. C'est une Commission instituée auprès du Conseil, qui veille à leur observation et sanctionne leur transgression[58]. Il est à noter que le droit néerlandais ne connaît pas encore la fusion juridique[59]; les concentrations d'entreprises s'y réalisent le plus souvent dans la pratique par l'acquisition de la totalité ou d'une très grande majorité des actions d'une société par une autre. Les deux sociétés subsistent en tant qu'entités juridiques, bien qu'il en résulte une dépendance economique de la première.

2.
Le Code contient des règles visant la protection des intérêts des actionnaires d'une part, et la protection des intérêts des employés d'autre part. Les règles concernant les employés - dont il sera ici question - sont applicables lorsqu'il s'agit de fusion impliquant au moins une entreprise établie aux Pays-Bas employant cent personnes ou plus[60]. A une telle entreprise est assimilée celle qui, sans répondre au nombre requis, fait

cependant partie d'un 'ensemble d'entreprises', qui, lui, emploie ce nombre. Par 'ensemble d'entreprises' l'on entend la situation de fait où le contrôle d'un nombre d'entreprises, sans égard pour leur structure juridique formelle, est exercé par la même personne physique ou morale[61]. Le Code définit la 'fusion' comme l'acquisition du contrôle, directement ou indirectement, des activités d'une entreprise ou d'une partie de celles-ci. Le cas suivant (à titre d'exemple) a été considéré comme fusion dans le sens du Code: une société-mère avait transféré le contrôle sur les activités d'une de ses sociétés avec personnalité juridique, à une autre entreprise; la société filiale n'avait pas d'employés; le transfert de ces activités a été tenu pour transfert d'une partie des activités de la société-mère. En d'autres termes, le travail lié à ces activités a été considéré comme étant exécuté par des employés au service de la société-mère ou bien au service d'une autre personne morale formant avec elle un groupe.

3.
Les entreprises impliquées dans une fusion sont obligées d'en informer à temps les organisations syndicales et de leur donner l'occasion d'exprimer leur point de vue sur l'intérêt des employés[62]. Cette obligation existe seulement envers celles des organisations syndicales dont les activités peuvent être directement influencées par la fusion[63]. L'existence d'un ensemble d'entreprises fournit - d'après la Commission - la présomption que même les entreprises qui ne sont pas parties à la fusion ou dont le contrôle n'a pas été transféré, doivent être considérées comme impliquées à la fusion; cette présomption cède toutefois le pas aux circonstances spéciales faisant clairement apparaître le contraire[64].

4.
L'obligation d'observer les règles de conduite incombe en premier lieu aux organes de direction des personnes morales (néerlandaise ou étrangère) concernées par la fusion (art. 16). Ceux-ci sont tenus de prendre part aux délibérations avec les organisations syndicales y relatives. Lorsqu'une entreprise appartient à une ou plusieurs personnes physiques, c'est sur elles que repose l'obligation d'observer les règles. En outre, le Code tient compte de la possibilité que d'autres personnes mènent les pourparlers de fusion, par ex. un commissaire, un actionnaire détenteur d'actions privilégiées, le syndic d'une entreprise en état de faillite; c'est à eux alors d'observer les règles. Ce qui est important: si l'organe de direction de la filiale, concernée par la fusion, néglige d'observer les règles, l'organe de direction de la société-mère est aussi responsable pour cette négligence. Ceci aura lieu notamment au cas où les règles de conduite trouvent application en raison du

seul fait que l'entreprise concernée par une fusion appartient à un groupe d'entreprises[65].

5.
D'après le Code, les règles de conduite ne trouvent pas application si la "fusion n'appartient pas à la sphère juridique néerlandaise" (art. 15, 3c). Les cas suivants (à titre d'exemples) ont été considérés comme appartenant à la sphère juridique néerlandaise: une personne étrangère avait fait une offre portant sur les actions d'une personne morale étrangère, laquelle était détentrice d'une participation à 100% dans un subholding néerlandais de filiales également établies aux Pays-Bas; la nationalité de la société-mère ne constitua pas, d'après la Commission, un obstacle à l'application des règles de conduite parce qu'une telle transaction concernait "intégralement un intérêt néerlandais". Dans un autre cas la Commission jugea que le fait qu'un droit étranger fût applicable à l'achat des actions, n'excluait pas purement et simplement que la fusion puisse être considérée comme appartenant également à la sphère juridique néerlandaise, du moins pour ce qui concernait l'applicabilité des règles de conduite. La Commission retint les points de rattachement suivants: la société absorbante était établie aux Pays-Bas; la personne morale étrangère avait un certain nombre de filiales et succursales établies aux Pays-Bas; la société absorbante exerçait entre autres des activités aux Pays-Bas par l'intermédiaire de filiales et succursales appartenant à la personne morale étrangère; le nombre d'employés travaillant aux filiales et succursales aux Pays-Bas était, par rapport au nombre total d'employés de l'ensemble d'entreprises absorbées, assez considérable.

V. REMARQUES FINALES

1.
Les questions de d.i.p. contenues dans le plan du rapporteur général M. A.F. Conrad, se résument, à notre avis, en la question de la loi applicable à la responsabilité de l'actionnaire (personne physique, société-mère) pour les obligations de la société par lui contrôlée, envers des tiers déterminés (créancier individuels). Eu égard à l'extrême pauvreté quantitative des matériaux sur ce sujet, il n'est pas possible de donner une réponse bien définie. Ce n'est qu'indirectement, en esquissant un tableau de la jurisprudence existante, qu'on y arrivera partiellement. Les décisions les plus anciennes rattachent la responsabilité *ex contractu* (dans tous les cas les associés ou actionnaires étaient des personnes physiques) à la loi du siège social de la société. La loi applicable au rapport litigieux n'est pas prise en considération[66]. A l'exception d'un cas où la source de la dette n'était pas clairement établie,

d'un cas où l'obligation découlait d'un contrat de prêt et d' un cas où il s'agissait d'un affrètement, tous les autres concernaient des obligations dérivant des contrats de vente. Une tendance différente se dessine, croyons-nous, dans les décisions les plus récentes: le juge n'opère pas avec une règle de rattachement unique mais il applique, problème par problème, des règles de rattachement différentes. On l'a vu à propos de la question de savoir si la société-mère représentait dans un cas concret la société filiale; à propos de relations de travail, où la responsabilité de la société-mère fut retenue ou refusée en vertu de la loi applicable au rapport litigieux et où pour déterminer cette dernière loi, le siège social de la société-mère fut employé comme une circonstance parmi d'autres; à propos d'un contrat d'agence où le tribunal a admis que l' intermédiaire avait une prétention contre la société-mère, bien que celle-ci ne fût pas formellement partie au contrat, cas dans lequel la loi du siège social de la société-mère, pas plus d'ailleurs que celle de la société filiale, ne joua aucun rôle.

2.
Sous condition que cette tendance s'affirme dans l'avenir, nous procéderons à quelques hypothèses - schématiquement formulées - se rapportant à certaines situations, tout en rappelant l'attitude flexible du juge néerlandais envers le système de l'incorporation[67].

a. La question de la responsabilité de l'actionnaire qui a participé à un contrat conclu entre la société filiale et un tiers, devrait être régie par la loi applicable au contrat. À défaut de choix du droit applicable, serait appliquée la loi ayant le lien le plus étroit avec le contrat. En l'occurrence cette solution conduirait à appliquer la loi du siège social de la société filiale à titre de loi de la partie effectuant la prestation caratéristique du contrat donné. Le même raisonnement vaudrait pour le cas où l'actionnaire n'est pas lui-même cocontractant mais a participé à la décision prise par la société filiale de conclure le contrat avec le tiers. La question de savoir si la société filiale représentant l'actionnaire, a le pouvoir de lier celui-ci, ne devrait pas être soumise à la loi régissant l'opération principale concrète (contrat avec le tiers), mais à la loi du pays où la société filiale a agi, ce qui conduirait en l'occurrence à la loi du siège social de la société filiale[68].
b. La responsabilité de l'actionnaire laquelle en droit matériel néerlandais, aurait été qualifiée *ex delicto* (abus de droit, abus de circonstances) devrait reçevoir cette même qualification sur le plan des conflits de lois. Ce qui conduirait à l'application de la *lex loci delicti commissi*[69], avec tous les aléas - admettons-le - que cela comporte, no-

tamment en ce qui concerne la détermination du *locus delicti* (lieu des agissements de l'actionnaire; lieu où les effets de ses agissements se sont fait sentir; éventuellement élaborer une nouvelle notion de *locus* pour cette sorte de délits[70]). Ainsi, le créancier d'une filiale étrangère qui invoquerait devant le juge néerlandais le comportement illicite de l'actionnaire néerlandais devrait être reçu dans sa demande indépendamment du fait que la loi du siège social de la société filiale connaît ou ignore pareils recours au droit civil pour juger de la responsabilité de l'actionnaire (agissements contraires à la bonne foi, acte illicite). Inversément, au cas où la *lex loci delicti commissi* étrangère ignore pareils recours au droit civil pour la responsabilité de l'actionnaire, ou bien au cas où le comportement de celui-ci ne saurait être d'après elle qualifié d' illicite ou de contraire à la bonne foi, le créancier de la société filiale néerlandaise pourrait alléguer devant le juge néerlandais que la loi néerlandaise devrait être appliquée. À cette fin deux constructions - au moins - seraient possibles: par ex. que les agissements de l'actionnaire étranger heurtent tellement les conceptions fondamentales de l'ordre juridique néerlandais, que le juge devrait apprécier l'illicéité et les conséquences selon son propre droit[71]; que d'après l'ensemble des circonstances du cas concret les Pays-Bas se présentent comme le pays le plus étroitement lié au rapport litigieux (pays où les effets se sont fait sentir; pays du siège social de la société diliale; éventuellement un comportement peu convenable de celle-ci également; pays du domicile du créancier). Notons encore qu'en d.i.p. néerlandais, la règle de conflit non-écrite en matière de délits, est de caractère facultatif; les parties peuvent s'entendre sur le droit à appliquer (ce sera le plus souvent au cours du procès[72]), ce qui élimine en pareil cas le problème de la détermination du *locus delicti*.

c. Une dernière hypothèse: dans l'état actuel des choses, le juge néerlandais pourrait refuser d'appliquer une loi étrangère en vertu de laquelle l'actionnaire devient responsable auprès du créancier de la société filiale dans d'autres cas que ceux admis par la jurisprudence dans les affaires purement internes[73].

NOTES

1. *Staatsblad* (*Stb*) 1959 no. 256. Cette loi se rapporte à la Convention de La Haye de 1956 concernant la reconnaissance de la personnalité juridique des sociétés etc., laquelle a été ratifiée par les Pays-Bas (la Convention n'est pas entrée en vigueur).
2. *Schip en Schade* (*SS*) 1980 no. 56. Candia, une *single ship company*, avait vendu son navire, immatriculé en Grèce et battant pavillon hellénique, à Delina. Le transfert avait eu lieu avant la saisie conservatoire du navire par une société japonaise. Cette dernière allégua que le droit hellénique était applicable à la question de la responsabilité, tandis que Delina invoquait le droit anglais en vertu d'une clause du *memorandum agreement* entre elle et Candia concernant la vente du navire.
3. *Tractatenblad van het Koninkrijk der Nederlanden* 1970 no. 166, p. 10.
4. Les articles relatifs à la constitution d'une société, S.A. ou S.à.R.L., parlent d'un acte multilatéral. Dans un projet de loi récent (v. sous II.2.e) le terme 'multilatéral' ne figure plus; par cette modification, lit-on dans l'exposé des motifs, on n'aura plus besoin de recourir à un homme de paille.
5. V. sous II.3.A, note 19.
6. Sur ce sujet en général v. M.J.G.C. Raaijmakers, *Over verschuivingen in het toerekeningspatroon bij rechtspersonen*, et H.L.J. Roelvink, *Door rechtspersonen heenkijken* (rapports rédigés en 1977 pour l'Association des Juristes Néerlandaise).
7. Pour d'autres exemples v. Roelvink, *op.cit.*, p. 88 et suiv.
8. *Stb* 1969 no. 267-268.
9. *Bijl. Hand.* II 1967/68, 9633.
10. Cet article a été inséré en 1976.
11. *Tweede Kamer* 1980-81, 16.631, nos. 1, 3, 4. L'exposé des motifs est publié sous le numéro 3; v. encore sous 16.631, A-C l'avis du Conseil d'Etat concernant le projet ainsi que la réponse du Ministre de la Justice.
12. Un autre projet de loi, également de date récente (v. 16.630), prévoit la responsabilité des dirigeants de la personne morale pour des dettes de la personne morale, entre autres, envers le fisc.
13. V. l'exposé des motifs, *op.cit.* p. 3.
14. D'après l'exposé des motifs - *op.cit.* - il en est de même si un des dirigeants est une personne morale; mais pareilles situations - lit-on dans l'exposé - ne sont pas susceptibles de se présenter souvent.
15. Parmi les mesures qui peuvent être prononcées en cas de 'mauvaise gestion' figurent l'annulation d'une décision des dirigeants, le licenciement d'un ou plusieurs dirigeants ou commissaires, la dissolution de la société (art. 356).
16. *Nederlandse Jurisprudentie* (*NJ*) 1980, no. 71 avec la note de J.M.M. Maeijer; v. aussi B. Geersing, dans *TVVS/Ondernemingsrecht* (*TVVS*) 1980, p. 249 et suiv., p. 277 et suiv.
17. Les organisations syndicales n'ont exercé jusqu'à maintenant que rarement leur droit d'enquête.
18. Il ressort du compte rendu du rapporteur que les sociétés établies hors des Pays-Bas ont prêté leur concours "volontairement et sans réserve".
19. C.A. Boukema (*TVVS* 1979, p. 244) écrit que la question fréquemment débattue par la doctrine, de savoir si la direction d'une filiale à 100% doit se comporter conformément aux instructions de la société-mère, a été résolue implicitement par la Chambre. Il lui paraît que cette décision fournit "au droit positif néerlandais le fondement juridique de la subordination d'une société filiale à 100%".
20. D'après Maeijer, *op.cit.* p. 229, une décision dans un autre sens n'aurait certainement pas contribué à inciter les entreprises internationales à investir dans l'industrie néerlandaise.
21. Le projet de loi visant l'adaptation de la réglementation néerlandaise des comptes annuels à la quatrième directive du Conseil des Ministres des Communautés Européennes fut soumis à la Deuxième Chambre le 8 septembre 1980.
22. La déclaration est déposée auprès du bureau du registre du commerce du lieu où la personne morale a son "domicile", "à l'inspection de toute personne". La déclaration peut être retirée (art. 343, al. 5).
23. V. note 2.
24. V. G.G.M. Bak et C.A. Boukema, *TVVS* 1977, p. 233; 1980, p. 148.
25. V. aussi la décision de la Chambre du 14 avril 1977 (concernant la Homburg BV), *TVVS* 1977, p. 227, et une autre décision de la même date (concernant Sekisui Systeembouw NV), *TVVS* 1977, p. 231.
26. *TVVS* 1980, p. 148; *NJ* 1981, no. 64.

27. Dans les autres décisions (par ex. celles citées sous note 25) la Chambre se contente du seul fait que les comptes annuels exprimèrent la "réalité juridique formelle". Et de remarquer que les demandeurs (syndicats, actionnaires minoritaires, etc.) avaient d'autres voies de recours à leur disposition pour contester certaines décisions ou agissements des organes de la société. Bak et Boukema (*TVVS* 1977, p. 231) les mentionnent: demande en annulation de la décision de la direction, en dommage-intérêts, en requête judiciaire.
28. Selon Bak et Boukema (*TVVS* 1980, p. 149) il n'est pas facile de déterminer quel est un prix 'normal' pour les voiliers livrés par la société-mère française à un bureau de vente aux Pays-Bas. "En outre", remarquent-ils, "on peut supposer que le fisc aussi prendra connaissance d'une telle information avec un intérêt particulier".
29. V. sur ce sujet en général Roelvink, *op.cit.* p. 85 et suiv., p. 138.
30. M.J.A. van Mourik (*Weekblad voor Privaatrecht, Notariaat en Registratie/WPNR* 1976, p. 533, note 19), remarque justement que dans le domaine des affaires civiles l'identification est admise par exception tandis qu'en matière fiscale les indentifications "fourmillent".
31. Une décision récente de la Cour de La Haye (du 11 avril 1980, *NJ* 1980, no. 604) refusa l'identification entre sociétés appartenant au même groupe, v. sous III. B.1.
32. V. quelques décisions citées par Roelvink, *op.cit.* p. 106, 109, 110; ce même auteur écrit (p. 139) que la jurisprudence néerlandaise ne se montre pas trop encline à identifier une société avec son actionnaire unique, lorsque c'est ce dernier qui y tient.
33. Par ex. un jugement du Tribunal d'instance de Groningue (cité par P. Vlas, *De Notarisklerk* 1980, p. 140) refusa l'assistance judiciaire à une association de propriétaires d'appartements au motif que ceux-ci n'étaient pas indigents et que par conséquent la personne morale elle aussi n'était pas indigente. D'après le tribunal la personne morale formait du point de vue économique une "unité" avec les personnes physiques.
34. Tribunal d'instance d'Amsterdam, jugement du 15 janvier 1975, *De Praktijkgids* 1975, p. 267.
35. *NJ* 1974 no. 396 où la décision précitée de la Cour d'appel est également publiée.
36. Jugement cité par Roelvink, *op.cit.* p. 114.
37. *Asser Kartotheek* (*AK*) no. 11.666; v. aussi *Netherlands International Law Review* (*NILR*) 1980, p. 252 avec une très brève note de Vlas.
38. No. du rôle 1851/1977.
39. No. du rôle 80/5046.
40. *NJ* 1940, no. 560.
41. Citons encore le jugement du tribunal de Rotterdam du 18 février 1964 (*SS* 1964, no. 43). Le demandeur soutint que le fréteur au voyage était son expéditeur, "auquel il devait être identifié". Des doutes existaient quant à la forme juridique des propriétaires: société en nom collectif ou copropriété de navire. Les parties au procès avaient pris comme "point de départ" que "la forme juridique de collaboration" devait etre jugée selon le droit néerlandais. Le tribunal attendit que les parties le renseignent sur cette "forme de collaboration" qui était établie à Dublin et sur la nationalité du navire.
42. Par ex. un jugement récent de la Cour d'appel d'Arnhem (du 19 novembre 1979, *NJ* 1980, no. 419) a retenu la responsabilité *ex delicto* des époux, seuls actionnaires d'une S.à.R.L., dont la femme était le directeur et le mari le conseiller: "les circonstances de fait éveillaient pour le moins l'apparence que toute possibilité de recouvrement par les créanciers de la société avait été ôtée par des dextérités juridico-techniques ... l'actif qui reste n'est pas suffisant pour le paiement immédiat de la réclamation de C." Cette dernière société avait fait effectuer une saisie conservatoire sur un immeuble des époux. Quelques jugements admettent que le dirigeant est personnellement responsable s'il savait, ou pour le moins il ne pouvait pas avoir des doutes au moment de la transaction, que la société ne pourrait pas honorer ses obligations; v. par ex. la décision de la Cour d'appel de Bois le Duc du 6 avril 1976, *NJ* 1978 no. 454; en l'espèce le dirigeant de la S.à.R.L. (en même temps détenteur de la moitié des actions) avait aussi éveillé l'apparence que la société était solvable. Dans le même sens la décision de la Cour d'appel de La Haye du 12 janvier 1972, *NJ* 1972 no. 221; en l'espèce le directeur de la S.A. était en même temps l'actionnaire unique.
43. *NJ* 1980 no. 604.
44. *Weekblad van het recht* (*W*) no. 7517.
45. *NJ* 1942, no. 242.

46. *NJ* 1916, p. 1110, jugement confirmé par la décision de la Cour d'appel de La Haye du 28 avril 1916 (*NJ* 1916, p. 1114) pour ce qui concernait la responsabilité.
47. *NJ* 1947, no. 229.
48. *W* no. 7736.
49. *W* no. 9009.
50. *AK* no. 5372. E.C. Henriquez (*WPNR* 1971, p. 42) est d'avis que l'art. 11 a trait plutôt à la responsabilité des représentants.
51. *AK* no. 5811 et les remarques de Henriquez dans *WPNR* 1974, p. 756.
52. *SS* 1974 no. 92.
53. *NJ* 1973, no. 400, avec la note de Hijmans van den Bergh. L'affaire *Mackay* a fait l'objet de plusieurs commentaires; v. parmi les plus récents ceux de C.J.J. van Maanen, Concernverhoudingen en individuele arbeidsovereenkomst, *Naamloze Vennootschap* (*NV*) 1978, p. 162-163; du même auteur, Intra-concern overplaatsing van werknemers, *NV* 1979, p. 86 et suiv.
54. *NJ* 1976, no. 566; sur cette décision v. Van Maanen, *NV* 1978, p. 158.
55. *NJ* 1978, no. 426; sur ce jugement v. Van Maanen, *NV* 1978, p. 158, 162.
56. *AK* no. 10.723.
57. V. aussi notre rapport publié dans *Rapports Néerlandais pour le Dixième Congrès International de Droit Comparé* (1978), p. 139-142. Parmi les publications récentes en langue néerlandaise v. P. Sanders, De Derde Richtlijn, *TVVS* 1979, p. 41-47 et p. 76-84.
58. Depuis l'entrée en vigueur du Code (1970) jusqu'au premier juillet 1980, la Commission a traité 4.432 affaires. Les règles de conduite furent considérées comme non applicables à 1.503 affaires. Dans 228 (sur 2.929) cas a été constatée une transgression des règles, v. H.W. Wertheimer, Tien jaren fusiecode, *TVVS* 1980, p. 221-223.
59. Les Pays-Bas sont obligés d'introduire cette figure en vertu de la Troisième Directive du Conseil des Ministres des Communautés Européennes (no. 78/855 du 9 octobre 1978). Un projet de loi est déjà soumis à la Deuxième Chambre.
60. En cas de convention collective de travail, les règles peuvent être déclarées applicables à des entreprises employant moins de cent personnes.
61. D'après le rapport explicatif de la Commission "l'ensemble d'entreprises" comprend plus que ce que l'on entend généralement par le terme *concern*: également la relation entre entreprises qui ne sont pas indépendantes du point de vue de la forme juridique; par ex. une personne morale avec des établissements dépendants.
62. Les entreprises sont tenues de fournir aux organisations syndicales des renseignements concernant les motifs de la fusion et leur soumettre un plan social.
63. Mentionnons que la protection des travailleurs en cas de fusion est également prévue par la loi sur les comités d'entreprise (v. sous II.2.d), laquelle prévoit que le comité a le droit de donner son avis, entre autres, en cas de fusion avec une entreprise établie à l'étranger, sauf si on peut raisonnablement s'attendre à ce que la fusion n'aura pas des effets préjudicieux pour les employés de l'entrepreneur aux Pays-Bas.
64. Sur la 'jurisprudence' relative de la Commission v. les brèves remarques de G.J.W. Arendsen de Wolff, *TVVS* 1978, p. 387-388.
65. V. A.M. Brenninkmeijer, *TVVS* 1978, p. 371.
66. Par ex. la Cour d'appel d'Amsterdam (v. note 47) avait fait catégoriquement la distinction entre droits et obligations des parties découlant du contrat (en l'espèce celui-ci était régi par le droit néerlandais) d'une part, et la question de la responsabilité des parties en tant qu'associés, d'autre part; cette dernière question fut régie par le droit anglais, droit du pays où la *partnership* était établie.
67. Nous croyons que les art. 138 et 248 du Second Livre CC, tels qu'ils seront modifiés (v. sous II.2.e), devraient être qualifiés de règles du droit des sociétés et non de règles du droit de la faillite. Cette qualification trouve, d'après nous, son appui dans l'exposé des motifs (v. sous note 3) où on lit, entre autres, que la responsabilité du dirigeant n'a pas son fondement dans la faillite, mais dans la responsabilité que le dirigeant porte envers la société dans l'accomplissement de ses tâches. Et encore qu'il n'y a pas de raison, pour ce qui concerne la responsabilité du dirigeant, de distinguer entre faillite et autres situations.
68. Cette solution découle de la règle de conflit non-écrite néerlandaise, concernant la relation entre le représenté et le tiers; v. de la jurisprudence la plus récente: Tribunal d'Amsterdam 18 juin 1975 (*SS* 1976, no. 51); 27 janvier 1976 (*AK* no. 10.458); 19 avril 1977 (*AK* no. 10.723).

69. Contra: Van Maanen (*TVVS* 1979, p. 333) qui se prononce pour l'application de la loi du siège social de la filiale. Henriquez (*Het vennootschapsstatuut*, 1961, p. 118 et p. 263, le resumé français) soumet la responsabilité de l'actionnaire qui a participé à l'acte illicite ou à la décision de le commettre à la *lex loci delicti commissi*; ceci comme exception à l'application de la *lex societatis*. Par ex. la Cour d'Appel d'Amsterdam (décision du 5 juin 1914, *NJ* 1914, p. 1115) a appliqué la loi allemande à titre de *l.l.d.c.*, à la responsabilité d'une société commerciale en nom collectif établie en Allemagne, pour l'acte illicite commis par son comptable. Par contre le Tribunal d'Almelo (jugement avant dire droit du 25 septembre 1975, *WPNR* avec les brèves remarques de Henriquez; v. aussi Vlas, *NILR* 1980, p. 250) appliqua à un différend entre une société en commandite allemande et son ex-actionnaire dirigeant, la loi allemande en faisant appel à plusieurs points de rattachement, entre autres, à la circonstance que la société était établie en Allemagne Fédérale; il s'agissait en l'espèce d'une amende pour un délit de circulation que l'actionnaire avait portée à la charge de la société.
70. Le droit néerlandais a été implicitement appliqué dans un cas où une circulaire contenant les raisons pour lesquelles la société avait perdu confiance en l'exploitant de sa succursale aux Pays-Bas, fut expédiée depuis la Tchécoslovaquie; v. l'arrêt de la Haute Cour du 19 décembre 1935, *NJ* 1936, no. 559.
71. Un raisonnement analogue a été suivi - hors du domaine du droit des sociétés - par la Cour d'appel d'Amsterdam dans sa décision du 6 juin 1957; v. le commentaire de R.D. Kollewijn, sous l'arrêt de la Haute Cour du 18 avril 1958, dans *Clunet* 1961, p. 892.
72. V. par ex. la décision de la Cour d'appel de La Haye (du 16 février 1977, *SS* 1978, no. 44) qui a accepté l'accord des parties que le caractère illicite des agissements ou de l'abstention d'agir, d'une entreprise établie en Uruguay (il s'agissait d'une question d'accréditif) soit jugé d'après le droit néerlandais.
73. Il en est de même dans le domaine de la reconnaissance et l'exécution des jugements étrangers, croyons-nous; v. aussi H.M. Alvares Correa, *TVVS* 1976, 132.

Le régime juridique applicable aux rapports de travail sur le plan international

C.J.J. VAN MAANEN

auditeur à la Cour d'Appel d'Amsterdam

II.B.3.

I. Introduction (nrs 1-6)
II. Droit du travail matériel néerlandais (nrs 7-11)
III. Conflits de lois (nrs 12-28)
- autonomie de la volonté (nrs 12-16)
- rattachement objectif (nrs 17-22)
- lois d'application immédiate (nrs 23-28)
IV. Procédure (nrs 29-37)
- droit interne (nr 29)
- compétence internationale (nrs 30-33)
- clauses d'élection de for (nrs 34-36)
- introduction de l'instance (nr 37)
V. Divers (nrs 38-41)
- détermination de l'employeur (nr 38)
- conflit mobile (nrs 39-40)
- grève (nr 41)

I. INTRODUCTION

1.
La pratique néerlandais du droit du travail international a produit des solutions qui, assurément, méritent l'attention du comparatiste. D'autre part, l'ensemble de ces solutions est trop fragmentaire que l'on puisse en déduire un "système du droit du travail international" comme il a été élaboré, en Allemagne, par M. *Gamillscheg*[1].
Dans cet état de choses, une réponse intégrale au questionnaire présenté par le rapporteur général contiendrait nécessairement beaucoup de spéculations subjectives de l'auteur accidentel. Or, le but de nos rapports étant la comparaison du droit positif des états rapporteurs, et non pas la comparaison des spéculations susvisées, l'auteur de ce rapport se restreindra dans l'exposition de ses vues personelles, et mettra l'accent sur les données fragmentaires du droit néerlandais qui sont plus ou moins sûres[2].

2.
Données fragmentaires, parce que la loi ne contient aucune règle générale pertinente, de sorte qu'il est au juge de trouver une solution acceptable dans l'espèce. Cependant, il convient de signaler d'emblée que le *Hoge Raad*[3], notamment depuis une quinzaine d'années environ, saisit presque toute occasion de guider la jurisprudence en matière du droit international privé par des (quasi-) arrêts de règlement. Le droit du travail international en a profité aussi, comme nous verrons tout à l'heure.

3.
Données fragmentaires, encore, parce que, dans la doctrine néerlandaise, le droit du travail international n'a été l'objet d'étude que dans un rapport, présenté en 1966 à la réunion annuelle de l'Association néerlandaise de droit international, par M. *Koopmans*[4]. Il vaut la peine d'y insister un instant.

4.
Les points de départ de M. *Koopmans* sont, dans le domaine des faits: la migration, croissante rapidement à l'époque, de la main d'oeuvre, et le trafic des frontaliers; et, dans le domaine socio-juridique: l'emprise des considérations socio-économiques et organisatoires dans le droit du travail. Cela conduit l'auteur à ne retenir que deux facteurs de rattachement, à savoir le lieu du travail et la localisation de l'établissement auquel l'employé appartient[5].
M. *Koopmans* pèse les titres respectifs de ces deux facteurs, en examinant de près les branches diverses du droit du travail matériel (néerlandais, surtout). Il en tire la conclusion suivante, pour l'hypothèse que le lieu du travail et l'établissement sont situés dans divers pays: en premier lieu, il faut respecter les délimitations explicites des dispositions matérielles en présence; à défaut de telles délimitations, c'est la loi du lieu du travail qui s'applique quant à ses dispositions visant la situation concrète du travail; au demeurant, c'est la loi de l'établissement qui s'applique.
A la fin du rapport, l'auteur reconnaît ce qu'il avait déjà impliqué: il rejet les méthodes de rattachement de contrats, courantes à l'époque (autonomie de la volonté, volonté présumée, détermination du lien le plus étroit en faisant la revue de toutes circonstances de l'espèce, etc.).

5.
Nous verrons que la jurisprudence ultérieure, dans ses résultats, cadre bien avec les idées avancées par M. *Koopmans*. En effet, on n'a retenu que les deux facteurs de rattachement proposés par lui; en effet, on a pratiqué un dépeçage analogue au sien, en reconnaissant l'application nécessaire de quelques dispositions du droit matériel néerlandais.

Cependant, ce qui frappa surtout dans le rapport, à savoir l'adoption (soit-elle tacite) de la méthode unilatéraliste pour l'ensemble de la matière, avec l'annexe du rejet de l'autonomie de la volonté, n'a pas été suivi dans la jurisprudence. Qu'il s'agît d'un contrat de travail ou d'un autre contrat quelconque, la méthode unilatéraliste n'est, encore, pratiquée qu'à titre d'exception à la méthode des conflits de lois, quoi qu'en disent les critiques de la méthode "savignienne" comme *Deelen*, *d'Oliveira*, *De Boer*, ou *Strikwerda*[6]. Toujours, ce sont les principes généraux de la méthode des conflits de lois en matière de contrats qui dominent la jurisprudence sur le droit du travail international.

6.
A l'avis de l'auteur du présent rapport, cela s'explique du fait que les points de départ de M. *Koopmans* ne cadrent pas avec la réalité (ou, si l'on veut: l'irréalité) de l'expérience judiciaire. Aucun plaideur n'a jamais contredit que le droit néerlandais s'applique au contrat de travail d'un travailleur migrant d'origine italienne, employé aux hauts fourneaux d'IJmuiden[7]; aucun exploitant d'hauts fourneaux n'a eu l'idée d'insérer un choix de la loi italienne dans un tel contrat. Les personnages principaux qui figurent dans les litiges sont, aujourd'hui encore, des individus comme les représentants de commerce, les cadres dirigeants, les techniciens spécialisés, et les guides touristiques. Les litiges s'agîssent des rapports patrimoniaux entre eux et leurs employeurs. De considérations socio-économiques ou organisatoires jouent un rôle très modeste.

II. DROIT DU TRAVAIL MATÉRIEL NÉERLANDAIS

7. *Sources.*
Le cadre juridique de la relation de travail est déterminé, en premier lieu, par la loi: le Titre VII A (articles 1637 à 1639x) du *Burgerlijk Wetboek*[8], complété par quelques lois non codifiées[9]. Surtout dans les relations internationales, les conventions collectives jouent un rôle secondaire, voire négligeable.

8. *Dispositions frappantes.*
Plus les systèmes juridiques en présence diffèrent, plus la question du droit applicable sera contestée. Ainsi, la jurisprudence néerlandaise en la matière concerne le plus souvent l'applicabilité ou la non-applicabilité d'une des dispositions suivantes, frappantes du point de vue comparatif: le *BBA*[10], l'article 1639s *BW*[11], la *Wet Minimumloon*[12].

9. *BBA*.
Selon l'article 6 du *BBA* il est interdit de mettre fin à une relation de travail sans l'autorisation préalable du Directeur du *GAB*[13], abstraction faite de quelques exceptions[14]. Selon l'article 9, un licenciement sans autorisation est nul. Par conséquence, le travailleur retient le droit à son salaire, même s'il n'accomplît pas son travail, sous condition qu'il soit disposé à l'exécuter. Cette réglementation constitue la clef de voûte de la protection contre le licenciement. Quelle que soit la décision du Directeur du *GAB*, la procédure menée devant lui prendra quelques mois, qui s'ajouteront à la durée du délai-congé; et, si le Directeur du *GAB* refuse l'autorisation, il ne reste l'employeur (persévérant) que de "acheter" le consentement du travailleur au licenciement.

10. *L'article 1639s BW*.
Outre le contrôle préventif du Directeur du *GAB*, il y a le contrôle rétrospectif du caractère raisonnable du licenciement, en vertu de l'article 1639s *BW*. Ces deux contrôles diffèrent en ce que le Directeur du *GAB* apprécie seulement la nécessité du licenciement projeté, alors que le juge civil, en appliquant l'article 1639s *BW*, apprécie le droit éventuel du travailleur déjà licencié à une indemnisation.
Le juge peut accorder une indemnisation "en équité" si le licenciement a été "manifestement déraisonnable". La jurisprudence n'a pas réussi à éclairer ces notions, mais quoi qu'il en soit, il y a eu des espèces où le juge a accordé des indemnisations de plus d'un million de florins. Assurément une perspective attrayante pour, disons, un employé américain d'une société multinationale d'origine américaine, détaché aux Pays-Bas, qui se voit licencié "à l'américaine", sans préavis, sans motivation, et, apparemment, sans autre motif qu'aux Etats-Unis le vent a tourné.

11. *Wet Minimumloon*.
Selon l'article 7 de cette loi tout travailleur est en droit de reclamer de son employeur le salaire minimum, fixé semestriellement sur la base d'un index déterminé par la loi. Au 1er juillet 1981, le salaire minimum d'un travailleur de 23 ans ou plus est de Fl. 1925,30 par mois.

III. CONFLITS DE LOIS

Autonomie de la volonté

12. *Contrats en général*.
Le *HR* a reconnu le principe de l'autonomie de la volonté dans le sens conflictuel dans l'arrêt *Alnati*, qui date de 1966[15]. Les maintes questions concernant les contours plus précis du-

dit principe, si vivement discutées dans la doctrine néerlandaise et étrangère, ne se sont guère présentées dans la jurisprudence. Il faut renvoyer l'intéressé à la littérature[16].

13. *Contrats de travail - position du HR.*
Pour le contrat de travail aussi, le *HR* a mis en avant la liberté des parties de choisir la loi applicable à leur contrat[17]. Dans l'espèce, cependant, un tel choix n'ayant pas été fait, le *HR* n'avait pas eu à y apprécier le bien-fondé.

14. *Suite - décisions conformes.*
Dans la jurisprudence ultérieure, il n'y a que deux décisions rapportées où il était question d'un choix exprès. Dans les deux cas, le juge a suivi ce choix comme tel; d'ailleurs, ni dans l'un ni dans l'autre la règle de rattachement objectif n'aurait conduit à un résultat différent[18].

15. *Suite - décisions contraires.*
Il y a deux décisions dans lesquelles le juge a nié que les parties puissent déroger aux dispositions impératives de la loi applicable en vertu du rattachement objectif. Cependant, l'une d'elles est antérieure à l'arrêt précité[19]; lorsque dans l'autre il était question d'un choix tacite, manifesté dans un litige connexe[20]. Il n'est pas évident que le juge a eu conscience qu'il touchait une question déjà décidée par le *HR*.

16. *Commentaire.*
Dans le système du *HR*, l'effet d'un choix choquant (fantôme de la doctrine) ne peut être redressé que soit par les correctifs de la théorie générale de l'autonomie de la volonté (l'exigence de "l'internationalité du contrat", celle de "l'intérêt raisonnable", *e.t.q.*), soit par celui du jeu des lois d'application immédiate. Or, il est concevable que le *HR*, plutôt que d'élargir la portée de ces deux correctifs (ce qui compromettrait la sécurité juridique dans le domaine contractuel entier) préfèrera réduire l'effet d'un choix de la loi applicable inséré dans un contrat de travail, comme le fait l'article 6 alinéa 1er de la Convention de Rome sur la loi applicable aux obligations contractuelles (selon lequel la loi choisie ne s'applique que dans la mesure qu'elle est plus favorable au travailleur que la loi applicable à défaut de choix). Quelques auteurs le recommandent[21].

Rattachement objectif

17. *Contrats en général.*
Au fil des années, le *HR* a élaboré un nombre de règles de conflit, différentiées selon le type de contrat. Ces règles mettent en avant un point de rattachement primaire pour le con-

trat visé , mais contiennent parfois d'exceptions ou de rattachements subsidiaires, et souvent une clause échappatoire. Les résultats du *HR* sont proches à ceux que produirait la théorie de la prestation caractéristique; cependant, le *HR* n'a jamais dit qu'il accepte cette théorie comme directive générale pour le rattachement objectif de contrats.
Les jurisdictions inférieures, à défaut d'un arrêt directeur du *HR*, se contentent généralement d'une solution casuîstique, en recherchant "le lien le plus étroit" dans l'espèce concret.

18. *Contrat de travail - position du HR.*
Après l'évocation du principe de l'autonomie de la volonté, le *HR*, dans l'arrêt précité[22], donne la règle de rattachement objectif suivante:

1. si un pays déterminé peut être désigné
   a) comme le lieu où la prestation de travail s'accomplit habituellement;

   ou bien, dans le cas où les activités de l'employé s'étendent à plus d'un seul pays,

   b) comme le pays où se trouve, en vertu du contrat, le poste central de l'employé,

   le contrat est régi par la loi de ce pays.
2. Si un tel pays ne peut pas être désigné, le contrat est régi par la loi du pays où l'employeur a son siège.
3. Dans les deux cas sous la réserve de circonstances particulières entraînant que la loi d'un autre pays doive régir le contrat.

Puisque le *HR* s'est prononcé dans un arrêt si récent, il est inutile de donner un aperçu de la jurisprudence des juges inférieures. Je passe à quelques précisions sur de catégories particulières d'employés.

19. *Suite - cadres dirigeants.*
L'arrêt précité poursuit:

> *La règle première (*no. 18 sous 1.*) s'applique aussi - sous ladite réserve (*no. 18 sous 3.*) - à des entreprises internationales avec des établissements en plusieurs pays; la circonstance que certains employés, occupés à l'étranger dans des établissements d'une telle entreprise, communiquent directement avec la direction centrale de celle-ci, qui leur donne d'instructions et reçoit leurs rapports, ne constitue pas, en soi, un lien suffisamment étroit avec la loi du pays où se trouve cette direction centrale, que l'on pourrait reconnaître, en règle générale, que le contrat de travail de tels employés soit régi par la loi de ce pays; non plus lorsque leurs activités ne se limitent pas au pays*

où ils ont leur poste central, mais s'étendent de là à plusieurs pays.

On le voit: pas d'exception pour les cadres dirigeants.

20. *Suite - employés détachés.*
L'arrêt précité poursuit (suite de la citation littérale précédente):

... sauf dans le cas que l'employeur ait détaché lesdits employés du pays où se trouve la direction centrale de l'entreprise, à un établissement à l'étranger.

Il s'ensuit du contexte que "lesdits employés" sont ceux qui (a) sont embauchés dans le pays de la direction centrale, et (b) durant leurs détachements à l'étranger, communiquent directement avec celle-ci.
La condition d'embauchage dans le pays de la direction centrale est au coeur de la notion de détachement. Par contre, la justification de l'autre condition, celle d'une communication continue de l'employé détaché avec la direction centrale, n'est pas aussitôt évidente. Pour autant que la continuation d'un lien entre l'employé et l'entreprise qui l'a détaché soit requise, c'est plutôt l'intention de retour qui me semble essentielle; retour, non seulement au pays d'origine, mais aussi au service de cette entreprise.

21. *Suite - directeurs de sociétés.*
Selon le Tribunal[23] de Rotterdam "la fonction de directeur d'une société néerlandaise, fonction exercée aux Pays-Bas, s'oppose - en vertu du droit de sociétés néerlandais, qui régit la société défenderesse - à l'application d'une loi autre que la néerlandaise"[24]. Cependant, cette décision ne semble pas un précédent incontestable[25].

22. *Suite - marins.*
La loi néerlandaise ne contient pas une règle de conflit impérative comme l'article 5 du Code du travail maritime français. Néanmoins, aux Pays-Bas aussi, le pavillon est retenu en point de rattachement primaire[26].

Lois d'application immédiate

23. *Contrats en général.*
Aux Pays-Bas, comme ailleurs, la doctrine montre un "renouveau de la tendence unilatéraliste". La version dominante est celle de M. *De Winter*, qui a proposé que:

"Une disposition qui ne fait pas partie du droit qui régit le contrat doit être prise en considération si elle

remplit, dans l'ordre juridique d'un état impliqué dans un contrat international une fonction d'une importance telle qu'on ne pourrait exiger de l'état impliqué qu'il sacrifie en l'espèce l'intérêt qui est protégé par la disposition en question."[27]

Dans cette proposition il est sans importance que la loi du contrat soit choisie par les parties ou bien déterminée par rattachement objectif; et il n'importe que la disposition en question fasse partie de la loi du for ou bien de la loi d'un pays tiers.
La possibilité de l'application d'une disposition étrangère qui ne fait pas partie de la loi choisie a été reconnue dans un motif surabondant de l'arrêt *Alnati*[28]. Cependant, dans l' arrêt *Sewrajsing*[29] le *HR* n'a pas pratiqué cette possibilité. Aussi, la position actuelle du *HR* est incertaine.
D'autre part, l'application immédiate d'une disposition de la loi du for est un phénomène bien connu dans la jurisprudence. Le droit du travail nous en montre l'exemple classique (*infra* no. 26).

24. *Contrat de travail - salaire minimum.*
Dans son article 4, la loi sur le salaire minimum détermine expressément son propre domaine d'application. La réglementation peut être résumée comme suit:
- tout employé a droit au salaire minimum; avec cette restriction que
- l'employé qui accomplît son travail hors du Royaume n'a droit au salaire minimum que si lui, ainsi que son employeur sont domiciliés dans le Royaume.

Cette réglementation a donné lieu a maints procès, entamés par de saisonniers de nationalité néerlandaise, qui remplissaient, à l'étranger, la fonction de guide ou d'hôtesse au service d' organisations touristiques néerlandaises; saisonniers qui, pendant les six mois environ de leur emploi, retenaient leurs habitations aux Pays-Bas, et maintenaient, là, leurs inscriptions au registre de la population. La question se posait si un tel saisonnier garde son domicile aux Pays-Bas, "domicile" entendu dans le sens de la loi sur le salaire minimum.
En 1980, le *HR* a répondu à cette question par la négative[30]. Le *HR* a considéré que le niveau du salaire minimum est lié à la "situation de prospérité" régnant aux Pays-Bas. Il s'ensuit qu'un employé qui accomplît son travail - presque totalement - à l'étranger, et qui séjourne donc durablement à l'étranger, hors de la "situation de prospérité" néerlandaise avec le niveau de prix annexe, n'est pas domicilié aux Pays-Bas dans le sens de l'article 4 de la loi sur le salaire minimum.

24. *Suite - commentaire.*
Puisqu'on peut supposer, avec raison, que le droit néerlandais régissait le contrat de travail (le *HR* en passe sous silence), la décision nous révèle un exemple d'une loi "auto-limitée". D'autre part il n'y a pas de doute que la loi sur le salaire minimum s'applique "immédiatement", quelle que soit la loi applicable au contrat, dès que les conditions de l'article 4 sont remplies. Donc, il y a unilatéralité parfaite. Enfin: bien que l'arrêt traite de l'interprétation d'une notion légale (celle du domicile) c'est bien "l'intérêt important protégé par la loi en question" (*supra* no. 23) qui décide l'affaire; le *HR* parle du but de la loi, à savoir de garantir l'employé un salaire qui est le minimum acceptable du point de vue social.

26. *Contrat de travail - BBA.*
La jurisprudence sur le domaine d'application du *BBA* nous montre un autre exemple d'unilatéralité parfaite.
En 1953, le *HR* devait apprécier l'allégation que l'applicabilité (incontestée) du droit néerlandais à un contrat de travail entraînait nécessairement l'applicabilité du *BBA*. Le *HR* rejetait cette allégation, en considérant que: si des intérêts du marché néerlandais du travail sont impliqués dans une relation de travail, à accomplir hors du Royaume, le *BBA* devra s'appliquer d'une façon qui peut servir la protection desdits intérêts, mais la seule circonstance qu'un contrat de travail est régi par le droit néerlandais n'a pas pour conséquence nécessaire que lesdits intérêts soient affectés[31].
D'autre part, en 1971, le *HR* a considéré que, quant à l'applicabilité du *BBA*, il est indifférent que la relation de travail soit régie par le droit néerlandais ou bien par le droit d'un autre pays; le *BBA* s'applique dès que le licenciement projeté affecterait les rapports sur le marché néerlandais du travail.
Il découle d'une douzaine de décisions des juridictions inférieures que l'on peut estimer le marché néerlandais du travail affecté si, dans l'espèce, il est à prévoir que l'employé, après son licenciement éventuel, postulera un nouvel emploi sur ce marché.[33]

27. *Suite - commentaire.*
Récemment, cette jurisprudence constante a été contestée par l'auteur de ce rapport[34]. La critique considère faux le point de départ du *HR*, à savoir l'allégation que le *BBA* contient une réglementation, dans l'intétêt public, du marché néerlandais du travail. Aujourd'hui, les Directeurs des *GAB*, en appliquant le *BBA*, ne prennent plus en considération l'intérêt public; l'équité dans la relation donnée entre employeur et employé est leur seule directive. Aussi, reprenant les mots de M. *De*

Winter (*supra* no. 23), on ne peut pas dire que le *BBA* protège un intérêt d'une telle importance que l'état (les Pays-Bas) ne puisse pas le sacrifier.

28. *Contrat de travail - art. 1639s BW.*
Comme on pouvait s'y attendre, il a été allégué que l'article 1639s *BW*, de même que le *BBA*, soit une disposition visant à régler les rapports sur le marché néerlandais du travail, et qu'il doive être, par conséquence, appliqué immédiatement dès que ce marché est en cause, quelle que soit la loi applicable au contrat.
Dans l'affaire *Mackay II*[35] le Tribunal d'Amsterdam, qui jugeait que le droit de l'état de New York régissait le contrat, et devait donc répondre à cette allégation, l'a rejeté. L'avocat-général, dans sa conclusion devant le *HR*, approuvait de la décision du Tribunal; le *HR* pouvait en passer parce qu'il jugeait que l'article 1639s *BW* s'appliquait en tant que partie de la loi du contrat qui était, contraire à l'opinion du Tribunal, la loi néerlandaise.
Le rejet par le Tribunal de ladite allégation était fondé sur le motif que l'article 1639s *BW* ne sert qu'à créer de meilleurs moyens de déploiement de l'équité concrète dans l'exécution du contrat de travail. M. *Van Rooij*, dans sa thèse, a appuyé ce raisonnement [36].

IV. PROCÉDURE

29. *Droit interne.*
Avant d'aborder l'aspect international, il faut signaler que le droit de procédure connaît un régime spécial pour les litiges en matière de travail:
- compétence absolue: en première instance, le juge de canton est compétent (art. 39 *RO*); sauf lorsque l'employé occupe le poste de directeur d'une société, auquel cas le Tribunal est compétent (*BW*, Livre 2, articles 131 et 241);
- compétence relative: l'article 125b *Rv* contient des règles spéciales pour les litiges en matière de travail; les règles communes s'appliquent à titre subsidiaire (art. 125 *Rv*); parmi ces règles communes, il convient de citer l'article 126 alinéa 3 *Rv* (*forum actoris*, cf. Convention de Bruxelles, art. 3 al. 2);
- introduction de l'instance: par requête, les parties étant convoquées par le greffier (art. 125b *Rv*).

30. *Compétence internationale - traités internationaux.*
Les Pays-Bas sont partie à la Convention de Bruxelles du 27 septembre 1968, dont le champ d'application matériel comprend les litiges en matière de travail[37]. Puisque le texte et la

jurisprudence sont accessibles en plusieurs langues, le présent rapport peut en passer sous silence.

31. *Compétence internationale - droit commun.*
Aux Pays-Bas, comme ailleurs, les règles de compétence internationale sont déduites de celles de la compétence relative du droit interne[38].
En droit interne, les principaux chefs de compétence sont le lieu du travail et le domicile du défendeur; à titre subsidiaire, le domicile du demandeur s'y ajoute. Sur le plan international, la réglementation se réduit au schéma suivant:

a. *travail aux Pays-Bas*
   1. principalement dans un seul canton: *forum loci laboris*[39] ou *forum rei*, au choix du demandeur, soit-il l'employeur ou l'employé (art. 125b al. 1er);
   2. travail s'étendant à plusieurs cantons: le demandeur étant l'employé, *forum rei* ou *forum actoris*, à son choix (art. 125b al. 2); le demandeur étant l'employeur, *forum rei* subs. *forum actoris* (art. 125b - 125 - 126 al. 3). Dans les deux cas, à défaut d'un domicile réel du défendeur aux Pays-Bas, le domicile élu, s'il y en a un, s'y substitue pour la détermination du *forum rei* (art. 125b al. 2, 2ème phrase).

b. *travail hors des Pays-Bas*
   Quiconque soit le demandeur, *forum rei* (art. 125b al. 1er) subs. for du domicile élu du défendeur (art. 125b al. 2, 2ème phrase) subs. *forum actoris* (art. 126 al. 3).

32. *Suite - commentaire.*
Cette réglementation contient une lacune et une exorbitance. Lacune, en ce que l'idée de base du *forum loci laboris* n'a pas été élaborée pour l'hypothèse que le travail s'accomplîsse dans plusieurs cantons, et que ni l'employeur ni l'employé soient domiciliés aux Pays-Bas. Exorbitance, en ce qui concerne le *forum actoris* au cas que le travail s'accomplîsse hors des Pays-Bas.

33. *Exception: directeurs de sociétés.*
Compétence absolue du tribunal, compétence relative de celui du domicile de la société[40]. Par anticipation sur le sujet que nous aborderons dans un instant, il faut ajouter que cette compétence relative est considerée comme exclusive[41].

34. *Clause d'élection de for - effet dérogatoire.*
Selon l'article 98a al. 1er *Rv*, à appliquer d'office selon al. 3 du même article, toute clause qui déroge aux règles légales sur la compétence relative du juge de canton, est nulle de plein droit.

La question se pose de savoir si cette disposition ne vise que le cas où la clause déroge à la compétence légale du juge de canton en faveur d'un autre juge de canton (néerlandais); ou bien qu'elle vise aussi le cas où elle déroge à la compétence de tout juge de canton néerlandais, en faveur d'un juge étranger.
Statuant sur une telle clause, insérée dans un contrat de travail, le Tribunal de Rotterdam a interprété l'article 98a dans le sens dernier nommé (acceptation de l'effet dérogatoire sur le plan international)[42].
En 1981, le *HR* s'est prononcé dans le sens contraire, mais il ne s'agîssait pas d'un contrat de travail[43]. L'énoncé de cet arrêt couvre toute compétence du juge de canton, donc y compris la compétence en matière de travail. Cependant, le *HR*, se référant au but de la loi, a fait une exception (qui, d'ailleurs, manque d'intérêt pour notre sujet).

35. *Suite - commentaire.*
Sur la base de cet arrêt, il semble loin d'être évident que le *HR* acceptera l'effet dérogatoire d'une clause d'élection de for, insérée dans un contrat de travail. D'autre part, il convient de rappeler qu'à l'occasion du réajustement de la Convention de Bruxelles, les contrats conclus par les consommateurs (grossement dit les contrats visés dans l'arrêt du *HR* de 1981) sont exclus de l'article 17, pendant que les contrats de travail y restent assujettis. Il est concevable que le *HR* adaptera le droit commun à ce modèle; ce qui serait possible sans revenir sur l'arrêt de 1981.

36. *Suite - effet prorogatoire.*
Selon un ancien arrêt du *HR*, ce n'est que le législateur qui attribue compétence au juge néerlandais; les parties ne le sauraient pas[44]. Cette jurisprudence a été critiquée avec l'argument que la loi reconnaît bien l'influence des parties sur la compétence internationale, en permettant que le demandeur saisisse le juge du domicile élu du défendeur. On comprend mal que l'effet prorogatoire de la volonté des parties dependrait de ce que cette volonté ait été exprimée sous forme d'une élection de for ou d'une élection de domicile.
Quoi qu'il en soit, aujourd'hui l'effet prorogatoire doit être reconnu dès que le défendeur respecte la clause d'élection de for, c'est à dire: comparait et ne soulève pas l'exception d'incompétence[45].
Quant au cas où le défendeur soulève l'exception d'incompétence, il est concevable que le *HR* adaptera le droit commun à l'article 17 de la Convention de Bruxelles, revenant à l'arrêt de 1915 susmentionné.

37. *Introduction de l'instance.*
Un litige en matière de travail est introduit par requête. Le

greffier convoque les parties par lettre recommandée à une date dans les quatorze jours après la réception de la requête (art. 126b al. 1, art. 125c al. 1-2 *Rv*).
En 1911, le *HR* a décidé que cette réglementation ne s'applique pas si le défendeur est domicilié à l'étranger; cela en vue du moyen de convocation et de la durée du délai prescrits[46].
Le défendeur domicilié à l'étranger doit être assigné par le demandeur, en observation des règles communes pertinentes, ainsi le *HR*.
En 1978, le juge de canton de Rotterdam s'est écarté de cet arrêt, se fondant sur de traités internationaux applicables dans l'espèce[47]. Si que le droit commun s'applique, il n'est pas évident à quel titre le juge puisse surseoir à statuer dans le cas où le défendeur ne comparaît pas dans les (courts) délais voulus; alors, le second motif de l'arrêt susmentionné tiendrait encore.
Quoi qu'il en soit, la controverse est d'un intérêt restreint, parce que le demandeur avisé élira toujours la voie de l'assignation; le pire qu'il lui peut arriver c'est qu'il doit en payer les frais[48].

V. DIVERS

38. *Détermination de l'employeur.*
Dans les groupes de sociétés, il arrive qu'un employé, notamment celui qui a été transferé de l'une à l'autre, ne saurait plus dire laquelle soit son employeur. Ce problème, bien connu en France[49], s'est posé au juge néerlandais aussi dans des litiges où la société défenderesse contredisait qu'elle était la co-contractante de l'employé réclamant des indemnisations de licenciement[50]. Les décisions n'ont pas produit une solution nette du problème.
Dans la doctrine, il a été proposé, pour le droit interne, d' accorder l'employé le bénéfice du doute, dans ce sens que soit considérée comme employeur toute société qui a créé l'apparence d'être la co-contractante par des actes qui ne sont, normalement, exécutés que par l'employeur. Ainsi, le problème de la détermination de l'employeur est qualifié comme une question de consentement.
Sur le plan international, suivant cette qualification, c'est la loi du contrat (présumé) qui décide si l'apparence puisse valoir consentement[51].

39. *Conflit mobile - position du HR.*
Selon le *HR*, la question de savoir si le transfert de l'employé à une autre fonction dans un autre pays implique un changement de la loi applicable, ne se prête pas à une réponse générale[52].
Dans l'espèce, le *HR* approuvait la décision du juge de fait, qui avait admis que la loi applicable avait changé, en considé-

ration de la différance de nature et d'importance des fonctions remplies successivement par l'employé concerné.
La prudence du *HR* a été critiqué sur le motif que l'emphase, dans la règle de conflit, au point de rattachement primaire du lieu du travail, devrait conduire à l'adoption, en règle générale, du système de l'application immédiate de la loi du nouveau lieu du travail; d'autant plus parce que l'exception évidente, à savoir celle du détachement temporaire, a déjà été incorporée dans la règle de conflit[53].

40. *Conflit mobile - effets.*
Un changement de la loi applicable conduit à des problèmes particuliers quant à la mise en oeuvre des dispositions matérielles qui attachent un effet juridique à des faits que se séparent dans le temps, ou bien à l'ancienneté de l'employé.
Dans la doctrine, il a été soutenu que ces problèmes, bien qu'ils résultent d'un phénomène de droit international privé, à savoir le changement de la loi applicable, n'en sont pas moins des problèmes de l'application du droit matériel applicable avant ou après. Aussi, la solution ne peut pas être générale, mais dépendra du contenu matériel des systèmes juridiques successifs. Plus la structure des règles successives diffère, plus une solution matérielle, visant la réalisation du but des règles successivement applicables, sera nécessaire[54].

41. *Grève.*
Aux Pays-Bas aussi, l'*ITF* (*International Transport Workers Federation*) a organisé des grèves visant la souscription de sa convention collective par les armateurs de navires battant un pavillon de complaisance.
Dans l'affaire *Tropwind* (navire battant pavillon singaporien, armé par une maison américaine, equipé, pour la plupart, par des marins philippiniens) les marins, licenciés à cause de leur grève, refusaient de débarquer. L'armateur et le propriétaire (suisse) du navire demandaient l'expulsion des marins, ainsi que l'abstention, de la part de l'*ITF*, de toute action qui empêcherait le départ du navire.
En référé, le Président du Tribunal d'Amsterdam[55], en examinant si la grève justifiait le licenciement, appliquait la loi singaporienne, choisie dans les contrats de travail (coïncidant, d'ailleurs, avec celle du pavillon). Selon le Président, cette loi s'appliquait aussi à la question de savoir si la participation à une grève, organisée par un syndicat, puisse valoir l'inexécution du contrat de travail individuel. La conformité du licenciement au droit singaporien n'étant pas établi, le Président rejetait la demande.
La demande formée contre l'*ITF* était fondée sur l'allégation d'un acte illicite. Suivant, d'ailleurs sans motivation, le point de vue commun des parties, le Président appliquait le droit néerlandais à cette partie de la demande. Cependant, considérant

que les règles néerlandaises du droit de grève reflètent la pratique néerlandaise des relations professionelles, le Président adaptait ces règles aux particularités des relations professionelles dans le secteur du transport maritime international. Sa conclusion était que l'action de l'*ITF* n'était pas illicite.
Ainsi ne se produisit pas le résultat boiteux que, d'une part, l'incitation à la grève par le syndicat, appréciée selon la loi du lieu de la grève, soit considérée licite lorsque, d'autre part, la participation à celle-ci, appréciée selon la loi du contrat, soit considérée comme une inexécution justifiant un licenciement. Peut-être c'était cette perspective qui conduisit le Président à considérer expressément qu'il pouvait laisser de coté l'éventualité que le résultat de l'application du droit singaporien soit incompatible avec les conceptions de base du droit de grève, régnantes aux Pays-Bas.

(juin 1981)

NOTES

1. Gamillscheg, *Internationales Arbeitsrecht*, Berlin-Tübingen 1959, 4. Kapitel.
2. L'étude du matériel s'est concentrée sur la période d'après-guerre.
3. Cour de Cassation, dorénavant abrégé *HR*.
4. Koopmans, De internationaalrechtelijke aspecten van de arbeidsovereenkomst, *Mededelingen van de Nederlandse Vereniging voor Internationaal Recht*, no. 53, 1966; compte-rendu du débat, no. 54 de la même série. Au demeurant, la doctrine n'a produit que quelques commentaires isolés sur des décisions judiciaires.
5. "Etablissement" compris dans le sens de "entité indépendante du point de vue technique et organisatoire"; cf. le terme allemand *Betrieb*.
6. V. notamment la thèse récente de Strikwerda, *Semipubliekrecht in het conflictenrecht*, Alphen a/d Rijn 1978.
7. Exemple tiré du rapport de M. Koopmans, p. 25.
8. Code civil, dorénavant abrégé *BW*.
9. Un aperçu du droit du travail néerlandais en français/allemand dans *Jura Europae, Droit du Travail*, München/Paris (feuilles mobiles) no. 60.
10. *Buitengewoon Besluit Arbeidsverhoudingen* 1945 (Arrêté extraordinaire sur les relations de travail); V. *Jura Europae* (note 9), no. 60.16-75.
11. V. *Jura Europae* (note 9), no. 60.16-89.
12. Loi sur le salaire minimum; V. *Jura Europae* (note 9), no. 60.42-10.
13. *Gewestelijk Arbeidsbureau* (Bureau régional du travail).
14. A savoir: consentement mutuel, faute grave, période d'essai, employé étant directeur d'une société.
15. HR 13-5-66, *NJ* 1967.3; *Revue Critique* 1967, p. 522, note Struycken.
16. Deelen, *Rechtskeuze in het Nederlands internationaal contractenrecht*, Amsterdam 1965; d'Oliveira et al., *Partij-invloed in het internationaal privaatrecht*, Deventer 1974.
17. HR 8-6-73, *NJ* 1974.400 (*Mackay/Amexco II*).
18. Ktr 's-Gravenhage 26-10-73, incorporée dans l'arrêt publié dans *NJ* 1976.2; Rb Arnhem 9-3-78, *AK* 11.210.
19. Rb Amsterdam 7-5-57, *NJ* 1957.646, *Clunet* 1961, p. 892.
20. Rb Amsterdam 24-12-75, *AK* 9758.
21. Henriquez, *WPNR* 5533; Van Maanen, Het BBA en het internationaal privaatrecht, *WPNR* 5584/5585.
22. V. note 17.
23. *Rechtbank*, première instance pour les litiges entre un directeur et la société qu'il gère. V. *infra* no. 32.
24. Rb Rotterdam 6-11-73, incorporée dans l'arrêt publié dans *NJ* 1976.566.
25. La décision part de l'idée d'une interdépendance ferme, quant au statut du directeur, des règles du droit des sociétés et celles du droit du travail. Quelques-uns préfèrent à distinguer ces deux aspects autant que possible. V., pour le statut du directeur d'une société en droit néerlandais: *Jura Europae*, *Droit des sociétés*, München/Paris (feuilles mobiles) no. 60.10.32-39.
26. Quelques décisions en matière de saisie sur navires.
27. De Winter, Dwingend recht bij internationale overeenkomsten, *NTIR* 1964, p. 329; reproduit dans le choix d'articles *Naar een sociaal IPR*, Deventer 1979, p. 182 (résumé en français).
28. V. note 15.
29. HR 12-1-79, *NJ* 1980.526, note Schultsz; *Revue Critique* 1980, p. 68, note Van Rooij.
30. HR 30-5-80, *NJ* 1980.634, note Schultsz.
31. HR 5-6-53, *NJ* 1953.613.
32. HR 8-1-71, *NJ* 1971.129 (*Mackay/Amexco I*).
33. Une analyse de cette jurtisprudence est présentée dans: Van Maanen, Het BBA en het internationaal privaatrecht, *WPNR* 5584/5585.
34. Dans l'article cité dans la note précédente.
35. V. note 17.
36. Van Rooij, *Publiekrecht en IPR*, Alphen aan den Rijn 1976, p. 16.
37. *CdJCE* 13-11-79, no. 25/79.
38. HR 5-12-40, *NJ* 1941.312.
39. J'évite les termes *forum solutionis* et *forum executionis* parce qu'il n'importe quelle obligation sert de base à la demande.
40. *BW*, Livre 2, art. 131 et 241. Cependant, dans le cas exceptionnel où le montant de la demande soit inférieur à Fl. 3.000, le régime normal (no. 31) s'applique.
41. Van der Heijden-Van der Grinten, *Handboek voor de naamloze en besloten vennootschap*, 9e éd., Zwolle 1976, p. 471.
42. Rb Rotterdam 19-2-71, *NJ* 1972.29.

43. HR 16-1-81, NJ 1981.663, note Heemskerk.
44. HR 24-12-15, *NJ* 1916.417.
45. Cela s'ensuit de l'article 18 de la Convention de Bruxelles, qui ne contient aucune condition de "intégration du litige dans la Communauté".
46. HR 29-9-11, *W.* 9256.
47. Ktr Rotterdam 16-11-78, *Praktijkgids* 1979, p. 269, note (approuvante) Sterk. Le juge appliquait la Convention de Bruxelles et la convention germano-néerlandaise.
48. HR 27-10-50, *NJ* 1950.760.
49. V. p. ex. A. Lyon-Caen, *Droit Social* 1978, p. 201 et les références.
50. Hof 's-Gravenhage 2-5-75, *NJ* 1976.566; Rb Amsterdam 14-12-77, *NJ* 1978.426.
51. Van Maanen, Concernverhoudingen en individuele arbeidsovereenkomst, *De Naamloze Vennootschap* 1978, p. 157.
52. Arrêt précité, V. note 17. La mutabilité de la loi du contrat était reconnue déjà dans Ktr Amsterdam 18-7-66, *NJ* 1968.240.
53. Van Maanen, Intra-concern overplaatsing van werknemers, *De Naamloze Vennootschap* 1979, p. 88.
54. V. l'article cité dans la note précédente, p. 88-90.
55. Prés. Rb Amsterdam 30-11-78, *NJ* 1981.65, note Schultsz. Je passe sur l'attendu où le Président constate son pouvoir de jurisdiction.

ABBREVIATIONS

AK	Fichier du T.M.C. Asser Instituut
BBA	*Buitengewoon Besluit Arbeidsverhoudingen* 1945/Arrêté Extraordinaire sur les relations de travail (Pays-Bas)
BW	*Burgerlijk Wetboek*/Code civil (Pays-Bas)
CdJCE	Cour de Justice des Communautés Européennes
Clunet	Journal du Droit International (France)
GAB	*Gewestelijk Arbeids Bureau*/Bureau Régional du Travail (Pays-Bas)
HR	*Hoge Raad*/Cour de Cassation (Pays-Bas)
Ktr	*Kantonrechter*/Juge de canton (Pays-Bas)
NJ	*Nederlandse Jurisprudentie* (Pays-Bas)
NTIR	*Nederlands Tijdschrift voor Internationaal Recht*/Revue néerlandaise de droit international
Rb	*Rechtbank*/Tribunal de première instance (Pays-Bas)
Rev.Crit.	Revue Critique de droit international privé (France)
RO	*Wet op de Rechterlijke Organisatie*/Loi sur l'organisation judiciaire (Pays-Bas)
Rv	*Wetboek van Burgerlijke Rechtsvordering*/Code de procédure civile (Pays-Bas)
W.	*Weekblad voor het Recht* (Pays-Bas)
WPNR	*Weekblad voor Privaatrecht, Notarisambt en Registratie* (Pays-Bas)

DOCUMENTATION

Le T.M.C. Asser Instituut, Alexanderstraat 20-22, 's-Gravenhage, centre d'étude du droit international fondé par les diverses facultés de droit, prend à tâche d'instaurer une documentation sur (entre autres) le droit international privé. On y maintient un fichier de décisions judiciaires, oui ou non publiées (*AK*).
De temps en temps, le *WPNR* publie des aperçus de la jurisprudence ainsi recueillie; l'institut lui-même publie des recueils de jurisprudence couvrant plusieurs années.

Le défaut et l'opposition

TACO STERK
Professeur à l'Université de Leyde

II.C.1.

'Il plaide bel, qui plaide sans partie'.

1. INTRODUCTION

1.1 *Le questionnaire*

Dans une procédure intentée entre deux ou plusieurs parties, chaque partie peut comparaître devant le juge et défendre son point de vue dans l'affaire; elle peut également s'abstenir. Une partie peut laisser la procédure totalement in foro en ne comparaissant pas dès le début et en s'obstinant à ne pas comparaître; elle peut aussi, en ayant d'abord comparu, s'abstenir après ajournement ou suspension et comparaître de nouveau au cours du procès. En fin de compte, il est possible qu'une partie qui a comparu au procès, laisse passer un ou plusieurs actes de procédure. Cela peut avoir lieu dans toutes les procédures où les parties sont désignées comme demandeurs et défendeurs, fidéjusseurs, requêrants et parties défenderesses. Ceci peut non seulement se produire en première instance, mais également après usage des voies de recours. Cela peut même avoir lieu dans la jurisdiction gracieuse à propos des tiers qui peuvent se mêler à un proces pour la défense.
Quelles sont les conséquences d'une telle abstention quant à la continuation de la procédure?
Est-ce qu'il y a de l'influence sur l'édification, le contenu et le caractère juridique des décisions par lesquelles l'instance se termine? Est-il possible de rétablir l'abstention avant ou après le fin de l'instance et est-ce qu'on possède des voies de recours à cet égard?
Dans un rapport plus principiel il est possible de rétablir la problématique en s'efforçant de vérifier le principe de respect des droits du défendeur. Il s'agit seulement de quelques unes des questions que l'on peut émettre à propos des termes 'défaut' et 'opposition' et auxquelques divers systèmes juridiques donnent des réponses opposées.

La definition du sujet de cette conférence ne possède vraisemblablement pas une base si vaste, mais vise la technique de cette procédure dans laquelle défaut et opposition sont mentionnés comme le plus important matériel de procédure pour pouvoir faire face aux questions signalées.
Pour la procédure néerlandaise, cela signifie qu'en tout cas un procès normal introduit en général par assignation dans des affaires contentieuses et également le référé, sont inclus dans le sujet. En dehors de celui-ci, demeuront alors les procédures moins formelles comme l'arbitrage, les procédures introduites avec une requête en matière gracieuse, mais aussi, pour des raisons économique de procédure, dans un nombre croissant d'affaires contentieuses, la procédure d'injonction de payer et autres de ce genre. Néanmoins, il faudra parfois choisir au hasard dans le dernier groupe, sinon la ligne de démarcation côtoyerait de trop près une limite incidentelle établie dans la procédure néerlandaise.

1.2 *L'importance relative du sujet*

Pour se faire une idée de l'importance relative du jugement par défaut dans la pratique juridique, le tableau 1 nous indique de quelle façon se sont terminées en 1977 des affaires traitées par les tribunaux selon la procédure normale. Les affaires de famille mentionnées sur le tableau sont surtout des divorces. Les affaires terminées par les juges de paix ne sont pas comprises dans ces chiffres (e.a. créances jusqu'à fl. 1.500,- et des affaires de loyer ou de travail.

TABLEAU 1 : affaires terminées

affaires qui se sont terminées devant les tribunaux en 1977 avec:		dont des affaires de famille	générales
radiation	9.442 (20%)	3.182	6.260
jugement par défaut	19.660 (42%)	9.500	10.160
jugement contradictoire	17.616 (38%)	12.680	4.936
	46.718	25.362	21.356

Source : Enquête des tribunaux par le Ministère de la Justice 1977.

1.3 *La procédure civile*

Si, à première vue, le code semble provenir d'une procédure orale, la procédure normale est principalement une procédure

de rôle par écrit. Le caractère en est formé par l'échange de conclusions écrites sur les audiences de la mise en état. L'élément oral ne s'exprime que lorsque le juge a ordonné que les parties comparaissent personellement pour procurer des informations ou bien pour tenter une réconciliation ou un autre opération de ce genre. Il va sans dire que l'on peut plaider oralement après l'échange de conclusions : cela arrive rarement en jugement de première instance. Dans les affaires contradictoires du tableau 1, on a constaté au total 632 plaidoiries (également au sujet de ce procès *T.A.W. Sterk*, Vrijmoedige procesvoering, 1979).
Il en va autrement dans les référés en première instance où, après la convocation, l'audience se passe entièrement oralement. Etant donné la très vaste interprétation que la justice a donné à la compétence du président du tribunal en référé, cette procédure est d'une grande importance pour la pratique juridique néerlandaise. Dans les procédures introduites avec une requête, la défense a lieu en livrant une mémoire de défense au greffier, après quoi on traite en général oralement la question au cours d'une audience à huis clos.

1.4 *L'assignation*

Le procès normal est presque toujours introduit par une citation qui, à la prière du demandeur est assignée au défendeur par un huissier (art. 1 Rv). On ne réclame, comme cela avait souvent lieu dans l'ancienne justice, une autorisation du juge - après une tentative de réconciliation - précédant la convocation que pour la procédure rare de la supprimation de la communauté conjugale à la prière de l'un des époux (art. 804 et 806 Rv). Une autorisation du juge précédant la convocation pour raccourcir les termes légaux de convocation (art. 7 Rv) et cela, jusqu'à l'établissement d'une saisie conservatoire, (e.a. art. 727 Rv) est bien entendu d'un tout autre ordre. La convocation est l'acte professionel d'un huissier nommé par la Couronne (art. 14 règlement des huissiers).
Il ne le peut accomplir que dans l'arrondissement où il est nommé. L'assignation, dans le sens d'un acte d'huissier de justice par lequel le demandeur cite son adversaire à comparaître devant le juge, est entièrement traitée dans les frontières nationales. Où que ce soit dans les frontières nationales, un exploit peut être signifié au défendeur en personne par un huissier nommé sur place.
On peut également signifier au domicile aux Pays-Bas, sans tenir compte du fait que le défendeur soit présent ou non.
On peut, si c'est nécessaire, remettre une copie à un membre de la famille (art. 1 Rv.), ou alors au service principal de la direction locale (art. 2 Rv). On appelle cette assignation: un 'par le maire'. Il n'est pas certain dans ce cas que le défendeur soit mis au courant de la convocation correctement et

à l'heure. Des méthodes similaires prennent place lorsque le défendeur n'a pas de domicile, ou pas de domicile ou résidence connu aux Pays-Bas (art. 4 Rv). Dans ces cas la signification est faite au parquet. Les conséquences de ce système sont parfois atténuées par des conditions des traités internationaux (vide *infra* sub 2.A.6.).
Les dernières années on est confronté à des problèmes particuliers occasionnés par des habitants clandestins de demeures et de bâtiments (squatters). Pour éviter l'évacuation par un procès, ils conservent souvent l'anonymat. La justice subalterne accepte à ce moment une convocation par description de la personne, quelquefois, avec une photo.
Le tableau 2 nous indique la façon de l'assignation, quels chiffres se rapportent à l'arrondissement d'Utrecht, qui est assez représentatif pour les Pays-Bas.

TABLEAU 2

	signification de l'assignation			
assignation dans des affaires patrimoniales de tribunaux procurées à	dans des affaires par défaut		dans des affaires contradictoires	
le défendeur (à personne)	131	(27%)	68	(35%)
membre de la famille	155	(32%)	46	(24%)
dirigeant ou associé	22	(5%)	3	(2%)
personnel	30	(6%)	20	(10%)
maire	140	(29%)	48	(25%)
d'une autre façon	7	(1%)	7	(4%)
	485	(100%)	192	(100%)

p = .0039
sans 'd'une autre façon' p = .007
Source : Enquête des archives du tribunal d'Utrecht 1.5.70/1.5.71

2. DÉFAUT

2.A.1. *Le terme 'défaut'*

Dans la langue néerlandaise, le mot *verstek* est généralement utilisé pour 'défaut', alors que sa véritable signification est : retrait du droit de se défendre ou forclusion (*A. Beets*, R.M. 1882, p. 262-270).
La signification ancienne se rapportait donc plutôt aux conséquences contemporaines du défaut. Néanmoins, dans le code de procédure civile paru en 1838, le législateur a utilisé le mot *verstek* comme traduction du mot français 'défaut' que l'on utilise également dans la langue juridique néerlandaise.

Le terme 'défaillant', dans l'article 89 Rv, n'est pas traduit. Est-ce que le mot *verstekeling* avait déjà la signification de 'passager muet'?

2.A.2 *Pas de défaut faute de conclure*

Depuis 1838 la procedure civile néerlandaise connait seulement le défaut faute de comparaître (art. 75 et 76 Rv); le défaut faute de conclure a disparu à ce moment sans aucun règlement suppléant explicite; en dépit de l'abstention d'actes de procédure d'une partie qui a comparu une fois au procès, le procès, et aussi le jugement, demeurent contradictoires.

2.A.3 *Représentation en justice*

Sans les procédures pour les cours de justice (tribunal, cour d'appèl et cour de cassation), les parties doivent se faire représenter. Pour les tribunaux et les cours d'appèl de l'arrondissement où les cours ont leur siège, ce représentant est un avoué inscrit; devant la cour de cassation, la partie est représentée par un avocat inscrit à La Haye.
La représentation obligatoire n'existe pas aux juges de paix; les parties peuvent comparaître devant le juge de paix selon leur préférence, en personne ou bien représentées par un mandataire majeur (art. 99 Rv).
Le juge peut encore décider, en ne s'opposant pas à ce qu'un représentant de la procédure entre en scène, si les parties, en personne ou avec leur représentant au procès, devront comparaître devant lui pour fournir des informations ou pour une tentative de réconciliation (19 a et 19 Rv); les parties ont cependant le droit de plaidoyer elles-mêmes au procès; généralement, c'est leur avocat qui s'en charge. Ceci n'a rien à faire à la validité de la comparution en justice et des actes de procédure.
Dans un référé établi par assignation pour le président du tribunal, le demandeur doit comparaître par un avoué, mais s'il le désire le défendeur peut également comparaître en personne (art. 290 Rv). En général, à l'exception de ces cas particuliers cités, la comparution en justice d'une partie ne peut exister d'une manière valable quand elle ne comparaît pas elle-même à l'audience mais que c'est le représentant au procès qui comparaît.
La règle de représentation obligatoire au procès qui, à l'exemple de *Van Boneval Faure* (tôme I, pag. 118) est considérée comme l'un des sept 'Eléments principaux du droit de procédure civile', a des conséquences importantes pour la déroulement du procès, qui, pour la plus grande partie, se passe loin des yeux des profanes.
Le monopole du barreau existe encore intégralement (généralement les professions d'avocat et d'avoué sont exercées toutes

les deux par la même personne). On décèle quelques critiques chez *G.R. Rutgers*, De verplichte procesvertegenwoordiging ('La représentation obligatoire au procès'), diss. VU Amsterdam, 1979 (avec un sommaire en français).

2.A.4 *Aucune des parties ne comparaît*

Si aucune des parties ne comparaît à la première audience, après la proclamation de l'affaire, le juge radie l'affaire. On trouve les rarisons de cette radiation dans l'application analogique ou extensive de l'article 42 Règlement I par la loi R.O. Cette disposition est prise lorsque toutes les parties s'abstiennent de comparaître à une audience après un ajournement déterminée à poursuivre l'affaire. Même sans ce règlement, le juge pourrait agir de cette manière dans les deux cas; en effet, on ne lui demande pas la moindre décision, même pas d'ajourner l'affaire à une audience ultérieure. Si le juge décide de ne pas ajourner, l'affaire est également rayée.
Beaucoup plus compliquée c'est la question de prévoir les conséquences de la radiation. Si une affaire est rayée du rôle accidentellement ou par abstention (p.e. lorsqu'on oublie de renvoyer de nouveau l'affaire au rôle après avoir ordonné une enquête, à la suite de suspensions (art. 254 e.v. Rv) ou même à cause d'une radiation donnée à la prière des parties (vide *Van den Dungen/Jansen*, note 4 de l'art 135, et *Van den Dungen/Sterk*, note 3 du Livre I, titre 3, Chap. 15 sub g), une poursuite de l'instance reste toutefois possible. Dans les deux premiers cas, c'est déjà dans la nature de l'intermittance. Dans le cas de la radiation demandée par les parties on doit généralement décider quelles étaient les intensions des parties durant l'application de cette mesure administrative. Doit-il en être autrement en cas de la radiation donnée d'office par le juge, si aucune des parties n'est comparue? La cour de cassation pense que oui (*HR* 4 mars 1929, *NJ* 1929, 829, *W* 11972 note *Star Busmann*). La cour de cassation compare cette radiation au défaut congé de l'article 75 en cas de défaut du demandeur (voir sub 2.A.5). On trouve la même interprétation chez *Star Busmann/Rutten* no. 389. L'opinion est tout autre chez *Van Rossem/Cleveringa* note 2 de l'art 75 et *Van den Dungen/Jansen* note 4 de l'art. 135.
La question est surtout importante lorsque l'instance est menée par voie de recours contre un jugement et quand, par exemple à la suite d'un terme d'échéance, il ne serait pas possible d'ériger de nouveau la procédure. La ligne sévère choisie par la cour de cassation favorise certainement les garanties légales; par contre, dans l'interprétation opposée, on s'abstient d'intervenir sans en avoir été prié dans le statut du demandeur. Pour ce problème peu courant il est cependant souhaitable que le législateur fasse un choix.

2.A.5 *Le demandeur ne comparaît pas*

Si le demandeur ne comparaît pas en justice, on constate le défaut (art. 75 et 139 Rv.). En cas de pluralité des demandeurs la même chose se produit à l'égard de chaque demandeur qui n'est pas comparu indépendamment (*Van Boneval Faure* Vol II p. 223 e.s.; *Van Rossem/Cleveringa* note 3 de l'art 75; *Van den Dungen/Jansen* note 3 de l'art. 75).
On soutient que le défaut contre le demandeur doit être constaté d'office déjà le premier jour du jugement (*Van Rossem/Cleveringa* note 3 de l'art. 75; *Star Busmann/Rutten* no. 390). Même dans le cas où cette interprétation aurait du succès, cela n'empêche pas qu'il n'y a pas de sanction pour cette règle. Pourquoi n'existerait-il pas de bonnes raisons d'ajournement? Il est fort possible que l'on doive encore vérifier lorsque l'on doute de la validité de la comparution du demandeur, p.e. parceque ce n'est pas la personne adéquate qui est comparu ou bien parce que l'on met en doute le mandat du représentant au procès.
Il est également possible que l'anticipation par le défendeur, par laquelle le jour d'audience intimé par assignation a été avancé, entraîne des recherches sur la validité de l'anticipation. Finalement, il ne semble pas d'exister de raison valable pour refuser en tous cas un ajournement quand la partie adverse le demande, peut-être pour économiser les frais, justement afin de donner au demandeur la possibilité de pouvoir de nouveau comparaître au procès.
Là où pour de raisons pratiques, l'audience est remplacée par un système dans lequel la comparution de l'avoué est supplée par un avis par écrit, on utilise les mêmes règles mutatis mutandis (cour de Bois-le-Duc, le 10 juin 1980, *NJ* 1981, 84).

2.A.6 *Le défendeur ne comparaît pas*

Le plus important est bien entendu le défaut d'un défendeur. Si le défendeur ne comparaît pas à la première audience, le juge décide à la prière de demandeur, de donner défaut (art. 76 et 139 Rv); *Van Boneveal Faure* tôme II p. 229; *Van Rossem/Cleveringa* note 1 de l'art 76; donner défaut d'office est défendu par *Star Busmann/Rutten* no. 390). Le but de donner défaut contre le défendeur est la continuation du procès afin d'obtenir un jugement sur le fond. L'importance de l'action du demandeur est en premier lieu. Le principe de respect des droits du défendeur nécessite, à l'opposé, que des mesures efficaces soient prises pour permettre au défendeur de défendre ses intérêts au cours du procès.
Le législateur a trouvé cette garantie dans l'art. 76, établissant qu'il faut respecter tous les termes et toutes les formalités, ce qui signifie que l'assignation doit être rédigée d'une façon valide.

L'article 92 Rv prévoit en outre de respecter la sanction de nullité de la convocation pour pratiquement chaque disposition légale. Le point faible se trouve dans le contrôle formel basé sur l'acte d'assignation. Si l'assignation est rendue publique à cause d'une pseudo ignorance du domicile du défendeur, il est possible que cet abus échappe à l'attention du juge. Ce genre d'abuse du demandeur peut quelquefois être la cause de la rétractation du jugement par défaut à la demande du défendeur par l'intermédiaire de la voie de recours extraordinaire de requête civile (*W.L. Haardt*, Fair Play, Leiden 1958, p. 9; *HR* 2 mai 1958 *NJ* 1961, 552).
Il n'existe pas d'autres conditions requises pour donner défait. L'incompétence du juge et l'irrecevabilité de la demande n'empêchent absolument pas de donner défaut, mais peuvent poser des problèmes après. Les règles de l'art. 15 de la Convention relative à la signification et la notification à l'étranger des actes judiciaires et extra-judiciaires en matière civile ou commerciale (La Haye 15 nov. 1975) et de l'art 20 de la Convention concernant la compétence judiciaire et l'exécution des décisions judiciaires en matière civile et commerciale (Bruxelles, 27 sep. 1968) procurent des garanties plus sérieuses pour le défendeur. Quand le défendeur ne comparaît pas, les deux clauses prescrivent au juge de surseoir à statuer aussi longtemps qu'il soit évident que la signification est bien faite et que la signification a eu lieu en temps utile pour que le défendeur ait pu se défendre. Il va sans dire que ces deux clauses ne se mêlent pas directement aux règles et aux usages nationaux quant à donner défaut, mais visent seulement à donner au défendeur la possibilité de comparaître au procès avant de statuer sur le fond de l'affaire.

2.B.1 *La procédure par défaut contre le demandeur*

Le but du défaut contre le demandeur est de mettre fin à l'instance (art. 75 Rv). Au contraire le défaut contre le défendeur rend possible une décision sur le fond en dépit du fait que le défendeur ne soit pas comparu.
Le défaut contre un demandeur permet le congé du défendeur de l'instance et la condamnation du demandeur aux frais de procédure provoqués par lui. Le demandeur ne peut faire commencer la procédure de nouveau qu'après avoir payé les frais (art. 75 et 139 Rv.). *Jansen* fait à juste titre remarquer que le défaut contre le demandeur est de compréhension plus limitée que le défaut contre le défendeur (*Van den Dungen/Jansen* note 3 de l'art. 75).
Au temps du droit ancien, pendant la République (jusqu'au 19ème siècle), c'était le contraire : le défaut contre le demandeur était considéré plus sérieusement que le défaut contre le défendeur (*Merula* I, p. 459).

A l'époque, le défaut contre le demandeur signifiait que son action était définitivement abolie. On a abandonné ce système depuis la codification.

2.B.2 *La procédure par défaut contre le défendeur*

Les suites du procès par défaut contre le défendeur sont déterminées par son but : un jugement sur le fond. Aussi bien le travail d'enquête du juge (vide *infra* sub C) que des complications d'autre nature, comme par exemple l'intervention d'un tiers, peuvent empêcher que le procès se déroule dans la forme la plus simple. Le plus souvent, il n'y a vraiment pas de raison d'actes de procédure ultérieures et il est généralement possible, après avoir donné défaut et l'introduction de la demande, de statuer sur le fond après un court délai. Les règles à appliquer dans la procédure sont mutatis mutandis les mêmes à celles d'une procédure contradictoire. L'article 134 Rv fait une exception en établissant qu'en cas de défaut du défendeur, une modification ou une augmentation de la demande, les moyens y compris, n'est pas permis.

2.B.3 *Pluralité des défendeurs*

La pluralité des défendeurs ne provoque un régime différent que si ce ne sont pas tous les défendeurs qui fassent défaut. Afin d'éviter des jugements incompatibles, l'affaire sera conclue par jugement reputé contradictoire contre tous les défendeurs. Il est prescrit, comme condition complémentaire pour pouvoir poursuivre le procès, de citer en justice le défendeur non comparu de nouveau (art. 79 Rv). En pratique, l'application de cette règle exige parfois beaucoup de virtuosité de la part du juge, particulièrement lorsqu'il n'a pas été établi à temps quels défendeurs sont représentés par un avoué comparu (Confer *Van den Dungen/Jansen* note 6 de l'art 79). On évite en général cette méthode de travail assez compliquée et coûteuse, en ajournant l'affaire, après quoi le défaillant peut encore comparaître. S'il ne se présente pas, il faudra énoncer la seconde citation.

2.C. *Rôle principale du juge sur le fond*

La loi laisse une grande mesure de liberté au juge lors de son instruction, en décrivant son rôle négativement dans l'art. 76 Rv : les conclusions du demandeur seront adjugées à moins que le juge ne les trouve pas justes et fondées. La même critère est appliqué dans quelques autres cas où il est possible de s'opposer à une décision du juge : dans la procédure de requête pour les actions alimentaires (art. 828 c Rv) et dans celle pour la promulgation d'une injonction judiciaire de paiement (art. 125 p Rv).

Le fait que le juge rejette une demande qui, selon la loi ne peut pas être fondée dans les moyens de l'assignation ne fait aucun doute. Si les moyens sont suffisamment proposés, il n'est pas obligatoire pour le juge d'attendre une preuve de ses propositions de la part du demandeur. Ce point de vue a eu de sérieuses conséquences sociales; il a permis d'obtenir plus facilement des divorces tant que (jusqu'en 1970) le divorce d'un commun accord était encore interdit (confer *HR* 21 juin 1883, *W.* 4924, où l'aveu était accepté en cas de divorce).
Même dans les procédures où l'aveu n'est pas accepté comme moyen de preuve, il n'est pas nécessaire pour le juge de charger le demandeur de fournir des preuves en cas de défaut du défendeur (*HR* 26 novembre 1979, *NJ* 1980, 487).
Jusqu'où, par contre, est-il permis au juge d'ordonner des mesures de preuve et dans quel cas pourrait il rejeter la demande comme injustifiée parce qu'il trouve que les faits établis ne méritent pas de crédibilité, sont des questions qui ont souvent posé des problèmes, surtout dans la pratique. Le plus souvent, les problèmes concernent les actions d'encaissements. Le juge peut-il par exemple ordonner qu'il soit prouvé que la somme des intérêts conventionels demandés reposent réellement sur un contrat? Peut-il ordonner d'être tenu au courant ou bien vérifier si le demandeur a violé des lois d'ordre public lors de la conclusions de contrat?
La cour de cassation a donné un indice clair dans son arrêt du 17 janvier 1969, *NJ* 1969, 112; on conseille au juge de ne pas rejeter trop précipitamment les demandes et il lui est signifié que s'il doute du bien fondé de la demande, il est raisonnable de ne pas la rejeter directement mais de bien se renseigner.
En ce qui concerne l'application d'office du droit, les limites sont à peu près les mêmes que dans un procès contradictoire. Cela a de sérieuses conséquences pour la compétence. Non seulement les règles non obligatoires de compétence territoriale des tribunaux entre eux, mais également les règles de compétence d'attribution dans lesquelles est établie la compétence d'exception du juge de paix, demeurent par défaut du défendeur en dehors de l'application d'office comme dans le procès contradictoire (*HR* 19 novembre 1976, *NJ* 1977, 151). Dans ce dernier cas, cela signifie la perte d'une instance pour le défendeur.

2.D *La nature juridique du jugement par défaut*

Les différences de caractère juridique du jugement par défaut et du jugement contradictoire sont plus de signification pratique que de signification principielle. Les deux jugements sont équivalents à titre exécutoire. Les mêmes règles au sujet de la possibilité d'exécution provisoire par anticipation,

pour priver la suspension d'exécution aux voies de recours ordinaires, existent pour tous les deux. Les moyens d'exécution, même l'astreinte, sont les mêmes. On constate une grande différence au moment où un jugement passe en force de chose jugée, c.à.d. qu'aucune voie de recours ordinaire ne peut plus lui porter atteinte. On ne sait jamais d'avance quand commence le délai d'opposition contre un jugement par défaut, car celui-ci est déterminé par la notification du jugement au condamné en personne ou également par sa connaissance du jugement (vide *infra* sub B). Cela provoque en outre une différence au sujet de l'autorité de la chose jugée, de la vigueur obligatoire entre les parties, également désignée par l'adagium '*res indicata pro veritate habetur*' et seulement octroyée à des jugements passés en force de chose jugée (*D.J. Veegens*, Het gezag van gewijsde, 1972, par.9;*Star Busmann/Rutten* no. 392; *Pitlo/Hidma*, p.106-107; *HR* 8 juin 1973, *NJ* 1974, 76).
Il n'existe non plus de différence au sujet du '*ne bis in idem*'.
Il en est de même pour la force probante d'un jugement dans un autre procès. Dans ce cas, le juge est libre de juger. Mais un jugement par défaut ne renfermera que rarement des éléments qui peuvent fonder une force probante. Il ne s'agit jamais de l'administration de la preuve sous surveillance convenable de la partie adverse. La force probante des jugements par défaut est donc pratiquement nihil.

2.E *Défaut après usage des voies de recours*

Les règles concernent le défaut en général; elles trouvent également leur application en appèl, en cassation, et même lors de la révision des arrêts du *Hoge Raad*, en tierce opposition et requête civile. Même alors, le défaut contre l'appelant signifie seulement qu'il n'a pas comparu à l'instance qu'il a commencé lui-même et le défaut de son adversaire ne veut que dire que celui ne comparaît pas malgré une assignation valide. Une jurisprudence sans ménagement ne trouve pas de réponse d'une autre façon.
La question de savoir quelles sont les conséquences du défaut du plaignant est sans problème : la partie adverse est toujours congée de l'instance. En attendant le délai du recours aura été terminé, de façon que le recours soit généralement épuisé.
De même, en cas de pluralité, les problèmes sont les mêmes que lorsque tous les alliés n'ont pas utilisé le recours. La tâche du juge est plus difficile par défaut de la partie adverse. Alors la formule simple de l'article 76 Rv n'est pas imputée pour vérifier la demande ou la défense de la partie qui a fait appèl. Le juge devra en tous cas tenir compte de ce qui a été établi au cours de l'instance antérieure et vérifier si les griefs ou les moyens invoqués sont bien fondés.

2.F. *Comment éviter le défaut?*

Affirmer qu'un jugement par défaut serait un mal à éviter est un peu excessif. Il s'agit, que les droits du défendeur ne soient pas piétinés : il doit, dans des limites raisonables, obtenir une possibilité convenable de comparaître au procès de préférence pour défendre son point de vue. Les clauses des traités nommées sub. 2.A.6, concrétisent cette idée.
La manière dont les assignations peuvent être établies aux Pays-Bas, autrement qu'en la personne du défendeur, est en grande partie responsable de ce que le défendeur ne soit informé pas du tout ou pas à temps de la première audience.
Le tableau 2 en donne un aperçu éloquent. On en déduit que surtout dans les affaires par défaut, on signifiait moins au défendeur en personne mais plus par l'intermédiaire d'un membre de la famille ou du maire.
Le degré de propabilité statistique de ces chiffres n'empêche pas de ne pas encore les considérer comme inquiétants. On peut évidemment affirmer d'un point de vue principiel, qu'il est quand même curieux de constater que tant de personnes dépendent de la minutie scrupuleuse des tiers avant de recevoir leur convocation.
Celui qui est au courant de la convocation encore avant que le jugement par défaut soit prononcé et qui veut se défendre, a deux possibilités d'éviter le défaut. Tant que la décision au sujet du défaut est conservée, n'importe quelle comparution empêche que le défaut soit donné. Après le défaut, même juste le jour du jugement, le défendeur peut encore purger le défaut avant le jugement (art. 89 a Rv). Par cette purge le défaut est aboli et l'affaire est poursuivie contradictoirement. La purge n'a été introduite dans la loi qu'en 1896 pour éviter certaines formes d'abus par lesquelles le condamné peut mettre hors de jeu le demandeur originel (vide *Hartogh et Cosman*, p. 29; *Star Busmann/Rutten* no. 340).

3. OPPOSITION

3.A. *L'opposition comme voie de recours*

L'opposition contre les jugements par défaut est généralement classée dans les voies de recours ordinaires comme le pourvoir en appèl et la cassation.
On considère surtout l'effet suspensif de jugements déclarés exécutables par anticipation. L'opposition partage avec les voies de recours extraordinaires (la tierce opposition et la requête civile) l'incertitude du délai, parce que celui-ci ne commence pas à partir du jugement et que l'affaire revient devant le juge qui a statué la première fois. La plus grave conséquence de l'opposition est que, différemment des autres

voies de recours, l'affaire est pour la première fois contradictoire. Effectivement, d'une façon plus imagée qu'historiquement juste, on appelle l'opposition une 'purge differée'.
La préexistance du jugement par défaut tant qu'il n'est pas annulé par un nouveau jugement demeure la différence importante avec la purge.
Des problèmes coincidents peuvent se présenter lorsque la partie adverse se sert également d'une voie de recours contre le jugement par défaut, p.e. le pourvoir en appèl ou la cassation. Par coïncidence de pourvoir en appèl et d'opposition l'art. 335 Rv choisit pour l'appèl et la possibilité d'opposition est éliminée. Si la partie adverse fait un appèl en cassation, le choix est en principe laissé au défendeur (art. 401 b et 401 c Rv).

3.B. *Opposition sur opposition ne vaut*

L'opposition contre un jugement par défaut ne revient qu'au défendeur. S'il fait défaut comme partie opposante, le jugement par défaut reste valable. Il ne peut y avoir opposition contre un jugement où l'on confirme le jugement par défaut (art. 87 Rv). Le demandeur originaire qui n'a pas comparu à l'opposition n'a pas le droit d'opposition contre le jugement prononcé à l'opposition (*HR* 23 juin 1905, *W* 8250). Ce jugement est toujours réputé contradictoire. L'opposition contre les arrêts de la cour de cassation, prononcés par défaut en cassation, est déterminée par l'article 425 Rv, tout aussi bien en ce qui concerne les moyens que les délais.

3.C. *Pas d'opposition par le demandeur*

Le défaut du demandeur met fin au procès (vide sub 2.A.5 et 2.B.1). Il n'est pas possible d'y faire opposition; le demandeur peut recommencer l'instance tant que les délais éventuels ne sont pas expirés.

3.D. *Délais et forme de l'opposition*

L'opposition doit s'effectuer dans quinze jours après le jugement par défaut ou bien un acte fondé sur le jugement est signifié au défaillant en personne. Le terme de l'opposition démare également à moins que le défendeur présente aucun signe de sa connaissance du jugement (art. 81 Rv). Ce dernier point a souvent crée des problèmes d'interprétation et de preuve.
Le délai d'opposition contre des arrêts de cassation commence au moment de la signification, même si celle-ci n'est pas adressée au défaillant en personne (art. 425 Rv).
Pour les jugements de divorce, le délai est un mois après la signification du jugement au défaillant en personne ou deux

mois après signification d'un autre genre et l'annonce publiée dans le Journal Officiel néerlandais (art. 825 Rv).
L'opposition n'est plus possible si le jugement a été executé. Pour d'autres jugements d'état que le divorce, il existe une fiction d'exécution (art. 82 Rv). Ces deux règlements de jugements constitutifs d'état comprennent sans doute quelques risques pour ceux des défendeurs pour qui les clauses des traités nommées sub 2.A.6 ne sont pas applicables. L'opposition est effectuée par assignation de façon courante. La défense, comme elle aurait été donnée par réponse, doit être indiquée dans l'assignation (art. 83 Rv).
Au cours de la procédure de requête concernant les actions alimentaires, le délai est de huit jours et l'opposition est effectuée par requête au juge.

3.E. *Le juge compétent*

Généralement un juge du degré supérieur est saisit s'il utilise une voie de recours normale. L'opposition y fait exception. Tout comme dans les recours extraordinaires, l'affaire revient devant le même juge qui a statué le jugement par défaut. Dans le cas d'opposition, c'est une conséquence logique de l'idée que l'opposition remet en route la véritable discussion contradictoire dans l'instance d'origine terminé par défaut. Une exception notable existe lors du référé. C'est le tribunal qui s'occupe de l'opposition du jugement par défaut du président. Il semble qu'en pratique ce soit souvent le même président qui traite de l'opposition, alors comme chambre à juge unique du tribunal.

3.F. *Les conséquences de l'opposition*

L'opposition occasionne encore une discussion contradictoire. En attendant, le jugement par défaut se maintient jusqu'au moment que le jugement contradictoire, à statuer sur l'opposition, le confirme ou annule. Si le jugement a été déclaré exécutoire par anticipation, le demandeur peut le mettre à exécution nonobstant l'opposition. Les frais supplémentaires à une seule procédure contradictoire occasionnés par la procédure par défaut et par l'opposition, sont toujours mis sur le compte de l'opposant, sauf lorsque la première convocation est annulée (art. 89 Rv; *HR* 11 décembre 1970, *NJ* 1971, 112).

3.G. *Le cours du procès et le rôle du juge*

Le cours du procès dans l'opposition n'est rien d'autre qu'une suite contradictoire du procès terminé prématurement avec le jugement par défaut. Le fait que les parties soient respectivement nommées opposant et opposé et que les conclusions portent également d'autres noms, ne peut qu'induire en erreur mais *'what is in a name?'*. De même le rôle du juge ne diffère pas de celle d'un procès rendu contradictoire dès le début, mais alors l'opposition peut se limiter à une partie du jugement par défaut, de sorte que, pour le reste, le jugement soit de toute façon confirmé.

4. APPRÉCIATION D'ENSEMBLE

4.1 *Questionnaire*

Est-ce qu'il faut dans l'avenir conserver le jugement par défaut et l'opposition? Le fait qu'il soit possible d'intenter un procès même si le défendeur ne donne pas sa collaboration au procès, ne fait plus le moindre doute. Les éléments de la question si justement formulée sont en rapport étroit, parce que l'importance de la distinction entre jugements par défaut et jugements contradictoires se trouve en grande partie dans la possibilité d'opposition contre des jugements par défaut. L'assimilation des deux sortes de jugement implique l'abrogation de l'opposition et ainsi empêche, la poursuite de l'instance contradictoire. Même s'il existait une autre voie de recours, comme le pourvoir en appèl, le défendeur perdrait quand même une instance.

4.2 *Pas d'abus de l'opposition*

Pour l'abrogation pourrait plaider un abus de l'opposition, à fin de retarder le payement. Il faut en effet lutter contre les impôts superflus du juge et de la partie adverse, contre un retard inutile de l'exécution et un gaspillage des frais. La fréquence de l'usage de l'opposition n'est absolument pas inquiétante.
On a constaté, au cours de l'enquête des archives d'Utrecht (1-5-1970/1-5-1971) que parmi les 1140 procès terminés par jugement contradictoire, 34 seulement concernaient une opposition contre un jugement par défaut, dont 23 étaient des divorces.

4.3 *Nature des requêtes dans les affaires par défaut*

Il est possible de se faire une idée plus claire de la désirabilité du droit nouveau, en recherchant quelle est la nature des demandes jugés par défaut. Le nombre important des divorces par défaut est évident parce que même si les époux sont d'accord pour se séparer, une sentence du juge est pourtant nécessaire. Le tableau 3 nous montre que parmi les affaires patrimoniales par défaut on trouve relativement beaucoup d'actions d'encaissements, c.à.d. des créances conventionnelles.

TABLEAU 3 encaissements

terminés par jugement	par défaut		contradictoire	
encaissements	554	(82%)	108	(36%)
autres actions patrimoniales	121	(18%)	193	(64%)
	675	(100%)	301	(100%)

Source : enquête des archives du tribunal d'Utrecht 1.5.1970/1.5.1971

On trouve certaines indications dans le nouveau des créances. A cet égard il faut tenir compte du fait que lors de la période d'enquête, la limite de la compétence des juges de paix a été élevée de fl. 500,- à fl. 1.500,- (et après élevée à fl.3.000,- à partir du 1.1. 1978).
Cela signifie que déjà au cours de la période d'enquête, un grand nombre d'actions jusqu'à fl. 1.500,- n'ont plus été présentés aux tribunaux. Parce que les procédures par défaut sont de plus courte durée que les procédures contradictoires l'enquête des jugements sur la période d'enquête procure un chiffre relativement trop bas pour pouvoir se rendre compte des actions les moins importantes.
Néanmoins, le tableau 4 indique clairement la différence entre les affaires par défaut et les affaires contradictoires.

TABLEAU 4 niveau de la créance

créances terminées par jugement	par défaut		contradictoire	
≤ fl. 1.500,-	293	(41%)	54	(25%)
≥ fl. 1.500,- à ≤ fl. 5.000,-	295	(41%)	74	(35%)
≥ fl. 5.000,-	129	(18%)	84	(40%)
	717	(100%)	212	(100%)

Source : enquête des archives du tribunal d'Utrecht 1.5.1970/1.5.1971

Les chiffres de base du tableau 4 peuvent être groupés différemment. Nous découvrons alors que dans 54% des jugements par défaut, la créance était inférieure à fl. 2.000,- et que dans 55% des jugements contradictoires la créance était supérieure à fl. 3.000,-. Il semble en tout cas que le défaut ait le plus souvent lieu pour les actions les moins importantes.
Si nous vérifions qui sont les parties et quelles sont les actions dans les affaires patrimoniales par défaut et dans les affaires contradictoires, nous constatons d'après les chiffres des tableaux 5 et 6 que dans les affaires par défaut, le demandeur est, - dans une mesure considérablement plus grande - une personne juridique (sociétés etc. y compris), le défendeur une personne physique et l'action un encaissement.

TABLEAU 5 créances et parties dans les affaires contradictoires

	demandeurs		défendeurs	
	personnes physiques	personnes juridiques société diverse	personnes physiques	personnes juridiques société diverse
encaissements	113 (22%)	92 (18%)	168 (30%)	46 (8%)
autre créance	92 (18%)	72 (14%)	152 (27%)	35 (6%)
divers	78 (15%)	63 (13%)	129 (23%)	35 (6%)
	283 (55%)	227 (45%)	449 (80%)	116 (20%)

Source : enquête des archives du tribunal d'Utrecht 1.5.1970/1.5.1971

TABLEAU 6 créances et parties dans les affaires par défaut

	demandeurs		défendeurs	
	personnes physiques	personnes juridiques société diverse	personnes physiques	personnes juridiques société diverse
encaissements	104 (15%)	455 (67%)	553 (72%)	81 (11%)
autre créance	23 (3%)	37 (5%)	59 (8%)	3 (-)
divers	19 (3%)	45 (7%)	61 (8%)	11 (1%)
	146 (21%)	537 (79%)	673 (88%)	95 (12%)

Source : enquête des archives du tribunal d'Utrecht 1.5.1970/1.5.1971

Des informations supplémentaires pris chez un certain nombre de ces défendeurs par défaut nous ont appris que dans bien des cas en effet, il s'agissait d'encaissements commercials concernant des prix d'achat, des travaux, services ou emprûnt à de petits patrons autonomes et à des particuliers.

4.4 *Quelques conclusions*

Les résultats de ces données en chiffres et de tout ce qui est mentionné ci-dessus, nous mènent aux conclusions suivantes:

1. L'opposition n'offre pas de problèmes sérieuses pour la pratique.

2. L'aggrandissement de la possibilité de la procédure la plus simple d'injonction de paiement peut conduire à une simplification considérable, même lorsque la limite financière à cet égard ne s'élève qu'à fl. 1.500,-.
3. La nature des affaires par défaut est telle que si l'on souhaite une amélioration du statut de défendeur, il faut, dans bien des cas, le rechercher plutôt dans des procédures du genre de litiges de consommateurs, '*small claims*' (plaintes sans gravité) et leurs pareils.
4. Il est possible d'offrir plus de garantie pour que la citation en justice parvienne effectivement à atteindre l'assigné; de même, on peut encore améliorer le contrôle à ce sujet.

La responsabilité des juges

H. WINKEL
Ancien juge à la Cour d'Appel d'Amsterdam

II.C.3.

TABLE DES MATIÈRES

I. Introduction
II. Remarques préliminaires
III. La responsabilité légale des juges (les trois formes de la r.d.j. externe)
  A. Responsabilité civile
    a. Responsabilité se rapportant à l'administration du droit civil
      1. Déni de justice
      2. Partialité
      3. Négligence de préserver les pièces de la procédure
      4. Injure
    b. Responsabilité se rapportant à l'administration du droit pénal
      1. Partialité
      2. Erreur judiciaire
  B. Responsabilité pénale
    1. Divulgation du secret du délibéré
    2. Injure
  C. Responsabilité disciplinaire
    1. Le contrôle présidentiel
    2. Le contrôle du H.C.
IV. La responsabilité interne
  A. Responsabilité des juges concernant la conduite de la procédure
    a. Conditions de leur fonctionnement
      1. L'enseignement professionnel
      2. L'indépendance des juges
      3. Le rôle des parties, maîtres de la procédure
      4. L'enchaînement des recours
      5. L'intérêt de mettre fin aux procès
    b. Arguments relatifs à l'extension de la r.d.j.
      1. L'affaire-Osterman et ses répercussions

2. La responsabilité du juge-commissaire dans la faillite
3. Discussion sur la r.d.j. en 1942
4. Discussion à l'occasion de la réforme de la cassation en 1962
5. Jurisprudence d'après-guerre
6. Doctrine d'après-guerre

B. Responsabilité des juges concernant l'évolution du droit
a. Les deux causes principales déterminant les changements actuels dans la réalisation de la r.d.j. concernant l'évolution du droit
1. Dépréciation de la valeur du droit
2. Manque de homonomie
b. Phénomènes accompagnant les activités des juges concernant l'évolution du droit
1. Exploration des limites de la fonction des juges
2. Théorie fonctionnelle de droit
3. L'affluence des référés
4. Le besoin de réponses aux questions fondamentales de droit
5. L'influence de l'emploi de formules vagues par le legislateur moderne
6. L'indépendance des juges
7. Les discours d'adieu

Notes
Bibliographie
Abbréviations

Wat te veel vergeten, althans te weinig gezegd wordt, is dat de rechter bij alle 'vrijheid' zich metterdaad voelt als een dienaar niet alleen van de samenleving, maar in het bijzonder van het recht (ce qu'on oublie trop, du moins ce qu'on dit trop peu, c'est que le juge, de quelle que 'liberté' qu'il dispose, se sent effectivement non seulement un serviteur de la société, mais particulièrement du droit). A.M. Donner : Macht en gezag van de rechter, R.M. Themis 1974, p. 4).

I. INTRODUCTION

En général on peut faire une distinction entre la responsabilité externe et la responsabilité interne. La première constitue la situation dans laquelle se trouve une personne qui peut être obligée de rendre compte de ses actes à une autorité supérieure, ayant pouvoir de lui appliquer des sanctions de caractère civil pénal ou disciplinaire. La seconde se rattache à la conscience personelle, le sentiment de devoir se comporter selon certaines normes reconnues comme obligatoires pour sa conduite. Rapportant ces définitions générales à la responsabilité des juges (r.d.j.) telles que le rapporteur général l'a proposé[1], on peut conclure que la 'legal (i.e. civil, criminal and disciplinary) responsability' de la formule *Cappelletti* correspond à la responsabilité externe. La responsabilité interne renferme les deux autres formes de la classification *Cappelletti* : d'une part les 'procedural responsabilities'[2], ou bien la responsabilité concernant la conduite de la procédure, et d'autre part la '(co-)responsability for the evolution, creation and/or modernization of the law'[3], ou bien la responsabilité concernant l'évolution du droit.

II. REMARQUES PRÉLIMINAIRES

Avant d'examiner ces trois formes de la r.j.d. il est utile d'insérer quelques remarques introductives :

a. Le rapport est intitulé : la responsabilité *des juges*, et non celle du juge. L'emploi du pluriel exprime la conception que la responsabilité judiciaire n'est pas seulement individuelle, mais qu'elle est aussi collegiale[4]. Le juge unique ainsi que la collectivité des juges délibérant comme membres d'un tribunal etc. sont responsables, de leurs décisions[5].
b. Selon les instructions du Comité néerlandais concernant l'élaboration du rapport le rapporteur doit se limiter en principe à l'état actuel du sujet[6]. Cependant en l'espèce il est impossible d'observer strictement ces instructions quant à la r.d.j. interne. C'est seulement en traitant ce sujet rétrospectivement qu'une idée suffissament complète peut être obtenue.
c. En général le rapporteur n'entrera pas en détails. Un tel examen renfermerait le danger de dépasser le nombre des pages disponibles. De plus, il encourrait le risque d'une doublure avec les rapports d'autres pays dont le droit en question est plus ou moins identique avec le droit néerlandais[7].
   D'accord avec cet effort de concision la jurisprudence ne sera citée que par des résumés des décisions.
d. Le caractère du rapport implique également que les citations littérales des auteurs qui se sont occupés du sujet seront limitées. Le plus souvent les auteurs seront cités dans les notes avec la référence des passages de leurs oeuvres. Parfois une simple mention de l'auteur dans le texte suffira pour désigner la teneur de son opinion.

III. LA RESPONSABILITÉ LÉGALE DES JUGES (les trois formes de la r.d.j. externe)

Il est question de responsabilité légale des juges, si à cause de leur violation d'une loi concernant leur fonctionnement, ceux-ci sont tenus responsables du préjudice causé par eux. Habituellement cette responsabilité est l'objet d'une procédure intentée soit par la partie victime de leur faute (par ex. le déni de justice), soit par l'autorité supérieure qui est compétante de leur demander justification de leurs actes et qui peut leur appliquer une sanction en cas de justification insuffisante. Les lois sur lesquelles la r.d.j. légale est fondée peuvent être des lois civiles, pénales ou administratives[8].

A. *Responsabilité civile*

Il y a une variété de sanctions dont les juges, tenus responsables civilement, risquent l'application. Il faut distinguer les sanctions qui sont appliquées à l'occasion de l'administration du droit civile et celles appliquées à l'occasion du droit pénal. Une particularité du dernier est que c'est l'administration (le pouvoir exécutif) qui indemnise le dommage causé par les juges responsables.

a. Responsabilité se rapportant à l'administration du droit civil

1. *Déni de justice*

Selon les articles 844 e.s. du code de procédure civile il y a déni de justice si les juges refusent de répondre des requêtes ou de décider un litige pendant devant eux. Le déni de justice est constaté par deux requêtes faites aux juges en la personne du greffier. Tenu compte du rang des juges en défaut, le procès contre eux est intenté devant un tribunal ou devant une cour par la partie victime du déni de justice. Les juges reconnus coupables commettent un délit civil[9]. La sanction consiste dans la condamnation à dommages et intérêts.
Les cas de déni de justice, rapportés dans la jurisprudence sont peu nombreux[10]. Le cas le plus frappant, datant de 1929, est celui du juge de paix auquel fut présentée une requête identique à celle qu'il avait rejeté auparavant.Il se borna à faire savoir au requérant par une simple lettre qu'il se refusa de prendre connaissance de sa seconde requête par le seul motif que sa requête précédante identique avait été débouté par lui. Le H.C. auquel l'affaire fut soumise jugea qu'il s'agit de déni de justice si un juge déclare expressément ne pas vouloir prendre connaissance même si une requête identique présentée auparavant est rejetée par lui[11].

Par conséquent l'arrêt de la Cour d'Amsterdam qui avait débouté l'action de déni de justice[12] fut cassé. Le H.C. renvoya l'affaire devant cette cour pour examiner l'éventualité d'une condamnation à dommages et intérêts[13].
Dans la doctrine les ouvertures limitées du déni de justice servent comme argument pour réfuter la possibilité d'étendre la r.d.j. hors des cas prévus par la loi[14]. D'autre part il y a des auteurs[15] qui sont d'opinion que le fait que le déni de justice est limité[16], empêche d'accepter la thèse de *Ter Heide* que dans des cas politiques et idéologiques - dans lesquels il est difficile de trouver une base légale pour un jugement - le juge peut se refuser à donner une décision.

2. *Partialité*

Tandis que dans le cas de déni de justice la r.d.j. est sanctionnée par la possibilité d'une condamnation du juge à dommages et intérets, la sanction de sa partialité consiste dans sa retraite forcée (art. 29 e.s. code de procédure civile). L'initiative pour cette éloignement peut être prise soit par la partie intéressée (récusation) soit par le juge lui-même (qui peut s'excuser). Les causes de la récusation sont énumérées dans l'article 30 du code de procédure civile. Elles se rapportent à des circonstances qui peuvent compromettre l'impartialité du juge[17].

3. *Négligence de préserver les pièces de la procédure*

On peut déduire de l'article 2011 code civil[18] que les juges sont responsables des pièces de la procédure, responsabilité qui prend fin 5 ans après le jugement des procès. Ce délai est considéré comme une déchéance.
Une sanction spéciale n'est pas prévue, de sorte que la règle générale concernant le délit civil est applicable, en d'autres termes le juge en défaut est responsable aux termes de l'article 1401 code civil[19].

4. *Injure*

Le code civil contient un article concernant l'injure comme délit civil (art. 1412). Ce n'est que dans la doctrine qu'est envisagée la possibilité que le juge se rend coupable d'un injure soit dans le cours d'une interrogation orale soit dans une pièce du dossier. Le seul écrivain qui s'est occupé de cette question en reconnaît la possibilité. Il est d'avis qu'il en est question si les termes employés par le juge sont manifestement grossiers. Si un juge est d'opinion qu'une partie manque d'honnêteté, il lui faut, selon *Van Oven*[20], montrer sa désapprobation sans émotion.

b. Responsabilité se rapportant à l'administration du droit pénal.

1. *Partialité*

C'est aussi dans la procédure pénale que la négligence d'observer l'impartialité est sanctionnée. Cependant, tandis que dans la procédure civile le moyen principal de garantir l'impartialité des juges est la récusation, invoquée par la partie intéressée - l'excuse du juge jouant un rôle subordonné - le code de procédure pénale (art. 512 e.s.) présume que l'initiative sera prise en premier lieu par les juges eux-mêmes; ils peuvent s'excuser afin de ne pas courir le risque de partialité, mais ils n'y sont pas obligés. Cela n'empêche pas que la récusation est également possible.
A l'opposé du code de procédure civile le code de procédure pénale ne contient pas une énumération détaillée des cas dans lesquels ces deux moyens peuvent être invoqués. La loi se contente d'une formule générale: la présence de circonstances ou de faits par lesquels l'administration de la justice pourrait être endommagée.

2. *Erreur judiciaire*

En principe l'erreur judiciaire au civil n'entraîne pas de r.d.j. légale, pas non plus qu'une responsabilité de l'Etat. Les moyens de recours ordinaires et extraordinaires sont censés être suffisants.
Quant au droit pénal la situation est différente. Quoique là aussi des moyens de recours soient disponibles, l'Etat assume dans certains cas une responsabilité pour les erreurs judiciaires concernant des décisions qui, après une investigation encore plus approfondie se révèlent comme erronées.
Il est vrai que les juges sont responsables de ces décisions, mais il faut prendre en considération que celles-ci sont souvent prises dans des circonstances insuffisamment claires au moment de la décision. C'est pour cela qu'il serait injuste de rendre les juges responsables personnellement des conséquences nuisibles pour le prévenu (inculpé). D'autre part il est indésirable que ces personnes en souffrent les dommages, à moins que leur propre faute n'ait pas contribué substantiellement à ces décisions. C'est là l'explication du fait que l'Etat a assumé cette responsabilité limitée.
C'est une responsabilité qui est liée aux conditions spéciales de la juridiction pénale. Celle-ci n'est pas la conséquence d'un délit civil[21]. Etant donné qu'il s'agit d'une responsabilité dérivée de celle des juges, les cas dans lesquels la loi a rendu possible 'une indemnisation raisonable, basée sur l'équité' (termes de la loi) sont brièvement numérés :

1. l'affaire est terminée par un acquittement ou par une ordonnance de non-lieu de l'inculpé détenu (art. 89 code de procédure pénale)[22];
2. la révision de l'affaire a fini par un acquittement (art. 481 code de procédure pénale);
3. la détention est terminée parce que les causes ne sont plus valables, de sorte que l'inculpé est mis en liberté (art. 550 code de procédure pénale).

B. *Responsabilité pénale*

1. *Divulgation du secret du délibéré*

Par l'article 272 du code pénal est sanctionnée l'infraction à un des devoirs professionnels des juges les plus importants, celui de l'observation du secret du délibéré.
Son observation est assuré également par une sanction disciplinaire (art. 11 e.s. loi sur l'organisation judiciaire).

2. *Injure*

Il peut arriver que les juges se rendent coupables d'une des formes du délit d'injure (art. 261 code pénal).
Ainsi que dans le cas précité (I) la condamnation peut impliquer une sanction disciplinaire.

C. *Responsabilité disciplinaire*

1. *Le contrôle présidentiel*

Le président d'un tribunal (cour) est compétent d'exercer un pouvoir disciplinaire envers les membres de son corps ou envers ceux qui sont assimilés à eux[23]. Il peut leur donner un avertissement à cause de leur négligence de la dignité de leur office ou de leur devoir (occupation) officiel, soit à cause de leur infraction à certaines règles de conduite officielle (entre autres l'observation du secret du délibéré et l'exercice de certaines professions considérées inconvenables pour les juges).

2. *Le contrôle du H.C.*

Malgré leur inamovibilité les juges peuvent être suspendus temporairement dans l'exercice de leur office ou même révoqués. Laissant de côté les détails on peut mentionner comme causes principales :
1. la condamnation par un jugement irrévocable à cause d'un délit/crime;
2. la déclaration en faillite;
3. l'interdiction judiciaire;

4. commettre ou omettre des actes qui causent un préjudice considérable soit au fonctionnement de l'administration de la justice soit à la confiance en celle-ci[24].

C'est le H.C. qui est compétent de prendre connaissance de ces affaires de suspension et de révocation[25]. Le H.C. n'est pas toujours obligé de prononcer la révocation. Seulement dans les cas considérés comme les plus graves la révocation est obligatoire.

IV. LA RESPONSABILITÉ INTERNE

A. *La responsabilité des juges concernant la conduite de la procédure.*

a. Conditions de leur fonctionnement

Pour évaluer l'exécution - et leurs défauts eventuels - de la tâche primordiale des juges, celle de prendre des décisions dans les conflits qui leur sont soumis, il faut examiner successivement les conditions de leur fonctionnement optimal. L'examen de ces conditions est d'autant plus actuel parceque dans la doctrine c'est un point controversé si ces conditions sont parfaites et ne doivent pas être complétées[26]. C'est qu' un nombre d'auteurs conteste que les juges puissent se considérer exempts de critique à condition qu'ils remplissent leur tâche par la seule application de la loi[27]. Ces auteurs sont d'avis que les conditions du fonctionnement de la r.d.j. en question sont insuffisantes pour garantir une administration du droit de façon telle qu'elle est adaptée aux besoins modernes de la société. Selon eux il faut que la r.d.j. embrasse également la solution des cas non prévus par la loi même si cela impliquait une aggrevation de cette responsabilité.
Les conditions du fonctionnement actuel des juges peuvent être divisées en deux catégories, celles qui se rapportent à la personne des juges et à celles des parties participant à la procédure (I/III) et celles qui ont trait au cadre dans lequel les décisions des juges s'effectuent (IV/V).

1. *L'enseignement professionnel*

Depuis 1956 des mesures ont été prises pour le recrutement des juges : les jeunes candidats qui aspirent à une carrière comme juge reçoivent une éducation théorique et pratique[28]. A côté de cet enseignement formalisé il y a une ouverture à la carrière de juge pour les juristes d'un certain âge, disposant d'expérience juridique (par exemple comme avocat ou dans la vie industrielle.
Le *Studiecentrum Rechtspleging* (centre d'études pour la juridiction), fondé en 1960 n'est pas seulement responsable de

l'éducation théorique des juges aspirants, mais il organise également des cours pour l'instruction supplémentaire des juges de carrière[29].

2. *L'indépendance des juges*

L'importance de l'indépendance des juges est estimée tellement supérieure que même ceux qui contestent la séparation des pouvoirs dans le sens strict du mot ou ceux qui y attribuent seulement une importance relative[30], sont d'accord que l'influence de l'Etat sur les décisions des juges doit être exclue. Egalement on est d'avis que le fait que l'Etat est, sous certaines conditions, responsable des dommages qui peuvent résulter des décisions des juges, ne lui permet pas d'influencer la teneur des décisions.

3. *Le rôle des parties, maîtres de la procédure*

Il y a une relation essentielle entre la r.d.j. et l'influence des parties sur la procédure. Au civil l'initiative est à eux. Les juges ne doivent répondre qu'aux questions qui leur sont posées par les parties et leur responsabilité ne peut s'étendre hors des conclusions des parties. Au pénal la r.d.j. est déterminée par la liberté dont la partie (l'inculpé ou le détenu) dispose pour sa défense.

4. *L'enchaînement des recours*

Selon les codes de procédure civile et pénale la grande majorité des affaires soumise aux juges peut être examinée de nouveau au moins une fois par des juges d'une instance supérieure. Il est évident que cela réduit la possibilité qu'à cause d'une faute des juges les parties soient préjudiciées.

5. *L'intérêt de mettre fin aux procès*

L'objet de la procédure consiste non seulement à trancher les questions du litige qui divise les parties. Il faut aussi restaurer la paix. La réconciliation peut être compromise si les procès peuvent être prolongés indéfiniment.

b. Arguments relatifs à l'extension de la r.d.j. dans la conduite de la procédure

La tendance des arguments sus mentionnés[31] est que le fonctionnement de la procédure n'exige pas une extension de la r.d.j. Le rôle des juges tel qu'il est défini par la loi garantit suffisamment l'administration de la justice.
Cependant - ainsi que le rapporteur a déjà relevé - cette opinion n'est pas partagée par tous les auteurs et dans la

jurisprudence il y a également des décisions qui font preuve d'une opinion contraire. Evidemment il est impossible d'en donner une idée complète. Dans la suite le rapporteur se bornera à rapporter les circonstances et faits les plus importants depuis 1924[32].

1. *L'affaire-Osterman et ses répercussions*

La date 1924 est choisie parce que dans cette année il fut prononcé un arrêt[33] qui produit une discussion sur la question dans quel degré l'Etat pouvait être tenu responsable non seulement à cause de délits civils commis par des fonctionnaires exécutifs, mais aussi à cause de ceux commis par des juges. Plusieurs auteurs (notamment *Meijers, Donker, Telders* et *Wolfsbergen* ont examiné l'influence de cette affaire sur la r.d.j. Ils sont presque unanimement d'avis qu'en principe les juges ne peuvent répondre personnellement de leurs jugements prétendus erronés. Ces auteurs empruntent leurs arguments aux conditions, mentionnées plus haut, concernant le fonctionnement de la procédure.
L'essentiel du pouvoir judiciaire - ainsi leur raisonnement - est qu'il est exercé souverainement. Les conditions sous lesquelles les juges exercent leur pouvoir (notamment l'enchainement des recours) garantissent que ce pouvoir n'est pas exercé d'une manière arbitraire. Seulement dans le cas de déni de justice [34] les juges peuvent commettre un délit civil. En dehors de ce cas *Donker* reconnaît la possibilité exceptionnelle d'une r.d.j. - à savoir quand il s'agit d'une erreur essentielle commise par les juges dans une procédure d'une extrême importance.
Du reste, il est significatif que dans les rapports de *Kamphuisen* et de *Westerouen van Meeteren* publiés en 1939 par la N.J.V. sur la responsabilité des fonctionnaires de l'Etat à cause de délits civils la r.d.j. n'est pas même mentionnée.

2. *La responsabilité du juge-commissaire dans la faillite*

La fonction du juge-commissaire dans la faillite est une des activités semi-administratives des juges. A côté des activités principales des juges, celle de rendre des jugements dans les procès dont ils sont saisis[35], la r.d.j. peut jouer là aussi un rôle modeste. Dans la jurisprudence ont eu lieu deux procédures [36] [37] dans lesquelles le syndic a entamé un procès contre un juge-commissaire et contre l'Etat à cause d'un délit civil commis par le premier, consistant dans la négligence de ses devoirs de surveillance. Ni dans l'un ni dans l'autre cas[38] le syndic n'a réussi dans son action. C'est aussi dans la doctrine que la responsabilité du juge-commissaire a été discutée. *Marx* et *Polak* sont d'avis que le juge est responsable si sa surveillance s'avère insuffisante[39].

3. *Discussion sur la r.d.j. en 1942*

En 1942 une discussion sur la responsabilité de l'avocat[40] provoqua également une discussion sur la r.d.j. à laquelle prirent part *Jansma, Duynstee* (I) et *Wolfsbergen* (I). Tandis que *Jansma* et *Wolfsbergen* nièrent en principe la r.d.j., *Duynstee* défendit la thèse que le juge qui 'foule aux pieds la loi' est responsable selon l'article 1401 du code civil (voir note 19).

4. *Discussion à l'occasion de la réforme de la cassation en 1962*

A l'occasion de cette réforme une question fut posée dans la IIme Chambre des Etats-Généraux concernant les frais de la procédure de la cassation qui montra que plusieurs députés furent d'opinion que la responsabilité pour la cassation n' incombait pas aux parties de la procédure, mais aux juges ou du moins à l'Etat. Selon eux il serait opportun de faire payer les frais par l'Etat parce que la cassation est en somme dans l'intérêt général, celui de l'unité de droit (dont les juges sont responsables), et non dans l'intérêt des parties. Le Gouvernement n'a pas accepté cette opinion. Sans tenir compte - ainsi fut sa réponse - que le but de la cassation sert également l'intérêt privé par la prévention de jugements erronés, il est uniquement cet intérêt privé qui contribue à l'intérêt général.

5. *Jurisprudence d'après-guerre*

A différentes occasions la r.d.j. a été l'objet d'une procédure. Aucune procédure n'a abouti à une acceptation de la r.d.j. En 1951 un procès fut intenté aux Antilles contre le Gouvernement de Curaçao[42], basé sur un délit privé dont le Gouvernement serait responsable. C'est que la Cour de Justice aurait suspendu (révoqué) à tort un juriste de Curaçao dans sa profession d'avocat. Dans la procédure intentée par celui-ci contre le Gouvernement la Cour n'exclut pas dans son arrêt la possibilité qu'un juge puisse se rendre coupable d'abus de pouvoir outre dans le cas de déni de justice. Cependant, en l'espèce il n'y avait pas été question d'abus de pouvoir, étant donné que les circonstances de l'affaire justifiaient amplement la suspension (révocation) du demandeur dans sa profession d'avocat.
En 1971 la question de la r.d.j. fut nettement posée dans un procès intenté contre un juge de paix qui, selon la demanderesse aurait prononcé un jugement erroné dans une procédure concernant un contrat de travail[43]. Le H.C. rejeta la cassation contre l'arrêt de la Cour d'appel d'Amsterdam déboutant l'action de la demanderesse.

Le H.C. jugea qu'étant donné le nombre limité des moyens de recours un examen réitéré par un autre juge était impossible, excepté dans le cas d'une violation des principes de droit fondamentaux d'une telle importance qu'il n'y avait pas eu un traitement intègre et impartiale.
En 1978 une question analogue fut posée concernant une plainte contre la Cour suprême administrative (*Centrale Raad van Beroep*). Ici le H.C.[44] a maintenu son point de vue précédant.

6. *Doctrine d'après-guerre*

Un nombre considérable d'auteurs s'est prononcé sur la r.d.j. soit dans des articles traitant le sujet[45], soit dans des annotations concernant les arrêts dans lesquelles le H.C. donna son opinion sur la r.d.j.[46,47].
Il a paru utile au rapporteur de donner une impression de leurs opinions par un résumé de leurs éléments essentiels plutôt que par une analyse de chacune de leurs opinions.
Voici donc la récapitulation :

- Il n'y a pas d'unanimité entre eux sur l'opportunité de limiter la r.d.j.;
- Parfois il n'est pas clair si les auteurs ont en vue la r.d.j. ou bien la responsabilité de l'Etat pour les délits civils (fautes) des juges;
- Tout en reconnaissant l'importance de l'enchaînement des recours qui rend indésirable une extension de la r.d.j., quelques auteurs sont disposés à rendre les juges responsables dans des cas de fautes manifestes, notamment si les moyens de recours ne peuvent pas être invoqués (par ex. dans la jurisdiction gracieuse);
- On se doute parfois si 'la sécurité juridique (garanti de la liberté individuelle), assurée par la restriction de la r.d.j. prime l'équité développé par extension de la r.d.j.;
- Il semble opportun d'assurer les juges contre les conséquences financières de leur responsabilité.

B. *La responsabilité des juges concernant l'évolution du droit*

Evidemment il est impossible de traiter ce sujet amplement dans le cadre du rapport présent. Pour cela il faudrait au moins jeter un coup d'oeil sur presque toutes les branches du droit pour montrer les activités des juges en regard de l'évolution du droit et l'influence des idées modernes sur ces activités. Le rapporteur se bornera de faire quelques remarques d'une part sur l'origine des changements actuels dans la réalisation de la r.d.j. en question (a) et d'autre part d'attirer l'attention sur un nombre de phénomènes qui accompagnent les activités des juges concernant l'évolution du droit, notamment sous l'influence des idées modernes (b).

a. Les deux causes principales déterminant les changements actuels dans la réalisation de la r.d.j. concernant l'évolution du droit:

1. *Dépréciation de la valeur du droit*

Depuis quelques dizaines d'années des auteurs[48] ont attiré l'attention sur ce phénomène qui peut être constaté non seulement parmi les laïcs moyens qui ont perdu leur confiance dans les forces régénératrices du droit, mais aussi parmi les juristes, devenus sceptiques par les réponses inadéquates des juges aux questions compliquées pour lesquels la société attend une solution. Cette foi diminuante dans le droit s'étend aussi aux juges auxquels on reproche parfois partialité, résultat prétendu de leur recrutement exclusif des classes priviligées.

2. *Manque de homonomie*

Un des buts principaux de l'administration du droit est la recherche de l'accord entre les besoins de la société d'une part et les solutions que le droit peut offrir d'autre part. Selon plusieurs auteurs modernes[49] c'est un trait distinctif de notre temps qu'il y a un désaccord croissant entre ces deux, en d'autres termes il y a une manque de homonomie[50].
Un corollaire de ce phénomène est un déplacement des formes hétéronomes de l'élaboration du droit aux formes autonomes[51]. On exige une liberté plus grande pour le juge pour des solutions équitables dans des cas non prévus expressément ou implicitement par la loi.

b. Phénomènes accompagnant les activités des juges concernant l'évolution du droit.

Ces phénomènes n'ont pas tous le même caractère : en partie ils touchent la doctrine (1/2), en partie la procédure (3/4) et en partie la personne du juge (5, 6 et 7). De plus, certains de ces phénomènes inventorient, pour ainsi dire, un certain aspect (1, 5 et 7), tandis que d'autres (2, 3, 4 et 6) sont des réactions aux changements actuels.

1. *Exploration des limites de la fonction des juges*

En 1974 la revue *R.M. Themis* a entamé ce sujet par la publication de cinq essais[52]. Dans son résumé des autres essais *Langemeijer* fait remarquer qu'en somme il s'agit de deux questions:
1. jusqu'à quel point le juge peut-il se libérer de la loi?
2. quelle décision doit-il prendre par manque de normes légales (la question nommée 'political question')?[53]. Ainsi qu'on pouvait s'y attendre, les réponses des auteurs varient.

Se servant de termes militaires *Langemeijer* résume les réponses de deux auteurs (*Enschedé* et *Leyten*) par le terme 'Halte!' sinon 'Demi-tour !', tandis qu'il indique que les trois autres auteurs sont plus enclins à déplacer les limites.
Drion limite la fonction des juges sous un angle différent. Le rôle du juge dans la formation du droit (surtout du droit civil) ne doit pas être exagéré. En particulier quand il s'agit de questions politiques la formation du droit par le législateur est préférable. Ce sont les membres du pouvoir législatif - et non les juges - qui sont responsables de la traduction des questions politiques en termes légaux dont les juges peuvent se servir.

2. *Théorie fonctionnelle de droit*

Cette doctrine, d'origine allemande (*Esser*), a été introduite notamment par *Ter Heide*[54]. C'est une doctrine sociologique selon laquelle les décisions des juges doivent correspondre avec les besoins de la société et avec les attentes de ses membres.
La doctrine a eu un retentissement considérable[55]. Plusieurs auteurs l'ont commentée, parfois avec sympathie, parfois avec réserve[56].
Naturellement il est impossible d'analyser ici l'influence de cette doctrine. Le rapporteur se borne à relever ce qui suit: il y a eu une discussion sur l'opposition entre l'interprétation praeter legem et interprétation contra legem, souvent à l'occasion d'arrêts du H.C. qui montrent une certaine hardiesse[57]. Egalement la 'political question' a reçu l'attention[58].
Langemeijer - à la recherche d'arguments selon lesquels les juges sont qualifiés de trouver des motifs pour leurs décisions ailleurs que dans la loi - a soutenu plusieurs fois que les décisions des juges doivent être 'acceptables' pour les membres de la société[59]. L'approbation que la théorie a reçue par un grand nombre d'auteurs ne veut pas dire qu'il n'y a pas eu d'opposants. Entre eux il faut nommer *Enschedé*[60], *Van Oosten* et *Pels Rijcken*[61]. Une de leurs objections est le danger de la disparition d'un des éléments principaux du droit, celui de la sécurité du droit.

3. *L'affluence des référés*

Si l'accroissement du nombre des référés n'est plus si spectaculaires que jadis[62], en tout cas l'importance des affaires a augmenté notamment à cause du nombre des procédures contre l'Etat[63]. L'intérêt public qui est en jeu dans ces procédures rend l'accomplissement de la r.d.j. d'autant plus difficils.

4. *Le besoin de réponses aux questions fondamentales de droit*

Le principe 'stare decisis' n'est pas un principe de droit néerlandais[64]. Néanmoins les arrêts du H.C. qui tranchent des questions de principe[65] ont une valeur éminente pour l'administration du droit. Ils doivent garantir selon la parole d'un ancien président du H.C.[66] que le droit reste un 'patrimoine paisible'.
Il y a des indications que dans la crise actuelle de la r.d.j. le besoin de réponses aux questions de droit fondamentales est d'une certaine urgence[67]. Par conséquent, c'est avec raison que ce besoin est relevé ici.

5. *L'influence de l'emploi de formules vagues par le législateur moderne*

Le législateur moderne se sert souvent de formules vagues. Suivant *Wiarda*[68] il y a trois causes qui expliquent cet emploi :
1. La complexité de la société moderne;
2. L'extension de la tâche de l'Etat moderne;
3. L'intérêt décroissant pour la sécurité du droit.

Il est évident que ce phénomène aggrave la r.d.j. considérablement. D'une part il est souvent difficile pour les juges de trouver une solution motivée par manque de données légales suffisamment claires, d'autre part les juges ont une plus grande liberté et l'emploi de cette liberté les rend plus susceptibles à la critique des parties et des tiers.
Enschedé[69] indique le même phénomène en ce qui concerne le droit pénal : le nombre croissant de définitions vagues de délits rend la tâche des juges de plus en plus difficile.

6. *L'indépendance des juges*

L'indépendance des juges est intimement liée à la r.d.j.. Si l'on défend l'indépendance absolue du pouvoir judiciaire, les juges ne sont responsables qu'à eux-mêmes.
Plusieurs auteurs ont signalé les implications, sinon la contestabilité de cette opinion[70]. Selon *Ter Heide* au contraire, l'indépendance du pouvoir judiciaire ne signifie pas que les juges ne sont responsables qu'à eux-mêmes.[71]
Plus la place qu'on veut céder aux juges dans la solution de conflits en absence de textes légales formelles est grande, est-on enclin davantage à rejeter l'indépendance absolue des juges. Naturellement le rapporteur ne peut que signaler ce problème qui culmine peut-être dans le problème de la relation entre le droit et la politique[72].

7. *Les discours d'adieu*

Il y a une certaine tradition selon laquelle les présidents des corps judiciaires et les procureurs-généraux du H.C. prononcent un discours à l'occasion de leur retraite. Le plus souvent ces discours ont un caractère rétrospectif, leur sujet étant un ou plusieurs aspects de leurs expériences de magistrat. On peut considérer ces discours comme des indices de la r.d.j. pour ainsi dire dans leur qualité de magistrat ils rendent compte de leurs faits et gestes[73]. C'est ainsi que ce rapport se termine en référant à ces discours d'adieu[74] dont le premier a été publié en 1952 et le dernier en 1980. Quoique la solution des problèmes examinés dans ces discours - souvent identiques à ceux traités dans ce rapport - ne soit pas toujours la même, ce qui inspire tous les orateurs c'est leur sollicitude persistante du perfectionnement de l'administration de la justice[75].

NOTES

1. Texte de la lettre circulaire du 11 décembre 1980 du rapporteur-général, M. le professeur *Cappelletti*, adressée au comité néerlandais de l'Académie Internationale de Droit Comparé : 'the traditional and more literal meaning of the topic'.
2. C'est à dire: '(a) direction of the proceedings, (b) search for the relevant facts and/or (c) determination of the contents of the case'.
3. Désignée par le rapporteur-général comme 'political responsability': les juges comme interprètes ou créateurs du droit. Evidemment le terme 'political responsability' est employé par le rapporteur-général dans le sens de la r.d.j. pour remplir les lacunes (réelles ou supposées) de la loi et non dans le sens de prendre parti dans des questions purement politiques. Tout de même il faut reconnaître qu'il est parfois difficile de distinguer l'une de l'autre.
4. Cette responsabilité collégiale est exprimé notamment par le secret du délibéré que les juges doivent observer (art. 828 loi sur l'organisation judiciaire).
5. *Crombag* (I) p. 44: un juge se forme une opinion personelle, mais il doit la justifier envers ses collègues, de sorte que le jugement est le produit de leur collaboration.
6. Le rapporteur ne rapportera pas sur la r.d.j. ni quant à l'application du droit communautaire de la C.E.E., ni quant à l'application de la convention européenne pour la protection des droits de l'homme et des libertés fondamentales. V. sur ces sujets *Kapteyn-Ver Loren* et *Alkema*.
7. Comp. *Crombag* (I) p. 55
8. Comp. *Langemeijer* (III) p. 87.
9. *Van Boneval Faure* p.282; *Van Rossem - Cleveringa* (art. 844 e.s.).
10. Outre le cas du juge de paix, mentionné dans le texte, on peut relever: Hof Amsterdam 20.6.1916, *NJ* 1917 p. 939 (cas concernant le service intérieur des tribunaux);
Hof Arnhem 16.11.1926, *NJ* 1927, p. 1480 (si les parties sont d'accord que la demande doit être adjugée, l'opinion contraire d'un tiers, le fiso, ne peut être invoquée comme motif pour provoquer un jugement concernant cette opinion); Hof van Justitie Nederl. Antillen 15.1.1963, *NJ* 1963 p.237 (cas marginal entre le déni de justice et l'abus de droit de procédure); Centrale Raad van Beroep 20.8.1969, *AB* 1970 p. 273 (dans le droit administratif une action en déni de justice est inconnue).
11. HR 8.4.1929, *NJ* 1929 p. 874 (note PS.) = *W* 11974 (note SB).
12. Hof Amsterdam 17.11.1928, *W* 1.1922.
13. Du reste le réquérant n'eut pas de succès, la Cour d'Amsterdam étant d'avis qu'en l'espèce il n'y avait pas de motifs pour allouer un dédommagement (Hof Amsterdam 25.6.1929, *NJ* 1929 p.1132), décision qui fut confirmée par le HC (HR 21.10.1929, *NJ* 1929 p. 1681, note PS).
14. Comp. *Van Zeben*, p. 209 e.s.
15. Comp.*Crombag* (I) p. 41
16. Selon *Star Busmann* nr. 353 la procédure du déni de justice est un moyen non seulement de garantir l'indépendance du juge, mais aussi son impartialité.
17. Comp. *Van Boneval Faure* p. 150; *Van der Burg* p. 33 et *Van Veen* (II) p. 286 e.s. Ce dernier auteur remarque que la récusation est strictement personelle et ne peut se rapporter à une instance comme telle. La récusation d'un juge de paix est également possible : Rb Breda 12.1.1953, *NJ* 1954 p. 489.
18. Comp. l'art. 2276 du code civil français
19. *Pitlo - Hidma* t. p. 256. L'article 1401 du code civil correspond à l'article 1382 du code civil français. La définition classique du délit est formulée dans l'ârret du HC 31.1.1919, *NJ* 1919 p. 161.
20. *Van Oven* p. 733
21. Comp. *Stellinga* (II) p. 200; *Wolfsbergen* (I) p. 245
22. Dans des conditions analogues des dommages et intérêts peuvent être alloués selon certaines lois de caractère sémi-pénal, à savoir : la loi concernant les délits économiques (art. 31), la loi sur les étrangers (art. 41) et la loi sur l'extradition (art. 59). Comp. sur ce sujet *Melai*.
23. Art. 14 loi sur l'organisation judiciaire. Le texte de cet article a été modifié par la loi du 7.9.1972. Voir sur cette dernière loi : *Giltay Veth* (I) et *Leyten* (I).
24. Art. II e.s. loi sur l'organisation judiciaire. Egalement le texte de ces articles a été modifié et amplifié considérablement par la même loi du 7.9.1972. V. outre l'article de *Leyten* (I) cité dans la note précédente : *Boas* p. 345 e.s.

25. Le contrôle sur les membres du Conseil d'Etat est exercé d'une manière analogue. C'est dans ce cas le vice-président ou son substitut qui fait fonction de procureur-général. V. sur ce sujet *Duynstee* (II) p. 53 et note 46.
26. Comp. *Asser-Rutten* p. 216 e.s.
27. Selon *Michiels van Kessenich-Hoogendam* p. 72 les frais de la procédure doivent être portés par l'Etat si les juges ont commis une faute qui doit leur être imputée.
28. Opleidings- en vormingsbesluit RO (décret royal concernant l'éducation et la formation des juges : KB 21.12.1956 (Stb. 643). Pour les détails v. *Giltay Veth* (II) et *Leyten* (II).
29. En 1972 la NJV s'est occupée de l'enseignement juridique en général (v. la bibliographie sv. De juridische opleiding). Les délibérations ont eu comme sujet entre autres la question spécifique de l'enseignement pour le pouvoir judiciaire.
30. Comp. par ex. *Van Asch van Wijck* p. 515 es.
31. Le rapporteur s'est borné à énumérer ces arguments et s'est abstenu de les adstruire par des références à la doctrine ou à la jurisprudence. C'est que plusieurs auteurs dont les publications ont été citées dans la bibliographie - notamment *Donker, Kortmann, Marx, Meijers* et *Wolfsbergen* (I) - ont déjà fourni l'argumentation.
32. Sur la responsabilité de l'Etat sous l'ancien régime v. *Hartog*.
33. Dans l'affaire *Osterman* le HC décida qu'un organe du pouvoir exécutif peut commettre un délit civil dont l'Etat est responsable : HR 20.11.1924, *NJ* 1925 p. 89.
34. Il est important de noter que dans le code de procédure civile, à l'exclusion des autres cas de la prise à partie, seulement le déni de justice a été emprunté au code de procédure civile français.
35. Avec raison *Langemeijer* (IV) p. 89 a fait remarquer qu'aucun des cas de la r.d.j. légale se rapporte à l'activité principale des juges, celle de donner des jugements dans des conflits. Comp. *Van Veen* (II) p. 291.
36. Rb 's-Gravenhage 12.1.1939, *Advocatenblad* 1939 p. 92. Sur la responsabilité du syndic : HR 10.6.1926, *NJ* 1926 p. 1049 et HR 26.5.1933 *NJ* 1933 p. 870.
37. Rb 's-Gravenhage 11.3.1957, *AB* 1957.398, cassation rejetée contre l'arrêt de la Cour de la Haye 22.5.1958 par HR 17.4.1959, *NJ* 1961.573 = *AA* 1959/60 p. 32 es (note WFP) = *AB* 1959, p. 316 es (note *Stellinga*). V. aussi *Stellinga* (I).
38. Dans le cas de 1957/59 l'action fut entamée par le syndic, successeur de celui qui avait fraudé.
39. *Beekhuis* dans son compte-rendu de l'ouvrage de *Polak* est d'un autre avis.
40. Rb Utrecht 28.10.1942, *NJ* 1943 p. 231.
41. Kamerstukken 2079 zitting 1963/64 (délibérations des Etats-Généraux 2079 session 1963/64). V. *Veegens* par. 164.
42. Hof van Justitie Nederl. Antillen 13.11.1951, *NJ* 1952 no. 322.
43. HR 3.12.1971, *NJ* 1972 no 137 (note G.J.S.) = *AA* 1973 p. 156 es (note *P.A.Stein*) = *AB* 1972 p. 65 es (note *Stellinga*) = Tijdschrift voor Privaatrecht 14 (1) 1977 p. 164 es (*G.J. de Groot*).
44. HR 17.3.1978, *NJ* 1979 no. 204 (note MS). Ainsi que le rapporteur a déjà remarqué (note 6) il laisse de côté la question, également soulevée dans cette procédure et dans la précédente, concernant la violation prétendue de la convention européenne pour la protection des droits de l'homme et des libertés fondamentales.
45. *Blomquist, Enschede* (IV),*Kortmann, Michiels van Kessenich-Hoogendam, Peters, Stellinga* (II), *Vranken* et *Van Zeben*.
46. Annotations sur les arrêts mentionnées dans les notes 32, 37 et 38.
47. Il faut mentionner aussi les conclusions du Ministère public précédant les arrêts du HC. V. également la conclusion de avocat-général *Berger* précédant l'arrêt 24.1.1969, *NJ* 1969 no. 316 (note HD) concernant la responsabilité de l'Etat commettant un délit civil par une mesure législative.
48. V. par ex. *Ter Heide* (II) p. 32 et note 8 (résumé d'une enquête de 1966); *Langemeijer* (I et II pass.); *Leyten* (I) p. 589; *Wiarda* (I) p. 161. Quant au droit pénal V. notamment *Feber*.
49. V. notamment *Ter Heide*
50. Comp. *Langemeijer* (II) p. 804 et (VII) p. 88.
51. *Wiarda* (II) p. 80 e.s.
52. Outre les publications mentionnées dans la bibliographie de *Enschedé* (III) *Langemeijer* (VI) et *Leyten* (III), il y a les essais de *W. van Gerven* et de *J. van der Hoeven* sur les limites de la fonction du juge resp. dans le droit européen et dans le droit administratif.
53. V. note 3.

54. V. *Ter Heide* (I/IV). C'est dans sa thèse de 1965 que cet auteur a publié son premier exposé.
55. En 1976 a paru un fascicule spécial de la revue Ars Aequi, dans lequel ont été publiés, outre l'article de *Ter Heide* (I) des articles de *Bloembergen* et d'autres.
56. V. sur la publication de *Ter Heide* (II) les réactions de *Van Dunné* (I), *Van Haersolte*, *Loeff* et *Langemeijer* (II).
57. Un exemple extrême : HR 3.3.1973, *NJ* 1972 no 339 = *AA* 1972 p. 328 (cas d'une assurance contre l'incendie) qui selon les commentateurs est un exemple explicite d'une interprétation contre legem.
58. V. notamment *Leyten* (III) pass. Dans les publications la signification du terme politique n'est pas toujours la même. Parfois (par ex. *Enschedé* (I) et *Feber*) on entend par politique des questions controversielles pour lesquelles il n'y a pas encore de solution légale, parfois (par ex. *Cnoop Koopmans*) on a en vue le phénomène que les juges ont des préjugés politiques à cause de leur recrutement restreint à certaines classes priviligées.
59. Entre autres *Langemeijer* (IV) p. 92.
60. *Enschedé* (II et III)
61. V. les Mélanges qui lui sont offerts sous le titre : De hanteerbaarheid van het recht (la 'maniabilité' du droit) Deventer 1980.
62. V. les interviews avec trois présidents d'un tribunal à la veille de leur retraite : NJB 1973 p. 1377 e.s.
63. V. *Zonderland*
64. *Crombag* (I) p. 65.
65. Comp. le réquisitoire du Ministère public précédent HR 3.7.1972, *NJ* 1973 no. 78 sur l'intérêt de résoudre des questions de droit fondamentales par le HC.
66. *De Jong* p. 578
67. Comp. *Rood - de Boer* et *Van Veen*
68. *Wiarda* (II) p. 39 e.s. et p. 64 e.s.
69. *Enschedé* (III) p. 611 e.s.
70. *Van Asch van Wijck* p. 518: dans le cadre de l'Etat indivisible l'indépendance du pouvoir judiciaire n'est pas raisonnable. Comp. le rapport récent *Trema Special* 79-2.
71. *Ter Heide* (II) p. 12.
72. Comp. *Enschedé* (I). La grande majorité des auteurs repoussent une responsabilité politique des juges.
73. Un auteur récent (*W.D.H. Asser*) défend l'opportunité d'un compte-rendu annuel de la magistrature à l'exemple de celui des procureurs-généraux.
74. Voilà la liste des orateurs en ordre alphabétique : *Feber*, *Van Houten*, *De Jong*, *Langemeijer* (V), *Van Oosten*, *Van Schaick Mathon*, *Schenk*, *Stheeman*, *Thöhe* et *Wiarda* (I). Comp. *Van Dunné* (I).
75. Motivé par cette sollicitude le président actuel du HC a publié en mai 1980 une lettre ouverte dans laquelle il met en demeure le législateur à cause de sa négligence d'actualiser la législation.

ABBREVIATIONS

AB	- Administratieve Beslissingen (décisions administratives)
HC	- v. HR
HR	- Hoge Raad der Nederlanden (Haut Conseil des Pays Bas)
KB	- Koninklijk Besluit (décret royal)
NJ	- Nederlandse Jurisprudentie (jurisprudence néerlandaise)
NJB	- Nederlands Juristenblad (journal des juristes néerlandais)
NJV	- Nederlandse Juristen Vereniging (association néerlandaise des juristes)
Rb	- Rechtbank (tribunal de première instance)
Stb	- Staatsblad (journal officiel)
WPNR	- Weekblad voor Privaatrecht, Notarisambt en Registratie (hebdomadaire concernant le droit privé, le notariat et la régistration)

BIBLIOGRAPHIE

Alkema,E.A. : Studies over Europese grondrechten (Etudes sur les droits fondamentaux européens) (Deventer 1978).

Van Asch van Wijck, L.H.K.C. : De onafhankelijkheid van den rechter (L'indépendance du juge), NJB 1939, p. 515 e.s., p. 545 e.s.

Asser, W.D.H. : Rechterlijke onafhankelijkheid en politiek (l'indépendance des juges et la politique), Trema 1981 p. 51/52.
Asser-Rutten : Verbintenissenrecht (le droit des obligations), t. III (Zwolle, 5me édition 1979).
Bloembergen, E. : Het belang van de rechter als persoon (l'intérêt du juge comme personne) contribution dans le no. de Ars Aequi XVI (1967) concernant : de functionele rechtsleer (la théorie fonctionnelle de droit) p. 129/132.
Blomkwist, J.W.H. : Over onrechtmatige rechtspraak (de la jurisprudence illégitime), Ars Aequi XXI (6) = 1972, p. 281 e.s.
Boas, S. : De voorgestelde bepaling i.z. ontslag ongeschiktheid rechterlijke ambtenaren (l'article proposé concernant le congé des fonctionnaires judiciaires à cause d'incapacité, NJB 1972, p. 435 e.s.
Van Boneval Faure : Het Nederlandsch Burgelijk Procesrecht (le droit de procédure civile néerlandais), t. 1 (Leyde 1893) t. 3 (ibidem 1901).
Van den Burg, F.H. : Het rechterlijk oordeel in de administratieve rechtspraak (le jugement judiciaire dans la jurisprudence administrative, contribution au recueil: Het rechterlijk oordeel (le jugement judiciaire), Zwolle 1973, p. 31 e.s.
Cnoop Koopmans, A.J. : Rechter en politiek (le juge et la politique), NJB 1973, p. 630 e.s. V. aussi la discussion sur ce sujet : N.J.B. 1973, p. 1201 e.s.
Crombag, C.A. : Over het legitimeren van rechterlijke beslissingen (de la légitimation de décisions judiciaires), contribution au recueil : het rechterlijk oordeel (v. Van der Burg) (Crombag I).
Idem : De juridische opleiding (Crombag II)
Donker, L.A. : De consequenties van het arrest HR 20.11.1924, NJ 1924 p. 89 (les conséquences de l'arrêt...) W.P.N.R. 2951/2953.
Drion, H. : Stellingen over rechtsvorming t.g.v. het 60-jarig bestaan van de Nederlandse Jurisprudentie, verdedigd op 19 okt. 1973 (thèses sur la formation du droit, défendues le 19 oct. 1973 à l'occasion de la 60me anniversaire de la Jurisprudence Néerlandaise) NJB 1975, p. 1035 (v. aussi NJB 1973, p. 1185).
Van Dunné, J.M. : De persoon van de rechter en de rechtsvinding (la personne du juge et l'invention juridique), Trema III (1980) p. 286 e.s. (Van Dunné I)
Idem : De zgn. functionele rechtsleer en Paul Scholten (la théorie prétendue fonctionnelle théorie et PS), NJB 1971, p. 813 e.s. (Van Dunné II).
Duynstee, F.J.F.M. : Aansprakelijkheid van den advocaat (la responsabilité de l'avocat), NJB 1943, p. 218/219 (Duynstee I).
Idem : Rechterlijke onafhankelijkheid (l'indépendance judiciaire, contribution au recueil : Rechtspleging, Opstellen rond het thema rechterlijke organisatie t.g.v. het 50-jarig bestaan van de Faculteit der Rechtsgeleerdheid van de Katholieke Universiteit Nijmegen), p. 35 e.s., Deventer 1974 (Duynstee II).
Enschedé, Ch. J. : Strafrecht en politiek (le droit pénal et la politique), Deventer 1970, (Enschedé).
Idem : Rechtsvinding en rechtsvorming (l'invention juridique et la formation du droit), Delict en Delinquent 1973 p. 513 e.s. (Enschedé II).
Idem : De grenzen van de functie van de strafrechter (les limites de la fonction du juge pénal, R.M. Themis 1974, fascules 5/6 (concernant les limites de la fonction du juge), p. 605 e.s. (Enschedé III).
Idem : De constitutionele positie van de rechterlijke macht i.h.b. van het O.M. (la position constitutionelle du pouvoir judiciaire, notamment du Ministère Public), Trema III (1980) p. 82 e.s. (Enschedé IV).
Feber, G.H.A. : Over strafrechtspraak (de la juridiction pénale), NJB 1970, p. 410 e.s.
Giltay Veth, D. : Disciplinaire rechtspraak over de rechterlijke macht? (la juridiction disciplinaire sur le pouvoir judiciaire ?), NJB 1970, p. 891 e.s. (Giltay Veth I).
Idem : De rapporten Bloemarts en Witsen Elias, NJB 1970, p. 1061 e.s. et p. 1120 e.s. (Giltay Veth II).
Van Haersolte, R.A.V. : Een nieuw rechts-theoretisch klimaat (un nouveau climat de la théorie de droit), rapport Vereniging Wijsbegeerte des Rechts (1970).
Hartog, R.H. : Onrechtmatige overheidsdaden in de Republiek der Ver. Nederlanden (délits civils sous la République des Provinces Unies, Thèse Leyde 1971.
Ter Heide, J. : Iudex viator. Probleem - of systeem-denken of gesystematiseerd probleem-denken (la pensée juridique comme problème ou comme système) dans le recueil Ars Aequi 1967 (v. Bloembergen, p. 3 e.s. (Ter Heide I).
Idem : De onafhankelijkheid van de rechterlijke macht (l'indépendance du pouvoir judiciaire), Amsterdam - Brussel 1970 (Ter Heide II).
Idem : Enige opmerkingen over het juridisch onderwijs en de rechtspraak als sociale functie (quelques remarques sur l'enseignement juridique et la juridiction comme

fonction sociale), Colloquium : Taak en opleiding van de magistratuur, Tijdschrift voor Privaatrecht 10 (1972) p. 322 e.s. (Ter Heide III).
Idem : Ontwikkelingen in de rechtspleging van de laatste 20 jaar (développements de l'administration de la justice dans les derniers 20 ans, contribution au recueil : Het rechterlijk oordeel (v. Crombag) (Ter Heide IV).
Van Houten, B.W.:Pers en rechtspraak (la presse et l'administration de la justice), NJB 1974, p. 18.
Jansma, K.J. : De aansprakelijkheid van de advocaat (la responsabilité de l'avocat) NJB 1943, p. 193/195.
De Jong, F.J. : Enkele aspecten van de civiele cassatie (quelques aspects de la cassation civile) NJB 1971, p. 572 e.s.
De Juridische Opleiding : rapports de Crombag, H.F.M. (Crombag II) - Heijder, A. - Koopmans, T. - Neeleman, P., HNJV 1972 (Enseignement juridique).
Kamphuisen, P.W. : Aansprakelijkheid onrechtmatige overheidsdaad (la responsabilité du délit civil du pouvoir public), rapport Nederl. Juristen Vereniging 1939.
Kapteyn, P.J.G., - Ver Loren van Themaat, P. : Inleiding tot het recht van de Europese Gemeenschappen (Introduction au droit de la Communauté Européenne (Deventer 3me éd. 1980).
Kort Geding : interviews van drie scheidende rechtbank-presidenten (F.P.E. Bloemarts, U.W.H. Stheeman, et W. Schenk) (interviews de trois premiers présidents de tribunaux à la veille de leur retraite), NJB 1973, p. 1377 e.s.
Kortman, C.A.J.M. : De aansprakelijkheid van de staat voor schade voortvloeiend uit rechterlijke uitspraken (la responsabilité de l'état du fait de dommage a la suite de jugements judiciaires), contribution au recueil : Rechtspleging (v. Duynstee II).
Langemeyer, G.E. : Discours à l'occasion du centenaire de la Nederl. Juristen-Vereniging (sur la dépréciation du droit) NJB 1970, p. 781 e.s. (Langemeyer I).
Idem : De onafhankelijke rechter op de schopstoel (le juge indépendant sous le feu des critiques, NJB 1971, p. 801 e.s. (Langemeyer II).
Idem : De taak van de rechter (la tâche du juge) (v. Ter Heide III), Tijdschrift voor Privaatrecht 1972, p. 299 e.s. (Langemeyer III).
Idem : De verantwoordelijkheid van de rechter (la responsabilité du juge) contribution au recueil : Het rechterlijk oordeel (v. Van der Burg) p. 87 e.s. (Langemeyer IV).
Idem : Wetgever en rechter (afscheidsrede als P.G. bij de HR) (le législateur et le juge), NJB 1974, p.1. e.s. (Langemeyer V.
Idem : De jurist op de terugtocht? (le déclin du juriste ?) (v. Enschedé III), R.M. Themis 1974, p. 591 e.s. (Langemeyer VI).
Idem : De creatieve rechter (le juge créatif), NJB 1980, p. 428 e.s. (Langemeyer VII).
Leyten, J.C.M. : De rechterlijke organisatie (l'organisation judiciaire), NJB 1971, p. 509 e.s., p. 639 e.s. (Leyten I).
Idem : De opleiding van de magistratuur in Nederland (l'instruction de la magistrature aux Pays-Bas) (v. Ter Heide III), Tijdschrift voor Privaatrecht 1972, p. 355 e.s. (Leyten II).
Idem : Over civiele rechtspraak en haar grenzen (de la jurisprudence civile et de ses limites) (v. Enschedé III), R.M. Themis 1974, p. 679 e.s. (Leyten III).
Idem : Taak en positie van de rechterlijke macht (la tâche et la position du pouvoir judiciaire), rapport Nederl. Juristen Vereniging 1975 (Leyten IV).
Loeff, J.J. : De list der rechtssociologie (la ruse de la sociologie du droit), NJB 1971, p. 258 e.s.
Marx, A.J. : De taak van de rechter-commissaris in het faillissement (la tâche du juge-commissaire concernant la faillite), R.M. Themis XCIX (1938), p. 16 e.s.
Melai, A. : Het Wetboek van Strafvordering (commentaire sur le code de procédure pénal) art. 89.
Meyers, E.M. : Onrechtmatige overheidsdaad (le délit civil du gouvernement), WPNR 2883/2884.
Michiels van Kessenich - Hoogendam, L.P. : Kostenveroordeling bij rechterlijke misslagen (la condamnation aux frais de procédure en cas d'erreurs judiciaires), NJB 1978, p. 72 e.s.
Van Oosten, M.S. : Verhouding rechter - wet (la relation entre le juge et la loi) NJB 1980, p. 517 e.s.
Van Oven, J.C. : Belediging door een rechter (l'insulte par un juge), NJB 1931, p. 733 (article non signé).
Pels Rijcken, L.D. : Rechtszekerheid. Assepoester van rechtstheorieën, in : Feestbundel G.J. Scholten, Zwolle 1979 (Sécurité du droit. 'La cendrillon' des théories du droit, contribution au recueil : Mélanges G.J. Scholten) p. 309 e.s.

Peters, A.A.G. : De veranderende rol van rechter, wet en proces (le rôle changeant du juge, de la loi et du procès), Mélanges J.J.M. van der Ven, Deventer 1972, p. 143 e.s.
Pitlo-Hidma : Het Nederlands Burgerlijk Wetboek (le code civil néerlandais), Arnhem 1981, t. 4
Polak, M. : Handboek van het Nederlands Faillissementsrecht (manuel du droit de faillite), Groningen 1972, 7me édition. V. aussi le compte-rendu par C.H. Beekhuis de la 6me édition, dans R.M. Themis 1962, p. 158 e.s.
Rood, M.G. : Taak en positie van de rechterlijke macht (v. Leyten IV).
Rood- de Boer, M. : Zijn alle beginselen beslecht ? (le HC et les questions de principe), NJB 1974, p. 89 e.s.
Van Rossem - Cleveringa : Verklaring van het Nederlands Wetboek van Burgerlijke Regtsvordering (Manuel du droit de procédure civile) 4me édition 1972.
Van Schaeck Mathon, E.H.F.W. : De appel-procedure in kort-geding-zaken (l'appel des référés), R.M. Themis 1967, p. 39 e.s.
Schenk, W. : Verantwoording en vooruitzicht (compte-rendu et perspective) NJB 1974, p. 6 e.s.
Schuyt, C.J.M. : Taak en positie van de rechterlijke macht (v. Leyten IV).
Stheeman, U.W.H. : Pers en Rechtspraak (la presse et l'administration de la justice) NJB 1974, p. 17
Star Busmann - Rutten : Hoofdstukken van Burgerlijke Rechtsvordering (commentaire du code de procédure civile), Haarlem 1972 (3me édition).
Stellinga, J.R. : Aansprakelijkheid van de staat en de rechter-commissaris in een faillissement t.z. van door de curator aan de boedel toegebrachte schade (la responsabilité de l'état et du juge-commissaire dans une faillite à raison de dommages causés par le syndic), Tijdschrift voor Overheidsadministratie nr. 709 (1959), p. 204 e.s. (Stellinga I).
Idem : Grondtrekken van het Nederlands administratief recht (les principes de droit administratif), Zwolle 1973 (2me édition) (Stellinga II).
Idem : Aansprakelijkheid voor onrechtmatige daden van de rechter (la responsabilité des délits civils du juge), Militair-Rechterlijk Tijdschrift LXXI (1978), p. 577 e.s. (Stellinga III).
Telders, B.M. : De aansprakelijkheid van publiekrechtelijke lichamen en hunne organen volgens het burgerlijk recht (la responsabilité des institutions publiques et de leurs organes selon le droit civil), Mélanges E.M.Meyers, Zwolle 1935, p.613 e.s.
Thöne, C.W. : Discours d'adieu, NJB 1952, p. 559 e.s.
Trema Speciaal 79-2 : De onafhankelijke rechter (le juge indépendant), Rapport Nederl. Vereniging voor Rechtspraak (commission Saelman).
Veegens, D.J. : Cassatie in burgerlijke zaken (la cassation civile), Zwolle 1971 (2me édition).
Van Veen, Th.W.: Moet de HR beginsel-vragen beslechten? (Le HC doit-il trancher des questions de principe?), NJB 1974, p. 669 e.s. (Van Veen I).
Idem : Wraking van rechters (la récusation des juges), Delikt en Delinkwent 1972, p. 286 e.s. (Van Veen II).
Vranken, J.B.M. : Beroepsaansprakelijkheid (la responsabilité professionnelle), Advocatenblad 53 (1973), p. 364 e.s.
Wedeven, H.L. : Taak en positie van de rechterlijke macht (v. Leyten IV).
Westerouen van Meeteren, F.M. : Aansprakelijkheid onrechtmatige overheidsdaad (le délit civil du pouvoir public), rapport Nederl. Juristen Vereniging 1939.
Wiarda, G.J. : Rechtsregels als houvast voor rechtspraak (les règles de droit comme appui de l'administration de la justice), NJB 1977, p.161 e.s. (Wiarda I).
Idem : Drie typen van rechtsvinding (trois types d'invention juridique), Zwolle 1980, 2me édition (Wiarda II).
Wolfsbergen, A. : Rechters aansprakelijkheid (la responsabilité du juge), NJB 1943, p. 243 e.s. (Wolfsbergen I).
Idem : Onrechtmatige daad (le délit civil), Leiden 1946 (Wolfsbergen II).
Van Zeben, C.J. : Onrechtmatige daad van de rechter (le délit civil du juge), Mélanges S.N. van Opstall, Zwolle 1972, p. 201 e.s.

Législation agricole des Pays-Bas

G. HEIDA
Professeur à l'Université de l'Agriculture, Wageningen

II.D.1.

INTRODUCTION

Bien que la population active agricole ait sensiblement diminué au lendemain de la deuxième Guerre mondiale, - en 1950 elle représentait quelque 17% de la population active globale des Pays Bas -, l'agriculture procure toujours du travail directement à 5 à 6% et indirectement à 13 à 14% de la population active globale des Pays-Bas.

La part de l'agriculture dans les exportations est d'environ 25%. La contribution nette de l'agriculture à la balance des paiements couvre à peu près 15% du total des importations. En 1978, l'excédent des exportations agricoles était de 8,3 milliards de florins: les exportations représentaient 26,5 milliards de florins, alors que les importations n'atteignaient que 18,2 milliards de florins. Par ailleurs, l'agriculture joue un rôle important dans de la gestion des terres en dehors des zones urbaines : 70% de ces terres sont des terres agricoles et 8% de celles-ci sont boisées.
Dès lors, il va de soi que l'agriculture demeure un secteur primordial pour l'emploi, l'économie nationale, la gestion des espaces verts et pour l'alimentation.
En outre, l'agriculture propre revêt une importance certaine pour l'approvisionnement en temps de guerre - régi par une loi spécifique, la *Noodwet Voedselvoorziening* (loi d'urgence sur l'alimentation) et la *Bodemproduktiewet* (loi sur les productions du sol), datant de 1939 - et en cas de calamités diverses. C'est là un facteur particulièrement important pour un petit pays à forte densité de population comme les Pays-Bas.
Dans le courant du 19e siècle, l'agriculture a connu de sérieux problèmes sociaux et économiques, notamment à la suite du développement industriel. Les régions rurales étaient menacées de paupérisation, situation encore aggravée par le fait que les importations de céréales résultant de la valorisation de l'Amérique du Nord perturbèrent les rapports sur le marché

intérieur. Les pouvoirs publics se virent contraints de promulguer des mesures légales draconiennes, qui - à l'origine - étaient axées principalement sur la formation, l'information et la recherche. Il importait avant tout de renforcer le pouvoir concurrentiel de l'agriculture, mais aussi d'améliorer la lutte contre les maladies des animaux et des végétaux et de promouvoir la qualité des produits agricoles. Cependant, ces mesures se révélèrent insuffisantes. Dans le courant du siècle présent - en particulier dans les années trente - les pouvoirs publics se virent obligés d'intervenir sur le marché en prenant des mesures au niveau des prix des produits agricoles et du volume de la production.
Un des problèmes majeurs auxquels l'agriculture était confrontée dans notre pays fort peuplé était la pénurie relative des terres, qui plaçait le fermier dans une position de négociation faible. Cette situation a donné lieu à des interventions visant à modifier la proportion des terres affermées. Actuellement, 40% des terres agricoles sont louées et 60% sont exploitées par le propriétaire, alors qu'en 1960, le pourcentage des terres affermées était encore de 54,4%. Il se produit donc un glissement au détriment de la superficie affermée. Apparemment la protection très étendue du fermier rend l'affermage moins attrayant pour les spéculateurs.
Un autre problème tient à la situation en matière de lotissements et à la taille des entreprises. En 1978, les 134.377 exploitations comptant plus d'une hectare de terres cultivées se répartissaient comme suit :

de 1 à 5 ha.	32.473
de 5 à 10 ha.	27.970
de 10 à 20 ha.	39.887
de 20 à 30 ha.	18.931
de 30 à 50 ha.	11.513
plus de 50 ha.	3.603

Selon les régions agricoles, la moyenne du nombre de lots par exploitation variait, en 1979, de 7 au maximum dans le Limbourg (région des "loess") et 5,3 dans les *Veenkoloniën* (exploitations des tourbières), à 1,6 dans les IJsselmeerpolders et 1,4 dans certaines régions de la Hollande méridionale.

Les pouvoirs publics n'ont pas hésité à prendre des mesures radicales en vue d'améliorer les structures agricoles, les unes prévoyant des aides financières, les autres ayant un caractère plus ou moins contraignant.

Afin de dissiper une impression qui risquerait d'être défavorable à cet égard, il convient de souligner que les entreprises ont elles-mêmes pris l'initiative, en créant des organisations

et des coopératives agricoles. Ces dernières ont connu un essor considérable. Ainsi, pour ne donner qu'un seul exemple, leurs registres généalogiques du cheptel bovin avaient - et ont toujours - une grande renommée internationale.
Par ailleurs, il y a lieu de relever le développement de la Communauté économique européenne. Le cadre tracé par la politique agricole commune, élaborée par la Communauté, impose des limites de plus en plus strictes à la politique nationale. Il ne me paraît pas utile de m'étendre sur la politique agricole européenne dans le cadre du présent exposé. Cependant, pour une bonne compréhension de la politique nationale, il est indispensable d'avoir des notions de la politique de la C.E.E. Ainsi, la politique du marché et des prix, qui relève essentiellement de la C.E.E. ne sera commentée qu'accessoirement dans la suite de cet exposé. Dans cette optique, nous ne parlerons pas de la loi relative à la production, aux débouchés et aux prix agricoles (*Landbouwwet betreffende de voortbrenging, de afzet en de prijsvorming van landbouwprodukten*). Même si la politique nationale revêt une importance vitale pour l'agriculture, elle présente dans ce domaine un caractère essentiellement exécutif. La politique du marché et des prix devrait éventuellement faire l'objet d'un exposé sur l'ensemble de la C.E.E. Il nous reste à relever une dernière délimitation du terrain. On peut en effet se demander ce qu'il y a lieu d'entendre par "agriculture". Ainsi, la question se pose de savoir s'il faut, oui ou non, traiter d'une loi qui, tout en revêtant une signification particulière pour les agriculteurs, s'applique aussi aux autres catégories professionnelles.
Pour éviter des développements théoriques au sujet de la délimitation, j'ai opté pour une approche pratique. J'essaierai donc de relever les dispositions légales qui ont une signification spéciale pour l'agriculture, soit parce que la loi s'adresse spécifiquement au secteur agricole, soit parce que sa mise en oeuvre comporte la possibilité de prévoir des modalités spécifiques.

Quelle que soit, pour l'agriculture, l'importance de la *Algemene ouderdomswet*, qui a instauré une pension de retraite pour tous les résidents néerlandais, sa portée générale l'exclut du champ de cet exposé. La *Veiligheidswet* (loi sur la sécurité du travail), par contre, qui est à la base de l'arrêté sur la sécurité dans l'agriculture, entre en principe dans le cadre du sujet qui nous préoccupe. Il faudra d'ailleurs empêcher que les arbres ne cachent la forêt, ce qui serait le résultat d'une énumération exhaustive des mesures légales. Un accent rélatif sera mis sur les mesures qui présentent le plus d'intérêt pour les juristes, bien que ce ne soit pas une donnée objective non plus. En conclusion de cette introduction, il peut être utile d'indiquer l'importance des différents secteurs de l'agriculture. En 1978, la superficie totale des terres agricoles, à l'exception des surfaces boisées, était affectée à raison de 34% aux cultures agricoles proprement dites, tandis que les prairies occupaient 60% de la superficie et l'horticulture 6%. La superficie arable était de 698.500 ha. au total. Par 1000 ha., les principaux produits se répartissaient comme suit : blé 121, orge 71, pommes de terre 162, betteraves sucrières 131 et maïs vert 118. L'élevage rapporte quelque 68% de la valeur brute de la production agricole totale des Pays-Bas. La superficie des herbages était de ± 1.240.000 ha. et, toujours en 1978, le nombre moyen de vaches laitières et nourriels atteignait presque 184 par ha. La production porcine est d'environ 15 millions de bêtes par an. La production annuelle d'oeufs est de quelque 7500 millions par an, tandis que la production de volailles représente environ 480.152 tonnes de poids brut par an. La superficie affectée à l'horticulture est de 112.000 ha., dont 8.185 ha. de cultures sous verre. La part de l'horticulture dans la valeur brute de la production agricole globale est de 22% environ. Relevons ici que la production agricole des Pays-Bas est, dans son ensemble, fournie par des exploitations familiales. S'il est vrai qu'un nombre croissant d'entreprises est exploité sous l'une ou l'autre forme juridique, telles l'association (*maatschap*) ou la société 'fermée' à responsabilité limitée, il s'agit généralement de formes de coopération dans lesquelles les actionnaires sont personnellement intéressés à l'entreprise. Il existe également des formes de coopération entre parents. En 1978, il y avait au total 1353 sociétés 'fermées', dont 989 dans le secteur horticole. Il existe en outre un grand nombre de formes de coopération partielle, par exemple l'utilisation en commun de machines et l'aide mutuelle.

II. ENSEIGNEMENT, INFORMATION ET RECHERCHE

Depuis les années quatre-vingts du siècle dernier, l'Etat stimule la fréquentation de l'enseignement agricole, il assure par le truchement d'un service spécial, l'information des agriculteurs et des horticulteurs, tandis que des instituts créés par l'Etat se livrent sur une grande échelle à des recherches en vue d'améliorer l'agriculture. Le pays est couvert par un réseau très dense d'écoles primaires, moyennes et supérieures d'enseignement agricole : 133 écoles primaires, avec un cycle d'études de quatre ans, comptant quelque 30.000 élèves; 50 écoles moyennes comptant quelque 11.000 élèves et 11 écoles supérieures, comptant environ 4.300 étudiants. A cet égard, on peut faire la distinction entre les écoles d'enseignement agricole, les écoles d'enseignement horticole et les écoles de technologie alimentaire. L'école supérieure d'agronomie de Wageningen constitue le sommet universitaire de la pyramide d'enseignement. Elle compte environ 5.300 étudiants. Toutes ces écoles sont financées par le ministère de l'Agriculture. Quant à la recherche, qui se développe indépendamment de l'enseignement sans toutefois pouvoir en être entièrement dissociée, elle est assurée notamment par une trentaine d'instituts créés et financés par l'Etat, dont la plupart sont établis à Wageningen. D'autres institutions et organisations font de la recherche, entre autres la *Organisatie voor toegepast natuurwetenschappelijk onderzoek* (organisation pour la recherche appliquée en physique), la *Landbouwhogeschool* (école supérieure d'agronomie et la faculté vétérinaire de l'Université d'Utrecht. La recherche couvre en fait l'agriculture sous tous ses aspects : les techniques culturales, l'amélioration des cultures, les méthodes de travail et la mécanisation, l'économie, la conservation des produits agricoles, la lutte contre les maladies des animaux et des végétaux, etc. L'information agricole, enfin, est assurée par le *Dienst bedrijfsontwikkeling* (service de développement agricole) du Ministère de l'agriculture. Pour réaliser sa mission, ce service dispose de 38 conseillers agricoles régionaux et un total de 1100 collaborateurs. A cet égard, relevons également les services d'information des organisations agricoles. Ces services emploient 215 personnes au total. Ils sont chargés en particulier de l'information économique et sociale. Ces services sont subventionnés par l'Etat, une partie des frais étant remboursés au gouvernement néerlandais par la Commission européenne.

III. LÉGISLATION RELATIVE A LA QUALITE DES PRODUITS

Très tôt déjà, l'Etat s'est préoccupé de la qualité des produits agricoles. Il est évident que son action dans ce domaine s'est faite en étroite concertation avec les associations agricoles, qui assurent même certaines tâches en toute indépendance. Relevons que si l'affiliation à ces organisations est obligatoire, cette obligation a été déclarée nulle par un arrêt récent de la Cour de Justice de la C.E.E. Parmi les mesures tendant à garantir la qualité des produits agricoles, il faut citer en premier lieu la *Landbouwkwaliteitswet*, suivie de près, en ordre d'importance, par la *Landbouwuitvoerwet* (exportations agricoles) de 1938, et la *Zaaizaad- en Plantgoedwet* (semences et plants). Reproduire le contenu de ces lois nous mènerait trop loin. Cependant, pour en donner une idée générale, nous donnerons brièvement quelques caractéristiques de la *Zaaizaad- en Plantgoedwet*. La loi actuelle date du 6 octobre 1966; elle règle le droit des obtenteurs de même que le commerce des semences et plants utilisés dans l'agriculture et l'horticulture. La loi protège l'obtenteur d'une nouvelle variété par l'octroi d'un droit d'obtention. Ce droit est attribué par un conseil ad hoc, le *Raad voor het Kwekers-*

recht. L'une des conditions pour obtenir le droit d'obtention, est que la variété obtenue se différencie suffisamment d'autres variétés. Le détenteur d'un certificat d'obtention a le droit exclusif de commercialiser le végétal protépé. Il est cependant tenu d'accorder les licences nécessaires pour permettre l'approvisionnement du marché en matériel de reproduction à des conditions raisonnables. La licence doit être délivrée moyennant une rétribution équitable. Toutes les variétés doivent être inscrites dans un catalogue. Le matériel de reproduction ne peut être commercialisé que sous la dénomination enregistrée. En vertu de cette loi, des dispositions peuvent être prises en rapport avec : la santé, la pureté et la qualité du matériel de reproduction, la classification, l'emballage etc., et également en ce qui concerne les documents administratifs.
L'exécution de la loi est confiée dans une large mesure à trois services de contrôle : le *Nederlandse algemene keuringsdienst* (contrôle général), le *Nederlandse algemene keuringsdienst voor groentezaden* (culture légumière) et son homologue pour les *boomkwekerij-gewassen* (arboriculture). Ces services sont des institutions de droit privé placées sous la tutelle des pouvoirs publics. Sauf stipulation explicite, les dispositions élaborées ne peuvent être contraires aux directives et règlements établis par la Communauté économique européenne. Toute infraction à la loi constitue un délit économique.
La *Landbouwkwaliteitswet* (loi générale sur la qualité des produits agricoles) précitée prévoit un système similaire en ce qui concerne le contrôle des produits. Ainsi, le commerce du beurre et du fromage est contrôlé par deux 'stations' d'expertise ad hoc, la *Botercontrolestation* (beurre) et la *Kaascontrolestation* (fromage).
Bien qu'elle occupe une place particulière, on peut également citer, dans ce contexte, la *Paardenwet*, qui tend à maintenir et améliorer la qualité du cheptel chevalin, en particulier la race des étalons reproducteurs. L'une des caractéristiques de cette législation est que l'exécution est confiée pour une large part aux *Stamboekverenigingen* (associations qui établissent les registres généalogiques, qui assurent notamment les expertises prescrites. Les associations en question doivent être agréées par les pouvoirs publics. En 1959, le *Landbouwschap* (fédération des professions agricoles) a édicté une réglementation complémentaire, prescrivant notamment que le propriétaire ou le détenteur d'un étalon reproducteur doit être en possession d'une licence.

IV. LUTTE CONTRE LES MALADIES ET LES FLEAUX

Outre la qualité, il importe de garantir la santé des végétaux et des animaux. A cet égard, il convient de citer en premier lieu la *Plantenziektenwet* (loi sur les épiphyties) et, pour

être complet, la *Bloembollenziektewet* (maladies affectant les bulbes). La première, comme son nom l'indique, tend à prévenir les maladies des plantes et à combattre les organismes nuisibles à l'agriculture. Ces mesures concernent notamment la lutte contre des fléaux comme le rat musqué, le doryphore, la mouche de la cerise ou celle de l'asperge. Une place très importante est accordée à la lutte contre la nématode de la pomme de terre. En vertu de cette loi, une certaine alternance de cultures peut être imposée. Il est même possible d'interdire une certaine culture dans une région déterminée. Dans certaines conditions, la destruction de plants peut être ordonnée. Dans ce dernier cas, une indemnisation peut être accordée.
Le contrôle est axé en partie sur les importations et les exportations. Des prescriptions peuvent régler ou limiter l'importation ou la culture de parasites d'organismes nuisibles. L'application de la loi est contrôlée par le *Plantenziektekundige dienst* (service phytosanitaire) qui est un organisme de l'Etat. Les travaux nécessaires, par exemple les expertises préalables à l'importation ou à l'exportation, sont portés en compte aux intéressés.
Comme c'est le cas dans divers domaines de l'agriculture, l'emprise de la C.E.E. se fait également sentir dans celui de la lutte contre les maladies des végétaux. A titre d'exemple, il suffit de signaler la directive du 8 décembre 1969 relative à la lutte contre la nématode de la pomme de terre.
Quant à la lutte contre les épizooties, elle est réglée dans une importante mesure par la *Veewet* (loi sur le bétail). Cette loi a notamment institué le *Veeartsenijkundige dienst* (service de médecine vétérinaire) qui est chargé du contrôle. Cette loi donne au ministre le pouvoir d'interdire ou de soumettre à certaines conditions l'importation et le transit d'animaux ou de produits animaux susceptibles de porter des virus. Le bourgmestre de la commune peut, lui aussi, et sur avis du service de médecine vétérinaire, prendre diverses mesures en vue de combattre une maladie contagieuse. Le cas échéant, le ministre peut intervenir.
Les mesures peuvent aller de l'isolement du bétail contaminé à l'abattage des bêtes malades. En cas d'abattage de bétail malade ou suspect, l'éleveur est indemnisé. Des mesures peuvent également être prises en ce qui concerne le transport du bétail et l'organisation de marchés et expositions, en vue de prévenir la propagation de maladies.

La promotion de la santé des animaux est en partie assurée par les associations agricoles. C'est notamment le cas de la lutte contre certaines maladies, qui est réglée par ordonnance du *Landbouwschap* (fédération agricole). Citons à titre d'exemple la lutte contre la brucellose. Dans le même contexte, il convient de citer les services vétérinaires régionaux.

Ces services, au sein desquels les pouvoirs publics collaborent avec les associations professionnelles, jouent un rôle important pour la protection de la santé des animaux.

Sur le plan législatif, relevons encore la *Vleeskeuringswet* (loi sur l'expertise vétérinaire) et la *Destructiewet*. La première règle l'inspection des viandes et des produits dérivés nuisibles à la santé publique. La deuxième règle la transformation de produits animaux impropres en produits utiles.

V. LA CHASSE

La réglementation de la chasse relève depuis toujours de la législation agricole. La loi sur la chasse (*Jachtwet*) tend à protéger d'une part l'agriculture contre les dommages provoqués par le gibier, d'autre part à protéger certaines espèces de gibier. Enfin, elle est également conçue dans l'intérêt de ceux qui pratiquent la chasse comme forme de récréation active. Il importe de concilier ces trois intérêts.
Cette loi règle notamment le droit de chasse du propriétaire sur ses terres, la délégation du droit de chasse à des tiers, la délivrance de permis de chasse (sans lesquels on ne peut chasser), l'ouverture de la chasse sur certains animaux pendant une période déterminée, l'interdiction de chasser dans certaines conditions (par exemple lorsque le gibier laisse des traces dans la neige), l'étendue minimale d'un terrain de chasse, le lâcher de gibier nuisible, la prévention de dommages provoqués par le gibier, la réparation de ces dommages par le titulaire du droit de chasse, la lutte contre le braconnage, etc. Il convient de citer en même temps la *Vogelwet*, loi qui organise la protection des oiseaux, et en particulier des oiseaux appartenant à une des espèces sauvages d'Europe. Il en résulte que les animaux de basse-cour ne comptent pas parmi les oiseaux protégés. Aux Pays-Bas, les poules ne parviennent pas à subsiter dans la nature. Sont entre autres exclus des oiseaux protégés, ceux qui sont classés parmi le gibier nuisible dans la loi sur la chasse. Cette loi tend également à concilier l'intérêt de la protection des espèces menacées et l'intérêt de la protection de l'agriculture contre les ravages provoqués par les oiseaux.
Au termes de cette loi, il est interdit de capturer, de détenir, de transporter ou de tuer des oiseaux protégés. Il est également interdit de ramasser des oeufs. Toutefois, lorsque les oiseaux provoquent des dommages ou deviennent une nuisance, l'autorisation de les capturer ou de les tuer, ou de déranger leurs couvées, peut être donnée. Pour le reste, la loi prévoit certaines exceptions, comme le ramassage des oeufs de vanneau pendant une période donnée.

VI. LOI SUR LES PESTICIDES ET LES PRODUITS PHYTOPHARMACEUTIQUES (*BESTRIJDINGSMIDDELENWET*)

De même que la loi sur la chasse et la loi sur la protection des oiseaux, la loi sur les pesticides relève à la fois de l'agriculture et de la protection de l'environnement.

Cette loi poursuit deux objectifs. En premier lieu, elle vise à garantir la conformité des pesticides. Ensuite, elle tend à assurer la protection des hommes et des animaux contre les effets dommageables pouvant résulter de l'utilisation de certaines substances. C'est ainsi que les insecticides doivent faire l'objet d'une autorisation avant de pouvoir être mis dans le commerce ou utilisés. La loi fixe également des critères quant à l'emballage, l'indication de la toxicité, l'enregistrement et la conservation du produit.

La mise en oeuvre de la loi est assurée conjointement par la ministère de l'Agriculture et celui de la Santé publique et de l'Environnement. Les pesticides et produits phytopharmaceutiques ne peuvent être délivrés qu'aux personnes agréées ou qualifiées ayant 16 ans au moins.
Quant à ses objectifs, la loi sur les antibiotiques présente une certaine ressemblance, lointaine il est vrai, avec la loi sur les produits phytopharmaceutiques. Dans l'intérêt de la santé des hommes et des animaux, cette loi apporte des restrictions au commerce des antibiotiques destinés à être utilisés chez les animaux. L'usage incontrôlé d'antibiotiques chez les animaux comporte le risque que la population absorbe trop d'antibiotiques à la suite de la consommation de viande de boucherie ou de produits animaux, de sorte qu'en cas de maladie le traitement au moyen d'antibiotiques risque de n'avoir aucun effet, ou de n'avoir qu'un effet insuffisant.
Dans la même ligne, l'administration incontrôlée de produits vétérinaires est limitée parce que, aux termes de la loi sur l'exercice de l'art vétérinaire, seuls les médecins vétérinaires sont autorisés à pratiquer cet art. L'éleveur lui-même ne peut avoir en sa possession ni sérums, ni vaccins, ni moyens permettant d'établir un diagnostic.

VII. LOI SUR LE BAIL À FERME (*PACHTWET*)

En abordant ici la loi sur le bail à ferme, nous apportons une césure profonde dans les sujets à traiter. Si toutes les lois citées plus haut relevaient du domaine du droit administratif, la loi sur le bail à ferme règle en premier lieu les rapports de droit privé entre le propriétaire et l'usager de la terre. En fait, cette loi règle une partie du droit des obligations. Cependant, elle est destinée avant tout à assurer la protection du fermier, ce qui lui confère un caractère éminemment social. En raison de cet objectif, la loi contient presque exclusivement des dispositions de droit impératif. Pour les praticiens du droit agraire, la loi sur le bail à ferme constitue indiscutablement le noyau dur du droit. Son importance du point de vue économique et l'intérêt qu'elle présente du point de vue législatif sont tout aussi indéniables. L'affermage n'est pas une espèce de location en général. La bail à ferme est régi par une loi spécifique. Par bail à ferme, on entend la convention par laquelle une partie s'engage à donner en usage à l'autre partie, moyennant paiement une ferme ou une terre pour y pratiquer l'agriculture. S'il n'est pas nécessaire, pour qu'il y ait bail à ferme, que l'agriculture soit pratiquée à titre d'exploitation, il faut cependant qu'elle ait un but économique. Aussi la loi sur le bail à ferme est-elle applicable aux droits de jouissance réels dont la durée ne dépasse pas vingt-cinq ans.

La bail doit faire l'objet d'une convention écrite, bien qu'une convention orale ne soit pas nécessairement nulle en soi. Les parties contractantes doivent soumettre la convention à l'approbation de la *Grondkamer* (chambre foncière). Celle-ci est un organe administratif du pouvoir central, qui dispose d'un large degré d'autonomie. Elle est composée de propriétaires terriens et de fermiers. La Chambre contrôle les fermages à la lumière de normes établies par arrêté royal. Par ailleurs, la Chambre doit apprécier, le cas échéant, si le bail n'entraîne pas des conséquences indésirables du point de vue de l'économie agricole ou s'il n'est pas contraire à la loi sur le bail à ferme. La Chambre est habilitée à modifier la convention. A la demande de l'une ou l'autre des parties, ou des deux, le fermage est revu tous les trois ans. En outre, le préneur peut demander la réduction du fermage pour un an si, à la suite de circonstances extraordinaires, la production est largement insuffisante. La bailleur, quant à lui, peut demander une augmentation du fermage pour un an, en cas d'exécution de travaux extraordinaires profitant au fermier. Le fermage ne peut être payé qu'en espèces.

La convention vaut de plein droit pour une durée de douze ans s'il s'agit d'une ferme, de six ans s'il s'agit d'une terre seule. Dans des conditions extraordinaires, l'autorisation d'affermer la terre pour une durée plus courte peut être donnée. A l'issue de la période convenue, la convention est prorogée de plein droit de six ans, à moins que le bailleur ait fait savoir qu'il ne souhaite pas de prolongation. Dans ce cas, le préneur peut demander à la *Pachtkamer* de la justice cantonnale (une chambre *ad hoc*, composée du Juge du canton comme président et d'un préneur et un bailleur comme assesseurs) de proroger le bail. Le juge décide en équité.

A moins que le bailleur lui-même ou l'un de ses proches parents ait l'intention d'exploiter le bien affermé. Dans ce cas, les intérêts du bailleur prévalent. La demande doit également être rejetée lorsque le bailleur veut utiliser la terre pour des fins non agricoles. Dans ce cas, le preneur a en principe droit à des dommages-intérêts. C'est également le cas lorsque le bailleur ne réalise pas son intention d'exploiter les terres lui-même. Toutefois, si les intérêts du bailleur en cas d'utilisation propre ne sont pas très substantiels, tandis que ceux du preneur en cas de poursuite de l'exploitation le sont, les intérêts de part et d'autre peuvent être appréciés.

La convention peut être résiliée avant terme en cas de mauvaise exploitation par le preneur ou en cas d'affectation du bien affermé à des fins non agricoles, par exemple dans le cadre d'une extension urbaine. Dans le premier cas, aucune indemnisation n'est due au preneur, dans le deuxième cas il a droit à une indemnité. Le décès du preneur ne met pas fin à la convention. Cependant, le juge peut résilier le bail à la demande des héritiers ou du bailleur. Un cercle restreint de parents, dont l'épouse et les enfants, ont le droit de demander à être substitués au preneur décédé. En outre, le preneur a le droit de transférer, après intervention du juge, les droits de fermage à ses plus proches parents. Le bien loué ne peut être vendu par le bailleur qu'après une offre préalable au fermier. Le fermier a un droit de préférence. En cas d'expropriation du bien loué, le bailleur a droit à une indemnité. En cas d'incendie, le bailleur est tenu de reconstruire les bâtisses. Si le fermier a apporté des améliorations au bien, il peut, dans certaines conditions, faire valoir ses droits à une indemnité à l'expiration du bail.

VIII. REMEMBREMENT

Après la loi sur le bail à ferme, la loi sur le remembrement (*Ruilverkavelingswet*) est la deuxième grande loi agraire de notre pays. Contrairement à la loi sur le bail à ferme en ce qui concerne la de bail à ferme, la loi sur le remembrement ne donne pas de définition de la notion de remembrement. Le remembrement s'est développé de l'échange de quelques parcelles à la restructuration complète d'une région. Outre les échanges de parcelles, le remembrement comporte actuellement la construction de routes, le creusement de canaux et fossés, le transfert de fermes, de même que la plantation de bois et l'aménagement de zones de récréation. Tous ces travaux, réalisés dans l'intérêt de l'agriculture, doivent permettre la création d'entreprises viables et bien désenclavées, de procéder à des lotissements et d'aboutir à la maîtrise du régime hydraulique. Le financement de ces travaux est assurée par l'Etat. Une partie des frais est recouvrée à charge des bénéficiaires, par le biais d'un système de paiements échelonnés. La principale forme de remembrement, le remembrement légal, se fait en vertu d'une décision de l'ensemble des propriétaires et des fermiers. La direction générale en matière de remembrement relève de la *Centrale Cultuurtechnische Commissie*, où le pouvoir central dispose d'une voix prépondérante. L'exécution du remembrement sur le plan local est assurée par des commissions locales, qui se composent généralement d'agriculteurs. Les membres sont désignés par les "Etats députés" de la province.

Les Etats députés sont en outre associés à la préparation du remembrement. Ils sont notamment chargés de faire voter le remembrement, d'établir les plans des routes et cours d'eau, de régler la propriété, d'assurer la gestion et l'entretien des routes et cours d'eau.

La commission locale est assistée par un certain nombre d'experts, dont un géomètre du cadastre et un ingénieur du service agronomique du ministère de l'Agriculture.

Une des principales activités de la commission locale consiste à établir les droits de chacun et à évaluer l'apport de chacun. En cas de litige entre l'intéressé et la commission, la décision appartient au juge. Les droits ainsi établis servent de base à l'attribution. Chacun doit retrouver un droit de propriété ou d'usage équivalent. Un écart maximal de 5% est cependant admis comme marge. La perte de terres à la suite de la construction de routes ou de creusement de cours d'eau, de même que du transfert à des organismes publics, donne lieu à une répartition égale entre tous les intéressés. 5% de la valeur au maximum peut être transférée aux organismes publics.

En général, on parvient, notamment par l'attribution de suppléments, à acheter assez de terres pour diverses fins. Ces terres peuvent servir pour l'agrandissement des entreprises, pour la plantation de bois, etc. Des réclamations contre le plan d'attribution établi par la commission locale peuvent être introduites auprès du tribunal. Outre les critères énoncés ci-dessus, il faut - pour établir le plan d'attribution - que chaque parcelle soit désenclavée.

Après que le plan d'attribution est établi, il est procédé à une deuxième estimation, afin de déterminer l'utilité que les intéressés ont retirée de l'exécution des travaux de remembrement. Le coût, diminué de la subvention de l'Etat, est réparti entre les lots en fonction de l'utilité que le remembrement a apportée au propriétaire. Les résultats de cette estimation sont consignés sur la liste des règlements pécuniaires.

Des réclamations contre la liste peuvent être introduites auprès du tribunal. Sur cette liste peuvent encore figurer des montants auxquels les intéressés ont droit à titre de dédommagement pour les travaux de remembrement réalisés. Le remboursement annuel à charge des propriétaires se fait à raison de 6% sur trente ans (annuités).
La phase le plus importante dans l'opération de remembrement est l'établissement du plan d'attribution. C'est à ce moment, en effet, que l'on a connaissance des parcelles qui devront éventuellement être cédées et de celles que l'on recevra en échange. Au milieu de l'année 1979, des remembrements étaient en préparation pour une superficie de quelque 424.000 ha., et en course d'exécution pour quelque 510.000 ha. Depuis le début du remembrement en 1925, l'opération a porté sur un total de 750.000 ha. environ.

IX. DEUX NOUVELLES LOIS

Actuellement, deux nouvelles lois sont en préparation. Il s'agit de la *Landinrichtingswet* (loi sur l'aménagement rural) et de la *Wet op het Agrarisch grondverkeer* (loi régissant les transactions foncières en zone rurale). Cette dernière loi a entre-temps été adoptée par le Parlement.
La loi sur l'aménagement rural est appelée à remplacer la loi sur le remembrement.
Une différence majeure entre les deux est que la nouvelle loi d'aménagement ne visera plus exclusivement à servir les intérêts agricoles. La loi tendra à l'aménagement des zones rurales conformément aux fonctions de ces zones, telles qu'elles sont établies dans le cadre de l'aménagement du territoire. Aussi, elle pourra contenir des dispositions relatives à la protection de la nature et des paysages, à la récréation, au patrimoine historique et culturel, etc. Un aspect important de cette loi est la coordination qu'elle établira entre l'aménagement rural et l'aménagement du territoire en général. Pour le reste, il sera créé la possibilité de procéder à des expropriations en vue de l'installation de certains équipements. De même, l'octroi de primes en cas de cession volontaire de terres recevra une base légale dans la nouvelle loi. La décision d'exécuter un projet d'aménagement rural, dans la mesure où il s'agit de réaménager les régions, sera du ressort de l'administration provinciale.

La loi sur les transactions foncières, quant à elle, régit de manière très stricte la vente de terres agricoles et de terrains naturels. Le but visé est de maîtriser les prix des terres. En 1970/1971, le prix moyen de terres non affermées était de ƒ 9.830 par ha., et en 1978/1979 de ƒ 55.370. Depuis lors, une baisse est intervenue.

Aux termes de la nouvelle loi, seuls les agriculteurs peuvent acheter des terres. Le cas échéant, des conditions particulières, notamment quant au lotissement éventuel, la taille de l'exploitation etc., pourront être fixées. Dans certaines régions, notamment celles où un remembrement est en préparation les pouvoirs publics auront un droit de préemption en cas de vente de terres. Les terrains acquis de la sorte pourront être utilisés pour agrandir des entreprises, mais ils pourront aussi être affectés à des fins récréatives, par exemple.

X. AUTRES MESURES TENDANT À AMÉLIORER LES STRUCTURES

Pour être complets, nous devons encore relever un certain nombre de dispositions touchant à la structure de l'agriculture et à la relation entre l'agriculture, d'une part, la nature et le paysage, d'autre part. Ainsi, une réglementation prévoit l'octroi d'une prime à l'agriculteur disposé à adapter son exploitation en fonction de conditions qui seront fixées du point de vue de la protection de la nature ou des paysages. Ces dispositions visent les terres situées dans des régions qui revêtent une certaine importance sur le plan de la protection de la nature. Les modalités sont fixées par convention. Un régime légal est également en cours d'élaboration pour les 'accords de gestion'. Actuellement, certaines questions sont réglées par une ordonnance du ministre de l'Agriculture et de la Pêche. L'agriculteur parce qu'il accepte de s'imposer certaines restrictions dans son exploitation, reçoit une subvention. Ainsi, dans certains cas, l'usage d'engrais chimiques est interdit.

Il convient de relever encore l'existence de nombreux régimes de subventionnement visant à améliorer la structure de l'agriculture, par exemple par l'agrandissement et la modernisation des entreprises. Ces régimes sont mis en oeuvre par un institut crée à cette fin particulière par le ministre de l'Agriculture : la *Stichting Ontwikkelings- en Saneringsfonds voor de Landbouw* (fonds de développement et d'assainissement agricoles). Les organisations agricoles sont représentées au sein de cette fondation et participent à sa gestion. Parmi les régimes ou formes d'aide prévues, citons : l'indemnité de sortie, les subventions-intérêts, les subventions pour certaines formes de coopération, les aides aux coopératives et les primes de reconversion.

XI. LOI FORESTIERE (*BOSWET*)

La loi forestière ne peut être omise dans une énumération des lois agraires. Cette loi tend à assurer la protection des forêts et autres régions boisées. Elle ne porte aucunement préjudice au pouvoir qu'ont les communes de prendre des mesures complémentaires, notamment dans l'agglomération. La plupart des communes ont d'ailleurs un règlement relatif à l'abattage. Cette loi impose à celui qui veut procéder à un abattage, l'obligation d'en faire communication préalable. Il est possible d'interdire l'abattage pour une période de cinq ans chaque fois. Le propriétaire de la surface boisée est obligé de replanter dans les trois ans. Pour les nouvelles plantations, après abattage, l'Etat peut octroyer un crédit, avec ou sans intérêt selon les cas.

XII. TRAVAIL ET SECURITE

Comme nous l'avons déjà relévé, la majorité des exploitations agricoles sont des entreprises familiales. Cela veut dire que tous les travaux sont exécutés par des membres de la famille. Cependant, dans une branche plus que dans l'autre, on trouve également des travailleurs salariés dans l'agriculture. Les conditions de travail proprement dites - salaires, heures de travail, congés ... - sont réglées par les associations professionnelles : des conventions collectives de travail sont établies sur la base de la législation générale. Dans la loi sur le travail (*Arbeidswet*) un paragraphe distinct est consacré au travail agricole. Elle laisse cependant la possibilité aux organisations professionnelles d'arrêter elles-mêmes les temps de travail et de repos par un régime de droit public. Depuis le 1er mai 1960, cette matière est régie par une ordonnance de la *Bestuur van het Landbouwschap*, une organisation professionnelle agricole de droit public, dans la direction de laquelle sont représentés les agriculteurs et les travailleurs agricoles.

La loi sur le travail comprend des dispositions interdisant le travail des enfants, et des mesures visant à protéger les jeunes travailleurs contre des travaux pénibles ou dangereux. Ainsi, il est interdit de conduire un tracteur au-dessous d'un certain âge et il faut être en possession d'un permis de conduire pour tracteur.
Sur le plan de la sécurité, il faut surtout mentionner le *Landbouwveiligheidsbesluit*, arrêté relatif à la sécurité du travail dans l'agriculture, pris en vertu de la loi générale sur la sécurité du travail. Cet arrêté comprend des règles en vue de prévenir les accidents, par exemple en prévoyant les dispositifs de sécurité dont doivent être munis certaines machines comme les meules et les scies circulaires.

Par ailleurs, il fixe des règles en ce qui concerne l'équipement (freins, etc.) des véhicules et en matière d'échafaudages, échelles, recouvrement d'ouvertures dans le sol, réfectoires, etc.
Ces derniers temps, une attention particulière est accordée à la prévention de dommages à la suite du renversement de tracteurs et à la prévention de troubles auditifs, provoqués par le bruit des tracteurs.

XIII. L'ORGANISATION DE L'AGRICULTURE

Les Pays-Bas connaissent une organisation très poussée et structurée de l'agriculture. Il suffira de relever les organisations générales, telles le *Koninklijk Nederlands Landbouwcomité* (comité royal agricole), la *Katholieke Nederlandse Boeren- en Tuindersbond* (ligue paysanne catholique) et la *Nederlandse (protestants) Christelijke Boeren- en Tuindersbond* (ligue protestante).
Ces trois grandes organisations paysannes collaborent avec les organisations de travailleurs au sein de la fédération agricole (*Landbouwschap*). Aux Pays-Bas, en effet, les différents secteurs économiques ont la possibilité de créer des organisations de droit public. En gros, on peut faire la distinction entre *Produktschappen* et *Bedrijfsschappen*. Les *Produktschappen* regroupent les entreprises associées aux phases successives de la production. C'est ainsi que relèvent du *produktschap* de l'industrie laitière : l'élevage, la fabrication de fromage, l'industrie du lait et des produits laitiers, les commerces de gros et de détail des produits laitiers.
Les *bedrijfsschappen* regroupent les entreprises qui remplissent des fonctions similaires. C'est ainsi que relèvent du *Bedrijfsschap voor de landbouw*, en d'autres termes le *landbouwschap*, les entreprises agricoles, les entreprises d'élevage et les exploitations horticoles, entre autres.
Les directions des *produktschappen* et *bedrijfsschappen* sont désignées par les organisations professionnelles libres, dont les trois grandes organisations paysannes précitées et les syndicats des ouvriers agricoles.
La tâche des *produktschappen* se situe principalement dans le domaine de la régulation du marché, celle des *bedrijfsschappen* s'inscrit notamment dans le cadre de la défense générale des intérêts de la branche en question. C'est surtout dans l'agriculture que cette forme d'organisation professionnelle de droit public a connu un tel succès.
Le *Landbouwschap* est devenu *le* grand organe de coopération de l'agriculture organisée, où se trouvent groupes des experts dans de nombreux domaines. Des commissions ont été constituées pour tous les aspects de l'agriculture et de l'horticulture; avec l'assistance des experts du sécretariat, ces commissions

conseillent le *landbouwschap*. En outre, l'organisation dispose de Conseils régionaux, qui se chargent notamment de défendre les intérêts de l'agriculture sur le plan de l'affectation des terres et de l'aménagement du territoire. Le *landbouwschap* joue également un rôle important sur le plan des relations agraires internationales, du fait que le secrétariat international des trois organisations paysannes précitées est attaché à cet organe. Enfin, le *landbouwschap* assume la fonction d'interlocuteur permanent du ministre de l'Agriculture et de la pêche. Chaque mois, les problèmes et les desiderata du monde agricole font l'objet de discussions entre le ministre et la délégation du *landbouwschap*. Parmi les *produktschappen* on peut relever le *Hoofdproduktschap voor akkerbouwprodukten* (organisation centrale pour les produits des cultures agricoles) et les *produktschappen* pour les pommes de terre, pour les céréales, les semences, les légumineuses à fruit sec, pour les fruits et légumes, pour les graines à semer, pour les espèces ornementales, pour le bétail et la viande, pour la volaille et les oeufs, pour les fourrages et enfin pour les produits laitiers. Les directions de ces organisations professionnelles de droit public définissent leur politique de manière autonome. Il va de soi que leur politique ne peut être contraire à la loi. Les règlements élaborés sont controlés par les pouvoirs publics. Les intéressés jouissent d'une protection juridique à l'égard des organisations en question par la possibilité d'appel auprès d'un Collège d'appel indépendant, le *College van beroep voor het bedrijfsleven*.

Le Ministère de l'agriculture est subdivisé en une série d'unités organiques à caractère général, une Direction générale de l'agriculture et de l'alimentation et une Direction générale de l'aménagement rural et de la gestion des terres et des forêts.

La Direction générale de l'agriculture et de l'alimentation a comme champ d'action :
- les questions relatives à la production, la transformation et la commercialisation des produits de l'agriculture;
- les questions relatives à la régulation du marché et la coopération internationale dans le domaine de la politique économique et commerciale générale et dans celui de la coopération au développement;
- l'information, la recherche et l'enseignement agricoles;
- les questions générales en matière d'alimentation et de qualité, les questions phytosanitaires et vétérinaires.

Le domaine de la direction générale de l'aménagement rural, de la gestion des terres et des forêts couvre les matières suivantes :
- l'aménagement ainsi que le développement technique des

zones rurales;
- les questions relevant de l'aménagement du territoire et de la gestion de l'environnement;
- l'acquisition et la gestion temporaire de terres pour l'agriculture et à des fins d'intérêt général;
- les questions en relation avec la banque foncière et la gestion des terres agricoles dont l'exploitation est adaptée en fonction des objectifs de la protection de la nature et des paysages;
- la gestion des fôrets et des parcs naturels;
- les questions relatives à la chasse et la protection de la faune;
- la pêche professionnelle et sportive.

XIV. OBSERVATION FINALE

Le présent exposé ne donne qu'un aperçu général de la législation agricole néerlandaise.

LÉGISLATION AGRICOLE

ÉNUMÉRATION DES DIFFÉRENTES LOIS AYANT UNE IMPORTANCE POUR L'AGRICULTURE:

Arbeidswet van 1919/Loi sur le travail de 1919
Wet op de Publiekrechtelijke Bedrijfsorganisatie/Loi sur les organisations professionnelles de droit public
Bestrijdingsmiddelenwet/Loi sur les pesticides et les produits phytopharmaceutiques
Bloembollenziektenwet/Loi sur les maladies des bulbes
Boswet/Loi forestière
Jachtwet/Loi sur la chasse
Landbouwwet/Loi agricole
Natuurbeschermingswet/Loi sur la protection de la nature
Natuurschoonwet/Loi sur les paysages et les sites naturels
Wet op de ontgrondingen/Loi sur les extractions
Paardenwet/Loi sur les chevaux
Pachtwet/Loi sur le bail à ferme
Ruilverkavelingswet/loi sur le remembrement
Veewet/Loi sur le bétail
Vogelwet/Loi sur la protection des oiseaux
Zaaizaad- en Plantgoedwet/Loi sur les semences et plants

SOURCES CONSULTÉES:

- Kernpunten uit de Memorie van Toelichting op de Begroting 1981 van het Ministerie van Landbouw en Visserij (Points fondamentaux de l'exposé des motifs du budget 1981 du Ministère de l'Agriculture et de la Pêche).
- Aspekten van de Nederlandse Landbouw en Visserij, Direktie Voorlichting en Externe betrekkingen van het Ministerie van Landbouw en Visserij, december 1979 (Aspects de l'agriculture et de la pêche des Pays-Bas, Direction Information et Relations extérieures du Ministère de l'Agriculture et de la Pêche).

Co-operation according to Dutch law

A.N. HUIZENGA
Barrister at Law, The Hague

III.A.1.

I. GENERAL REMARKS

1. The first act on co-operations dates from November 17, 1876, which was replaced in 1925. Since July 27, 1978 the law on co-operations is part of the Civil Code, in which the co-operative society is dealt with in Book 2, Title 2, Section 2. As the co-operative society is a *species* of the *genus* association, Section 1 of Title 2 C.C. also applies. The association is a legal entity and therefore Title 1 of Book 2, which contains general rules regarding legal entities is likewise applicable. Of course, general rules are overridden by special rules.

2. The Civil Code distinguishes between co-operative societies working in the insurance-business - which are designated as *onderlinge waarborgmaatschappij* (mutual guarantee association or mutual insurance company) - and all other co-operative societies - designated as *coöperatieve vereniging* (co-operative association or society).

3. In general the law does not distinguish between the co-operative association and the mutual guarantee association. Therefore I shall only mention the special rules for the mutual guarantee association and, if these do not exist, I shall refer to co-operative associations generally.
I shall use the following abbreviations: (a) *c.a.* (short for co-operative association) if the same rules apply to the mutual guarantee association and the other co-operative societies; (b) *m.g.a.* for mutual guarantee association; and (c) *c.s.* (short for co-operative societies) for co-operative associations which are not mutual guarantee associations.

4. In the second half of the nineteenth century the need for co-operations arose, mainly on economical grounds. Originally co-operations made use of the then existing legal possibili-

ties, mainly the common association. In 1874 the Minister of Justice refused to grant legal personality to a co-operative credit association as in his opinion the draft-rules were contrary to the Act on Associations of 1855. This act required that an association may not have a material aim. This resulted in the Act of 1876 (see under 1).
This act soon proved to be insufficient: it contained juridical imperfections and barred the development of *c.s.* The main objections were that even small defects in the establishing-act of *c.s.* made the *c.s.* void, and that the general meeting of all members of the *c.s.* could not be replaced by a meeting of representatives. The new Act of 1925 (see under 1) met these objections and cleared the way for further developments.
The recodification of the civil and commercial law brought the law of *c.s.* (and also of *m.g.a.*) into the (new) Civil Code. This did not imply a great deal of change for *c.s.* The most important alterations were: (a) that every modality of association which answers to the definition of the *c.s.* (see under 8) in the Civil Code cannot chose any other form of legal personality than a *c.s.*; and (b) that the *c.s.* is a modality of the common association.

5. The above shows that, although the need for co-operations was originally economic, the emergence of legal rules regarding the *c.s.* was brought about by juridicalities, which also dictated the development towards the present system of legal rules.

6. The *m.g.a.*, is, at least in the Netherlands, older than the *c.s.* The *m.g.a.* was already known before the enactment of the Commercial Code in 1838. Paragraph 286 of the Commercial Code dealt in a very summary way with the *m.g.a.*: it referred to the rules and regulations of the *m.g.a.* and, in the case that these were incomplete, to the principles of law. Shortly after the introduction of the Commercial Code the Supreme Court held that a *m.g.a.* could be a legal entity.
Until the re-codification the legislator did not interfere with the *m.g.a.*, but in the process of re-codification the legislator came to the conclusion that the *m.g.a.* and the *c.s.* were very much akin. They have in common that they intend to meet the material needs of their members by the running of a business. The legislator did not see sufficient reason why it should not apply the rules of the common association to the *m.g.a.* Very important was the democratic principle that in an association the general meeting must have final power, which is the more important for associations running a business for the benefit of their members. Therefore the legislator decided not to give opportunities to organizations not being proper associations to present themselves as *m.g.a.* In due course the *m.g.a.* has been regulated in the same Section

of the Civil Code as *c.s.* The same rules are applicable, with a few exceptions brought about by the special character of the *m.g.a.* Only a real mutual insurance company now has the right to possess the legal personality of *m.g.a.* It is also obliged to be a *m.g.a.* (see under 8 for its definition).

7. The same applies for the *m.g.a.*: it has been juridicalities that led to the present legal system concerning *m.g.a.*

II. LEGAL MODALITIES

8. The *c.a.* is a special kind of the (common) association and it has two modalities: (a) the *m.g.a.* which is an association having as its purpose to enter into insurance-agreements with its members; and (b) the *c.s.* which is an association having as its purpose to meet the material needs of its members by entering into agreements with its members through the business which it runs for the benefit of its members.

9. An association can be defined as a legal person with members who co-operate for a purpose and according to rules laid down by the members. Therefore, the *c.a.* also has legal personality, provided that its rules and regulations have been laid down in an instrument drafted by a notary (see under 14).

10. In the original draft-bill for the Act of 1876 (see under 1) the co-operation was juridically defined as a partnership with limited liability. On initiative of Parliament the legislator finally chose for the also new form of *c.s.*, since a co-operation generally has the structure of the common association. (For *m.g.a.*, see under 6.) The fact that in the process of re-codification it has been decided to continue the existence of the *m.g.a.* as a special form of *c.a.*, is based on historical arguments: the *m.g.a.* is older than the *c.s.* and does not use the word *coöperatief* (co-operative) in its name.

III. ALLIANCE COOPÉRATIVE INTERNATIONALE

11. The Dutch law does not respect the principles of the *Alliance Coopérative Internationale*, neither those which are in effect, not those which have been established by the Congress of Vienna of 1966. I have found no reference to it, neither in literature, nor in the parliamentary documents on *c.a.*

IV. SOME GENERAL RULES

12. The *c.a.* is a legal entity and has full capacity to possess legal rights.

13. The *c.a.*, its members and the members of its committees must behave towards each other reasonably and fairly. This means that the (objective) good faith governs the relations within the *c.a.*

V. ESTABLISHMENT OF THE C.A.

14. The establishment of a *c.a.* is a multilateral legal act, to be performed by a notarial instrument which must contain the rules and regulations of the *c.a.* If a *c.a.* has been established without a notarial instrument or if the instrument does not answer to the requirements of the Civil Code, the *c.a.* does exist, but not as a legal person. The Court can dissolve the *c.a.*, but it must grant the *c.a.* the opportunity to comply with the legal requirements.

15. The *c.a.* has to be registered under the Business Names Act and has to file its rules and regulations. As long as this has not been done, the person who performs any legal act on behalf of the *c.a.* is severally liable with the *c.a.*

VI. THE RULES AND REGULATIONS

16. Every *c.a.* established by notarial instrument has written rules and regulations. Such rules must contain the following terms (I leave out minor points):
(a) its name; (b) its purpose; (c) rights and obligations of the members; (d) the procedure of calling the general meeting of members; (e) the procedure of appointment, suspension and dismissal of members of the managing committee; (f) the appropriation of a surplus after dissolution of the *c.a.*

17. The name of a *c.a.* must indicate the character of its business, and in case of a *c.s.* the word *coöperatief* must be added, and in case of a *m.g.a.* the word *onderling* of *wederkerig* (both meaning: mutual). At the end of the name of a *c.a.* the liability of the members must be indicated by the letters *W.A.*, *B.A.* or *U.A.* (see under XI).

18. In the rules and regulations of an *m.g.a.* the following important points must be also settled:
(g) the term of existence (which may be indefinite); and (h) provisions on the guarantee capital.

19. Whereas the Civil Code in the greater part of its paragraphs concerning the *c.a.* may be set aside only by the rules and regulations, these always contain many deviations from the not mandatory statutory law. If deviation is allowed, I shall mention such hereafter by the words "not mandatory" between brackets.

20. The rules and regulations can only be changed by a decision of the general meeting (with a more complicated calling-procedure than usual).
If the calling-procedure has not been observed, an alteration of the rules is unimpeachable if such has been unanimously decided upon in a general meeting where all the members are present or represented. In other cases the decision has to be taken with two thirds of the votes (not mandatory). The rules may exclude the possibility of their alteration, but even then the general meeting, where all the members are present or represented, can unanimously decide to alter such.
An alteration of rules becomes effective as from the moment of its execution by the notary. A copy of the instrument must be filed with the Business Names Register.

VII. THE ORGANIZATION

21. The *c.a.* must always have: (a) a general meeting of members (which may be replaced by a meeting of representatives); and (b) a managing committee (sometimes split up in an executive committee and a general committee).
The Civil Code does not object to other committees, e.g. a balloting committee, a supervisory committee, a committee of appeal.

VIII. THE MEMBERS

22. Natural and legal persons and organizations without legal personality may be members of a *c.a.*

23. The ways of becoming member of a *c.a.* are: (a) the founder-members by and through the act of establishment of the *c.a.*; (b) by admission, on which the managing committee has to decide (not mandatory) and with the right for the general meeting to decide otherwise in case of non-admission (not mandatory), which does not imply a formal right of appeal for the applicant; and (c) in case of a *m.g.a.*, by entering into an insurance agreement with the *m.g.a.* if the rules and regulations provide for such a way of admission.
The rules may provide that everyone who expresses his wish to join the *c.a.* is thereby admitted. They also may provide that

members must satisfy certain conditions. The membership of a *c.a.* *W.A.* or *B.A.* (see under 33 and 34) must be applied for in writing. The decision of admission must also be in writing.

24. The rules may provide for suspension of members and the applicable procedure.

25. The membership terminates: (a) by death of the member (not mandatory) or by termination of the member; (b) by giving notice by the member or the *c.a.* (see under 26); (c) by expulsion (see under 27); and (d) by law in the case that between the member and the *m.g.a.* no insurance-contract is in existence anymore (not mandatory).

26. A member can always terminate on at least four weeks' notice. The *c.a.* can only terminate in the cases provided for in the rules and regulations or in case a member no longer satisfies the conditions for membership; here again the term of notice is at least four weeks. Both parties must give notice towards the end of the financial year. (The term of notice and the termination date are not mandatory.)
Both parties have the right to terminate without a term of notice, if it may not reasonably be required from the member to continue the membership.
The rules and regulations may attach conditions to a resignation so long as these are in compliance with the purpose of the *c.a.* (e.g. payment of a resignation penalty; limitation of the amount of members who may leave per annum). In general, such conditions intend to safeguard the continuity of the *c.a.* Conditions going farther than allowed are in so far regarded as non existent.
For the *c.a.* *W.A.* and *B.A.* (see under 33) the termination must be signified in writing.

27. Expulsion of a member by the *c.a.* is only possible in the case the member behaves contrary to the rules and regulations or decisions of the *c.a.*, or if he harms the *c.a.* unreasonably. Expulsion is decided upon by the managing committee (not mandatory). If the member has not been expelled by the general meeting of members, he has the right of appeal to the general meeting. The member is suspended pending the (term of) appeal.

28. The legal relations between the *c.a.* and its members are established by statute law, the rules and regulations and the decisions of the *c.a.* Commonly, the most important right of the members is the right to vote. Their most important obligations are often to pay a subscription, and to do all that is necessary to guarantee that the *c.a.* continues its business on an acceptable level (e.g. to deliver or to take off goods).

If so allowed by the rules and regulations, the *c.a.*-decisions may create rights for or obligations of the members towards the *c.a.* If by a *c.a.*-decision the obligations of the members are increased, each member - even those who have voted in support of the increase - has the right to terminate his membership towards the first possible ordinary termination day. Consequently the increase of obligations does not apply for him. The rules may exclude this right of liberation with regard to subscriptions and other obligations which according to the rules may be imposed.

29. The membership does not pass by inheritance and it is not transferable (not mandatory). For the *m.g.a.* the following exception exists: if the membership is linked to the insurance-contract, then transfer of the contract also causes transfer of the membership (not mandatory).

30. If the rules and regulations do not stipulate otherwise, the *c.a.* may obtain rights vis-à-vis third parties for its members, and, if the rules expressly allow, it may bind the members to third parties. The *c.a.* has the right to sue third parties in the name of its members, and also to claim damages.

IX. THE LIABILITY OF THE MEMBERS

31. The members are never directly liable to third parties which have contracted with the *c.a.*, not even after the dissolution of the *c.a.*

32. If the rules and regulations do not stipulate that its members have only a limited liability (*B.A.*) or even no liability at all (*U.A.*) (see under 33 and 34), the legal system of liability is applicable. If such is the case, the letters *W.A.* are added to the end of the name of the *c.a.* (see under 17). This legal system is as follows.
After the general meeting has decided to dissolve the *c.a.* or the *c.a.* has been declared bankrupt, the (official) liquidator - a plurality of liquidators is possible - estimates the deficit and claims from those who are member at the moment of the dissilution decision or the declaration of bankruptcy, and those who terminated their membership within one year before that moment (the rules may lengthen this period) their shares in the deficit augmented with, at the most, 50% for costs of liquidation and provision for bad debts. Such persons are obliged to pay at once. Everyone is liable towards the *c.a.* for equal shares (not mandatory).

33. The rules may limit the liability of the members to a maximum in two ways: (a) only a maximum deficit can be recover-

ed from the (former) members; or (b) every (former) member is only liable for a maximum amount. If the *c.a.* has chosen for such limited liability, the letters *B.A.* (*beperkte aansprakelijkheid*, meaning: limited liability) must be added to the name of the *c.a.* (see under 17).

34. The rules may also exclude every personal liability of the members. In this case the letters *U.A.* (*uitgesloten aansprakelijkheid*, meaning: liability excluded) must be added to the name of the *c.a.* (see under 17).

35. By way of alteration of the rules and regulations the system of liability can be changed. Doctrinal writing accepts that this is also valid vis-à-vis third parties, but it is clear that creditors of the *c.a.* can resist to such an alteration by means of the *actio Pauliana* on the grounds of defraudation of the creditors in case the *c.a.* could foresee that it would not be able to pay its creditors.

X. THE GENERAL MEETING OF MEMBERS

36. The general meeting (g.m.) has all the powers which have not been attributed by law or by the rules to any committee. Commonly the g.m. has the right to appoint, suspend and dismiss the members of the managing committee (and other committees provided for by the rules). The g.m. must have the following powers: (a) to appoint, suspend and dismiss the majority of the members of the managing committee; (b) to alter the rules; (c) to control the financial course of events; and (d) to dissolve the *c.a.*

37. Every (not mandatory: not-suspended) member has admittance to the g.m. and has (not mandatory) one vote. The rules may provide for admittance and voting rights for persons who are no member of the *c.a.* but are member of one of its committees, but their votes can never surpass one-third part of the total amount of the number of votes totally cast.

38. The rules may provide for a meeting of representatives instead of a g.m. If such is the case, every member must have the right to take part - directly or indirectly - in the election of the representatives. The representatives have to be member of the *c.a.*
The meeting of representatives is common for the larger *c.a.*
The rules may prescribe that all representatives have the same amount of votes or bind the amount of votes to the amount of members represented by every representative.
The rules may provide for binding instructions (mandates).

39. The president and secretary of the managing committee are also president and secretary of the g.m. or the meeting of representatives (not mandatory). The president decides whether a decision has been taken and to which extent (not mandatory). The members present at the g.m. have the right to contest his decision immediately after it has been taken, in which case a new vote must be taken.

40. The greater part of decisions only need a simple majority. For important decisions (dissolution, alteration of rules) the law prescribes a larger majority, but the rules may provide otherwise.
The rules may stipulate that after certain decisions of the g.m. a referendum must be held among the members. Pending the referendum the decision of the g.m. may not be executed.
It is possible to take decisions outside the g.m., but only with previous knowledge of the managing committee and unanimously by all members. Such decisions have the same legal force as formal decisions of the g.m.

41. Decisions of the g.m. can be annulled: (a) if they have come into existence contrary to the statutory regulations on the powers of the g.m. and the procedure of deciding; (b) if they are contrary to the rules; and (c) if they are not in compliance with good faith.
The members, members of the managing committee and interested third parties may invoke the above grounds for annulment within one year after sufficient publication of the decision or after the moment they had knowledge of the decision or after the moment such decision had been brought to their attention, whichever is the earlier, but only if they have a reasonable interest. This prescription does not apply in case a person is sued by the *c.a.* under such decision and he invokes the annulment to resist its claim.
A voidable decision may be confirmed by a new decision of the g.m., but only if the g.m. had the power to take such a decision and if nobody has started a lawsuit based on the annulment in the meantime.
If the Court declares the decision annulled or void, the judgment is of effect *erga omnes*.

42. The managing committee has the right to call the g.m., and it has to do so on request of a certain amount of the members. If the committee does not call on request of the members, they themselves have the right to call. This right of the members cannot be excluded.

XI. THE MANAGING COMMITTEE

43. Except for limitations by rules and regulations the managing committee (m.c.) has the right to administer the affairs of the *c.a.* and to represent the *c.a.* (also in the Court). The rules may state that the power of attorney does not (only) belong to the m.c., but to one or more members of the m.c. separately or jointly, or even jointly with other persons. Third parties nor the *c.a.* can invoke an excess of the power of attorney which is not based on the statutory regulations. The m.c. has no power to enter into agreements to buy, sell or mortgage real property, or to guarantee obligations of third parties, or to make the *c.a.* severally liable for debts of third parties, or to give any other security for such (not mandatory).

44. The members of the m.c. must be appointed by the members from the group of the members (not mandatory), but they always have the right to appoint more than the half of the members of the m.c. The appointing persons have the right to suspend and dismiss the members of the m.c. appointed by them (not mandatory).

45. If the rules provide for an executive committee, they must also state the division of tasks between the committee and the m.c.

46. With regard to the decisions of the m.c. or other committees the same annulment rules as for the decisions of the g.m. apply (see under 41).

47. The m.c. is responsible to the g.m. and is answerable for its financial conduct. In the case of a *c.a.* with more than Dfl. 3.000.000 asset value the annual statement of accounts must be checked by a chartered accountant.

47a. The supervision of the m.c. can be transferred to a supervisory committee. It does not seem essential to deal with this committee here.

XII. DISSOLUTION

48. The dissolution of a *c.a.* is caused by: (a) occurrences provided for in the rules and regulations (very seldom); (b) a resolution for the dissolution of the *c.a.* taken by the g.m. (on which in general the same regulations as for alteration of the rules and regulations are applicable); (c) insolvency after bancruptcy of the *c.a.* or the stay of bancruptcy procedures for want of assets; (d) by Court order in the follow-

ing cases: (1) the *c.a.* is a prohibited legal person (if its purpose or activities are contrary to the public order or good morality); (2) the *c.a.* acts to a considerable extent contrary to its rules and regulations; (3) the *c.a.* does not answer to the statutory definition of a *c.a.* and (4) the act of the establishment does not meet the requirements (see under 14); and (e) by total absence of members.
The above enumeration is exhaustive. On request of the managing committee, interested (third) parties and the Public Prosecutor the Court shall issue a statement that and as from which moment the *c.a.* is dissolved. This statement is binding for everybody.

XIII. LIQUIDATION

49. After its dissolution the *c.a.* continues its existence but only as far as is necessary for the liquidation of its estate. In case of a dissolution order the Court appoints at least one liquidator. In case of bankruptcy the Court appoints at least one official liquidator who has to perform his task. In other cases the rules and regulations may provide for (the appointment of) liquidators. If no liquidators have been appointed, the m.c. has to liquidate the *c.a.*

50. The surplus, if any, belongs to the members (not mandatory). See for the procedure in case of a deficit under 32.

51. The *c.a.* is terminated by completion of the liquidation. If thereafter a new creditor appears, the Court may re-open the liquidation procedure on request of any interested party and appoint new liquidators if necessary.

XIV. PUBLIC SUPERVISION

52. No general public system of supervision of the *c.a.* is in existence in The Netherlands. For the *c.a.* working as a credit institution the general laws of supervision of such institution, and for *m.g.a.* the supervision laws concerning insurance companies, are applicable.

53. A credit-*c.a.* has to have a license of the *Nederlandsche Bank N.V.* (the central bank). The *Nederlandsche Bank* also exercises the monetary and business-economical supervision on the credit-*c.a.* and has the right to withdraw the license. The *c.a.* is obliged to file periodically financial reports with the *Nederlandsche Bank* and to give information as is asked for. The *Nederlandsche Bank* has the right to give instructions to the credit-*c.a.* If the *Nederlandsche Bank* observes developments

dangerous for the solvency and liquidity of the *c.a.*, it draws the attention of the *c.a.* to these and orders a course of conduct, if necessary. If this fails to have effect, the *Nederlandsche Bank* can resort to more severe measures, e.g. the publication of its instructions or appointment of at least one official who has to approve every act of the credit-*c.a.* before the *c.a.* may exercise its powers.
There is also an emergency regulation for cases that solvency or liquidity of a credit-*c.a.* shows dangerous developments and no improvement is to be expected. Then the Court may on request of the *Nederlandsche Bank* declare that the *c.a.* is in a condition for which, in the interest of the whole body of creditors, special provisions are necessary. The Court appoints at least one trustee who exercises all the powers of the *c.a.* and safeguards the interests of the creditors.
After such a declaration the credit-*c.a.* is in a condition which is very similar to the temporary suspension of payment.

54. The supervision of the *m.g.a.* is exercised by the *Verzekeringskamer* (Insurance Controlling Board), which has powers similar to those of the *Nederlandsche Bank*. I shall therefore not go into detail, but only mention that the regulation in emergency situation cases is different for *m.g.a.* working in the indemnity insurance business. Then the Court may enpower the *Verzekeringskamer* to liquidate partly or fully the insurance portfolio or to transfer the insurance contracts to other insurance companies.
For *m.g.a.* working in the life insurance business similar emergency rules as for banks apply.

XV. THE SOCIAL SIGNIFICANCE

55. Outside of the agricultural sector the *c.a.* has nearly no importance, except for the *m.g.a.* insuring costs of medical care. Former *c.a.* have been replaced by other legal constructions (mostly incorporated companies with limited liability).

56. The *c.a.* is a common phenomenon in the agricultural sector where they often have strong market positions. I mention the following (data from January 1, 1981):

- 978 farmers' loan-banks (united in the *Centrale Coöperatieve Raiffeisen-Boerenleenbank*) give about 90% of the total amount of bank-credit in the agricultural sector (and form together the third ranking bank in The Netherlands);

- 245 *c.a.* have a market-share of more than 50% in fertilizer and mixed food;

CO-OPERATION

- more than 90% of the milk-production goes to the 41 co-operative dairy factories and more than 80% of the milk-products are made by these;

- all industrial patatoes are processed by only one *c.a.*;

- 56% of the seed-patatoes and slightly under 30% of the patatoes fit for consumption is traded by *c.a.*;

- the trade in vegetables, fruits, flowers and plants is for at least 80% in the hands of *c.a.*;

- more than 60% of the sugar-beet harvest goes to co-operative sugar-factories;

- nearly 50% of the business assistance is rendered by *c.a.*

57. Only 8 *m.g.a.* operate in the life insurance branch. All other 450 *m.g.a.* deal with indemnity insurance. About 150 of these are subject to the supervision of the *Verzekeringskamer*. The other 300 are so small that supervision is not of public interest.

58. The Dutch legislation is adequate. It allows for developments within the framework of a few mandatory statutory laws, which are considered to be essential to the public interest. No need for alteration is felt nor is the legislator preparing any alteration.

Abus d'information préalable en droit néerlandais

B. WACHTER

Professeur à l'Université de l'Etat à Utrecht

JOS NETTEN

Collaborateur scientifique à l'Université de l'Etat à Utrecht

III.A.2.

I. SOURCES DU DROIT RÉGISSANT LA MATIÈRE

Jusqu'à présent il n'existe en droit néerlandais aucune réglementation spécifique en matière de lutte contre l'abus d'information préalable relative à des transactions de titres[1]. S'il est vrai qu'en juillet 1973, la Commission du droit des sociétés[2] avait, à la demande émis à ce sujet du Ministre de la Justice, un avis[3], comportant notamment deux propositions de réglementation, dont l'une relevait du droit pénal et l'autre du droit des sociétés, ce document n'a cependant pas été suivi d'initiatives législatives. L'absence d'une réglementation légale spécifique ne signifie pas que le phénomène dénoncé ne se produirait pas aux Pays-Bas[4], ni que, le cas échéant, il resterait sans suite, voire qu'il serait impossible d'y attacher des conséquences juridiques. Les auteurs sont unanimes à considérer comme répréhensible tout abus de connaissances privilégiées au s jet de transactions de titres. En vue de lutter contre cette pratique, et notamment quant à savoir quel genre d'action il y a lieu d'intenter contre celui qui a vendu ou acheté des titres, alors qu'il disposait d'informations préalables, l'on se réfère aux possibilités découlant des principes généraux du droit des obligations tels que l'erreur, le dol, l'abus de droit , l'inexécution et l'acte illicite, ce dernier permettant notamment d'intenter une action contre les personnes qui "bien que non dirigeantes" auraient acquis des informations préalables de façon illicite, ou qui en auraient en connaissance en raison de leur position - par exemple en qualité d'expert comptable externe ou de banquier - alors qu'ils étaient censés, en raison de cette connaissance même, s'abstenir de procéder à l'achat ou à la vente de certains titres, ou même de conseiller des tiers à ce sujet[5]. Outre ces principes généraux il y a lieu de se référer, en cette matière, aux mesures prises par la *Vereniging voor de Effectenhandel* (Association pour le commerce des valeurs) et à celles qui émanent du Conseil Economique et Social (C.E.S.).

Avant de nous étendre sur le fond de ces réglementations et sur les possibilités qui en découlent en vue de combattre les abus d'information préalable, il convient de situer brièvement la *Vereniging voor de Effectenhandel* et le C.E.S., afin de mieux apprécier l'importance que nous devons accorder aux réglementations émanant de ces institutions.

La *Vereniging voor de Effectenhandel* est une organisation de droit privé bénéficiant de la personnalité juridique. Elle centralise aux Pays-Bas l'ensemble des transactions de titres en bourse. Cette centralisation est rendue possible par le fait que cette association assure la gestion des transactions de titres en bourse, dont l'accès est exclusivement réservé aux membres de l'association. En outre, il est interdit, en vertu de l'article 2 de la *Beschikking Beursverkeer* 1947 (arrêté relatif aux opérations en bourse) d'acheter ou de vendre des actions autrement qu'à l'intervention des membres de l'association[6]. L'intervention obligatoire de commissionnaires vaut également pour les transactions hors bourse. La régularité des transactions de titres est ainsi assurée depuis longtemps par l'Association, ce qui explique pour une bonne part que l'on ait pu se passer d'une réglementation spécifique de cette matière[7]. L'intervention des autorités publiques se limite à la *Beurswet* 1914[8] (loi portant organisation de la bourse) et à l'arrêté de 1947 réglementant les opérations boursières - *Beschikking Beursverkeer*. (Depuis de nombreuses années une nouvelle réglementation relative au marché des valeurs et aux opérations en bourse est en préparation au Ministère des Finances.)
La centralisation par cette association des transactions de titres cotés en bourse a eu pour effet que cette organisation, au départ un organisme privé visant essentiellement à la défense des intérêts de ses membres, est devenue une organisation poursuivant des objectifs plus larges et plus généraux, à savoir la défense des intérêts du commerce des valeurs au sens le plus large du terme[9].

La régulation du commerce des valeurs s'opère sur la base des statuts de l'association, ainsi que des réglements et des prescriptions qui découlent de ceux-ci[10]. Ces dispositions réglementaires permettent à l'association de prévenir, bien que modestement, les abus possibles d'information préalable et de les réprimer. L'association étant toutefois un organisme de droit privé, il en découle que les mesures qu'elle serait amenée à prendre dans le domaine des abus d'information préalable, n'auront forcément que le caractère de dispositions de droit privé.
Ces dispositions relèvent tantôt du droit des associations, tantôt du droit des obligations. En effet la société, qui désire que ses titres puissent faire l'objet de transactions of-

ficielles en bourse, devra accepter un certain nombre d'obligations à l'égard de l'Association. Celles-ci concernent notamment les prescriptions en matière de publicité, destinées à éviter les abus éventuels d'information préalable[11]. Bien que ces limitations relèvent du droit privé, le monopole de fait de la *Vereniging voor de Effectenhandel* ainsi que l'intervention obligatoire de commissionnaires prévue par l'article 2 de la *Beschikking Beursverkeer* 1947, font que les mesures prises ou à prendre par l'association en matière d'abus d'information préalable frappent en principe toutes transactions de titres et revêtent dès lors un importance considérable. Le contrôle du respect des statuts, règlements et toutes autres prescriptions est assurée par l'association elle-même conformément à une règlement de contrôle, en vertu duquel un "bureau de contrôle" a été créé. La Commission d'Ordre dispose d'un arsenal de mesures disciplinaires pour pénaliser les infractions aux règlements ainsi que les actes considérés comme contraires aux usages de la profession[12]. Ces sanctions varient, selon la gravité de l'infraction, de l'avertissement à la réprimande, et de l'amende ou de la suspension pour une durée maximum de six mois à la radiation.

Outre la *Vereniging voor de Effectenhandel*, le Conseil Economique et Social (C.E.S.) joue un rôle important dans le domaine qui nous occupe. Le C.E.S. est un organisme de droit public, créé par la loi et ayant pour tâche de donner des avis au gouvernement et d'assister celui-ci[13]. Le C.E.S. est composé de 45 membres, dont 15 sont désignés par les organisations de travailleurs, 15 par les organisations patronales et 15 par la Couronne. Outre sa fonction consultative, le C.E.S. a pour mission "de promouvoir les activités économiques dans l'intérêt du peuple néerlandais et de veiller aux intérêts de la vie économique et des personnes participant à celle-ci"[14]. En octobre 1968, le Ministre de la Justice a demandé avis au C.E.S. au sujet d'une réglementation relative aux fusions d'entreprises. Cet avis a abouti à l'arrêté du C.E.S. de 1970 relatif aux règles de conduite en matière de fusions, entré en vigueur depuis le 19 juin 1970 en vertu d'un arrêté du C.E.S. Cette réglementation a été revue à deux reprises pour aboutir à l'arrêté C.E.S. de 1975 relatif aux règles de conduite en matière de fusions, en vigueur depuis le 1.4.1976. Dans cet arrêté, qui n'a pas cependant force de loi[15], le C.E.S. a introduit une série de dispositions tendant à éviter les abus d'information préalable. Le contrôle de l'application des règles de conduite en matière de fusions, prescrites par l'arrêté du C.E.S., est assuré par la Commission des Fusions. Les conséquences d'infractions éventuelles à cette réglementation seront examinées ultérieurement.

II. LES TECHNIQUES PAR LESQUELLES SONT EMPÊCHÉES LES OPÉRATIONS INDÉLICATES

L'absence en droit néerlandais d'une réglementation spécifique en matière d'abus d'information préalable, n'est pas due au fait que ce phénomène n'aurait pas retenu l'attention dans notre pays. Des solutions diverses, parmi lesquelles certaines s'inspiraient de réglementations étrangères, ont été proposées et examinées. Un certain nombre de celles-ci furent concrétisées sous la forme de réglementations extra-légales. Nous examinerons à présent les solutions ainsi retenues ainsi que la façon dont elles ont été traduites en droit néerlandais.
Les auteurs font généralement une distinctions entre les transactions de titres à l'amiable et celles qui sont réalisées en bourse. En ce qui concerne les transactions de gré à gré, l'on admet qu'on devrait pouvoir se défendre sans difficultés majeures contre un abus éventuel d'information préalable, en invoquant les principes du droit des obligations, notamment l'erreur, le dol et l'abus de circonstances[16].

La règle de l'erreur est définie par l'article 1358 du Code Civil. A ce sujet l'on se réfère à deux arrêts rendus par la Cour supérieure *(Hoge Raad/HR)*, le premier datant du 19 juin 1959 (*NJ* 1960.59, nt. H.B.) et le second du 30 novembre 1973 (*NJ* 1974.97, nt. G.J.S.).
Le premier arrêt concerne la question de savoir si le vendeur d'un objet - il s'agissait d'une coupe ancienne en argent - peut invoquer l'erreur à l'égard de l'acheteur lorsqu'il apparaît, après la conclusion de la vente, que la valeur de l'objet est largement supérieure à celle sur laquelle les parties en cause s'étaient basées pour fixer le prix. Dans son arrêt la Cour considère notamment que dans ce cas une action basée sur l'erreur n'est pas fondée en raison du fait que "conformément à l'opinion générale et au sens de l'équité, celui qui vend un objet contre une prestation contraire dûment convenue, renonce par le fait même à l'éventualité que ledit objet se révélerait par la suite posséder des qualités dont il ne pouvait présumer l'existence au moment de la transaction". La Cour poursuit toutefois en soulignant que "cette considération n'exclut pas que dans des cas de ce genre, l'annulation de la convention peut être justifiée par des circonstances accessoires, notamment dans le cas où l'acheteur aurait pu informer le vendeur des qualités de l'objet, ce à quoi il était tenu en vertu de la bonne foi ...". En vue de l'application de cette dernière considération il y a lieu de se référer aux motifs invoqués par le même collège dans un premier arrêt rendu sur un cas d'erreur, stipulant notamment que "les parties, en engageant le négociation au sujet d'une convention à conclure, se mettent mutuellement dans une position juridique spéciale régie par la bonne foi, entraînant pour elles l'obligation

de tenir compte également des intérêts légitimes de la partie co-contractante"[17]. Un autre arrêt auquel il est référé dans le cadre de l'application de principe de l'erreur, concerne le cas d'une erreur de la part de l'acheteur, dans lequel la Cour a également admis l'existence d'un certain devoir d'information. A ce sujet il est à noter d'ailleurs qu'au cours des 10 à 15 dernières années, la législation et la jurisprudence néerlandaises non seulement admettent dans des cas de plus en plus nombreux l'existence d'une certaine obligation d'information, mais tendent aussi à concrétiser celle-ci par des exigences plus strictes à cet égard[18].

Outre l'erreur, le dol est un autre moyen permettant d'intenter une action pour dol dans le domaine des transactions de titres à l'amiable en cas d'abus d'information préalable. Cette action fondée sur l'article 1364 du Code civil, permet également de demander l'annulation de la convention. Une des conditions pour faire aboutir cette action est qu'il y ait eu recours à des "artifices" de nature telle que, sans eux, la partie co-contractante n'aurait pas conclu le contrat. Au sujet de cette action les auteurs se réfèrent généralement à l'arrêt de la Cour supérieure (*HR*) du 2 mai 1969 (*NJ* 1969.344, nt. G.J.S.), dans lequel il est observé "que l'omission intentionnelle d' information constitue un artifice au sens de l'article 1364 du Code civil, mais non l'omission involontaire".

Examinons enfin les possibilités offertes par le principe de l'abus de circonstances, tel qu'il a été établi par la jurisprudence, en vue notamment de lutter contre d'éventuels abus d'information préalable[19]. L'on considère en effet qu'il est contraire aux bonnes moeurs d'abuser de certaines circonstances lors de la conclusion d'une convention, et que dans ce cas il peut en résulter la nullité de la convention en application des articles 1356 et 1373 du Code civil. L'enseignement de la jurisprudence[20], consacré d'ailleurs par l'article 3.2.10, 4me alinéa, du nouveau Code civil, est qu'une action fondée sur l'abus de circonstances s'indique dans les cas où quelqu'un, au moment de conclure une convention, tire profit de circonstances particulières, tenant à la personne même du co-contractant, telles une situation de besoin, de dépendance, d' inexpérience, l'acceptation de charges excessives sous la pression des circonstances, etc. Il en résulte, comme le relève *Uniken Venema*[21], que cette action - en cas d'abus d'information préalable - est moins efficace qu'on ne peut l'attendre des actions citées en premier lieu.

En ce qui concerne les transactions de valeurs cotées en bourse, il est considéré que les actions civiles précitées et d'autres actions civiles ne peuvent apporter de solution pour combattre l'abus de connaissance préalable. Cette thèse est étayée par divers arguments[22]: il n'existe pas de relation contractuelle directe entre celui qui s'est rendu coupable de l'abus et la personne qu'il a lésée; la "partie" opposée à celui qui a abusé d'une information préalable ne subit pas de dommage. Dans le même ordre d'idées, on avance que la personne lésée aurait tout aussi bien acheté ou vendu les titres si la personne qui a abusé s'était abstenue de toute action: le préjudice qu'il a subi n'est pas une conséquence de l'abus de connaissance préalable et n'est donc susceptible d'aucun recours en droit civil, telle une action fondée sur l'acte illicite (art. 1401 Code civil). À ce raisonnement, *Uniken Venema* a opposé que si le lien causal entre l'abus et la conclusion de la convention est inexistant, le sort de toute action en dédommagement n'en est pas pour autant scellé. Il fait à cet égard l'observation suivante:

> *"Lorsqu'on se demande si en droit néerlandais les* insiders *sont effectivement tenus par un devoir d'information à l'égard des parties anonymes participant aux opérations boursières, on pourrait, à mon avis, selon le droit actuel, considérer pareil devoir d'information comme découlant de la convenance sociale",*

et, plus loin:

> *"Je suis d'ailleurs d'avis que, même dans l'état actuel du droit, une action en dédommagement peut être introduite, dans certaines conditions, contre ceux qui ont abusé d'information préalable."*[23]

Le fait que - pour autant que nous ayons pu le vérifier[24] - des jugements font défaut dans ce domaine, ne peut manquer de convaincre quiconque s'occupe de la problématique de l'abus de connaissance préalable, de la nécessité de prévoir à cet égard des sanctions pénales[25].
Outre l'effet préventif qu'aurait pareille sanction, elle permettrait de faire verser à l'Etat, sous forme d'amende, le bénéfice réalisé par l'usage abusif d'une information préalable. Dans ce pays, la cession de gains à l'Etat est considérée comme une solution préférable à la cession à la société, sanction qui est prévue par certaines réglementations à l'étranger. En effet, comme objection contre cette sanction, on avance que la société n'a pas subi de préjudice à la suite de l'abus de connaissance préalable, outre le fait que cette forme de cession profite également à la personne qui a commis l'abus, dans la mesure il a des actions dans la société concernée. *Uniken Venema*, qui fait siennes ces objections formulées par la *Commissie Vennootschapsrecht* (Commission pour le droit des sociétés), fait en outre observer que même si la société devait subir un préjudice quelconque du fait de l'abus d'information préalable, par exemple une atteinte à sa renommée, ou des dommages résultant d'une action qui serait intentée contre la société, avec

succès, par des acheteurs ou vendeurs anonymes, un régime de cession est superflu parce que dans ce cas, la société pourrait se retourner contre celui qui a commis l'abus par une action pour acte illicite ou pour inexécution[26].
Van der Grinten relève encore que la jurisprudence n'a pas encore eu à s'occuper de la question de savoir si un administrateur d'une société anonyme ou d'une société "fermée" à responsabilité limitée peut être tenu responsable, en vertu de l'article 8 du Livre 2 du Code civil de l'usage abusif à son propre profit, de connaissance préalable[27].

III. ORGANES CHARGÉS DE VEILLER AU RESPECT DES RÈGLEMENTS, VISANT À LA PRÉVENTION DES OPÉRATIONS INDÉLICATES PAR VOIE DE DÉCLARATION

Il est évident que l'abus d'information préalable n'est possible qu'aussi longtemps qu'un nombre restreint de personnes dispose d'une information donnée. L'avance de ce groupe par rapport à l'extérieur peut être éliminée si l'on impose l'obligation de rendre publiques au plus tôt les données relatives à la société qui ont habituellement une certaine influence sur les cours des valeurs émises. La publication rapide de ces données limite la période pendant laquelle l'abus d'information préalable peut se produire, et limite donc l'étendue du phénomène lui-même. C'est précisément cette corrélation entre l'abus d'information préalable et la publicité qui a amené la commission parlementaire chargée de préparer la discussion en séance publique du projet de loi relatif aux comptes annuels des entreprises, de demander l'avis du Ministre de la Justice quant à la suggestion de compléter cette réglementation légale par une disposition aux termes de laquelle les sociétés anonymes seraient tenues de publier des propositions de dividendes et des chiffres annuels provisoires le jour même où l'organe compétent a pris une décision en la matière[28]. L'avis du Ministre revenait à ceci, que la prévention d'abus d'information préalable étant devenue à présent un sujet qui n'est plus uniquement considéré en relation avec les comptes annuels, il était provisoirement plus sage de demander l'avis de la *Commissie Vennootschapsrecht* (Commission du droit des sociétés)[29]. Cette demande d'avis a donné lieu au rapport prérappelé du 5 juillet 1973, dans lequel la commission suggérait de prévoir une disposition comportant pour la direction d'une société anonyme dont les actions, les créances (ou certificats de celles-ci) sont cotées en bourse, l'obligation légale de publier, dès l'instant où une décision est intervenue, la proposition de dividende, de même que les chiffres trimestriels, si ceux-ci sont fournis par la société[30]. Bien qu'*Uniken Venema* se rallie à la portée de ces dispositions, il estime que la proposition de la Commission ne va pas assez loin; il préconise pour sa part l'obligation de publier toutes informations dont on peut raisonnablement attendre que, dès leur publication, elles influenceront sensiblement le cours des titres émis par la société[31]. Le gouvernement n'a pas voulu aller aussi loin, mais à la suite de l'avis émis par la Commission du droit des sociétés, il a proposé, dans le cadre du projet de loi tendant à adapter la législation à la quatrième directive du Conseil des Communautés Européennes relative au droit des sociétés, de compléter l'article 103 existant du Livre 2 du Code civil (disposition qui fait partie de la section "Le patrimoine de la société anonyme" - *Het vermogen van de naamloze vennootschap*) en y ajoutant un alinéa de la teneur suivante:

> *"Si les actions de la société, les titres de créance ou les certificats de ces actions et créances, émis avec sa collaboration, sont repris dans le prix-courant d'une bourse quelconque, la société publie ses chiffres semestriels et trimestriels dès qu'ils sont disponibles. Cette obligation ne vaut pas si les chiffres sont communiqués uniquement aux administrateurs, aux commissaires et au conseil d'entreprise.*
> *Pareille société publie immédiatement la proposition de dividende sur les actions ou autres titres, de même que les décisions de liquider des dividendes intérimaires."*[32]

En vertu de l'article 1, 4e, de la Loi sur les délits économiques[33], le non-respect de cette obligation est considéré comme un délit économique et passible de peines en tant que tel. Il en résulte que pour les sociétés anonymes au moins, en ce qui concerne les valeurs cotées en bourse visées par la disposition proposée, notre droit contiendra dans un avenir assez proche un régime légal tendant à prévenir et à réprimer les abus d'information préalable.
Il serait faux d'affirmer que cette disposition légale apporte une réglementation dans un domaine encore entièrement inexploité. L'Association du commerce des valeurs (*Vereniging voor de Effectenhandel*) et le C.E.S. avaient déjà, en l'absence de dispositions légales, imposé des règles similaires aux intéressés.

L'Association du commerce des valeurs s'est occupée de la question dès 1970[34]. Dans le règlement des fonds (*Fondsenreglement*) l'Association a fixé comme condition pour la reprise de fonds dans la cotation[35], que les directions des sociétés doivent s'engager par écrit vis-à-vis de l'Association, pour autant que la demande se rapporte à un fonds intérieur:

a. à faire, au plus tard dans le courant du 9me mois de chaque exercice comptable, une publication comprenant outre les informations publiées antérieurement, suf-

fisamment de données pour permettre au public d'apprécier la situation de son patrimoine et sa situation financière, de même que ses résultats d'exploitation pour la première moitié de l'exercice en cours;

b. si les données particulières visées ci-après n'apparaissent pas dans des publications antérieures, tels les comptes annuels, à faire - aussitôt après que les commissaires ont approuvé le compte annuel de l'exercice antérieur - une publication reprenant les principales données particulières des documents annuels, dont en tout cas une éventuelle proposition de dividende;

c. de faire immédiatement une publication au sujet de tout fait ou événement se produi nt au sein de la société et dont il faut considérer qu'il aura une influence notable sur les cours;

d. de porter à la connaissance de l'Association du commerce des valeurs, immédiatement, par la voie la plus rapide et si possible avant 11h30 ou après 13h30 du jour de la publication, toute communication destinée à publication ayant de l'importance pour les détenteurs d'actions de la société;

e. en cas d'extension de la part placée du capital social par placement de gré à gré, ou en cas de placement de gré à gré de titres convertibles en valeurs faisant partie du capital social, à en informer l'Association du commerce des valeurs au plus tard le deuxième jour ouvrable après celui où le placement s'est opéré et - pour autant que ce ne soit pas encore chose faite - de faire une publication, si l'Association du commerce des effets le juge souhaitable.[36]

Dans une communication récente de l'Association à ses membres, la possibilité a été créée de suspendre la cotation officielle, et ce afin d'empêcher "que l'inégalité d'information des parties prenant part au commerce n'influence défavorablement le cours"[37]. L'arrêté du C.E.S. relatif aux règles de conduite en matière de fusions comprend également une disposition ayant une portée similaire, prévoyant l'obligation de publier au plus tôt toute information susceptible d'influencer les cours. De par sa nature, cet arrêté a cependant un champ d'application plus restreint que les prescriptions de l'Association. En effet, l'arrêté du C.E.S. se limite à un seul domaine, à savoir la fusion ou la reprise d'entreprises (ou l'intention d'y procéder).
L'arrêté relatif aux règles de conduite élaboré par le C.E.S. (1975) est subdivisé en quatre chapitres. Le premier, qui traite de la matière qui nous intéresse, prescrit les règles de conduite à observer en vue de protéger les intérêts des action-

naires; il est d'application lorsqu'une société anonyme ou une société "fermée" à responsabilité limitée prépare ou lance une offre publique sur des actions, sur des certificats de ces actions, de même que sur les obligations d'une société anonyme convertibles en actions ou en certificats d'actions, lorsque ces actions etc. sont cotées en bourse ou traitées couramment aux Pays-Bas[38].
Le champ d'application du premier chapitre de l'arrêté du C.E.S. relatif aux règles de conduite en matière de fusions est étendu aux offres non publiques, préparées ou lancées par une S.A. sur des actions nominatives, lorsque pareille offre est ou sera portée à la connaissance de plus de la moitié des détenteurs des actions de la catégorie qui fait l'objet de l'offre, inscrits au registre des actions visé aux articles 85 et 194 du Livre 2 du Code civil. Si les conditions d'application du chapitre premier de l'arrêté du C.E.S. se trouvent réunies, il importe de connaître - pour le sujet qui nous intéresse - la teneur de l'article 3, dont l'alinéa 1er est libellé comme suit:

> *"Lorsqu'une offre publique est préparée ou lancée, les directions des S.A. concernées sont tenues, dès que surviennent des circonstances qui requièrent la publication d'un communiqué en vue de sauvegarder l'évolution normale du cours des actions, de procéder immédiatement à une telle publication."*[39]

De l'avis de la Commission pour les fusions[40], cette norme générale de publication doit permettre d'informer immédiatement les actionnaires d'une société faisant ou ayant fait l'objet d'une offre, de tous les éléments de fait déterminants pour la formation du choix en rapport avec l'offre et, partant, pour la formation des cours des actions en question[41]. Comme circonstance requérant un communiqué public, l'article 3, 2me alinéa c, indique:

> *"Une évolution de cours ou un autre développement susceptible d'indiquer que l'existence de négociations relatives à une offre publique ou l'intention unilatérale de faire une offre publique est connue par des tiers, qui pourraient faire usage de cette connaissance."*

Selon le commentaire de la Commission pour les fusions, cette disposition tend à obliger ceux, qui sont associés à la préparation d'une offre publique, à faire une publication dès qu' existe ne fût-ce que la moindre possibilité d'abus d'information préalable[42]
Notamment dans le but de prévenir pareil abus, l'arrêté du C.E.S. précise aux articles 5 et 6 que le prix et le rapport d'échange doivent être rendus publics au plus tôt. L'article 8

de l'arrêté relatif aux règles de conduite en matière de fusions s'applique également de manière spécifique à la matière qui nous intéresse, bien qu'elle ait un caractère quelque peu différent des dispositions citées plus haut. Cette disposition est libellée comme suit:

> 1. *Tout directeur et administrateur de chacune des S.A. concernées par une offre publique est tenu de fournir à la Commission, au moment de la publication de l' "avis d'offre", un relevé précis des transactions effectuées, au cours des six mois précédant la première communication publique en matière de prix ou de rapport d'échange, par lui-même, son épouse, ses enfants mineurs et des personnes morales dans lesquelles ces personnes ont la maîtrise, et portant sur:*
> *a) des titres de la S.A. visée, et*
> *b) si l'offre tend exclusivement ou accessoirement à la remise en échange des titres offerts de titres émis ou à émettre par la S.A. offrante.*
> 2. *Tout directeur et administratuer de la S.A. visée est tenu de fournir à la Commission, au moment où l' "avis d'offre" est publié, un relevé précis du nombre et de la catégorie des actions et autres titres émis par la S.A. visée détenus par lui-même, son épouse, ses enfants mineurs et des personnes morales dans lesquelles ces personnes ont la maîtrise.*

On peut observer que d'une part, la notion de communication obligatoire est très large, en ce sens qu'elle se rapporte à tous les "titres" et qu'elle ne se limite donc pas à des titres spécifiquement désignés; d'autre part, cet article prévoit uniquement cette communication obligatoire, sans interdire ou sanctionner autrement les transactions qui en font l'objet et qui pourraient avoir été faites à la suite d'un abus de connaissance préalable[43]. Le nonrespect des règles de conduite énoncées par l'arrêté du C.E.S. peut avoir pour effet que la Commission des fusions prononce un blâme public ou publie un communiqué[44]. La publication se fait par le truchement de l'organe d'information du C.E.S. Aucune suite juridique directe n'est attachée à cette sanction, étant donné que les règles de conduite établies par l'arrêté du C.E.S. constituent des normes n'ayant pas force de loi. En tant que tel, l'arrêté du C.E.S. n'a donc aucune force impérative à l'égard des directions d'entreprises auxquelles il s'adresse[45].
Le caractère non-impératif de l'arrêté du C.E.S. n'implique cependant pas que dans la pratique il n'aurait pas plus d'effet que celui que peut avoir d'ordinaire tout code de conduite élaboré avec la participation des membres du groupe même ou de leurs représentants. La force de loi indirecte de l'arrêté résulte pour une bonne part de l'influence de l'Association pour

le commerce des valeurs, qui dans une communication du 9 septembre 1971 a imposé à ses membres un certain nombre d'obligations en rapport avec l'arrêté du C.E.S.[46]. Cette communication est rédigée comme suit:

1. *Si avant le lancement d'une offre publique sur actions, ou avant la réalisation d'une fusion ou d' une reprise, un membre est informé par l'une des sociétés intéressées d'une telle intention ou s'il est associé à des discussions à ce sujet, le membre en question est tenu de veiller à ce que les sociétés observent le code de conduite en matière de fusions 1971.*
2. *Si une société concernée par une offre publique sur actions demande la collaboration d'un membre pour la composition de l' "avis d'offre" à publier, le membre en question est tenu de veiller:*
   a) à ce que le contenu de cet avis d'offre réponde aux normes fixées en la matière dans la Code de conduite en matière de fusions 1971 et aux autres conditions fixées à cet égard par l'Association pour le commerce des valeurs;
   b) à ce que soient respectées les règles du Code de conduite en matière de fusions 1971 imposant la communication de certains relevés à la Commission pour les fusions au moment de la publication de l'avis d'offre.
3. *Si dans l'un des cas visés sub 1 et 2 il apparaît au membre que la société concernée - ou l'une des sociétés concernées - entend ne pas observer, ou n' observer qu'en partie, les règles de conduite en matière de fusions 1971, le membre est tenu de refuser sa collaboration ou d'y mettre fin, sauf évidemment dans le cas où la Commission pour les fusions a accordé une dérogation aux règles susdites.*

(...)

En ce qui concerne les sanctions - communiqué et blâme publics - pouvant être prononcées par la Commission pour les fusions, on peut dire que leur impact réside dans l'*effet du pilori*[47]. Dans la communication citée ci-dessus l'Association pour le commerce des valeurs avait à l'origine attaché une conséquence indirecte à un blâme prononcé par la Commission pour les fusions, en ce sens que dans ce cas, les membres étaient tenus de refuser toute collaboration à l'exécution et la réalisation de l'offre, et le cas échéant d'y mettre fin. Or, eu égard notamment à l'intervention obligatoire d'un commissionnaire, conformément à l'article 2 de la *Beschikking Beursverkeer* 1947, la non-intervention des membres de l'Association comporte que l'offre ne peut être effectuée[48]. Après quelques années d'expérience, la commission chargée de contrôler l'application de l'arrêté relatif aux règles de conduite en matière de fusions, en est arrivée à rompre l'automatisme entre les sanctions qu'elle prononce et celles de l'Association pour le commerce des valeurs. Dans des cas exceptionnels, notamment lorsque des intérêts supérieurs requièrent que l'offre publique soit faite en tout état de cause, la commission compétente du C.E.S. peut non-obstant le blâme public qu'elle aurait prononcé, demander à l'Association de laisser à ses membres la liberté d'accorder leur collaboration à la poursuite de l'offre publique[49].

Certains auteurs considèrent qu'à une infraction au code de conduite du C.E.S. est attaché un autre effet juridique, indirect il est vrai, du fait qu'elle constitue un acte illicite au sens de l'article 1401 du Code civil[50]. Le raisonnement tenu est que la violation du code de conduite constitue un acte ou une omission qui est "contraire ... à la convenance sociale qui veut que l'on respecte la personne ou le bien d'autrui"[51]. *Wijckerheld Bisdom* fonde ce raisonnement sur la considération que l'arrêté du C.E.S. relatif aux règles de conduite - puisqu'il résulte d'un consensus au sein de C.E.S., organe dont on peut attendre qu'outre les intérêts des personnes intéressées directement, il ait également pris en considération les intérêts des clients et des consommateurs, l'intérêt général en somme - que ce code, donc, peut être considéré comme un ensemble de normes qui répondent à la convenance sociale[52]. La jurisprudence n'a toujours pas apporté de réponse à la question de savoir si un actionnaire, lésé par le fait de ne pas avoir reçu les informations indispensables au sujet d'une offre publique projetée - dommage dont on peut considérer qu'il résulte d'un abus de connaissance préalable - peut se retourner contre la société sur la base de raisonnement précité concernant l'acte illicite.
Dans le rapport de la Commission pour le droit des sociétés, il a été envisagé de suggérer au Ministre de prévoir, outre la disposition pénale proposée, l'obligation légale pour les administrateurs et commissaires, leurs épouses et enfants mineurs, de faire communication des actions, certificats d'actions et obligations convertibles en actions qu'ils détiennent. On a exclusivement songé à une communication obligatoire, sans envisager d'interdire en même temps certaines transactions dans des périodes "critiques". Bien que l'on considérait que l'introduction d'une telle obligation légale présente certains avantages, notamment celui d'appuyer la sanction pénale proposée par la Commission[53], la majorité des membres de la Commission n'a pas jugé souhaitable de prévoir une disposition de ce genre.

Un des arguments invoqués contre pareille obligation était que ceux, qui veulent abuser de leur connaissance préalable, ne se laisseraient pas intimider par une obligation de communication, mais qu'ils essaieraient de s'y soustraire par le truchement d'hommes de paille ou par le biais de banques étrangères. Par ailleurs, il fut observé que cette disposition porterait atteinte à la vie privée des personnes astreintes à la communication. Enfin, la mesure pourrait amener les personnes visées à se défaire des actions qu'ils détiennent dans leur propre société, ce qui ne profitereait guère à la stabilité au sein de l'assemblée générale des actionnaires[54]. *Uniken Venema*, qui partageait l'opinion majoritaire de la Commission, fit observer qu'une disposition visant à soumettre à une communication obligatoire des situations déterminées, critiques dans le cadre de l'abus d'information préalable, aurait plus d'effet qu' une obligation générale[55]. A cet égard, on s'est référé à la communication obligatoire "spécifique" prévue à l'article 8 de l'arrêté du C.E.S. relatif aux règles de conduite en matière de fusions, et qui vise une situation concrète pouvant être considérée comme critique sous l'angle de l'abus de connaissance préalable.

NOTES

1. Conformément à l'article 1 de la *Beschikking Beursverkeer* 1947 (arrêté relatif aux opérations en bourse) il y a lieu d'entendre par titres: actions, obligations, lettres de gage, parts de fonds de placement, actions de jouissance ou parts de fondateur, certificats d'option et toutes autres valeurs similaires, les inscriptions dans les registres de créances et d'actions et tous autres droits similaires.
2. La Commission pour le droit des sociétés est une commission consultative créée par le Ministre de Justice (*Staatscourant* 1968.138) ayant eu notamment pour tâche d'émettre un avis au sujet du présent problème.
3. Rapport relatif à l'abus d'information préalable d 5 juillet 1973, *Staatsuitgeverij* 1973, également repris dans le fascicule *N.V. en B.V.*, p. VII, a-1.
4. Cfr. C.AE. Uniken Venema, Voorwetenschap, *TVVS* 1964, p. 4; F.W.C. Blom, Misbruik van voorwetenschap, *TVVS* 1970, p. 58; Th.S. IJsselmuiden, Witteboorden criminaliteit in ondernemingen, *RMTh* 1973, p. 104/105.
5. Cfr. également Nederlands Genootschap voor Bedrijfsjuristen, *De Naamlooze Vennootschap* 1981, p. 57.
6. Arrêt du 27 mars 1947, *Stb.* H 105.
7. B. de Smalen, *Effectenbeurs, effectenbedrijf en effectenverkeer*, 1975, p. 30.
8. Loi du 4 septembre 1914, *Stb.* 445.
9. Article 3 des statuts de l'Association.
10. Pour une énumération des règlements voir B. de Smalen, Effectenbeurs in nieuwe stijl, *Serie Bank- en effectenbedrijf* nr. 2, 1974, p. 14/15.
11. Cfr. Annexes J et K du *Fondsenreglement*, publié dans *Rechtspersonen*, J.G.N. de Hoop Scheffer.
12. Article 5, al. 1, du Réglement d'Ordre.
13. *Wet op de bedrijfsorganisatie* du 27 januari 1950, *Stb.* K 22.
14. Art. 2 de la *Wet op de bedrijfsorganisatie*.
15. Cfr. D. Kokkini-Iatridou, Rapports néerlandais pour le Dixième Congrès International de Droit Comparé, p. 139.
16. *Handboek voor de naamloze en besloten vennootschap*, revu par W.C.L. van der Grinten, 1976, no. 178.2 et 257; Rapport de la *Commissie Vennootschapsrecht*, 1973, no. 5; C.AE. Uniken Venema, *Misbruik van voorwetenschap*, 1974, p. 22 et 28.
17. HR 15 novembre 1957, *NJ* 1958.67, nt. L.E.H.R.
18. Cfr. HR 7 décembre 1979, *NJ* 1980.290, nt. G.J.S.
19. L'article 3.2.10, al. 4, du nouveau Code civil, qui sera instauré probablement d'ici quelques années, prévoit explicitement l'abus de circonstances.
20. Cfr. HR 11 janvier 1957, *NJ* 1959.37, nt. H.B.; HR 29 mai 1964, *NJ* 1965.104, nt. G.J.S.; HR 29 avril 1971, *NJ* 1972.336, nt. E.A.A.L.; HR 15 novembre 1974, *NJ* 1976.122, nt. E.A.A.L.; HR 13 juin 1975, *NJ* 1976.98, nt. G.J.S.
21. *Misbruik van voorwetenschap*, 1974, p. 28, nt. 38.
22. J.H. Maschhaupt, Misbruik van voorwetenschap, *TVVS* 1969, p. 294; *Handboek voor de naamloze en de besloten vennootschap*, 1976, nr. 178.2.; *Rapport van de Commissie Vennootschapsrecht*, 1973, no. 3.
23. *Misbruik van voorwetenschap*, 1974, p. 48 et 54.
24. Dans l'affaire "Erdal", la seule question soulevée était le caractère licite d'une indemnisation globale - HR 24 septembre 1976, *NJ* 1978.135, nt. B.W. On trouve un exemple très clair d'un usage considéré comme abusif et illicite de connaissance préalable en dehors du domaine de la vente et de l'achat d'actions dans HR 27 février 1970, *NJ* 1970.239, nt. G.J.S. Cfr. pour les aspects fiscaux de l'abus de connaissance préalable: Langereis, *Weekblad voor fiscaal recht* 1978, p. 969 e.s.
25. J.H. Maschhaupt, Misbruik van voorwetenschap, *TVVS* 1969, p. 294; Th.S. IJsselmuiden, Witteboorden criminaliteit in ondernemingen, *RMTh* 1973, p. 100 e.s.; *Rapport van de Commissie Vennootschapsrecht* 1973, no. 7; C.AE. Uniken Venema, *Misbruik van voorwetenschap*, 1974, p. 19 et 20; Nederlands Genootschap voor Bedrijfsjuristen, *De Naamloze Vennootschap* 59me année 1981, p. 59.
26. *Misbruik van voorwetenschap*, 1974, p. 57.
27. *Handboek voor de naamloze en de besloten vennootschap*, 1976, no. 257.
28. Voorlopig Verslag, Bijl. Hand. Tweede Kamer, zitting 1968-69, 9595, 9596 (nr. 5) p. 13.
29. Memorie van Antwoord, Bijl. Hand. Tweede Kamer, zitting 1968-69, nr. 9595, 9596 (nr. 6), p. 12.
30. *Rapport Commissie Vennootschapsrecht* 1973, nr. 10.
31. *Misbruik van voorwetenschap* 1974, p. 71-74.
32. Bijl. Hand. Tweede Kamer, zitting 1979-80, 16 326 (nr. 2).

33. Loi du 22 juin 1950, *Stb.* K 258.
34. *TVVS* 1970, p. 314-315.
35. Il s'agit en l'occurrence d'actions, d'actions de jouissance, de parts de fondateur et de certificats d'actions.
36. *Fondsenreglement* (règlement des fonds), publié dans: *Rechtspersonen*, J.G.N. de Hoop Scheffer.
37. Communication du 19 mai 1981.
38. On parle de commerce courant, tant en bourse qu'hors bourse, lorsque les titres font l'objet de plusieurs transactions par trimestre chaque année, selon le *Commentaar op het SER-besluit fusiegedragsregels*, 1975, 2me éd., p. 6.
39. Pour l'application de la publication obligatoire de cet article, tel qu'il était rédigé dans l'arrêté relatif aux règles de conduite de 1971, voir G.J.W. Arendsen de Wolff, Publiciteit bij openbare biedingen, *TVVS* 1973, p. 315-318.
40. Blâme public du 27 août 1973, *Commentaar op het Ser-besluit fusiegedragsregels* 1975, 2me éd., p. 11.
41. Par actions, on entend toujours les titres cités antérieurement dans le texte: art. 1, al. 1 et 2, de l'arrêté du CES relatif aux règles de conduite en matière de fusions 1975.
42. Cfr. *SER-besluit fusiegedragsregels* 1975, p. 35.
43. Au sujet de l'absence de sanction, voir C.R.C. Wijckerheld Bisdom, Bij de derde versie van hoofdstuk 1 van de Fusiegedragsregels, *TVVS* 1975, p. 234 et 235; 14e Verslag van de Commissie voor Fusieaangelegenheden, 4me trim. 1973, p. 8/9.
44. Art. 32 *SER-besluit fusiegedragsregels* 1975.
45. Au sujet du caractère juridique de l'arrêté du CES relatif aux règles de conduite en matière de fusions, voir C.R.C. Wijckerheld Bisdom, De Nederlandse Fusiegedragsregels, dans: *Recht in beweging, Opstellen aangeboden aan Prof. Mr. Ridder R. Victor*, II, Anvers, p. 1358 et 1359.
46. Communication 342 du 9 septembre 1971.
47. Voir à ce sujet C.R.C. Wijckerheld Bisdom, l.c., p. 1360.
48. Sur l'effet de cette non-intervention, voir *TVVS* 1971, p. 223.
49. *Commentaar op het SER-besluit fusiegedragsregels* 1975, 2me éd.,p. 100/101.
50. G.J.W. Arendsen de Wolff, *De informatieplicht van de onderneming*, 1976, p. 310-312 (avec bibliographie étendue).
51. HR 31 janvier 1919, *NJ* 1919.161.
52. C.R.C. Wijckerheld Bisdom, l.c. p. 1366.
53. Au sujet de cette fonction d'appui, voir également C.AE. Uniken Venema, *Misbruik van voorwetenschap*, 1974, p. 65-68.
54. *Rapport Commissie Vennootschapsrecht* 1973, p. 8.
55. *Misbruik van voorwetenschap*, 1974, p. 68.

Piped transportation in the Netherlands

Ch. P. VERWER
III.A.3.
Civil servant Dept. of Economic Affairs, Directorate-General for Energy, The Hague

INTRODUCTION

This study comprises a survey of the (procedural) laws which have a direct influence on the installation and exploitation of pipelines in the Netherlands.
The survey is preceded by a brief consideration of the transportation by pipeline already existing in the Netherlands.

I. Transportation through pipelines can be classified in two ways:

a. *on the basis of the products transported;*
b. *on the basis of the pipeline's purpose.*

a. *Products transported*

The rough distinction that can be made on the basis of products transported by pipelines is as follows:
1. drinking and waste water
2. natural gas, oil and chemical products.
This classification has various consequences for the laws which (can) apply to the different pipeline systems.

Drinking water and waste water pipes

Water has been piped over great distances since the beginning of this century; particularly for the purpose of providing drinking water for Amsterdam, a pipeline was installed to transport water from the Rhine to the dunes lying to the west of the capital. This water is then piped on to Amsterdam after a natural filtration process in the dunes. This transportation is not dealt with in this article, as the pipes concerned are usually used for the public benefit by (lesser) authorities.

To these pipelines apply provincial regulations, insofar as they exist. For the law applicable to the municipal distribution of drinking water, see p. 5.

(Natural) gas, oil and chemical products

The discovery of a large source of gas in the north of the Netherlands in particular has led to the construction of an entire network of pipelines, specifically for the transportation of gas, in the last twenty years. The concentration of petro-chemical industry in the western districts of the port of Rotterdam and in the industrial area on the Westerschelde is the reason for the existence of an extensive system of pipelines in these areas and of some pipelines, both single and in groups from Rotterdam and Zeeland respectively to the hinterland, viz. the Ruhr and Antwerp. In addition, the development of the chemical industry in the former coal mining area of Limburg has led to piped transportation there, with connections to Rotterdam.

b. *The pipeline's purpose*

The pipelines transporting products can be classified into three categories, related to the purpose of the pipeline. I will briefly indicate below that there are also legally relevant differences. The classification is as follows:
- *production lines* : lines which form part of a product extraction installation
- *transport lines* : lines which are intended or used for the transportation of a product, usually over great distances
- *distribution lines*: lines which are intended for the transportation of a product to individual consumers within a particular area (especially a municipality).

Examples of these three different types of pipeline can be found in the Netherlands for the transportation of natural gas. There are *production lines*, connecting the point of extraction to the transportation network. This type of pipeline is dealt with from a legal point of view by the *mining legislation*. The 1903 Mining Act[1] contains a general directive measure consisting, inter alia, of provisions for the transportation of explosive products "to ensure safety in mining operations.... and of .... minerals".
The Mining Regulations[2] contains rules for "Pipelines for the purpose of extracting minerals" in chapter 8a (articles 143a-d). These rules cover the procedure for laying pipelines "intended for the transportation of the extracted minerals"; the installer is obliged to submit plans for installation, and if there is any possibility of danger, the Minister of Economic Affairs

has the power to prescribe the route and the method of installation (art. 143b). The other two articles (143c and 143d) urge the installer to take adequate measures for the prevention of any danger, when laying the pipeline.
The gas is then transported through the *transportation lines* of the transportation network, from the connection points on the production network to the connection points of the distribution networks. These are characterised, inter alia, by a higher diameter, higher pressure and the exploitation by the N.V. Gas Unie (Gas Board). They are not subject to specific legislation as regards the exploitation, nor as regards installation.
The *distribution lines* transport the gas from the transport line to the individual consumers and are characterised by a fine network of pipes with a relatively small diameter, lower pressure etc. They are controlled by the municipal and district energy companies.
The distribution and transportation of drinking water is subject to separate legislation, the Waterworks Act[3]. This act is predominantly concerned with the hygiene aspects of the provision of drinking water, and its organization. The Provincial Executive Committee has a great deal of responsibility in this respect and it can impose an obligatory concession (art. 26). However, the concession conditions can be concerned only with tarif levels, the obligation to supply and co-operation with other boards (art. 30).

II. INSTALLATION OF PIPELINES

N.b. Unless stated otherwise, the pipelines mentioned hereafter refer to the transportation lines.

Amicable settlement

In the Netherlands it is possible to arrive at an agreement with landowners whose property is affected by the installation of a pipeline, on the basis of agreements in private law. The effect may temporarily be significant - during the installation - but during the exploitation of the pipeline the effect need not be very extensive. This depends particularly on the depth at which the pipe has been laid, the composition of the soil etc.

Concession

If it is not possible to agree with a landowner on the basis of an agreement in private law, on the installation of a pipeline, the pipeline cannot be installed. However, this can be undesirable for a number of reasons. The government may

consider the installation of a pipeline for the transportation of a product for a particular connection.
The installer can obtain a "recognition" of his intention from the government by being granted a concession for "the installation and maintenance of a pipeline"[4]. With this concession the installer can tackle many problems for which there was no solution on the basis of agreements in private law with the landowners.
It is strange that there is no legislation provided for the authority to grant the concessions for this form of transportation. The concession is granted by the Crown on the recommendation of the Minister of Economic Affairs. The granting of concessions is specifically dealt with by law[5] for a form of transportation with comparable infrastructural consequences, resulting from the installation: the railways. It should be noted that these concessions for the installation of an infrastructure for transportation are granted by the Crown on the recommendation of the Minister of Transport and Waterworks.

Indirectly the requirements for a concession have been laid down in law: in the Act on Hindrances in Private Law[6] and in the Act regulating statutory instruments on Hindrances[7], the acquisition of a concession can be a condition for a temporary lifting of a hindrance of private or public law on the basis of these acts.
In addition, a declaration in law that the installation would be in the public interest, can have the same consequences.
As the granting of concessions for (the installation and maintenance of) pipelines has not yet been laid down in law, the question is whether conditions may be imposed on the concessions. Current practice shows that conditions are imposed on the concessions, and anyone requesting a concession will probably not get very far by objecting to particular conditions. In this respect legislation is desirable. As far as I know, there is no case law on this question.

Expropriation

The application of the two acts on hindrances can result only in landowners having to submit to orders, while being accorded damages (Act on Hindrances in Private Law) or granting permission to act contrary to statutory instruments or to obtain the requisite licence. Although this will often be sufficient for the exploitation of a pipeline, it is conceivable that particularly when a number of pipelines have to be laid close together it might be necessary to have complete control over the land where the lines run. The Expropriation Act deals with this. For its application a declaration of public interest is requested, on the basis of a provision in the constitution[8].

PIPED TRANSPORTATION

As regards (pipelines for) the supply of drinking water, art. 72b of the Expropriation Act provides that a Royal Decree is sufficient for the declaration of public interest on which the expropriation is based.
The provision does not distinguish between pipelines for distribution and those for transportation, and this leads to the conclusion that this article will also apply to the transportation lines as indicated above.
A similar "simplified" procedure for expropriation applies to the contents of a development plan (art. 77); this may also be the case for a pipeline. I will continue the discussion of development plans under III.
In principle, the installation of the proposed pipeline can commence if the restrictions on the plan have been cleared up in one of the ways described above. However, some legislation must be taken into account, which, although not specifically aimed at the installation of pipelines, does have consequences for the installation. In the first instance, there is the Environment Act[9]. This act is responsible for the optimal use of space, which is so limited in the Netherlands. The installation of a pipeline should therefore be incorporated into the intended planning under this act.

A brief survey of the Environment Act follows below. In the Environment Act there are three levels of plans :

municipal	-	development plan
provincial	-	district plan
central government	-	government policy laid down in structural plans.

The development plan regulates the allocation of space at a municipal level. This type of plan can provide the permission required for the installation of a pipeline. The completion of a development plan can take a considerable length of time, for in the preliminary decision there is a possibility of a Crown appeal after approval from the Provincial Executive Committee, and this in itself may take a few years. The Crown appeal has a delaying effect. The higher government levels may give instructions regarding the contents of a development or district plan. The provincial authorities can give instructions in advance regarding the contents of a development plan under the conditions of art. 37, and on the basis of art. 38, the Minister of the Environment can give the provinces instructions concerning the district plan or instructions which the provinces must give the municipality concerning the development plans. These procedures are extremely time consuming, considering that the normal course of a district or development plan, including the possibilities of appeal, remains unaltered.

In urgent cases, however, the Government can bypass all this on the basis of art. 65 of the Environment Act[10], which provides the possibility of exemption for certain procedural elements. However, this procedure is rarely used, as it disrupts the normal context of decision making in a rather radical way, totally discounting local interests. Even though this is a procedure for urgent cases, it still usually takes about a year, mainly because the Minister has to discuss the matter with the lesser authorities involved.

In this legal system, the municipality plays an important role: it draws up the development plan in which the municipality lays down the plans for the allocation of its area. The development plan has some normative value: in an area destined for housing, no industry may be introduced, and vice-versa. The planning of roads, railways etc. is also included in a development plan.
In determining the plan of the pipeline to be installed, the installer must take the development plans into account, and if necessary, make alterations if there is no room in the existing plan for a pipeline.
In the event that a pipeline cuts across a number of municipalities, the procedure may be time consuming and complicated, for the plans of two neighbouring municipalities have to be altered along the same lines. If this does not happen, it is impossible to achieve a co-ordinated plan.
In addition to the acts discussed above, the installer is also concerned with other legal provisions with a general application concerning the construction of installations and the protection of the environment. Examples include the Public Nuisance Act[11], the Noise Pollution Act[12] (pumping installations) to the extent that the pipeline (or parts of it) of the installations belonging to it fall within the criteria of these acts' scopes of operation. Of the legislation referred to, the Noise Pollution Act is most of all a law for the protection of the environment. There is also a bill pending in parliament concerning the protection of the soil, which will have consequences for the installation and exploitation of pipelines. At present it is not possible to predict whether, or in what form, this bill will become law, and when this regime will enter into operation.

III. EXPLOITATION OF PIPELINES

Part I has shown that there is transportation through pipelines for various purposes on a fairly considerable scale in the Netherlands. The exploiters of pipelines have come together in the Association of Pipeline Owners in the Netherlands (VELIN), which discusses common problems concerned with

exploitation, and prepares recommendations for the government. Apart from the Gas Board and *Defensie Olie Centrale* (Oil Transport Section of the Ministry of Defense), the members include many companies active in the (petro) chemical production sector which have to use large pipelines or networks of pipelines for this purpose. The owners of the water pipelines in the Netherlands have their own organization, entirely independent of that industrially based association.
In view of the fact that their interests are completely different, it is understandable that the common pipeline exploiters fall into these two distinct groups.

With regard to the pipelines which are not situated in the pipeline route Pernis - Klundert, general provisions of law apply regarding installation and control. This means that the liability towards third parties of the pipeline exploiter and the owner for the products transported falls under art. 1401 CC. In the event of damages to third parties resulting from the specific use of a pipeline, it is not possible to determine who is primarily liable for the damages caused, as in the manner indicated in the Act on Matters of Public Interest of 1972[13]. This clearly shows that it could be extremely difficult to determine whether the owner of the product transported, or the exploiter of the pipeline, would be wholly or partially liable.
These are questions of proof regarding the causality between the damage and the product or between the damage and the transportation by pipeline.

The exploiter of a pipeline is free to undertake transportation for others. There are a few exploiters who do nothing else, as the sole purpose of their company is to undertake transportation. A closer look reveals that this type of exploiter forms an economic unit with the company for whom he is arranging transportation. One suspects that the division into legally independent units has only been arranged to spread financial risks. If injured parties do not suffer as a result, there is no objection to this kind of division.
There are also pipeline exploiters who produce and export products themselves, in addition to transporting them for third parties.
However, it is virtually impossible to transport individually determined amounts, and the solution for this sort of transportation has been found in agreements on purchase and supply. An amount 'A' with a value 'B' is received, and an amount 'X' with a value 'Y' is supplied, so that this can be seen in the context of A x B = X x Y. In fact, this is a matter of sales and purchase agreements which facilitate production processes in various disparate companies in the context of multinational enterprises.

During the session 1979 - 1980 a bill was submitted to parliament aimed at guaranteeing the efficient and, above all, safe transportation for the large scale importation of LPG. For this purpose it has been decided that a permit will be required for the importation and exportation and in the conditions, one method of transportation is described. This refers particularly to transportation by pipeline.

However, this policy is difficult to achieve because of the lack of a legal procedure which could achieve the advantages of the application of the Act on Matters of Public Interest (see chapter IV) for the installation of a single pipeline. The procedure for the installer is complex and full of pitfalls (see chapter II) because of the existing legislation, particularly in the area of town and country planning.
In addition, the installer needs a great deal of patience to see the procedure through. This makes it very unattractive for industry to think about using pipelines in a hurry, as an alternative to large scale transportation. It is up to the government to clarify the situation so that pipelines can function as an equal alternative to transportation by road, rail or waterways.

IV. THE PIPELINE ROUTE[14]

Towards the end of the 1960s it became necessary to connect the port areas of Rotterdam, Moerdijk, Antwerpen and Zeeland by a network of pipelines.
The proximity of water reservoirs for the supply of drinking water also put pressure on this area for the installations of pipelines for drinking water. There seemed to be advantages in grouping together in the plans all the pipelines that were expected to be required within a particular area. These advantages could be expressed in the construction of a pipeline system capable of being crossed by waterways, railways and roads.
This might encourage future installers to use this existing plan for other pipelines because of a centralised control of the route. In view of this large scale plan, expropriation of the land seemed the best solution, so that a so-called Act on Matters of Public Interest was required in accordance with the Expropriation Act (see chapter II.3).
The bill developed into its present form particularly as a result of parliamentary suggestions : a bill incorporating a regulation for the control of the pipeline route, liability towards third parties and an obligation to insure for this liability, as well as the technicalities concerned with expropriation.

PIPED TRANSPORTATION

This act contains a basic regulation for some aspects which arise in the exploitation of pipeline routes; it is conceivable that a legal arrangement for the exploitation of single pipelines could deal with the subject in an analagous fashion.

Before discussing the act in more detail, I would like to make one remark concerning government policy with regard to transportation by pipeline. On 26 January 1972 it was agreed at the plenary meeting in the Second Chamber of the Parliament that there would be a structural scheme for transportation by pipeline. Up to now no structural scheme has been submitted, although this was once more agreed to in the answers to questions from the Chamber on 29 May 1979[15].

As indicated earlier, the aim of the subject was initially limited to a declaration of public benefit that a pipeline route was needed in the interests of the public, and that expropriation should be carried out for this purpose. The first first two articles of the act concern this question exclusively. In fact, this aim of the act has been achieved now that the provisions of the act have entered into force
Arts. 5 and 6 deal with procedural requirements incorporated for the achievement of the pipeline route dealt with in this act. The practical importance of this lies in the other provisions of the act. These empower the Minister of Transport and Waterworks to establish a legal person in private law together with the other signatories[16]. This legal person will be concerned with "the installation and furnishing, maintenance and control of the pipeline route"[17]. In addition, other infrastructural waterworks constructions can be transferred to the controlling body and it is charged with the obligation to reimburse any "damage inflicted upon persons or other things which are not pipelines or establishments connected with pipelines within the pipeline route, or materials within this area, and which is a result of the ignition, explosion or escape of products which are found in one or more of the pipelines or establishments along the route on the grounds of the sole fact that such damage was caused by this" (Art. 4, par. 1).
This puts liability for risks on the controlling body which does not apply for natural disasters "of an exceptional nature", terrorism or sabotage. The question is, when can a natural disaster considered to be "exceptional"? Would the floods of 1953 warrant consideration as an exception to the obligation to compensate for damages, while a single break in the dyke at the level of the pipeline would not? There is also a possibility of moderation in the case of deliberate damage or gross neglect for the injured party.
In my opinion, it is very important that art. 4 also provides that, with the exception of deliberate damage or gross neglence, no liability should be attributed to "the owner or user of the

products transported by the pipeline which caused the damage, the user of a pipeline, the subordinates of the controlling body, or contractors not subordinated to it, which the controlling body causes to carry out work, in accordance with its task". This provision attributes a large measure of responsibility to the controlling body, which should, after all, offer a guarantee towards the party wishing to transport products through a pipeline which it does not own.
The controlling body will then have to impose requirements for technical qualities in order to give substance to "the obligation for a guarantee" required by law.

Finally, as a last consideration, in the liability for risk of the controlling body, the law incorporates a duty for the body to insure itself against "liability in accordance with the regulations in pursuance of this act" (art. 3, par. 6).
This provision has been sanctioned in two ways :

a. the Minister of Transport and Waterworks can stop transportation by pipeline along the route, if this obligation has not been met (art. 3, par. 6 in fine) and
b. the party accepting insurance as a guarantor of the controlling body is not free to terminate the cover without giving at least two months' notice.

The further elaboration of the obligation to insure can be carried out as a general directive measure (par. 8); as far as I know up to this moment, no substance has been given to this elaboration.

Meanwhile a controlling body as prescribed in the 1972 Act on Matters of Public Interest was set up on 21 December 1978. One year later the Foundation for the Pipeline Route of the Southwest Netherlands had virtually completed everything for the takeover under a long term lease granted to the Foundation by the State of the Netherlands, which now owned all land acquired by means of expropriation on the basis of the Act on Matters of Public Interest. The exploitation[18] is by the Foundation, started in 1979, and it has made a report on this[19].
The current procedure is for a delegate to draw up an agreement with the Foundation in order to install a new pipeline in the pipeline route, and if the parties can agree, install the pipeline. The agreement incorporates a number of requirements concerned with reciprocal rights and obligations.

PIPED TRANSPORTATION

NOTES

1. The Act of 27 April 1904 containing further provisions concerning mining, with the amendments of the Act of 21 April 1980, *Stb.* 73.
2. Royal Decree of 21 December 1964, *Stb.* 538.
3. Act of 6 April 1957 containing provisions regarding the control of waterworks companies and the organization of the supply of public drinking water. *Stb.* 150.
4. E.g. Concession of 8 May 1969, *KB* no. 25.
5. Act on the reorganization of the railways, 26 May 1937, *Stb.* 520, art. 6.
6. Act of 13 May 1927 for the abolition of hindrances in private law (*Stb.* 159).
7. Act of 23 April 1899 for the abolition of hindrances in the execution of works ordered or carried out for the public benefit and resulting from provisions in regulations, *Stb.* 129.
8. Art. 165 of the Constitution reads :
   1. Expropriation in the public interest can occur only after a prior declaration in law that expropriation would benefit the public interest, and after damages have been guaranteed or awarded in advance in accordance with the provisions of the law.
   2. The law determines the cases in which the above-mentioned declaration in law is not required.
   3. ....
   4. ....
9. Act of 5 July 1963, containing the definitive version of new provisions concerning the environment, *Stb.* 286.
10. This article states :
    1. With regard to works or activities in which speedy execution would benefit the public interest, our Minister can, upon request, grant exemption regarding provisions which are part of a development plan, the provision of art. 46, par. 2 and 5 of this act (...).
    2. Before arriving at a decision the Minister hears the municipal council and the provincial executive council as well as the State Planning Commission. If exemption is granted for the provisions of art. 46, par. 5 of this act, (...) the Minister also consults the Minister of Education, Arts and Sciences.
11. Act of 15 May 1952 containing new regulations for the prevention of establishments causing serious damage or hindrance (*Stb.* 274).
12. Act of 16 February 1979 containing regulations concerned with the prevention or restriction of noise pollution, (*Stb.* 99).
13. See Chapter IV.
14. The Act of 11 March 1972 containing a declaration of public interest of expropriation of plots of land, rights of way and other rights in rem for installing a pipeline route from Pernis through Klundert to the Schelde near the Dutch/Belgian border.
15. See Chamber records, session 1979 - 1980, *TK Appendix* 1553. April 1982 the scheme is published.
16. Ministry of Housing (of the people) and Environment of Affairs, Ministry of Justice, Ministry of Agriculture and Ministry of Finance.
17. Art. 3, par. 1 in fine.
18. 589 km. pipeline per ultimo '79.
19. Annual Report, 1979.

Computer programs as subject matter of intellectual property rights

D.W.F. VERKADE

Professor of Law at the University of Nijmegen,
Attorney, member of the Amsterdam Bar

III.B.1.

A. INTRODUCTION / HISTORY OF THE QUESTION

It cannot be said that legal protection of computer programs is a topic with an important history in The Netherlands, if it could be considered as a topic at all in this country. One important decision of our Patent Office excepted, court decisions are still lacking. Marked pressure from the side of interested circles being absent, there is for the time being no occasion for actual legislative activity, although the Dutch Government shows its interest in the discussions on the subject within the framework of WIPO/OMPI.
Probably like in other countries, in The Netherlands the first lawyers facing intellectual property problems relating to computer programs, during the nineteen-sixties, have been those who had to draft software development, sale, or leasing contracts, or who had to consider possible patent claims. Wider attention to this problem - and to legal problems arising from computer usage in general - has, as far as I know, for the first time been drawn by my colleague Dr. Alida Bos in 1968[1]. The first essay on possibilities and impossibilities of computer program protection under Dutch positive law was published in 1969[2]. It has not been followed up by literature, taking a different view on substantial points.

In the 19-seventies, the question was put on the agenda of the AIPPI (IAPIP). The position of the Dutch Group has been embodied in two reports, to which I will return below.
In the meantime, in 1970, the Dutch Patent Office had issued its - in general negative - decision as to the patentability of computer software. I will discuss this decision in paragraph C.
Although the software business is relatively important in The Netherlands, more 'history' than this - apart from some discussions in various associations - can hardly be reported here.

The practical experience with computer programs *thus far* in The Netherlands - and, as far as I can see, also in various other western European countries - do not urgently evoke statutory regulations for better protection, at least seen from the point of view of the software creators. Cases of misappropriation of computer programs have frequently been imagined, but thus far seldom been reported. The only issues which seem to occur with some frequency are those due to insufficient regulation of the contractual relationship between a (custom building) software supplier and its customer. Contractual regulation could preclude - but does not always preclude, due to insufficiency - serious and in practice occurring disputes on the position of the client after (possible premature) termination of his relationship with the supplier; on the position of the leased or hired, standard or custom-built software in cases of bankruptcy of one of the parties; and with regard to third-party-utilisation of software, developed in various forms of cooperation between the software firm and the client. But, as said, real 'computer program piracy' has thus far not become a burning problem. There are, in my opinion, two major reasons to explain this present situation.

In the first place there is a practical reason. To operate or at least to maintain the good working of a computer requires as yet a certain degree of specialized skill. Theft of a computer program is not enough to have this program operated, and much less to have this program revised, updated, etc. Of course, a 'thief' could be a skilled computer programmer or operator. But cases in which a skilled programmer, or a firm employing skilled programmers, really will be tempted to have a computer program stolen instead of buying it or developing such a program by himself or itself will be exceptional.
The other reason is a moral one. Fortunately, in many circles and more particularly in the specialized world of computer owners and programmers there is a strong common feeling that, even if the law would perhaps not prohibit computer program misappropriation or program piracy, such piracy is 'not done'. Under these circumstances one could argue - and it has been argued - that the need for legislation in order to improve computer program protection is lacking. However, even though there are at this moment various other features of greater importance in the field of international intellectual property, neglect of the legal protection of computer programs would not be wise. Circumstances may change and, especially in the field of computers, they may change rather fast. Computer program piracy could become realistic in a fast growing market for computers that are ready to operate, in particular smaller types, and a growing market for smaller and bigger standardized software packages and chips.

There is a more basic reason for a good legal protection of - not only but also - computer programs. Protection of intellectual and industrial property does not serve, and should not serve, the interests of the proprietors only.
A better legal protection for computer programs could encourage creativity and investments in this field of technology and could promote the dissemination of and trade in programs. This is a general interest and simultaneously it could be the justification for a better fitting legal protection: fitting better than the existing patent, copyright and trade secret law systems do now.

B. DEFINITIONS

In the absence of any special legislation, a legal definition of 'computer program' or 'computer software' does not exist in The Netherlands. Neither is there an 'official' definition, adopted e.g. by some Dutch governmental or judicial body.[3]
For the purposes of this report, I may understand by computer program and computer software the same as is understood by these terms in the WIPO Model Provisions on the protection of computer software[4].

C. PRESENT STATE OF LEGISLATION, CASE LAW AND JURISPRUDENCE; AVAILABILITY OF PROTECTION UNDER PATENT LAW, COPYRIGHT LAW AND THE LAW ON UNFAIR COMPETITION

1. *Patent law*

As regards the Patents Act, the situation seems still to be governed by an interim ruling (November 21, 1969) and a final decision (December 16, 1970) handed down by the *Octrooiraad* (Patent Office), *Afdeling van Beroep* (Board of Appeals)[5]. It should be noted that, in The Netherlands, the Patent Office Board of Appeals is the final instance to grant a patent; a judicial remedy after refusal is not available.
The application in this case concerned a telephone connecting system, but thanks to the broad and fundamental considerations the decision is of wider importance. Its essence and its underlying philosophy can be briefly summarized as follows[6].

A computer program is neither a product nor a method within the meaning of the Patents Act, but an instruction for causing a machine to operate or for carrying out a method. As such, it is therefore not patentable, any more than mathematical or physical theories or methods of calculation or design. This is, by itself, insufficient for a categorical denial of the possibility of patenting; we have to investigate whether a 'disguise'

as a product or as a method renders the grant of a patent possible.
As a product (e.g. magnetic tape, memory, computer provided with the program), however, a program is not considered patentable, because a product that is distinguished from a known product in its information content only is not a different (new) product within the meaning of the Patents Act (cf. books, gramophone records; according to case law the information contents are not protected by the Patents Act). In other words, a computer does not become a different product by loading the computer with a different program. At best, this amounts to a different use.
As a method a program is not patentable unless the method lies in the field of industry (material production); only then can using a product or 'operating a computer' be patentable. A further requirement is for the method to amount to more than just the normal operation of the apparatus concerned. Otherwise a patent should be directed not to a method but to the apparatus, and as stated above, this is not allowed in the case of software. However, provided these requirements have been satisfied, a computer program can be patentable as a method, provided also, of course, that the other conditions for the grant of a patent (novelty, inventiveness) are satisfied. Examples of basically patentable methods are a method of cutting turbine blades or of producing a chemical (respectively using a milling machine and a reactor controlled by a computer, and characterized by the program used in it). Examples of not-patentable methods are computer programs for calculating a square root, for controlling traffic lights or a telephone exchange, or for directing artillery.
The decision of the Patent Office seems to be in line with (and could be inspired by) the then draft of the Convention on the Granting of European Patents, Article 52, Section 2 - litt. d, and Section 3. Although the strong link to technology, required now, could perhaps be loosened to a certain degree (e.g. for telephone connecting systems), one should be aware of the general requirements for patentability in the sphere of the level of novelty and inventiveness, which will anyhow limit the possibilities of patenting software to a very small percentage.[7]

2. *Utility Model*

In The Netherlands legislation with regard to so-called utility models does not exist.

3. *Copyright Law*

Any affirmation by a Dutch court on the eligibility for copyright protection of computer software is still absent. But the

applicability of copyright law has been upheld in literature[8]. Like in most other countries, the eligibility for copyright protection does not require that the created work appear in a certain form. A sufficient amount of originality - in the fulfillment of the task to find a solution for a problem - by creation of a computer program seems to be present, except of course the basic standard instructions[9].
It is, of course, understood that the rights under the Copyright Law do not extend to the basic concepts on which the computer software is based. On the other hand, protection is not restricted to identical copies; the concept of 'plagiarism' is applicable.
Under Copyright Law, protection is available against 'publication' and 'reproduction'. To fight 'computer program piracy' in the sense of the reproduction and marketing of standard and system software, Copyright Law seems to be a useful instrument. However, the existing Copyright Law is not an adequate means against singular - but possibly very important - '(mis-)appropriation'. Not only are the basic concepts unprotected by Copyright Law, nor can the sale of a computer program to and its use by third parties be controlled by the copyright holder.
In this connection it should be noted that Copyright Law allows 'some' copies to be made for internal use, by buyers as well as by borrowers and third parties, and Dutch Copyright Law does perhaps not exclude enterprises and corporations from this facility.

4. *Trade Secrets, 'Know-how' Protection and Unfair Competition Law*

Within the limits of labour law and antitrust law - which cannot be discussed here - the limitation to exclusive internal use, secrecy, a non-competition clause, etc., can be agreed upon by parties. In general, however, such contractual obligations should be stipulated expressly; statutory provisions inferring such obligations do not exist; judicial construction of such obligations from general rules of 'good faith' and 'care' is probable only in exceptional cases.
Protection against third party utilization, based upon the general rule forbidding unfair competition, would in general presuppose secrecy of the program. Furthermore, to take advantage of the efforts and investments by another, and even to take advantage of breach of contract by another is, as such, not 'unfair competition', according to the standing doctrine of the Supreme Court[10]. The provocation of a breach of contract or bribery may constitute unfair competition and thus result in a tort.
If the courts would take the view - contrary to the point of view expressed under C.3. - that a computer program (or, less improbable, a chip) is not eligible for copyright protection

at all, protection against piracy in the sense of systematic duplication and marketing, based upon unfair competition might be available as a substitute[11].

D. PROPOSED SYSTEMS FOR LEGAL PROTECTION

In the Netherlands, neither official, nor unofficial proposals for a law reform in respect of computer programs have been introduced[12]. I may give my personal comment on some - not all, of course - foreign proposals together with my comment on the WIPO Model Provisions. I may abstain from suggestions as to the elements of a different *sui generis* system, since any strong feelings for such a system seem to be absent in The Netherlands.

E. WIPO MODEL PROVISIONS

The WIPO proposals are interesting, also from a point of view of international law, as they can be seen as an endeavour to find a solution for a common problem in a way which should be deemed to be feasible in most countries of the world, provided an actual need and political will exist.
I may make a few comments on the proposed 'model law'. In my opinion WIPO chose the right way in seeking a solution in a copyright approach and rejecting a patent approach. An adapted patent system would involve a far-reaching monopoly for patented software, enabling the proprietor to prevent others from using a program in a different form and/or a program created independently but constituting basically the same process. Such far-reaching monopolization for all programs, without examination, is not justified. Maintaining the principle, the great mass of blood-, sweat- and tears programs would not be protected under this system, and expensive examination of novelty and inventivity would be necessary.
An advantage of the patent approach is, of course, the mandatory publication of the patent matter in a way understandable to skilled people in this field, inseperably connected with the patent concept. Apart from the costs of such a system, particularly in the field of software, it could be argued that the higher degree of protection of a patent law, connected with the mandatory publication, might in practice prove to be rather meaningless since the use - often internal - of basically similar processes is very difficult to discover. Add to this that a public description as required under the patent concept would often require the description of know-how which should be matter of the computerized process, but which cannot be subject to the protection of the patent applied for. Therefore, the patent approach cannot be recommended generally and interna-

tionally as the way to solve the problem. This should not prevent States from granting patents for certain kinds of computer programs (cf. section 9 of the model law), but for the great majority of programs a different approach is to be preferred: a copyright approach.
Whereas patent protection is so far-reaching that only very few programs, meeting the standard of an 'invention', would be patentable, the much less far-reaching copyright(-like) protection could be applied, in principle, to all original software creations, without examination and even without the requirement of deposit or registration.
Lacking such examination, deposit or registration, for all originally created computer programs (see model law, sections 1 and 3) a protection against real misappropriation or piracy for a certain, not too long duration (section 7: 20-25 years) could be considered justifiable. Protection to be obtained so easily and for such a large number of programs, should not include the protection of the basic concept itself (see section 4 of the model law), nor should it protect against the use or reproduction of programs appearing to be similar but developed independently (see section 6, paragraph 2). It may, however, and - in my opinion - should protect against various forms of real misappropriation and piracy: section 5 items III to VIII describes a series of acts which can be considered to constitute such misappropriation or piracy. Section 8 entitles the proprietor to injunctions and damages. Items I and II of section 5 add protection against unauthorized disclosure of computer software.
In my opinion, the copyright-style WIPO Model Provisions could be welcomed in The Netherlands as a good means for a well-balanced protection (offering neither too little, nor too much) of computer software as defined in section 1 of the model law.
The expediency of introducing provisions like these in the national legislation will vary from one state to another. At the beginning of this report I wrote that cases of real 'theft' or piracy seem to occur very rarely thus far, and that protection against them under the existing copyright law (or unfair competition law) has in most states not been tested thus far. As soon as undesirable acts actually occur and existing laws fail to provide adequate remedies, introduction of a law like the WIPO model should be considered indeed.
Notwithstanding my positive attitude towards the WIPO proposal, I would add some critical remarks.

1. Section 5, items I and II could be deemed to be too far-reaching. These provisions based not on copyright but on trade secrets prohibit the disclosure of a program and do not allow or facilitate access by any person to any object storing or reproducing computer software before the computer software is made accessible to the public with the consent of the proprietor.

In my opinion, such acts should be prohibited by statutory provisions only, provided that the secret nature of the software is notified to the persons concerned or is otherwise apparent to them.

2. Although the extension of copyright-like protection to the 'use' of reproductions (copies) should be welcomed in principle, it should be made clear that, in the absence of different agreement, normal forms of use and 'personal' reproduction of a legally acquired program should not require further consent, and that in principle a package of computer software, paid by a user, could be transferred without the consent of the copyright proprietor, the right to use included. In this connection, I would refer to the CONTU proposition for a new section 117 in the U.S. Copyright Act (Final Report, July 31, 1978).

3. Section 2 of the WIPO model law deals with the proprietor of the protected software in accordance with generally accepted copyright law principles. As stated earlier in this paper, the most frequent practical problems with regard to rights to computer software thus far are connected with the question whether a program developed by a software house and paid for by a computer user may be 'commercialized' afterwards by the software house or by the principal. The frequency of conflicts in this field could be a reason for a special legal provision, e.g. allowing, unless otherwise agreed, commercialization by the principal, under the obligation to pay an equal profit share to the software house.

4. My final remark in this paper concerns the question whether dissemination and easier access to existing computer programs, in the interest of the general public, will indeed be promoted by a law as proposed by WIPO. Of course, a better protection decreases the proprietor's problems as to description, publication, public offer and dissemination in general. In this respect the WIPO proposal meets one of its objectives. However, taking away some risks connected with dissemination and publication is not the same as requiring publication or at least registration and cataloguing in order to facilitate access to information on existing computer software.

WIPO did study the arguments for and against deposit and/or registration systems, both mandatory and optional. It could be regretted that the International Bureau and its Advisory Committee did not succeed in finding a solution guaranteeing at least some sytematical form of registration and cataloguing and a minimum of disclosure in return for a better protection. However, the 1977 WIPO Report (sections 9-21) does convince me of the fact that in the field of software a deposit system really enabling access to existing software would involve extremely high costs - apart from political and legal protection problems. Any 'second best' or 'third best' deposit system, lowering such costs, will devaluate the deposit system more than proportionally. Under such circumstances, access to computer software and the practical availability of computer technology for people or countries needing support in this field could better be served within the framework of technical cooperation and assistance programs to be undertaken by United Nations, WIPO, EEC and other international bodies and/or individual States.

F. CONCLUSIONS

1.
Sofar, the absence of appropriate legal provisions with regard to computer programs, has not been viewed as an urgent problem in The Netherlands.

2.
Patent protection seems to be available only insofar a computer program has been implemented in a process in the field of material production (and will be restricted to such a process) provided, of course, that the other conditions for the grant of a patent (novelty, inventive step) have been met.

3.
Copyright and/or unfair competition law will probably be suitable to prohibit computer program piracy on a wider scale. Legal protection against simple copying and use as such is basically missing, apart from contractual provisions which however in principle do not offer protection against third parties taking advantage of a breach of contract.

4.
The copyright-style approach to improve the protection as proposed in the 1977 WIPO Model Provisions seems to be a good solution, although some details do not satisfy completely. Provisions as to the relationship between a software firm and its customer, now lacking, could be considered.

5.
A deposit and registration system with maximal dissemination advantages seems to evoke insurmountable (financial and other) problems; a less ambitious system, reducing costs and protection problems, will probably devaluate its dissemination capacity more than proportionally. Dissemination of software knowledge and international cooperation and technical assistance in this field could, however, and should therefore be promoted by other means.

NOTES

1. Cf. *Ars Aequi*, Vol. XVII (1968), p. 47.
2. D.W.F. Verkade, Bescherming van computerprogramma's, *Intermediair* Vol. 5 (1969), October 31 p. 49, November 7 p. 57, November 21 p. 27; also in *Bijblad bij de Industriële Eigendom* (*BIE*), Vol. 38 (1970), p. 58. By the same author: *Softwarebescherming*, Alphen aan den Rijn 1972.
3. In the 1975 Report on question 57 B in the name of the Dutch AIPPI-Group (*Annuaire* 1975/I, p. 430), the authors suggested the following definition: In the context of automatic data processing, a "computer program" is "an amount of information consisting of a collection of instructions, definitions, expressions and related data, written in a program language, and specifying operations applicable to informations, which collection defines a contemplated and more complex operation on said information and is suitable for execution by a computer, either direct, or after conversion into another program language". In this connection, by "program language" is understood "a language suitable for use in writing a computer program, and consisting of a formalized collection of a number of symbols and rules determining the manner and order in which the symbols can be assembled to form a computer program".
4. Published in *La Propriété Industrielle* (*Prop.Ind.*), Vol. 93 (1977), p. 259; also in *Industrial Property* (*Ind.Prop.*), Vol. 16 (1977), p. 259. Separate edition: *OMPI/WIPO Publication* No. 814 (1978).
5. *BIE*, Vol. 39 (1971), p. 54; english translation: *IIC*, Vol. 2 (1971), p. 308.
6. In the following text I may quote on a large scale from the 1972 Report on question 57 B in the name of the Dutch AIPPI-Group by M.L. Bazen, L.B. Chavannes, J. Dekker, J.E.M. Galama, A.M.C. Helmer and D.W.F. Verkade, *Annuaire* 1973/I, p. 427.
7. Cf. Report Dutch Group AIPPI 1972, *Annuaire* 1973/I, p. 430.
8. See notes 2 and 6.
9. A particularity of Dutch Copyright Law should be noted in this connection: *writings* - at least those destined for dissemination - are protected even without meeting the standard or 'originality' or 'personal character' (e.g. telephone directories).
10. Cf. Ter Horst, item 'Interference/Netherlands' in Pinner's *World Unfair Competition Law*, 2nd ed., Alphen aan den Rijn 1978.
11. Cf. (in a case concerning duplication of 'musicassettes', in that particular case not protected by copyright): Court of Appeals of Arnhem January 18, 1972, *Nederlandse Jurisprudentie* 1972.297, *BIE* Vol. 40 (1972), p. 132.
12. A comment on some alternatives has been given by the authors of the reports in the name of the Dutch AIPPI-Group (see notes 3 and 6), however without recommendation for law reform for the time being.

Use of industrial property as a clandestine cartel

M. VAN EMPEL

Professor at the University of Groningen

III.B.2.

PART ONE - THE NETHERLANDS

I. INTRODUCTION

Anybody who has to report on this subject in 1981 must necessarily start off with the *caveat* that Dutch law as such is only part of the story, and a fairly minor part at that. Indeed, Dutch law is no longer alone to govern the issue, but it co-exists with the law of the European Communities, which also is "the law of the land" within the territory of the Netherlands. In this of course the Netherlands are in the same position as the other Member States of the European Communities. Nevertheless, their respective positions differ as to the relative impact of their national rules as compared to the European rules. Indeed, the more lenient national law is on the subject, the more attention - both in theory and in practice - will focus on the European regime, with its more critical and negative bias.
In this connection it is submitted that the frasing of the subject-title as such implies a certain bias against "cartels", which may be held to be good policy and law, but which is not necessarily shared by all systems of law. In a country where cartels are viewed with an indifferent or even benevolent eye, "clandestine cartels" can be deemed a non-issue, because there is no need for cartels to be "clandestine".
It is against the background of these general observations that the following summary of Dutch law on the subject should be seen. This report will be concerned with patents and trade marks. For both it will be examined whether they entitle the proprietor to ensure "orderly marketing" of the products covered by the right concerned. Basically and very broadly speaking such "orderly marketing" can be achieved by two, complementory means. On the one hand there is the question of

access to the national market as such. On the other hand it must be examined to what extent the proprietor of the patent or trade mark is in a position to regulate production of, and trade in, the products concerned *within* the national territory by imposing certain conditions within the framework of a licence-contract.

II. PATENTS

1. *Access to the Dutch market*

The crucial provision in this regard is Article 30 (4)[1] of the Dutch Patent Act. According to this provision, if a product covered by the patent has been lawfully put on the market in the Netherlands, then the patent is not infringed by actions with regard to that product which otherwise would amount to infringement (the so-called "exhaustion principle"). It follows therefrom that the patentee who himself has marketed the product abroad, or who has licensed a third party to do so under a corresponding foreign patent, may nevertheless oppose his Dutch patent to the importation and marketing of that product on the Dutch market. Indeed, under the Dutch Patent Act that product has not been "lawfully put on the market in the Netherlands".

It is noteworthy that this specific reference to the Dutch market has been enacted at the 1977 - revision of the Patents Act. This is not to say that this is new law. Even under the old text of the Act which merely referred to "lawfully put on the market" without specific reference to the Dutch market, it was nevertheless firmly established at least as from 1943[2] that this restriction should be read into this provision. Doubt voiced incidentally as to whether this traditional approach was still in line with modern opinions on competition law were firmly rejected by the Dutch Supreme Court[3]. Having recalled both the territoriality of Patent Law and the spirit in which the Act had been drafted back in the early 20th century, the Court pointed out moreover that doing away with the "Dutch market" - criterion without any further restriction would open the flood-gates in a way never intended by the national legislation. However, nowhere in the law, the Court said, any clue was to be found as to where to draw the line for such further restriction. Thus, rather than to impose a wholly arbitrary new criterion the Court stuck to the time-honoured and firm criterion of the Dutch market.
It should be noted that in the meantime E.E.C.-law has provided just that distinguishing criterion - viz. "put on the market within the E.E.C." -[4] which the Dutch Supreme Court could not find in the mere framework of Dutch law.

Here there is an instance of the phenomenon mentioned above of Dutch law being completed - corrected if one wishes - by European law. Today the former cannot be understood without the latter (nor the reverse, for that matter). It is in this light that the new text of the Dutch patent Act has to be seen : accepting the exception that has to be made for intra-Community trade, the Dutch legislator wishes to emphasize that that is indeed an exception, justified by the particular closeness of the E.E.C.-countries, but that otherwise the rule still stands - and thus applies to imports from third countries - that a patentee may freely oppose his patent to importations of products, notwithstanding the fact that he himself has been instrumental to their marketing abroad.

2. *Operation on the Dutch market*

It seems a fair statement that under Dutch law as such - again not taking E.E.C.-law into account - the patentee is free to use his exclusive right as a basis and the licence as the tool to regulate production and trade in the products concerned on the Dutch market according to what he sees as his interest. The Patent Act and the Civil Code allow him to split up the monopoly and allot each part as he pleases. And for the licensee to transgress the metes and bounds so imposed upon him as a condition for the licence, will incur the penalty linked to infringement of the patent, not merely to breach of the (licence) contract. In other words, products so manufactured and/or sold will be deemed infringing products, also vis-à-vis third parties.
Whilst thus patent law provides the patentee with the necessary tools to organize the manufacture and/or marketing of products covered by his patent on the Dutch market, hardly any fetters are put on the actual use of those tools.
In particular the Competition Act (*Wet Economische Mededinging*) which, at first blush, could have been expected to impose certain limits, has proved very innocuous in practice. This notwithstanding the fact that a licence-contract as such can certainly be deemed to be "an agreement....by which competition between owners of enterprises is regulated" within the sense of Article 1 of that Act. It should be noted, however, that the Dutch Competition Act is based on the so-called "abuse"-approach, which implies that such "competition-regulating-agreements" - or, in other words, "cartels" - are not forbidden and illegal *per se*, but rather are basically left alone by public policy. Only if a "cartel" is found to operate against public interest, counter measures are envisaged. The practical result of this approach is that it requires concrete action by public authority in a particular case to bring the cartel to the fore.

As it is, it so happens that in the 25 odd years during which the Competition Act has been on the books no such action has been taken against a patent licence-agreement.

3. *Conclusion*

By way of conclusion it can safely be said that Dutch law proper - as distinguished from E.E.C.-law also applicable on the Dutch territory - leaves the patentee a completely free hand to organize the "orderly marketing" of products concerned, as he sees fit. To be sure this conclusion should be set in the actual context of the Dutch market, which to a very large extent is intrinsically open to international trade. The Dutch legislator may therefore be lenient to the patentee, the latter's monopoly nevertheless can never be more than a fairly relative one in real terms.

III. TRADE MARKS

Apart from the proviso for E.E.C.-law, which applies also here of course, a further distinction should be made in historical terms between the situation up till 1971 when trade mark law in the Netherlands was based on the Dutch Trade Mark Act of 1893, and the period thereafter where trade mark law has become a common matter to the three Benelux-countries (Belgium, the Netherlands and Luxemburg) based on the Uniform Benelux Trade Mark Act[5]. Although therefore an exclusively Dutch approach to the problems at issue is a thing of the past, it appears nevertheless useful to give a short outline of Dutch law as it stood in 1971.

1. *Access to the Dutch market*

Dutch law

Contrary to the Patents Act the Trade Marks Act of 1893 provided no clue as to how to answer the question whether and if so to what extent the proprietor of the Dutch trade mark had to allow imports of products carrying that trade mark if he had been instrumental in the marketing of that product abroad. In a land-mark decision - the first in a series involving the German Grundig-company - the Dutch Supreme Court found the law therefore not on the basis of any particular provision, but rather by reasoning from what it held to be the basic objective of trade mark law, viz. "the protection against confusion as to the origin of the goods". And the Court to deduce therefrom the fairly simple yardstick : infringement in the Netherlands is found where the product concerned does not originate with the proprietor of the Dutch trade mark.

On the one hand this ruling implied that the "territoriality" of the trade mark had no rôle to play here : provided the product originated with the Dutch trade mark owner there was no infringement, regardless where it had been first put on the market. On the other hand the ruling gave rise to a formalistic approach : the criterion was strictly whether the product had been marketed by the Dutch trade mark owner as such; no attention at all was paid to possible concern-relations between proprietors of the same trade mark in different countries. At the same time marketing by a licensee was deemed to be comprised in the marketing by the trade mark owner as such. The incongruous differences in outcome between concern-situations where trade marks were owned by different concern-subsidiaries, as opposed to having a licence can easily be imagined[6].

Benelux-law

The recent Benelux-law on the subject has continued the line developed under national law. Article 13A, para 3, of the Uniform Benelux Trade Mark Act (BMW) provides that the trade mark owner cannot oppose his trade mark to imports of products which have been marketed by himself or his licensee, be it in the Netherlands or abroad.
However, the issue of concern- and other trading organization links has been taken further within the Benelux-framework. Indeed for trade between the various Benelux-countries Article 33 BMW adds to the rule of Article 13A the criterion of "economic link relating to the products concerned" : the trade mark owner in Holland has to live with imports in Holland of products marketed in Belgium or Luxemburg by a "concern-affiliated" company or by his Belgian or Luxemburg sales agent.
It is so far uncertain whether the same rule would apply as far as imports from third (non-Benelux) countries are concerned. It could be argued that the philosophical and economical reasoning is the same, from whichever country the products are coming. On the other hand, one cannot be really sure that the specific Benelux-context should not be decisive here. At any rate, in the absence of a court ruling - preferably by the Benelux Court of Justice[7] - no real certainty is to be had.

Operation on the Dutch market

Whereas the old Dutch Trade Mark Act only allowed for trade mark licences as from 1956, the Benelux Act provides for them as a matter of course (Article 11 BMW). Basically partners to the agreement are left completely free as to the terms and conditions. It should be noted however, that only for restrictions as to time and to product-scope transgression by the licensee carries the penalty of trade mark-infringement.

Non-respect of other restrictions merely amounts to breach of contract, to be sorted out between the parties thereto.
Thus, on that score the trade mark-owners in the Netherlands has slightly less freedom to impose "orderly marketing" of "his" products than his patent-counterpart has. With regard to the Competition Act their situation are similar in theory and practice.
And again, of course, the overriding factor of the "open economy" of the Netherlands makes itself felt in the trade mark field as it does in the patent field.

PART TWO - THE EEC

I. INTRODUCTION

As suggested by the *General Rapporteur* this report centers around two major issues of competitive use of industrial property rights. On the one hand: to what extent can the proprietor of such rights bar imports of allegedly infringing products in the country concerned? On the other hand: what scope of freedom has he to mould licence-conditions so as to suit his concepts how to exploit his rights to his best advantage?

Before trying to present a picture of the state of the art on these two questions, attention should be drawn to the particular aspects of EEC Law on the matter. Indeed, the EEC presents itself in a somewhat twilight situation, about mid-way on the road towards a simple, unified market. This reflects not only upon the objective situation of the question, in the sense that specific rules apply to intra-community trade, which differ both from national trade and from international trade. It also affects the spirit in which specific questions which arise in this connection, are discussed: the frame of reference is explicitly dynamic; interpretation and application of the rules should promote - or at least not hinder - an ongoing process of change. And the objective of that process is the creation of a unified market comprising the whole of the Community-territory. It should be stressed that this objective - albeit ambitious enough - is a limited one. It does not speak out on the basic economic philosophy which is to reign on that market. Whether this will be dominantly "free market" or rather "planned economy" can be merely guessed at. This implies that one should be wary of too easy parallels with the U.S. where - at least historically - "free trade" has been interpreted as to mean not only free movement of goods throughout the territory, but also an unequivocal choice against trade regulation on that territory at the hands of either private parties or public authority. Inevitably, anti-trust "*à l'américaine*" has been coloured by that fundamental choice throughout. Thus also the interference of public policy with industrial property as a tool of private trade regulations in the US is not merely a matter of securing free movement of goods but also of fighting private "kingdom". The same simply is *not* true for the EEC. Free movement of goods is the paramount objective, contributory to the overall aim of economic integration between Member-States. Any other objective of present EEC industrial property-policy lacks the legitimation of consensus, explicitly sought and obtained, from the body politic within the EEC.

In the light of the foregoing it should not come as a surprise that actual development is geared to the free movement of goods within the EEC, whilst other issues are being dealt with in a rather piece-meal - and therefore hardly consistent-fashion.
Taking the two chapters distinguished by the *General Rapporteur*, this has resulted by now in a fairly clear and cohesive doctrine on *parallel imports* as opposed to a muddled, hesitating and unconvincing set of precedents in the field of *licensing*.

II. PARALLEL IMPORTS

A. *Intra-Community Trade*

The question as to the possible use of industrial property rights as a means for the blocking of "parallel imports" between Member States has to be answered on the basis of Articles 30 and 36 of the EEC-Treaty. These provisions are worded as follows :

Article 30 : *Quantitative restrictions on imports and all measures having equivalent effect shall without prejudice to the following provisions, be prohibited between Member States.*

Article 36 : *The provisions of Articles 30 to 34 shall not preclude prohibitions or restrictions on imports, exports or goods in transit justified on grounds of public morality, public policy or public security; the protection of health and life of humans, animals or plants; the protection of national treasures possessing artistic, historic*

> *or archeaeological value; or the protection of industrial and commercial property. Such prohibitions or restrictions shall not, however, constitute a means of arbitrary discrimination or a disguised restriction on trade between Member States.*

To be sure, article 36 is indeed the only specific reference in the EEC Treaty to industrial property. As long as the Community Patent Convention and Community Trade Mark Regulation, both of which will come up for discussion below, have not entered into force, the question of parallel imports is not addressed within the autonomous framework of patent law and trademark law, respectively. Rather it has come to be posed in terms of conflict between national industrial property law of each individual EEC Member State concerned, on the one hand, and the EEC law-rule of free movement of goods between the Member States, on the other hand. This conflict between two sets of rules situated at two different levels may have contributed to a certain sense of frustration which apparently was felt sometimes in industrial property circles, who felt that their realm was invaded by single-minded agnostics. Be that as it may, it was obvious from the start of the Common Market that one way or the other policy decisions had to be taken on the issue. Accordingly, at a very early stage a fairly ambitious program of legislation by convention was undertaken[1]. These efforts which for long seemed to have been in vain, now have at least resulted in two complete drafts, the Patent Convention and the Trade Mark Regulation already mentioned before[2]. On the question at issue, however, the development of legislative thought has been overtaken by case-law at the hands of the Court of Justice at Luxembourg.

At this point, attention must be drawn to the position of this Court. It is called to apply and interpret Community law, whilst it has no power on matters of national law of the respective Member States. National law, therefore, it has to accept as it finds it. Thus, in the present context, if the national patent law of a Member State has it that "parallel imports" can be blocked by the patentee, that is a fact in court at Luxembourg. At the same time, however, the Court can - and must - apply Community law. Again in the present context, this means in the first place that it has to decide what "free movement of goods" actually means under the EEC-Treaty. And it also means, in the second place, that, as the guardian of the jurisdictional cohesion of the Common Market, it is called upon to indicate how conflicts between Community law and national law of one or more of the Member States should be solved in a particular case.

Occasionally, this is done within the framework of Article 169 EEC which provides for court action by the Commission against Member States for non-respect of their treaty obligations on one point or the other[3]. Of much more practical importance, however, is Article 177, which allows national courts faced with a question on EEC-law to ask for a preliminary ruling by the Court of Justice on that question. As has been the case elsewhere, for the issue of parallel imports it is this "Article 177 procedure" which has allowed for development of a set of case-law, which gives us a fairly clear answer to our questions.
The by-now almost traditional sequence is for a patentee or trade mark owner to start proceedings for infringement against certain imports, for the importer then to retort that if allowed the claim would hurt the free movement of goods, for the national court then to find that indeed the claim should be allowed under its national law, but before handing down final judgement to ask the Court of Justice how this judgement would tally with EEC law. The Court then gives its opinion, certainly against the background of the case at hand, but still always leaving final judgement on the merits to the national court.

It should be stressed that in this dialogue between the national and the Community Court, the former "talks industrial property" and the latter "free movement of goods". It is only in so far as industrial property interferes with free movement of goods that the former comes to the attention of the Luxembourg Court in the first place. Its interest in it is an indirect, a derived one, it is not a prime object of concern. It is in this light, it is submitted, that one should see the so often repeated and quoted distinction which the Court makes in this connection between the "existence" and "the exercise" of industrial property-rights. It has been mistakingly been taken to refer to a "hard core" of the industrial property right as opposed to more ancillary rights. And on that basis it was then sought to argue, of course, that whereas Community law could, if need be, impinge upon the ancillary rights, it should leave the "hard core" untouched.
Again, it is submitted here that the starting point of this argument is wrong and the argument itself therefore illusory. The Court's position, it would seem, really is very simple and straightforward. It merely states that it is not prepared - even not entitled - to discuss industrial property rights as a legal institution as such, but rather must confine itself to judge the institution upon its effects on a particular point, viz. the free movement of goods between EEC States.
It accepts the institution of patent law etc. as a fact, but at the same time tells us that under the EEC Treaty it cannot accept certain particular implications of that law.

And that, given the rules of precedence within the EEC, those implications of a particular national law institution which EEC law cannot live with, have to go.
The logical consequence of this approach is that it proceeds essentially on a case-by-case basis: if one does not go for the roots there is no way of telling where the next erring branch will show. Of course, this is by no means meant as a criticism, on the contrary! But this being so, one should not seek to read into the Court's opinions more than they are meant to render.

This limited scope of the Court's action in this field was somewhat confused by the word "justified" in the first sentence of Article 36. It led the Court to draft its views of the interference between industrial property and free movement of goods in more general terms: for import-blocking by industrial property to be "justified" it should be in concurrence with the "specific subject matter" of the industrial property right concerned. Whereupon the Court apparently sought to define - in general and abstract terms - what that "specific subject matter" was. Thus in *Centrafarm v. Sterling Drug*[4] it held that

> *"in relation to patents, the specific subject matter of the industrial property is the guarantee that the patentee, to reward the creative effort of the inventor, has the exclusive right to use an invention with a view to manufacturing industrial products and putting them into circulation for the first time, either directly or by a grant of licences to third parties, as well as the right to oppose infringements."*

In the parallel trademark case *(Centrafarm v. Winthrop)*[5] one reads :

> *"in relation to trademarks, the specific subject-matter of the industrial property is the guarantee that the owner of the trademark has the exclusive right to use that trademark, for the purpose of putting products protected by the trademark into circulation for the first time, and is therefore intended to protect him against competition wishing to take advantage of the status and reputation of the trademark by selling products illegally bearing that trademark."*

By so venturing into general and sweeping definitions the Court inevitably came in for a certain amount of criticism from those who felt that that was not *the* definition of a patent, or trademark respectively. It is submitted here, however, that it was not - and could not have been - the Court's intention to give *the* definition for all countries

and all times. Rather, it should be stressed again, the approach was a functional one, viz. to find the scope and purport of the word "justified" in Art. 36. Thus, the Court sought to indicate what sort of patent-rights, respectively trademark rights, Art. 36 allowed for as an exception to the principle of the free movement of goods. (In this connection one may note that in later cases the Court added the characteristic words "in particular" to the "definitions".[6]
At any rate, providing a "definition" of the specific subject-matter did not absolve the Court from the task of establishing whether a particular action was indeed "justified" under Art. 36. The question of "repackaging" under trademark-law - which was submitted to the Court a few years ago[7] - is a case in point. Therefore, it may well be argued that even without the benefit of general "definitions" of the industrial property rights concerned, the Court could have built up a satisfactory set of rules as to whether a particular "exercise" of such rights can be deemed justified or not.
As it is, such set of rules now indeed appears available. Having dealt with a certain member of specific issues in different cases, the Court summed up its views in the *Terrapin-Terranova* case[8] :

> *"As a result of the provisions in the Treaty relating to free movement of goods and in particular of Article 30, quantitative restrictions on import and all measures having equivalent effect are prohibited between Member States. By Article 36 these provisions nevertheless do not preclude prohibitions or restrictions on imports justified on grounds of the protection of industrial or commercial property.*
> *However, it is clear from that same article, in particular the second sentence, as well as from the context, that whilst the Treaty does not effect the existence of rights recognised by the legislation of a Member State in matters of industrial and commercial property, yet the exercise of those rights may nevertheless, depending on the circumstances, be restricted by prohibition in the Treaty. In as much as it provides an exception to one of the fundamental principles of the Common Market, Article 36 in fact admits exceptions to the free movement of goods only to the extent to which such exceptions are justified for the purpose of safeguarding rights which constitute the specific subject matter of that property.*
>
> *It follows from the above that the proprietor of an industrial or commercial property right protected by the law of a Member State cannot rely on that law to prevent the importation of a product which has lawfully been marketed in another Member State by the proprietor himself or with*

his consent[9]*. It is the same when the right relied on is the result of the subdivision, either by voluntary act or as a result of public constraint, of a trademark right which originally belonged to one and the same proprietor. In these cases the basic function of the trademark to guarantee to consumers that the product has the same origin is already undermined by the subdivision of the original right. Even where the rights in question belong to different proprietors the protection given to industrial and commercial property by national law may not be relied on when the exercise of those rights is the purpose, the means or the result of an agreement prohibited by the Treaty. In all these cases the effect of invoking the territorial nature of national laws protecting industrial and commercial property is to legitimise the insulation of national markets without this partitioning within the common market being justified by the protection of a legitimate interest on the part of the proprietor of the trademark or business name.*

On the other hand in the present state of Community law an industrial or commercial property right legally acquired in a Member State may legally be used to prevent under the first sentence of Article 36 of the Treaty the import of products marketed under a name giving rise to confusion where the rights in question have been acquired by different and independent proprietors under different national law.
If in such a case the principle of free movement of goods were to prevail over the protection given by the respective national law, the specific objective of industrial and commercial property rights would be undermined. In the particular situation the requirements of the free movement of goods and the safeguarding of industrial and commercial property rights must be so reconciled that protection is ensured for the legitimate use of the rights conferred by national laws, coming within the prohibitions on imports 'justified' within the meaning of Article 36 of the Treaty, but denied on the other hand in respect of any improper exercise of the same rights of such a nature as to maintain or effect artificial partitions within the common market."

It is submitted here that, as long as there have been no substantial legislative changes at Community level (mark the words "in the present state of Community law" in *Terrapin*), this ruling is a reliable guide for the border land between industrial property and free movement of goods within the EEC. It seems a fair guess that, barring new legislation, new developments will not take place within the framework of the

first sentence of Article 36, with certain general categories of cases being "justified", where others are not. Rather - as appeared in later cases[10] - attention will concentrate on the second sentence of Art. 36.
As interpreted by the Court, this provision constitutes a barrier against abuse in specific cases of what on a general level is a "justified" exercise of the industrial property-right concerned. This is of course essentially a case-by-case approach, which, as explained earlier here, suits the particular repartition of rôles in this border land, between community law and national law, between the European Court of Justice and the national courts. To be sure, it appears that, after some hesitation, the Court has now firmly come down in favour of a decisive rôle for the national court dealing with the merits of the case at hand. Indeed, it found that under Community law it is up to the national court to check whether there is abuse in the sense of Article 36, second sentence, not for the Court of Justice[11].

New Community legislation in the offing

In developments above frequently a proviso was introduced concerning the eventuality of changes in legislation on the present subject at Community level. It seems appropriate therefore now to turn to those possible future developments. It should be stressed that indeed we are looking into the future here: at the time of writing none of the legal instruments to be discussed here (briefly) seems likely to enter into force before long.
First then, there is the *Community Patent Convention* of 1975.[12] The issue discussed here is addressed in its Articles 32, 81 and (indirectly) 93. Article 32 provides that

> *"the rights conferred by a Community patent shall not extend to acts concerning a product covered by that patent which are done within the territories of the Contracting States after that product has been put on the market in one of these States by the proprietor of the patent or with his express consent, unless there are grounds which, under Community law, would justify the extension to such acts of the rights conferred by the patent."*

Attention should be drawn to the fact that "exhaustion" by virtue of this provision takes place only where the product has been marketed in one of the Contracting States, i.e. within the EEC, that the "consent" must be "express", i.e. "explicit" and finally that a proviso is made for exceptions by virtue of "Community law". According to the - authoritive - "General Report" on the Convention[13], this expression "Community law" should be taken here as to refer "to the

provisions of the Treaty of Rome itself and the supplementory provisions thereto, the jurisprudence of the Court of Justice of the European Communities and the principles of national law common to all the Member States." It would seem that what it all boils down to is that the Convention takes the outcome of Community law on industrial property *versus* free movement, as it is spelled out by the Court of Justice, but does not want by any means to add itself a new bias against industrial property on top of that. In other terms, it is essentially a consolidating exercise.
The same holds true for Article 81 which essentially gives the same rule for national patents as Article 32 does for Community patents. For good order's sake Article 81 adds that a national patent is also "exhausted" when the product concerned has been marketed within the EEC by an "economically connected" party. Whereupon it is specified that for this purpose

> *"two persons shall be deemed to have economic connections where one of them is in a position to exert a decisive influence on the other, directly or indirectly, with regard to the exploitation of a patent, or where a third party is in a position to exercise such an influence on both persons."*

Finally, to avoid any possible doubt on this score, Article 93 of the Convention specifies that "no provision of this Convention may be invoked against the application of any provision of the Treaty establishing the European Economic Community."

Whereas the form of an international convention - albeit confined to EEC States - was chosen for the "Community patent", for the "*Community Trade Mark*" the form of an *EEC Regulation* was preferred. A draft for such regulation has been published in 1978. More recently (November 1980) the European Commission tabled still another proposal, viz. a draft *Directive* for the harmonisation of national trademark-law of the EEC Member States.[14] To be sure, both Article 14 of the Draft-Regulation and Article 6 of the Draft Directive aim at consolidating Community law as it stands. Particularly illustrative in this regard is the reference in the Draft-Directive, to the "repackaging"-issue, which had come to the fore in the two most recent "Centrafarm"-cases before the Court of Justice. It should be noted, however, that in both drafts we miss the specification that for the consent of the trademark-owners to bring about "exhaustion" such "consent" must be "express" and "explicit". One guesses that the European Commission felt this might prove too restrictive in practice.

On the other hand, no reference - similar to Article 81 of the Patent Convention - is made to "economically connected" parties in the Draft Directive. Judging by the spirit in which the document has been drafted, this should not be taken, however, as a more lenient approach towards the exercise of the trade-mark-monopoly. It seems more probable that this situation is now deemed to be covered by the notion of "consent".
Finally still another point of difference with the Community Patents is that marketing *anywhere* - not just within the EEC - can cause "exhaustion" (provided, of course, this is done by the trademark owner or with his consent). This takes us to the next point of this exposé, namely trade between the EEC and third countries.

B. *Trade with third countries*

It has been found above that the case-law of the Court of Justice relating to industrial property in the EEC was based on the provisions of Articles 30 and 36 EEC. To be sure, this was quite logical for intra-community trade. The question now is, to what extent this case-law can be applied also to trade with third countries.
The landmark here is the decision which the Court of Justice handed down in the three parallel "Columbia"-cases[15]. With commendable straightforwardness and clarity the Court found that

> *"neither the rules of the Treaty on the free movement of goods nor those on the putting into free circulation of products coming from third countries nor, finally, the principles governing the common commercial policy, prohibit the proprietor of a mark in all the Member States of the Community from exercising his right in order to prevent the importation of similar products bearing the same mark and coming from a third country. Nor may the provisions of the Treaty on the free movement of goods be invoked for the purposes of prohibiting the proprietor of the mark in the territories of the Member States from exercising his right in order to prevent another proprietor of the same mark in a third country from manufacturing and marketing his product within the Community, either himself or through his subsidiaries established in the Community."*

As mentioned already, the decision in itself is very clear: what applies in intra-Community trade does *not* apply in trade with third countries. In other terms, national industrial property law in the various EEC-countries need not suffer the same encroachments by "free movement"-rules here as is the case in intra-Community trade.

At the same time, it should be stressed that the decision does not say more than that. One should beware of the pitfall which has bedevilled early discussions on intra-Community trade, viz. that of an alleged "immunity" of industrial property.

In the first place, of course, it is up to industrial property law to establish what is the scope of the monopoly, in the first place. In this regard the difference between patents and trademarks is instructive. Whereas patent law in most countries allows the patentee to block "parallel imports" of infringing products whether he himself has been instrumental to their marketing abroad, or not, in trademark law on the contrary it is now by and large accepted as a defence that the trademark owner himself was - directly or indirectly - at the source of the "infringing" product. This difference is clearly evidenced in the Community Patent, as opposed to the Community Trade Mark, as envisaged at present (see supra): the latter is "exhausted" by marketing anywhere, the former only by marketing within the EEC.
Be that as it may, neither patents nor trademarks are, of course, immune to the possible application of Articles 85 EEC, or as it is put in the *Terrapin*-case[16]:.."the protection given to industrial and commercial property by national law may not be relied on when the exercise of those rights is the purpose, the means or the result of an agreement prohibited by the Treaty". This is as true for imports from third countries as it is for intra-Community trade.

Finally, attention should be paid to a somewhat particular situation, viz. that of imports into the EEC from "Associated Countries", which share with the EEC a "free trade area". Now, the treaties with those countries - of which Portugal is one - contain provisions which are almost chinese copies of Articles 30 and 36 of the EEC Treaty. The question therefore is : do those imports share in the legal regime applicable to third countries, or rather in that of the EEC States amongst themselves. It is submitted here that the answer to this question was by no means a foregone conclusion. Be that as it may, it has now been dealt with by the Court of Justice, which came down in favour of the former alternative. Indeed, in a judgement handed down on February 9, 1982, the Court held i.a.:

> *"The Treaty, by establishing a common market and progressively approximating the economic policies of the Member States, seeks to unite national markets into a single market having the characteristics of a domestic market.*
>
> *Those considerations do not apply in the context of the relations between the Community and Portugal as defined by the Agreement. The Agreement makes provision for the*

abolition of certain restrictions on trade between the Community and Portugal but does not seek to create a single market.

It follows that in the context of the Agreement restrictions on trade in goods will be considered to be justified on the ground of the protection of industrial and commercial property in circumstances in which their justification would not be possible within the Community."

Such a distinction is all the more necessary inasmuch as the instruments which the Community has at its disposal in order to achieve the uniform application of Community law and the progressive abolition of legislative disparities within the Common Market have no equivalent in the context of relations between the Community and Portugal. The Court therefore ruled that :

"The enforcement by the proprietor or by persons entitled under him of copyrights protected by the law of a Member State against the importation and marketing of gramophone records lawfully manufactured and placed on the market in the Portuguese Republic by licensees of the proprietor is justified on the ground of the protection of industrial and commercial property within the meaning of Article 23 of the Agreement between the European Economic Community and the Portuguese Republic of 22 July 1972 (Official Journal, English Special Edition 1972 (31 December)(L301), p. 167) and therefore does not constitute a restriction on trade such as is prohibited by Article 14 (2) of that Agreement. Such enforcement does not constitute a means of arbitrary discrimination or a disguised restriction on trade between the Community and Portugal within the meaning of the said Article."[17]

III. LICENSING

It has been submitted in the introductory remarks of this exposé that Community law in the field of licensing is a fairly muddled affair. It is time now to substantiate this somewhat harsh statement.
Before setting out on this discussion, however, an important *caveat* should be made: at the time of writing not a single decision in this field has been handed down by the Court of Justice.[18] Of necessity therefore the discussion is based upon broad statements of policy, on the one hand, and unconfirmed - albeit also uncontested - individual decisions by the Commission.

This being so, one has to start with the time-honoured basis of EEC competition law, viz. Regulation 17/62[19]. It may be recalled that in its Article 4 it operates a distinction between so-called "light" and "heavy" cartel-agreements, the latter being susceptible of being given the "green light" by the Commission only as from the date of notification, whereas "light cartels" may be so authorised with retro-active effect beyond that date. This seemingly procedural provision is of course of considerable practical importance. It means that parties to such an agreement need not bother about notification thereof at all, up until the moment doubt is cast on the validity of the agreement by either of them, or possibly by a third party. And as - as sometimes seems forgotten - the major part of agreements happens to operate to the reasonable satisfaction of the parties thereto, this means that by far the most of "light" cartel agreements in fact never come to the fore at all, in terms of EEC competition law.

As it is, by virtue of Article 4, para 2, of Regulation 17, licence agreements (industrial property and know how) are classified as "light cartels" in this sense. To be correct, this applies only to one side of the coin: conditions and restrictions accepted by the licensee. By implication, conditions and restrictions accepted by the licensor are deemed to be "heavy" cartel-provisions. This is only so, of course, in so far as it is presumed that the condition or restriction concerned falls within the ambit of Article 85 EEC in the first place. Obviously, beyond that line there is no question of "cartel-agreements", "light" or "heavy", at all.
As to this ambit of Article 85 as such, we still have with us on the books the "Notice on patent licensing agreements" which, due to its date of publication - 24 December 1962 - is frequently referred to as "Christmas Message".[20] It does not seem worthwhile to enter into the precise details of this "Notice". Suffice it to mention that here also the main emphasis is on conditions and restrictions accepted by the licensee. Indeed the Commission - in what really is a "policy statement" on its own behalf, which of course can bind neither the courts nor private parties - states that in its view certain of such conditions which relate to restrictions in time, space, quantity, field of use etc. "are not caught by the prohibition laid down in Article 85(1) of the Treaty". The same for that matter - albeit somewhat hesitantly[21] - was held with regard to the best known among restrictions on licensors, viz. exclusive and sole licences.
As of the end of 1962 therefore, private parties with industrial property interests could feel that they were on reasonable safe ground. Most frequent licence-conditions were deemed either completely out of the ambit of Article 85, or reasonably

inoffensive as "light cartels."
To be sure, all this applies only to bilateral licence-agreements between individual parties; "patent-pools", "cross-licence"-agreements and the like were - and are - a different story, which - it is generally accepted - can only be told on a case-by-case basis. It would seem, however, that this does not take away the fact that for by far the greatest number of licence agreements there was hardly any practical problem in sight.
It is submitted here that in the subsequent years ever since, the Community-authorities have succeeded merely in casting doubt upon this reasoning, thus jeopardizing legal security, without having been able to put new firm rules - be they more strict ones - in its place.

In 1965, on the proposal of the Commission, the EEC Council enacted Regulation 19/65, whereby the Commission was authorised to grant "block exemptions" by virtue of Article 85(3) EEC for certain categories of agreements.[22] One of those categories was: bilateral agreements with restrictions imposed in relation to the acquisition or use of industrial property rights and know-how. Obviously, such "block exemption" should enable the Commission to do away at one stroke with great numbers of cases. And indeed it appears that by that time a great number of i.a. patent licence agreements had been notified with the Commission with a view to obtaining an exemption under Article 85(3) EEC. One may wonder whether in the light of Regulation 17 and of the "Christmas Message" as discussed above, there was really much practical need for those notifications in the first place. Anyway, had the Community authorities been consistent with themselves, most of those notifications could have been passed by in silence, with a mere broad reference to those 1962-texts. Instead, the Commission - and the Council in its wake - have opted for the hard - if not impossible - way. Assuming that at least certain amongst such licence-agreements might be caught by the prohibition of Article 85(1) EEC, they set out to specify the criteria for a block exemption. In other words, having (needlessly) taken all those agreements in, they then had to justify getting them out again. And, it should be stressed, all this on a generic, abstract basis, with the discussion concentrating, not on real agreements taken as a whole and in their context, but rather on individual clauses, isolated and examined *in vaso*.

It may well be argued that in asking for, and obtaining, this "enabling regulation", the EEC Commission has presented itself with a poisoned present - a "*cadeau empoisonné*. Indeed, sixteen years have lapsed since Regulation 19/65 without seeing the Commission able to deliver the envisaged "block exemption". It is true that an official draft implementing regulation has

been published by the Commission in early 1979[23], but this has met with such criticism, that at the moment of writing it seems at least doubtful whether this draft will be enacted in substantially the same form.
Under these circumstances it does not seem worthwhile to go into the details of the draft. Attention should be drawn to its structure, however, in particular to the respective positions of its Articles 1, 2 and 3. As a matter of fact, it should be noted that the prime provision is in Article 1: there, some six licence-contract clauses are granted a "block exemption" by virtue of Article 85(3). As for Articles 2 and 3, they are tributary to Article 1 : the former lists 9 clauses which do *not* block application of Article 1, whereas inclusion in a licence contract of one of the clauses mentioned in Article 3 means that Article 1 shall not apply. To be exact, article 2 of the draft goes further than that in so far as it provides that the clauses mentioned therein are exempted from Article 85(1) anyway, regardless of whether they are combined with "Article 1-clauses", or not. The reverse is *not* true, however, for Article 3: its one and only effect is to take away the exemption provided in Article 1 for the six specific clauses mentioned in Article 1. It is therefore utterly erroneous and misleading to refer to Article 3 as a "black list", suggesting thereby that clauses mentioned therein would be prohibited *per se*. As mentioned earlier, the draft as it stands has - rightly - drawn much criticism. It would be still more serious to read into it sweeping implications which are still less justifiable.

Any discussion of the draft therefore, should concentrate first and foremost on the six clauses of its Article 1. As it is, these clauses refer to exclusive/sole licences, to territorial restrictions (manufacture and/or sales), to tie-in clauses and, finally, to minimum performances by the licensee (royalties, licenced production etc.). If the Regulation were to be enacted in this form, these clauses would then be granted a "block exemption". However, clauses whereby licensor and/or licensee should refrain from direct sales to a certain territory, would be so exempted only under certain fairly strict conditions. E.g. the "protected" party should not be "big business", the licensee should manufacture himself, not merely trade; and independent trade channels should be available.
This latter condition draws attention to a consideration of paramount importance. Whatever the fate of this draft-regulation, there can be no doubt whatsoever about the illegality under EEC law of export bans affecting the intermediate trade. Discussions on "territorial restrictions" in this context therefore only concern *direct* exports from one territory to the other. As soon as a product has been sold in a particu-

lar territory within the EEC to a third party, that third party cannot be blocked by licence-clauses or other contractual instruments when he wants to take the product and sell it elsewhere in the EEC.

This is what the case law of the Court of Justice, discussed earlier here, really is all about. It is against this background that one should see the balance which the draft regulation seeks to strike on the nevralgic point of territorial restrictions on sales within the EEC. It means that in the Commission's thinking a block exemption can be given for "orderly marketing" within the framework of a licence contract provided that the licensee has his own independent source of supply, and that independent trade can take the products concerned freely from one part of the EEC to another. Thus, whilst allowing for a certain amount of territorial protection - without which certain licenses would simply not be worth their while - the Commission, understandably, wants to avoid "absolute territorial protection", the EEC bogey *par excellence*. Whereas one can sympathise with this approach, the additional condition of a maximum turnover of the "protected party" - be he licensor or licensee - is of course arbitrary in its actual limit, but, it is submitted, also in its principle. Indeed, in a framework of licenses for individual products or processes it is hard to see with what justification one should distinguish along lines of concern-turnover.

In comparison with territorial limits on (direct) sales, the other clauses mentioned in Article 1 of the Draft would seem much less controversial.
Territorial limits on manifacture, on the one hand, may well be to the clear advantage of all concerned as a vehicle for orderly investment for the product concerned, and on the other hand, of course, do not provide anything like "absolute territorial protection" on the market.
Mutatis mutandis the same holds true for exclusive and sole licences. As the Commission has found in a number of individual cases, this may prove an essential condition for a potential licensee in the first place - again as a vehicle for the protection of investment - and thus stimulate industrial enterprise. At the same time the combined effect of the Court's case law and the qualified approach to limits on sales in this Draft Regulation should make sure that exclusive/sole licenses cannot evolve into "absolute territorial protection".

This leaves us with still two clauses, "tie-in" and "minimum performance by licensee". One can easily agree with the Commission that these clauses should not be hurt by the prohibition of Article 85(1) EEC.

It could be argued, however, that an exemption by virtue of Article 85(3) EEC is rather superfluous, as there seems to be much doubt as to whether Article 85(1) EEC would apply to them in the first place. "Minimum performances by licensee" really are hardly a matter of limiting competition. As for "tie-in", it should be noted that in the spirit of the Draft Regulation a block-exemption would be granted only "so far and so long as this obligation is indispensable in the interests of a technically unobjectionable exploitation of the invention". It would seem that indeed this proviso rather than providing a mere justification for Article 85(3), would take the clause out of the ambit of Article 85(1) altogether. As a matter of fact, this is precisely the line taken by the Commission's own "Christmas Message" of 1962.
But then, when publishing this Draft Regulation the Commission at the same time let it be known that it intended to withdraw its "Christmas Message". To be sure, most of its contents are regrouped, one way or the other, in the Draft Regulation and would therefore benefit by the block exemption. Nevertheless, one may doubt whether there is indeed good policy in this move, whereby the practical outcome is essentially the same - the Commission would not dream of taking up again any of those exempted agreements on an individual basis! - but whereby certain clauses are stigmatized all the same, thus lending a hand to irritating, while finally fruitless, and drawn out discussions between potential partners to licence-agreements.

By way of conclusion it is indeed submitted here that not much would be lost really if the Commission were never to enact this "Block exemption-Regulation". Trade and industry could well live with the mere combination of Regulation 17/62 (Article 4) and the "Christmas Message", and indeed would be better served that way in terms of legal security. As for the safeguarding of the free competition-regime in the EEC, not much would be contributed by a "block exemption" along the lines of the Draft Regulation, which - due to its generic and abstract approach - is condemned to give at the same time too little and too much. As a matter of fact the Commission's rôle as "guardian of the Treaty" would be better served by concentrating on the real facts in their actual context as they present themselves on a case-by-case basis.

The EEC Council when adopting Regulation 19/65 was indeed quite right in insisting that the Commission should only try its hand at a block exemption-regulation "after sufficient experience (had) been gained in the light of individual decisions".

Some experience certainly has been gained, as is evidenced by the some dozen individual decisions taken since then,[25] and by the various "amicable settlements" to which parties concerned have consented under more or less pressure from the Commission[26].

Nevertheless, those involved in the daily practice of licensing contracts probably cannot avoid the feeling that it takes more than that to claim such "sufficient experience".

INDUSTRIAL PROPERTY

NOTES

PART ONE - THE NETHERLANDS

1. Before 1977 substantially the same provision was to be found in Article 30 (2) of the Patent Act.
2. H.R. 25-6-1943, *NJ* 1943, no. 519 ("Philips/Mebius")
3. H.R. 1-3-1974, *NJ* 1974, no. 329 ("Centrafarm/Sterling Drug")
4. Cf. Articles 30 and 36 of the EEC Treaty.
5. This Uniform Act is an annex to the Benelux Trade Mark Convention of March 19, 1962, which in its Article 1 stipulates that that Act should be enacted as the national trade marks act in each of the three countries involved.
6. Cf. H.W. WERTHEIMER, *Droit des marques et concurrence*, CDE 1970, p.438 et seq.
7. Cf. Article 10 of the Benelux Trade Mark Convention, according to which questions on interpretation of the Uniform Trade Marks Act can be submitted to the Benelux Court of Justice.

PART TWO - THE EEC

1. As from November 19, 1959, three EEC Working Groups were entrusted with the task of preparing three draft Conventions relating to Patents, Trade Marks and Designs, respectively.
2. To be sure, the most substantial result of those efforts is the European Patent Convention (1973), which entered into effect in 1977. This latter Convention, however, is not confined to EEC Member States.
3. The parallel provision of Article 170 which provides for similar proceedings to be initiated by another Member State is hardly ever used in practice.
4. Case 15/74, Centrafarm B.V. and Adriaan de Peijper v. Sterling Drug Inc. (1974) E.C.R. 1147.
5. Case 16/74, Centrafarm B.V. and Adriaan de Peijper v. Winthrop B.V. (1974) E.C.R. 1183.
6. See infra footnote 7.
7. Case 102/77, Hoffmann-La Roche & Co. A.G. v. Centrafarm Vertriebsgesellschaft Pharmazeutischer Erzeugnisse m.b.H.(1978) E.C.R. 1139; Case 3/78, Centrafarm B.V. v. American Home Products Corporation (1978) E.C.R. 1823.
8. Case 119/75, Terrapin (Overseas) Ltd., v. Terranova Industrie C.A. Kapferer & Co. (1976) E.C.R. 1039.
9. See also Case 187/80, Merck & Co., Inc. v. Stephar B.V. and P.S. Exler, Judgement of July 14, 1981 (not yet published).
10. See supra footnote 7.
11. See Case 3/78 (supra footnote 7)
12. See OJEC, January 26, 1976, No. L17.
13. See 7 IIC 91 (1976) at p. 97.
14. Both the draft - Regulation and the draft - Directive have been published in EC Bulletin, Supplement 5/80.
15. See in particular Case 51/75, EMI Records Limited v. CBS United Kingdom Limited (1976) E.C.R. 811.
16. See supra footnote 8.
17. Case 270/80, Polydor Limited and RSO Records Inc. v. Harlequin Record Shops Ltd. and Simons Records Ltd. (not yet published).
18. Case 258/78 ("Maize Seeds" case), which is an appeal from a Commission-decision on the Eisele-INRA Agreement (OJEC 1978, L286/23), is still pending before the Court of Justice.
19. JO(EC) No. 13, February 21, 1962, p. 204; OJEC (Special Edition 1959-1962) p. 87.
20. JO(EC) No. 139, December 1962, p. 2922.
21. ..."Leaving out of account the controversial question whether such exclusive undertakings have the object or effect of restricting competition, they are not likely to affect trade between Member States as things stand in the Community at present"...
22. JO(EC) No. 36, March 6, 1965, p. 533; OJ (Special Edition 1965-1966),p. 35.
23. OJEC, March 3, 1979, No. C58/12.
24. Limit proposed is total annual (group)turnover of 100 million units of account. (A unit of account roughly corresponding to an "old" US dollar).

25. - Burroughs - Delplangue, OJEC 1972, L13/50
- Burroughs - Geha, OJEC 1972, L13/53
- Davidson Rubber Co, OJEC 1972, L143/31
- Raymond - Nagoya, OJEC 1972, L143/39
- Advocaat Zwarte Kip, OJEC 1974, L237/12
- Sirdar - Phildar, OJEC 1975, L125/27
- Kabelmetal - Luchaire, OJEC 1975, L222/34
- Bronbemaling, OJEC 1975, L249/27
- AOIP - Beyrard, OJEC 1976, L6/8
- Penney, OJEC 1978, L60/19
- Campari, OJEC 1978, L70/69
- Maize Seeds, OJEC 1978, L286/23
- Vaessen - Morris, OJEC 1979, L19/32.

26. Summaries of those "amicable settlements" are given in the EEC Bulletin and in the Reports on Competition Policy published on a yearly basis by the European Commission.

The legal status of Hovercraft in the Netherlands

WYBO P. HEERE

Assistant Professor at the University of Utrecht

III.D.1.

On 11 June 1959 the first experimental flight of an Air Cushion Vehicle (*ACV*), or hovercraft, took place and now, 23 years later, many of these vehicles can be found all over the globe.

The *ACV* was an invention of Chistopher Cockerell, United Kingdom, and the manufacture of *ACV*'s has been mainly confined, untill now, to the U.K. It is somewhat surprising that especially the United States have shown so little interest in this extra-ordinary contraption which has done much to revolutionize transport over water and over land, and which could have done much more if, for instance, the U.S. aviation industry should have taken up, and developed the new idea. Outside the U.K. we have also French and Japanese small industries, and even the United States have become active in the field because of the military aspects of hovercraft transport.[1] Still, for the greater part, *ACV*'s are a typical British product, and British legislation for *ACV*'s is the only well developed legislation for the subject under study.

As far as the Netherlands are concerned, *ACV*'s have played a very small role.[2] In 1971, an industry in the centre of the country tried to develop a design of its own, but the product never reached the point where it was manufactured for sale. In 1969 during the summer season, an experimental hovercraft service was set up between Den Helder in the North and the island of Terschelling, and between Harlingen and Terschelling. After the season, the service was suspended because of a too low passenger-rate. Before the service started, the municipality of Den Helder asked the Directorate of Inland Shipping (Department of Transport) to test and inspect the craft; after having received a positive advice, the municipality gave an operating permit based on the Public Means of Transport Act of 1880.

Since 1969 *ACV*'s have visited Dutch harbours on several occasions, in transit from Great Britain to Northern Germany or Scandinavia, for naval exhibitions, for demonstration flights, but no regular hovercraft services have been started anymore. In the summer of 1979, the Rotterdam Port Authority bought four Hovermarines built for police, controle and fire fighting purposes. These four sidewall craft have been in active service in the Rotterdam harbour ever since.

THE LEGAL STATUS OF ACV's

As early as 1962 the ICAO undertook studies to decide whether *ACV*'s should be included in Annex 7 of the 1944 Chicago Convention on International Civil Aviation.[3] After extensive discussions, the ICAO Council decided on 8 November 1967 to redefine the notion of aircraft as follows:

> *"Aircraft: any machine that can derive support in the atmosphere from the reactions of the air other than reactions of the air against the earth's surface."*

Thus, *ACV*'s are now excluded from the ICAO notion of aircraft.

The Netherlands legislature followed suit: it decided, by Order in Council of 15 January 1969, that *ACV*'s are not aircraft within the meaning of the Netherlands Civil Aviation Act.
The *ACV* is defined as:

> *"a craft designed to move on an air pad which is maintained between the craft and the surface of the earth."*

This way we knew that *ACV*'s are no aircraft. Neither did we get any further with a judgment of the Utrecht District Court of 2 December 1975[4] which held that

> *"an ACV is not a motor-, speed- or raceboat as meant in Article 40(c) of the General Police Order of Vinkeveen and Waterveen."*

In this case a private person was hovering on one of the Utrecht lakes in a two-seater *ACV* and was fined, in first instance, for using a "too noisy and too fast motorboat". As the judgment in appeal was formulated as a factual statement, it was not possible to appeal, once more, to the Supreme Court to obtain a decision on the principles. The Utrecht District Court followed the opinion of the present writer in *Netherlands Yearbook of International Law* 1971, that the *ACV* is neither an aircraft nor a ship, but a means of transport *sui generis* for which no specific legislation was available yet.

When the Rotterdam Port Authority began its Hovermarine services in the port area, it asked learned advice how to legally treat its craft.[5] Rotterdam was adviced (by a famous local lawyer) to equate the Hovermarines with rivercraft (see Arts. 310 and 748 Netherlands Commercial Code):

> *"rivercraft are vessels used in, and intended for inland navigation, and not for sea navigation ."* (Art. 748 (a)).

Also, where a ship makes one or a few trips across the sea, this does not change a rivercraft into a seagoing vessel.[6] The fact that the Hovermarines crossed the Channel to reach Rotterdam, did not turn them into seagoing vessels: they are used in, and intended for, inland navigation.
When *ACV*'s are regarded as rivercraft - and the fact that Hovermarines are sidewall craft helped, perhaps - then the inland navigation rules apply. They have no nationality, and Art. 778 Netherlands Code of Commerce declares most of the first chapter on inland navigation not applicable to the Hovermarines, because they are "vessels used in the public service of the State or any other public agency". This means, *inter alia*, that the Hovermarines do not have to be registered in the inland shipping register, that therefore liens are not possible nor hire-purchase; these restrictions seem not to worry the Rotterdam Port Authority unduly.
The inland shipping rules on the transport of persons and goods, towage and salvage, general average, etc., are also applicable to the Hovermarines - as long as one is willing to subsume *ACV*'s under rivercraft. The CLN Convention of Geneva, 1 March 1973, plus its Protocol of 5 July 1978, allow the liability for the above mentioned Hovermarines to be limited to about 443.500 Dutch guilders (ex Art. 6bb) or to about 666.666 guilders (ex Art. 6d).[7]

Netherlands legislation has not defined the legal status of *ACV*'s , nor does it declare applicable Acts or parts of them to *ACV*'s - with one exception.
The only national law which mentions hovercraft - though indirectly - is the Act for prevention of collisions at sea (*Zeeaanvaringswet*) of 21 March 1979[8], an Act implementing the Convention on the International Regulations for Preventing Collisions at Sea (London, 20 October 1972).[9] The Netherlands Act speaks of "*vaartuigen zonder waterverplaatsing*", clearly referring to Rule 3(a) of Part A as annexed to the 1972 Convention where it concludes under "vessels": "non-displacement craft ..., used or capable of being used as a means of transportation on water".
Early in 1982, the *Wet voorkoming verontreiniging door schepen* was sent to Parliament[10], an Act to implement the International

Convention for the Prevention of Pollution from Ships (London, 2 November 1973), and its Protocol of 17 February 1978 (London)[11]. The Netherlands Act mentions, *expresso verbo*, in Article 1(c) *"luchtkussenvoertuigen"* (*ACV*'s).
Other Acts (*Wetboek van Koophandel, Zeebrievenwet, Meetbrievenwet*) speak only about *"vaartuigen"* (vessels) without indicating whether *ACV*'s should be included in this general term. See, for instance, Articles 309 and 310 of the Netherlands Code of Commerce.
Neither are *ACV*'s mentioned in the text of Book 8 of the new Netherlands Civil Code which, *inter alia*, replaces the old Code of Commerce. Article 8.1.1.2 leaves open the possibility of including *ACV*'s under *"vaartuigen"* (vessels), but does not mention them.

CONCLUSION

In the Netherlands there is no specific legislation for *ACV*'s. Their legal status has never been defined, and the only at tempts that have been made to find some applicable law have centered exclusively on the possibility of including *ACV*'s under vessels. Negatively, the legislator has excluded *ACV*'s from the notion of aircraft, and a District Court refused to consider *ACV*'s as motorboats.

According to the present author, *ACV*'s are *ACV*'s, and are neither aircraft nor ships.[12] Perhaps the Netherlands legislator is waiting for an international convention as such a convention has been in the making for many years.
In 1966, at Helsinki, the International Law Association charged the Air Law Committee to prepare a draft convention on the legal status of hovercraft, which was duly produced by Paul Chauveau at the Buenos Aires session of 1968; this draft was further discussed at the sessions of The Hague, 1970, and New York, 1972. In the meantime Emmanuel du Pontavice had taken over from Paul Chauveau, and Du Pontavice presented a draft convention at Madrid, 1976.[13] In this Draft Convention for the Unification of Certain Rules relating to Hovercraft both public and private law aspects of *ACV*'s are regulated. The Draft was officially adopted by the International Law Association.
In 1971 the International Institute for the Unification of Private Law, UNIDROIT, decided to draft a statute also. In 1975 and 1976 three Preliminary Draft Conventions were finished[14], on registration and nationality, on the international carriage of passengers and their luggage, and on civil liability for damage caused to third parties. These drafts were handed over to IMCO which has repeatedly announced a diplomatic conference for the conclusion of a convention on hover-

craft, but this conference has not been realized yet. Therefore, we have no uniform rules for a very special vehicle which very definitely cannot be identified with the older, more traditional means of transport. The world, and it seems the Netherlands legislator also, is still waiting.

NOTES

1. Peter Mantle, *Air Cushion Craft Development* (first revision), Washington DC, USGPO, 1980. See pp. 15-32.
2. W.P. Heere, 'Air cushion vehicles, a legal puzzle', in 2 *Netherlands Yearbook of International Law* 1971, pp. 108-121.
   For a bibliography on the legal status of hovercraft, see Wybo P. Heere, *International bibliography of air law 1900-1971*, plus the supplements for 1972-1976 and 1977-1980, under no. 71d.
3. *Ibid.* pp. 114-115.
4. 24 *Verkeersrecht* 1976, pp. 259-260.
5. Not published.
6. Arbitration, 22 February 1967, *Schip & Schade* 1967, no. 45; District Court of Alkmaar, 25 June 1970, *Schip & Schade* 1970, no. 93; Court The Hague, 7 October 1970, *Schip & Schade* 1971, no. 29.
7. CLN Convention of 1973, *Uniform Law Review* 1974, II, pp. 102 e.s.; *Transport*, ed. by prof. Schadee (Deventer, The Netherlands), pp. 1064/1069. Protocol of 1978, *Uniform Law Review* 1978, I, p. 231; *Transport*, pp. 1293/1296.
8. *Stb.* (Official Gazette) 1979, no. 196.
9. London Convention of 1972, *Trb.* (Netherlands Treaty Series) 1974, no. 51.
10. Handelingen Tweede Kamer der Staten-Generaal, zitting 1981-1982, no. 17320, nos. 1-2.
11. London Convention of 1973, *Trb.* 1975, no. 147; 12 *I.L.M.* 1973, p. 1319. London Protocol of 1978, *Trb.* 1978, no. 188; 17 *I.L.M.* 1978, p. 546.
12. See note 2, at p. 110.
13. I.L.A., *Report of the 75th Conference held at Madrid, 1976*; see pp. XI-XXX, and 39 e.s., 51 e.s., and 65 e.s.
14. 'Le statut des véhicules à coussin d'air (aéroglisseurs)' and 'The legal status of air-cushion vehicles (hovercraft)', in: *Revue de Droit Uniforme/Uniform Law Review* 1974, II, pp. 16/17 e.s.
    Preliminary Draft Convention on Registration and Nationality of Air-Cushion Vehicles, Etude LII, Doc. 10, Unidroit 1975; *Uniform Law Review* 1975, II, p. 238.
    Preliminary Draft Convention relating to the International Carriage of Passengers and their Luggage by Sea and by Inland Waterway in Air-Cushion Vehicles, Etude LII, Doc. 18, Unidroit 1976; *Uniform Law Review* 1976, II, p. 54.
    Preliminary Draft Convention on the Civil Liability of Owners of Air-Cushion Vehicles for Damage caused to Third Parties, Etude LII, Doc. 19, Unidroit 1976; *Uniform Law Review* 1976, II, p. 108.

The role and powers of the council of ministers

INGE C. VAN DER VLIES
Assistant Professor at the University of Amsterdam

IV.B.3.

I. Introduction

II. Structure and organization of the council of ministers
1 Appointment and dismissal of the ministers
1.1 The Monarch
1.2 The Second Chamber
1.3 The Premier-designate
2 Installation of the council
3 Departments
4 The rules of procedure of the council of ministers
4.1 The task of the council of ministers
4.2 Relationship council of ministers - ministers
4.3 The sub-councils

III. Powers of the council of ministers
1 General remarks
2 Derived from the government
3 Derived from an individual minister
3.1 Legal power
3.2 The Budget
3.3 Head of the department
4 Tasks special to the council of ministers
4.1 Governing body
4.2 Legal tasks
4.3 Other powers
5 Responsibility to the Second Chamber
6 Conclusion

IV. The rôle of the council of ministers
1 Problems and forms of policy
2 The relation to the Chambers
3 In relation to the media

V. Conclusions

I. INTRODUCTION

The Dutch constitution does not specify what is to be understood by 'government', 'cabinet' or 'council of ministers'. In the constitution the Monarch is designated as the executive. The term 'Monarch', in the sense of executive power, should not be understood to mean the Queen or King in person. It is: the Queen acting under ministerial responsibility. The council of ministers is not mentioned in the constitution. The real significance of this board cannot be derived from written law. This board - originally founded as a personal body of advice for the King - has, in practice, developed into the most influential council of policy.
In Holland a general revision of the constitution is in preparation. The terminology defining Monarch and ministers will be brought more in accord with the real and constitutional meaning of these organs and with their meaning in common parlance. The draftbill for section 2.2.1, par. I of the constitution is worded as follows: *'The government is composed of the Monarch and the ministers'*. The draft for section 2.2.4, par. I of the constitution reads: *'The ministers together constitute the council of ministers'*. In the same section, par. III one of the tasks of the council of ministers is specified: 'The council of ministers deliberates and decides on the general government policy, and promotes the unity of that policy'.

First we will consider how the formation of the council of ministers is brought about. The way in which this happens has gradually developed in the course of the one and a half centuries of the existence of the Dutch state and it bears the marks of the past decades.
Then the relation between the government and the council of ministers will be discussed. In principle the execution of power in legal provisions is in the charge of the government. But, generally, the ministers or the council of ministers have the charge of this execution.
In the third section of this article we will consider the various powers of the council of ministers and their particular positions in constitutional law.
Finally the rôle of the council of ministers will be examined. This is a difficult question, as the way in which this organ acts in public is not too explicit; a statement, corroborated by 'the secret of the council of ministers'.

II. STRUCTURE AND ORGANIZATION OF THE COUNCIL OF MINISTERS

The following topics are concerning the council of ministers of the State of the Netherlands. Apart from that we have a Council of ministers of the Kingdom. The latter consists of members of the council of ministers plus the Minister Plenipotentiary of the Dutch Antilles, who participates in matters of the Kingdom touching the Antilles. Within the scope of this article, a conference of the Council for the Kingdom should be regarded as a special conference of the council of ministers.
The council of ministers must also be distinguished from the cabinet. The cabinet consists of all the ministers (± 15) and ministers of state (± 15). We have no regulations about these matters. And the cabinet has no special power.

1. *Appointment and dismissal of the ministers*

Both appointment and dismissal is done by the Queen, on the authority of section 86 of the constitution. In this case the term 'Queen' must be understood to mean: 'the Queen, acting under ministerial responsibility'. A letter of appointment and a discharge certificate must be signed by both the Queen and the minister.
Only a few formal hindrances can hamper the eligibility for the appointment of a minister. Chief among them is that a minister is not allowed to be a member of a representative college.

1.1 *The Queen*

The Queen plays an active part in the formation of a cabinet. She chooses a premier-designate (*formateur*, not exactly in the British sense; though he does attempt to form a cabinet and will often head it as Prime Minister, he may not be successful, nor need he become Prime Minister) and she asks him to form a government. Both the choice of this premier-designate and the formulation of the instructions for the formation is at the discretion of the Queen. The issue of the elections for the Second Chamber are, however, essential in these matters.

1.2 *The Second Chamber*

Considering the great number of parties, it will not be easy for any of them to obtain a majority in the Second Chamber. The Queen aims at organizing the formation in such a way that an optimal relation between the Chamber and the cabinet will be the result. So her first choice has to be a political objective one, only made for that end.

The new-appointed ministers will account for the formation to the States General.

2. *Installation of the council*

Once it is clear that their political parties will raise no objections to their appointment, the premier-designate will summon all the eligible ministers to attend a constitutional assembly. Then he will recommend their appointment to the Queen's consideration. The Queen appoints the ministers to their offices. The Queen also appoints the Ministers of State.

3. *Departments*

The highest echelon of officialdom is formed by one or more secretaries-general. They hold permanent appointments and serve cabinets of various colours. There are no political advisers. (They do occur nowadays, be it disguised)

4. *The Rules of Procedure of the council of ministers*

The rules of procedure of the council of ministers have been settled by Royal Decree. Voices are heard, demanding to lay down these rules by Act of Parliament in order to draw the States General into the debates. The fact that in these rules the procedural methods of one of the most important public boards are laid down, argues in favour of this point of view. The relationship among the various ministers is also defined and a number of powers is conferred on the Prime Minister. In 1979 the rules were rearranged in the usual form. No fundamental alterations have been carried through in this amendment. Below we will discuss a number of important provisions from the regulations.

4.1 *The task of the council of ministers*

The task of the council of ministers is to deliberate and decide on the general policy of the government and to promote its unity. Explicity *not* defined is the idea that the council should *determine* the general policy of the government.
Then an enunciative list is drawn up of subjects which do, in any case, belong to the general policy of the government, on which the council will deliberate. A selection from these subjects may give an impression of their nature: draft bills; drafts of general royal decrees, agreements with other powers, memoranda to the States-General, the promulgation of proposed policies, important subjects concerning foreign policy.
Other subjects may be entered on the agenda after consultation with the Prime Minister.

After having been arrested, the minutes will be sent to the Queen alone. The members are sworn to secrecy with respect to what has been discussed in the council.

4.2 *Relationship council of ministers - minister*

The rules of procedure demonstrate neither a purely individual, nor a purely collective, nor a purely hierarchical principle. It is an established fact that the Prime Minister is *primus inter paris*. In his capacity of chairman he has every authority with respect to order and co-ordination. But he has no special authority to concern himself with the content of a colleague's policy.

There is no provision whatsoever to say that the council may decide on the policy of an individual minister. The power of the council is limited to decisions on the general government policy. Only if the ministerial policy is part of government policy, a minister can be committed to decisions made by the council. Eventually the council will decide with a majority of votes. Therefore an individual minister will have to adapt his policy to the general government policy.

An individual minister is bound never to act in contravention of a decision of the council. Whenever a minister should consider a decision to be contrary to his own responsibility, he must notify the council. In case the decision should be sustained by the council, he will be left with two alternatives; either to act upon the decision of the council of ministers or to offer his resignation (for further information see section III.3). To show the more clearly that collective responsibility is all-important, the draft of the new constitution mentions specifically that the council of ministers decides in matters of the general government policy.

4.3 *The sub-councils*

In the rules of procedure of the council of ministers it has been laid down that the council may form sub-councils out of its own members, in order to prepare and to decide on matters concerning particular aspects of the general government policy. The Prime Minister is chairman of the sub-councils. Whenever a minister asks the sub-council to refer a case to the agenda of the council, this will be done immediately.

We have about ten sub-councils. Examples: the Council for Town and Country Planning and Environment Protection, the Council for General Defence, the Council for Welfare. Apart from these councils special committees may be formed out of the council of ministers. These committees need not be permanent and they will deal with the less important matters. Finally we have consultative groups, which are formed spontaneously. For instance, we once had a socio-economic triangle, which

consisted of three ministers under direction of the Prime Minister, to adjust the most pressing predicaments in the socio-economic field.
The institution of sub-councils aims at relieving the council. The institution of too many sub councils, however, could cause co-ordination problems.

III. POWERS OF THE COUNCIL OF INISTERS

1. *General remarks*

Except in the rules of procedure of the council of ministers (RoPoCoM) the council is vested with relatively little power. But the council does have a decisive influence of the way in which other organs exercise their powers: with the government and the individual ministers.
Moreover, the council of ministers has monopolized a number of tasks which had not been committed to the care of any other authority. In this field the council has more and more come to manifest itself as an organ as defined in constitutional Law.

2. *Derived from the government*

In the constitution and in a great number of Acts of Parliament the government (the Queen acting under ministerial responsibility) is granted many powers. To a great extent these powers belong to the *general* government policy, as meant in section 4 of the RoPoCoM. Therefore the council of ministers will have to deliberate these matters. The council of ministers will decide on the contents of the policy assigned to the government; the government will only establish it. This is one of the most important tasks of the council of ministers.
In many cases the influence of the council of ministers will go further than this; and will the government not be involved at all, though sometimes nominally entitled. The explicit co-operation of the Queen is only required in classical juridical forms. But, in the rules of procedure of the council of ministers certain cases are also labelled as belonging to the government policy, which are not dealt with in the classical juridical forms. The adoption of memoranda's is an instance of this. Although nominally the government is entitled to adopt memoranda's they are not involved in these matters. As we still label these cases as 'belonging to general government policy', we keep (where possible) one and the same name in reserve for the highest administrative policy.
On the authority of section 4 par. 2 of the RoPoCoM the council will eventually deliberate and decide on *promulgation* of proposed policies which may influence the position of the *cabinet*, which may have important financial consequences or

which may affect the policy of another minister and on which, up till then, the responsible ministers will have reached no agreement. Not specified is which particular organ should provide the proposed policies as meant in this section. This comprehensive section puts the cabinet in a central position, but - and this is a limitation - only as far as the promulgation is concerned.
An enigmatic section. With respect to another question the government has determined that 'legal power' implies the way in which this power is exercised. This then, seems to be the main implication of this section. If a proposed policy should not be promulgated, or in a distorted way, this would necessarily recoil on the policy itself. Due to this section almost any power of the government of any importance has, via this interpretation, been reduced to the same denominator, namely 'general government policy' and in this way everything has been merged into the council of ministers.

3. *Derived from an individual minister*

Various powers may be assigned to a minister, either in his capacity of a member of the government or of a minister.
By virtue of the rules of procedure the council is in any case involved in the exercise of powers by the minister as a member of the government, whenever this exercising should affect the *general* government policy (For further information, see III.2)
The position of the council towards the minister will be more difficult if the minister should be granted a power by means of a law in so many words. Formally regarded the exercise of this power will fall outside the scope of the government policy. Consequently, the council will have no formal authority to concern itself with the policy of the minister in these matters.
The formal line of argument can be sustained by the following points. It would seem to be in the nature of things to lay down in the RoPoCoM that the council should be granted the authority to concern itself with such a policy of the minister. Yet this is far from easy. The RoPoCoM is a Royal Decree, which is of a lower legal order than an Act of Parliament by virtue of which a minister is generally granted his powers. Such a lower rule should not run counter to the higher regulations. In the prevailing rules this has therefore not been done expressis verbis. But two provisions have been made, and in view of the foregoing we may say that their relationship with the principle of legal supremacy is rather strained.
The first provision is to the effect that a minister may not act in contravention with a decision of the council. In practice this means that a minister is bound nearly almost to act upon any decision made by the council though individual views on policy are respected.

The second provision is to the effect that the promulgation of every proposed policy which may influence the general government policy, must first pass the council.
The greater part of the power of the council of ministers flows from the fact that the council possesses ministerial power. We will mention some of these powers:

3.1 *Legal power*

In many laws one or more ministers are granted the power of legislation in a material sense or else the power of disposition. This will affect all possible subjects.

3.2 *The Budget*

The technical powers granted to the minister in the Budget and the Acts of Parliament concerned were accountable for the fact that the minister could independently grant dispositions. At first this power was undisputed, as it was to concern mainly beneficiary dispositions. The ministers may also independently enter into transactions of civil law. On this account we now find, side by side with the classical administration, a new administration, whose legality is not very clear.

3.3 *Head of the Department*

The minister will either be appointed as head of a certain department or as a minister without portfolio.

4. *Tasks special to the council of ministers*

We can distinguish various kinds of tasks that are special to the council of ministers. On the one hand there are tasks flowing from, or only connected with, the rules of procedure; on the other hand tasks flowing from legal obligations. The phenomenon that the council of ministers can be commissioned with certain tasks by or in virtue of the law is fairly recent.

4.1 *Governing Body*

Nowadays the formulation of a governmental programme is regarded as one of the first tasks of a cabinet on its accession to power. In the council of ministers it will be the guideline in establishing all further policies. (for further information see IV).
In view of section 11 RoPoCoM the council has an important task in settling conflicts among the ministers themselves. Although generally no votes are taken, a reference to this section makes it possible for the council to decide entirely

against the wish of the minister who is most of all concerned. Apart from a co-ordinating function in the field policy, the council of ministers also has an administrative-technical co-ordinating function. This function is mainly important during preliminary work in the field of the policy. There are hundreds of committees of officials, instituted by a number of ministers or by the council of ministers, to co-ordinate the activities of the various departments. This important administrative task of the council of ministers is getting more and more attention.
There is a great number of committees and advisory bodies, and a sharp line of demarcation cannot be drawn between them. Formally advisory bodies should be instituted by law. This roundabout course is not always taken. The council and the ministers will often institute their own advisory bodies, under a slightly different name. The council is at the head of all these advisory bodies.

4.2 *Legal tasks of the council of ministers*

The council of ministers is mentioned in a limited number of laws. These laws, however, are those concerning either the advisory bodies or extraordinary circumstances. In the latter the Prime Minister is often mentioned as well.
Often the advisory bodies are charged to give advice not only to the government, but also to the council. Such a law may prescribe, for instance, that a particular advice must be discussed in the council of ministers. This is a legal acknowledgement of the function of the council within the government.
Before long the council will, by virtue of the constitution, get the power to decide on the general government policy.

4.3 *Other powers*

Occasionally circumstances may arise in which the council of ministers will combine a number of powers in one decision. For instance, it has occurred that the council, as council, was compelled to withdraw a promise of a subsidy. This happened at the insistence of the Second Chamber and it concerned foreign policy. Never before had the council granted a subsidy, let alone withdrawn a decision taken by one of its ministers. Another instance of similar behaviour is the reaction on petitions. These are often presented to the States General, but quite a few of them to the council of ministers, where they are most often dealt with by a minister.
Another instance is to be seen from the attitude of the council when international contracts are to be concluded.

5. *Responsibility to the Second Chamber*

Who is to render accountability to the Second Chamber: the minister or the council?
On the one hand the minister is curtailed in the way in which he may render his accounts; he must keep within the bounds of the cabinet-policy (section 11 RoPoCoM). On the other hand he may rely on his colleagues: the whole council of ministers will support the policy which the minister is at that moment defending. If the Chamber should consider the answer of a minister to be unsatisfactory, the Chamber will know that if the consequences are to be taken seriously, a cabinet-crisis may be risked.
The council of ministers will always commit itself to one particular line of policy. Therefore it is not uncommon for a minister to offer his resignment, either because he cannot comply with the policy of the council or on account of a political conflict in the Second Chamber. Examples of resignments on account of internal conflicts:

1971 - the minister for economic affairs resigns, because he disagrees with a decision of the council concerning the collective labour agreement of the metal industry.
1972 - two ministers resign on account of the retrenchment-policy of the council of ministers
1978 - the minister for defence resign, on account of the policy of the council of ministers with respect to the nuclear bomb.
1980 - the minister for defence resigns, on account of the policy of the council with respect to the financing deficit and the development of income.

In 1977 the *Den Uyl*-cabinet fell on account of such an internal conflict, when one minister was in danger of dropping out. There is no saying how often the opposite case may occur; of a minister who, in the Chamber, will uphold the point of view of the council instead of his own. The ministers are sworn to secrecy with respect to the course of events in the council. Sometimes this duty will not be fulfilled too scrupulously. In such a case the outcome will entirely depend on the position of the minister. A strong or indispensable minister will take care that the cabinet will firmly stick to its own line (*Van Agt* in the affair of the *Bloemenhove*-clinic); others will beg pardon (*Vorrink* in the affair of the *Bloemenhove*-clinic). In general we may say that in essential moments the council of ministers will present itself collectively to the Second Chamber. Differences of opinion will be dealt with internally, either beforehand or afterwards. This rule may either mean that all of them will have to tone down to one point of view or that some ministers, or the whole council (and as in such

a case the ministers of state will resign their seats: the whole cabinet) will offer their resignation. Just as the policy-making, is shifting, the way of accepting responsibility is shifting from individual to collective.
The tendency to intensify the collective responsibility has been laid down in the proposed constitution. The new provisions are meant to establish, among other things, that the council of ministers will in the first place be the responsible body to the Chamber.

6. *Conclusion*

Formally the number of tasks of the council of ministers is limited. But the term does occur more and more in written law. The powers explicity granted to the council concern mainly internal relations. An important fact is that the council of ministers is more and more getting into the way of presenting itself collectively to the Second Chamber. The original individual duty to accept responsibility is mainly practical; a minister will defend those points of the policy of the council which fall within the scope of his portfolio and on which he is the preeminent expert.
For the rest the council of ministers will mainly exercise the powers of other organs: on behalf of the government or the minister(s). The government has only given them the authority to debate on the general government policy. In practice, however, the council is the institution which will determine the policy. One cannot draw a sharp line between the exercise of the powers of others and the exercise of their own powers. As in both cases the council will determine the content of the policy and as the open summary in the rules of procedure allows that all policy may be labelled as general government policy, this obscurity will, in practice, present no difficulties.
Apart from this task towards third parties, the council has the internal task to settle differences of opinion among the ministers. It is hard to say how important this particular task may be.
Finally the council also has an administrative task: the coordination of the staff of government officials.

IV. THE ROLE OF THE COUNCIL OF MINISTERS

Only little is known about the internal significance of the council of ministers. The members are sworn to secrecy; the minutes and the list of decisions are secret. The curious observer will only incidentally perceive a slight outbreak of fire, caused by an intentional or unintentional leak.
The rôle of the council in the formation of its policy could be specified, by the council itself, in either of two ways.

On the occasion of its accession to power the council may lay down the main lines of its policy-programme, which they may further elaborate during their reign. But the council may also dispense with this procedure and have the aim to make the best possible decisions ad hoc. In practice the councils will compromise between these two principles, generally inclining to the latter.
It is true that every cabinet will formulate a programme for its own policy. But this has only actual political significance. In the daily practice, which will set in immediately after the governmental statement to the Second Chamber has been made, the council of ministers will be overburdened with urgent matters and questions of detail. Soon the cabinet will lose sight of the main lines that had been established and while instituting advisory bodies on a long-term basis, they will switch over to crisis-management, apart from those matters that had already been arranged in so many words. This does not alter the fact that by means of these decisions, made under compulsion of the circumstances, the policy will be formed.
In 1969 the Rotterdam professor *Van Maarseveen* discussed the domination of the council of ministers in a startling speech. He drew attention to the power exercised by the council of ministers and to its imperfect juridical design. In his opinion the council was the highest policy-formulating body. In a report issued about ten years later, the domination of the council of ministers was disputed; a conclusion drawn from the decisions of the cabinet, which mainly settled various conflicts. This conclusion seems to be wrong. The only conclusion we may draw is that in Holland we are ruled via incidental solutions.

1. *Problems and forms of policy*

In Western Europe the last hundred years have shown a greater or less degree of change from a liberal state to a state of social welfare. Often the regulating of the desiderata in the social welfare state took place outside the bounds of classical jurisdiction. The granting of favours was mainly regarded as a political or ideological, and very rarely as a juridical problem. Those who had the means would determine the policy: the ministers. This does not mean that the policy was not given juridical shape at all. The juridical shaping - especially legislation - often did not occur before the policy had long since been completed. The then formulated so-called 'frame-laws' are often drafted so widely that within the framework of one and the same law a great many lines of policy may be marked out.
An example of the ample space in which the council of ministers can determine its policy is given now that the welfare of the

state must be curtailed. It is the council of ministers which, within the scope of the existing legislation, will determine the adjustment-policy. Possibly the rôle of the council of ministers is even stronger than when our prosperity was increasing. Each of the ministers must defend his own portfolio against the others. Especially the ministers for economic and social affairs will often be sharply opposed to each other. The rôle of the council of ministers will gain in weight along with the amount of unemployment, the difficulties in the monetary policy, the scarcity of energy, and along with the relation of the problems and the fundamentality of the necessary decisions.
This conclusion is even enforced by the relation between national and international politics. Almost every decision in the international field can affect the domestic economic situation. This means that the council of ministers must be able to back the foreign policy of the ministers who are most concerned. In Holland this became apparent in an affair about a licence for the export of two submarines to Taiwan. Legally a licence will be granted or not by one certain minister, viz. the minister for economic affairs. However, on account of various complications, it was finally, probably against the wish of the minister for foreign affairs, determined collectively by the council.
The significance of the policy of the council of ministers appears from new forms of policy. The formulation of memoranda (often replacing legislation) and especially of plan-memoranda concerns the ministers and the council. In the RoPoCoM has explicitly been determined that memoranda which are to be submitted to the States General must be brought up for discussion in the council of ministers.

2. *The relation to the Chambers*

Of the two Chambers of the States General the Second Chamber plays the most important part with respect to the duty of the ministers to render accountability, though in principle, the two are equivalent.
Which particular juridical form the council of ministers may choose for the proposed policy appears to be of little consequence to the effect of the efforts of the Second Chamber to co-determine the policy; legislation or not. Statements as the latter must be made and regarded with some caution: it is hard to ascertain the influence of the Chamber.
In the first place it is a fiction to speak of the 'Chamber'. In practical politics the Chamber is subdivided into a Chamber-majority and a Chamber-minority. The majority is clearly more successful than the minority. Proposals of the majority are always passed by that same majority. But, if the approved proposals will bring about any change in the policy of the govern-

ment is hard to check. The execution of a motion may often take years. On the other hand there is no saying how many preliminary consultations will be carried on between the representatives of the cabinet on the one side and representatives from among the members of Parliament of the parties in government on the other side. These consultations may either be carried on as preliminary work for the parliamentary party representations or as preliminary work for the council of ministers. This does not alter the fact that confrontations between political associates from the government and from the parties do occur in the public assembly of the Chamber.
The Chamber, or parts of it, generally addresses itself to the cabinet as a whole. (For further information see III.5)
Briefly summarized we may say that the Second Chamber has accepted that the policy is primarily constituted by the council of ministers and not by the minister(-ial council) in co-operation with the Second Chamber.
To this we must certainly add that from this remark should not be inferred that the Second Chamber should have no influence. Especially the majority of the Chamber can assert itself: but there is no saying to which degree the majority will actually do so.
Besides, the majority of the Chamber will most of the time address a minister as a member of the council of ministers. This cannot only be explained by the entanglement of the problems, through which the modification of part of the policy may have consequences for the whole policy, but especially by the unstable equilibrium of the usual coalition cabinet.

3. *In relation to the media*

The public authorities are fully alive to the fact that there must not only be a good policy, but that this policy must be promulgated in the best possible way. Consequently, in 1979 a provision was laid down in the rules of procedure, saying that the promulgation of the policy must be brought up for discussion in the consultations of the council of ministers. This does not concern all sub-divisions of the policy; only for those proposed policies which may have effect on the position of the cabinet, or the ones that may have important financial implications, or those concerning the policy of more than one department, about which the ministers in question have as yet reached no agreement. Before 1979 this question was only indicated in internal guidelines.
The presentation in the media has certainly contributed to the development of a council of ministers. The policy of the cabinet will be proclaimed and defended by the Prime Minister. When proclaimed, the policy will immediately become the object for public discussion. The point of view of the cabinet, which is proclaimed immediately after the assembly of the council of

ministers, is set off against the views of the political parties, the trade unions, the employers' unions, all other pressure groups, and of the commentators of the media themselves. Often letters are sent to the States General. But these have lost the right to bring off a scoop. Moreover, they will only after a day or so be able to react on the proclamation of the council of ministers.
Whether a remark made by a minister will fall under the publishing prohibition is often hard to ascertain. Sometimes it will be an open secret that there are internal differences of opinion. In principle the ministers will not show them. But once a decision has been taken, there will, under certain circumstances, be no harm in disclosing which differences of opinion there were and what exactly has been the main determinant to a particular point of view. This may happen in the form of an extensive motivation of the decision. What exactly will be tolerated will depend, among other things, on the attitude of the council of ministers towards the openness to the public.
The possibilities of sanctions against a minister who has gone beyond the limits of permissible openness are limited. He or she may be hold responsible by the Chambers. This happened repeatedly. In such cases the Chambers are mainly interested in the question whether a standpoint, as voiced by a minister, should be taken as expressing a personal view, or the opinion of the minister himself, or a standpoint of the cabinet. Undoubtedly the too frank minister will be hold responsible for the controversial remarks in the council of ministers. Unknown is what will be said about it in the council. The measure of last resort (dismissal) will - among other things in view of the above mentioned difficulties of a coalition-cabinet - be very rarely applied.
In proportion to their positions and to the matter in hand, the ministers will therefore be enabled to show (their) differing opinions. As long as they will not defy the unity of the council of ministers, they can regulate the degree of their own liberty. The unity of the council of ministers will always remain the standard in such publications. Whether this weapon will be wielded against the minister or against the council of ministers, depends on the strength of the minister himself. Since the council of ministers or its members have often been presented by the media, their importance is growing in the eyes of the voters. The cabinet-policy will be the issue at the elections as it has been propagated by the best-known ministers. In Holland we seldom see one minister - for instance the Prime Minister - acting as the only representative. The cabinet will be opposed not so much by the Second Chamber as by the leader of the opposition.

V. CONCLUSIONS

The Council of ministers has developed into the most important organ to determine the policy. The rules determining its position are still too much dependent on its origin: personal body of advice to King William I. Though we may expect that on this point a modification in the constitution will be carried through one of these days, we know that this modification will not go beyond a formal acknowledgement of the council of ministers.
In terms of law the government and the ministers are growing in significance. In terms of practice the significance of the council of ministers is increasing, for it is the council of ministers which exercises the powers of the government.
Moreover, the council of ministers is gaining importance in an independent way. The council as such will take the many decisions concerning the policy. It is exactly in a period of declining prosperity, in which socio-economic decisions are highly fundamental, that this administrative task of the council is keenly felt.
Besides, the council is acting more and more collectively. The council acts as a single unit with respect towards the States General (at any rate towards the opposition) and also towards the public in general. Unification is fostered by the secret character of the assemblies of the council. Moreover, the council, as highest echelon of the public authorities, has the disposal of the most technical help and assistance. The influence of officialdom on the policy has been left out of consideration.
There is a growing tendency to accept the council as a political fact. The decisions of the council are directly related to the legal position of citizens. The shift in accent of the legislation of government and States General to the establishing of the policy by the council of ministers under supervision of Parliament (that is to say: the opposition) is a hazardous speculation on the strength of the ministerial responsibility.
For the distribution of powers the ministerial responsibility is no longer a very suitable instrument, because it happens very rarely that only one or just a few ministers are responsible. By making the cabinet into the issue of the elections, the voters are enabled to give their opinion about it. They opt for the present policy or for that of the opposition.
The rôle and powers of the council of ministers have increased. The possibilities to supervise the council have not increased on a corresponding scale.

The unique Dutch broadcasting system on the eve of the revolution in teletechnics and the freedom of information

HERMAN COHEN JEHORAM
Professor of law at the University of Amsterdam

IV.C.1.

I. INTRODUCTION

If one speaks of the revolution in teletechnics, which is largely still to come as far as the actual application of these technics is concerned, and the freedom of information one is first and foremost obliged to sketch the situation as it still exists, more or less on the eve of this revolution. The precise manner in which this structure will be changed is still unclear. In every country this mere technical revolution will hit a different cultural and political situation as far as the media are concerned. In all probability the technical revolution will work out somewhat differently in different countries, according to existing infrastructures. National differences are especially to be found in the national broadcasting systems. The emphasis in this article will therefore be on the unique Dutch broadcasting system on the eve of the revolution in teletechnics and the freedom of information. Its final effects on the other media should not be underrated, but as these influences will make themselves be fully felt only after the revolution in broadcasting has been realised, speculations in this field may be too risky at this moment.

II. GOVERNMENTAL MEDIA POLICY

Governmental policy with regard to the media must limit itself to the creation of general means and facilities. It cannot interfere with the messages to be communicated nor with the choice of the messengers. This principle follows directly from the Western interpretation of the freedom of expression, which includes the freedom of information.
In general this principle has also been observed by Dutch authorities, with only one important, but narrowly defined, exception, which has lastly been laid down in the draft of a newly worded Dutch Constitution. Art. 7 of this draft, dealing

with the freedom of expression, reads in its second paragraph: "The law provides for rules concerning radio and television. There is no preceding supervision over the content of a radio- or television-broadcast." This is in conformity with art. 10 of the European Convention for the protection of Human Rights and Fundamental Freedoms, which also states that the freedom of expression, laid down in this article "shall not prevent States from requiring the licensing of broadcasting, television ... enterprises".
This specific restriction of the freedom of expression/information is based, in Dutch[1] as in other decisions, on the scarcity of the means of radio and television broadcasting. This scarcity makes it inevitable that the government, by a licensing system, distributes broadcasting time and facilities. With regard to the non-scarce printed media a similar licensing system would be regarded as an intolerable infringement on the freedom of expression/information.

III. THE CULTURAL AND POLITICAL BACKGROUND OF THE DUTCH BROADCASTING SYSTEM

In many countries the government has solved the problem by simply creating a broadcasting monopoly for some governmentally controlled license holder. Sometimes an oligopoly is created of public but not governmentally controlled broadcasting organisations. We also find systems of governmentally licensed private commercial broadcasting organizations or a combination of these and public broadcasting organizations.
The Dutch system does not fit into any of these categories. It is closely linked with the whole organization of Dutch society, at least as it existed in the 1920's when radio broadcasts started. The present Broadcasting Law of 1967 is in fact the somewhat belated fixation of a historic situation.

In the early twenties a fierce political battle had just been fought between on the one side Protestant and Catholic parties against on the other side non-confessional "liberal" forces, but the positions of these political sides were still deeply entrenched. The confessional block, and especially the leading group of calvinists were still convinced of the validity of their old antithesis: the irreconcilable opposition between christian and neutral, liberal groups in society. The two main christian groups, Protestants and Catholics, felt they had to protect themselves against contacts with liberals (and also each other) and the ensuing dangers of ideological contamination. Therefore, the Catholics and Protestants each organized a whole self-contained society for their flocks, with each their own universities and schools, newspapers, sportclubs, hospitals, unions, political parties and every conceivable

sort of organization. This social system was also to determine the coming Dutch broadcasting organization.
The first broadcasting organization in the Netherlands started in 1923, originally under the auspices of the hard ware industry (Philips). This still existing private association, *AVRO*, called itself "general" and "neutral" in character. It sought membership among listeners in all denominations and groups of Dutch society, as a private but *national* Dutch broadcasting organisation.
Those terms "general" and "neutral" were already an ideological provocation of the confessional groups in the Netherlands who could not accept such a "liberal" broadcasting organization as a national organization which would also represent themselves. Therefore the Catholics started their own private foundation *KRO* and the Protestants their private association *NCRV*. The social-democrats also could not identify with the "national" *AVRO* and created their own association *VARA*. A fifth and very small association, the *VPRO*, was formed by liberal Protestants.
Those four big private "pillars" of the rising broadcasting system, the *AVRO*, *KRO*, *NCRV* and *VARA*, each with their members or patrons were to dominate the entire broadcasting scene in Holland before and long after the Second World War. The fifth one, the small *VPRO*, was tolerated.

As indicated above, the fragmentation of Dutch society along religious and political dividing lines in general was mainly a result of the desire of religious or political groups to protect their own constituency against influences from the outside. As far as especially radio was concerned, however, the stakes were even higher for many political and religious leaders. To them the new medium seemed to offer splendid opportunities for mission, for propaganda among potential adherents outside the direct circle of the faithful. Radio differed from the traditional printed media to the extent that it reached an audience that was not so committed to the respective good cause that it had paid for any subscription to one of the ideologically coloured papers. One did not at first perceive all the consequences of exactly this last characteristic. It also meant of course, that every group was more than ever exposed to the ideas of others. And indeed, the crumbling of the ideological ghettowalls which has occurred in the Netherlands in the last 50 years has certainly been influenced by radio and later television.
The phenomenon can also be viewed in the light of a struggle for emancipation. Three of the five groups who had created their own broadcasting organization, the Protestants, the Catholics and the Socialists were, though in different ways, involved in certain emancipatory struggles. Also in this respect the respective broadcasting organizations have done their work.

Not only for these reasons the Dutch broadcasting system as such has very deep roots in Dutch society. The picture would be incomplete without a short indication of the very direct connections between the private broadcasting organizations and the political parties. Just as religion, ideology and emancipatory struggle had been the basis for all those countless organizations in Dutch society which had formed themselves along roughly the same dividing lines, so also for the political parties. With some, but not too much, simplification and generalization it can be said that the present four big political parties in the Netherlands have their respective counterparts (and aids!) in the five old and still existing broadcasting organizations I have mentioned. The biggest political party, the Christian-Democrats (48 seats in the Second Cahmber of 150 seats), a recent merger of the former Catholic and two Protestant parties, find their broadcasting equivalent in *KRO* (Catholic) and *NCRV* (Protestant). The Socialist party (44 seats) has its strong links with the *VARA* (Socialist), the right-wing Liberal party (26 seats) is by many observers seen as in sympathy with the *AVRO* (neutral). The left-wing Liberal Party (17 seats) seems to be of the spirit of the small *VPRO* (undogmatic left).

IV. THE BROADCASTING LAW

Because of these strong political affiliations of the broadcasting organizations which started their activities in the early twenties, the government at the time could do little but legitimize, in its ensuing broadcasting regulations, the existing situation. The idea of a non-governmental national broadcasting system, propagated in several circles, was politically defeated. The Broadcasting Regulation of 1930 distributed 20% of all the available broadcasting time to each of the four big private broadcasting organizations, 15% was reserved for a so-called general program, in turn provided for by each of the same Big Four (a symbolic shadow of the national broadcasting idea) and a small remainder was offered to the *VPRO*.

After the Second World War everything in Holland had to be rebuilt from scratch and many people had the euphoric opinion that a new and better society should be started where the old dividing lines had vanished. Then the idea of a non-governmental national broadcasting system came up again, only to be defeated anew by all the restaurative forces which soon made themselves felt in all segments of Dutch society. The five old broadcasting organizations reconstituted themselves. After a long political battle, in which even one government fell over the issue of also opening the possibilities for commercial broadcasting, finally the Broadcasting Law of 1967 passed parliament. The new law was again tailormade for the existing organizations. Access to the ether was reserved for private non-commercial organizations (associations or foundations) with a minimum number (since 1980: 150.000) of members or contributors. Their main purpose should be the broadcasting of a radio- or televisionprogramme which in principle would comprise all categories of programming material. Finally (and here I quote article 13 section 2 § 4 of the Broadcasting Law in its 1980 version)

> *"they have to be representative for a specific social, cultural, confessional or spiritual current in the population and aimed, to such a degree and in such a way, at the fulfilling of in the population existing cultural, confessional or spiritual needs, that their broadcasts for this reason can be deemed to be for the general good."*

Apart from this remarkable prose the law made a few concessions to more openness in the system, most of which seemed to be rather symbolic in 1967. Access to the ether for new upcoming (cultural, confessional, spiritual) broadcasting organizations was facilitated by the introduction of the phenomenon of provisional "aspirant broadcasting organizations", with a lowered minimumstandard of membership (60.000). These "aspirants" get for a few years some broadcasting time. This had indeed served as a steppingstone for three new broadcasting organizations among which two neutral ones. In 1980 the opening in the system has therefore been narrowed down by an amendment to the Broadcasting Law which now prescribes (art. 14, sect.3) that the aspirants must "set themselves the goal to broadcast a programme which differs to such a degree, as far as the choice of parts of the programme, their subject matter and their tendency is concerned, from the programme broadcast by the organizations which (already) have been allotted broadcasting time, that it enhances the pluriformity in broadcasting."

Also much more important than it had seemed to be in 1967 was the introduction of the new organization *NOS*, the Board of which is nominated partly (½) by private broadcasting organizations, partly (¼) by representative cultural and social organizations after consultation with the Minister of Culture and partly (¼) by this Minister himself, who also appoints the chairman. The *NOS* serves in the first place as an umbrella organization of all the existing and future private broadcasting organizations. It takes care of all the matters of common interest of the organizations, it coordinates their activities and represents them and last but not least it runs a complete technical studio system for the organizations. On top of all

that the foundation *NOS* is also itself entitled to broadcasting time. It broadcasts a "joint programme". According to the law (art. 36) this *NOS*-programme must, together with the programme of the private organizations, furnish "a balanced total image". Furthermore the *NOS* must "give opportunity for self-expression to those social, cultural, confessional or spiritual currents in the population, which are not represented" by one of the private organizations. The *NOS* is indeed the ever-growing offspring of the old ideal of a national broadcasting system.
The *NOS* also differs from the private broadcasting organizations to the extent that it does not need any members or contributors for its existence or amount of broadcasting time.
As already said above, the private organizations must have at least 150.000 members to get any broadcasting time at all. Also their amount of time is allotted according to certain progressive minima of membership. For this purpose three classes of organizations , A - C, were created which get broadcasting time to the ratio 5 : 3 : 1. The lowest class organization (C) has between 150.000 and 300.000 members, B between 300.000 and 450.000 and finally A any number over 450.000. The purpose of the introduction of the scale A-C in 1967 was to give A-status to the existing Big Four broadcasting organizations.
The B-status was academic and the C-status was a reserve for the small *VPRO*, of old the conscience of the system: the *VPRO* had to be able to continue without it having to be taken seriously.

V. THE BROADCASTING-GUIDE LAW

The financing of the entire radio- and television broadcasting which at this moment costs about 800 million Dutch guilders a year, is for three quarters provided for by the broadcasting fees the public has to pay, through a government-run collection system. The remaining 200 million Dutch guilders are paid with the net result of advertising spots, which are broadcast in small blocks around the news, not by any private commercial organization, but by a public foundation, the *STER*.
The private broadcasting organizations themselves are strongly forbidden to make any profit or to help third parties in making profit. This non-commercial character of the Dutch broadcasting organization is indeed a central feature of the whole system as it existed and could exist before and years after the Second World War and as it was finally codified in the Broadcasting Law 1967. It rested on a certain characteristic element in Dutch society which seemd stable but which was already crumbling in 1967, i.e. the ideological segmentation of the populace as indicated above.
The license to broadcast and also the amount of broadcasting

time depended on membership (and according to the law a paying membership) of private ideological broadcasting associations. But why did these associations find a paying membership at all? Originally, in the twenties, the socialist, Catholic, Protestant etc. organizations could indeed reckon on a faithful audience which was willing to contribute to the voicing of its own opinions. But when the ideological borders began to be less heavily guarded and finally the whole justification of their existence became an object of spreading doubt, also the selfevidence of a paying membership decreased. People needed other incentives to continue those memberships which were the basis for the broadcast licenses. These were found in the subscriptions to radio/tv-guides.

The broadcasting organizations had, of old, not only occupied themselves with their primary task - broadcasting -, they also had published each their own weekly radio/tv-guide for their members. These weeklies offered lists of all the programme data of the Dutch radio and television stations and - abridged - also the main foreign stations. Because of a peculiar provision in the Dutch Copyright Law of 1912, the organizations enjoyed a copyright on these listings of their programme data. This copyright they used to bar any publisher from competing in the field by way of bringing out an independent radio/tv-guide or even republishing the lists in a newspaper or magazine. The result at this moment is, that the four million Dutchmen who want to have a weekly survey of radio and television programmes are forced to subscribe to one of the radio/tv-guides of the broadcasting organizations.
The Broadcasting Law 1967 has made use of this situation by linking the subscription to such a monopolized radio/tv-guide to the *membership* of the publishing broadcasting organization. This in effect means that the organizations do not attract or hold their members primarily by the way in which they fulfill their primary task - broadcasting -, but by the attractiveness and cheapness of their radio/tv-guides. The Dutch Broadcasting Law is in reality a Broadcasting-*guide* Law, a cause for serious fictions and ensuing distortions as far as licensing *and* allotting broadcasting time is concerned.

A most telling example was furnished just before and immediately after the enactment of the new law. It had to do with the old copyright protection of lists of programme data, which was based on art. 10 of the Copyright Act 1912 stating that *all* writings are protected by copyright. This means protection not only for writings which show some "personal character", the customary criterion for any work to be protected by copyright, but also for writings which are completely devoid of any personal character, like telephone directories and indeed lists of radio and tv programme data. This copyright of the broadcasting organizations on lists of radio & tv programme data has been upheld against publishers who tried to bring these lists independently, in some fifteen final court decisions, among which four Supreme Court decisions[2]. But beginning with the second Radio-programme-data-decision, in 1961, the Supreme Court also had to reckon with the argument of the defenders, that such a monopoly of information might infringe the right to freedom of information as laid down in the European Convention on Human Rights. This led the Supreme Court to distinguish between the normal full copyright as it exists on works with a personal character and a somewhat lesser, *pseudo*-copyright on writings which lack this personal character. This pseudo-copyright now differs for instance from the full copyright in that it only gives protection against the actual copying of the written or printed lists of the copyright owners. This pseudo-copyright would not prevent the independent publishers from seeking the information in other ways than by this mere copying of written lists.

The last case that came for the Supreme Court concerned the independent commercial publisher of the radio/tv-guide *Televizier*. Here it was decided (in 1965) that the plaintiffs, the broadcasting organizations, had to prove the infringement of their pseudo-copyright. This meant they had to provide the nearly impossible proof that *Televizier* had actually copied their written or printed lists without resorting to the free seeking of the information. This would have been the end of the copyright-based radio/tv-guide monopoly of the broadcasting organizations, had not the government reacted. The Broadcasting Law was just in preparation and when it was sent to parliament in April 1966, it contained two articles on the copyright on lists of radio & tv programme data. Art. 22 of the Broadcasting Law 1967 now shifts the burden of proof to the defenders. Independent publishers of radio/tv-guides now have to prove they have *not* actually copied written lists, i.e. they have to mention the names of their informants within the broadcasting organizations themselves by whom they have freely sought the desired information: an effective deterrent for the then still flourishing *Televizier*.
At this juncture the oldest existing broadcasting organization, the *AVRO*, had lost so many members that it would soon lose its cherished A-status. *Televizier*, on the other hand, would soon have to stop its activities because of the new law with its fatal strengthening of the pseudo-copyright on lists of programme data. *AVRO* and the publisher of *Televizier* made a profitable deal: *Televizier* simply became a second radio/tv-guide of the broadcasting organization *AVRO* and the subscribers to *Televizier* were "sold" as members to the *AVRO*. *Televizier*, now sharing the monopoly status of a radio/tv-guide, stopped the lawsuit it had started in Strasbourg for the European Commis-

sion of Human Rights against the Dutch government, which by monopolizing radio/tv-guides would infringe the right to freedom of information[3].

VI. THE EROSION OF THE BROADCASTING SYSTEM

The task of broadcasting on political and ideological basis became more difficult when television was simply added to radio and licensed to the same existing broadcasting organizations. Many license-holders who could perhaps still keep their ideological profile for radio were really at a loss the moment they had to do the same with the medium television and its tendency to entertain the public rather than to inform it. These eroding factors led to the birth of two new broadcasting organizations which do not have any ideology and whose purpose is solely to entertain. They started to broadcast commercial programmes from the sea outside any territorial waters but beamed to Holland, one with television from a former oil-platform and the other with radio from a ship. After the law had been changed and measures taken, these "pirates" had to stop. It only meant that they came ashore and founded private "non-commercial" broadcasting organizations, *TROS* and *VOO*[4], with their own pop- or what-have-you culture, because the Broadcasting Law demanded at least the fulfilling of cultural needs. In no time at all they had enough subscribers/members to start as aspirant-broadcasting organizations, then as C-broadcasting organization, with in the meantime the *TROS* already enjoying the A-status and the *VOO* now claiming B-status. They began to broadcast extra popular programmes which attracted such a huge audience that the ideological broadcasting organizations, afraid of losing an even highly fictional membership and with that their license, only began to imitate the *TROS* and *VOO* programmes. At present the Dutch television (radio to a much lesser degree) shows a continuing competition between broadcasters on the most popular level. Needless to say, the already declining ideological content of the programmes of the old organizations is further diminishing. The residue of really motivated members of these organizations can only feel estranged.
A countercurrent is only to be found in the two smallest broadcasting organizations, the nonconformist *VPRO* and the new ultra-orthodox Protestant organization *EO*. But then both these opposite organizations have an amount of broadcasting time limited enough to enable them to maintain a specific profile.

The really big flaw and curse of the Dutch Broadcasting Law is its absurd strengthened pseudo-copyright on lists of programme data and the ensuing monopolizing of radio/tv-guides for the broadcasting organizations (which in itself might already infringe the freedom of information[5]). This then serves as the basis for the fictional linkage of subscription to a radio/tv-guide to membership of a broadcasting organi ation. By the further linkage of these memberships of organizations to their amount of broadcasting time the final result is a fierce competition for sheer survival between all the broadcasting organizations on the most popular level.

VII. CABLE TELEVISION

Some revolutionary inventions in teletechnics like viewdata- and teletext systems and direct satellite broadcasting are only beginning to be introduced and their application is still in an experimental stage to such an extent, that their social and legal impact cannot yet be assessed.
One new technique which is really operating on a large scale at this moment especially in the Netherlands, is cable radio and television. More than 60% of the households which receive television programmes in Holland do so by means of the cable, and in 1985 this is expected to be increased to 85%.

Cable television at this moment can be used for two different activities. In the first place the cable-operator can retransmit radio and television programmes which are originally broadcast by "Hertzian" broadcasting stations, and in the second place the cable-operator can distribute his own "original", i.e. self-originated programmes. The latter is regarded as "broadcasting" and the Minister of Culture has to issue broadcasting licenses for this activity. Apart from some minor local experiments in this field, the cable-broadcasting has not yet come off the ground. All the emphasis in the rise of the cable at this moment is on retransmitting programmes, originally broadcast by Dutch, German and Belgian radio and television stations. As far as television is concerned, the actual number of channels is about 6 to 8, but the *PTT* (the governmental agency for Post, Telegraph and Telephone) has plans to supply facilities to raise this number to 16.

The old and hotly debated question whether the present capturing of broadcast signals "out of the air" and the distributing of the programmes to cable-subscribers without the consent of the authors amounts to a copyright infringement, is answered in the affirmative by a Supreme Court decision[6] of October 30, 1981. A special committee of the Netherlands Ministry of Justice had already given as its opinion that pending this ruling of the Supreme Court it would be wise to adopt the working assumption that retransmission by cable television falls within the scope of copyright. It then further assumes that the government will make use of the possibilities which art. 17a of the Copyright Act already provides for : a system of compulsory

licenses for cable-retransmission[7]. At the beginning of cable television plans existed for one large national cable network in which government and broadcasting organizations would take part. The initiative has however been taken out of the hands of a hesitating and inactive government by local authorities, who started to set up their own cable systems, with the help of a very eager hardware-industry. A little political pressure in parliament led to the abandonment of the national plan. The government now issues cable-licenses to the municipalities, which have entered into all sorts of joint ventures with industry for the installation and operation of local cable networks. The *PTT* occasionally takes care of connecting local systems with each other by relay.
The private Dutch broadcasting organizations have very mixed feelings about the cable retransmission of foreign programmes because of the competition this brings before their own audience and the ensuing dangers for the number of their own memberships of which their license depends. At present this danger is still a minor one, because the retransmitted foreign stations do not use the Dutch language which restricts their Dutch audience considerably. One does fear, however, the coming of teletext which might be used to subtitle foreign broadcasts. Especially urgent is the question of the commercial Luxemburg station *RTL*, which might very easily start a programme, interspersed with Dutch commercials, in the Dutch language. A curious political incident may highlight this.

In the fall of 1979 a commercial cable-operator in Sluis, a hamlet near the Belgian border, who had a connection with a Belgian cable system which did carry the Luxemburg *RTL*-programme, asked the Dutch *PTT* to relay his captured *RTL*-signal nation-wide to other local Dutch cable-operators. He made use of the fact that the Broadcasting Law had just been amended to the effect that the Minister of Culture had no responsibility anymore for the mere retransmitting of broadcast programmes, but only for the distribution of self-originated cable-programmes. The Sluis cable-operator - or his legal adviser - was a few months early though. The amendment would enter into force by the 1st of January 1980. The Sluis plans caused uproar in the Dutch broadcasting establishment. And this succeeded, by its faithful Christian Democrat and Socialist representatives in parliament, in getting an immediate and full parliamentary debate on the matter in the Second Chamber. The outcome was a resolution carried by the same faithful majority (one big government-party and one big opposition-party) that the (Christian Democrat) Minister of Culture should as yet have a task in judging, against the background of the guiding principles of the Dutch broadcasting system, the access to the cable of foreign television programmes. The entering into force of the contrary amendment of the Broadcasting Law was "postponed", and the Minister was invited to send a Note to parliament about new criteria to be set and implicitly to refute the criticism, also voiced in parliament, that this entire operation amounted to putting a glass cover over the country to isolate it from undesirable foreign information, an infringement of the right to freedom of information.

In the resulting Note of the Minister the preparation of a new amendment of the Broadcasting Law was announced. The Minister of Culture would have to give his consent to the cable retransmission of at least those foreign broadcast programmes which cannot be received directly by the Dutch public but are nevertheless destined for this public. A criterium to judge this last characteristic would especially be the use of the Dutch language in the programme, spoken or subtitled, eventually through teletext. Also the contents of programmes could be relevant here, for instance the broadcasting of commercials for products on the Dutch market or of events mainly of importance for the Dutch public. The proposed restrictive measures would only affect those foreign programmes which do not satisfy the demands of the Dutch Broadcasting Law concerning the non-commercial character of national broadcasts. This new "*RTL*-law" would be in conformity with the right to freedom of expression/ information as laid down in the existing treaties, especially with art. 10 of the European Convention of Human Rights where it is expressly said that this freedom shall not prevent states from requiring the licensing of broadcasting and television enterprises. In a heated and often confused discussion about this Note in the standing Committee for Culture the opponents remarked that a cable retransmission enterprise was something different from the broadcasting or television enterprises mentioned in art. 10 European Convention, and that anyway the whole legitimation of restrictions of this kind, scarcity, had disappeared. The most forceful (Christian Democrat) defender of restrictions accused his opponents of pleading for an unnational policy ...

The whole issue seemed to be of very temporary importance. The government's Note itself remarked that the proposed licensing system for foreign programmes, which could not be received directly by the public, would become meaningless the moment these programmes would be broadcast by direct reception satellites. But then the proposed measures would at least create an interim period in which the national broadcasting system could recover its breath to develop adequate answers to the threats of a new technology. High hopes were set on the Scientific Council for Government Policy which had been requested to report to the government (probably in 1982) about the consequences of technological developments for the mass media and society at large. Already for years this request has served as an alibi for a completely inactive government, as if the time for our broadcasting system "to recover its breath" did not run out fast.

VIII. REGIONAL, LOCAL AND PIRATE BROADCASTERS

One of the possibilities opened by new technology is regional and local radio and even television by Hertzian broadcasting as well as by original cable broadcasting. The Broadcasting Law provides for a government licensing system for regional or local broadcasting along somewhat the same lines as exist for national broadcasting. Regional or local broadcasters should be representative for the region or town and non-commercial, not to forget the existing cultural and social needs to be fulfilled again by the regional or local programmes.
A difference with the national system is that regional or local advertising is completely forbidden. Proposals to abolish this difference meet, of course, strong opposition among organisations of local press, who argue that their ensuing loss of advertisements would push many local papers out of existence, an irreplacable loss of pluriformity. Years ago exactly the same reasoning on a national scale, i.e. for national papers, had not been able to stop the introduction of commercials in the national broadcasts though; it has only led to a transitional financial compensation scheme for the press.

The pressure for regional broadcasting up till now has led to the existence of four semi-regional stations and two really regional stations, one in Amsterdam and one in the south of the country. Plans exist to enlarge the number to twelve, one for each province. Their broadcasting time is very limited and their financing, which on a provisional basis has been provided for by the state, will probably - according to a pending bill - be largely dependent on provincial funds, much to the annoyance of the organizations which run the existing stations or prepare new ones. They fear undue influence of the provincial or local powers that be on the contents of the programmes. Also the number of twelve regional stations is thought to be largely insufficient. Finally there is pressure for local stations.
In the absence of legal local stations, the initiative has been taken over by illegal local broadcasters. Thousands of *etherpirates* are operating at this moment in the Netherlands. The occasional tracing and closing down of an illegal station by the authorities seems to be insignificant in this massive current of illegal broadcasting. The pirates mainly operate on a commercial basis. They broadcast commercials for local business, interspersed with popular music.

Television pirates have detected a very inexpensive means for their broadcasting by making use of the local cable network. Around midnight, when the official Dutch and German television stations have ended their programmes and the cable retransmitting system is "empty", the pirates beam, from very nearby, a

weak television signal to the big aerial of the cable system and this is sufficient to make the cable transmitter operate. Especially in Amsterdam the cable-subscribers can now receive late shows on a number of cable television-channels. The programmes consist mainly of commercials for local business and videotapes of films, sometimes films which are still showing in cinemas, sometimes even films which have not yet reached the Dutch cinema circuit, but then also many B- and some pornofilms. In no time at all these illegal late shows have become immensely popular, their very illegality enhancing their attractiveness for Amsterdammers. Indeed, everything here is illegal: the unlicensed broadcasting, the commercials, the videotaping and broadcasting of films without the consent of the copyright owners, the breaking in into the cable system[8] and maybe also the broadcasting of pornography[9].
A special radio/tv-guide "The Pirate" has been founded (circulation 50.000) to carry the lists of pirate broadcast programme data. It also published the lists of programme data of official Dutch television. The publishers/editors declared in press-interviews that they acted as a "NOS" for the (then) five "big" Amsterdam pirate stations. A kind of illegal replica of the Dutch broadcasting system. The real *NOS* and the Dutch Cinema Association asked the President of the Amsterdam High Court for injunctions against the publishers of "The Pirate". The court proceedings were chaotic and hilarious, an anonymous pirate broadcaster having been given permission by the President to film these proceedings for his pirate broadcasts, and many pirates being present. The outcome, however, was the issuing of 19 injunctions against publishing the lists of pirate-broadcast films (which amounted to promoting the pirate broadcasters' infringement on the copyright on the films) and against the publishing of the lists of official Dutch tv-programme data (an infringement of the pseudo-copyright on lists of programme data)[10]. This meant the end of the radio/tv-guide "The Pirate", an outcome which might still raise questions in the field of the right to freedom of expression/information[11]. The pirate broadcasters themselves of course continued.

Columbia Pictures Industries Inc. and ten other big American film companies took the next step. They brought a lawsuit, based on copyright-infringement, against the Amsterdam cable company, which was not prepared to close the cable channel at night (after the regular broadcasting stations had stopped) and thus enabled the pirates to break in into the cable system. After a first set-back[12], the Amsterdam Court of Appeal decided[13] on 17 September 1981 that the cable company had to refrain from infringing the copyright of the plaintiffs: the company had indeed to shut the channel as soon as a film of one of the plaintiffs was broadcast by the pirates. An appeal

to the Supreme Court is pending. After this Amsterdam Court of Appeal decision other lawsuits had to be brought by other copyright owners against the same and other cable-operators to achieve the same result with respect to their films[14]. So for instance the Amsterdam cable company now has to refrain from retransmitting films of all those producer- and distributor-members of the all encompassing Dutch association of holders of filmrights: the *Nederlandse Bioscoopbond*. This *Bioscoopbond* is now threatening to sue the other Dutch cable-operators who still do not comply to the Amsterdam decisions.
The latest development is the Supreme Court Decision of October 30, 1981[15], which said that cable companies who transmitted programmes (in this case official broadcasting stations), were not mere *antennae* of the subscribers to the cable system, but companies, which made use of copyrighted works and therefore had to ask the author's permission for this retransmission. With this decision the cable-operators lost an important copyright case, but they were recognized as persons in law. All of a sudden now hundreds of Pinocchio's are flexing their muscles in the Low Countries with reasonings like: if we have to pay royalties for our activities, why then restrict ourselves to mere retransmitting of programmes of others? For the same money we could just as well have fun and make our own programmes: we want to become local broadcasters, the "we" in reality being the Dutch municipalities and some commercial concerns.

IX. LIBERALIZE OR PERISH

Against the background of pressures of this kind in the broadcasting situation, a number of reports has recently been published by commissions of the four big political parties[16], of two broadcasting organizations[17] and of the largest federation of workers' unions[18] to propose amendments to the frozen Dutch system in order to rescue it.
In this context one should not forget that apart from the big flaw, based on the pseudo-copyright on programme data (which could rather easily be removed), the system has in the past nevertheless realized an access, pluriformity and freedom of expression/information in radio and television which is perhaps unique in the world. It would be difficult to name any group or current in Dutch society, which cannot express itself in the broadcasting system, if not before the microphones of one of the eight private broadcasting organizations, then at least via the semi-public *NOS*, which by law is obliged to give access to groups not represented in the private organizations. Finally nobody is obliged to give "objective" or "balanced" information as is required in many countries. On the contrary: from the start in the twenties all the broadcasting time was allotted to ideological groups to enable them to voice their

convictions. The purpose of the whole system was unchecked expression for every creed, and the "neutral" *AVRO* (later also *TROS* and *VOO*) was often frowned upon for its very lack of ideological engagement. The "balancing" in broadcasting had to come about by the confrontation of all the unrestricted expressions of faith or political creed. It was up to the listener/viewer to "balance" the conflicting informations in his own mind: an inherently democratic ideal which is not always attained but on the other hand cannot be abandoned.

To save all this, proposals have been made to mend the big flaw of the existing system, the distorting linkage of the more or less forced subscription to a radio/tv-guide to the membership of a broadcasting organization[19], and to loosen the restricted system, without however abandoning the idea of private ideological broadcasting organizations. In a time of increasing technical possibilities also new categories of potential broadcasters should get a chance. Indeed, the right to freedom of expression/information might require such a liberalization. One could think of access for new ideological inspired and emancipatory groups, like feminists, the gay liberation movement, Moslems and Molukkans. The biggest controversy however is concerned with the question of access for commercial broadcasters. Opponents take the view that commercial powers would then take over completely and thus form the most important threat for pluriformity and freedom for others. Partisans of mixed systems, where industry would also have its, guarded, place, point out that with the increase of technical means the broadcasting inevitably enters an open-market situation. That same situation for other media like publishing, the press and filming has not led to the end of the freedom of expression in these fields. More effort should be made in providing guarantees against a commercial take-over of broadcasting than in a futile attempt to block the road to commercial broadcasting altogether.
The demise of the unique Dutch broadcasting system is unavoidable, if the government continues to ignore all proposals which aim at liberalizing it[20]. Already on the present eve of the revolution in teletechnics the scarcity of the means of broadcasting has diminished to such a degree that a mere clinging to the old restrictions amounts to an infringement of the right to freedom of information.

(November 1981)

NOTES

1. KB 9 August 1972, *AB* 1973.194 and KB 26 August 1975, *AB* 1977.29.
2. Radioprogramme data I: HR 17 April 1953, *NJ* 1954.211; Radioprogramme data II or *Explicator*: HR 27 Jan. 1961, *NJ* 1962.355; Radioprogramme data III or *Televizier* I: HR 25 June 1965, nr. 9836, *NJ* 1966.115, and Radioprogramme data IV or *Televizier* II: HR 25 June 1965, nr. 9843, *NJ* 1966.116.
3. *Yearbook of the European Convention on Human Rights* 1966, p. 512, and *Yearbook* 1968, p. 782. See also the report of the European Commission of Human Rights 6 July 1976 (*De Geïllustreerde Pers NV* vs. The Netherlands), *Decisions and Reports* December 1977, p. 5, which should have decided exactly the same issue, but unfortunately did not really do so: see annotation Cohen Jehoram under this Report, *Ars Aequi* 28 (1979), p. 145-153.
4. Considerable doubt over this non-commercial character of *TROS* and *VOO* has been raised by the recent report (March-May 1981) of the first research in this matter conducted by the Governments Superintendant of Broadcasting. Also the still existing connection between the *AVRO* and the commercial publisher of *Televizier* has been criticized in this report.
5. Cohen Jehoram, *Ars Aequi* (1979), p. 145-153.
6. *Auteursrecht* 1981/5, p. 111. In the first two instances of the case the courts had given negative answers to this question: High Court Amsterdam 19 June 1978, *Auteursrecht* 1979/1, p. 10, and Amsterdam Court of Appeal 12 June 1980, *Auteursrecht* 1980/4, p. 77.
7. Memorandum from the Committee on Collection, Administration and Distribution of Royalties of the Netherlands Ministry of Justice (*Commissie 'Incasso, beheer en repartitie auteursgelden'*), Document Council of Europe, Committee of Experts on Legal Protection in the Media Fields, *MM-PJ* (80)7, also published in *Auteursrecht* 1979/4, p. 83.
8. It should be mentioned, however, that the Amsterdam cable-television company did not seem to mind at all this breaking in by the pirates.
9. This is somewhat questionable after HR 28 Nov. 1978, *NJ* 1979.93 (Deep Throat).
10. Pres. High Court Amsterdam 25 June 1981, *Auteursrecht* 1981/4, p. 84.
11. See note 3.
12. Pres. High Court Amsterdam 26 Febr. 1981, *Auteursrecht* 1981/3, p. 69.
13. Court of Appeal Amsterdam 17 Sept. 1981, *Auteursrecht* 1981/5, p. 118.
14. Pres. High Court Amsterdam 22 Oct. 1981 and Pres. High Court Utrecht 23 Oct. 1981.
15. See note 6.
16. *Van grottekening tot satelliet*, een liberale media-nota door Wim Keja (VVD); *Van schaarste tot overvloed, omroep in tachtig*, rapport van de Kommissie Omroeppolitiek van de Partij van de Arbeid, Den Haag, Febr. 1980; *Landelijke en regionale omroep*, Stichting Wetenschappelijk Bureau D'66, March 1980; *Massa- of Kassacommunicatie?*, rapport van een commissie van het Wetenschappelijk Instituut voor het CDA, Den Haag, April 1981.
17. *Aanbevelingen voor een toekomstige omroepstructuur - Nieuwe ontwikkelingen vragen om een ander bestel*, VPRO, Febr. 1981; *Enkele grote lijnen voor de struktuur van de Nederlandse Omroep in de komende jaren*, notitie t.b.v. de informateurs drs. R.F.M. Lubbers en drs. J. de Koning, TROS, Hilversum, June 1981.
18. *Media en werknemer*, een aanzet tot discussie, FNV, March 1981.
19. Even in the report *Massa- of Kassacommunicatie* (see note 16) of a commission of the Christian-Democrat Party, the defender most in armour for the status-quo, this linkage has been called "one of the big flaws of the present system".
20. Cohen Jehoram, Overheid en Omroep, *Auteursrecht* 1980/3, p. 47.

SUMMARY

The Dutch broadcasting system is a result of the peculiar historical, cultural and political situation of the Netherlands. The license to broadcast are reserved for non-commercial private organizations, which operate on ideological basis. The erosion of these bases, new teletechnics, the rising pressures of regional, local and pirate broadcasters and of commercial interests call for a liberalization of the frozen and restricted system, which nevertheless in the past has realized an access, pluriformity and freedom of expression/information unique in the world.

Conscientious objections in the Netherlands

E.A. ALKEMA

Professor at the Universities of Amsterdam and Groningen

IV.C.2.

I. DEFINITION

For the purpose of this study we consider as conscientious objections: those objections against legal obligations raised by a person following his moral or religious sense of right or wrong. The concept encompasses two categories. Some objections will make a person disobey the law or act contrary to it; other objections do not provoke illegal acts, since they have been recognised within the law and special exemptions have been provided for. Especially the latter are of great importance in Dutch law.
In order to distinguish the first category of ordinary offences and of some forms of so-called civil disobedience it should be added that the moral or religious urge must be essential and even existential to the person concerned and, further, that the violated legal obligation should be directly connected with his convictions[1].
This definition mentions side by side religious and moral motives. It is indeed difficult to discern between religion on the one hand and creed, belief and conviction on the other hand. Besides, as will be seen later such a distinction is rarely made in the Dutch legislation or jurisprudence.

II. HISTORICAL AND CONSTITUTIONAL BACKGROUNDS

Through its linkage with the freedom of religion the freedom of conscience is rooted deeply in the Netherlands' history. At the origin of the Dutch State, during the secession from the Spanish kingdom at the so-called "Pacification of Ghent" in 1576 and in 1579 at the occasion of the confederation of the northern Dutch provinces the freedom of religion was formulated and laid down in official acts.
During the centuries religious freedom and tolerance have been one of the finest though not always spotless traditions

of the Netherlands. It no doubt is linked with the great religious variety within the Dutch society. Freedom of religion was expressly included in the constitution of 1798 and has been elaborated in later constitutions. Since 1815 one chapter, now chapter nine (Articles 181-187) is devoted to the freedom of religion.

Yet, the freedom of conscience as a separate right was only introduced in 1922. Article 183 (now Art. 196) provided for statutory recognition of conscientious objections against military service. It confirmed a practice already in existence since 1917 permitting conscripts to enter into a contract for non-military service in lieu of their military duty. It is highly unlikely that a more comprehensive provision will be included in the Constitution in the near future. In the Royal Commission, set up in 1967 for the revision of the Constitution and the Ballot Act, only one member, *D.H.M. Meuwissen,* pleaded for such a provision[2]. That proposal has not been endorsed by the Government when introducing the now pending bills to amend the Constitution. The idea of a general provision recognising conscientious objections was rejected for two reasons[3]. On the one hand it was considered unacceptable to allow everybody to shirk his legal obligations (an argument already developed in the jurisprudence). On the other hand a severely restricted freedom of conscience - in the alternative - would affect unfavourably it was argued other connected freedoms such as the freedom of religion. Therefore, the new Constitution will continue to recognise conscientious objections only with respect to military service[4].

Persons who want to invoke the Constitution to found their conscientious objections, therefore, will have to rely (as they actually do) on the general provision in the Constitution concerning freedom of religion Art. 181 ssqq. In the now pending proposals to amend the Constitution this Article on the freedom of religion has been extended; it also guarantees the philosophy of life ("*levensovertuiging*"). This is, of course, a much wider concept.

It is worthwhile to repeat the double argument advanced by the drafters of these amendments. The Explanatory Memorandum points out that the inclusion of philosophy of life is wholly in line with the international treaties, which extend the protection of the freedom of religion also to the freedom of philosophy of life. Moreover, the Memorandum states, within the Netherlands a general conviction has developed over the years, that there should be no distinction between the two elements in the relation of the State with the justiciables[5]. This picture, however, is not complete. Within the Dutch legal order the Constitution is less predominant than in most other legal systems. Article 131 par. 2 of the Constitution provides that statute law (i.e. Acts of Parliament) are "inviolable". This means that the courts may only review the constitutionality of ordinances and delegated legislation but not of statutes. Of course, the legislator i.e. the Crown (the Head of State and the Ministers of the Cabinet) and the Parliament are bound to comply with the Constitution, but the legislator's interpretation of the Constitution is final.

III. OBLIGATIONS UNDER INTERNATIONAL LAW

The Netherlands is a party to both the European Convention on Human Rights (since 1954) and the International Covenant on Civil and Political Rights (since 1979). These instruments guarantee (in Art. 9 and Art. 18 respectively) the freedom of thought and conscience. Both provisions are considered as self-executing. Consequently they take - in virtue of Arts. 65 and 66 of the Dutch Constitution - precedence over all statutory law (including the Constitution itself!), whether enacted before or after the ratification of the international instrument. The courts are obliged to apply the self-executing treaty provisions and to set aside any contrary municipal law[6].

IV. LEGISLATION

a. *Oaths*

The Dutch legislation is characterised by the provision of either an alternative or a dispensation in case of conscientious objections. The legislation with respect to oaths is an example of the former. At numerous occasions Dutch law prescribes an oath. In criminal and civil lawsuits witnesses and experts are sworn in; oaths are also means of evidence; they are prerequisite for the entrance into several offices e.g. for police, judicial and military officers; for members of representative bodies and cabinet ministers and further for certain professions e.g. for medical doctors and lawyers. Several groups both religious and non-religious e.g. Baptists and atheists are opposed to swearing oaths referring to God; they prefer a solemn promise. From the beginning of this century on a gradual equalization has taken place, which was completed in 1971. Since that year such a promise is equally valid as an oath and the breaking of the promise is equally punishable as perjury (Art. 207 Criminal Code).

b. *Military service*

As mentioned before the only constitutional provision with respect to conscientious objections concerns military service.

The provision, Article 196, reads:

"The conditions upon which exemption from military service may be granted on account of serious conscientious objections shall be stated by law."

The first Act executing this provision was adopted in 1923[7]. It was replaced by the Act of 27 September 1962[8] now in force. Through an amendment in 1978[9] the definition of conscientious objections was widened. Originally only persons[10] whose religious or moral convictions forbade them to participate in any violence of war were recognised. Nowadays it suffices that a person objects to personal military service "with respect to the use of means of violence in which he may be implicated through his serving in the Dutch armed forces" (Art.2)
This marks the official recognition not only of general but also of socalled selective or specific objections e.g. objections against the use of nuclear weapons or the participation of the armed forces in a particular international armed conflict. The broadening of the definition was no doubt the outcome of criticism in literature[11] and also of forceful protests of some conscripts against the American intervention in Vietnam. The latter considered the armed forces of the Netherlands accessory to those actions through the Dutch membership of the North Atlantic Treaty Organization (NATO).
It is for the Minister of Defense to judge the soundness of the objections. For this purpose the Minister is advised by a special committee of independent experts. If the conscript's objections are not accepted as valid he may appeal to the Crown.

As is demonstrated by the statistics over the period of 1975 through 1979 (see Annex) about 1,8 - 2,5% of those registered for military service invoked conscientious objections and over 90% of these requests were granted.
If recognised the objector is obliged to fulfil other, non-military service during a period as long as the ordinary military service.
The incumbents of religious or religious-humanitarian offices and persons, who are being schooled for such offices are exempted also from this substitute service. However, in February 1981 the Government announced its intention to abolish this exception[12]. The amendment was introduced because in some ecclesiastical circles the exception was considered as an outdated privilege.
In spite of the apparent liberal practice of recognition of conscientious objections against military service by the law some groups are still opposed to it. They either object to *any* public service (notably the Jehovah's witnesses) or they are motivated by a radical anti-militarism and refuse to avail themselves of the exemption offered by the law[13]. The latter consider the non-military service unfit to disseminate their anti-militaristic principles. Those who refuse to make

use of the law and to obey orders when drafted are convicted for insubordination and have to serve cellular detention for a period as long as the ordinary conscripts (i.e. at least 12 months)[14].
A somewhat related form of conscientious objections concerns the obligatory civil defence. These objections have not been recognised in the law. Consequently conscientious objectors were turned down by the courts[15].
Lately conscientious objections have also been voiced by some professional - and thus originally voluntary - members of the armed forces. These objections are directed against the use of nuclear weapons. At first the Minister of Defense reacted by announcing that the officers concerned would be dismissed, but under parliamentary pressure he retracted that threat and promised to consult with the officers' unions and the officers themselves before taking any official steps against them[16].

c. *medical interventions*

Dutch law does not recognise conscientious objections against blood tests. Such tests are not obligatory with respect to inquiries into paternity, but only- in a certain manner - compulsory for the control of alcohol use in traffic. A driver suspected of being under the influence of alcohol can be ordered by the police or prosecuting authorities to undergo a test. Refusal is an offence punishable with detention of three months at most[17].
Members of some ecclesiastical denominations and groups have objections against prophylactic medical interventions e.g. vaccinations. They consider such interventions to be derogatory to Providence or a negation of the predestination. Others object to *any* medical intervention including surgery and blood-transfusion.
The latter objections have become especially acute with respect to the medical treatment of minors, but are nowadays rejected in court. Interventions which are medically indispensable for children cannot be stopped by the parents. If necessary the parental power may be suspended for the time of the medical treatment. Usually a suspension is initiated by the local board for children welfare[18].
The former objections against vaccinations, however, are generally recognised. A case in point was the *Inentingswet* 1939 (Act concerning vaccination)[19] repealed in 1975 [20] prescribing vaccination against smallpox for children under the age of twelve months. These vaccinations could be opposed according to the law either on medical or on moral grounds.
For the armed forces there is a special act concerning immunisation[21]. It covers the vaccination against smallpox and other contagious diseases.
Dispensation is provided for in case of conscientious objections

of either the military man himself or - if still a minor - of his parents. Originally only religious grounds were recognised but in 1975 moral grounds were included as well[22].
No official coercive measures were taken when in 1978 an epidemic of poliomyelitis broke out in an area where many parents were opposed to vaccination on religious grounds[23]. Consequently, some of these children actually were struck by the disease. Yet, such objections may have negative consequences in other respects. An example is the decision by the administration that a couple of Jehova's witnesses was not eligible to adopt another[24] child, because of their objections against a possible necessary bloodtransfusion. As a consequence a proper medical treatment of the child would not have been guaranteed.

d. *Social security*

Most major statutes in the field of social security contain provisions for conscientious objections. As was mentioned before some religious groups oppose any form of insurance on principle. Here those objections concern i.a. statutory insurances with respect to unemployment[25], sickness[26], disability to work[27], old age pensions[28], pensions for widows and orphans[29], and family allowances[30].
Without going into details the system may be described as follows[31]. Eligible for exemption are persons who have conscientious objections and corporate bodies which employ such persons or which are owned or run by such persons. Exemption is only granted on condition that a person has *general* objections against *any* insurance whether concerning himself, his property or a third person for whom he is responsible[32]. When his objections are recognised a person is exempted from the payment of the periodic premiums. He is, however, assessed for the same amount in the income or wage tax.
This round-about way of payment does not affect the right to benefits under the various Statutes. Only with respect to the Old Age Pensions Act the benefits are paid out in a somewhat different manner[33]. Further, special arrangements are provided for for married couples in case of the husband's death, separation or divorce.
The authorities charged with the payment of the benefits also decide on the requests for exemption. Any refusal or withdrawal of an exemption can be submitted for appeal to the National Social Security Council.
At many instances the social security legislation requires potential beneficiaries to subject themselves to a medical test[34]. In general there are no exemptions to this requirement. In case of unemployment, however, a person may refuse i.a. for conscientious objections to undergo a medical test. But then he will lose the benefits of the Unemployment Act[35].

e. *Civil liability for traffic accidents*

A system somewhat similar to the one just described prevails for the legally obligatory insurance with respect to civil liability for damage caused by motor-vehicles[36]. Conscientious objectors can be exempted from this legal obligation. In lieu, they have to pay annually a certain amount of money for which the Ministry of Finance provides them with an exemption certificate. This contribution is paid to a special fund. Victims of traffic accidents caused by not insured persons may receive an indemnification from this fund. In view of the millions of motor-vehicles in use the number of exemptions is small indeed. During the eight months' period from January 1st till September 1st 1981 only 1910 exemptions were granted[37].

f. *Shops early closing and compulsory education*

The Shops Early Closing Act 1951 grants an exemption to shopkeepers adhering to a religion according to which the weekly day of rest is not held at Sundays[38]. The authorities deciding on the exemption may attach special conditions to it.
The Compulsory Education Act 1969[39] exempts parents who have all-important objections against the way of teaching in any school in their neighbourhood (i.e. within a reasonable distance from the place where the family resides). It suffices to give the local authorities notice to that effect[40].

g. *Ritual slaughtering*

At the end of this not exhaustive review of legislation providing for dispensation or exemption mention should be made of the Act concerning Inspection of Butcher's Meat 1919 and the Decree based thereupon of 1957[41]. It provides for exemptions for slaughtering in accordance with Israelite and Islamite rites. These exemptions are granted if the (representatives of the) religious groups concerned can demonstrate adequately that there is a demand for such ritually slaughtered meat[42].

V. CASE-LAW

This paragraph describes some general features of the case-law with respect to conscientious objections. It is divided into five parts: cases in which conscientious objections were raised
a) in spite of the legal exemptions provided for;
b) with respect to factual obligations;
c) with respect to contractual obligations;
d) against legal obligations;
e) cases concerning conscientious objections submitted to the European Commission of Human Rights against the Netherlands State.

a. *Objections in spite of legal exemptions*

A first general trend of the jurisprudence is that the courts are used to reject any claim based on conscientious objections to legal obligations if the law provides for an exemption. Two decisions with respect to the General Old Age Pensions Act may illustrate that. In both cases it was alleged that the Act was contrary to Art. 9 of the European Convention on Human Rights guaranteeing freedom of religion and conscience.
In the first case a clergyman objected to this form of insurance *specifically* whereas the Act only allows for dispensation in case of *general* objections[43]. The clergyman advanced the opinion that according to the Bible it was for the parish to sustain clergymen and retired clergymen and not for the State. The Court found that the statutory exemption was not intended by the legislator to constitute the fulfilment of obligations undertaken in pursuance of Art. 9 and generally that "the freedom to manifest one's religion or beliefs guaranteed in that Article is not the same thing as freedom to oppose one's own religious ideas or beliefs to the provisions of the law".
The latter argument was also used by the Court to reject the defence in the other case[44]. There it had been alleged that the additional assessment in the income-tax imposed in lieu of the premiums was contrary to "the freedom to manifest one's religion or belief, in worship, teaching, practice and observance".
These negative decisions show that the courts do not accept objections against either the legal construction and form of the exemption or against the criterion laid down in the law (i.e. that only general and not specific objections entitle to dispensation).
As for remedies the General Old Age Pensions Act also offers an interesting example[45]. It was claimed that contrary to Art. 13 of the European Convention the Act had excluded any remedy with respect to the additional assessment in the income-tax. The Court did not review the Act under Art. 13, for it found that Art. 13 was not self-executing. It is curious to note that the European Commission of Human Rights also rejected that claim. The reason being that the Dutch courts, although they had formally declared themselves incompetent in this matter, in fact had paid due attention to the arguments based on conscientious objections[46].

b. *Decisions with respect to factual obligations*

Two decisions entering into this category concern the fluoridation of drinking water. The "compulsory" character of this interference with private life is a consequence of the monopoly that local authorities usually have regarding the provision with water.

In the first decision (on administrative appeal and decided by the Crown) the objections of some citizens were rejected, but the authorities were at the same time obliged to offer adequate alternative facilities (public taps), where those interested could fetch unfluoridated water[47].
In the second decision it was the Supreme Court who accepted the objections and declared the fluoridation illegal since it lacked a proper base in an Act of Parliament required for such a drastic interference into private life[48]. When the Administration next submitted a bill in order to empower the water companies to fluoridate the water it met with so much opposition in Parliament that the bill was dropped and fluoridation had to be stopped[49].
In a third case about the monopolistic role of public utility services the claimant had been cut off from electricity because he was in default paying the entire electricity bill[50]. He had refused to pay an additional levy for reasons of conscience. That levy was meant to finance a nuclear electricity plant in Kalkar (Germany), a common project of the German Federal Republic, Belgium and the Netherlands. Again the courts turned down the objections. Yet, the Government, in order to meet the conscientious objections created a special fund for the research of alternative ways for energy generation. Conscientious objectors could contribute to this fund instead of paying the contested levy[51].

c. *Contractual relations*

A recent judicial decision concerned the effect of conscientious objections on private legal relations[52]. Two nurses were transferred within a hospital from the gynaecological department to other departments, because they had conscientious objections against assisting in abortions even if these were carried out on medical indication. When they opposed their transfer the judge ruled that it was legitimate since the nurses' material interest had been taken into account properly. He thus rejected the nurses' claim that they should be maintained in their original positions and that, consequently, the hospital should change its policy with respect to abortions.

d. *Against legal obligations (no legal exemptions being provided for)*

Where the law does not provide for exceptions the courts also as a rule reject especially in penal law conscientious objections. They may, however, be a ground for mitigation of punishment[53]. In the literature the question has been discussed at length if and to what extent the defence of conscientious objections could be considered as superior power removing the criminal character of a violation of the law so as to discharge

the person concerned[54].
The courts competent in ordinary penal matters are used to decline such claims. Apparently two lower military courts have admitted an exception[55]. But on second view these decisions are no proper exceptions. In both cases the defendant had requested before - but in vain - to be exempted according to the law (from military service and from the obligation to be vaccinated respectively). These exemptions had not been granted. Yet, the military men refused to act against their conscience. In construing their defence as superior power the courts, so to speak, recognised their conscientious objections as yet.
Other examples are the rejection by the courts of claims of cattle-breeders, who were opposed to the obligation to vaccinate their life stock against tuberculosis[56] and people who had conscientious objections against traffic safety measures, notably against the obligation to wear crash helmets for drivers and passengers of motorbikes and motorized bikes and against the duty to wear safety belts at the front bench of motor-vehicles[57].

e. *Cases submitted to the European Commission of Human Rights*

At some occasions the Dutch legislation and court decisions have been challenged under the European Convention, but without success. The applications concerned i.a. the Old Age Pensions Act[58] and the Act for the Prevention of Tuberculosis among Cattle[59] The Commission declared these applications "inadmissible" after it had established that the domestic law was an interference compatible with par . 2 of Art. 9 of the Convention.
In some other applications against other States parties to the Convention traffic measures such as obligatory crash helmets and safety belts were tested against the Convention[60] and declared inadmissible. This jurisprudence thus indirectly confirmed the Dutch courts' view.
In general the Commission's jurisprudence underscores the impression that the Dutch municipal law is rather "liberal" as far as the freedom of conscience is concerned.

VI. CONCLUSIONS

In conformity with a long standing tradition Dutch law recognises at many instances conscientious objections. Gradually religious and conscientious objections are being equated in the law.
So far, international treaties on human rights have had hardly any impact. Only the just mentioned equalization of religious

and conscientious objections may be - at least partially - a consequence of the international treaties.
In order to maintain equality among the justiciables before the law and also "*devant les charges publiques*" conscientious objectors usually are obliged to make special contributions or to pay additional taxes instead of the disputed payments. The criteria for these objections are, of course, vague. Sometimes the law requires that the person concerned is generally opposed to certain legal measures, but with respect to military service and the extra duty on electricity fares specific objections also have been acknowledged.
The test of the truth of objections often is and must be very superficial. In some instances it even suffices that a person states his objections and gives notice thereof to the authorities. Often the decisions on requests for exemptions are taken by an administrative organ. Sometimes a special appellate administrative remedy is provided for.
In view of the rather "liberal" approach of the legislature of the conscientious objections the courts did not feel free to accept conscientious objections *praeter legem* or *contra legem*; they were not prepared to accept other objections than those officially and legally recognised.
The administration and the legislature, however, are inclined to consider such objections favourably and (try to) take appropriate measures.
In practice the treatment of conscientious objectors in Dutch law seems to be satisfactory. It depends, however, on two conditions being fulfilled.
Firstly, that the persons with conscientious objections will continue to accept the often rather artificial alternatives to the legal obligation objected to. Secondly, that where the objections concern certain physical duties e.g. military service or specific military or police tasks, enough volunteers are available to take the places of those who refuse and want to be exempted. The Dutch legal order does not answer the question of principle what should be done in case these conditions are not met. But is there any other State whose municipal law does?

NOTES

1. J. Remmelink, "De overtuigingsdader", in *Honderd jaar rechtsleven*, Zwolle 1970, p. 181.
2. Tweede Rapport Staatscommissie van Advies inzake Grondwet en Kieswet, 's-Gravenhage 1969, p. 63.
3. Bill 13872 No. 3 p. 4 - 5.
4. Bill 15467 (R 1114).
5. Bill 13872 No. 3, p. 28 - 29.
6. See E.A. Alkema, "The Application of Internationally Guaranteed Human Rights in the Municipal Order", in F. Kalshoven e.a. ed., *Essays on the Development of the International Legal Order in memory of Haro F. van Panhuys*, Alphen a/d Rijn 1980, p. 181-198.
7. *Stb.* 357.
8. *Stb.* 370.
9. *Stb.* 694.
10. Including minors.
11. P.J. Boukema, *Het geweten als staatsrechtelijk probleem*, Alphen a/d Rijn 1972.
12. Bill 16608.
13. HR 4 Dec. 1979, *NJ* 1980, 157; HMG 3 April 1974, *Militair-rechtelijk Tijdschrift* 1974, 280.
14. HR 4 May 1981, *NJ* 1981, 464.
15. HR 30 May 1967, *NJ* 1968, 64; see also Boukema o.c. (supra n. 11) n. 46.
16. Cf. Stichting Maatschappij en Krijgsmacht, *Dienstweigeren en gewetensbezwaren*, 's-Gravenhage 1981.
17. Wegenverkeerswet (Traffic Code) 13 Sept. 1935, *Stb.* 554, Arts. 33a and 35. The European Commission of Human Rights rejected an application against the Netherlands alleging that the compulsory blood test would be contrary to Art. 8.(the right to protection of private life): 8239/78 *Decisions & Reports* 16, p. 184.
18. Rb. Dordrecht 27 June 1973, *NJ* 1973, 432; see H.J.J. Leenen, *Rechten van mensen in de gezondheidszorg*, Alphen a/d Rijn 1978, p. 115 ssqq.
19. *Stb.* 805.
20. *Stb.* 606.
21. 7 Aug. 1953, *Stb.* 432.
22. 12 Nov. 1975, *Stb.* 649.
23. Hand. II 1977-78 Aanhangsel (Appendix to the Official Records of the 2nd Chamber of Parliament) No. 1499.
24. Judicial Section, Council of State, 2nd Ch., 22 June 1981, *Weekoverzicht Raad van State*, 2e halfjaar 1981, 2.269.
25. Werkloosheidswet 10 Dec. 1964, *Stb.* 485.
26. Ziektewet 5 June 1913, *Stb.* 204.
27. Algemene Arbeidsongeschiktheidswet 11 Dec. 1975, *Stb.* 674.
28. Algemene Ouderdomswet 31 May 1956, *Stb.* 281.
29. Algemene Weduwen en Wezenwet 9 April 1959, *Stb.* 239.
30. Algemene Kinderbijslagwet 26 April 1962, *Stb.* 160.
31. See Art. 17 Coördinatiewet Sociale Verzekering (Statute coordinating some matters of social security) 24 Dec. 1953, *Stb.* 577.
32. With respect to minors the conscientious objections of the parents or guardians prevail unless the minor himself declares to have a different conviction, R.A.F. de Guasco e.a., *Het sociale verzekeringsrecht in Nederland*, Alphen a/d Rijn 2nd ed. 1979, p. 153.
33. Ibidem p. 379 - 380.
34. H.J.O. Martens, "De medewerkingsplicht bij een geneeskundig onderzoek of een geneeskundige behandeling in het sociale verzekeringsrecht", *Sociaal-Maandblad Arbeid* 1976, p. 763-769 and J.K.M. Gevers,"Het verplicht geneeskundig onderzoek in de arbeidswetgeving", *Soc. Maandblad Arbeid* 1979, p. 387-400.
35. Art. 31 Werkloosheidswet (see supra n. 25).
36. Wet Aansprakelijkheid Motorrijtuigen 30 May 1963, *Stb.* 228.
37. See Annex.
38. Winkelsluitingswet 24 Jan. 1951, *Stb.* 38.
39. Leerplichtwet 30 May 1968, *Stb.* 303.
40. Ktr. Groningen 20 April 1979, *NJ* 1979, 382.
41. Vleeskeuringswet 25 July 1919, *Stb.* 524; Vleeskeuringsbesluit 24 Jan. 1957, *Stb.* 29.

42. Cf HR 4 Nov. 1969, *NJ* 1970, 127 concerning an offence of this Act. The Supreme Court rejected the defence based on Art. 9 of the European Convention on Human Rights, but thereupon the Decree was amended so as to create more opportunities for ritual slaughtering.
43. HR 13 April 1960, *NJ* 1960, 436.
44. HR 13 March 1963, *NJ (AB)* 1963, 610.
45. HR 24 Febr. 1960, *NJ* 1960, 483.
46. Appl. 2065/63 *Yearbook* VIII (1965) p. 266.
47. Royal Decree 14 Aug. 1970, *Staatscourant* 1970, 172.
48. HR 22 June 1973, *Rechtspraak van de Week* 1973, 50.
49. Bill 12738.
50. HR 20 Dec. 1974, *NJ* 1975, 221; see H. Besselse, "De Kalkarheffing en gewetensbezwaren", *AAe* XXIII(1974) p. 353-364.
51. See *Staatscourant* 19 Dec. 1974, 247.
52. Hof 's-Gravenhage 24 June 1981, *NJ* 1982,6.
53. N. Keijzer, *Military Obedience*, Alphen a/d Rijn 1978, p. 275.
54. D. Hazewinkel-Suringa, *Inleiding tot de studie van het Nederlandse strafrecht*, 7th ed., revised by J. Remmelink, Alphen a/d Rijn 1981 p. 242-244; see also the reports of J. Remmelink and D. van Eck, "Behoort de wetgever nadere regels van algemene of bijzondere aard te stellen betreffende het beroep op gewetensbezwaren tegen de naleving van door het strafrecht gesanctioneerde normen?", *Hand. Ned. Juristenvereniging* 1960 I, p. 3-79 and p. 81-154 respectively.
55. Remmelink (at p. 36) and Van Eck (at p. 147) (o.c. n. 54 supra) quote both Court Martial (south) 17 Aug. 1948, *NJ* 1948, 813 (quashed by HMG on 17 May 1949) and Court Martial (east) 1 Aug. 1957 (unpubl.).
56. Wet Bestrijding Tuberculose onder Rundvee 23 June 1952, *Stb.* 352, repealed 10 April 1964, *Stb.* 120; HR 22 March 1955, *NJ* 1955, 305.
57. HR 20 Sept. 1976, *NJ* 1977, 28 (crash helmet);
HR 16 Jan. 1979, *NJ* 1979, 200 (safety belt). In both cases Art. 8 of the European Convention on Human Rights had been invoked.
58. Appl. 1497/62, *Yearbook* V (1962), p. 288 and
Appl. 2065/63, *Yearbook* VIII (1965), p. 267.
59. Appl. 1068/61, *Yearbook* V (1965), p. 278.
60. Appl. 7992/77 X v. U.K., *Decisions & Reports* 14, p. 234 (crash helmet/compatible with Art. 9); Appl. 8707/79 X v. Belgium, *Decisions & Reports* 18, p. 255 (safety belt/compatible with Art. 8).

ANNEX

EXEMPTIONS FROM MILITARY SERVICE

1. *Annual number of requests for exemption* (1975-1980) *)

	1975	1976	1977	1978	1979
number of requests	2117	2227	1999	2432	3091
withdrawn	573	677	542	337	162
prima facie declared inadmissible	170	101	110	134	16
decisions pending	17	54	135	1321	2873
decisions taken	1357	1395	1212	640	40
recognised (*general* objections)	1195	1234	1147	622	36
recognised (*specific* objections)	70	93	31	2	-
recognised (*totals*)	1265	1327	1178	624	36
not recognised	92	68	34	16	4
percentage not recognised of decisions taken	0.677	0.487	0.281	0.250	1.00

*) situation at January 1st, 1980.

2. *Number of exemptions compared to number of conscripts*

(1975-1980)	1975	1976	1977	1978	1979
Conscripts	117,912	122,121	116,506	121,822	122,324
Requests for exemption	2117	2227	1999	2432	3091
Percentage	1.795	1.823	1.715	1.996	2.527

3. *Breakdown of requests according to religion* (1979)

Roman Catholic	427
Nederlands Hervormd (Reformed)	173
Gereformeerd (Calvinist)	156
Doopsgezind (Mennonite)	8
Zevende Dags Adventisten (Adventists)	15
Baptists (Baptists)	9
Jehova's Getuigen (Jehovah's Witnesses)	35
Luthers (Lutheran)	2
Miscellaneous	171
Humanist (Humanist/member Ethical Union)	12
No religion	2083
TOTAL	3091

Number of certificates handed out to conscientious objectors with respect to insurance for civil liability for damage caused by motor-vehicles

(period: January 1st, 1981 - September 1st, 1981)
(source : Ministry of Finance)

passenger cars	942
motorized bikes	515
tractors	217
vans	69
trailors	85
trucks	54
trucks with trailor	11
sundries	17
TOTAL	1910

La commune néerlandaise

WILLEM KONIJNENBELT
Professeur à l'Université de Tilbourg

IV.D.2.

I. INTRODUCTION: L'ORGANISATION POLITIQUE DES PAYS-BAS
   1. Vue d'ensemble
   2. Les trois niveaux du pouvoir politique
      - Le pouvoir central
      - Le pouvoir provincial
      - Le pouvoir municipal

II. SIGNIFICATION DU POUVOIR MUNICIPAL
   1. La décentralisation territoriale
      - La décentralisation sur le plan politique
      - Aspects économiques de la décentralisation
      - Compétences municipales
   2. La notion d'autonomie locale

III. RAPPORTS ENTRE LES COMMUNES ET LES AUTRES COLLECTIVITES PUBLIQUES
   1. Les rapports de la commune avec la province et avec l'Etat
   2. Rapports entre les communes

IV. LES COMPETENCES LOCALES
   1. Critères d'attribution des compétences municipales
   2. Valeur et portée des compétences municipales
      - Pouvoirs discrétionnaires et pouvoirs liés
      - Contrôle et garantie des compétences municipales

V. QUELQUES EXEMPLES DE RÉPARTITION DES COMPÉTENCES ENTRE L'ÉTAT, LES PROVINCES ET LES COMMUNES
   1. La police
   2. L'éducation primaire
   3. La santé
   4. L'urbanisme

I. INTRODUCTION : L'ORGANISATION POLITIQUE DES PAYS-BAS

1. *Vue d'ensemble*

Avant d'entrer dans les détails du pouvoir local aux Pays-Bas et ses rapports avec les organes qui se trouvent "au-dessus" de la commune, je veux tracer en grandes lignes l'organisation du pouvoir politique aux trois niveaux les plus importants: niveaux central, provincial et municipal.
Cette description devra être forcément simplifiée. Déjà dans le système des pouvoirs centralisés et décentralisés selon la formule de la (dé)centralisation territoriale, l'image est extrêmement compliquée. La quasi-totalité des communes participent chacune à plusieurs syndicats de communes, à vocation unique ou multiple. Le chaos de ces syndicats a engendré des projets de réforme du système de l'administration intérieure du pays (la *réorganisation administrative*).
On a vu des projets pour l'implantation d'un niveau d'administration entre la province et la commune: le "district" ou l'agglomération. Un autre projet a voulu partager la majorité des provinces en deux ou trois parties, si bien que le pays connaîtrait 24 mini-provinces au lieu des onze provinces actuelles. Mais l'opposition qui s'est produite contre cette opération énergique a eu pour résultat que, le plus vraisemblablement, une seule nouvelle province verra le jour: Rijnmond (Bouches du Rhin), pour l'agglomération de Rotterdam; l'agglomération dispose déjà d'un statut particulier.
Quant à l'administration au niveau "régional" - c'est à dire le niveau entre les provinces et les communes -, deux tendances se dessinent. L'une veut que la majorité des pouvoirs pour lesquels l'échelle communale est devenue trop petite, soient déférés aux provinces; l'autre courant proclame la coopération intercommunale mieux structurée pour ces compétences.

A part de la décentralisation territoriale, il y a plusieurs formes de décentralisation fonctionnelle. La forme la plus ancienne, qui remonte du moyen-age, est celui des polders: collectivités publiques pour l'administration des eaux, qui fonctionnent sous la surveillance des provinces. Puis, il y a les organisations publiques professionnelles et industrielles; tels les ordres des avocats et des experts-comptables; les organisations publiques pour l'agriculture, pour les détaillants, le syndicat hôtelier "Horecaf", e.t.q. Je les passe sous silence.

2. *Les trois niveaux du pouvoir politique*

Le pouvoir central

Les principaux organes du pouvoir central - sans compter les organes judiciaires - sont le Parlement et le Gouvernement.
Le *Parlement*, qui porte le nom historique d'Etats Généraux, comprend deux chambres.
La première chambre (le Sénat), composée de 75 membres, est élue au suffrage indirect. Le corps électoral se compose des membres des Etats provinciaux, qui élisent les sénateurs d'après un système de représentation proportionnelle[1].
Les 150 membres de la seconde chambre, élus au suffrage direct, sont également élus d'après un système de r.p. Aussi les deux chambres ont-elles une composition presque identique en ce qui concerne la répartition des sièges parmi les partis politiques.

> *Des deux chambres du Parlement, la première n'a qu'un intérêt réduit. Elle n'a pas le droit d'amendement ou d'initiative, elle ne joue guère un rôle dans la formation d'un nouveau cabinet, elle n'engage pas la responsabilité capitale du Gouvernement. Le Sénat est une chambre de réflexion avant le droit d'approuver ou de rejeter les projets de loi.*

Le *Gouvernement* comprend environ seize ministres; le Premier Ministre, président du Conseil des Ministres, est, légalement, *primus inter pares*. Tous les ministres ont le même rang et les mêmes pouvoirs. A part d'une ou deux exceptions (les ministres sans portefeuille), ils se trouvent à la tête d'un ministère.
Un ministre peut être assisté d'un ou deux secrétaires d'Etat; ceux-ci exercent des pouvoirs ministériels dans un domaine limité mais ils ne siègent pas dans le Conseil des Ministres. Un secrétaire d'Etat souffre d'une double responsabilité: il est responsable devant son ministre et devant le Parlement.
Le Gouvernement comme tel et les ministres sont responsables devant les deux chambres des Etats Généraux. Le système de gouvernement est un système parlementaire; par conséquent, le ministre ou le Gouvernement ayant perdu la confiance du Parlement, doit démissionner.

Les décisions formelles des ministres et du Gouvernement sont prises tant dans la forme d'arrête Royal (c'-à-d. signé non seulement par un ou plusieurs ministres ou secrétaires d'Etat mais aussi par la Reine), tant dans la forme d'arrêté ministériel ou interministériel. L'acte du Gouvernement ou du ministre qui doit être pris dans la forme d'un arrêté Royal, s'appelle acte de la Couronne.

En ce qui concerne les pouvoirs législatifs du Gouvernement il faut remarquer qu'ils sont limités:

a.
Le Gouvernement ne possède pas en propre un pouvoir réglementaire général pour assurer l'exécution des lois; il ne dispose d'un tel pouvoir réglementaire que sur la base d'une disposition explicite de la loi qui confère ce pouvoir, par voie de délégation, à la Couronne ou à un ministre.

> *Sur le terrain du droit administratif la vaste majorité des lois donnent des pouvoirs législatifs délégués au Gouvernement ou au ministre. Dans ces cas les règlements d'exécution sont déterminés, selon la disposition légale, comme arrêté Royal réglementaire (délibération en conseil des ministres avis du Conseil d'Etat, publication dans le Journal officiel; cf. le règl. d'adm. publique français), ou comme simple arrêté (inter-)ministériel.*

b.
Néanmoins, le Gouvernement possède un pouvoir réglementaire autonome qui est en fait très limité. L'article 57 de la Loi fondamentale dit que le Gouvernement a le droit d'établir des arrêtés Royaux réglementaires sans base légale, à moins que ces arrêtés ne créent pas de délits. De tels arrêtés autonomes sont extrêmement rares; il y en a deux exemples récents qui déterminent la repartition des fonds parmi les provinces et les communes pour quelques activités sur le terrain socio-culturel.

c.
Il y a davantage; c'est la '*pseudo-législation*' (env. les directives du droit administratif français), dont on distingue trois catégories:
- directives des ministres à leurs fonctionnaires, surtout pour les services déconcentrés,
- publication de la façon dont un organe public usera d'un pouvoir discrétionnaire,
- publication des conditions à remplir afin de pouvoir prétendre à une subvention (dans les cas où manquent des dispositions légales pour l'allocation des subventions).

Cette pseudo-législation n'a pas force de règle de droit, mais elle a environ la valeur juridique des promesses ou des précédents.

Le pouvoir provincial

Depuis des siècles, les Pays-Bas connaissent des provinces; d'abord comme entités souverains, depuis 1814 comme des collectivités décentralisées.

Maintenant on compte onze provinces; bientôt Rijnmond verra le jour comme la douzième province du Royaume.
Les organes du pouvoir provincial sont au nombre de trois: Les Etats provinciaux, les Etats députés, et le Commissaire de la Reine.

Les *Etats provinciaux* - ancien nom qui rappelle l'époque où cet organisme était composé par les représentants des classes, des 'états' - font le parlement ou le conseil de la province. Parmi les membres des Etats provinciaux sont élus six députés, qui forment - avec le Commissaire qui les préside - les *états députés*, bureau de la province.
Enfin, le *Commissaire de la Reine* est nommé par le Gouvernement. Il préside aux Etats députés (dont il est membre) et aux réunions des Etats provinciaux, où il n'a cependant pas le droit de vote.

Le Commissaire, comme le maire français, a une tête de Janus: il est à la fois agent du pouvoir central et organe du pouvoir provincial.
En tant que représentant du pouvoir central il surveille les bourgmestres dans la province (qui ne lui sont cependant pas sub-ordonnés!) et donne des conseils au Ministre de l'Intérieur concernant les nominations des bourgmestres; pour ceci, il est subordonné à la Couronne (au Ministre de l'Intérieur).
En tant qu'organe provincial il a certaines responsabilités dans le domaine de la surveillance de la sécurité publique dans la province, il doit concourir à l'exécution de quelques lois, et il préside aux deux autres organes de la province. Pour tout celà, il est responsable devant les Etats provinciaux.
En pratique, le Commissarie est surtout considéré comme organe de la province; il n'agit qu'exceptionnellement comme servant le pouvoir central.

Les députés sont uniquement responsables devant les Etats provinciaux, qui, eux, ne peuvent pourtant pas les révoquer.
Les organes provinciaux ne sont jamais responsables devant le Gouvernement.

Le pouvoir municipal

Les plus de 800 communes sont toutes organisées de façon pareille. A quelques rares exceptions près, les dispositions du Code des communes sont les mêmes pour Amsterdam et Rotterdam d'une part, et pour les petits villages de mille habitants d'autre part.
L'organisation du pouvoir local est très voisine de celle du pouvoir provincial. On y retrouve les trois organes: conseil municipal, municipalité, bourgmestre[2].

Le *conseil municipal* compte sept membres pour les petites communes (moins de 3.000 habitants) jusqu'à 45 membres pour les quelques communes avec plus de 200.000 habitants. Le conseil est présidé par le bourgmestre, qui n'a le droit de vote que s'il a été élu comme membre du conseil, cas extrêmement rare.

La *municipalité*. Les conseils municipaux élient parmi eux deux à huit échevins, qui restent membres du conseil. Les échevins forment, sous la présidence du bourgmestre, le collège des bourgmestre et échevins (la municipalité), dont le bourgmestre est membre avec droit de vote. La municipalité est le bureau de la commune.

Dans les communes de plus de 30.000 habitants les échevins sont considérés comme des professionnels; leur rémunération est calculée à partir d'une fonction à temps plein. En réalité déjà l'échevin de la commune de 20.000 habitants trouve une occupation à temps plein dans sa fonction.

Le *bourgmestre* est nommé par arrêté Royal, sur proposition du Commissaire de la Reine. Avant de faire sa proposition au ministre, le Commissaire est tenu de consulter le conseil municipal.

Le bourgmestre est toujours fonctionnaire professionnel. Il peut combiner sa fonction avec la participation à un organe représentatif, comme les Etats provinciaux ou le Sénat. Mais il est formellement interdit d'être à la fois bourgmestre et député (membre des Etats députés) ou bourgmestre et ministre.

D'habitude, les bourgmestres sont des hommes de carrière. Souvent anciens fonctionnaires publics ou échevins, ils ont coûtume - une fois nommé bourgmestre - de rester dans leur office; mais ils ne restent pas toujours dans la même commune. Normalement le bourgmestre se voit octroyé une autre poste tous les huit ou dix ans, et de temps en temps il cherche l'office dans une autre commune. Mais il y a aussi l'exemple du bourgmestre qui est déplacé après quatre ans; ou l'autre, qui occupe une seule poste quasi-éternellement - cas beaucoup pire.

Le bourgmestre n'agit jamais comme agent du pouvoir central: il est organe de la commune et il n'est que cela. Aussi est-il responsable de tous ses actes devant le conseil municipal. La même chose vaut pour les échevins et la municipalité en tant que collège: ils sont entièrement et uniquement responsables devant le conseil municipal, qui peut même faire démissionner un échevin (le bourgmestre ne peut être révoqué que par la Couronne).

Bien que le conseil soit l'organe suprême du pouvoir municipal, le collège des bourgmestre et échevins (la municipalité) en est l'organe central, il est l'exécutif municipal.
Il est à noter que tous les pouvoirs de la municipalité sont des *pouvoirs collégiaux*; les membres de cet organe n'ont pas de pouvoirs propres, à exercer par eux seuls. Cependant le Code des communes ne connaît pas seulement la responsabilité collective de la municipalité, mais également la responsabilité individuelle de ses membres. Ceci reflète la réalité: comme dans le Gouvernement, chaque membre de la municipalité a sa 'portefeuille', pour laquelle il a donc une responsabilité spéciale.

La *répartition des pouvoirs* parmi les organes locaux se trace ici en grandes lignes. Le conseil municipal a le pouvoir réglementaire dans la commune; il vote aussi les plans (d'urbanisme, de subventionnement pour quelques secteurs...) et le budget municipal, il établit les impôts locaux, il décide de l'achat ou de la vente des biens immobiliers de la commune.
Le bourgmestre est chargé de la défense de l'ordre public (aussi est-il le chef de la police dans la commune) et il assure l'exécution des lois qui concernent l'ordre public et des règlements de police municipaux, votés par le conseil.

Les autres tâches incombent à la municipalité. C'est elle qui assure l'exécution d'un grand nombre de lois de cogestion (v. Ch.2, par. 1), des règlements et des autres arrêtés décidés par le conseil; elle prépare les déliberations du conseil. C'est sous les ordres de la municipalité, enfin, que travaille le corps des fonctionnaires municipaux.

II. SIGNIFICATION DU POUVOIR MUNICIPAL

1. *La décentralisation territoriale*

La décentralisation sur le plan politique

Le concept de la décentralisation territoriale comprend deux notions, intiment liées l'une à l'autre:

a.
Un *système politique* où les pouvoirs publics sont répartis entre le Gouvernement central (y compris le législateur) et les collectivités locales ou régionales; il peut y avoir des

rapports de tutelle entre ces pouvoirs, mais ils ne sont pas subordonnés de façon essentiellement hiérarchique.

b.
Le *transfert des pouvoirs publics*, dans un système de décentralisation au sens sus-indiqué, des organes 'supérieurs' à des collectivités 'inférieures'.
Le terme est également utilisé dans un sens plus large; alors on entend par 'décentralisation' tout changement dans les rapports des forces entre les collectivités publiques en faveur des collectivités inférieures, p.e. une atténuation de la tutelle administrative ou financière.

Dans le présent article, le terme décentralisation est utilisé dans les deux sens sans distinction précise; la signification exacte dépendra chaque fois du contexte.

L'idée de la décentralisation est profondément enracinée dans la culture politique néerlandaise. D'une part, parce que l'organisation politique la plus ancienne était l'organisation sur le plan local: les polders (v. Ch. 1, par. 1), les communes[3]; d'autre part - et voici un trait original de notre pays - parce que les provinces furent, pendant des siècles, des états indépendants et souverains. Après la déchéance de Philippe II d'Espagne, en 1581, les sept provinces néerlandaises du nord formèrent la République des Pays-Bas Unis; la République fut, avec l'Helvétie d'avant 1828, l'exemple classique d'une confédération. Pendant la période napoléonienne de 1795 jusqu'à 1813, le pays fut purement unitaire pendant quelques années; mais après la reprise de l'indépendance, le pays - devenu monarchie - choisit pour un compromis entre la confédération d'antan et le centralisme français; ce fut un état unitaire décentralisé, où 'tout ce qui tient à l'administration et à l'économie intérieure de leur Province' incombait aux Etats provinciaux, et où 'la direction pleine et entière de leurs intérêts particuliers et domestiques' (Loi fond. de 1814) était confiée aux administrations locales.
L'histoire a montré, dès le commencement, de très fortes tendances centralisatrices, en raison d'un certain nombre de circonstances auxquelles je n'insisterai guère; des développements similaires se sont produits partout en Europe. Il n'en reste pas moins que, dans la culture politique des Pays-Bas, celui qui fait appel au principe de la décentralisation, fait toujours bonne figure; les ministres et les membres du Parlement ont l'agréable coutume de claironner leur amour de la décentralisation. A l'heure où l'opération de la conversion des provinces en agglomérations ou en 'mini-provinces' est au point mort (v. Ch. 1, par. 1), le Parlement exige et le Gouvernement donne les promesses les plus solennelles que toute une série de transferts de compétences en faveur des

provinces et des communes (la 'décentralisation matérielle') aille être élaborée; mais la matière est rude et les ministères (qui risquent de voir diminuer leurs pouvoirs) se montrent réticents.

Cependant, il existe un groupe de pression qui est très puissant et qui ne cesse de réclamer la décentralisation: c'est l'Association des Communes Néerlandaises, association de droit privé qui réunit toutes les communes; elle défend et plaide les intérêts des communes auprès du Gouvernement et du Parlement[4].

Aspects économiques de la décentralisation

En ce qui concerne l'aspect économique de la décentralisation, deux sujets seront abordés: l'intérêt économique de l'action communale et les ressources financières des communes.

I n t é r ê t é c o n o m i q u e

Pour indiquer l'intérêt économique de la vie communale, comparé à celui de l'action de l'Etat, je donne ici, à titre d'illustration, un tableau chiffré sur l'année 1980.

Dépenses	x 1 000 000
Total des dépenses de l'Etat (subsides aux provinces, aux communes et aux polders inclus)[5]	Hfl. 110 000
Total des dépenses des communes	35 000
Total des dépenses de la ville de Tilbourg[6]	250
Personnel	
Nombre des personnes engagées par l'Etat militaires exclus	160 000
Total des personnes engagées par les communes	210 000
Nombre des personnes engagées par la ville de Tilbourg	2 700

R e s s o u r c e s f i n a n c i è r e s

Les ressources des communes se divisent en trois catégories. Chaque catégorie contribue aux finances municipales pour le taux approximatif indiqué ci-dessous.

a.	allocation générale du Fonds des communes	35%
b.	subsides dits 'spécifiques', accordés par l'Etat	55%
c.	revenus propres des communes	10%

a : allocation générale du Fonds des communes.
Le Fonds des communes est un fonds, créé par la loi et géré par les Ministres de l'Interieur et des Finances. Il est alimenté selon un pourcentage, prévu par la loi (env. 12%), par les produits fiscaux directs et indirects les plus importants du Trésor.
Le Fonds se répartit selon des critères objectifs. Les critères les plus importants sont la population, le surface, le nombre des habitations et les coûts des services sociaux de la commune. L'allocation générale n'a pas de buts spéciaux auxquels elle devrait être destinée; elle est à la libre disposition de la commune. En revanche, il y a maintes lois de cogestion (v. infra, par. 1) qui obligent les communes de remplir des engagements très coûteux sans que ces frais soient remboursés, ou contre des remboursements insuffisants.

b : subsides 'spécifiques'.
Le monde des subsides 'spécifiques' que l'Etat (c'-à-d. les ministères, indépendants l'un de l'autre) accorde aux communes est un vrai chaos d'env. 530 sortes différentes. Ce chaos est pourtant, nous l'avons vu, la source la plus importante des finances municipales.
Les subsides 'spécifiques' ont pour trait commun qu'ils sont accordés pour des buts précis et qu'ils ne peuvent être dépensés que pour ce but. Par conséquent, ils laissent très peu de pouvoir discrétionnaire, de pouvoir d'appréciation aux organes municipaux. Quand elle dépense de l'argent, provenant de l'allocation générale, la commune peut donner la priorité relative ou absolue à tel ou tel but; quand elle bénéficie d'un subside spécifique, elle n'est plus libre d'agir selon ses propres préférences.
Presque tous les subsides dits spécifiques ont un autre trait commun: ils sont accompagnés de toute une gamme de conditions, de prescriptions et de directives souvent très minutieuses.
En principe on peut distinguer dans ces subsides deux sub-catégories:
- dédommagements (totaux ou partiels) des frais que la commune doit faire à la suite d'un devoir lui imposé par la loi; p.e. éducation, constructions des chemins;
- offres de payement partiel des frais que la commune *peut* faire pour un but spécial; p.e. subventionner des musées, les arts, des cours d'application.

La seconde sous-catégorie n'est pas aussi innocente qu'elle pourrait paraître à première vue; bien au contraire, elle est trop séduisante. Le gouvernement a trouvé ici une méthode fort effective pour influencer ou diriger l'action municipale sans qu'il ait besoin d'une base légale; un simple article du budget lui suffit.

c : revenus propres des communes.
Ici la source principale est la fiscalité municipale. Le Code des communes donne la possibilité aux conseils municipaux de mettre en oeuvre quelques impôts; le plus important est la taxe immobilière, pour laquelle sont contribuables les propriétaires et les usagers (locataires etc.) de l'immobilier.
Enfin, il y a les revenus patrimoniaux, peu importants pour la majorité des communes. Il s'agit des profits, tirés du commerce foncier par les communes, et des revenus de quelques entreprises d'utilité publique (gaz, électricité).

Insuffisance des ressources locales

Les ressources financières des communes correspondent-elles aux compétences retenues? - Voici un grand problème. Régulièrement les communes manifestent leur mécontentement; et elles n'ont pas tort.
Le problème n'y paraît pas quand on consulte les chiffres des budgets: le total des budgets municipaux pour l'année 1980 ne montre qu'un déficit d'environ 1%. Ceci s'explique par le jeu de la tutelle: le budget municipal avec un grand déficit n'obtiendra pas l'approbation des Etats députés.

Sur le terrain de la cogestion il y a plusieurs tâches pour lesquelles les communes reçoivent trop peu d'argent. Les 'malfaiteurs' les plus importants sont:

- l'enseignement primaire et les jardins d'enfants
- le coût de la réhabilitation des quartiers anciens
- la construction et l'exploitation des habitations populaires (H.L.M.)
- le transfert des pouvoirs de subvention aux communes sur le terrain socio-culturel; l'Etat récompense les subventions payées, mais ne récompense pas les frais de la planification obligatoire, extrêmement compliquée et les salaires des fonctionnaires, chargés de l'exécution de cette nouvelle tâche.
- les conséquences de la politique d'immigration
- le coût des services sociaux; ici, comme sur le terrain socio-culturel, l'Etat rembourse les paiements versés par les communes à leurs clients; mais les frais de 'l'appareil de gestion' ne sont couverts que partiellement; le nombre des fonctionnaires travaillant dans ces services s'est fort accrû à la suite de l'extension de la clientèle: ce sont les années maigres.

En revanche, le pourcentage des produits fiscaux du Trésor qui alimentent le Fonds des communes, environ 14% pendant des années, a récemment été réduit d'environ 2%...

C'est la loi qui fixe le régime du Fonds des communes; dans plusieurs cas c'est la loi qui détermine les subsides spécifiques. Mais les montants accordés aux communes ont tendance à être adaptés aux besoins de l'Etat. Ceci est déjà le cas de l'allocation générale - le pourcentage alimentaire du Fonds des communes change au moins une fois par an -; pour les subsides spécifiques, on n'en rate pas là.

Compétences municipales

Pour indiquer l'intérêt de la notion de la décentralisation sur le plan juridique, il est nécessaire de consacrer quelques mots à la répartition des compétences entre les trois niveaux de l'administration; j'y reviendrai ultérieurement dans le chap. IV.
L'attribution des compétences publiques aux organes municipaux - je n'insisterai pas sur les provinces - se fait selon un double principe, que l'on retrouve dans la Loi fondamentale.

Le premier principe, exprimé par l'article 153, al. 1, c'est celui de la *clause générale*, ou le principe du *pouvoir autonome* de la commune. La disposition constitutionelle dit 'Tout ce qui concerne la réglementation et l'administration des intérêts domestiques de la commune, est confié au conseil municipal'.
Question: que sont les intérêts domestiques de la commune? L'expression veut dire: toute chose que le conseil entend entamer, à moins que le sujet ne tombe pas dans les domaines déjà couverts par les pouvoirs central ou provincial.

Le second principe, celui de la *cogestion*, nous le trouvons dans l'alinéa 3 de ce même article 153 de la Loi fondamentale: 'Lorsque les lois, les arrêtés Royaux réglementaires ou les règlements provinciaux le prescrivent, les administrations locales concourent à leur exécution'.[7]
Le mode classique de ce concours est celui de l'exécution par voie d'actes administratifs individuels (octroi de permis, d'exemptions de subventions, taxes...) ou d'actes de fait (constructions, etc.). Depuis le commencement de notre siècle on connaît également des actes réglementaires en cogestion (règlement municipal de voirie, de clôture des magasins...) et des plans arrêtées à l'exécution d'une loi de cogestion (plans d'urbanisme, plan pour le subventionnement des bibliothèques, des musées...).

L'histoire fournit d'innombrables exemples de changement du

domaine autonome à celui de la cogestion. La réglementation de la route par exemple, de la clôture des magasins, de l'urbanisme, de la construction: tout cela a commencé dans des règlements municipaux autonomes, tandis que maintenant on trouve des lois sur tous ces sujets; mais (presque) toutes ces lois invoquent le concours de tel ou tel organe provincial ou municipal, comme nous le verrons plus loin.
Mais si une loi invoque le concours de la commune ou non, la commune retient toujours, à titre de son pouvoir autonome, une *compétence complémentaire*: les aspects d'un sujet qui échappent aux clauses de la loi (ou, le cas échéant, de l'arrête Royal réglementaire ou du règlement provincial) sont, en principe, à la libre disposition du conseil municipal: ils peuvent être saisis par un règlement municipal.
Pour les communes, il s'agit ici d'un principe non-écrit. Pour les provinces, le Code des provinces - qui est plus récent que celui des communes - le dit expressément dans l'article 80 : 'Le pouvoir réglementaire des Etats provinciaux reste intact à l'égard des sujets, réglés par une loi ou un arrêté Royal réglementaire, pour autant que les règlements n'y soient pas contraires'.

Il en résulte que les communes ont une compétence quasi-intégrale: elles s'occupent de presque tous les terrains d'intervention publique. Ce '*wide range of action*' est considéré comme un caractère essentiel du pouvoir local. Ceci n'empêche pas, bien entendu, qu'une importante partie de l'action municipale est controlée ou même maîtrisée par le Gouvernement ou, le cas échéant, par la province (surtout les Etats députés), comme nous le verrons ultérieurement.

2. *La notion d'autonomie locale*

L'expression d''autonomie locale' est employée dans deux sens: au sens juridique et au sens politique. Le terme ne signifie pas exactement la même chose dans les deux cas.

l'autonomie locale comme *notion juridique* indique le pouvoir, confié à la commune, de faire tout ce que lui paraît utile dans 'l'intérêt domestique de la commune'; v. supra, par. 1. C'est la Loi fondamentale même qui, comme nous l'avons vu, a chargé les communes de ce pouvoir autonome, et le Code des communes donne des dispositions plus détaillées. Il s'agit ici d'un pouvoir général, ne dépendant pas d'une loi spéciale qui donne aux communes tel ou tel devoir, ou des compétences spéciales pour un terrain limité. Autrement dit: l'autonomie, comme notion juridique, s'oppose aux pouvoirs de cogestion. Les actes autonomes n'échappent pas à la tutelle administrative. Le règlements autonomes qui créent des délits, doivent être communiquées aux Etats députés, qui en peuvent demander

l'annulation dite 'spontanée' à la Couronne, s'ils les jugent contraires aux lois ou à l'intérêt général. La Couronne dispose d'ailleurs d'un pouvoir général d'annuler toute délibération du conseil municipal ou de la municipalité pour ces mêmes raisons[8].
Puis, le budget municipal, voté par le conseil, le transfert des pouvoirs à une commission (v. Ch. 1, par. 2, n.2), la création de ou la participation à une personne juridique de droit privé (fondation, S.A...) ou de droit public (syndicat des communes), et la vente et l'achat des biens immobiliers par la commune, sont soumis à l'approbation des Etats députés. Au cas où ceux-ci refusent leur approbation, le conseil peut en appeler à la Couronne[9].

Comme *notion politique*, l'autonomie locale vise le degré d'independance vis-à-vis des autorités provinciales et centrales; autrement dit, le pouvoir d'appréciation ou le pouvoir discrétionnaire des organes municipaux. Pour éviter la confusion, je parlerai ici de (degré de) *discrétion*. Donc l'autonomie comme notion politique s'exprime en compétences discrétionnaires; elle s'oppose aux compétences liées ou à l'absence de compétences.
Le degré de discrétion d'une compétence dépend essentiellement de trois facteurs:

a : de la terminologie de la loi qui donne la compétence ('la municipalité peut'/'la municipalité doit';'à l'avis du conseil'/définition précise de la compétence du conseil; termes vagues/termes précis);
b : du régime éventuel de tutelle administrative;
c : des possibilités financières de la commune.

Par conséquent, le couple des termes 'autonomie - cogestion' n'est pas parallèle à l'opposition entre compétence discrétionnaire et compétence liée; les rapports sont beaucoup plus compliqués. Il y a des pouvoirs autonomes qui sont discrétionnaires dans les trois sens; il y en a d'autres qui ne le sont en aucun de ces sens. Il en va de même pour les pouvoirs de cogestion; il y en a qui sont libres, discrétionnaires, dans plusieurs sens; et d'autres sont fort liés. S'il est impossible d'indiquer une relation fixe entre les deux notions sur le plan qualitatif, on peut bien faire une remarque quantitative. Quand on laisse à part le critère financier (c), on constate que la majorité des compétences autonomes sont plus ou moins discrétionnaires, tandis que les compétences de cogestion sont en général plus liées.

III. RAPPORTS ENTRE LES COMMUNES ET LES AUTRES COLLECTIVITÉS PUBLIQUES.

1. *Les rapports de la commune avec la province et avec l'Etat*

Le système de décentralisation territoriale comprend les trois niveaux d'administration, mais aussi trois niveaux de démocratie.
Les deux mots, administration et démocratie, reflètent deux caractères de la décentralisation, c'est-à-dire le caractère technique (la décentralisation comme variante de la déconcentration) et le caractère politique (les rapports tendus entre les nécessités de l'état unitaire et les demandes pluriformes des collectivités locales).
Cette ambigüité des valeurs de collaboration ou opposition entre la commune et les deux administrations 'supérieures', se retrouve dans les deux sujets traités ici:
a. les rapports de tutelle,
b. la notion d'administration complémentaire.

a. *La tutelle administrative*

Chaque loi de cogestion a son propre système de tutelle. C'est pourquoi il y a toute une panoplie de formes de tutelle et de rapports analogues entre les différents niveaux. On peut faire plusieurs subdivisions.

1e D'une part les droits de tutelle, des moyens d'influence des organes supérieurs à l'égard des organes d'une administration inférieure. D'autre part les moyens de modération de ceux-ci, c'est-à-dire des moyens pour se défendre contre la tutelle ou pour modérer ses effets; p.e. droit de recours, droit de consultation préalable.
2e La tutelle préventive (approbation) ou répressive (annulation a posteriori).
3e Moyens de tutelle légaux et moyens extra-légaux. Les moyens extra-légaux sont extrêmement divers: persuasion personelle; contrats de droit privé; offres de subside avec un régime de conditions; composition des gremiums de préparation ou de consultation....
4e Moyens forts (approbation, annulation) ou faibles (devoir de communication).
5e Moyens négatifs et moyens positifs. En utilisant un moyen négatif, l'organe de tutelle peut seulement mettre obstacle à une décision qui ne lui plaît pas; par un moyen positif il peut assurer que sa volonté soit faite (directives, prendre la décision au lieu de l'organe surveillé...).
6e La tutelle *in rem* (visant les actes) ou *in personam* (frappant les personnes; p.e. révocation d'un bourgmestre[10]).

Le 5e nous confronte très clairement avec le problème de l'opposition ou la collaboration entre les niveaux. La théorie et la pratique s'opposent fort aux moyens de tutelle positifs, ces moyens étant considérés comme contraires au principe de décentralisation au sens politique; ils sont de nature beaucoup plus menaçante à l'égard de la discrétion municipale que les moyens négatifs. En pratique, les moyens positifs sont assez rares, leur application est même exceptionnelle[11]; la seule existence de cet instrument suffit.

Encore exige-t-on que les moyens de tutelle soient utilisés de manière restrictive; l'organe de tutelle ne saurait 'occuper la chaise' de l'organe surveillé. Le plaidoyer pour l'usage réservé de la tutelle s'explique aussi par le fait que l'organe de tutelle ne juge pas uniquement la légalité (la juridicité) des actes surveillés mais encore leur opportunité. Au titre du contrôle de l'opportunité, l'organe supérieur a, en principe, toutes les possibilités d'imposer sa propre volonté, des propres opinions politiques - et voilà le rapport tendu avec la décentralisation au sens politique, qui exige que ce soit la démocratie locale qui décide, et non pas un organe provincial ou gouvernemental.

b. *L'administration complémentaire*

L'idée de l'administration complémentaire est née il y a une douzaine d'années; à cette époque on entendait par ces mots l'action concertée des communes, des provinces et du Gouvernement. Née dans des milieux communaux, l'idée était plutôt d'inspiration défensive: l'Etat devait se rendre compte qu'il ne lui faut pas dominer les communes, mais, au contraire, collaborer avec elles et leur fournir les moyens d'action nécessaire.
L'idée était séduisante, même trop séduisante. Le Gouvernement a vite compris comment il pouvait abuser de la notion de l'administration complémentaire. En chantant sur ce ton, en invitant les communes aux consultations mutuelles, les ministères avaient trouvé une méthode très efficace pour imposer aux communes leurs demandes.
Depuis lors, la notion a changé de visage. Maintenant on entend par 'administration complémentaire' une méthode d'administration communicative, avec possibilités de consultation, voire d'accords entre des organes publics sous la forme de contrats administratifs[12]. Mais tout cela avec des garanties pour l'indépendence, pour la discrétion réelle des communes et pour l'influence des conseils municipaux. Il y a, dans ce cadre, des propositions menant à atténuer les moyens de tutelle dans les cas où la loi prescrit une consultation entre organe surveillé et organe de tutelle.

2. *Rapports entre les communes*

Les communes désirant coopérer, peuvent créer un Syndicat de communes. Il y a des syndicats à vocation unique et à vocation multiple. Le syndicat chargé d'une compétence des conseils municipaux, est créé par les conseils; s'il est chargé de quelques compétences des municipalités, ce sont eux qui doivent fonder le syndicat; les bourgmestres aussi peuvent créer des syndicats pour l'exercice commune d'une compétence bourgmestrielle.

Le transfert des compétences est soumis à l'approbation des Etats députés. Aujourd'hui il existe env. 1.500 syndicats de communes sur 810 communes, dont env. 50 à vocation multiple. Voici une des raisons pour lesquelles on a essayé de réorganiser l'administration intérieure du pays; cf. ch. 1, par. 1. Sur quelques terrains la loi ouvre la possibilité de la coopération forcée. Alors les Etats provinciaux ou députés peuvent obliger les communes indiquées par eux, de fonder un syndicat. La coopération forcée figure surtout dans des domaines techniques; p.e. les services des sapeurs pompiers, l'organisation des ambulances, les services municipaux pour l'inspection des constructions et des habitations.

IV. LES COMPÉTENCES LOCALES

1. *Critères d'attribution des compétences municipales*

Comme nous l'avons vu, deux types d'attribution des compétences aux communes figurent dans le droit public néerlandais; la clause générale, en ce qui concerne les pouvoirs autonomes, et l'énumération pour les pouvoirs en matière de cogestion; v. ch. II, par. 1.
Je rapelle que l'énumération, pour les pouvoirs de cogestion, ne se fait pas au moyen d'une liste; au contraire, chaque loi de cogestion - dont il y a des centaines, sinon des milliers - donne des pouvoirs spécifiques à un ou plusieurs organes municipaux. Le plus souvent, les pouvoirs réglementaires et la fixation des plans sont attribués au conseil municipal; les pouvoirs autres que réglementaires concernant l'ordre public sont confiés au bourgmestre, et les autres compétences sont données à la municipalité.

Dans le cadre de la réorganisation administrative, le Ministre de l'Intérieur s'est efforcé d'imposer aux communes une 'liste *négative*', c'est-à-dire une liste (brève) de sujets, tabous pour l'intervention municipale. Sous la pression unanime du Parlement et des communes, le ministre a dû retirer la proposition.

2. *Valeur et portée des compétences municipales*

Pouvoirs discrétionnaires et pouvoirs liés.

Sur le terrain de l'autonomie locale, il n'y a que des compétences de décision. Ce sont les organes de la commune qui décident s'ils veulent agir ou non, ou de quelle manière ils entendent le faire; toutefois, ils se trouvent soumis à la tutelle administrative pour un certain nombre de catégories de décisions autonomes[13].

Quant aux pouvoirs de cogestion, on trouve toutes les variétés des compétences discrétionnaires et liées. Traditionnellement, les pouvoirs de cogestion sont divisés en quatre catégories.

pouvoirs facultatifs : a. discrétionnaires,
b. liés;

pouvoirs obligatoires: c. discrétionnaires,
d. liés.

Sur le chemin qui conduit de la discrétion à l'exécution pure et simple, nous rencontrons les catégories dans l'ordre suivante : a, c, b et d. En voici quelques exemples:

a.
Le conseil municipal peut désigner des terrains ayant des installations, classées pour le risque, l'insalubrité ou l'incommodité qu'ils représentent, et n'ayant pas le permis normalement requis par la loi.

c.
La municipalité est chargée de régler les demandes de permis de logement; la loi leur accorde un pouvoir très discrétionnaire d'accorder ou de refuser ces permis.

b.
Le conseil peut déléguer à la municipalité le pouvoir d'élaborer en détail un plan d'urbanisme; s'il le fait, le conseil est obligé d'indiquer le plus exactement possible les limites de la discrétion de la municipalité; la municipalité doit obéir, en outre, aux dispositions de l'arrêté Royal portant règlement d'urbanisme (règlement, donné à l'exécution du Code d'urbanisme).

d.
La municipalité est chargée de l'administration de l'état civil, de l'organisation des élections, etc. Ici il s'agit des compétences presque absolument liées, des compétences d'exécution quasi-mécaniques.

Contrôle et garantie des compétences municipales

a. *C o n t r ô l e*

Quant au thème du contrôle des compétences des organes locaux, on a déjà parlé du système de tutelle administrative; v. supra, ch. 3, par. 2.
A côté de la tutelle, il y a le contrôle judiciaire et quasi-juriciaire. Mais ici, le contrôle n'est plus systématique: le juge ne peut intervenir que si quelqu'un le saisit d'un recours contre un acte administratif.
Remarquons d'abord que, en droit public néerlandais, le recours ne joue jamais contre les actes réglementaires; seuls les actes individuels et - le plus souvent - les plans sont susceptibles d'un recours en annulation devant une juridiction administrative. Puis, le système de la juridiction administrative est extrêmement compliqué.
Dans plusieurs cas, la loi donne un recours quasi-hiérarchique contre des actes administratifs; dans cette hypothèse, un acte municipal peut être contesté devant les Etats députés ou devant la Couronne[14]. D'une part, ce n'est pas un juge indépendant qui statue; mais du jugement des Etats députés on peut en appeler, le cas échéant, à la Couronne ou à la Section de la justice du Conseil d'Etat. D'autre part, non seulement la légalité, mais encore l'opportunité de l'acte peut être contestée.
Dans d'autres cas, on peut s'adresser à un juge administratif spécialisé. C'est le cas notamment dans le domaine des impôts, de l'assurance sociale, de l'organisation industrielle et de la fonction publique.
Enfin, la Section de la justice du Conseil d'Etat peut recevoir des recours en annulation contre tout acte administratif individuel qui ne tombe pas dans la compétence d'une autre juridiction.
Toutes les juridictions mentionnées peuvent contrôler la compétence de l'agent public dont l'acte est attaqué.

b. *G a r a n t i e*

Comment est garantie la répartition des compétences et, surtout: comment sont garanties ces compétences en ce qui concerne les infractions de la part de l'Etat ou de la province?
Avant tout, c'est le champ de la politique. La loi peut régler presque tout, de la manière qui lui plaît. Elle peut notamment convertir des pouvoirs municipaux, autonomes jusqu' ici, en pouvoirs de cogestion, c'-à-d. réglementés par la loi (et munis, le plus souvent, d'un système de tutelle). Ici, le Ministre de l'Intérieur doit veiller au centralisme des ses collègues, et le Parlement doit vaincre ses propres inclinations centralisatrices.

Puis, tous les projets de loi qui touchent les pouvoirs des provinces ou des communes doivent être soumis à l'avis du Conseil pour l'Administration Intérieure[15]; les avis du Conseil sont publiés.
Et enfin - l'Association des Communes Néerlandaises est toujours vigilente.
Quant aux garanties juridiques, il faut examiner quelques détails du système de tutelle administrative. D'abord, les moyens de tutelle sont essentiellement des moyens de caractère négatif; par conséquent, ce ne sont guère des outils aptes à l'intervention proprement dite.
En second lieu, la tradition veut que la tutelle soit exercée d'une façon assez restrictive. Les cas de refus d'approbation ne sont pas très nombreux; les annulations spontanées sont même très rares: on en compte env. 20 par an.

La loi connaît quelques entraves. Quant à l'annulation spontanée on a déjà vu que l'avis du Conseil d'Etat est obligatoire (Ch. II, par. 2, note 9). Le Code des provinces prescrit l'avis de la Section du contentieux du C.E. pour chaque refus d'approbation d'un acte provincial. Pareille disposition n'existe pas dans le Code des communes; mais il y a une proposition récente qui veut que l'approbation ne pourra être refusée qu'après consultation préalable de l'organe concerné.

En réalité, le danger le plus perfide c'est celui de la manipulation financière. Que peut on espérer pour la liberté des communes si elles manquent d'argent, si pour chaque initiative elles sont obligées de tendre la main à tel ou tel ministère, ou du moins si elles sont dépendantes d'un subside 'spécifique'[16] pour grande partie de leurs actions?
Depuis longtemps on entend des plaidoyers qui veulent que le volume des subsides spécifiques soit réduit au profit de l'allocation générale; qu'une loi donne des règles générales pour tous les subsides spécifiques. La 'décentralisation matérielle' dont on parle tant de nos jours, nous apportera-t-elle la réalisation de ces désirs?

V. QUELQUES EXEMPLES DE RÉPARTITION DES COMPÉTENCES ENTRE L'ÉTAT, LES PROVINCES ET LES COMMUNES

1. *La police*

La police est chargée de plusieurs devoirs. Ils se répartissent en deux catégories: le devoir dit *judiciaire* (la recherche des infractions et des crimes) et les devoirs dits *administratifs* (défense de l'ordre public, assistance publique).

En ce qui concerne les devoirs judiciaires, la police est l'instrument du Ministère Public, subordonné au Ministre de la Justice. En ce qui concerne les devoirs administratifs, la police se trouve sous les ordres du bourgmestre; le bourgmestre, lui en est responsable devant le conseil municipal.

Dans les petites communes (moins d'env. 15.000 hab.) on trouve des corps de la police nationale; dans les autres communes, il y a la police municipale. La description qui vient d'être donnée ci-dessus vaut pour les deux catégories.
Les dépenses de la police municipale sont, en principe, à la charge de l'Etat. Aussi le Ministre de l'Intérieur détermine-t-il, après consultation du bourgmestre, le nombre des fonctionnaires de police dans la commune, aussi bien que leurs rangs. En outre, les commissaires de police sont nommés par la Couronne, après consultation du bourgmestre; les fonctionnaires subalternes sont nommés par le bourgmestre.

Le conseil municipal vote les règlements de police, c'-à-d. les règlements municipaux concernant l'ordre public; le bourgmestre (aidé de ses policiers) est chargé de les appliquer.

2. *L'éducation primaire*

Aux Pays-Bas, la plupart des écoles primaires se trouvent entre les mains des institutions privées. Parmi ces écoles libres on distingue trois grandes catégories: les écoles catholiques, protestantes et 'neutres'[17].
Les écoles primaires publiques sont gérées par les communes; elles sont neutres du point de vue religieux et politique.
La Loi fondamentale garantissant la liberté et l'égalité financière de l'enseignement primaire, les écoles jouissent du même régime financier; elles sont toutes financées intégralement par les communes, qui sont remboursées par l'Etat.
Les écoles enseignent les mêmes matières obligatoires, mais les écoles libres nomment leur propre personnel et choisissent leur matériel scolaire.
La commune est obligée de 'reconnaître' (et de subventionner) toute école libre qui a un nombre suffisant d'élèves, fixé par la loi. La loi détermine les autres conditions techniques etc. des écoles et des enseignants. En principe, il n'y a pas de distinction quant au 'niveau' entre les catégories d'écoles; en général, cette conception est conforme à la réalité.
La commune a le devoir légal de veiller à ce qu'il y ait un nombre 'suffisant' d'écoles sur son territoire.
Il en résulte que le pouvoir local revêt le rôle de pouvoir public à l'égard des écoles privées, tandis que, à l'égard des écoles publiques, il assume également le rôle de direction.

3. *La santé*

En ce qui concerne la santé, il convient de distinguer deux échelons: l'échelon hôpitalier et le 'premier échelon'.
La plupart des hôpitaux sont des hôpitaux privés; la loi n'oblige aucun pouvoir public à exploiter un hôpital. Néanmoins, dans plusieurs grandes villes, on trouve des hôpitaux municipaux.
Les hôpitaux sont soumis à l'approbation du ministre; ils sont soumis à la surveillance de l'inspection de la santé, service national déconcentré. Une loi récente a créé les 'plans des hopitaux provinciaux' qui doivent être votés par les Etats provinciaux et approuvés par le Ministre de la santé publique; les hôpitaux qui ne figurent pas sur le plan devront disparaître. Les communes ne figurent dans ce système qu'à titre consultatif ou, le cas échéant, comme objet: ceci est le cas des communes qui ont un hôpital municipal.

Quant au premier échelon, la plupart des communes disposent d'un service de santé publique - ou d'un service commun, dans le cadre d'un syndicat de communes -, qui est géré en vertu du pouvoir autonome de la commune.

4. *L'urbanisme*

Le Code d'urbanisme connaît en principe deux niveaux de décisions: la province et la commune; le Ministre de l'aménegement du territoire ne dispose que de quelques pouvoirs de tutelle.
Les conseils municipaux sont obligés de voter des plans d'urbanisme, qui déterminent la destination du terrain. Les plans sont fixés après une procédure de participation, ouverte à chacun. Le plan est soumis à l'approbation des Etats députés; toute personne ayant participé à la procédure préalable, peut attaquer la décision des Etats députés devant la Couronne.
Le plan d'urbanisme municipal a un caractère impératif: les permis de construire ne peuvent être accordés que si le projet est en accord avec le plan d'urbanisme (et avec le règlement de voirie).

Au niveau de la province, il y a des plans dits régionaux, fixés par les Etats provinciaux. Théoriquement ces plans ne sont pas impératifs; leur valeur juridique consiste en cela que les Etats députés ne peuvent donner des directives à une commune que sur la base d'un plan d'aménagement du territoire régional. Cependant, à part cela, ces plans déterminent la politique d'approbation des Etats députés; c'est ainsi que le plan régional fixe les grandes lignes de l'aménagement du territoire par les communes.

Le ministre peut donner des directives aux Etats provinciaux pour les plans régionaux; il ne se sert que rarement de cette compétence. Cependant, le ministre prépare maintes décisions planologiques; pour ce faire, il va jusqu'à consulter la Seconde Chambre du parlement. Résultat pratique: les décisions du ministre sont suivies 'spontanément' par les provinces.

Les plans d'urbanisme municipaux ne sont pas nécessairement rigides. La loi prévoit une procédure spéciale pour les projets non conformes au plan, que la commune voudrait cependant admettre. Alors le conseil doit prendre une 'décision préparatoire', déclarant qu'un nouveau plan va être préparé; puis, les Etats députés doivent approuver la décision d'accorder le permis de construire à l'encontre du plan qui est encore en vigueur.

Les décisions concernant les permis de construire peuvent être contestées devant le conseil municipal et devant la Section de la justice du Conseil d'Etat.

NOTES

1. Cependant la première chambre ne représente pas les provinces mais 'la nation entière'.
2. Je laisse de côté les commissions que peut créer le conseil municipal et auxquelles il peut déférer des pouvoirs.
3. 'Commune' au sens original du mot: l'administration de la terre commune par l'assemblée des alleutiers, des propriétaires héréditaires du sol.
4. N.B. Le droit public néerlandais ne connaît pas de disposition correspondant à l'art. L. 121-29 du Code des communes français. ('Il est interdit à tout conseil municipal soit de publier des proclamations et des adresses, soit d'émettre des voeux politiques, soit, hors les cas prévus par la loi, de se mettre en communication avec un ou plusieurs conseils municipaux'). Bien au contraire, l'art. 157 de la Loi fond. stipule: 'Les administrations municipales peuvent appuyer les intérêts de leurs communes et de leurs administrés près du Roi, des Etats Généraux et des Etats de la province à laquelle elles appartiennent'.
5. J'ai employé les termes wallons. Dans le droit administratif belge, le mot *subside* désigne une subvention de l'Etat à une collectivité décentralisée, tandis que l'expression de *subvention* est généralement réservée pour l'aide financière, accordée à une personne privée.
6. 150 000 habitants.
7. Des dispositions analogues s'appliquent aux provinces.
8. La même chose vaut pour les délibérations des Etats provinciaux et députés; les décisions du maire et du Commissaire d'autre part ne sont pas susceptibles de cette annulation spontanée. La Couronne ne peut annuler une délibération qu'après avoir demandé l'avis du Conseil d'Etat.
9. Comme dans tous les cas où quelqu'un peut faire appel à la Couronne, celle-ci ne statue qu'après avis de la Section du contentieux du C.E. Théoriquement, le C.E. a la justice retenue ici. En pratique, c'est la justice quasi-déléguée: seulement dans 0,06% des cas l'avis du Conseil d'Etat n'est pas suivi (moyenne de 2 fois par an).
10. En fait la possibilité de révocation d'un bourgmestre est plutôt théorique.
11. Exemple: une commune dans la région de Tilbourg, refusant d'adapter son plan d'urbanisme pour rendre possible le prolongement d'une autoroute, a récemment été obligée, au moyen d'une directive ministérielle, d'adapter le plan.
12. N.B. Jusqu'ici, le droit néerlandais ne connaît qu'un seul contrat public: le syndicat des communes (avec participation éventuelle d'une province ou de l'Etat); du reste, il n'y a que les contrats de droit privé. Des propositions récentes veulent créer des contrats administratifs pour les accords entre des organes publics.
13. V. supra, ch. 2, par. 2.
14. C'-à-d., pratiquement devant la Section du contentieux du Conseil d'Etat; cf. supra, ch. 2, par. 2, note 9.
15. Le Conseil est un organisme consultatif du Gouvernement. Il est composé d'une trentaine de membres: bourgmestres, échevins, membres des Etats députés, quelques Commissaires de la Reine, et quelques professeurs en droit public ou en sciences administratives.
16. V. supra, ch. 2, par. 1, fin.
17. En principe, les écoles ne sont pas gérées par les églises.

Tax avoidance in international transactions

CHRISTIAN M. STRIK

Assistant Professor at the University of Nijmegen

IV.E.1.

INTRODUCTION

Considering that the French version most probably is the original one, considering as well that the subject of tax avoidance in international transactions would be much too broad to be treated at the Congress in all or at least most of its aspects, the General Reporter suggested to take as a basis the French version, i.e. to confine the subject to situations arising from income or capital being withdrawn from taxation - definitely or temporarily - in the state of source, residence or taxpayer's nationality.

I. BACKGROUND

1. QUESTION :

Does your country export or import capital on a considerable scale? Is there a danger of an exodus of capital?

ANSWER :

There is a capital export (flow of capital abroad), but there is also a capital import to the Netherlands on a considerable scale. This open movement of capital is a characteristic of the Dutch economy and has to be maintained in opinion of the Dutch Central Bank. There is no danger of an exodus of capital.

2. QUESTION :

Please give a general description of your country's system op income taxation and, if existing, taxation of capital (wealth tax etc.). Give names of all relevant codes, acts etc., which you are going to refer to in answering the following questions

CAPITAL MOVEMENTS OF NON-MONETAIRY SECTORS IN INTERNATIONAL RELATIONSHIP

(in millions of guilders)

	1974	1975	1976	1977	1978	1979	1980
Import	16.179	22.664	22.534	30.736	34.439	39.984	46.299
Export	18.963	25.742	29.368	33.627	36.537	40.597	45.075
Balance	-2.784	-3.078	-6.834	-2.891	-2.098	- 613	1.224

DIRECT INVESTMENTS

(in millions of guilders)

	Total					Capital participations				
	1976	1977	1978	1979	1980	1976	1977	1978	1979	1980
Dutch investments abroad (-)	-2.967	-3.715	-3.791	-4.361	-5.321	-1.365	-2.465	-2.694	-1.645	-1.749
Foreign investments in the Netherlands	936	883	1.449	2.402	2.492	627	743	607	1.198	979
Balance	-2.031	-2.832	-2.342	-1.959	-2.829	- 738	-1.722	-2.087	- 447	- 770

as well as their date of enactment and their official reference (place of publication in an official journal, number of the act, or the like).

ANSWER :

Successively we discuss the Income Tax, the Net Wealth Tax, the Corporate Income Tax and the Dividend Tax.

2.1 *The income Tax*
Income Tax is levied on individuals. The place of residence is the only criterion in determining the tax liability. If a person concerned has his residence in the Netherlands he is considered to be a domestic taxpayer. A domestic taxpayer is liable to tax on his world-wide income (income originating in any place or country). In the case a person doesn't have his residence in the Netherlands, but has income earned in the Netherlands he is considered to be a foreign taxpayer. Thus, - in principal - nationality and domicile are irrelevant. However, there are some treaties in which nationality and domicile become relevant in the case the taxpayer has his residence in both countries. The General Act on State Taxes (*Algemene Wet inzake Rijksbelastingen,* Act of July 2, 1959, *Stb.* 301, Article 4) gives a rather broad definition of residence for tax purposes : residence shall be determined according to the circumstances. Because of the lacking of a specific definition of 'residence', the case law on the subject of residence is very casuistical. However, the existence of a personal and durable connection between the person concerned and the Netherlands is required. In this matter importance is attached to : the location of the dwelling; the duration or the time spent in the Netherlands; the place where his wife (the family) lives; the location of employment.
In order to prevent the possibility of a person having no residence anywhere because of differing foreign and domestic legislation, Art. 2 in the Income Tax Act of 1964 provides that a taxpayer who has left the Netherlands, giving up his Dutch residence, but returns to reside again within a period of 1 year, without having established residence abroad, shall be asumed not to have left the Netherlands.

The Basis of Income Tax charged on Domestic Taxpayers

For domestic taxpayers - residents in the Netherlands - income tax is calculated on the so-called 'taxable income' of a calender year. Three sources of income are laid down in the Income Tax Act 1964 as follows :
a. profits derived from enterprises;
b. net income from labor or from personal wealth, or received in the form of periodic payments;

c. income derived from a so-called substantial share-holding interest.

The sum total of income obtained from these three sources is the so-called 'gross income' (*onzuiver inkomen*) from which the so-called 'personal liabilities' (e.g. interest on private debts and premiums paid for life annuities), 'extra-ordinary charges' (e.g. high medical expenses and support of relatives in need), the 'deductible gifts' (e.g. gifts to churches, charitable institutions, cultural and scientific institutions and those of public usefulness in general) and donations to the old-age reserve are subtracted.
This results in what in the Income Tax Act is called 'the income'. The taxable income is obtained after the further deduction of any outstanding losses carried forward from previous years and backward from succeeding years.

a. The source : profit redived from enterprise.

According to article 7 of the Income Tax Act profit comprises the sum total of the advantages and benefits of whatever nature of description, realized by the conduct of a business enterprise.
The total profit made during the life span of the enterprise is taxable. Income Tax is levied on a yearly basis and therefore the profit must be determined every year. Article 9 of the Income Tax Act provides that yearly profit shall be determined to so called 'sound commercial usage' (*goed koopmansgebruik*) and accordingly to a set method which is independent of the expected results and which may be modified only if sound commercial usage so warrants. Case law has made it clear that the principles of business economics can be followed closely. The entrepreneur has thus great latitude within this framework.

If the enterprise is sold or liquidated previous not taxed benefits are added to the profit and taxed. The same applies to the case of decease of the entrepreneur. In both cases special rates are applicable : in case of take-over or liquidation : 20% - 54%, in case of decease : 20%.
If the entrepreneur emigrates, taking his enterprise with him, a settlement has to be made as well.

b. The source : net income from labor or from personal wealth, or received in the form of periodic payments.
Net income means : income minus deductible charges.

b.1 Income from labor includes pensions obtained from prior employment. Net income from labor is subject to the tax on earnings by virtue of the Wage Tax Act 1964 (*Wet op de loonbelasting* 1964).

This tax is credited against the Income Tax.

b.2 Income from private wealth includes for example dividends, interest, rents obtained from the hire of movable goods and life annuities. Dividend is subject to the Dividend Tax Act 1965 (*Wet op de dividendbelasting* 1965). Dividend Tax is credited against the Income Tax.

b.3 Income from periodic payments includes for example payments in accordance with the Old Age Pension Act (Act of May 31, 1956, *Stb* 281), and the Widow's and Orphan's Pension Act (Act of April 9, 1959, *Stb* 139). Furthermore periodic payments by the government like scolarships and payments in accordance with family law (alimony) are also considered as periodic payments.

c. The source : profit from Substantial Shareholding Interest

Substantial interest exists of the person concerned either alone or with his wife or next-of-kin and at any time during the past five years, possessed more than one third, and if the person either alone or with his wife possessed more than 7% of the paid-up capital (Art 39 Income Tax Act 1964). Substantial shareholding interest profit is taxed at a special rate of 20%. The ratio of the concept of the substantial shareholding interest is to provide for the possibility of levying taxes on the profit reserves of the corporation at such time as the corporation's shares are sold. In case of a take-over by acquisition of shares a substantial interest shareholder may ask to shift the arised profit caused by selling the shares to the new shares. Then the substantial shareholding interest profit is taxed when the new shares are sold (art. 40 Income Tax Act 1964).

The basis of Income Tax charged on Foreign Taxpayers

For foreign taxpayers - non-residents of the Netherlands - income tax is calculated on the so-called domestic income. Three sources of domestic income are laid down in article 49 of the Income Tax Act 1964 :

a. Profit from a domestic enterprise;

b. Net income derived from :
   - labor, with relation to an existing or previous employment held in this country, or earnings subject to deduction of Wage Tax, resulting from employment or previous employment not filled in this country;
   - Real estate situated in the Netherlands and credits secured by mortgage on Dutch real property;
   - Profit sharing in the profits of an enterprise with management in the Netherlands;
   - Shares or "actions de jouissance", debentures or claims

emitted by or held against corporations, established in the Netherlands and in which the beneficiairy holds a substantial shareholding interest;
- Periodic payments or provisions made by Dutch public corporations.

c. Profit obtained from a substantial shareholding interest in a corporation established in the Netherlands.

The sum total of all income derived from all or any of the three sources mentioned above constitutes the so-called 'gross domestic income' (*binnenlands onzuiver inkomen*), from which may be deducted :
(1) interest payable on mortgage secured on real property in the Netherlands;
(2) premiums paid in compliance with National Insurance.
The taxable income is obtained by the further deduction of negative income of other years.
This series is limitative : revenues or income derived from other Dutch sources are not liable to Income Tax. Exempted, therefore, are interest and dividends received from corporations established in the Netherlands but in which the beneficiairy does not hold a substantial shareholding interest, royalties. On the other hand dividends and interest received from profit sharing debentures are subject to Dividend Tax only.

Tax rates of the Income Tax

The Income Tax is levied on the so called 'taxable amount' (*belastbare som*), reduced with the 'tax free amount' (*belastingvrije som*), depending on personal criteria as married or single, aged, disabled etc. The scale of tax rates has been constructed in accordance with the 'bracket-system'; the highest marginal rate is 72%. Income derived from a 'substantial shareholding interest' may be taxed at a fixed rate of 20%.
The income of the children for which the parent is entitled to a child allowance is added to the income of the parents.
The wife pays her own taxes on earnings (not on income from private wealth) independently of the husband.
To avoid imposition of double taxation in respect of foreign income relief is granted through a proportional reduction in Dutch taxation (See III.3)

2.2 *The net Wealth Tax*

Net Wealth Tax is levied on individuals. Concerning the idea of the place of residence is referred to the Income Tax.
The Net Wealth Tax is laid down in the '*Wet op de Vermogensbelasting* 1964' (Net Wealth Tax Act 1964) and is complementary to the Income Tax. For domestic taxpayers the Net Wealth Tax is based on the wealth of an individual (not a corporation)

at the beginning of each year wherever situated in the world. Later alterations in the wealth of the individual don't have any significance in determining the taxable wealth.
For foreign taxpayers taxable wealth consists of the value of their property in the Netherlands (domestic property) reduced with the amount of their domestic debts as enumerated in the Act. Domestic property is defined as any property belonging to an enterprise estableshed in the Netherlands, real estate owned in the country, credits secured by mortgage on domestic real property and claims to a share in the profits of a Dutch enterprise where these do not result from a shareholding or employment relationship. Exempted from taxation is the value of shares held in a corporation. The value of property is determined by economic criteria.
The present rate of the Net Wealth Tax is 0.8% and like the Income Tax the Net Wealth Tax also has some deductable amounts. To avoid imposition of double taxation in respect of wealth situated abroad relief is granted through a proportional reduction in Dutch taxation (see III.3)

2.3 *The Corporate Income Tax*
The Corporate Income Tax is laid down in the *Wet op de vennootschapsbelasting* 1969 (Corporate Income Tax Act 1969) and is levied on entities enumerated in this Act.
The Act distinguishes entities established in the Netherlands and entities with the place or establishment outside the Netherlands. In the first case the entity is to be considered as a domestic taxpayer and as such it is liable to pay tax on its profit, irrespective of where the profit is earned, its so-called 'world-wide profit'. In the second case the entity is to be considered as a foreign taxpayer and as such it is liable to pay taxes on profits earned in the Netherlands (domestic profit). The place of establishment is important and is exactly defined in the *Algemene wet inzake de rijksbelastingen* (General Act on State Taxes). In this matter importance is attached to : the location of top management, the place where production or commercial centres are located and the place where the annual shareholder's meeting is held, or the accounts are kept.

Basis of charge to Corporate Income Tax levied on Resident Taxpayers

For resident taxpayers - entities established in the Netherlands - Corporate Income Tax is calculated on the so-called taxable amount. This amount is obtained by subtracting from the yearly taxable profit losses not previously compensated. The Dutch Corporate Income Tax is based on the 'classical system', and is maintained in spite of the fact that the Corporation Income Tax rate is 48% and the rate of the Income

Tax levied on paid dividend can rise to 72%.
Benefit derived from shares in other corporations is also added to the profit. However, dividend and other benefits received from a substantial holding privilege are excepted. The substantial holding privilege is granted if the tax-paying entity has held shares to the value of 5% of the paid-up capital of a corporation. The substantial holding privilege covers all advantages derived from the shareholding, including the profits resulting from the disposal of the shares. Losses cannot be subtracted from the profit, except in case of dissolution of the company whose shares were held.
Concerning mergers of enterprises taxation may be postponed. In case of foreign-source profit a proportional reduction in Dutch taxation may be granted.

The basis of Charge to Corporate Income Tax levied on Foreign Taxpayers

For foreign taxpayers - entities not established in the Netherlands - Corporate Income Tax is calculated on the so-called 'taxable domestic amount'. This amount is derived from the domestic sources of income as laid down in the Income Tax Act 1964.
The special regulations for the computation of the profit of entities established in the Netherlands are also applicable to entities established abroad. Thus the regulations about substantial shareholding, mergers etc. are also applicable to the latter entities. To compute the taxable amount the total earnings derived from domestic sources are reduced by subtracting the interest paid on domestic real estate and the outstanding losses.

2.4 *The Dividend Tax*
Dividend Tax is imposed on the dividends of shares, profit-sharing notes and profit-sharing debenture bonds issued by corporations resident in the Netherlands. An exemption is granted if the shareholder is a company to which the exemption for 'substantial holdings' applies.
The rate of taxation is 25 per cent; the tax is withheld by the distributing corporation. Usually the dividend tax is credited against the Income Tax due from the share-holding individual or corporation. For non-resident shareholders, the dividend tax is normally a final tax without further liability to individual or corporate income tax. Under the treaties concluded between the Netherlands and several other nations to prevent double taxation, foreign shareholders pay a reduced rate on the dividends they receive.
In terms of Income Tax, the notion of 'dividend' comprises any amount transferred to the shareholder, provided the amount transferred is not a refund of capital. Therefore

every payment out of the profit to the shareholder of the corporation is dividend. In this view dividend is also what the shareholder receives more than the paid-up capital on the shares in case of liquidation of the corporation.
In case the corporation buys his own shares, the payment has to be split up in a refund of capital and a payment out of the profit (dividend). Bonus-shares issued against reserved profits are also considered as dividends of their nominal value; but if the bonus-shares are issued against the Share Premium Reserve, they are not counted as dividends. If preferential claims are awarded to the shareholders, then these claims are not counted as income.

2.5 *Relevant Acts*
Wet op de Inkomstenbelasting 1964, Wet van 16 december 1964, Staatsblad 519 (Income Tax Act 1964);
Wet op de Vermogensbelasting 1964, Wet van 16 december 1964, Staatsblad 520 (Net Wealth Tax Act 1964);
Wet op de Vennootschapsbelasting 1969, Wet van 8 oktober 1969, Staatsblad 469 (Corporate Income Tax Act 1969);
Wet op de Loonbelasting 1964, Wet van 16 december 1964, Staatsblad 521 (Wage Tax Act 1964);
Wet op de Dividendbelasting 1965, Wet van 23 december 1965, Staatsblad 621 (Dividend Tax Act 1965);
Algemene Wet inzake Rijksbelastingen, Wet van 2 juli 1959, Staatsblad 301 (General Act on State Taxes).

3. QUESTION :

Give name, date, and reference of exchange control regulations and similar provisions.

ANSWER :

The guilder is a strong currency and one of the currencies in the joint European float known as 'the snake' arrangement, whereby the countries concerned (the Netherlands, West Germany, Belgium, Luxembourg and Denmark) maintain 'spot' exchange rates with each other within margins of 2¼% above and below parity rates. The Netherlands will also participate in the proposed new European Monetary System.
The policy of the Netherlands Bank is to maintain national liquidity within reasonable boundaries and to prevent the guilder from appreciating unduly against other currencies.
To achieve these aims, the Bank has power to restrict imports and exports of capital, but at present in most cases, it merely requires that transactions be reported to it for statistical purposes so that it may take regulatory action if the need arises. What restrictions there are relate largely to

borrowing and lending rather than to movements of equity capital, although administrative procedures must be complied with in all cases.
If an exchange licence is required, it is usually applied for through one of the banks, or through a professional office familiar with exchange control procedures.
International receipts and payments must be made through authorized institutions - in practice, the commercial banks operating under general license from the Netherlands Bank.
Transactions between the Netherlands and other countries can in general be carried out in any currency, whether convertible or not. The main foreign exchange market is in Amsterdam, with another in Rotterdam. Rates for spot transactions and forward deliveries in the principal currencies of Western Europe, North America and Japan are published daily in these markets.

Relevant Acts :
Wet Financiële betrekkingen buitenland, Wet van 28 mei 1980 Staatsblad 321 (Foreign Financial Relationship Act 1980);
Uitvoeringsvoorschrift Buitenlands beroep op de Nederlandse kapitaalmarkt (UV 1981/3). (Execution Direction Foreign Demand on Dutch Capital Market);
Uitvoeringsvoorschrift Ter beschikking krijgen van gelden van niet-ingezetenen (UV 1981/4). (Execution Direction Dutch Demand on Foreign Capital Market).

II. EXPORT OF CAPITAL - DEFINITIVE.

1. QUESTION :

Is emigration of natural persons and/or legal entities limited generally or with regard to their property by administrative measures, especially exchange control regulations?
Please give a description of the law and how it is applied.

ANSWER :

The emigration of individuals.
In principal there are no administrative measures focused on the disability of emigration of individuals, and equally there are no cramping exchange control regulations.

The emigration of legal entities.
Legal entities established in accordance with Dutch law remain subject to Dutch tax laws irrespective the place of the real seat and irrespective the place of the activities. A Dutch legal entity cannot have its place of residence outside the Netherlands. Dutch law, however, can allow transfer of the place of residence abroad. The Voluntary Transfer of Residence

Act (Act of May 9, 1967, *Stb.* 161) and the Governmental Transfer of Residence Act (Act of May 9, 1967, *Stb.* 162) give a limited possibility to transfer the place of residence abroad. In accordance with these acts transfer of the place of residence to the Netherlands Antilles may take place in case of war, danger of war, revolution or comparable circumstances. When there is talk of emigration of a legal entity established in accordance with Dutch law this means in practice transfer of the real seat and/or transfer of the activities of that legal entity abroad.

Indeed there are some special cases in which tax problems may occur because the legislator dictates a settlement of the present reserves and goodwill (emigration is seen as a realisation). These cases will be discussed in paragraph 3.

2. QUESTION :

Is there a special tax on emigration of capital ('flight tax')?

ANSWER :

In the Netherlands no special tax is levied on emigration of capital.

3. QUESTION :

In the course of capital exportation there is often a problem of unrealized capital gains or other 'hidden reserves' (e.g.: as a consequence of depreciation allowances) which might escape taxation definitively unless they are taxed at the moment of their exportation. To attain such taxation export of capital assets in some countries is treated as a mode of realization. Does this problem exist in your country? If affirmative, please give a detailed description of the problem and the way it is handled.

ANSWER :

Concerning capital exportation we distinguish the export of private capital and the export of capital of an enterprise.

Export of private capital.
In the Netherlands capital gains on private capital are not texed. Excepted are capital gains on shares belonging to a substantial shareholding interest (see I.2.1).
In case of emigration no settlement has to be made, but the emigrating person who has a substantial shareholding interest in a Dutch resident legal entity, will still be subject to the Dutch tax laws concerning realized substantial shareholding

profit. In tax treaties the Netherlands, however, mostly insert the paragraph which confines taxation on substantial shareholding to profit arised within 5 years after emigration, as far as it concerns substantial shareholding interest in a Dutch resident legal entity.
Another tax burden may be created by the Inheritance Tax Act 1956 (Act of June 28, 1956, *Stb.* 362). This tax (*Successierecht*) is levied when property is inherited from either a resident of the Netherlands or a non-resident Dutch national who dies within ten years of his departure from the Netherlands.
Partial relief is granted for inheritance taxes paid abroad. Acquisitions from a spouse are exempted up to Dfl. 250,000.- Exemptions for minor children range from Dfl. 11,250.- to Dfl. 56,250.- depending on their ages.
There are further exemptions, for example in respect of adult children, parents and charities.

Export of capital of an enterprise.

1. As long as the entrepreneur has his residence in the Netherlands it is not relevant whether his enterprise is moved abroad or brought from abroad to the Netherlands. In both cases no profit realisation is taken. The consequences will appear when the entrepreneur emigrates.
   Distinction has to be made between :
   a. A domestic taxpayer emigrates. This means he gives up his Dutch residence;
      (aa) he continues his domestic enterprise (In the Netherlands remains also a permanent establishment). In this case the enterprise remains in the Netherlands. The entrepreneur becomes a foreign taxpayer: profits from the domestic enterprise remain taxable by the Dutch Income Tax. In the fiscal point of view domestic taxable profit is made. This is also the case in business economic point of view. If a person emigrates without taking his domestic enterprise with him, nothing changes in the economic point of view. There is no reason to state that according to good commercial usage the continuity of the balance sheet is interrupted. What difference would it make in this point of view where the entrepreneur lives. In this case there is no need to stop a 'loop-hole'. In the fiscal point of view, however, the domestic tax liability finishes and the foreign tax liability begins. Does this mean profit realisation? The termination of the domestic tax liability doesn't imply the enterprise to cease to be a source.
      The real profit calculation doesn't induce a fictious termination or a fictious begin of a respecti-

vely old and new source. In case of emigration, the source remains the same. The technical mutation of a domestic taxpayer into a foreign taxpayer doesn't have any effect on the profit figure of the enterprise.
The effect is merely of a fiscal nature, namely specific profits don't count anymore after emigration for the calculation of the taxable profit.
In the year of emigration this will lead to the fiscal technic of two assessments. But, in spite of it, the enterprise remains the same.
When, in case of emigration, the enterprise remains in the Netherlands, the bookkeeping has to be balanced. Because the enterprise doesn't terminate and the entrepreneur remains the same, the balance continuity will not be interrupted. The only thing the law orders in case of emigration is a separate calculation of the profit in the period before emigration.

(bb) he takes his enterprise abroad.
In this case he ceases his activities in the Netherlands: a settlement has to be made and realized profit is taxed.

(cc) he emigrates and continues his foreign enterprise.
The year of emigration is also the last year in which profit from the foreign enterprise can be taxed in the Netherlands, so profit realisation has to be taken.

(dd) he continues both his foreign enterprise and his domestic enterprise.
If an entrepreneur has a domestic enterprise (this means in the Netherlands remains a permanent establishment) and a foreign enterprise while the enterprise remain where they are, then profit realisation has to be taken concerning the foreign enterprise.
For every separate enterprise an investigation has to decide whether profit realisation has to be taken. Does this entrepreneur bring his domestic enterprise abroad after his emigration, then profit realisation has to be taken concerning this enterprise.

b. A foreign taxpayer 'emigrates' his domestic enterprise abroad.
Concerning this situation the same rules are applicable as in case 1.a.(bb). Tax will be levied on the surplus value of the capital.

2. Concerning the Corporate Income Tax we distinguish legal entities established in accordance with Dutch law and legal entities established in accordance with foreign law.
   a. Legal entities established in accordance with Dutch law are always domestic taxpayers and therefore subject to Dutch tax law for their world-wide profit.
      In case a legal entity established in accordance with Dutch law transfers its real seat abroad, for the levy of the Dutch Corporate Income Tax the place of residence however, remains in the Netherlands, except for deviating clauses in tax treaties.
      Transfer of the real seat abroad has no impact on the levying of Dutch taxes. In these cases no settlement has to be made, because the capital assets are not withdrawn from the Dutch Corporate Income Tax. The total profit is and will be taxed by Dutch tax.
   b. A legal entity established in accordance with foreign law, but with the real seat in the Netherlands, is a domestic taxpayer and therefore subject to Dutch Corporate Income Tax.
      (aa) In case of emigration of the real seat and with transfer of the enterprise a settlement has to be made : profit realisation has to be taken.
      (bb) Is only the enterprise transferred abroad, but remains the real seat of the legal entity in the Netherlands, then there are no fiscal consequences: no capital is withdrawn from the levying of Dutch taxes.
      (cc) Is only the real seat transferred abroad, but remains the enterprise in the Netherlands, then there are no fiscal consequences either : no capital is withdrawn from the levying of Dutch taxes.

3. Export of individual capital assets of an enterprise.
   A Dutch enterprise is, as already stated (see I.2.3) subject to Dutch tax law for its world-wide profit. The place where the profit is made is not relevant in principle.
   Export of individual capital assets to foreign branches doesn't imply profit realisation of hidden reserves and goodwill.
   In case an individual capital asset is transferred abroad to a foreign permanent establishment the calculation of the world-wide profit has still to be based on the Dutch bookkeeping value. The calculation of the profit of the permanent establishment (exempted from taxation in the Netherlands), however, will be based on the real value of that asset.
   Besides the tax burdens already mentioned before, another tax burden may be created in case an investment bounty was obtained and the enterprise or a part of it emigrates, a

settlement takes place when tax cannot be levied anymore on the profit of that enterprise. This occurs when the enterprise or the taxpayer/entrepreneur emigrates. In those cases these assets are deemed to be withdrawn from the enterprise, so that the obtained investment bounty has to be paid back.

4. QUESTION :

Are there any other important tax burdens on capital being exported definitively?

ANSWER :

Besides the tax burdens already mentioned (II.3) no other tax burdens have been created.

5. QUESTION :

How does the opinion prevalent in your country evaluate the measures described under nos. II.1 to II.4., especially under the aspects of economic policy and tax equity?

ANSWER :

As already stated above there is a capital export and a capital import on a considerable scale. This open movement is a characteristic of the Dutch economy and has to be maintained in opinion of the Dutch Central Bank.
Concerning the present-day actual situation the fact can be established that there is a far-reaching liberalisation. Real restrictions exist still in the movement of short-term capital in the private sector, while non-residents are not allowed to invest in the internal money market.
Measures have to take away the fear that our open economy leads to a loss of means of expenditure in favour of foreign countries.
The Dutch Central Bank warns against the thought of introduction of investment regulations. The offer of means of the capital market is not increased by it and there exists a considerable change the offer will be discouraged.The policy concerning the movement of capital abroad has an essential function for both the control of the growth of liquidity in the economy and the stimulation of the equilibrium of the balance of payments. In a sound balanced economic situation a structural balance on the current account has to compensate a shortage in the developing capital movement. A situation of shortage on the current account makes import of capital necessary.
A very fundamental objection against investment regulation is the replacement of the market mechanism of a larger part

of the financial markets by the budget mechanism. Moreover, investment regulations are in contravention of the genius of the EC-Treaty and Directives.

III. EXPORT OF CAPITAL - TEMPORARY

1. QUESTION :

Is transfer of capital to foreign countries, especially investment in foreign countries, limited by administrative measures (exchange control et al.) in your country? Please give a description of the law and how it is applied.

ANSWER :

There is no control on direct investments abroad. Concerning indirect investments, however, there are some restrictions. A resident may not lend to a nonresident by taking up bonds without an exchange license. In practice, a license will be granted readily if the transaction fits into the Netherlands Bank's timetable for the raising of capital.
A resident may make loans to any one or more nonresidents, who are permitted to borrow up to Dfl. 10 million each per calender year from that resident without a license being necessary. For larger amounts licenses are required, although at present they are readily granted. This Dfl. 10 million limit does not apply to authorized Dutch banks. Shares in nonresident companies may normally be acquired by residents or resident companies without restriction.
In general, current transactions by Dutch residents or resident companies may be effected without limitation through the authorized banks on production of a simple reporting from to the bank concerned.
Residents may also effect settlements through accounts at foreign banks or by book entries in current or intercompany accounts, provided that The Netherlands Bank is informed in writing of the existence of such accounts; this rule also extends to nonmonetary transactions, even if of a capital nature, such as the subscription of share capital by the delivery of inventories or equipment.

Imports and exports of goods or services are free of controls except for certain strategic goods and works of art. The granting of credit in respect of imports and exports should be reported to the Netherlands Bank when payment is to be made, in full or in part, 12 months or more before or after delivery, respectively. If such long credit is not the usual practice in the trade concerned, an exchange license must be obtained.

2. QUESTION :

If investment consist in material assets : does the problem of taxation of 'hidden reserves' as described above (no. II.3) arise and how is it dealt with?

ANSWER :

As in case of definite capital exportation in this situation distinction can be made as well between :

a. Export of private capital.
   No Dutch tax is levied on temporary transfer of private capital (wealth) abroad.
b. Export of capital of an enterprise.
   If an asset is transferred temporary to the permanent establishment, it will still belong to the head-office. If the asset is sold after the temporary transfer the possible profit made by selling the asset is considered as domestic profit and fully taxed in the Netherlands.
   The only fact an asset is temporary transferred abroad does not cause profit realisation.

3. QUESTION :

Does your country tax income from foreign investments and, if your answer is in the affirmative, how?

ANSWER :

The Netherlands taxes income from foreign investments. Either by the Income Tax or by the Corporate Income Tax (see I.2). However the Dutch tax system includes an absolute tax exemption (and not a tax-credit) for profits made in other countries by branch-offices or subsidiairies. This means that for holding companies there is a tax system which is very favourable compared to most other countries.
The main characteristic of the Dutch holding company system is the participation exemption (*deelnemingsvrijstelling*), a complete tax exemption for dividends, capital gains and losses.

3.1 QUESTION :

Is income from foreign investments taxable and under which presuppositions? Please give a detailed specification.

ANSWER :

See III.3.

3.2 QUESTION :

How are taxes in the country of investment allowed for in the absence of a tax treaty, simply as cost, by giving a credit or in any other way?

ANSWER :

To avoid imposition of double taxation in respect of foreign income, relief is provided by :
1. Unilateral measures - Royal Decree of April 7, 1965;
2. A comprehensive network of double taxation agreements.

Unilateral measures for avoiding double taxation apply only to those elements of income specifically defined in the 1965 Royal Decree as amended, provided that they were subject to a tax on income levied by another sovereign power. In principle, it is sufficient that the foreign-source income is subject to such a tax; it is not necessary for the tax to have been actually levied or paid. For instance, it may be that the income is so low that it is below the relevant tax exemption limit. Unilateral provisions apply only where no treaties exist or no other relief measures are applicable.
If the above condition is met, relief is granted through a proportional reduction in Dutch taxation according to the following formula :

$$\frac{\text{Foreign income}}{\text{Total taxable income}}$$

x Dutch tax on total taxable income

= Amount of tax reduction.

Dutch tax on total taxable income is thus reduced by Dutch income tax attibutable to the foreign-source income. As corporate income tax rates are progressive only to a small degree, unilateral relief for corporations in most cases effectively represents a total exemption of foreign-source income.
When there is a loss from foreign sources, such loss can be set off against domestic profits. However, to avoid relief for foreign losses being given twice, relief for foreign income is reduced by any foreign losses incurred in the preceding six years. Where, however, there is a domestic loss and a foreign profit in one year, relief cannot be granted in respect of the full amount of foreign profit. In such circumstances the excess foreign profit may be carried forward for offset in any of the following six years.
Any foreign taxes suffered that are not eligible for relief under either unilateral provisions or the terms of a double

taxation agreement may be deducted from Dutch taxable income and treated as an expense.
As from 1976 the taxpayer may elect to deduct foreign withholding taxes from Dutch taxable income as expenses even when the unilateral provisions or a double taxation agreement provide for a tax credit against Dutch income tax. Such election is useful, for instance, when the Dutch taxpayer is not in a position to claim a tax credit.

3.3 QUESTION :

Has your country concluded any tax treaties?
Following the credit or the exemption method?
Do they contain tax sparing clauses (generally, or in which cases)?

ANSWER :

Double taxation agreements concluded by the Netherlands generally provide for the avoidance of double taxation in a manner comparable to the unilateral measures that have been described above. Almost all agreements provide for reduced rates of foreign and Dutch withholding taxes. In addition, some treaties provide that foreign withholding taxes on dividends, interest and royalties are to be allowed as credits against the Dutch tax arising on such income. This is accomplished in basically the same way as unilateral relief for interest and royalties received from developing countries.
Most general double taxation agreements negotiated by the Netherlands relating to income and capital gains have followed the draft model published by the Organization for Economic Cooperation and Development in 1963 and replaced by the 1977 OECD Model Convention.
General agreements are in force with Australia, Austria, Belgium, Canada, Czechoslovakia, Denmark, Finland, France, Germany (Federal Republic), Hungary, Indonesia, Ireland, Israel, Italy, Japan, Luxembourg, Malta, Morocco, Norway, Singapore, South Africa, Spain, Surinam, Sweden, Switzerland, Thailand, U.K. and U.S.A. Double taxation in relations with the Netherlands Antilles is avoided by a special law.

Tax sparing credit-method

By the tax sparing credit-method a higher credit is given by the country of residence than the real tax burden in the developing country. In this way the tax incentive given by the developing country is not undone by the taxation system in the country of residence. The Netherlands give tax sparing credit in the tax treaties with : Indonesia, Israel, Korea, Malta, Singapore, Spain, Surinam and Zambia.

3.4 QUESTION :

Summing up the last two questions : if a tax advantage is granted in the country of investment (a lower tax rate, a tax incentive etc.), will an investor residing in your country be able to retain this advantage or will it be consumed by domestic taxation (as it normally is in the case with the credit system)?

ANSWER :

Because of the several systems to avoid double taxation in answering this question a distinction has to be made between:

(1) profit derived from a foreign investment under the Royal Decree 1965 : proportional reduction is granted;
(2) profit derived from a foreign investment under a tax treaty : proportional reduction is granted;
(3) profit derived from a foreign investment under a tax treaty : tax sparing credit-method.

ad (1) and (2) : In these cases the amount of the reduction is independent of the tax paid abroad (see 3.2) A granted tax advantage abroad is retained by the investor.

ad (3) : As stated before (see 3.3) the tax sparing credit-method gives a higher credit than the real tax burden abroad. The granted tax advantage abroad is not consumed by domestic taxation.

3.5 QUESTION :

Can taxation of foreign income be avoided by founding a separate legal entity (corporation, trust or the like) in the country of investment or in a third country, as long as the earnings are not repatriated? Are there rules designed to combat such avoidance or rules designed for other purposes but apt to be used for this special purpose (like rules about sham transactions)? Please give a not too extended description.

ANSWER :

The concept of management and control is fundamental to Dutch tax legislation. This concept, central to anti-avoidance legislation, is that if one company is so managed and controlled by another that it cannot be considered to have a separate identity, then, similarly, it cannot be considered to be taxed separately : instead, its income will be included in the controlling company's income for tax purposes. Thus, if a Dutch company, for example, decides to reduce its domestic tax burden by establishing a Hong Kong company which then levies tax at the rate of 17% on profits instead of the 48% Dutch tax otherwise payable, it would do so in the hope that profits could be shifted from a high-tax regime and that tax is avoided thereon. It may well be that the directors of the Dutch company have never been to Hong Kong, that trade is still carried on by the staff or the Dutch company and that, to all intents and purposes, it is still the Dutch company carrying on trade throughout the world; the only difference is that the invoices are made out in the name of the Hong Kong company, which is in fact therefore only a paper organization. It is clear that the management of the Hong Kong company is effected in the Netherlands and that control of the Hong Kong company is also in the hands of the Dutch company. Such a blatant 'tax avoidance scheme' is clearly unacceptable, and the profits of the Hong Kong company will be subject to tax in the Netherlands.

If, however, there is a commercial reason for incorporating a Hong Kong company to trade in the Far East and if the Hong Kong company is properly constituted with directors who are active in the day-to-day management of the company, then the management and control of the Hong Kong company is vested in Hong Kong. It does not matter that the Dutch company has control or the Hong Kong company : *any* parent company has ultimate control of its foreign subsidiary if it has a majority interest in it. In this latter case, management of the Hong Kong company is local and, although the Dutch company's directors may be involved in the management of the Hong Kong company, the individuality of the foreign company is still preserved. Hong Kong tax is therefore levied and, if dividends are remitted to the Dutch parent, this income will be tax exempt in the Netherlands as a result of the qualifying participation privilege.

It is not always cristal clear whether management and control is vested locally or with the parent company; it may often be the case that management and control is not entirely local and that the foreign parent may be held to administer the affairs of the local subsidiairy. However, if the two countries involved have entered into a double tax treaty, it should be easier to decide under the relevant provisions of the treaty which country has the right to impose its taxes on profits earned. If the two countries have not entered into a double tax treaty - and this may signify that one country has a high-tax regime and the other a low-tax one - then a case may be brought by the tax authorities of one country to impose its taxes on foreign profits, in which case consideration must be given to the reason why the foreign company was formed.

If no commercial reason can be attributed to the formation or the foreign company other than tax avoidance, the plaintiff tax authorities may be successful. If other reasons exist, then a succesful defence may be made. Thus, the principle of management and control, although the basis on which the above claims may be made, is a flexible one.
It should be noted that it may not only be the parent company that manages and controls the subsidiairy, but a subsidiairy company that manages and controls its parent. Thus, the shareholders of the company may divest their shares to a foreign entity to avoid tax on dividend income; however, such an attempt to avoid tax would be unsuccessful if the management and control principle held that the parent had no separate identity apart from the fact that it had been legally constituted.
Considering another aspect of the above example of the Hong Kong subsidiairy and the Dutch parent : there is no double tax treaty between the Netherlands and Hong Kong and, therefore, the question of management and control of the Hong Kong company is vital in determining whether or not the Dutch authorities will tax the profits earned by that company. If Dutch taxation is imposed, the taxpayer will end up paying 17% Hong Kong tax plus Dutch tax at the rate of 48% on the net profit received or receivable by the Dutch company i.e. the gross profits of the Hong Kong company less 17% tax. The total tax rate is therefore approximately 57%, leaving only 43% of gross income after tax, as opposed to 52% had no foreign subsidiairy been incorporated.
If the Dutch company had incorporated a foreign subsidiairy in a country which has a tax treaty with the Netherlands - such as Switzerland - even though Switzerland has a lower tax rate than the Netherlands, the Swiss company may still be held to be a separate entity in accordance with the tax treaty and Dutch tax may not be imposed on the Swiss company's profits. However, íf the Swiss company has earned income at the expense of the Dutch company, which would not have been the case of there were no special relationship between the Swiss and the Dutch companies (i.e. parent and subsidiairy), then the profits of the Swiss company may be adjusted to reflect what would have been earned on a purely arm's-length basis and, likewise, the profits of the Dutch company would be adjusted and Dutch tax would be payable on the undisclosed income.
The incorporation of a foreign company in order to save tax, where that foreign company is obviously only incorporated for tax avoidance reasons and has no substance in actual effective management, will often not be successful. If the foreign company is incorporated in a country which has a double tax treaty with the domestic country, then the foreign company may be taxed separately but, even so, the absence of effective

management may negate successful tax avoidance. For example, a Dutch holding company of a Swiss subsidiairy, which has been formed purely to obtain the benefit of the 35% refund of the Swiss anticipatory tax withheld on dividends remitted to Dutch parents, will not receive the full refund of it was incorporated solely to take advantage of the tax treaty provisions (article 9(2)(a) of the 1966 Switzerland/Netherlands Double Tax Treaty).
Double taxation in relation with the Netherlands Antilles is avoided by a special law (see 3.3) In several cases foreign profit is leaded through a Netherlands Antilles subsidiairy in order to save tax using the low tax regime of the Netherlands Antilles.

4. QUESTION :

Does your country give tax incentives for investing abroad (generally or in certain cases as, e.g., for investment in developing countries)?

ANSWER :

In general the Netherlands doesn't give any tax incentives for investing abroad.
An exception is made for investments in developing countries. A Royal Decree amending the Decree of 1965 has provided special relief from double taxation in respect of dividends, interest and royalties received from residents in developing countries by way of tax credit.
Where dividends, interest and royalties received from residents of such countries have been subject to a local income tax, either by way of assessment or as a withholding tax, such tax may be credited directly against Dutch tax payable on such income. The relief granted in the lower of the foreign taxes paid or the Dutch income tax on the related income less costs. If the effective rate of Dutch income tax is lower, than the foreign taxes paid, any difference may be credited in any of the next six years against Dutch tax arising in that period. However, the credit against Dutch tax in these years cannot be higher than the relevant Dutch tax on the foreign-source income in those same years.

5. QUESTION :

What does the opinion prevalent in your country think of the rules described under 3 and 4 under the aspects of economic policy and tax equity? If there are important voices, please give citations. Please give your personal judgement and reasoning too.

ANSWER :

The systems described under 3 and 4 are fully accepted in the Netherlands. It is not disputed and one may count on it that the systems will prevail until maybe some EEC directive will forсe us to abandon it. However, the Dutch try to interest the other EEC countries to adopt the system in the whole EEC.

IV.

1. QUESTION :

What is your country's position with regard to investment of foreigners in your country?
If there are official statements, please give citations.

ANSWER :

Foreign investments are welcomed in the Netherlands.
Usually, the status of a foreign-owned company is exactly the same as that of a purely Dutch enterprise. There are no special rules to be followed by foreign-owned business, apart from a few exchange control formalities.
With only minor exceptions, there are no rules requiring Dutch participation in capital or management of any enterprise registered in the Netherlands, nor are there usually any restrictions on foreign companies operation in particular places or trades, or owning real estate. No objections are normally raised to the employment of skilled foreign managers or specialist staff, provided that entry requirements have been complied with.
Moreover, some of the rules restricting the powers of shareholders in large enterprise have been specifically relaxed for foreign-owned enterprises.

1.1 QUESTION :

Are there administrative regulations to control or prevent investment ?

ANSWER :

Short-term financial loans from abroad are not allowed (UV 1981-4 art. 2 etc. See I.3).

TAX AVOIDANCE

Concerning investments on long-term basis liberal measures are taken by EEC and OECD.
The Netherlands is even more liberal than the OECD-code dictates.

1.2 QUESTION :

Are there tax incentives for or against investment of foreign capital? Please give a detailed description.

ANSWER :

Dutch tax legislation contains many provisions that can operate to the significant advantage of a foreign investor, the most important being :

1. Advantageous computation rules :
   (a) Ability to use LIFO and base stock methods in valuing inventories, thus avoiding taxation of inflationary inventory increases. (The FIFO methods may also be used if appropriate).
   (b) Deferral of tax by the use of tax-free reserves. The principal reserve of this type is that used to hold gains from sales of fixed assets until they are replaced, but reserves for future asset maintenance and self-insurance may also be established.
2. Exemption from Dutch tax on a Dutch company's dividend income and capital gains arising from substantial participations in Dutch or foreign companies.
   This important provision is known as the 'participation exemption' or 'affiliation privilege'.
3. Ability to carry forward losses for six years or carry them back for two years. Losses incurred in the first six years of trading may be carried forward indefinitely.
4. Ability to file a consolidated tax return to combine the profits and losses of Dutch companies that are members of a group in which the subsidiaries are wholly-owned by their Dutch parent company. This is known as a 'fiscal unity'. It is also sometimes possible to obtain relief for losses in foreign subsidiaries by writing down loans to those subsidiaries .
5. A comprehensive tax treaty network that largely eliminates double taxation.
6. A complete absence of withholding taxes on interest (except interest on profit-sharing bonds), royalties, management fees and branch profits.
7. Rules on intercompany pricing helping to eliminate problems concerning the deductibility of expenses.

8. A rate of corporate tax of 48% with no additional city or state taxes on income.
9. No tax on capital gains as these are either taxed as income or exempt (See point 3 above). Conversely, capital losses unless they arise from substantial participations.
10. No disadvantageous treatment of foreign investors compared with Dutch resident investors. Companies are taxed under the 'classical system' rather than by the 'imputation' system found in some neighbouring countries, which may be discriminatory against foreign investors.
11. A system of substantial tax-free bonuses (known as 'WIR') that take the place of the investment allowances and accelerated depreciation deductions granted in other countries.

1.3 QUESTION :

Is repatriation of income received from such investment subject to control and/or restrictions? Please give a detailed description.

ANSWER :

Repatriation of income received from investments in the Netherlands is not limited neither by control regulations nor by restrictions of any kind.

2. QUESTION :

Does the opinion prevalent in your country feel that desirable investment in your country is hampered by tax measures of capital-exporting countries which are unfavourable to importing countries? If possible, please give a specification of such measures and of the countries applying them.
What is your personal judgement ?

ANSWER :

Investment in the Netherlands is not hampered by tax measures in other countries.

V. ADDITIONAL INFORMATION

QUESTION :

Please give any additional information which in your opinion might be useful to the General Reporter for understanding the problems treated, especially the legal and economic situation of your country, the measures adopted, and so might give additional help to him in preparing his report.

ANSWER :

International groups of companies very often find it convenient to have a centralized finance company through which all group financing is arranged. The participation exemption mentioned earlier is of great importance to an international holding company in the Netherlands.
No withholding tax is levied on interest paid.
The Netherlands has a network of tax treaties that regulate the restitution of advance levies abroad.

Aut dedere, aut judicare

NICO KEIJZER

Professor of criminal law at the Free University, Amsterdam

V.A.2.

I. GENERAL OBSERVATIONS

The idea behind the maxim *aut dedere, aut judicare* originally stems from Grotius. He wrote in 1625 :

> "... *since the organization of states, it is agreed that the crimes of individuals, in so far as they properly concern the community to which they belong, should be left to the states themselves and their rulers, to be punished or condoned at their discretion. But so comprehensive a right has not been granted to states and their rulers in the case of crimes which in some way affect human society, and which it is the right of other states and their rulers to follow up ...*
> *Much less do states and their rulers possess this full authority in the case of crimes by which another state or its ruler is in a special sense injured, and on account of which that ruler or state, for the sake of dignity or security, has the right to exact punishment, in accordance with our previous conclusions. Therefore, the state in which the guilty person dwells, or its ruler, ought not to interfere with this right. Since as a matter of fact states are not accustomed to permit other states to cross their borders with an armed force for the purpose of exacting punishment, and since such a course is inexpedient, it follows that the state in which he who has been found guilty dwells ought to do one of two things.* When appealed to, *it should either punish the guilty person as he deserves, or it should entrust him to the discretion of the party making the appeal. This latter course is rendition, a procedure more frequently mentioned in historical narratives.(...) All these examples nevertheless must be interpreted in the sense that a people or king is not absolutely bound to surrender a culprit, but, as we have said, either to surrender or to punish him.*" [1]

In the present day, his words possess an astonishing actuality. During the 18th and 19th centuries, under the influence of the idea that the law of a state resulted from a social contract between its members, prosecution of foreigners for offences committed abroad was not very common and, unless their own direct interests should be affected by the offence, states often did not even establish jurisdiction over such acts. A change has occurred, however. By the tremendous growth of international communication and by the increasing consciousness of planetary limitations, the family of nations is now more tied together than ever before, notwithstanding the hostility existing between some of its members. Under these circumstances there are many offences which "affect human society".
Accordingly, the rule *aut dedere aut judicare* has nowadays been laid down in a number of international conventions that have been made in order to improve the suppression of offences that are a common threat to mankind, such as the counterfeiting of currency, the misuse of narcotic drugs, or acts of terrorism. In several of those conventions, the participating states have undertaken to make certain conduct a criminal offence under their own criminal law[2]. On the other hand, provisions were adopted in order to make such offences extraditable offences between the participating states[3].
They further undertook to establish the jurisdiction necessary for having the suspects of such offences, even if they were foreigners who committed their acts abroad, prosecuted before their courts if they should not be extradited[4], and, for that purpose, to submit such cases to their competent authorities[5].
By these means, the perpetrators of such offences have to an important extent been deprived of their possibilities of finding in countries other than those in which they committed their offences, a safe refuge from prosecution. Therefore, these treaties must be welcomed as an important step forward in giving effect to the solidarity among nations.
Two caveats must however be made.

In the first place, attention should be drawn to the fact that this development tends to over-ride national differences in criminal policies. Unrestricted introduction of the rule *aut dedere aut judicare* could in effect imply that a state would be obliged to prosecute any offence at any place committed by any suspect found on its territory, unless he should be extradited for it. This would, of course, be unacceptable to states that are jealous of their own ideas of a just criminal policy in accordance with their national traditions and circumstances. Therefore, unless certain restrictions are made that prevent undue foreign interference in national criminal policies, the achievement of a common suppression of offences which are a common threat may be jeopardized by states being

hesitant or averse to unnecessarily giving up their national identities in the field of criminal law.
In this respect, the following restrictions should be taken into account.

A. The scope of offences to which the rule *aut dedere, aut judicare* is made applicable should be restricted to those offences that indeed are commonly perceived as serious offences. Important differences in the national tolerances occur in certain fields, such as those of pornography, homosexuality, the use of soft drugs, etc. Such differences should be respected[6].

B. There are also differences, among states, concerning the discretionary power that is given to the prosecuting authorities for deciding whether or not to prosecute a case, taking regard of the public interest. In treaty provisions, the rule *aut dedere, aut judicare* should therefore be laid down in such a way that they remain acceptable to states that believe in vesting their prosecuting authorities with that power of discretion. For *judicare* the wording "submit to its competent authorities for the purpose of prosecution" is preferable to "prosecute", if only for the reason that it avoids making prosecution obligatory in cases where it would be bound to fail for the very reason that blocked the extradition, such as prescription, or an earlier conviction for the same fact[7].
The discretion granted to those authorities does not necessarily make the treaty provision an idle clause, because they can be obliged to take their decision in the same manner as in the case of any offence of a serious nature[8].

C. Furthermore, differences among states exist with regard to the principles according to which criminal jurisdiction is established. For example, according to the Anglo-American tradition, application of any other than the territoriality principle is exceptional, while many countries on the European continent have adopted more far-reaching possibilities of prosecuting offences that have been committed on the territory of other states.
By undertaking the obligation of establishing representative jurisdiction concerning any person found on their territory who is suspected of a certain offence and whose requested extradition cannot be accorded, states would force themselves to represent the requesting state in applying jurisdiction principles, such as the protective principle or the active or passive personality principle, in which they possibly do not believe themselves.

> In order to prevent states from renouncing participation for this reason, it is advisable that treaty provisions are worded in such a way that the representative jurisdiction, that parties undertake to establish, concerns only those cases of refused extradition requests that are based on a principle of jurisdiction equally existing in the law of the requested state[9].

In the second place, it should be taken into account that extradition and prosecution are not equal alternatives. Apart from exceptions, such as the case of a political offence, trial in the state where the offence has been committed is generally preferable to trial in the state where the suspect has been captured, evidence normally being better available in the first state. If prosecution by the state where the suspect has been found results in an acquittal because of lack of evidence, this verdict may even block a later prosecution by the state where the evidence is available, by force of the rule *ne bis in idem*.[10] For this reason, a requesting state whose request for extradition has been denied might prefer awaiting the moment that the person claimed may come within its reach, to seeing that person prosecuted by the requested state. Therefore, the maxim *aut dedere, aut judicare* should be construed in such a way that the state on whose territory the offence has been committed has the primary responsibility for prosecuting the case, while prosecution by the state where the suspect has been found is only a secondary duty. Accordingly, the latter states obligation to submit the case to its prosecuting authorities should be made subject to the condition that, extradition having been requested and refused, the requesting state has made an application to that effect[11].

Although these observations may seem to be inspired by a certain provincialism, the present author hopes, to the contrary, that they may add to a convinced and fruitful cooperation between nations, in criminal matters, where their common interests are at stake.

II. ANSWERS TO THE QUESTIONNAIRE

Q. 1. : What are the bases of extradition in your state?

The bases of extradition by the State of the Netherlands are the extradition treaties, bilateral or multilateral, that have been made with other states[12]. The Extradition Act (1967) holds rules of procedures, guide lines to be followed by the government when making extradition treaties[13], and guide-lines for the interpretation of certain provisions made in those treaties, such as the requirement of double criminality. Consequently, in case of conflict between a provision of an extradition treaty and the Extradition Act, the treaty provision prevails[14].

Q. 2. : Is there a duty to extradite?

In the extradition treaties, the contracting parties undertake to extradite all persons whose extradition is requested by the (or an) other contracting party, subject to the conditions laid down in the treaty. Therefore, if those conditions are fulfilled, there is a duty to extradite.

Q. 3. : Is there a duty to prosecute as an alternative to extradition?

In a number of treaties to which the Netherlands are a party, the maxim *aut dedere aut judicare* has been incorporated[15]. If it does not extradite an alleged offender[16], the State of the Netherlands is obliged, under the provisions of those treaties, to submit the case to its competent authorities for the purpose of prosecution.
Under the law of the Netherlands[17], however, and the treaty provisions just mentioned do not interfere with that rule[18], the prosecuting authorities have the power of waiving any case whose prosecution is not deemed to be in the public interest.

Q. 4. : Is the duty to extradite or prosecute if it exists alternative or coexistent?

According to most extradition treaties to which the State of the Netherlands is a party, the alleged offender shall [19] not be extradited if he is being prosecuted by the requested state for the same offence for which extradition was requested[20].
On the other hand, the case against an alleged offender whose extradition has been granted will normally be waived, prosecution not being in the public interest. The duties are therefore not coexistent.

Q. 5. : Under which of the bases of extradition does the duty to extradite or prosecute arise?

The duty to extradite or to submit the case to the competent authorities for the purpose of prosecution only arises under the relevant treaties[21].

Q. 6. : If a duty to extradite or prosecute exists, how does it arise and how is it applied procedurally?

According to the procedure laid down in the Extradition Act, if a person who is being suspected of having committed an offence abroad has been caught on the territory of the State of the Netherlands, and a request for his extradition has been received, the Minister of Justice will have the case brought before a Court which must investigate whether the legal conditions for extradition have been fulfilled.
If the Court decides that the requested extradition is inadmissible, or if the Minister of Justice refuses the extradition on other grounds (such as a special hardship resulting from the requested person's age or state of health, or the well-founded belief that the request was made for the purpose of prosecuting or punishing a person on account of his religious or political conviction, or the nationality, race or population section to which he belongs[22]) extradition will not be granted. Should the request concern an offence to which the rule *aut dedere aut judicare* applies, then the state (i.e. the Minister of Justice) would, normally from that moment on, be obliged to submit the case to the prosecuting authorities, if this had not already previously been done.
Under the Hague and Montreal Conventions, however, which do not contain the condition of an extradition request actually being made and refused, the duty to submit the case to the prosecuting authorities exists from the very moment that the suspect has been found.
The same is true for the Geneva convention for the suppression of counterfeiting currency (1929), as far as nationals are concerned[23].

Q. 7. : If such a duty exists, what is the legal position or responsibility of the state that fails to carry out such a duty?

If the state should fail to carry out an extradition to which it is obliged, it would violate the extradition treaty and expose itself to any diplomatic steps or measures the requesting state might choose to take.
Eventually, the Minister of Justice would have to answer in Parliament for having caused a diplomatic incident. If the State, when obliged to submit a case to its prosecuting authorities, should fail to do so, the same would, in theory, apply. If this obligation would indeed have been fulfilled, however, but the prosecuting authorities (who are ultimately subordinate to the Minister of Justice) waive the case for preponderant reasons of public interest, the effect would in practice be the same, but no international obligation would

have been violated[24]. Again, the Minister is answerable in Parliament for his policy in criminal matters.

Q. 8. : If the duty to extradite, or the duty to extradite or prosecute, does not exist, is there any other legal obligation incumbant upon the state denying extradition?

In general, no other obligation rests on the State of the Netherlands denying extradition or prosecution to which it is not obliged. However, under circumstances, international custom perhaps requires precautionary measures to be taken[25]. The Aliens Act (1965) provides for the possibility of aliens being taken into custody pending their expulsion if public order or safety so require[26].
The problem of disguised extradition will not be dealt with in this paper.

Q. 9. : See Q. 10.

Q. 10. : What substantive or procedural rights or remedies does a requesting state have vis à vis a requested state that denies extradition and fails to prosecute?

If the requested state fails to fulfil its international obligation under the extradition treaty in force between the two states, the requesting state may take recourse to any peaceful means of settling the dispute such as degrading its diplomatic representation in the requested state, or bringing the case before the International Court of Justice.

NOTES

1. *De jure belli ac pacis*, Liber II, Caput XXI, para III-1,2, IV-1,3; Translation F.W. Kelsey, ed. The Classics of International Law, Oxford/London 1925 (italics added, N.K.).
2. E.g. Convention for the suppression of counterfeiting currency (Geneva 1929), Art. 3; Red Cross Convention (Geneva, 1949), Art. 49, 50, 129, 146 respectively; Single Convention on narcotic drugs (New York, 1961) Art. 36-1; Convention on Psychotropic substances (Vienna, 1971) Art. 22-1(a); O.A.S. Convention to prevent and punish the acts of terrorism taking the form of crimes against persons and related extortion that are of international significance (Washington, 1971), Art. 1,8 d; Convention on the prevention and punishment of crimes against internationally protected persons, including diplomatic agents (New York, 1973) Art. 2; International Convention against the taking of hostages (New York, 1979) Art. 1,2; Convention on the physical protection of nuclear materials (Vienna, New York, 1980) Art. 7.
3. E.g. Convention for the suppression of counterfeiting currency (Geneva, 1929) Art. 10; Convention for the suppression of unlawful seizure of aircraft (The Hague, 1970) Art. 8; Convention for suppression acts against the safety of civil aviation (Montreal, 1971) Art. 8; Convention on the prevention and punishment of crimes against internationally protected persons, including diplomatic agents (New York, 1973) Art. 8-1; European convention for the suppression of terrorism (Strasbourg, 1977) Art. 4; International Convention against the taking of hostages (New York, 1979) Art. 10.
4. Convention for the suppression of unlawful seizure of aircraft (The Hague 1970) Art. 4-2; Convention for the suppression of unlawful acts against the safety of civil aviation (Montreal, 1971) Art. 5-2; Convention on the prevention and punishment of crimes against internationally protected persons, including diplomatic agents (New York, 1973) Art. 3; European Convention on the suppression of terrorism (Strasbourg, 1977) Art. 6; International Convention against the taking of Hostages (New York, 1975) Art. 5.
5. Hague Convention (1970) Art. 7; Montreal Convention (1971) Art. 7; New York Convention (1973) Art. 7; Strasbourg Convention (1977) Art. 7; New York Convention (1979) Art. 8. Similar provisions have been laid down in: The International Convention for the suppression of counterfeiting currency (Geneva, 1929) Art. 8,9; the Red Cross Conventions (Geneva, 1949) Art. 49, 50, 129 and 146 respectively; the Single Convention on narcotic drugs (New York, 1961) Art. 36-2 (iv.); the O.A.S. Convention to prevent and punish the acts of terrorism taking the form of crimes against persons that are of international significance (Washington, 1971) Art. 5.
6. Unlike, for example, the Convention on psychotropic substances (Vienna, 1971) Art. 2, by which the power of determining which psychotropic substances should come under the criminal law is delegated by the participant states to an international organization. The State of the Netherlands is not a party to this convention.
7. A similar result is reached by adopting a provision such as Art. 36-4 of the Single Convention on narcotic drugs (New York, 1961): "Nothing contained in this article shall affect the principle that the offences to which it refers shall be defined, prosecuted and punished in conformity with the domestic law of a Party".
8. See for example, the provisions mentioned in note 24.
9. E.g. Art. 6 of the European Convention on the suppression of terrorism. See also the Explanatory Report to this convention, par. 55, 56.
10. Autrefois acquit, or autrefois convict.
11. Examples of treaty provisions that do not make this condition are the Hague Convention (1970) Art. 7; the Montreal Convention (1971) Art. 7; the New York Convention (1979) Art. 7. To the latter convention, the State of the Netherlands is not yet a party.
12. "No extradition will take place unless on the basis of a treaty", is stated in art. 2 of the Extradition Act. (1967).
13. ".... and the general conditions under which treaties with foreign states concerning the extradition of aliens can be made .... shall be laid down by statute". (Art. 4 of the Netherlands Constitution, to which the opening words of the Extradition Act refer).
14. Supreme Court decisions HR 13-3-1973, *NJ* 1973-289 and HR 22-7-1974, *NJ* 1974-501. Under the Netherlands Constitution, ratification of treaties is subject to parliamentary approval (Art. 60). In case of conflict between a self-

executing treaty provision and an Act of Parliament, the treaty provision prevails (Art. 66).

15. - The Convention for the Suppression of Counterfeiting Currency (Geneva, 1929) Art. 8, 9.
    - The Red Cross Conventions (Geneva, 1949), Art. 49, 50, 129, 146 respectively.
    - The Single Convention on narcotic drugs (New York, 1961), Art. 36-2 (iv).
    - The Convention for the suppression of unlawful seizure of aircraft (The Hague, 1970), Art. 7.
    - The Convention for the suppression of unlawful acts against the safety of civil aviation (Montreal, 1971), Art. 7.
    - The International Convention against the taking of hostages (New York, 1973) Art. 8.
    - The European Convention on the Suppression of Terrorism (Strasbourg, 1977), Art. 7. Ratification of the latter convention is still pending.

    The Geneva Convention (1929), the Red Cross Convention (1949) and the New York Single Convention (1961) do not contain provisions obliging the parties to establish the jurisdiction, necessary for prosecution as an alternative to extradition.
16. The condition that extradition should have been actually requested has neither been made in the Red Cross Conventions, nor in the Hague and Montreal Conventions mentioned in the previous reference. In the Geneva Convention for the Suppression of Counterfeiting Currency (1929), it has only been made in relation to offences committed by foreigners abroad (Art. 9).
17. Art. 167-2 and Art. 242-2 of the Netherlands Code of Criminal Procedure.
18. According to Art. 36-2 (iv) of the Single Convention on narcotic drugs (New York, 1961), serious offences shall be prosecuted. See, however, note 7.
19. Under the European Convention on Extradition (Paris, 1957), Art. 8, and under the extradition treaty with Belgium and Luxemburg (Brussels, 1962), Art. 7, this provision is optional.
20. The prosecution may, for this reason, be suspended by order of the Minister of Justice. Art. 9 (2), Extradition Act.
21. See note 15.
22. Art. 10, Extradition Act.
23. See note 16.
24. The convention for the suppression of unlawful seizure of aircraft (The Hague, 1970), Art. 7; the Convention for the suppression of unlawful acts against the safety of civil aviation (Montreal, 1971), Art. 7, and the European Convention on the suppression of terrorism (Strasbourg, 1977), Art. 7, require that the prosecuting authorities shall take their decision in the same manner as in the case of any offence of a serious nature.
25. When the Netherlands government, in 1920, refused the extradition of the German ex-Emperor, it assumed the duty to take the necessary measures of precaution and of submitting his liberty to limitations in order to safeguard international security. (Diplomatic note to the British government, 2nd March 1920, published *W* 10529).
26. Art. 26, Aliens Act.

The problem of the lawyer and client in criminal cases

G. SPONG

Lawyer, member of the Bar, The Hague

V.B.1.

Introduction.
I. General considerations on the position of the counsel.
II. Stages of criminal procedure and the related problems of the counsel/client.
III. The counsel in juvenile criminal cases.
IV. Defence in political criminal cases.

INTRODUCTION.

A great deal has been written in Dutch legal literature about the problems of the lawyer in criminal cases. In 1921 the idea was prevalent that a lawyer with a good reputation would not act in a criminal case on principle, except in special circumstances; by 1950 the function of the counsel in criminal cases was being described as such a lofty and worthy thing, *provided that it was properly performed*, partly because of its social aspects, that any lawyer who realised this and had any experience of it would have discovered a sense of great fulfilment in dealing in particular with criminal cases. It is not immediately apparent what the majority of members of the bar think about criminal law in 1981 - for the number of civil lawyers is still greater. However, it is certainly the case that the practice of criminal law increasingly attracts interest. According to practising lawyers in Amsterdam, there are not even enough cases in their district for all of them to have a share.

In this article we will discuss the way in which the counsel can fulfil his task. In the defence of a criminal case Dutch criminal law refers to the lawyer as *raadsman* (counsel) (cf. Art. 28, 37 Sv). When instigating legal proceedings the law refers to the *advocaat* (lawyer) (Art. 450 Sv.) This is correct, for even a lawyer who was not the counsel in a case may instigate proceedings on behalf of the defendant, if requested to do so. The above shows that there is a difference between the position of the lawyer as counsel and the lawyer as legal representative in a case. If the lawyer is the legal representative in a case, his actions, though carried out independently, are attributed to the defendant because he is identified with the latter[3]. If he acts as counsel, this is not the case. For example, a statement made by the counsel in session cannot be used as evidence[4].

The problems which can arise for the counsel in the context of legal assistance for criminal cases are in the first place, closely linked with his position in criminal law. On the one hand, his position is limited by a number of legal provisions concerned with his competence and obligations, and on the other hand, by his own individual views on the ethics of criminal law. After all, the way in which the counsel should function in a criminal case, depends on the case's position in a social context, and thus on the question of the role which should be played by the counsel. Therefore, in chapter I we will put forward some general considerations on the position of the counsel.
A number of problems are closely related in the second place with the current position of criminal law. Consequently we will discuss one problem which affects the counsel's function with reference to the different stages of criminal law.
Finally, a mention should be made in the third place of the fact that a number of problems are closely related to the type of criminal law. The defence in juvenile cases and so-called "political" criminal cases in particular poses specific problems for the counsel. The following discussion will be based on criminal law in which detention is given.

I. GENERAL CONSIDERATIONS ON THE POSITION OF THE COUNSEL.

There is some difference of opinion about the question of the counsel's function or role. It is obvious that there will be different views on the desirable role of lawyers in a criminal case when there are different views of the objectives of criminal law. If criminal law is seen predominantly from the point of view of purposeful crime prevention, the counsel (lawyer) will be assigned a considerably less important role, both quantitatively (for whom and from when does he act?) and qualitatively (what powers does he have?), than if a criminal case is considered from the point of view of defending the individual - the defendant - against the authorities[5]. With reference to H.L. Packer[6], it is important to determine whether the counsel is acting in a Crime Control Model, in which the primary aim is the prevention of crime, or in a Due Process

Model, in which an attempt is made to achieve a procedural balance between the counsel and the defendant, on the one hand, and the public prosecutor on the other hand, and in which, moreover, the elementary principles of criminal law such as the *presumptio innocentiae* principle and the prohibition of self-incrimination are respected.
The history of Dutch criminal law has shown that opinions on the proper process of criminal law have developed from a predominantly inquisitorial approach, corresponding to the Crime Control Model, into a more moderate accusatory approach corresponding to the Due Process Model. In the latter an attempt has been made to achieve a compromise position between crime prevention and a guarantee of the rights of the individual[7]. The Criminal Code, in which the powers of the counsel are set down, is therefore not an elaboration of a single principle, but rather a compromise between two conflicting ideas. The way in which it is interpreted is often a question of personality and individual preference[8].
It is almost self-evident that in this atmosphere of tension the counsel's function will be set with problems. No doubt it is to some extent for this reason that the legislator has given the counsel a separate title in the Criminal Code, with the aim of avoiding misunderstanding as far as possible. In addition, the whole Code contains provisions concerning the counsel's powers. One of the most striking is Art. 331 Sv., which proides that with regard to the way in which the case proceeds in court, every power accorded the defendant under this title (title 6), is also accorded to his counsel.

Meanwhile it seems that a number of essential tasks of the counsel can be observed which occur in every criminal case, despite the differences in approach of criminal law and the role played by the counsel in this. The counsel's function in criminal cases is to provide legal assistance for his client and to exercise control over the case.
In his work on the sociology of law, C.J.M. Schuyt[9]gives a clear analysis of the two functions and notes that they can be in conflict with each other. Controlling the case means, first of all, that the counsel makes sure that the case is proceeding in accordance with the applicable rules of law, and also checks whether the statements and reasons given by the public prosecutor or judge are relevant. This means that in order to exercise control over a case the counsel may sometimes have to say sharp and unpleasant things, and this implies an antagonistic attitude. However, presumably his function as a legal assistant, viewed as obtaining the best possible results for the client, requires a more co-operative attitude. These tasks, which conflict on the most basic level, are an essentially insoluble problem for the counsel. According to E. d'Oliveira-Prakken this fact is counterbalanced by the fact that the

concept of legal assistance for criminal cases can be seen in a wider sense than the mere obtaining of the most favorable possible verdict for the client. In her opinion, legal assistance should entail that the counsel helps his client to analyse the problem concerning his criminal case, informs him of the possible attitudes and points of view that can be adopted, and about the probable consequences of these, leaving the choice as far as possible to the client. The defendant should be the central person, assisted but not manipulated, by his lawyer[10]. Dutch law illustrates how important the advisory function described above can be in the Supreme Court's opinion that in dispensing punishment the court can take into account the fact that the defendant, possibly to his own disadvantage, has made use of his right not to give evidence[11]. An accompanying function could be added to the functions already mentioned. According to P.J.W. de Brauw, the defendant might feel the need for moral support at any stage of the trial. For many defendants the feeling that nobody can, or wishes to understand their deed, is the most frustrating part of the whole of their trial and sentencing. Neither the prosecuting parties nor the judge can provide this support. In addition to the rehabilitation services, the counsel is in a position to be a great moral support to the client[12].

The problem described above of the conflict between exercising control over the case and providing assistance means that there should be close contact between the counsel and his client, at the very least. It often happens that the counsel, in view of the position of case law, cannot always predict with 100% certainty that indicating a formal deficiency as to the form, or not taking into account a particular rule of law, will be to his client's advantage in the end.
For example, when a counsel advises a client to make use of his right not to give evidence during court proceedings, it may well be that this would not guarantee his acquittal. If this attitude is actually condemned by the judge in pronouncing his verdict, many counsels will be faced with the question whether to ignore certain matters in exercising control over the trial so that the aim of "obtaining the best possible result" is not necessarily endangered.
In this case it is necessary for the contact between the client and his counsel to be good, so that the client can eventually take the best possible decision with regard to his attitude during the trial. The counsel should be aware that in many cases his advice can be the decisive factor. In giving his advice, the counsel should therefore not hesitate, where necessary, to inform his client of his own uncertainty regarding the effect of the attitude to be adopted in the trial. An example of this is the difficult advice that it may sometimes be necessary to give on the question of whether or not

to appeal to a higher court, for there is the possibility of a more severe sentence if the case goes to appeal. Another striking example of the tension between exercising control over the trial and providing assistance in the sense described above, results from the provisions of Art. 302 Sv. Art. 302 Sv. provides that neither the president nor any of the judges must reveal any opinion regarding the defendant's innocence or guilt while the court is in session. This article is an expression of the principle of presumptio innocentiae, which was mentioned above.
Insofar as the article lays down rules of conduct for judges, it forbids them to express themselves in such a way that indicates that they have an opinion regarding the defendant's innocence or guilt[13].
When a defendant recognises the prescribed procedure, every time the judge makes a statement indicating that he is convinced of the defendant's guilt, this should certainly not lead to the counsel's interceding. However, it often happens that judges seriously violate this provision, particularly when the defendant has pleaded not guilty. One judge might do this by making cynical jokes about the suspect's version of events, another by stating bluntly that the suspect is not very credible. J. Remmelink has furnished a number of striking examples of this[14].
These statements, and particularly the cynical jokes indicating that the judge is convinced of the defendant's guilt, pose a problem for the counsel when he has to act in the capacity of exercising control over the proceedings, and point out to the judge that he has violated the prohibition. Acting in this way may be desirable from the point of view of exercising control over the proceedings, but it has such a negative influence on the atmosphere during the course of court proceedings, and possibly on the sentence - an irritated judge is unlikely to give a mild verdict - that many counsels for this reason often decide not to intervene. In this respect it is difficult to indicate the limits for the counsel regarding the question of what is acceptable.
In my opinion, one of the limits is certainly that the defendant must be treated with dignity and should not be ridiculed.

The counsel's position has three dimensions. P.J.W. de Brauw has explained concisely and lucidly that two dimensions are determined by the functions and rights accorded him by law, while the third dimension can be described as "obligations", because it is largely concerned with the integrity of his professional conscience.

> "*In the execution of his task the counsel is continually exposed to demands from two sides.*
> *On the one side there is the defendant, who expects him*

to do everything possible and make the fullest possible use of his rights as a counsel; while on the other hand there are, firstly, the prosecuting parties, and later the judges, who consider that the counsel has only been accorded these rights in the confidence that he will use them only in cases where the correct course of law, as they see it, is not made more difficult.
The conflict situation in which the counsel therefore almost always finds himself to a greater or lesser extent, is made more difficult by the fact that both parties often ask him for more than he can give in view of his position of trust towards the other side".
This position of trust comprises various elements which should be clearly distinguished .
This is by no means a solution to the ever present conflict situation .
The analysis of these situations is sometimes simplified by making these distinctions."

In this context De Brauw refers to the distinction between the use of rights which the counsel has per se, and the rights which he shares with the defendant. The right to free and unrestricted communication and correspondence with the defendant and the right to exemption resulting from the obligation to secrecy belong to the first category. The right to look at the records of the case and to use them, is typical of the second category.
The counsel may not, in any circumstances, abuse either the first or second category, which is to use them for any purpose other than what is strictly concerned with the defence and personal support of the defendant. For the second category De Brauw considers that there is no reason to make use of the rights accorded the defendant as well, in a more restricted capacity than the defendant would have himself, though it is advisable to proceed cautiously. De Brauw correctly points that it is necessary to proceed cautiously because the counsel, unlike his client, is bound to a number of rules of conduct which may be sanctioned by disciplinary tribunals.

Thus Art. 2 of the 1980 Rules of Conduct provides that the lawyer must abstain from making any statement which could mislead the judge or the other party. It is clear that this obligation for the counsel to avoid making any misleading statement will result in even more difficult decisions with regard to advising the defendant. In this context De Brauw notes:

"He must point out to the defendant what rights he has, including the right to plead not guilty.
He must go through the defendant's statement to the court with the defendant, and in doing this he must limit his

advice to counselling that the defendant does not declare everything: he may never give advice to the defendant to tell untruths or make use of other improper means.
He does not have to prevent the defendant from telling a lie he has made up, if he has to admit that this might benefit the case, but he must warn that he cannot appeal to this[15]*".*

From these comments of De Brauw I conclude that the counsel must inform his client about the consequences of giving information with regard to his legal position. It is obvious that the counsel must not come up with this sort of proposal of his own accord. According to De Brauw, the obligation of the counsel described above to inform the client regarding his legal position does not apply vis-à-vis witnesses. In preliminary discussions with witnesses the counsel must do everything possible to prevent his reaction revealing to the witness that the latter's false statement (perjury) could benefit the defendant's case. In this context De Brauw even considers that the counsel should attempt to prevent the witness from committing perjury. I cannot agree with De Brauw on this point. Insofar as the counsel has a duty to find the truth, he must still certainly not exercise any influence on the contents of a witness's statement. However, he would be doing so if he attempted to prevent the witness from making a perjured statement, however noble this might seem. In this context I would like to state, for the sake of clarity, that the counsel's task with regard to discovering the truth, does not lie in assisting to solve a crime, but in making sure that the evidence is collected in an orderly way and, if necessary or desirable, to furnish contrary evidence. He is responsible for seeing that the "equality of arms" principle is applied. It is also possible to argue that the counsel should not prevent a witness from committing perjury from an entirely different point of view. A witness who commits perjury is committing a crime. In general, lawyers have no obligation to prevent crime. That is the job of the police. There is no reason why the lawyer, even when acting as counsel in a case in which the crime of perjury is committed, should suddenly be assigned this policing function. If he were, the counsel's role would be only that which belonged in Packer's Crime Control Model. In my opinion, this is not the function which members of the legal profession should perform in criminal law.

In conclusion, I agree with De Brauw that the limit of a counsel's acceptable task in this advisory capacity should be the invention of a false statement or the advice to make it. Moreover, he may not make an appeal to a perjured statement.

The above shows that I consider the defence to have a subjective character. The counsel puts forward his client's version of events, translated o not into legal jargon, for example in the arguments put forward as defence.
For this reason there is no possibility for a counsel to be objective, contrary to the idea put forward by the General Council in 1969[16]. What is meant by the rather vague term "objective counsel" has not been clearly described anywhere, as far as I know. The importance for a counsel to be subjective whilst still serving the cause of justice follows from the view to which I subscribe, and which entails that modern criminal law can also be considered as a constant attempt to use reason and intellect to prevent the rough, arbitrary and inhuman qualities of primitive punishment and revenge found in blood feuds, lynch justice and the sheer usurpation of power by the strong from the weak[17].
After all, the process of criminal law as a result of political process - for criminal laws are products of "past politics" - is potentially conflicting and open[18]. Nor can it be denied that the development of Dutch criminal law is influenced by the dominant morality[19].
Legislation on public decency is a striking example of this. Given the excessive demands made on criminal law, it seems impossible to me that the counsel should try to be objective in the sense described above, when acting on behalf of his client. If he does so, he is guilty of moralising and this must be just about the last thing a client expects from his counsel. Moreover, his so-called objective attitude, which actually amounts to an uncritical positivistic frame of mind, would make him incapable of preventing the rough and arbitrary elements and usurpation of power which unfortunately still occur in the execution of our criminal law.

In this context it is necessary to refer to the interesting comments of Han Janse de Jonge and Ties Prakken. They view the development of methods of conducting the defence in the Netherlands in the twentieth century from the point of view of constitutional law. They point out that the processes of criminal law are dominated by a liberal philosophy of truth, which is expressed in the dialectic structure of criminal law. This can be seen even in the way in which a court is furnised: two parties stand opposite each other (the public prosecutor and the defendant) with the judges behind a green table, arriving at their verdict in a neutral and independent manner on the basis of what the parties produce with regard to the facts and the law.

> *"By taking the side of his client in a totally one-sided way the lawyer serves the cause of truth, in a legal sense, and contributes to the quality of justice[20]."*

However, no matter how desirable it is to have a subjective attitude, it should not be forgotten that the objective of obtaining the best result, often in terms of the least severe punishment, does not always benefit so much from an antagonistic attitude. Even if there are conflicts of interests or values at stake, this does not mean that they should dominate every criminal case. Thus it is not so much the extent to which a conflict is a conflict of interests or values which largely determines the strategy of a trial[21], but the client's desire to raise this matter. If he does not wish to do so, it is not so necessary to focus the client's vision on events.

Finally, it should be mentioned that the subjective counsel relates better to his position as a representative in the case. As I remarked in the introduction, there is a formal difference between the two positions, but it cannot be denied that both positions are aimed at serving the client's interests. If the lawyer acts as a representative in the case, he is identified with his client. In this context, German law refers to the *höchstpersönlicher Verbundenheit mit dem Beschuldigten* [22] (the extremely personal connection with the accused party).
In Dutch law this identification even means that mistakes made by the counsel (lawyer) in his use of legal methods are attributed to the defendant. Because of this the Solicitor General very recently remarked to the Supreme Court that the counsel's behaviour must be faultless : there is no legal possibility of putting right his mistakes[23].

It seems extremely complicated on the one hand, to identify the counsel with his client in certain circumstances, and on the other hand, to oppose this identification and argue that there should be a distance between them by assigning the counsel an objective role.

For the sake of clarity it ought to be noted that subjectivity need in no way affect the counsel's independence nor imply that the counsel feel obliged to do everything his client considers necessary. A subjective attitude does mean that a counsel's conduct during the trial is based on his client's views and, at the very least, the counsel does not openly maintain a distance from his client.

II. STAGES OF THE PROCESS OF CRIMINAL LAW AND THE RELATED PROBLEMS OF THE COUNSEL/CLIENT.

A. *Preliminary enquiry*

The investigations preceding the course of the court proceedings are termed "preliminary enquiry" (Art. 132 Sv.). These investigations can consist of detection carried out by the police and /or the preliminary legal enquiry by the *Rechter Commissaris* (the judge charged with the preliminary enquiry, hereafter "Judge Commissary")(Art. 168 in conjunction with Art. 181 Sv.). During this stage the role of the counsel is to be an accessory to the client.
Very recently a report was given by F.H. Koster regarding the counsel's role during the preliminary enquiry, with respect to the situation in the Netherlands, on the occasion of the meeting of the Association for the comparative study of Dutch and Belgian law, held on 21 November 1980 in the Hague. P. van den Noortgaete gave a report for Belgium. The legislator's aim of assigning the counsel a task even during the preliminary enquiry is not only expressed in the rather detailed regulation of his powers during the preliminary legal enquiry, but also in the provisions ensuring the unrestricted communication between the counsel and his defendant and his right to see the written documents related to the case[24]. In his report Koster discusses in detail a number of the counsel's rights, such as the right to unrestricted communication with the defendant, the right to see the written documents related to the case, the right to attend the hearings and other rights the counsel has during the detection and preliminary legal enquiry.
This chapter will not deal with these matters, but an attempt will be made to highlight some of the problems facing the counsel in exercising his rights. In this respect I have not attempted to cover every aspect.

Choice and assigning of a counsel

In the first instance, a defendant can get a counsel by choosing one. He also has the right to do so at any time, even when a counsel has already been chosen or assigned him: he can even choose more than just one counsel (Art. 38 Sv). If the defendant is being detained, the president of the court (or court of appeal) where the case for which the defendant is being detained is being held, officially assigns a counsel when the detention commences. Since the Act of 26 October 1973 (S.509), which entered into force on 1 January 1974, defendants who have been detained are also assigned a counsel by the Dean of the Order of Advocates of the district where the defendant has been detained (Art. 40 Sv.). The detention is a way in which the (auxiliary) officer of justice can detain the defendant for a

maximum of four days after he had been detained for a maximum of six hours for questioning.
Immediately after detention, the counsel, who was appointed by the Dean is informed of it. In practice the Dean draws up a list of lawyers who will represent the defendant who has been detained: the counsel who undertakes this representation is sometimes known as the *piket advocaat* (the lawyer on duty). The latter not only represents the defendant when he is detained at the police station, but also when he appears before the Judge Commissary, if the public prosecutor has ordered that he will be taken into custody.

The first problem which could face the piquet lawyer, is the fact that in this capacity he may be confronted with more than one suspect in a particular case, and these suspects may all have been taken into custody at the same time. In general the police adopt the position in this situation that a different counsel should act on behalf of each of the defendants. This view results from the fear of collusion though, as M. Wladimiroff has correctly remarked, it does not have a basis in law.[25] The police do not have the power to determine whether or not a counsel can act on behalf of a particular defendant. Only the public prosecutor may be able to take this decision under certain circumstances on the basis of Art. 50, par. 2 Sv.). Meanwhile, the piquet lawyer is best advised to be aware of possible complications which might arise if he were to take on the defence of a number of clients in a case. The possibility that there might be conflicting interests is a particularly convincing argument for having a separate counsel for each defendant[26].
There is a difference of opinion in Dutch case law about the question whether, when a counsel does act on behalf of a number of defendants, the fact that one defendant remains ignorant of statements made by others, justifies a restriction of the unrestricted communication described in Art. 50, par. 2. The Arnhem Court answered this question affirmatively in its judgment of 2 March 1979, *NJ* 1979, 298, and a similar response was given by the Leeuwarden Court on 15 March 1978, *NJ* 1978, 429. The Alkmaar Court, on the other hand, considered as follows in its verdict of 30 April 1974, *NJ* 1975, 316, with regard to the problem outlined above, and in particular with regard to the possibility that a lawyer might inform a defendant of another defendant's statement in good faith, though in good faith he should have remained ignorant of it.

> *"This possibility exists in every case where a number of defendants plead not guilty, and where one counsel acts on behalf of more than one defendant.*
> *However, this circumstance by itself is insufficient for imposing restrictions on the free communication between*

the counsel and one or more of the defendants. There was no evidence in the case in question of the existence of particular, i.e. concrete circumstances leading to the serious suspicion that the unrestricted communication between the counsel and defendant M. will have the consequences feared by the Public Prosecutor".

Another fairly serious problem during the stage of piquet service is the problem of information. Art. 30, par. 1 Sv. provides, inter alia, that the public prosecutor can give the defendant permission to look at the written materials related to the case, if the defendant so requests. Art. 51, Sv. also provides that, as regards the counsel's right to look at the written materials related to the case and obtain copies of these, Art. 30 Sv is also applicable.
Thus, from a formal point of view, the counsel is able to look at the written materials related to the case, i.e. official minutes, even during the piquet stage. Art. 30, par. 2 also provides that, to the extent that they apply to the stage where the defendant is taken into custody (the piquet stage), before a judge has entered the case, the public prosecutor can deny or prevent the defendant from looking at particular written materials, if this is in the interests of the investigation. In this case the defendant is informed in writing that the documents he has been given are not complete.
In view of the above-mentioned Article 51 Sv, the question arises whether the lawyer - in the above case, the public prosecutor - who takes the decision described above, is able to allow or forbid either the counsel alone or the defendant alone, or both together, to look at particular documents related to the case. In view of the texts of Arts. 50 and 51 Sv, an affirmative answer is out of the question.[27]
Duisterwinkel and Melai point out that conceivably the unfortunate situation might arise in which the counsel's request is not met, but the defendant's request is. During criminal proceedings one may assume that the counsel should perform his function in accordance with the powers and requirements laid down and prescribed in the Criminal Code, and will not abuse his position by attempting to hinder the pursuit of the truth. It is only in the event of his so doing, and Art. 50 Sv is applied (which provides that the unrestricted communication between counsel and client can temporarily be partially of entirely rendered impossible) that there is any reason to deny the counsel the right to look at the written materials while the measures of Art. 50 apply[28]. However, this is all very well in theory, but it does not work in practice.
If a counsel asks the detective on the case if he can look at the written materials related to the case, during the stage where the defendant is put into custody, he is usually told that no written materials have yet been drawn up, and there

are only ideas, or that the written materials related to the case are not yet complete.
Art. 152 Sv, however, provides that the written materials related to the case should be completed as quickly as possible. Nevertheless, in theory a record of the minutes counts as a written material related to the case, if it is signed and, according to Wladimiroff, the right to look at the contents should not depend on whether or not the record of the minutes is completed. The only criterion is the question whether a record has been made[29]. However, this is more difficult in practice than in theory. It very rarely happens that a counsel has seen the written materials related to the case before visiting his client during the piquet stage. At best the detective on the case might give him some brief information regarding the extent of the crime and whether the client has confessed. This means that the counsel is hardly in a position to advise his client with regard to his legal position vis-à-vis the evidence. It may be possible to assess the available evidence on the basis of the information that has been given or is assumed. The client can be advised with regard to his position on this basis. It is therefore important to proceed with caution[30].
For the benefit of foreign readers, I would like to add that although prominent Dutch legal experts consider that the counsel has the right to attend the police examination in pursuance of the applicable legal provisions[31], the police always argue that the counsel does not have this right, referring to Art. 50 Sv. In practice, the counsel is rarely admitted to the police examination.
The very fact that the counsel is not permitted to attend the eximination makes the lack of information during the stage where the defendant is taken into custody, extremely pressing. In this situation the counsel obviously has to point out to his client during the piquet service that, in pursuance of Art. 29, par. 2 Sv., he is not obliged to answer the questions put to him.
When the defendant has been taken into custody, the public prosecutor can enter an order for a custody lasting six days to the Judge Commissary. (Art. 63 et seq. Sv.)
In practice the counsel will have looked at the written materials related to the case and will possibly have obtained a copy of them before the Judge Commissary hears the defendant, in pursuance of Art. 64, par. 3 Sv. Thus he is better able to inform his client and advise him with regard to his position on the evidence prior to the commencement of the hearing before the Judge Commissary. In fact, the practical implications of this are that the counsel once again faces considerable problems.
In pursuance of the above-mentioned Art. 51 Sv, copies of the written materials related to the case are given to the counsel

in most districts, immediately prior to the commencement of the hearing before the Judge Commissary. However, from my own experience this rule is not kept in the district of Amsterdam, the largest district with the highest number of Judge Commissaries. It is strange that this has not led to vehement protest from the local legal practitioners. In this district the counsel may look at the written documents related to the case, but he only receives copies of them weeks after the hearing, and after the defendant has been taken into custody.
In this context it should be mentioned that the procedure by which the counsel may look at the written materials related to the case, is laid down by a statutory instrument (Art.34, par. 1 Sv.). This has been further elaborated in Art. 9 of the Tarif Decision in Criminal Cases of 27 November 1963 (S. 469).

As I have shown, the counsel is only able to advise his client properly when he has looked at the written materials related to the case. Viewed in this light it seems rather strange that Art. 34. par. 2 Sv. provides that the defendant (and therefore his counsel), can obtain from the court a copy of the written materials related to the case which he is permitted to look at, though this must not delay the investigation. Meyer rightly considers that it is extremely difficult for the counsel to advise his client properly if no records are available, or there is no opportunity for going through them with the client just prior to the hearing before the Judge Commissary. The statement made by the client before the Judge Commissary is extremely important in many cases. It is reported on the record and counts as legal evidence in accordance with Art. 344, par. 2, Sv. If the judge is in some cases susceptible to the defence's arguments that the contents of the written materials drawn up by the police have been obtained by illegal methods, these arguments will generally carry little weight with regard to the written materials drawn up by the Judge Commissary, particularly if the counsel was present at the hearing.
If the written materials are lacking or there is no opportunity of going through them with the client, it is a good idea to advise the client of his right not to answer the questions put to him. This can result in the atmosphere becoming rather strained, but the counsel can explain this attitude in a friendly and non-aggressive manner.[33] If the public prosecutor considers a preliminary legal enquiry to be necessary, he can demand that the Judge Commissary initiate this immediately (Art. 181, par.1 Sv.).
In many, though by no means all cases, the public prosecutor will demand of the Judge Commissary that the defendant be detained, in accordance with Art. 63, par.1 Sv.). As mentioned above, the Judge Commissary is obliged to hear the defendant on this order. The defendant is entitled to the support of a coun-

sel during this hearing (Art. 64, par. 3 Sv.). Even if there is no demand for the defendant to be taken into custody, the Judge Commissary must hear the defendant. In no event may the preliminary legal enquiry be closed before the defendant has been heard, or at least summoned. Art. 258, par. 2 concerns the public prosecutor's notification of the summons to the Judge Commissary, and is an exception to this, while Articles 241, par. 2 Sv and 316, par. 2 Sv. contain a separate regulation.

B. During the stage of the preliminary legal enquiry a problem arises resulting from the provisions of Art. 172 Sv. Art. 172, par. 1 Sv. provides that the Judge Commissary request the clerk of the court to draw up an accurate report of what has been said during the enquiry. Art. 172, par. 3 provides that if the defendant, a witness, expert witness or counsel requests that any statements are noted in the speaker's own words, this should happen whenever possible, provided that it does not exceed the limits of reason. This restriction, within reasonable limits, does not automatically apply for the defendant's statement, if this contains an admission of guilt. For Art. 29 par. 3 Sv. provides that the record of the hearing contain the defendant's admission, as far as possible in his own words.
It is the counsel's function to see that the defendant's statements, both admissions and denials, are noted in the records in his own words as far as possible. A slight nuance can easily shed a different light on a case. It often happens that a Judge Commissary still insists on going his own way and is not inclined to meet the defendant's and/or counsel's desires on this point. As it is the Judge Commissary who has the clerk of the court make the records, in accordance with Art. 172, par. 1 Sv., he makes the final decision about what the record reports. The counsel and/or defendant have no legal recourse whatsoever against a displeasing decision of the Judge Commissary. The counsel can advise his client not to sign the statement. Admittedly this has no effect on the legality of the record[34], but later on it could show during the court proceedings that the record does not contain the client's own words as far as it possibly could. In fact, the Judge Commissary who has the record drawn up is obliged to state the reason for the refusal or the omission if the record is not signed (Art. 174, par. 2 Sv.).
In practice the Judge Commissary usually states only that the defendant has refused to sign the record. It is obvious that a Judge Commissary of integrity should also mention the reason for this, so that there can be no misunderstanding or doubt at a later stage of the trial concerning the way in which the evidence has been obtained. Even if neither of these steps have been taken, an unsigned statement might have less value as evidence for the judge; the record in which it is included

does have evidential value if the judge is convinced that the statement recorded in the record was made as it is reported[35]. The question is whether Art. 256 Sv. can provide a solution in this case. In pursuance of this provision, the court can order that the shortcoming be rectified. There is some doubt that it could, because even if Art. 172, par. 3 were considered a substantial formal provision, the completed record remains available to the public prosecutor and can therefore be used as evidence in the case. In a similar question, regarding the statement of a witness, the Zutphen Court remarked in its decision of 19 March 1981 that the above consideration would be of more then theoretical significance if the "witness" (for our purposes read : "defendant") were to make an entirely different statement in another hearing. However, we are now concerned with an entirely different statement because the argument in the situation I have described above usually concerns only a few words or slight nuances[36]. In the current state of jurisdiction the counsel is well advised to use this violation as unlawful evidence for the defence. In this case the Judge is obliged to react to this when giving his verdict.

The counsel in court

One of the problems confronting the counsel both in the preliminary enquiry and during the court enquiry is the question what he should do if the client admits his guilt to him, but continues to deny this in court. At the 1939 General Meeting of the Dutch Association of Advocates (now the Dutch Order of Advocates) this question was answered in the sense that the counsel who has been assigned may not give up the defence. During this meeting the majority (27) of the votes was based on the view that justice is violated to a lesser extent when a guilty party is released because of insufficient evidence of his guilt than if a defendant is sentenced on the basis of insufficient evidence. A minority (24 votes) thought that the counsel would not be morally justified in preventing the truth from being revealed.
Langemeijer considers that the question posed above only concerns cases in which there is some doubt that there is sufficient evidence in law to convince the judge to pronounce sentence when the defendant pleads guilty. This assumption does not always work in practice because the problem frequently arises in cases in which the statement of evidence depends on an admission. Langemeijer considers that "*...it is not always acceptable for a counsel to argue a position which is aimed at preventing the judge from forming a conviction which corresponds with the truth and which he would presumably deduce from the available evidence if the counsel did not intervene.*" In his opinion, "*...the lawyer who is faced with this unpleasant adventure must make his client realise that he will not*

continue to help him and must withdraw from the case in a way which is not to the client's disadvantage".[37]
Beekhuis, his co-author for the introduction, does not go so far. In his opinion the counsel may not argue that his client has not made the statement concerned. I consider this to be right. However, Beekhuis leaves open the question whether the counsel is better advised to seek a replacement, as there are arguments both in favour and against. Beekhuis is particularly concerned with the fact that the judge must always be confident that the counsel's positive statements do not conflict with the counsel's knowledge of the facts, and that an expression of his own beliefs does actually concur with his real beliefs.[38]
However, if we assume that the counsel's function is to control the case, then in this context he need only check whether the evidence produced by the public prosecutor is sufficient to sustain a finding of the court that there has been proof. If it is not, the counsel can declare that the evidence is insufficient without being in conflict with his conscience or any ethical considerations and without making a statement about his client's innocence or guilt.
The counsel's own belief is irrelevant, and he does not therefore need to express his views on this point, and thus his conscience need not bother him. There is also the point that expressing his own belief makes little impression, unless the counsel concerned is exceptionally highly regarded by the presiding magistrates. This is another reason why I consider that he should not do so. The judge should arrive at his own conclusions on the basis of the contents of the legal evidence. The counsel should restrict himself to a discussion of the persuasive power of the evidence, and not of his own beliefs. The only thing the counsel is not permitted to do in this context is to mislead the judge. I therefore wholeheartedly agree with the opinion that the counsel is not obliged to prevent the defendant from being untruthful, though he must warn the defendant that he cannot appeal to this[39].

III. THE COUNSEL IN JUVENILE CRIMINAL CASES.

When the court comes across juvenile criminal cases, the law stipulates compulsory legal assistance, whereas it does not in the case of adults. This does not apply in district court cases (Art. 218g, par. 1 Sv.). Obviously minors can also choose a counsel themselves, as can their legal representative. If they disagree on the choice, the minor's choice is decisive. Defendants who are minors but are over sixteen years old, have the same rights in criminal law as defendants who have attained the age of majority; they can therefore enter into appeal themselves. However, defendants who are minors, but under sixteen, cannot act independently in criminal proceedings; their counsel acts on their behalf and decides whether or not to enter into appeal (Art. 504, par. 1 Sv.) If the legal representative does not agree with the counsel concerning the use, decision not to use, withdrawal or abandonment of any legal means, the former cannot lodge an objection with the president of the court concerned (Art. 504, par. 2 Sv.). The latter decides whether the counsel has acted correctly. Furthermore, a counsel who has employed a legal procedure in accordance with Art. 504, par. 2 Sv., should make sure that the clerk of the court who is recording the proceedings concerned, erases the words from the record which refer to the defendant's express authorisation of the counsel to use this legal procedure. If this has not been done, the appeal is not considered to have been made.

For juveniles under sixteen years of age only juvenile criminal law applies (Art. 77b, Sr.). In general, juvenile criminal law is also applied to juveniles between sixteen and eighteen years of age. However, the judge can apply adult criminal law to this category of minors, if he considers that there are sufficient grounds because of the serious nature of the act and the perpetrator's personality (Art. 77c, Sr.). The starting points of juvenile criminal law in which the personality of the defendant is used as an indication of whether or not juvenile criminal law should be applied, show that it is predominantly concerned with pedagogic considerations[40].

In juvenile criminal law, the child's interests have a central place. In this system the magistrate in the juvenile court is at "the heart" of the case. Apart from the fact that he has a wide range of punishments and measures at his disposal (cf. Art. 77g, Sr. and h, Sr.), he retains all sanctions to impose admonition, a declaration of confiscation and probation in a conditional form (Art. 77w, x Sr.). The importance of the magistrate in a juvenile court as the best judge of "the child's interest", is shown in Art. 77x, Sr., which provides that conditional release is possible at all times, unlike in adult criminal law, and that it can be ordered by the magistrate who has pronounced sentence. In adult criminal law the Minister of Justice is charged with granting conditional release. One thing is clear from this whole system, and that is that the fundamental rule in juvenile criminal law for the magistrate in the juvenile court is the interests of the child[41].

Anyone who takes part in many juvenile criminal cases knows that the magistrate assigns such a high priority to the child's interests that the rules of the applicable criminal law are not always correctly applied. For example, I remember one case in which the magistrate in the juvenile court, who also acts as the Judge Commissary, ordered a provisional detention for a minor on the grounds that this was absolutely essential in the interests of the child, who was an habitual drug addict.

I remember that the magistrate in the juvenile court put a great deal of pressure on me as the counsel not to make use of

the legal possibilities of obtaining a release for my client from this provisional detention. After consulting with my client and explaining his legal position, I decided not to use the legal procedures against the provisional detention. I must admit that it was a very difficult choice.
This was only one example of many in which the counsel is faced with the difficult question whether the child's interests should weigh as heavily for him as for the magistrate, in the sense that even the rules of criminal law should yield to this. In my opinion, this is not the case. At the very least the counsel must consult with his client and explain to him the different interests at stake. In some cases, as in the example above, the client is desperate for a solution to his problems and is prepared to accept the criminal law as being in his interests, despite the fact that the legal measures at first glance seem rather disagreeable. In this case there is no reason for the counsel to insist that criminal law must prevail. However, it is not so easy to know what to do in the not infrequent cases where the young client simply fails to understand what is at stake, either because of his deplorable psychological condition, or for some other reason. In this case, consulting with the client produces very few results.
To the same extent as for adult criminal law, the counsel is obliged to see that the individual's protection against the authorities and their law enforcement, comes first and foremost. In this it should not be forgotten that even if the child's interests are central in juvenile criminal law, the enforcement of the law takes place because justice appears to have been violated. It is this justice which requires a sense of loyalty with regard to criminal law and criminal proceedings.
This loyalty cannot be reconciled with the fact that the interests of the correct application of criminal law must yield to the child's interest, no matter how predominant this consideration is in juvenile criminal law. Thus the aim does not justify the means, which is the reason why, in view of the above, the counsel cannot tolerate the application of law enforcement which does not entirely comply with the requirements of criminal law, in the case described above.

IV. DEFENCE IN POLITICAL CASES.

Although, strictly speaking, there is no difference between political criminal cases and "ordinary" criminal cases - the dispensation of punishment even in an ordinary criminal case is a social and therefore political activity[42] - it is often argued that the *position* of the counsel in political criminal cases is more difficult or more delicate than in "ordinary" criminal cases[43]. The term "position" obviously refers to his function as counsel. I should like to question this assumption.

With regard to the term "political criminal cases", this usually refers to cases in which the culprit is someone who consciously defies the current system of justice and is a criminal of conscience, concerned with the recognition in the legal system of the norms he advocates.[44] If the political case is one in which the safety of the state is at stake, e.g. in so-called "terrorist" cases, the defence may find himself in the public dock. Normally a lawyer is not publicly asked about his own opinions, but in the defence of political criminal cases, this question is all too common[45].
The counsel is frequently under pressure from public opinion, influenced by the press, during his defence of political criminal cases. As I said above, the defence is often put in the dock, suggesting a sort of "political" complicity, which affects the relationship between the counsel and his client because the legal authorities are inclined to assume certain matters are definite (which are actually uncertain) as a result of this public suspicion. Consequently the unrestricted communication between the counsel and the detained client is viewed with "Argus eyes". I recall, for example, that during my visits to a client, who was a member of the *Rote Armee Fraktion*, I had to sit in a room behind a window with the curtains drawn and the plant-pots removed so that the guard, who was watching us from another room, had the best possible view. The defence in these political criminal cases is furthermore characterised by an enormous number of activities in the field of detention law. There are usually non-stop problems with regard to detention.
In short, though the amount of work in a political case may differ from that in an "ordinary" case, I believe that the position of the counsel remains the same, regardless of the pressure of public opinion and/or justice.
As a subjective counsel, the counsel must put forward the (political) motives and background of the political criminal case, in which the conflict of norms and values is central, just as he would in any other criminal case. It is no more relevant whether the counsel is in political or ideological agreement with a client on trial on suspicion of a crime of violence or conspiracy, than it is whether he is in agreement with a client in an ordinary case of shoplifting, which his politically motivated client might refer to as "an act of proletarian shopping". De Brauw considers that a counsel who does not agree with his client's politics should adopt an objective attitude. He is faced with a difficult decision, because the airing of his client's political views is not his concern[46]. From what I have already said, it should be apparent that I do not share this opinion as it does not do justice to the client's views, which should be expressed by his counsel. The explanation of political motives or the counsel's bringing them to the attention of the judge is all too often seen simply

as an expression of the counsel's *own* views. The role of the public prosecutor in criminal law clearly demonstrates that the judge cannot ignore politics. As the informant of the judge and the bench, the representative of the public prosecution brings the judge into contact with politics[47].
As I remarked in chapter I, the control over the case also means that the statements and reasons given by the public prosecutor and the judge are appraised for their relevance. Therefore the counsel should thoroughly question any argument that a case is not a political criminal case, and that the political motives should not play a dominating role in assessing the culpability and/or punishment. In doing so, his client's opinions will be scrutinised automatically. The only problem for the counsel in this respect is whether he should translate his client's views into legal terms. Han Janse de Jonge and Ties Prakken think he should[48]. Personally, I am not convinced. There seems to be little point in speaking in legal terms in a case where the client does not recognize the whole system of justice. In order to preserve his political identity it may even be essential to abandon any attempt at translating his interests into legal terms. Thus appealing to self-defence may be considered to be in conflict with the political ideology, which does not recognize applicable law. The fact that the defendant can be detained in a police barracks for preventative purposes, even though no legislation states that the barracks is a legal place of detention, can support the argument that the case has, and must have, a political character; the consequence of appealing against this has an undesirable depoliticising effect. I have already pointed out that the counsel for the defence cannot ignore the political background in these cases. Contrary to popular belief, the defence in this context is not predominantly concerned with using the law as a platform for propaganda. In a political defence, as in any other defence, the central issue is to consider how everything happened. This means that the defence must point out the class-related character of criminal law procedure in accordance with his client's wishes and with reference to the political attitude adopted during the trial by the public prosecution or the legal system as a whole. In the opinion of some political theorists, this will lead to an accusation, made by the public prosecution, containing fuel for political resentment, being considered as self-incrimination[49]. It is obvious that the defence can easily serve a political objective in the above procedure. The defence, which can be noteworthy by virtue of the client's consistent attitude, will certainly have some influence.
This will be a secondary consideration for a counsel who is not in political agreement with his client and may not openly maintain a distance from him. For a counsel who is in political agreement with his client, the means and aims of the defence thus coincide. The defence and propaganda are one, which in no

way need detract from the integrity of the defence.
Finally, the problem of the common abuse of the privilege of unrestricted communication with the client should be considered when discussing the defence in political criminal cases. There is the question whether the defence of political criminal cases can lead to different detained clients belonging to a group, making use of the unrestricted communication between a counsel and his client to pass (political) information from one detainee to another. The possibility of furnishing his client with information from books, newspapers and magazines will not be discussed here: with very few exceptions, these are always permitted. In other words, is the counsel entitled to set up a so-called "information system"? Han Janse de Jonge and Ties Prakken consider that this is permissible:

> *"The political opinion on the defence held by the lawyers in this case entails that they can see the defendants as collective in a political sense.*
> *This, in its turn, entails that they make use of the unrestricted communication between the counsel and his client to pass political (but not evidential) information from one detainee to another."*

The aim of all this is to preserve the political identity of the client. De Jonge and Prakken also point out that two general Deans of the Dutch Order of Lawyers have taken up this matter, without explaining clearly what is meant by the term "abuse", though this is precisely the central issue.
It is strange that De Jonge and Prakken also fail to qualify in more detail the term "abuse"; Van Haersolte does, however.[51] In his opinion, a counsel does not have the right to further the mutual solidarity of his clients by what he does, or even as a verbal "middle man". He considers that using his position for this purpose counts as abuse in the sense of *"détournement de pouvoir"*, an aspect of public law: the use of a privilege for another purpose than that which it was given.
Not without justification, De Jonge and Ties Prakken reply to this that citizens - lawyers and clients alike - never have to account for their objectives. They can only be called to account for the methods they use.[52] It is a fact that there are hardly any positive legal indications which clearly demonstrate what the essence of the defence should be.[53] Neither the Criminal Code nor the Code of Conduct for Lawyers provides an answer to this question. In general, the only indication given refers to what the counsel may not do. Thus a counsel is not forbidden to place the preservation of his client's political identity in the foreground as the aim of the defence. To this extent I consider that Van Haersolte is incorrect. Thus a great deal depends on the assessment of the means employed, and a description of the term "abuse" is unavoidable.

According to De Brauw, abuse is any other use than that which is directly related to the actual defence and personal support of the defendant.[54] Any other use should be avoided, even when the counsel considers that it can in no way influence the prosecution or sentence, or conflict with the rules of the institution where the client is detained. If this influence is absent and there is no conflict with the rules, there are other means available for meeting the defendant's wishes. Unfortunately De Brauw does not indicate what he means by "actual defence". Obviously he believes that there is such a thing as an unreal defence. He too, fails to describe what other means are available. With regard to this subject - the information system - it seems to me that abuse is certainly made when the privileges are used in such a way that they are in conflict with the law. Thus the question whether an "information system" organized by lawyers in this context, leads to the question whether it is possible to justify a restriction of the constitutional right to free opinion, association and meeting. This constitutional right also applies to detainees of the legal authorities, in pursuance of Art. 91 of the rules of imprisonment. If this is not the case, then an information system such as that described above cannot be considered to conflict with the law; if it is the case, the opposite applies. Art. 91, par. I of the rules of imprisonment provides, inter alia, that written correspondence between detainees is under the control of the director of the penal institution concerned. Regarding the restriction of the above-mentioned constitutional right, Art. 11, par. 2 of the European Convention for the Protection of Human Rights and Fundamental Liberties and Art. 22, par. 2 of the International Convention on Civil Rights and Political Rights provide that the restrictions are permissible only if they are provided for by law and (this law) is necessary in a democratic society. In this context the European Commission and the Court accepted in 1965 that internal prison regulations, frequently based on laws in a substantive sense, are "law" in the sense of the Convention.[55] Dutch case law has also accepted that where the above-mentioned European Convention says "prescribed by law" and "*prévues par la loi*" in Arts. 9 and 10 (this obviously also applies to Art. 11), this in no way refers exclusively to provisions which should be described as laws in a formal sense, according to Dutch law.[56] On the basis of the above-mentioned provisions of the Convention and case law, it must be assumed that Art. 91, par. 1 of the rules of imprisonment forms a permissible violation of the constitutional right to free speech, unless one were to consider that Art. 91, par. 1, mentioned above, is not necessary in a democratic society. In view of the European court's minimal questioning of this field, it is evident that the provision will not be disqualified as being unnecessary in a democratic society.

The result of this is that an information system must be in conflict with the law. As a counsel may not act in conflict with the law, whatever the aims of the defence, he cannot be permitted to organise an information system as described above.

NOTES

1. Van Kuijk, *Advocatenblad* 1921, p. 42.
2. C.H. Beekhuis, *Advocatenblad* 1950, p. 201.
3. H.R. 13 February 1951, *NJ* 1951.476, and Duisterwinkel/Melai note 3 on Art. 37 Sv.
4. H.R. 15 September 1980, *NJ* 1981.13.
5. P.H. Bakker Schut, Kanttekeningen bij een rapport, *Delict en Delinquent* 1972, p. 452-463.
6. H.L. Packer, *The Limits of the Criminal Sanction*, Stanford 1968.
7. P.J. Bauw, Raadsman in kritieke fase, *Advocatenblad* 1975, p. 650-664.
8. A. Minkenhof, *De Nederlandse strafvordering*, 3rd ed., p. 1-9.
9. C.J.M. Schuyt, *Rechtssociologie een terreinverkenning*, Rotterdam 1971.
10. E. d'Oliveira - Prakken, De rol van de avocaat in het strafprocesrecht, *Proces* 1973, Vol. 52 no. 3.
11. H.R. 18-11-1980, *NJ* 1981.134; H.R. 3-3-1964, *NJ* 1964.1980; H.R. 12-11-1974, *NJ* 1975.41.
12. P.J.W. de Brauw, Algemene beschouwingen over de positie van de advocaat in strafzaken, *Advocaat en Praktijk*, Alphen a/d Rijn 1979.
13. Duisterwinkel/Melai, *Het wetboek van strafvordering*, note 1 on Art. 302 Sv.
14. J. Remmelink, Verhoor in strafzaken, *R.M.Themis* 1966, p. 327-328.
15. P.J.W. de Brauw, o.c.
16. *Advocatenblad* 1969, p. 421 e.s.
17. Cf. Ch.J. Enschedé, Ethiek en Strafrecht, *Speculum Langemeijer*, Zwolle 1973.
18. Cf. Ch.J. Enschedé, o.c. p. 85.
19. H.L.A. Hart, *Law, Liberty and Morality*, p. 1.
20. Han Janse de Jonge & Ties Prakken, Politieke Verdediging: een rechtsstatelijk dilemma, *NJB* 1978 p. 328.
21. E. d'Oliveira-Prakken, o.c. p. 81.
22. Kleinknecht, *Strafprozessordnung*, 34th ed., p. 408 sub 1L.
23. Conclusion of the *Advocaat-Generaal* in H.R. 17 June 1980, *NJ* 1980.571, with annotation of Th.W. van Veen.
24. P. Koster, De rol van de advocaat in het vooronderzoek, preadvies Vereniging voor de vergelijkende studie van het recht van België en Nederland, The Hague 1980, p. 12.
25. M. Wladimiroff, De advocaat tijdens het opsporingsonderzoek, *Advocaat en Praktijk* 1979.
26. M. Wladimiroff, o.c.
27. Duisterwinkel/Melai, note 7 on Art. 30 Sv. in *Het wetboek van strafvordering*.
28. Duisterwinkel/Melai, o.c.
29. M. Wladimiroff, o.c.
30. M. Wladimiroff, o.c.
31. J. Remmelink, *R.M.Themis* 1966, p. 307, 308; E. Myer, *Delict en Delinquent* 1976, p. 17-33; Duisterwinkel/Melai, o.c., note 5 on Art. 28 Sv.
32. O.E. Meijer, De advocaat tijdens het gerechtelijk vooronderzoek, *Advocaat en Praktijk* 1979.
33. O.E. Meijer, o.c.
34. Duisterwinkel/Melai, o.c.,note 1 on Art. 174 Sv.
35. Duisterwinkel/Melai, o.c., note 5 on Art. 199 Sv.
36. Rechtbank Zutphen, decision 19 March 1981, *NJCM*, Bull. May/June 1981, p. 180 e.s.
37. J.E. Langemeijer, De positie van de advocaat in strafzaken, *Advocatenblad* 1950, p. 165.
38. C.H. Beekhuis, De positie van de advocaat in strafzaken, *Advocatenblad* 1950, p. 196, 197.
39. P.J.W. de Brauw, Algemene beschouwingen over de positie van de advocaat in strafzaken, *Advocaat en Praktijk* 1979.
40. *N.L.R.* note 6, bijzondere bepalingen voor minderjarigen.
41. Hazewinkel/Schuringa, *Inleiding tot de studie van het Nederlandse strafrecht*, 8th ed., p. 572.
42. A.L. Cnoop Koopmans, Rechter en Politiek, *NJB* 26 May 1973, p. 630 e.s.
43. P.J.W. de Brauw, o.c.; Beekhuis, o.c. p. 208.
44. J. Remmelink, Politieke delicten, in the collection of essays: *Vrijheid en Recht*, p. 177.
45. Han Janse de Jonge & Ties Prakken, Politieke Verdediging: een rechtsstatelijk dilemma, *NJB* 1978, p. 327.

46. P.J.W. de Brauw, o.c.
47. A. Herstel, *Twee geloven op één kussen, het O.M. zit er tussen, Rechter en Politiek*, Vereniging de Jonge Balie te Utrecht, 1978, p. 77.
48. Han Janse de Jonge & Ties Prakken, o.c. p. 334.
49. Schily/Ströbele, Plädoyers einer politischen Verteidigung, Internationale Marxistische Diskussion, *Arbeitspapiere* no. 11, Berlin 1973, p. 6.
50. Han Janse de Jonge & Ties Prakken, o.c. p. 337.
51. R.A.V. van Haersolte, Politieke verdediging in rechte, *NJB* 1978, p. 605.
52. Han Janse de Jonge & Ties Prakken, *NJB* 1978, p. 607.
53. F. Kuitenbrouwer, De politieke strafzaak: een fundamenteel dilemma, *Proces* 1978 no. 1, p. 1-8.
54. P.J.W. de Brauw, o.c.
55. X van Duitsland 1860/63 *Ann.* VIII p. 205 (217); Wallace van Nederland 1983/63 *Ann.* VIII p. 228 (246 en 264).
56. H.R. 25 June 1963, *NJ* 1964.239; H.R. 24 January 1967, *NJ* 1967.272.

ABBREVIATIONS

H.R.	*Hoge Raad der Nederlanden*/Supreme Court of the Netherlands
O.M.	*Openbaar Ministerie*/Public Prosecutor
NJ	*Nederlandse Jurisprudentie*/Netherlands Law Reports in civil and criminal cases
NJB	*Nederlands Juristenblad*/Netherlands Law Review
N.J.C.M.	*Nederlands Juristencomité voor de Mensenrechten*/Netherlands Lawyers Committee on Human Rights
Sr.	*Wetboek van Strafrecht*/Netherlands Criminal Code
Sv.	*Wetboek van Strafvordering*/Netherlands Code of Criminal Procedure
N.L.R.	*Noyon, Langemeijer & Remmelink: Het Wetboek van Strafrecht*/Comment on the Criminal Code

GPSR Compliance

The European Union's (EU) General Product Safety Regulation (GPSR) is a set of rules that requires consumer products to be safe and our obligations to ensure this.

If you have any concerns about our products, you can contact us on ProductSafety@springernature.com

In case Publisher is established outside the EU, the EU authorized representative is:

Springer Nature Customer Service Center GmbH
Europaplatz 3
69115 Heidelberg, Germany

Batch number: 10830943

Printed by Printforce, the Netherlands